DISCARDED

ESSAYS IN ANTHROPOLOGY

ALFRED LOUIS KROEBER

ESSAYS IN ANTHROPOLOGY

Presented to
A. L. KROEBER
IN CELEBRATION OF HIS SIXTIETH BIRTHDAY
JUNE 11, 1936

↑ 942440

Essay Index Reprint Series

LIBRARY OF
LAMAR STATE COLLEGE OF TECHNOLOGY

BOOKS FOR LIBRARIES PRESS, INC.
FREEPORT, NEW YORK

COPYRIGHT, 1936, BY THE
REGENTS OF THE UNIVERSITY OF CALIFORNIA

Renewed 1954 by Luella Cole Lowie

Reprinted 1968 By Arrangement With
The University of California Press

LIBRARY OF CONGRESS CATALOG CARD NUMBER:
68-20297

PRINTED IN THE UNITED STATES OF AMERICA

HONORARY COMMITTEE

PRESIDENT ROBERT G. SPROUL
PROVOST MONROE E. DEUTSCH
PROFESSOR FRANZ BOAS
PRESIDENT LIVINGSTON FARRAND

GUARANTORS

MR. AND MRS. SIDNEY M. EHRMAN	GLADYS AYER NOMLAND
MR. CHARLES DE YOUNG ELKUS, JR.	DR. ELSIE CLEWS PARSONS
MR. JULIUS GOLDMAN	MR. JOSEPH M. PROSKAUER
DR. HENRY HARRIS	MR. JAMES N. ROSENBERG
MISS ELSBETH KROEBER	MR. W. EGBERT SCHENCK
JUDGE IRVING LEHMAN	DR. ALFRED M. TOZZER
MRS. ROBERT H. LOWIE	MR. MAXWELL UPSON

MR. HUTTON WEBSTER

CONTENTS

	PAGE
Preface	xi
CARL L. ALSBERG and ROBERT H. LOWIE, *Alfred L. Kroeber: Personal Reminiscences and Professional Appreciation*	xiii
S. A. BARRETT, *The Army Worm: A Food of the Pomo Indians*	1
RALPH BEALS, *Problems in the Study of Mixe Marriage Customs*	7
FRANZ BOAS, *The Relations Between Physical and Social Anthropology*	15
FAY-COOPER COLE, *Family, Clan, and Phratry in Central Sumatra*	19
JOHN M. COOPER, *Scapulimancy*	29
JUAN DOLORES, *Papago Nicknames*	45
CORA DU BOIS, *The Wealth Concept as an Integrative Factor in Tolowa-Tututni Culture*	49
A. H. GAYTON, *Estudillo Among the Yokuts: 1819*	67
E. W. GIFFORD, *Californian Balanophagy*	87
Alexander A. GOLDENWEISER, *Loose Ends of Theory on the Individual, Pattern, and Involution in Primitive Society*	99
ERNA GUNTHER, *A Preliminary Report on the Zoölogical Knowledge of the Makah*	105
E. S. CRAIGHILL HANDY, *Dreaming in Relation to Spirit Kindred and Sickness in Hawaii*	119
ISABEL T. KELLY, *Chemehuevi Shamanism*	129
A. V. KIDDER, *Speculations on New World Prehistory*	143
E. M. LOEB, *The Distribution and Function of Money in Early Societies*	153
ROBERT H. LOWIE, *Lewis H. Morgan in Historical Perspective*	169
J. ALDEN MASON, *The Classification of the Sonoran Languages (with an Appendix by B. L. Whorf)*	183
N. C. NELSON, *Notes on the Santa Barbara Culture*	199
RONALD L. OLSON, *Some Trading Customs of the Chilkat Tlingit*	211
LILA M. O'NEALE, *Wide-Loom Fabrics of the Early Nazca Period*	215
ELSIE CLEWS PARSONS, *The House-Clan Complex of the Pueblos*	229
PAUL RADIN, *Ojibwa and Ottawa Puberty Dreams*	233
GLADYS A. REICHARD, *Attitudes Toward Avoidance: A Suggestion*	265
EDWARD SAPIR, *Hupa Tattooing*	273
CARL SAUER, *American Agricultural Origins: A Consideration of Nature and Culture*	279
W. SCHMIDT, *Donner und Regenbogen beim Höchsten Wesen der Yuki*	299
HARLAN I. SMITH, *The Man Petroglyph Near Prince Rupert; or, The Man Who Fell from Heaven*	309
FRANK G. SPECK, *Inland Eskimo Bands of Labrador*	313

	PAGE
JULIAN H. STEWARD, *The Economic and Social Basis of Primitive Bands*	331
M. W. STIRLING, *Florida Cultural Affiliations in Relation to Adjacent Areas*	351
WILLIAM DUNCAN STRONG, *Anthropological Theory and Archaeological Fact*	359
JOHN R. SWANTON, *Early History of the Eastern Siouan Tribes*	371
RICHARD C. THURNWALD, *Sozialpsychische Abläufe im Völkerleben*	383
C. F. VOEGELIN, *Productive Paradigms in Shawnee*	391
W. LLOYD WARNER, *The Social Configuration of Magical Behavior: A Study of the Nature of Magic*	405
T. T. WATERMAN, *The Great World Theater*	417
Bibliography of Alfred L. Kroeber	423

ILLUSTRATIONS

Alfred Louis Kroeber . . . . *Frontispiece*

PLATES

1: fig. 1. Ash saplings stripped by army worms; fig. 2, sand-lined pits for catching army worms, surrounding the base of a tree . . . *facing* 4
2: fig. 1. Live army worms crawling on the inner surface of a basket; fig. 2, Pomo woman sifting worms in an openwork basket to separate them from ashes after roasting . . . . *facing* 5
3. Near view of man petroglyph near Prince Rupert, B.C. . . *facing* 312
4. Bird's-eye view of man petroglyph . . . . *facing* 313

TEXT FIGURES

1. A system of sand-lined pits for catching army worms 3
2. The family of Datu Sati 20
3. Unique or rare implements and ornaments from the Santa Barbara culture area 205
4. Draft of the Cahuachi Nazca mantle 216
5. Motives A, B, and E of the mantle 220
6. Motives F, D, C¹, J, and C of the mantle 222
7. Motives H and G of the mantle 224
8. Detail of motive B at the point of color change, and of interlocking yarns on the reverse side at the point of color change 226
9. Chin tattoo designs of the Hupa and neighboring tribes 274
10. Chin tattoo designs of the Hupa and neighboring tribes 276

MAPS

1. Locations and movements of Eastern Siouan tribes 372
2. The world, on Goode's Polar Equal Area Projection *following* 422

PREFACE

IN THE SPRING of 1934 several of Professor Kroeber's one-time students conceived the project of an Anniversary Volume in honor of his sixtieth birthday and requested me, as his senior associate, to undertake the relevant editorial work. After a period of discussion as to the scholars who might reasonably be approached, it was decided to limit the number to those who had had definite personal contacts with Professor Kroeber. Thus, Father Schmidt was included because of Professor Kroeber's visit to him in Mödling in 1915, his recent return visit in 1935, and the correspondence, extending over many years, resulting from Father Schmidt's interest in Californian ethnography. Again, Professor Thurnwald has repeatedly sojourned in Berkeley and participated in discussions organized by the anthropologists residing there. Even with the limitations imposed, the editorial correspondence developed on a formidable scale, with the results herewith presented.

I should like to express my indebtedness to Dr. Carl L. Alsberg, a lifelong friend of Professor Kroeber's, for many practical suggestions in the launching of this enterprise; to Dr. Cora Du Bois for her unflagging zeal in promoting it; and to Mrs. Gwendoline Harris Block for generously devoting much time to correspondence and the inevitable drudgery of technically preparing the manuscripts for the press.

ROBERT H. LOWIE
Editor

ALFRED L. KROEBER

I. PERSONAL REMINISCENCES

By Carl L. Alsberg

THROUGH THE ACCIDENT that Alfred Louis Kroeber's parents and mine employed the same German pedagogue to begin their children's education, I became acquainted with him when he was seven and I was six. Our parents seem to have regarded the New York public schools of that day as inferior and to have believed that the first few years in primary school largely determine children's attitudes toward learning for the rest of their lives. Therefore, instead of sending their children to school at six years, they had us taught at home. The two families were but slightly acquainted and quite by chance chose the same teacher, Dr. Bamberger, the first principal of the Ethical Culture School, though only the Kroeber family had any direct contact with the Ethical Culture Society. The Ethical Culture School had been but recently founded through the efforts of the late Felix Adler and was regarded as a pioneer in American elementary education. Dr. Bamberger was a trained German pedagogue of outstanding ability who was later called to organize the Ethical Culture Society's school in Chicago. The school was in session from nine A.M. to one P.M.; its teachers therefore had their afternoons free, and Dr. Bamberger spent a part of every school-day afternoon and of Saturday with the Kroeber and a part with the Alsberg children. This was possible because the two families lived just east of Central Park within six city blocks of each other.

It was Dr. Bamberger's custom, whenever the weather at all permitted, to take us for a walk in Central Park or on excursions into the environs of New York. We learned to read on a park bench. Very soon on good days Dr. Bamberger took the Kroeber and the Alsberg boys out together. It was in this way that we came together. I still distinctly remember the first occasion: the four little boys, Alfred and Eddie Kroeber and Carl and Julius Alsberg, and the German teacher, red-bearded, gold-rimmed bespectacled, stout and huge—or at least he seemed huge to a little boy. I also remember how shy we little boys were and how inferior I, for one, felt at first toward the Kroeber boys. They seemed to me so well dressed and perfectly turned out: well-blacked shoes, undarned black stockings, knee pants (the baggy knickerbocker of the golf course had not yet come to America), and light tan, spring-weight overcoats of the type then known as "box coats," which did not quite reach down to the knee. I felt they were quite the little gentlemen and I a roughneck. I did not realize that there is something in Alfred Kroeber's make-up which renders him orderly, systematic, and neat in his thoughts as well as in handling his possessions. I was to have many evidences of this as we grew up together. Perhaps also the rather old-fashioned strict discipline and order which prevailed in the Kroeber household played a rôle in the development of these traits.

I dwell upon the influence Dr. Bamberger had upon us, for I believe it was in very large measure determining for the careers we ultimately chose. For example, I remember distinctly our first geography lesson: We were taken to the center of the span of Brooklyn Bridge, then only a few years completed; our teacher took a compass and a map of New York harbor out of his pocket, spread the map out and explained north and south, east and west to us and how to read a map. For most children—and adults too, for that matter—north is up and south is down because that is the way maps are hung on walls—but not for us. Also we were told about birds and beasts and plants, often with their scientific names, and about rocks and geological formations. The glacier scratches on some of the outcroppings in Central Park were shown to us. Naturally, we soon got the collecting fever. We collected many things—fossils and minerals, but principally beetles and butterflies. We learned not a little of systematic entomology, of the host plants and life histories of insects.

But our education was not limited to reading, writing, arithmetic, and natural history. We were given some idea of the classical world. Our teacher began telling us stories of the ancient world beginning with the siege of Troy, down to the decay of the Roman Empire. The story of the Iliad and the Odyssey appealed to us especially. The Greeks and Trojans were to us what Indians, trappers, cowboys, and Jesse James were to many other boys of that time. Achilles, Hektor, Agamemnon, and Odysseus were real personalities to us and we quarrelled about who should play the rôles of Achilles and Hektor in our games, for we played Greeks and Trojans as many boys then played Indians—and I suppose still do. Helen and Brisëis did not interest us.

The Kroebers had a summer home at Sheepshead Bay, one of a group including the country homes of the Zinsser families. The two or three occasions when I was invited for a fortnight's visit belong to my brightest memories. We boys, Alfred and Eddie Kroeber, Eddie Grelle, their cousin, Hans Zinsser, who was Eddie Kroeber's age, Gus Zinsser, who was somewhat older than any of us, and I built in the sand what we called the City of Troy,—for us quite an elaborate structure with a moat and walls and attempts at gates and a drawbridge. Then we fought the siege of Troy over again. Our lances were the spent rockets from Paine's pyrotechnic displays across the bay at Brighton Beach. Our missiles were the pop- and beer-bottle corks from Coney Island washed up in windrows at every tide. Evenings we watched the fireworks at Brighton Beach across the bay and on one for me never-to-be-forgotten occasion we were taken over to sit in the audience and see the fireworks from near by. This was even more memorable than the occasion when we were taken for an all-day fishing trip for sheepshead, though I don't remember that we caught anything but a few sea robins and butterfish.

After three years under Dr. Bamberger, we were sent to different schools. The Kroeber boys went to Sachs' School, probably the best college-preparatory school in New York at that time. The Alsberg family had in the meanwhile moved to Harlem, and so I went to a school there. Nevertheless, we saw much of each other Saturdays, holidays, and vacations; probably our common interest in collecting natural history specimens held us together. It was during this period that we formed a "scientific society," so-called, the principal purpose of which was to go on collecting excursions on Saturdays and holidays. We went into the Bronx Park region, which was then largely open country, to collect beetles and butterflies, to an iron-smelting furnace where we collected fossils from the limestone used in smelting, to Staten Island where we collected serpentine and related minerals, to the Franklin Zinc Smelter where we collected minerals, to the Palisades, to Snake Hill in the Jersey marshes, to such factories as would let us in, and, when we were older, we had winter-evening meetings at which we read "papers" and had heated discussions on many subjects we really knew very little about. These meetings lasted until well into our sophomore year at college. First and last, about fifteen boys were involved.

About his fourteenth or fifteenth year, Alfred Kroeber was sent to a boarding school in Connecticut, because it was thought he was growing too fast and needed more of an outdoor life. He entered Columbia College in 1892. He and I in the class of '96 and James N. Rosenberg of the class of '95, with whom Kroeber had become intimate at boarding school, formed a little group of our own, to which Joseph M. Proskauer of the class of '96 was soon added. There were, of course, others in our crowd, but the four of us have always hung together. This was perhaps because Columbia College had no dormitories in those days, so that friendships of school days were not disrupted by dormitory life. We all lived at home. In consequence, Kroeber was not subjected to the "polishing" which comes to the dormitory freshman from living in close quarters with unsympathetic personalities and which tends to force him into the stereotyped mould of the day. Kroeber never became a typical undergraduate.

At that time, Kroeber was perhaps the shyest and most diffident one of us, yet at heart the boldest and least hampered by convention or fear of consequences; so he got rather deeper than usual into freshman escapades. One scrape in particular seemed to us at the time serious. The statuary in Central Park had always offended our aesthetic senses. That we had every ground for our annoyance, any one may see for himself, if he will examine some of the survivors of that day still on view on "The Mall" or now considerably hidden away in inconspicuous nooks amid obscuring foliage. Much of the sculpture was bad, even for the Grantian period of American culture. It was of a piece with the cast-iron columns of A. T. Stewart's Department Store on lower Broadway or the State-War-Navy building in Washington. The difference between Kroeber and the rest of us was that it never occurred to us to act; he, however, did something about it. With one or two others—I have long since forgotten who they were—he decorated the statuary as a symbol of his scorn. Smooth-shaven gentlemen of bronze or marble received walrus mustaches in red paint; gentlemen in knee breeches were given stockings in the Columbia colors—transverse stripes of pale blue and white; and certain bronze dogs grew raccoon ring-tails over night. Unfortunately, the boys had been careless in buying the paint and were caught. At the time, I was shocked at my own father's levity. He seemed to take it as a great joke—a joke of which on the whole he rather approved. I thought it most inconsiderate that, for years thereafter, he and some of his friends should bring up what seemed to me a painful subject by addressing Alfred on occasion as Rembrandt or Van Dyke or Velazquez.

As Kroeber had daring to the point of what seemed to the rest of us recklessness, so he was the best of us at planning, but his shyness often prevented his playing the leader in the execution of his own plans. In the carrying out of what we undertook—oftenest something he had originated—it was not usually he who led. And so, while he did stand out in our own small group, he was not at all conspicuous in the social life of the college as a whole or of our class. Just as he was the one in our group least hampered by convention, so he was also the most critical. In our interminable debates he was the doubting Thomas, the asker of the uncomfortable question, the pricker of the other fellow's bubble.

There is little else to say of Kroeber's freshman year; it passed without much intellectual stimulus from our teachers. The course was prescribed: Latin, Greek, modern languages, mathematics, history—all mere continuation of subjects we had had before in preparatory school. The preparatory training of most of our classmates seemed to us incredibly poor; we wondered how they had passed the college entrance examinations. For most of them the courses may have been fruitful; but for a freshman like Kroeber, who not merely had an unusually clear head but also an adequate preparation, the freshman year would have been sterile scholastically, if it had not been for the university library. In those days, nearly all the stacks in the library were accessible to every student. After the library attendants had come to know you, you simply walked in and browsed as long as you liked. Kroeber was a voracious reader and his freshman year offered the opportunity to read widely and to think.

The sophomore year was different; it was then we came in contact with the poet and critic, George E. Woodberry, who lectured to us on English literature, dealing particularly with Coleridge, Shelley, Keats, Wordsworth, and their contemporaries. He was not merely a great man, but also a great teacher. His teaching went beyond the classroom and Kroeber came to know him well and to be greatly influenced by him—as indeed were all of us. Kroeber and the rest of us acquired an intense interest in literature, in literary criticism, and in art; and some of us, though not Kroeber, so far as I recall, even took to writing poetry. It was Woodberry's influence no doubt that led our group to establish a new undergraduate literary magazine, *The Morningside,* for we were dissatisfied with the existing undergraduate papers. We thought them stodgy and dull.

In the launching of this venture, Kroeber played a leading rôle. I'm afraid Swinburne, Aubrey Beardsley, Gelett Burgess, Oscar Wilde, O. Henry, and Kipling were among our models. The name, *The Morningside,* we chose because it anticipated the removal of Columbia University to Morningside Heights. We thought it oriented us toward the future, but Woodberry told us the name sounded like that of an apartment house. Among others besides Kroeber who were associated as editors or contributors in this venture during its beginnings were H. M. Birckhead, W. A. Bradley, J. Erskine, V. Gildersleeve, F. P. Keppel, J. M. Proskauer, E. C. Ropes, J. N. Rosenberg, E. R. Sackett, J. E. Spingarn, G. W. Wharton, H. W. Zinsser. This undergraduate monthly lasted for some years after Kroeber graduated—always unorthodox by undergraduate standards and often attacking the way undergraduate and even university affairs were managed. In senior year, largely due to Kroeber's influence, it criticized undergraduate instruction in history and pleaded for the teaching of cultural history. Just before the class of '96 was graduated, James Harvey Robinson was appointed to the Department of History. *The Morningside's* plea, which was really Kroeber's idea, perhaps had a little to do with this appointment.

In junior year we were permitted to choose a part of our courses, and our senior year was wholly elective. During this period, our little group began to drift apart in intellectual interests. It was then that Kroeber worked in the fields of philosophy, history, anthropology, and psychology, and came under the influence of Franz Boas. His final decision to study anthropology came as a shock to me; and many an argument did we have about it. I must confess that I did my best to dissuade him. We were both determined to devote ourselves to research. If, I argued, he wanted to spend his life in scientific investigation, why devote it to so vague, inchoate, and intangible a subject as anthropology in which clean-cut and definite conclusions were impossible; why not take some field you could get your teeth into, in which you knew where you stood and got a result or didn't. Kroeber's answer was to ask what you had when you did get a result in chemistry or physics. It was not likely to affect men's thinking and to make for progress in the only way that was worth while: to free man intellectually. The confused thinking about religions was perhaps the most important bar to man's progress and freedom. Anthropology was, he thought, capable of bringing some degree of clarity into the confused thought of men, and of freeing them to some degree from hoary tribal taboos. And so he proposed to see what he could do as an anthropologist. This presumably was not his only or his major reason for choosing anthropology, but it is the one argument in our discussions that remains with me after the lapse of these many years.

As a graduate student, he first had to face adversity; the Kroeber family suffered severe financial reverses. He had to decide between continuing in his chosen career as a scholar and going into some business that offered better prospects of immediate income but for which he felt himself fitted neither by temperament nor training and in which it was certain he would not be happy. The other stroke of fate he had to face was the death of his younger brother, Eddie, during the summer while Alfred was away on a field trip among the Arapaho in Indian Territory. He was miles away from a railroad or even a telephone at the time, and the message had to be taken to him by pony rider. Eddie Kroeber was very different in appearance, in temperament, and in interests from Alfred, but perhaps for this very reason they had been closer to one another than two brothers usually are.

Soon after receiving the doctor of philosophy degree from Columbia, Kroeber went to the University of California as an instructor in anthropology. In those days, he was a rather quiet young man, never a great talker, never trying to dominate his environment; but neither was he a follower of the crowd. He rarely had much to say except to his intimates, but he thought his own thoughts and went his own way. He could listen long without interjecting more than an occasional trenchant, provocative observation to egg the speaker on. Like many good listeners, he has the capacity to be objective, to see the other point of view, to penetrate behind another person's behavior to his underlying thought. He has always been good at divining motives. These traits indicate a sincerity and simplicity of character that primitive peoples sense at once and to which they respond by giving their confidence.

This interest in individuals as individuals, not merely as entities in a social group, probably accounts for his excursion into fields which would seem foreign to cultural anthropology, for example, psychiatry. He has made a serious study of abnormal psychology, especially of psychoanalysis. He actually did much clinical work and treated cases by psychoanalysis. Thirteen or fourteen years ago, he even made a serious trial at taking it up as a profession. The decade before had been a time of stress for him. The death of his first wife; the delay, due to the war, in the publication of his Handbook for seven years after it was finished; tardy recognition at his own institution and the financial worries thereby entailed—all these could not have made the war period and the years just before a particularly happy time. He perhaps felt himself in a blind alley, and his excursion into psychoanalysis was a fumbling for a way out. But he soon saw that he lacked utterly any trace of the charlatan's gift, without some measure of which only a limited success can be achieved in this sort of practice.

Gradually, however, recognition came and he again felt sure of himself. Though he had long demonstrated that he was a sound scholar and brilliant teacher, academic advancement was slow from his own institution and he was elected president of the American Anthropological Society (1917) before he was advanced to a full professorship (1919).

His is an essentially modest personality; he has too sound a sense of proportion to deceive himself in regard to values; he is too honest to deceive others. He is not the sort of person to take pride in the machinery of university administration, to push himself forward into the chairmanship of administrative committees—in short, to play a conspicuous rôle in university politics. He has preferred to make his way through the originality of his scholarship and the soundness of his teaching.

II. PROFESSIONAL APPRECIATION

By Robert H. Lowie

INTIMATELY as Kroeber's name is linked with California, he won his spurs in the Plains area, among the Arapaho and the related Gros Ventre, whom he studied under the auspices of the American Museum of Natural History. The papers growing out of this experience foreshadow the breadth of his professional approach with its felicitous blending of theoretical and empirical interests. So far as circumstances permitted, he slurred over no phase of tribal life. Trained in the severe school of Franz Boas, he studied the languages, recording myths in aboriginal texts, and in collaboration with George A. Dorsey published one of the most substantial collections of Plains Indian tales (Dorsey and Kroeber, Traditions of the Arapaho, FMNH-PAS 5, Chicago, 1903). In the period of Kroeber's novitiate, primitive art was the cynosure of anthropological eyes, in America as well as abroad; and Professor Boas' relevant interests impressed themselves upon his students and assistants. Kroeber revealed the amazing subjectivism and wealth of Arapaho design and interpretations, thereby illuminating the basic problem of conventionalization from a realistic model versus secondary attachment of meaning (The Arapaho, Part I, AMNH-B 18, 1902). Equally important was his definition of tribal styles of decoration (Ethnology of the Gros Ventre, AMNH-AP 1:158–177, 1908). Using the scanty material then accessible, Kroeber characterized not only the Arapaho and Gros Ventre, but practically all Plains peoples and evinced his distinctive ability of extracting significant results from refractory and elusive raw data. The second part of his Arapaho monograph (1904) had an equally decisive effect on subsequent research. It was for the first time that anything like so detailed a report had appeared on the age societies of the Plains. Schurtz's theoretical treatise on Altersklassen und Männerbünde had appeared two years previously and lent special piquancy to the new account. Kroeber himself sensed the inherent problems and outlined them in the light of the material then extant (The Ceremonial Organization of the Plains Indians of North America, ICA, 15th Session, Tome II, Quebec, 1907). He thus blazed the trail for one of the American Museum's major research projects—the intensive investigation of age societies (see AMNH-AP 11:1–992, 1912–1916).

While Kroeber never joined the permanent staff of the American Museum of Natural History, contacts with that institution stimulated his work in two directions, leading him in one case to a new area for field investigation, in the other to intensive library research. With the renaissance of sociological interest in kinship nomenclatures through Rivers' Kinship and Social Organization (1914) came the discovery that data needed for testing these theories were lacking for the Southwestern United States. Kroeber had already published a strikingly original paper on Classificatory Systems of Relationship (JRAI 39:77–84, 1909), which shifted the emphasis to the nonsocial factors determining the evolution of relationship terms. When, therefore, Dr. Wissler offered the opportunity to determine the kinship facts among a typical Pueblo tribe, Kroeber readily grasped it. The results are embodied in his Zuñi Kin and Clan (AMNH-AP 18:39–205, 1917), a paper that not only bore on the immediate goal of the expedition but set new problems as to the structure of Pueblo society. The other task assumed for the Museum was the study of its Philippine collections and the consequent writing of a volume for its Handbook Series entitled "Peoples of the Philippines" (1919).

Kroeber's versatile mind has concerned itself with a greater variety of subjects than probably any of his coevals. *Nullum fere anthropologiae genus non tetigit, nullum quod tetigit non ornavit.* He has dealt with racial bloodgroups and Australian languages, with pottery sherds and secret cults, with forms of arrow release and the most basic questions of anthropological method (e.g., History and Science in Anthropology, AA 37:539–569, 1935). To use the familiar pigeonholes, he has worked in linguistics, in archaeology, in ethnography and general culture history, as well as in theory. He has even shown a definite interest in physical anthropology, though of late mainly through intelligently following the achievements of others and assimilating them for the light they may shed on borderline problems. To linguistics he has devoted considerable energy, recording, analyzing, and classifying American Indian languages, as well as studying the reports on other aboriginal stocks. His tendency has been to substitute major units for the traditional families recognized in the American field; and he thus allies himself with such scholars as Dixon, Swanton, and Sapir. Archaeologically he has himself directed excavations in Mexico and Peru, the latter under the auspices of Field Museum, Chicago, though the stimulus doubtless came from the excellent collections made for the University of California by Max Uhle and deposited in our Museum of Anthropology.

Archaeology differs from Ethnology only in technique and the range of subjects explorable by it; and Kroeber's achievement is clearly greatest in what constitutes their common denominator, the field of Culture. Circumstances have made him an Americanist—specifically, *the* undisputed authority on California. Conspicuously successful as Kroeber has been in building up one of the largest schools of anthropology in the world, it must not be forgotten that the University of California created its Department of Anthropology for research, instruction developing later and at first slowly. When Kroeber came to California in 1901 it was to organize an archaeological, linguistic, and ethnographic survey of the state. For many years he lived in San Francisco, with the center of his activities at the University Museum in the Affiliated Colleges group of buildings there rather than on the Berkeley campus. Technically, the Department was at first headed by Professor F. W. Putnam of Harvard, who spent part of his vacations in California; but the planning and execution of the gigantic project, the garnering of raw data and the interpretation of their broader significance devolved wholly on Kroeber. Dr. Pliny Earle Goddard joined the staff for several years, and produced a valuable description of the Hupa, but his interests during this period were riveted to the Athabaskan stock. Kroeber, on the other hand, very soon came to organize the chaotic maze of facts, summarizing his major findings for the benefit of his colleagues. As the spirit moved him he would define regional types of culture, the morphological peculiarities of native tongues, or the essence of aboriginal beliefs. Since the political boundaries of the state did not coincide with ethnic divisions, he was inevitably drawn into intensive consideration of other geographical units. Thus he came to conceive the Basin Shoshoneans as Californian hinterlanders; the Northwest California group of Indians as the southernmost outposts of coastal British Columbian cultures; Southern California as part of a "major Southwest" that embraces northern Mexico no less than Arizona and New Mexico.

These studies finally crystallized in the monumental Handbook of the Indians of California (BAE-B 78, Washington, 1925), the manuscript of which was complete in 1918. Its sole predecessor was Stephen Powers' Tribes of California (1877), a book to which Kroeber pays characteristically generous praise in the preface to his own, but which in no way serves the specialist's needs. For a proper appraisal, it is also necessary to remember that Dixon's outstanding monographs on the Maidu (1905; fieldwork begun in 1899) and Shasta (1907) represent very nearly the only investigations conceived independently of the Department of Anthropology of the University of California that do measure up to modern standards. N. C. Nelson's researches on shellmounds and R. L. Olson's excavations on the southern islands; Barrett's work among the Pomo; T. T. Waterman's ethnogeographic discoveries in the northwest; J. A. Mason's recovery of Salinan culture fragments; and E. W. Gifford's expeditions to various parts of the state, were all executed as parts of Kroeber's major scheme of Californian work.

The plan of the Handbook is in the highest degree characteristic of Kroeber's mental processes. There is no formal Introduction: the author plunges at once into a description of the northwestern Yurok, whence he proceeds in geographical order toward each of the tribes to the south and east; there follow three topical chapters—Arts of Life, Society, Religion and Knowledge—which succinctly summarize the essence of what precedes; and after further chapters on Population, Race Names, and Culture Provinces comes the concluding treatment of Prehistory. When the Handbook was written, definitive tribal studies were far fewer than today, with inevitable unevenness of treatment: the practically unknown Washo could not be described on the same scale as the Yurok or Mohave. But wherever the data sufficed, Kroeber created tribal pictures of rare lucidity. Characteristically, he plays no topical favorites: basketry and bows loom as large in their appropriate niches as marriage customs and ceremonialism. Finally, this ostensibly descriptive account is pervaded throughout by theoretical points, which however, *more suo,* grow directly out of Kroeber's inductive findings. Given the local exogamy of the Yurok, there naturally rises the question of the clan concept; but the author indulges in no abstract discussion of the Platonic idea of a "clan." Similarly,

Pomo boats prompt a wise digression on geographical determinism, but it is only such specific cases that evoke theoretical argument.

Kroeber's Handbook has remained *sui generis*. No Americanist colleague has ventured to compress the material on a comparable area within correspondingly grand compass. Yet he remains unsatisfied, and the Californian work proceeds under his guiding hand, with one model monograph succeeding the next, from Wm. D. Strong's papers on South Californian society and A. H. Gayton's on the Yokuts to Cora Du Bois' and D. Demetracopoulou's reports on the Wintu. What is more, the neighboring Basin area, thirty years ago a terra incognita, is rapidly becoming well known through Kroeber's students—Julian H. Steward, Isabel T. Kelly, and others.

Characteristically, Kroeber, the founder of probably the largest undergraduate courses in anthropology in the world, long fought shy of writing any general book. When he finally produced his Anthropology (1923), it promptly became one of the outstanding texts in the subject—notwithstanding its extraordinary organization from the angle of classroom use. It is a work representative, indeed, of the width of his interests, but also of his repugnance to systematic treatment—the same trait, we surmise, that makes him avoid courses on, say, Religion or Social Organization, though he has recently yielded to the demand for a semester's lectures on Primitive Art. His Anthropology is thus in the highest degree eclectic, dealing with such problems of method, human biology, prehistory, and culture history as appealed to the author at the time and deliberately avoiding explicit exposition of others, such as religion. Kroeber evidently prefers solving the varied problems that spontaneously arise in his fertile mind.

Not that Kroeber closes his mind to new ideas—quite the contrary. Ever ready to grapple with more and more ranges of fact, he also avidly seeks novel avenues to the arcana of Culture. At one stage of his progress he brings Dr. Lila O'Neale's expert knowledge to bear on the significance of Peruvian textiles; at other times he tests the psychoanalytic, the ecological, the statistical approach. Thus it is not inertia that makes him eschew new tasks but a repugnance to being coerced into a preordained scheme.

Yet one form of system lures him, and the exception is a vital one. Classifying himself as a historian, Kroeber naturally arranges phenomena in coherent chronological wholes, and it is the lack of the historical flavor that he finds distasteful in the writings of others. In a recent paper (AA 37:545, 547, 556, 558, 566, 1935) he has advanced to a metachronological concept of history that is not wholly clear to me—stressing its "descriptive integration" rather than its time sequences. However that be, his pictures of the Yurok and the Mohave exemplify his descriptive skill, his capacity for throwing into bold relief tribal individualities, while his "historical" outlook in the conventional sense places him among the outstanding contemporary diffusionists. Some of us are charier of invoking diffusion to explain parallels in culture, some of us are inclined to sketch the historic process with less heroically sweeping lines. For my part, Kroeber's most characteristic performance in this field—

his reconstruction of Californian culture strata—forcibly recall's Haeckel's genealogical trees. Both schemes emerged from a potent urge to see a developmental series with a maximum of concrete detail; both are preëminently provocative and by the very opposition they arouse have stimulated further research.

Throughout his career Kroeber has been attracted by the ultimate riddles of anthropology. How is culture related to race? What is the bearing of psychology on ethnology? How does ethnology fit into the hierarchy of learned disciplines? On these questions and their correlates he has again and again risen to give testimony, as witnessed by his Eighteen Professions (AA 17: 283–288, 1915), The Superorganic (*ibid.*, 19:163–213, 1917), and his recent discussion, History and Science in Anthropology (*ibid.*, 37:539–569, 1935). His explicit credo reveals a deep sense of the uniqueness of cultural happenings, and would seem to imply an aversion to the laboratory scientist's "proofs" and "laws." But Kroeber's mind is happily not cribbed by a formal confession of faith. He has often enough demonstrated the validity of his views—even if he avoided syllogisms; and while deprecating the formidable title of "laws," he is now as he has been in the past on an eager quest for cultural regularities (see his Principle of Order in Civilization as Exemplified by Changes of Fashion, AA, 21:235 ff., 1919).

An insatiable and omnivorous seeker of knowledge, a rare observer of aboriginal life, equally skillful in delineating and interpreting its manifestations, Kroeber has created for himself a place not only of honor but of distinction in the history of his chosen science.

THE ARMY WORM: A FOOD OF THE POMO INDIANS

By S. A. Barrett

Among the Pomo, as among most Californian tribes, practically everything in nature was called upon to furnish its quota of foods. Insects were not omitted from the dietary of this tribe, grasshoppers, angleworms, yellow-jacket grubs, and various others being esteemed.

Perhaps the most interesting insect used as food by the Pomo is the so-called army worm [li' (C)]. Like certain other insects this worm has a cycle which causes it to appear in vast numbers once every several years. The exact periodicity is not known and could not be determined by questioning the Indians.

It happened to be the writer's good fortune to drop in at the Yokaia rancheria on the morning of May 15, 1904, only to find that the entire village was deserted except for two of the very aged. From these he learned that the entire population had moved down to a certain grove on the eastern bank of Russian river, where the army worms had suddenly appeared in hordes, the first time since 1898. Taking one of these old men along in the buggy, for he was too feeble to walk the several miles, the author immediately joined in the "hunt" and spent the entire day observing the gathering of this, the rarest, of all Pomo foods. The following statements are not, therefore, mere hearsay but direct personal observations confirmed by photographs, four of which are reproduced here in plates 1 and 2.

The army worm is a caterpillar which is almost hairless, having not to exceed half a dozen hairs on its entire body. It is about 2½ inches in length and is a general brownish color with Indian red stripes along the sides. The male [li'baiya (C)] is distinguished, according to the Indians, from the female [li'mata (C)] by the fact that it has a pinkish white belly, while the belly of the latter is always yellow in color.

According to the Indians' statements this worm comes only for at most a few days, in the early summer and only in years when there is a great deal of fog. It is said to belong to Thunder and to travel on the fog from the west. It feeds exclusively on the leaves of the ash [kala'm (C)], and when an army of these worms finishes with a grove of this species there is not a vestige of green to be seen. Plate 1, figure 1, shows some very small ash saplings at the edge of an opening and immediately adjacent to the larger ash trees of a grove. These had been completely stripped by the army worms so that they looked like the naked branches of deciduous bushes in the winter time.

It is an interesting fact that these worms move from tree to tree or from grove to grove chiefly in the afternoon. From observations made, this fact may be explained as due to the sun's heat. Eating during the night and early part of the day, the worms divest the trees of their leaves and the sun's rays pour in upon them, causing them to drop to the earth and seek the shelter of the leafy canopy of another ash which has not been disturbed. There is of course more or less movement of the worms all day long for, regardless of the hour, if a tree has been stripped of its leaves the worms descend to earth in search of a new food supply. However, by far the greatest number move in the afternoon. Their descent from the tree is as a rule most precipitate. They simply let go and drop, and this apparently without harm to themselves, regardless of the height. Almost never is one seen to descend the trunk of a tree. During the day the author spent in this ash grove, he was subjected to a continuous hail of falling army worms and a shower of leaf fragments dropped by the worms from their lofty dinner table.

The Indians know very well the route the worms will take when they do drop to the ground and move on to the next ash tree or grove. They prepare for this advance by digging large numbers of pits and trenches across the line of march of the worms and by encircling the bases of the ash trees toward which they are moving. These pits are of various sizes and shapes, circular, square, or rectangular. Each is about 6 inches in width and rarely more than 2½ feet in length. They are always from 4 to 6 inches in depth, and are vertical-walled little moats dug in the solid damp sand. As the worms race over the ground, with incredible rapidity, they fall into these little moats in large numbers. Yet seeing that they can ascend the vertical trunk of a tree, surely a vertical wall of solid damp sand proves no obstacle and they will climb out of this prison with the utmost ease. And so they would if it were not for the clever device employed to prevent just that kind of escape. When the little moats are dug the Indians bring over a quantity of fine, dry sand, with which they line the edges of the tops of these pits. The captive caterpillar finds no difficulty whatever in ascending the vertical wall of his prison, but when he reaches the edge of the pit his feet encounter the line of shifting, dry sand so that he loses his balance and topples over backward to the bottom of the pit again. Try as he may, he never can get out so long as the line of dry sand lasts at the edge of the pit. For this reason fresh dry sand is added from time to time. Also this line of dry sand serves another purpose. While it is true that these worms race along at great speed they are cautious to a certain extent. When they reach the edge of such a pit they could easily turn aside. They, however, are on the dry sand which shifts and rolls them headlong to the bottom of the pit.

There is one means of escape, however, which must be carefully watched. When a pit is fairly well filled with worms, the topmost ones can make their escape fairly easily. Therefore pits must be emptied quite frequently to prevent this.

In plate 1, figure 2, we have a very characteristic set of these sand-lined pits completely surrounding the base of a tree. In this particular instance, there were fourteen circular pits each about 6 inches in diameter and together making about 120 degrees of the circle. There were also six rectangular pits varying from 9 to 30 inches in length. These finished the line which completely encircled the base of this tree, and which formed a circle about 5½ feet in diameter. The spaces between successive pits is not to exceed an inch in each case, a space too small to allow a worm much chance to slip by on the dry rolling sand.

Another tree had a circle about 25 feet in diameter encircling its base and made by only eighteen pits varying in length from 1 to 3½ feet. Each had a width of about 6 inches and was 6 inches in depth.

Other such pits are arranged in straight or curved lines many feet in length across the general line of march of the army worms. One such set of

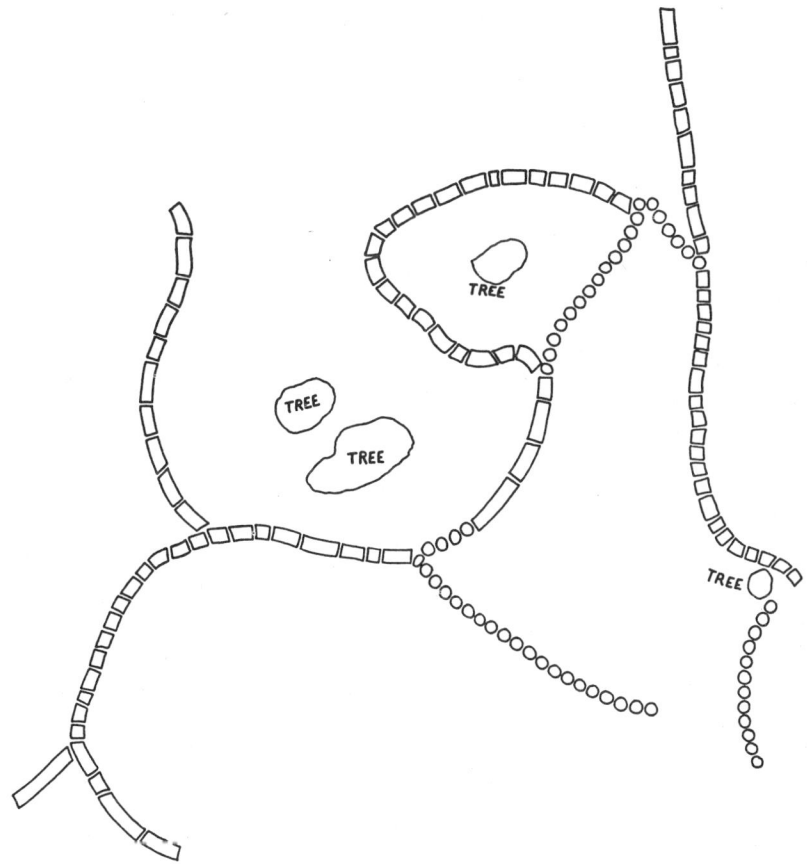

Fig. 1. A system of sand-lined pits for catching army worms.

pits numbered forty-two. They were rectangular and varied from 6 to 15 inches in length. Another line of thirty-seven pits measured nearly 50 feet in length. Another rather intricate pit system is shown in figure 1.

With all these deadly pitfalls we might think that no worms could possibly escape. However, some do, and to insure the fullest possible harvest, the Indians place girdles or collars [lī hubeu (C)] of ash leaves about the bases of the trees, 3 or 4 feet from the ground, as shown in plate 1, figure 2. The worms that do run the gauntlet and escape the pits start to ascend the tree, are arrested by the fresh ash leaves, and are easily collected by hand.

EXPLANATION OF PLATES

Plate 1: fig. 1, ash saplings stripped by army worms; fig. 2, sand-lined pits for catching army worms, surrounding the base of a tree.

Plate 2: fig. 1, live army worms crawling on the inner surface of a basket; fig. 2, Pomo woman sifting worms in an openwork basket to separate them from ashes after roasting.

ASH SAPLINGS; SAND-LINED PITS.

LIVE WORMS; POMO WOMAN SIFTING ROASTED WORMS.

Other workers also obtain quite a harvest by hand-picking worms from the low young ash saplings.

When the worms are obtained, whether it be from the pits, from the collars, or from the saplings, they are immediately placed in a vessel of ordinary cold water, where they quickly drown.

They are then roasted in hot ashes or are boiled and are devoured in large quantities on the spot. When everyone has satisfied his appetite, the cooked worms are spread out in the sun to dry for winter use.

Plate 2, figure 1, shows some of the live worms crawling about on the inner surface of a basket before being placed in the water. Plate 2, figure 2, shows a Pomo woman sifting out some of the army worms. They are first placed, with live coals and hot ashes, in a tightly woven basket to roast, after which they are placed in an openwork sifting basket, to separate them from the ashes. This method of cooking turns the worms a reddish color and is said to produce a very excellent sweet flavor.

Custom requires that conversation shall be carried on in low tones and that no undue noise shall be made by those gathering the army worms, because it is said that the worms become alarmed and leave. If any noise is made the army worms in the immediate vicinity will stop eating, raise the forward half of their bodies at an angle of about 30 degrees and sway the elevated part of the body rapidly back and forth in agitation for some time.

No one may speak crossly to another under penalty of being bitten by a rattlesnake.

Loeb,[1] in speaking of the army worm, states that they are gathered with much ceremony and great solemnity. His information comes from the Northern Pomo and is undoubtedly merely a statement made by an informant. It does not correspond with the above direct observations among the Central Pomo. In our work we found no solemnity; on the contrary we found much joy, though not boisterous, for reasons already stated. There was no singing of ceremonial songs and no idea that this food must be kept and treated with special respect. It was eaten on the spot and handled in every way just as any other food might be.

Just as the army worm appears, so suddenly and mysteriously does he disappear. Without warning of any kind he is gone and does not reappear again for several years.

It was really a red-letter day in any Pomo community when this little caterpillar made his appearance, and the Indians made this the occasion not only of an immediate feast but they stored for winter use as large quantities as possible of the dried caterpillars. No opportunity presented itself to check the amount dried upon this particular occasion, but certainly several hundred pounds of the dried product were garnered by the inhabitants of this relatively small village.

---

[1] Pomo Folkways, UC-PAAE 19:164.

MILWAUKEE PUBLIC MUSEUM,
MILWAUKEE, WISCONSIN.

PROBLEMS IN THE STUDY OF MIXE MARRIAGE CUSTOMS

By Ralph Beals

A BRIEF SURVEY of the marriage practices of the Mixe Indians will be used in this paper to suggest the complexity of problems which surround the study of many of the surviving native peoples of Mexico. The single institution of marriage is selected as an illustration because in the case of the Mixe it lends itself readily to a brief exposition of some of these problems. Not only may one describe a living institution, but also survey the variety of its social functions, analyze to some extent the processes by which the institution is changing and has changed, and finally one may arrive at certain historical deductions regarding past developments and the influences to which the Mixe have been subjected.

The Mixe inhabit an extremely rugged area extending about seventy miles westward from the Isthmus of Tehuantepec in southern Mexico. They are located almost entirely along the north side of the continental divide. Their numbers are somewhat under 40,000, distributed in between 40 and 45 villages which vary in population from 350 to 3000.

The study upon which this discussion is based was confined to the westernmost group of Mixe, inhabiting some eighteen villages located on or very close to the enormous mountain mass of Zempoaltepec. The elevation of these villages varies from 4500 to 9500 feet. Practically all are located in or near the rain forest belt, which shows marked variations in altitude between the limits just given. Rainfall is very heavy and the climate foggy and cold, although frost and snow are rare in the inhabited areas. The soil is poor and the majority of the cultivated fields are too steep to admit of plowing. Agriculture is therefore still largely by primitive *milpa* methods. Corn, a few beans, and still fewer watery squash were, until recently, the only plants raised. They are supplemented in the diet by coffee, chile sauce, and small quantities of meat, the latter usually on ceremonial occasions only.

The meagerness of the diet reflects the poverty of the material culture, certain aspects of which nevertheless show considerable variation from village to village. There is a slight degree of village specialization in handicrafts. Social organization and religion, although richer than the utilitarian aspects of culture, are still relatively simple, with occasional rather surprising elaborations. Between villages, there is considerable differentiation which needs further study and the significance of which cannot be entirely clear until knowledge of the remaining Mixe as well as of the surrounding native groups is available.

Among the more complex nonmaterial aspects of the culture are the customs surrounding marriage. Nevertheless, a socially recognized and approved mar riage may consist simply of a man and woman living together for a reasonable length of time. This is paradoxical only when viewed as an isolated statement. While the simple act of living together is certainly considered entirely valid, it is neither the only form of marriage nor the one most frequently practiced. Nevertheless, it must be emphasized that it is a socially recognized institution of thorough respectability.

The existence of this simple form of marriage makes it necessary to consider the Mixe attitude toward sex relations. Are more casual sexual encounters institutionalized? To a certain extent they are, depending upon the surrounding circumstances, but whether merely tolerated or institutionalized, none are classed as marriage and none receive social approbation.

The Mixe attitude toward sex matters is extremely lenient. Chastity is not particularly expected, although it may return a woman very definite rewards in social recognition. Casual sexual encounters are fairly frequent, particularly among unmarried people. Illegitimate children are not discriminated against in any way. The unmarried mother may or may not have social stigma attached to her, depending entirely upon the circumstances. In a case in point, a wealthy man forbade his daughter to marry the man of her choice. When the girl had a child by her lover, censure was voiced for the family but not for the girl, although it was rumored that she still maintained secret relations with the father of the child.

On the other hand, women may go about alone freely, even on the loneliest trails, without fear of molestation or comment, with one exception. If a woman have the reputation of being free with her favors, she may be accosted. Cases of rape are virtually unknown.

For the most part irregular sexual relations do not receive community recognition unless they follow a certain pattern. The woman who lives with a man for a month or two, then leaves him and is found living with another man a short time later, is in danger of incurring a real social stigma. One separation may be put down to an error in choosing her partner, but should she leave the second man in an equally short time, she is almost certain to be classed as a *soltera,* a "bachelor girl." She is then a member of an institutionalized group where her chances of marriage are very slim, far less, in fact, than those of the girl whose casual sexual encounter has left her with a child to advertize the fact but who has not lived with a man. The latter may marry fairly well; no man seriously looking for a wife would choose a soltera. Moreover, the soltera has her position advertised by being forced to attend certain portions of the town fiesta where instead of mingling with the women in the kitchen she sits with other solteras among the men and is treated with an attitude of levity never accorded other women.

The shield is two-faced, however. Although a man who acts in the same way is never thus publicly set apart, his chances of marriage are equally ruined. Let him live briefly with several women and he is known throughout the community as a soltero, one whom no sensible woman would think of marrying.

It is evident from these attitudes that the essential factor in marriage for the Mixe is intent. If a couple makes a serious effort to set up a permanent relationship, raising children and establishing an economic partnership, this is regarded by the Mixe as a marriage. If an honest effort fails, separation may occur without noticeably injuring the standing of either party. However, unless obvious incompatibility is involved, there is apt to be an assumption that one of the parties failed to live up to the implied terms of the marriage. The wife may be suspected of laziness or the husband of being a wife-beater. Consequently divorce is generally avoided as long as possible, for such a reputation would make remarriage difficult for the party deemed responsible.

Although marriage may be such a simple affair, in most towns a more elaborate form is more commonly observed. A man will go with his father or some old man to ask the consent of the girl's parents. Her own wishes are invariably consulted, her negative being final although her consent may be overridden by the parents. Even though everyone is agreeable, tradition prescribes three visits before consent is given.

Shortly after an affirmative reply (but sometimes as much as a year later), the young man gives a one- to three-day ceremony in his father's house or, more commonly, in one which he has built himself. Should he be unable to pay for this ceremony, he may work for the girl's parents for a year instead. The ceremony is rather complex, involving formal speeches, presents, and feasting with certain ceremonial foods. Usually the groom gives the bride a small present, from which evidently comes the only name applied to the affair, the Spanish word *prenda* (gift). There is dancing, and the guests are expected to drink all that is offered to them.

This form of marriage, with variations in detail, occurs in all of the nine western Mixe towns in which I made inquiries, although it is beginning to disappear in three villages at present most subject to Mexican influence. It may or may not be succeeded by a civil or church marriage. In any case such would not normally occur until a year or more after the prenda.

It is very clear that the Mixe regard the prenda as the essential wedding ceremony in point of social recognition. In case of marriage without the prenda, a couple's intentions require the proof of time. A young man who gives the prenda, on the other hand, may be praised publicly by the municipal officials as one who recognizes his responsibilities, the marriage being immediately socially acceptable.

Church weddings are most frequent in towns with resident priests, but even here it is resorted to by only a small portion of the population. One bar is the question of cost. Even the prenda involves the aid of relatives to meet the expense; the church wedding usually will run over sixty pesos, a sum almost no Mixe can secure without borrowing.

Church marriage serves a twofold purpose. It advertises to the community the ability of the family to pay for such a marriage, thus placing them in the upper social stratum insofar as any stratification exists in Mixe society. (Economic superiority and the holding of certain offices are practically the only recognized social distinctions. The holding of the really important offices is itself dependent upon economic status, as such offices always involve sacrifice of wealth.) Furthermore, it is a public affirmation that the woman has faithfully performed her part of the marriage duties. She has retained the admiration of her husband and has won the respect of his family to the extent that they are willing to help pay for the ceremony.

In recent years civil marriage has shown a marked increase, since it became largely a matter of registry. Almost all people who have a church wedding also observe the civil marriage. In towns without resident priests there is a definite tendency to attach to civil marriage the sort of social implications elsewhere attached to a church wedding.[1]

The vitality of the marriage institutions, coupled with their current tendency to alter, is a common characteristic of much of Mixe culture and parallels the situation existing in most of the native cultures of Mexico. Even in the most remote portions of the Mixe area, one encounters villages in which there is a tendency to look toward a new kind of life, and often a conscious effort to reform village life along more modern lines.

In accordance with this movement, Mixe villages may be classed rather readily as progressive or conservative, plus a certain intermediate group. In the progressive villages a considerable portion of the men speak Spanish; the government schools, established in 1928, are larger and more effective; non-Christian rituals are discouraged and in some places carried on only secretly by a conservative minority. Generally these progressive towns are those which have had a resident Catholic priest for many years, and they frequently lie on the borders of Mixe territory, where they are more exposed to outside influences. None of them, however, is nearer than a long day's travel on foot (about 25 miles over mountain trails) to either a Mexican village or a road.

Certain differences in marriage customs conform to the distinction between progressive and conservative. Church marriages are very rare in conservative towns, while in the progressive towns the prenda is obviously on the decline. Church marriages are not on the increase, however: rather is civil marriage becoming a substitute.

Variations of this type seem largely connected with the matter of progressiveness and conservatism. Other distinctions between towns are of a different order. In most of the towns service for the bride's family is a recognized but rarely used substitute for the prenda. In the progressive town of Juchila, however, service for the bride's family is obligatory for a year before marriage and the prenda is lacking. Elaborate gifts are given throughout the period in addition to the service. After marriage, residence as elsewhere is customarily in a house built by the husband, but if he have no house of his own, the couple will never reside with the husband's family. Instead, residence is temporarily with the bride's family, a complete reversal of the practice in near-by villages.

---

[1] This is a most meager statement of the social functions of the various types of marriage. Individual significances, psychological attitudes, problems of property and social stabilization, and the matter of prestige values are all much more complex than indicated.

This distinction cannot be associated with the difference between conservative and progressive towns. As Juchila is the most easterly of the villages visited, it may represent a regional distinction, possibly of ancient antecedents. This question cannot be answered until further study is made, and is raised here only to show the type of problem encountered.

The variation in marriage customs and the distinction between progressive and conservative towns suggest that the Mixe would be an ideal group for the type of study carried on in several recent investigations of native groups in Mexico. These studies have assumed that comparable differences indicate the degree of change from the traditional and illiterate folk-culture to the more sophisticated culture of the cities. In some cases a certain "stratification" has been postulated, a series of cultural horizons, which appear as a result of the comparison of villages in various stages of development or change from the folk-culture.[2]

In line with such a study, one might take Oaxaca, oldest and first Spanish town in the state and terminus of the railroad from Mexico City, as the focal center of the region. Next in order would be the subsidiary Indian towns of the Valley of Oaxaca, connected with the capital by branch railroads or primitive roads. Third might come the progressive villages in the Mixe Sierra, with succeeding series of the intermediate and conservative villages. The various types and conditions of marriage would then presumably be open to explanation in terms of the transition from a folk-culture.[3]

There is, indeed, a certain validity in this approach. The progressive villages are indubitably those which have been most in contact with the outside world through the presence of resident priests and, in some cases, through their location with reference to good trails. It is there that the church wedding is most common and the prenda is tending to disintegrate. Civil marriage likewise, in recent years, has become relatively frequent.

On the other hand, there are difficulties in the way of wholesale interpretation by this method, particularly if consideration of the historical and comparative aspects of the study is reduced to a minimum, as has been the case in past studies of this type. An avowed lack of interest in any effort to approximate the nature of the pre-Spanish culture has marked studies of the folk-culture in transition. Conclusions as to the nature of the contemporary changes cannot achieve the soundness that comes from the fullest possible understanding of the background of the folk-culture, which is to be attained by intensive use of the historical and comparative approach. Only in this way can inter-

---

[2] This reference is obviously to Redfield's viewpoint. Cf. Robert Redfield, Culture Changes in Yucatan, AA 36:57–69, and Redfield and Villa, Chan Kom, A Maya Village, Carnegie Institution of Washington, Publication 448. All such efforts stem primarily from Gamio's work at Teotihuacan, even though the ancestry is not always recognized. In general it is felt that such approaches slight the historical and comparative background. The first paper by Redfield, cited above, ostensibly deals with the historical changes, but it actually outlines the "stratification" theory and the analysis of historical change is submerged in his interest in the contemporary process as first evinced in his work at Tepoztlan.

[3] This statement is perhaps unfairly oversimplified, as the actualities are much more complex. Essentially, however, it summarizes the situation for such an approach.

pretation of any current process take into full account the possible significances of acceleration and lag in different aspects of the culture.[4]

Naturally, it would not be feasible to give a complete analysis of the situation with regard to the Mixe now, even though the studies so far carried on in the region were adequate. Nevertheless, a few pertinent suggestions may reasonably be made within the limits of this paper.

Perhaps the most significant problem in connection with marriage customs concerns the nature of the prenda and its present tendency toward disintegration, particularly in certain of the progressive villages. The prenda itself is a puzzling institution. It is known only by a Spanish name, yet it is in no discernible respect Spanish in origin. Without fully reviewing the evidence, it may be said that light appears only when comparative and historical sources are fully reviewed over a large area.

A ceremony, essentially the same as the prenda except for its much greater elaborateness, is found in a number of Zapotec villages, for example, Mitla. Here it passes under a native name and is viewed as a betrothal ceremony, to be followed perhaps a year later by a church wedding, although the marriage is usually consummated at once. In effect, it is a trial marriage which, if it proves unsatisfactory, will never be completed by a church wedding. Again, both in its elements and in its purpose, the ceremony cannot be considered of Spanish origin.

Although historic sources on the Zapotec give no light on the origin of the institution, a passage in Burgoa describing the wedding of a Mixtec chieftain, makes it highly probable that the Mitla betrothal ceremony is but a somewhat simplified version of the ancient Mixtec, and by inference, the ancient Zapotec marriage ceremony.[5]

The Mixe prenda, then, appears to have been borrowed from the Zapotecs, but borrowed within historic times and given a Spanish name, Spanish being the principal medium of communication between Zapotec and Mixe. The adoption of the prenda, however, must have been without benefit of Spanish influence, since the principal white contacts of the Mixe until the last eight years have been almost entirely with the priests and missionaries, who would have had no interest in transmitting a ceremony which in its entire social functioning did not conform to Catholic usage. This inference is borne out by numerous other indications that not only were many Zapotec customs borrowed, but many purely Spanish items in the present Mixe cultural inventory were borrowed from the Zapotecs after undergoing a degree of acculturation.

The present decline in the prenda is, then, the decline of a Zapotec custom borrowed by the Mixe in post-Conquest time. It is being replaced by a less

---

[4] Thus Sr. Gamio, in conversation with the writer in 1933, made it quite clear that he retained little interest in what the native cultures had been or how they had arrived at their present development. His expressed interest at the time was purely in the elements which could be best utilized in accelerating the incorporation of the Indian culture into the larger Mexican civilization. Mr. Redfield throws a sop to history, but essentially his interest is the same, even though not associated with the nationalistic and patriotic ideals of Sr. Gamio.

[5] Francisco de Burgoa, Palestra historial, 2:176, Mexico, 1670–74.

complex marriage more in accord with the basic simplicity of Mixe culture, perhaps approximating an earlier marriage form.

The influence of the modernization movement is to be discerned, not in the decline of the prenda, but in the tendency to eliminate from this early simple marriage, the scanty surviving ceremonial associations of turkey sacrifice and meal offerings and in the increasing importance of civil marriage. Certain developments in the latter, however, are definitely not due to the breakup of the folk-culture. Rather is civil marriage being absorbed into the folk-culture.

This process of absorption is well demonstrated in the ultra-conservative village of Yacoche. Civil marriage here occupies a place comparable to church marriage in the progressive towns. It is gradually being integrated, however, with a common form of marriage in which a pseudo-church ceremony is performed by the *capillo,* leader of the band and of course a Spanish importation. In addition there is feasting with ceremonial foods and the offering of turkey sacrifices. This incorporation is strictly comparable to the early introduction of the prenda. The culture has been slightly altered by the intrusive element. It has not changed, however, from a folk-culture to any perceptible degree. The new element has rather been modified to fit logically within the framework of the folk-culture without distorting the basic pattern.

The influence of the progressive party may well wane in time in view of the enormous economic obstacles to raising living standards and the futility of inculcating literacy among a people who live under conditions where it serves no useful function. If this occurs, a future generation of ethnographers may find themselves faced with the puzzling situation of an official of obviously Spanish origin playing the central part in a wedding ceremony whose principal elements consist of ritual feasting and the offering of sacrificial turkeys and maize foods. No amount of explanation in terms of the disintegration of a folk-culture will be of any assistance to them.

The plurality of problems suggested in connection with the study of Mixe marriages represents to some extent the various possible methods of approach at present in good standing in anthropological literature. The legitimacy of these approaches in themselves is unquestioned, but the fullest possible interpretation should be the objective sought by any method of approach. It is believed that consideration of Mixe marriage customs indicates that dedication to a single objective should be accompanied by a thorough exploration of the possibilities offered by other methods.

University of California at Los Angeles,
Los Angeles, California.

THE RELATIONS BETWEEN PHYSICAL AND SOCIAL ANTHROPOLOGY

By Franz Boas

DURING THE LAST DECADES physical anthropology and social anthropology have drifted more and more apart. This seems unavoidable on account of the difference in subject matter and the necessity of a thorough biological training for the one branch, while the other requires a knowledge of ethnological methods. With the wide extent of either field it is hardly possible to combine the two adequately.

Nevertheless some method must be found, if the important borderland between the two is not to be neglected—much to the detriment of either.

It may be conceded that the purely morphological study of early forms of man and of races is a matter that should be treated by the morphologist. It is more doubtful whether the study of living races can be left entirely to him. He must include in his study the determining factors that stabilize or differentiate racial types: heredity, environment, and selection as well as the occurrence of mutations. The social anthropologist is interested in the history of society and for this reason he has to know the origin and history of each type. Its distribution may throw important light upon historic events. The physical anthropologist has to answer many questions of the student of society. Is the similarity of two types living in remote countries due to genetic relationship or to parallel mutations? Is, for instance, the type of the Ainu due to an old genetic relationship with Europeans, or is it a spontaneous mutation in the Mongolid race? What rôle has domestication played in the development of races? In how far have anthropometric measures a taxonomic value showing genetic relationship, or in how far are they determined by environment or selection? When the biologist—for so we may call the physical anthropologist—wants to answer these questions, he must be familiar with ethnic data. The attempts of certain anthropologists to analyze on the basis of measurements and observations a population and to discover the constituent races is, at present at least, a hopeless task. Without the most detailed knowledge of the laws of heredity of each feature considered, as well as of the effects of environment, the task is like that of a mathematician who tries to solve without any further data a single equation with a large number of unknown quantities. If anything is to be done on these lines the historical composition of the population has to be known in detail.

Any attempt at a morphological classification of races, excepting the very largest groups, like Negroes, Mongolids, Australians, does not lead to satisfactory results without knowledge of the conditions that have made the type what it is. A purely taxonomic description of local types determined by means of those traits that strike the observer as most frequently occurring in the population in question, or that may be proved to be so, do not clear up the history of the population. We might claim that the frequency of various values of the head index in southern Italy indicates descent from distinct hereditary groups and state that a certain percentage of "Alpine" types have intermingled with the "pure" Mediterranean strain; or we might claim that the frequency of blue eyes in Sicily corresponds to the amount of Norman blood. These conclusions are valueless if it cannot be shown that the cephalic index is solely determined by heredity and that in a "pure" race its variations do not exceed very narrow limits, and that blue eyes may not originate by mutation, as they certainly must have done at one time, and that this mutation may not occur again in any one of the strongly depigmented European populations.

Added to these difficulties is that of an adequate definition of type. Actually the type of a population is always an abstraction of the striking peculiarities of the mass of individuals which are assumed to be represented combined in a single individual. What the striking peculiarities are depends largely upon the previous experiences of the observer, not upon the morphological value of the observed traits. This explains the diversities of opinion in taxonomic classification. They all contain so many subjective elements without necessary morphological checks that conclusions based on them have slight value. A result of historical significance can be obtained only by a study of the many genetic lines constituting the population, not selected from the arbitrary point of view of which is "typical," but with due consideration of the variety of forms that occur, of their frequencies in succeeding generations, and of their response to varying environmental influences.

Classifications made on the basis of a selected number of traits, like those of Deniker and many others, have an interest from a purely statistical point of view, showing how certain traits are distributed, but they do not give us any right to differentiate between racial strains.

These difficulties are the greater the less marked the difference between two populations, either on account of their genetic relationship or on account of intermingling of types. They disappear only in those cases in which no overlapping of types occurs.

A purely subjective selection of racial types according to their local distribution, and even more so the attempts to select by subjective judgments typical forms as constituent elements of a population will never give us a true picture of racial history.

Where it can be proved historically that a population is mixed, such as the American Mulattoes, the half-blood Indians, or the half-castes of the Orient, biological questions arise that require a thorough knowledge of social conditions. If it were true, as has been claimed so often, that mixed bloods are inferior in physique to their parents of pure stock, or that disharmonies of forms will develop that have detrimental effects, it must still be asked who were the parents? Were they of normal value, or of inferior strains in the race to which they belong, and are the conditions under which the mixed population live equal to those of the two parental stocks? Without an answer to these questions, which require sociological knowledge, the biological inferences have little value. Data like those available on American Negroes show the strong influence of unfavorable social conditions, while those obtained from Pitcairn Island, from the South African Bastards, from Kisar, or from North American Indians show that mixed populations may preserve full vigor.

The considerations relating to the significance of taxonomic differences are the more important the greater the environmental influences upon the feature studied. Among bodily traits this is true, for instance, of stature and weight, which are quite variable under varying conditions. Still more significant is this variability in the study of physiological and psychological functions.

While the physical anthropologist is liable to look at functional phenomena as expressions of structure, the ethnologist will bear in mind the varying conditions influencing functions. Undoubtedly these are, to a certain extent, determined by structure, but they vary in the same individual according to conditions, so that in a large population, containing many distinct lines, similar outer conditions may produce functional similarities that may give the impression of being determined by racial descent, while actually they are due to similar conditioning. The interpretation of such phenomena requires the greatest caution, on account of the constant danger of considering as causally related anatomical and functional characteristics that are only accidentally related. This is particularly true of the attempts to correlate mental characteristics of populations and bodily form. It may be that differences in personality exist in races fundamentally distinct, but no convincing proof has been given so far that the observed differences are actually structurally determined, while the modification of various aspects of personality of members of the same race who live under changed conditions has been proved.

In this field particularly a clear understanding of the meaning of social conditions is essential if the grossest errors are to be avoided. Sameness of conditions is altogether too readily either assumed or overlooked. If Davenport and Steggerda assume equality of all social groups in Jamaica they overlook group differences which can be evaluated only by those intimately familiar with the social life of the people. On the other hand the experimentally determined similarities in very simple reactions of identical twins are overvalued when applied to complex activities dependent upon cultural situations.

COLUMBIA UNIVERSITY,
NEW YORK CITY.

FAMILY, CLAN, AND PHRATRY IN CENTRAL SUMATRA

By Fay-Cooper Cole

IN THE YEARS 1922 and 1923 the writer spent five months in the Padang Highlands of Central Sumatra in the interests of the Field Museum of Natural History. In that region live the Menangkabaú, one of the largest and in many ways the most advanced of Malayan peoples. Although several Dutch publications have dealt with their interesting and complex culture, it is only recently that an adequate review and compilation of the situation appeared in an American journal.[1] The present paper is an attempt to clear up some obscure points and apparent contradictions in the earlier discussions of the social system of this people.

Debate and contradiction begin with the mention of the name. To one group of natives this is derived from a nine-pointed iron spike attached to the head of a mythical buffalo which their ancestors pitted against the prize bull of a Javanese prince. The name of the spike, they say, was minang, hence the people were called Minangkabaú. A second group of local historians agree on all details up to the final name, which they say is Menangkabaú, "won karbau" or "winning karbau." Loeb credits it to the archaic expression pinang kabhu, "original home" of the Malays.[2]

Despite the fact that in physical type and language the population conforms to that branch of mankind known as Malay, their own traditions carry them back to Roman colonists or to Alexander the Great. They first appear in literature in the fourteenth century as a vassal state of the Hindu-Javanese empire of Madjapahit,[3] but it seems certain that Indian influence entered the region much earlier. For a time they exercised considerable power as an independent state or kingdom under the reigning group of Indian origin. In 1511 an embassy—said to be pagan—was sent to Abuquerque at Malacca,[4] but soon after that time the kingdom was converted to Mohammedanism. From the seventeenth century the power and influence of the native state declined, while at the same time the influence of the Dutch became increasingly strong. Each of these outside influences resulted in some changes, but the old life and customs still continue probably much as they were before the establishment of Indian rule. Beneath the veneer of Mohammedanism the people are essentially pagan. The power of the magician is still very great, while a belief in magic, in dreams, and in spirits of the ancient faith dominates the acts of the bulk of the population. Proper acts and sayings bring rain and sunshine; the flight of birds and the entrails of slain animals furnish omens; while tiger protectors and holy tigers roam the jungle near every settlement. High-sounding titles, relating to offices long since obsolete, add to the importance of families and individuals in a community which prides itself on its democracy.

---

[1] Loeb; see Bibliography at the conclusion of this essay, p. 27.
[2] *Ibid.*, 26.   [3] Encyl. Ned. Ind., 4:200.   [4] *Ibid.*, 207.

In an attempt to see the social organization as it is understood by the natives themselves I have sought to outline, so far as possible, the family of Datu Sati and to amplify with statements from other men of importance in the group.[5]

The smallest unit recognized in this society is the rumah or house, the members of which all trace their origin back to a single woman. In the case of Datu Sati we have eliminated from this discussion all generations above his mother and have ignored her sisters and their offspring. Her sisters and brothers would, of course, occupy the same position in her generation that Datu Sati and his sisters occupy in his. For our present purpose then, Datu Sati and his sisters are all descended from one woman, a (see fig. 2), who is called nīnī, oldest woman, ību, mother, or inú^k (induk), head woman. Had we included

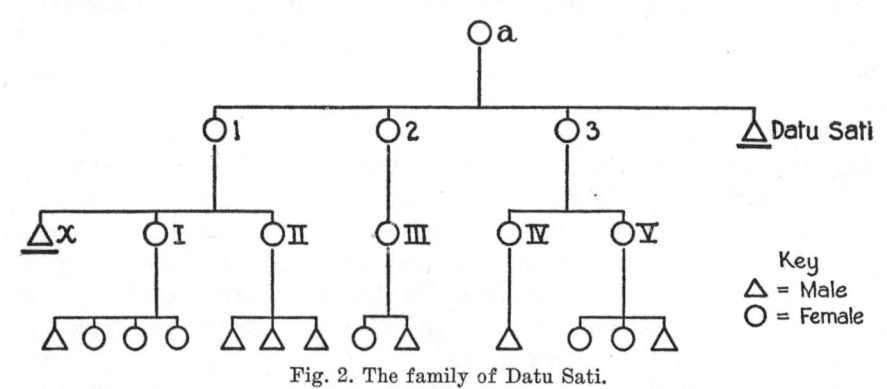

Fig. 2. The family of Datu Sati.

the offspring of her sisters they would have addressed her in the same manner as Datu Sati and his sisters, and they would have had equal rights in the house and lands.

Thus the family is made up of a head woman, her sons, her daughters and their children, and so on to succeeding generations. Her sons always retain their rights in the family property and may sleep in the general room at any time. However, they seldom live in the mother's house after about the age of fifteen; at that time they begin to spend their nights at the religious house near the mosque and continue this until marriage. It seems probable that this religious house is a perpetuation under Mohammedanism of a form of men's house so common in the southeastern Orient.

The daughters remain in the mother's house and when married are visited there by their husbands. Marriage is outside the house and clan, and the husband never acquires any rights in the house or property of his wife and children. The husband is called orang samando, or "borrowed man," a clear indication that he is not considered as a full member of the wife's group. His relationship to his children is recognized but is belittled; for, as the proverbs say: "A rooster can lay no eggs." "A mother is to her children as a hen to her chickens."

[5] The chief informants were Datu Sati of Suku Sikumang and Demang Tilatang of Pakan Kamis, but much additional material was gained from Lani Gelar Datu Serano and Ibrahim Gelar Datu Orang Kayo Besar of Batu Pelano (Sarik).

Each daughter has a room or compartment, in the long house, which is for the exclusive use of herself, husband, and children. All residents of the house frequent the common room at the front, and if all are on good terms they may use one cooking room and eat together. If, however, family differences or numbers make this arrangement difficult, a separate kitchen may be built for each daughter and her family.

All land and most other property belong to the rumah or house. When a girl marries, a plot of land is assigned to her and her husband to work. They have complete control of the products derived from it, except as they are called upon to share in the rumah expenses. But if the woman dies or is divorced, her husband's interest ceases at once. Goods accumulated by a married couple may be disposed of by gift while the owners are living, but if no provisions have been made for such personal belongings, the woman's share goes to her house, and the husband's to the house in which he was born.

A man never loses membership in his rumah. He has a right to return there at any time and partake in its food. He is nursed there when ill and takes part in its deliberations. In return he renders some service in the fields, in house building and repairs. All his privileges and loyalties are centered here, for, as the proverb says, "The carabao may roam but the pool remains."

An adult man, theoretically the brother or son of the nīnī, is chosen to be the head of the house and he then bears the title of mama^k rumah[6] or tuganai rumah. This selection is supposed to be made by all members of the house—male and female—but actually they usually give assent to a selection made long in advance. Only in the case of immaturity or incapacity of the regular claimant would the house assert its rights.

In figure 2 we find that Datu Sati, the son of *a*, is serving as mama^k rumah, and although there are actually other men of his age group—cousins—belonging to the house, he has in training his nephew, the son of his eldest sister 1. This boy acts as his assistant and in all probability will be chosen to succeed him.

In spite of the fact that the women and their children occupy the house and that inheritance is through them they are not all-powerful as has often been stated. The men have equal voice in all deliberations and one of them is chosen to represent the family.

The mama^k must keep in close touch with his nephews and nieces, to see that they are properly educated, to correct their faults, to assist in their undertakings. He must see that they are well married and that everything pertaining to the wedding goes according to the adat (customary law). He must look to the welfare of his people, to see that none of the family property becomes lost. He must keep watch that all live within the income of their property and that any surplus be added to the family wealth.

If property has been pawned he must know all the details and all the boun-

---

[6] Loeb (*ibid.*, 30) translates mama^k as mother's brother and traces it to a Tamil origin. In actual usage it may be applied to mother's brother, mother's son, to eldest sister's son or even to any son of any daughter of the house, if elected.

daries. With the consent of all the heirs he may arrange to pawn or lease land or other wealth. He uses family funds to make necessary replacements or he may demand service for such repairs. He receives complaints and gives judgment but he may be overruled by the family council. Finally he must always set a good example. For his services he receives no pay, other than his share in the family possessions, but he bears the additional title of gadang barliga, hereditary great, and on festive occasions wears a distinctive headdress. He is held in high esteem by his family and with their help may hope to gain a post of even greater honor.

Returning to Datu Sati: we learn that at the time he was chosen mama^k rumah, his mother and his sisters all lived in one house. His eldest sister 1 married and had three children—a son X, and two daughters, I and II. Sister no. 2 married and had one daughter, III; while sister no. 3 had two daughters, IV and V. These daughters married and had sons and daughters, as indicated in figure 2. This increase in the family led to the building of two additional houses on the lands of the original rumah. Such a grouping of relatives is called satu parui[7] or paruk, from one womb. If the grouping is large it is known as parui gadang, big womb, if small as parui ketek, small womb. Despite the fact that the family now lives in three houses they have all chosen to remain under Datu Sati and so are called sarumah, one house, as though they were still under one roof.

It frequently happens, however, in such a case that each house will select a mama rumah and it then becomes necessary for the whole family or parui to select one of these to represent the larger unit. This representative then bears the more distinguished title of pungulu, leader, and the whole group may then be called satu nīnī, one descent.

Since the rumah and parui are exogamous and matrilocal, the children of Datu Sati and the other males do not appear in figure 2. Their children belong to the families of their wives and are under the supervision of their maternal uncles. Despite the fact that mother's family and clan are considered more closely related to the child than are those of the father, the terms of address are similar. Thus a male child applies one general term to his mother and all the other women of her age group, in the rumah, but he also applies this term to father's sister. He can, however, use distinguishing terms for his real mother and her sisters. Likewise he uses one term for mother's mother and father's mother. Special terms may be used to indicate actual brother and sister and mother's sister's children but the child usually applies one term to all members of his own group in the rumah.[8]

As the community of Datu Sati grew, it attached to itself outsiders: friends, servants, people without families—mostly former slaves—until a considerable number have come to dwell on the lands of the original family. These outsiders own no land and have no voice in the government, but the adat says that the interests of all must be safeguarded. The pungulu usually adminis-

---

[7] The term hindu^k or satu indu^k, one head woman, is also used.

[8] Loeb (*ibid.*, 37) gives relationship terms in considerable detail.

ters the affairs of this larger group, but another male member of the rumah may be selected for the post. The division is known as a payung and its head then bears the title of capella payung or pungulu capella payung. According to a native saying, "the payung is a great tree in the middle of a plain, where you seek shelter from the rain and shade from the heat. You sit at the roots and lean against the trunk." "The pungulu should be wise and just, generous, patient and a good speaker. If he is not, the people under him are sheltered by a leaky roof." Hence all should be concerned in the training of his nephew so that he may become a good successor.

Several adjoining payung, each with its chief, make up a division known as suku. One of the payung chiefs is usually selected as chief officer and representative of the suku and is then known as pungulu adat, chief of customary law.

It seems probable that the suku is an outgrowth of the rumah and that most of its members are at least distantly related. It is so considered by the Menangkabaú and no marriage is supposed to take place within it. In ancient times death or expulsion was said to be meted out to any who violated the rule of suku exogamy. Today some of the suku are so large that the rumah most distantly related and those most closely associated are classed as "upper and lower suku" and marriage may be arranged between them if the consent of all the chiefs is obtained. Despite this growing laxity the feeling for exogamy is very strong. Its chief cause is blood relationship, real or assumed, but other causes are given. If a woman belonging to a suku with which marriage would normally be permitted were to serve as a wet-nurse in a house, she immediately would set up marriage barriers between her offspring and those of the family she serves, for according to the adat "those who draw from the same breast may never marry." It sometimes happens that several houses belonging to different suku are built so close together that all draw water from the same well or spring. This circumstance at once establishes marriage prohibitions between them for "those who draw from the same well may never marry." Despite these restrictions in marriage as it relates to the mother's suku, no such rules apply to blood relations on the father's side. Since the Menangkabaú are all now Mohammedans, four wives are permitted. The first wife should preferably be chosen from the father's suku and father's sister's daughter is a suitable match.

Property belonging to the various rumah within a suku is considered the property of the larger group. This is particularly true of real property, none of which can be alienated without the consent of all the suku chiefs. Theoretically one must be born into the suku and rumah, but adoption is possible. When this occurs the newcomer pays a price for his rights in the suku and family property. Once accepted he enjoys all the privileges of the old settlers.

The next larger unit is the negari. Theoretically it should consist of four suku,[9] but at the present time it may be made up of any number—thus the negari of Sarik has eleven suku. All suku in the negari are supposed to have

---

[9] Suku means "one-fourth" or "leg."

the same customary law and any outsiders dwelling there must conform. In sharp contrast to the exogamy of the suku, which constitute it, the negari is endogamous. It is explained that husband and wife with different customs are sure to quarrel, so that marriage is confined to the negari. So strong is this feeling that no man is allowed to marry into a negari not his own, and should a girl leave her negari she loses all rights in it. If her children come back they may share in her family rights.

Each negari has a council house called balei where the suku heads gather to discuss matters of mutual interest. It is said that formerly all the pungulu were equal. But in some districts where the autocratic party (see p. 25 below) is in control, these suku headmen are now graded, the most important often being called pungulu capella, head or chief pungulu. According to the adat such a chief comes from the parui and not from the suku, for "the people of ancient times had only rumah and parui, but no suku." Also the Dutch government has found it convenient to deal with this larger unit and has increased the power of its representatives.

The negari has clearly defined territory both of cultivated and forest lands. With the consent of the suku heads, which make up its council, the unoccupied lands can be assigned to families or suku, or can be leased or pawned to outsiders. Land of a family (rumah) can, with common consent, be sold to another family in the negari but not to outsiders.

It is said that the negari were formerly at war with one another and that this led to some of the larger settlements being surrounded by ditches and bamboo thickets. Between these unfriendly negari were stretches of neutral land which no one was supposed to cultivate. Even today the Dutch have difficulty in getting people to settle in these zones since "there is no adat or customary rights there."

According to the adat each negari should have (1) a limit or boundaries; (2) a balei (council house); (3) a mosque (this, of course, is a late introduction); (4) a galeng gang (fighting-ring for birds); (5) a main road.

It must also have the following "decorations": (1) rice fields; (2) a pungulu's house (the big house of the pungulu's family); (3) rice granaries; (4) gold and silver; (5) abundant rice. When it has these decorations it is clear that the people are industrious, that they have a leader, that they are guarded against famine and want, and that they have evidence of their labor.

The "pillars" of the negari are: (1) the pungulu, who is its soul; (2) those who conduct the wars of the negari, for they are its bones; (3) the officers, who are its limbs; (4) wise people, who are its tongue; (5) the populace, who are its substance. To prosper, the negari must have union of all its parts. A perfect negari should have four suku, each suku should have many parui, every kampong (village) should have its own chief, every rumah must have its mama[k]. Since the members of the parui are of one descent, they should not marry; since the people of a kampong live together, they should not marry.

Mention has been made of the kampong or settlement. It sometimes happens that a village springs up on the borders of two or more payung, suku, or negari. Since it contains people of each and hence has more than one adat, it has its own officers. The head of these is called capella kampong or pungulu kampong. He presides over all assemblies of the village but has no authority beyond its borders. While many of the people of the kampong may have the right to marry, there is a strong sentiment against such unions. The saying that "those who live on the same ground should never marry" seems to be as binding as that which prohibits those who draw from the same well from being united.

Two more institutions are met with in Menangkabaú society.[10] The first is the luá (or luha[k])—an administrative division which probably dates back to the days of Hindu-Javanese rule. Each had an administrative head and other officers paid by the radjah and appointed by him. With the fall of the empire these offices disappeared except for the titles which are retained in certain families. The districts are still recognized as Tanah Data, Agam, and Lima Pulu. The Dutch government has also established district officers known as Demang, with territories smaller than the luá. Since both these organizations are outside the adat (customary law) and have little importance in the social system, we pass them with this brief mention.

The last, and perhaps the most controversial institution is the laras. According to tradition the ancient kingdom of Menangkabaú was once divided by two powerful rulers—Datu Ketamang-goengan and Datu Perpatik nan Sebatang—into sections known as laras. That of the first ruler was known as Koto Piliang and was larger than Bodi Chinágo—the territory of the second. In addition to these there was a third called laras nan Pandjang, since it contained Periangan Padang Pandjang, the first permanent settlement in Menangkabaú lands. Of the people of this place it has always been said, "Kota Piliang he is not, neither is he Bodi Chinágo."

The unequal division of the land, we are told, led to bitter dispute and open strife between the larger laras. But when the two Datu were about to die they counseled the people to live together in peace and to aid one another.

According to Lamster[11] the names of these two laras come from four original clans called Koto, Piliang, Bodi, and Chinágo. These divided two and two and combined their names to give Koto Piliang and Bodi Chinágo. Each division, he says, had its own customs, usages and customary law.

Loeb[12] calls the laras "moieties" and says that at the time of conversion of the people to Muhammedanism they were already territorial units, each with a slightly different adat. Today these units appear as two systems or political parties and their members are found in every negari. Whichever party is dominant in a district imposes its system, but the people may change their allegiance at will. Thus, for example, Sarik formerly belonged to Koto Piliang but has now adopted the tenets and practices of Bodi Chinágo.

The major differences between the two parties can be summarized as follows: Koto Piliang emphasizes rank. A chief (pungulu) must always come

---

[10] Westenck; see Bibliography, below.
[11] Lamster, 105. See Bibliography, below. [12] Loeb, *ibid.*, p. 29.

from an original (first) family. His office is so exalted that he cannot give it up. Important chiefs occupy elevated seats in the balei, while lesser chiefs sit below. Final decisions rest with the higher chiefs whose verdicts are harsh and actions prompt.

In contrast to this autocratic party the aims of Bodi Chinágo seem most democratic. Where it is in control all people are equal. A chief may come from another than the first family if the people desire. He may resign in favor of another but his choice must be accepted by all. In the council house all are equal; a fact emphasized by the flat, level floor without seats of any kind. All matters of importance are discussed openly and the decisions are unanimous. Every attempt is made to right wrongs without resort to summary action.

A group of sayings or proverbs gives sanction to the attitudes of the two parties. A few examples will suffice. Koto Piliang says: "If he steals, cut off the beak." "He who is bitten bites back; he who is killed, murders." "If a dam holds back the water, cut it through with a single stroke."

Bodi Chinágo replies: "Fling from you that which is stolen. Spit up what has been wrongfully swallowed" (i.e., return the stolen goods). "If you hurt, repay. If you kill, pay blood money."

It seems probable that these laras represent a cleavage which goes far back in Menangkabaú history. Whatever may have been their origin or earlier functions, they seem at present to be much like political parties in western lands.

We have now reviewed the various units in the Menangkabaú system. The administrative divisions, or luá, being foreign, need not be considered here. The laras, or political parties, play an important rôle, especially in the election of chiefs. On the other hand, the system would function with little change if the laras were to disappear. The kampong, or settlement, has been fitted into the adat to meet a condition brought about by a concentration of population in certain localities. It adheres to the social scheme rather than forming an essential part of it.

It thus appears that the Menangkabaú system consists of the rumah, suku, and negari. One or more rumah (houses) make up a parui or lineage, which is, in fact, a joint family. This parui with its servants and other followers forms a payung. Several lineages constitute the suku or clan. It has no totemic features but is exogamous. Judging by the name, suku, or one-fourth, there probably were four original clans in a negari or phratry. Today many suku are found in each negari. In sharp contrast to the exogamous clan the phratry is endogamous.

Each phratry has its own adat or customary law. It controls the property of the clans and lineages within it, to the extent that it must sanction all exchanges between its members. However, lands belong first of all to the lineage and cannot be sold or leased without the consent of its members. Once that consent is gained, the clan must give its approval before the matter can be brought to the attention of the council of the negari.

There is no native unit above the negari, or phratry. In times of stress the phratries unite for common action, but such unions are short-lived. Under Hindu-Javanese rule a semblance of unity was achieved through the administrative divisions under the radjah, but these made little lasting impression on the system.

The similarities between the Menangkabaú parui and the taravad or matrilineal lineage of the Nayar caste of Malabar, and of both of these to certain other tribes of the mainland, have been noted by other writers. The archaeology of the southeastern Orient likewise gives hints of an early south Indian influence which antedated the coming of the Hindus.

Further research may afford a historical explanation for the social system now found among the Menangkabaú and their kinsmen in the Malay State of Negri Sembilan.

BIBLIOGRAPHY

Encyclopaedie van Nederlandsch Oost Indie, Gravenhage, 1917.

LAMSTER, J. C., The East Indies (Haarlem, 1928).

LEKKERKERKER, C., Landen volk van Sumatra (Leiden, 1916).

LOEB, E. M., Patrilineal and Matrilineal Organization in Sumatra, AA 36 (no. 1), 1934.

MAAS, A., Durch Zentral Sumatra (Berlin, 1910).

RADCLIFFE-BROWN, A. R., Patrilineal and Matrilineal Succession, Iowa Law Review, vol. 20, no. 2, January, 1935.

WESTENEK, L. C., De Minangkabausche Nagari (Weltevreden, 1918).

WINSTEDT, R. O., Journal Federated States Museum, vol. 9, pt. 2, 1920.

UNIVERSITY OF CHICAGO,
CHICAGO, ILLINOIS

SCAPULIMANCY

By John M. Cooper

TWENTY-NINE YEARS have gone by since the publication of Andree's survey of scapulimancy.[1*] During these years the field evidence for its occurrence in the Old World has not greatly expanded, but a mass of new information has accumulated upon its occurrence in the New World. The present writer in 1928 gave a brief review of the North American evidence as it then stood.[2] Since 1928 much more information from North America has come to light. The present paper is an attempt at a world survey of the evidence as it stands today in 1935 and at a reinterpretation of this evidence in the light of our newer knowledge, particularly of our newer knowledge from the North American continent.

As a provisional definition of scapulimancy, the following may be proposed: Divination by the shape, color, or other characters of, or by the marks, veins, burns, or cracks in, shoulder blades, or other flat or flattish bones, or tortoise shells. The two more important types of scapulimancy we shall call pyro-scapulimancy and apyro-scapulimancy. In pyro-scapulimancy, that is, scapulimancy by roasting or scorching, the bone is put in or near fire or embers, or fire or embers are applied to the bone, and the resulting fractures, cracks, or burns are read. In apyro-scapulimancy there is no such roasting or scorching, no use of fire at all; divination is from the shape, color, veining, and other natural peculiarities of the bone.

Other common names for scapulimancy are omoplatoscopy and spatulamancy; less common ones, spatulancy and osteomancy. As is obvious from the definition, none of these terms is quite satisfactory from the etymological standpoint, but, in view of established usage, the retention of the current word, scapulimancy, seems advisable, until the etymologists can find us a better one.

Pyro-scapulimancy in America

At the time Andree wrote in 1906 there were, so far as I can discover, only three extant published clear references to scapulimancy on the American continent. Faraud had found it among the Chipewyan; Casper Whitney, among the Dogrib. More than two centuries earlier, in 1634, Father Paul Le Jeune reported it among the Algonquian-speaking natives around the settlement of Quebec: "Ils mettent au feu vn certain os plat de Porc épic, puis ils regardent à sa couleur s'ils feront bonne chasse de ces animaux."[3]

As for the present-day Montagnais, Dr. William D. Strong, of the Smithsonian Institution, tells me he found scapulimancy among the Davis Inlet and Barren Ground bands of northeastern Labrador during his stay with them in 1927–28.[4]

Dr. Frank G. Speck of the University of Pennsylvania has found it widespread among the Naskapi-Montagnais of the Labrador peninsula, including

---

* Superior figures refer to notes at the end of this essay, p. 41.

the following bands: Lake St. John, Mistasini, Nichikun, Ungava, Michikamau, Moisie, and St. Marguerite.[5]

I have personally found it in present or former use among the following Montagnais bands of southern, central, and western Labrador: Lake St. John, Mistasini, Waswanipi, Neoskweskau (probably), Rupert House, Eastmain, Fort George, and probably too at Little Whale.[6]

As regards the Cree-speaking peoples, I have also personally found scapulimancy among the following tribes or bands: Northern Tête de Boule and southern Tête de Boule, Kesagami, Moose Factory, Albany, and Atawapiskat-Opinaga, as also among the Western Woodland Cree of the Fort McMurray (Alberta) and Lake Athabaska regions. Dr. Irving Hallowell of the University of Pennsylvania tells me he has recorded it among the Cross Lake Cree of Manitoba.[7] Inquiries made by me in 1931 among the Plains Cree of Rocky Boy Reservation in Montana brought negative replies.

Dr. Speck has reported scapulimancy from the Algonquian-speaking bands of River Desert and Timiskaming, and I have found it among the Abitibi band.[8]

The custom is widespread among the Otchipwe. Dr. Speck informs me that it is practiced at Timagami. I have found it at Ogoki on the middle Albany River. At Fort Hope and Lake St. Joseph on the Albany River, I was informed that scapulimancy was not in use, but that shoulder blades should not be thrown on a fire lest the figure of a man burn thereon and a Windigo put in an appearance. A little further west in the Thunder Bay district, Waugh found it in 1916, and both at Thunder Bay and at Lac Seul there was the taboo on burning animal bones, especially shoulder blades, lest a human figure or face burn on the bones and the one looking at it should turn into a Windigo. Mr. Lester Vincent of Fort Hope, Albany River, informed me that he once saw scapulimancy practiced by Indians a little north of Minaki on the Canadian National Railroad. I have personally found it in use among the Ojibwa of both the Lake of the Woods and the Rainy Lake districts.[9]

Dr. Hallowell informs me that he has found it among the Berens River Saulteaux [Ojibwa]. Mr. David G. Mandelbaum of Yale University writes me that an old Saskatchewan Cree on the Sweet Grass Reserve near Battleford told him: "I knew a Saulteaux who could foretell the future by heating an animal shoulder blade and reading the cracks," but that this old Cree informant had never seen any Cree do this. The Saulteaux here referred to "probably are Plains Ojibwa who traded at old Fort Ellice."[10]

In 1931 I made some inquiries among Plains Ojibwa informants of Montana, with, however, negative results. Fairly full inquiries made the same year among the Blackfoot of northwestern Montana and among the Gros Ventre of the Fort Belknap district, Montana, brought the same negative replies.

Miss Regina Flannery of the Catholic University informs me that she has found no clear evidence of scapulimancy in any of the published sources for the Algonquian-speaking Indians south of the St. Lawrence.

Dr. Speck writes me that the Penobscot read the blood-clots on shoulder blades. This is the only case of apyro-scapulimancy I know of on the American continent. I should be inclined to suspect possible European influence.

So far as I am aware, there is no evidence for scapulimancy among any of the other Algonquians, nor for that matter among any of the other Indian groups on the North American continent south of the Canadian border, nor have I come across any hint of scapulimancy anywhere in Central or South America.

The Crow used to take some blood from the shoulder blade of a buffalo, spill some badger blood over it, and look at themselves in the mixture, to see how they would meet their death.[11] But this particular method of divination, reported also from other Plains tribes and without any mention of shoulder blades, seems to be a fundamentally distinct thing from scapulimancy. Incidentally, I have found this identical type of divination rather widespread among the James Bay Indians, otter grease being substituted in the east for the typical badger blood of the Plains.

This completes our survey of Algonquian scapulimancy. It is now definitely established among most of the Algonquian-speaking peoples north of the line represented by the St. Lawrence, the Great Lakes, and the Plains, but, so far as our information goes, does not occur south of this line, except perhaps in the Minnesota and adjacent regions.

We may now pass to the northern Athapaskan-speaking peoples. There are only two records of it, so far as I can find, in our literature on them: Whitney's statement on the Dogribs, cited above, and Faraud's on the Chipewyan. Birket-Smith did not find it among the Chipewyan of Churchill during his short visit there.[12]

In spite, however, of the relative silence of our written sources on the northern Athapaskan area, scapulimancy is very widespread among the Mackenzie and neighboring peoples. I suspect it is or was of well-nigh universal distribution. During a rather rapid reconnaissance down the Mackenzie in 1931, I found scapulimancy perfectly well known to and practiced by all the peoples for whom I could find satisfactory native or other well-equipped informants: the Chipewyan of Lake Athabaska and of Great Slave Lake, Caribou Eaters, Dogrib, and Hare. I also obtained seemingly reliable information that it was or is practiced among the Slavey and Sikani trading at Fort Nelson in northern British Columbia.

Dr. Cornelius Osgood of Yale University writes me: "Of all the informants in Alaska of whom I have asked questions concerning scapulimancy, only two have recognized this custom, and they both belong to the Peel River groups of Kutchin. In short, all the informants among the tribes of the Alaska Indians on the Pacific watershed were not acquainted with this practice."[13]

There seems to be no record of scapulimancy among any of the Eskimo groups, including the inland Caribou Eskimo. Dr. Henry B. Collins, Jr., of the United States National Museum, tells me that in his Alaskan archaeological work he has been on the lookout for any evidence of scapulimancy in the scapulae dug up, but has never seen any that showed definite signs of having been burnt for this purpose.[14]

To sum up, as our North American evidence stands at present, we have established a continuous distribution of scapulimancy among the northern Algonquians and Athapascans, from extreme eastern Labrador, through the woodland area and to a certain extent out into the tundra, down the Mackenzie to its mouth and up the Peel River.

The dominant traits of the scapulimancy complex as found in the northern Algonquian and northern Athapaskan areas may be briefly outlined as follows: Except for the Penobscot case, pyro-scapulimancy is the exclusive form found. The bones more commonly used are the shoulder blades of moose, caribou, hare, and beaver; the shoulder blades of other animals, such as lynx, fox, or porcupine, are less frequently utilized, except here and there locally or by individual diviners. In many bands the sternum, usually of grouse or ptarmigan, is in even greater favor than are shoulder blades. I have come across, too, one band, the southern Tête de Boule, among whom a beaver hip bone was seemingly used.

Over most of the area, to judge from personal field experience, interpretation is by the location or shape more of burned spots than of cracks or fissures, thus contrasting with the uniform Asiatic method of interpretation by cracks. However, Speck and Comeau, Mandelbaum, and Osgood report interpretation by cracks, in the extreme eastern, south central, and extreme western sections respectively of the Canadian area.

As regards the more precise methods of interpreting the burns or fractures, I have found no elaborate conventional systems such as are reported from parts of Asia. The technique appears much simpler and less conventionalized. Nor is there any one method that is uniformly followed over the whole northern Canadian area. Certain vague resemblances occur. For instance, both among the Dogrib and among the Rupert House Montagnais and Kesagami and Moose Cree, so my native informants have advised me, parallel or branching lines may be drawn on the bone before it is scorched: among the Dogrib these lines signify hunters; among the other three groups they signify localities. In general, however, methods differ widely, it seems, from band to band, and even, as for instance at Rupert House, from diviner to diviner within the same band.

In one respect, the Algonquian practice differs appreciably from the Athapaskan. Over most, and perhaps all, of the Algonquian area, children are forbidden to play at scapulimancy, for, if they do, a human-like figure may burn on the bone and a Wihtiko (Windigo) or cannibal monster will come after them or they will turn into Wihtikos. The seeming absence of this particular trait from the Athapaskan scapulimancy complex is apparently due to the absence of the Wihtiko belief proper from Athapaskan culture.

Over the general Algonquian-Athapaskan area, scapulimancy is the more often resorted to in connection with game-finding. It may be and is, however, practiced for other purposes.

This ends our review of the New World. As is evident, a very much wider distribution is now established than was known to us even in 1928. The gap between the Labrador-Quebec-Ontario area and the Siberian area is now practically filled up.

Pyro-scapulimancy in the Old World

We may now turn to the Old World. I have not attempted to cover the whole vast literature of the Old World, nor even that of Asia, but have merely tried to fill out a little the distribution as traced in 1906 by Andree.

It may be well to begin with the records that are chronologically the earliest, namely, those from China. The inscribed bones and tortoise shells, found in 1899 in Honan and clearly used for pyro-scapulimancy, seemingly date from the Shang (or Yin) Dynasty of the latter half of the second millennium B.C. The method of divining from the cracks produced by fire applied to the shells and bones has been reconstructed and described in detail by Chavannes. While in later historic times only the tortoise shell was used in China for scapulimantic divination, the Honan finds seem to show quite clearly that earlier the shoulder blades, leg bones, and pelvis of ruminants (presumably of sheep and oxen) were also used.[15]

The most important and earlier mode of divination practiced by the primitive Japanese was the scorching of the shoulder blade of deer. In later times, however, by the eighth or even sixth century A.D., the tortoise shell was in use, seemingly from influences spreading through Korea from China. In the country districts divination by deer shoulder blades persisted long after. Munro ascribes deer shoulder-blade divination to the Ainu.[16]

The occurrence of pyro-scapulimancy by use of sheep shoulder blades is reported by Rockhill among the Mongols and the non-Mongolian K'amba of eastern Tibet. It is also reported among the Lolos, with the use of the scorched shoulder blade of a goat or sheep.[17]

Andree has summed up the main evidence for the occurrence and characteristics of scapulimancy among the Kalmuk, Kirghiz, Buriat, Tungus, Chukchi, and Koryak, and has cited or quoted in considerable detail the descriptive data from the respective sources. I may merely add in a footnote a few sources not utilized by him.[18] To this list of tribes we may now add the Tungusic Golds, and the Chuvantzy and Lamut.[19]

I have found no mention of the custom, in the sources accessible to me, among the Yukaghir proper or Gilyak. Scapulimancy is seemingly absent too among the Lapps, Samoyeds, Finns, and Wotjak. At least I have not found it recorded in the many sources I have consulted; and, as for the Lapps in particular, the older writers, Scheffer, Leems, and Regnard, who dealt in considerable detail with magical practices and divination, say nothing of shoulder-blade divination, nor does the more recent Lapp writer, Turi. These negatives are here set down with hesitation, particularly as I have been unable to cover the literature thoroughly, much of it being inaccessible and a great deal more of it being in Russian.

Attention may be called in passing to the fact that the earliest unmistakable reference to Siberian scapulimancy is the one in William of Rubruck's Itinerarium of 1253. He found sheep shoulder-blade pyro-scapulimancy a chief divinatory rite at the palace of the Mongol Khan Mangu.[20]

In a short treatise, probably but not certainly by Michael Psellus, the great Byzantine statesman and scholar (d. prob. 1078 A.D.), pyro-scapulimancy is described in some detail. Andree relying upon Pervanoglu's citation of Politis' account of Psellus' description, attributes scapulimancy to the Byzantines of the eleventh century. Psellus' original text, however, refers to scapulimancy as "the barbarian and strange method of omoplatoscopy"—"barbarian" in the case meaning specifically *non*-Greek, *non*-Byzantine, and "strange" implying the same. By what "barbarians" it was practiced at the time, Moslem or others, is not stated. But Psellus obviously means to say the custom was not a Byzantine one. He describes the technique as follows:

Now those who intend to obtain an oracle, having selected a sheep or lamb of the flock, first put in their minds or even declare with the tongue that which they wish to learn about. Then having sacrificed [not just "killed"] (the animal) they separate the shoulder blade from the whole body as (being) the instrument of oracular response, and having roasted this with charcoal and having stripped off the flesh they then have visible signs of the issue of their questions. But they foretell the future with other members also. Accordingly they put judgment of life and death in the excellence of the sharp projection in the middle of the shoulder blade. And if this is white and pure on either side, then they accept this as a symbol of life; but if it is burned up, they take this as a token of death. In the middle part of the shoulder blade they put judgments of calamities from the air. For if in the middle of the shoulder blade the two thin plates on both parts of the sharp projection should appear white and pure, they foretell a peaceful condition for the air; but if they are spotted, they prophesy the opposite. If anyone asks about war, if in the right part of the shoulder blade a red cloud-like spot should appear or in the other part a long and dark line, give response that there will be a great war. But if you should see both parts white according to nature, declare as the oracle that there is to be peace. And in brief in all questions, what is rather red and dark and burned up is connected with the more unfavorable issue of events, while the opposite of this is connected with the more favorable issue.[21]

Arabian and western scapulimancy is and has been almost exclusively apyro-scapulimancy, so far as our records go. This would suggest that Psellus' "barbarian and strange" scapulimancy was not Arabian. It may be recalled that it was just during the period of Psellus' life and literary activity that the Seljuk Turks first came into close contact with Byzantium. In the half century from 1021 to 1071 A.D., they made themselves masters of most of Asia Minor, and extended their sway practically to the gates of Byzantium. There is at least a reasonable possibility that the "barbarian and strange" custom described by Psellus was one he had learnt about among these new invaders from the Asiatic steppes.

This about completes our information on the Asiatic distribution of pyro-scapulimancy, except for one rather cryptic reference thereto by Wellsted, who mentions divination by "the burning of blade-bones" as practiced by the Arabs of Oman.[22] All other records I have found of scapulimancy among the Arabian peoples refer, where sufficiently clear, to apyro-scapulimancy.

To sum up, pyro-scapulimancy is distributed almost continuously over much or most of northeastern, eastern, and central Asia. Apart from its early occurrence in China and Japan and its presence in Tibet and among the Lolos and Ainu, it is largely confined to the northeastern Paleo-Siberians and to the Turk, Mongol, and Tungus branches of the peoples of Altai speech. It is seemingly absent from the Finno-Ugrian-speaking peoples and the Samoyeds.

The dominant traits of the scapulimancy complex as found in northeastern, eastern, and central Asia may be briefly outlined as follows:

Pyro-scapulimancy is the exclusive form found. The shoulder blades of sheep are the more often used among the sheep-raising peoples of the central Asiatic regions; reindeer and seal blades among the Paleo-Siberians; in later times tortoise shells in China and Japan. Use of the sternum is not reported.

Interpretation is dominantly, and it would seem almost exclusively, by cracks and fissures, rather than by spots or marks scorched on the bone. The technique in the eastern and central areas tends to be more elaborate and conventionalized than it is in the northeastern area or in North America.

Over most of Asia, the practice is not so largely associated with game-finding as it is in America.

So much for pyro-scapulimancy and its eastern distribution over northern North America and Asia. Now for apyro-scapulimancy and its western distribution over southwestern Asia, northern Africa, and Europe.

Apyro-scapulimancy

Our earliest record of apyro-scapulimancy appears to be that in Jordanes written around 551 A.D. He attributes what appears to be apyro-scapulimancy to the Hun leader, Attila: "Statuit [Attila] per aruspices futura inquirere. qui more solito nunc pecorum fibras, nunc quasdam venas in abrasis ossibus intuentes Hunnis infausta denuntiant."[23] "Looking at certain veins in stripped bones of sheep" to foretell the future, certainly sounds like scapulimancy, although no mention is made of shoulder blades. The more probable implication of "looking at certain veins" is that no fire was used.

Our next reference in chronological order is the statement by Margoliouth that scapulimancy is mentioned in the writings of Jāḥiẓ, who died A.H. 255 or 250 (869 or 864 A.D.).[24] Margoliouth gives no details, and I have been unable to locate the passage in any of the few published works of Jāḥiẓ accessible in other than Arabic.

Haskins refers to two medieval treatises or translations on scapulimancy, still in manuscript, by the early twelfth-century writer, Hugh of Santalla. Thomas Aquinas (13th cent.) knew of the custom, probably from Arabic or Jewish sources, and has a brief mention of it.[25] I can find no mention of scapulimancy in the Etymologiae of Isidore of Seville (6th-7th cent.), or in the patristic writings as indexed by Migne. The twelfth-century reference to the custom by Giraldus Cambrensis will be given when we come to the distribution of scapulimancy in northwestern Europe.

So much for the early and late medieval European and Arabic references to scapulimancy. We may turn now to the more recent distribution of apyro-scapulimancy. The farthest eastern occurrence of apyro-scapulimancy seems to be among the Sindhi and Belochi, the Persians and Afghans. Whether the Hazarahs used pyro-scapulimancy or apyro-scapulimancy is not clear from Masson. The Circassian usage is seemingly apyro-scapulimantic.[26] Apart from the one Oman Arabian exception noted above, all sufficiently clear descriptions I have come across of scapulimancy among the Arabs of Arabia and the Arabic-speaking peoples and Berbers of northern Africa, particularly of Morocco and Algeria, refer to apyro-scapulimancy, not to pyro-scapulimancy.[27]

Andree gave a review of the evidence for scapulimancy in southeastern, central, and southern Europe: Greece, Rumania, Southern Slavs, Bosnia, Serbia, Lithuania, Germany, Corsica, and Spain. Considerable further evidence is now available for its occurrence in Albania (Montenegro), Macedonia, Crete, Thessaly, and Pindus.[28] There is some question whether the attribution of the custom by Andree to France is fully justified; but the point is probably not important. In all these cases from Europe where the description is sufficiently clear and detailed, the reference is to apyro-scapulimancy, as it is in the following case from Albania.

To the published and accessible evidence I may add the following data very kindly sent me, in May, 1935, by Dr. Carleton S. Coon, of the Peabody Museum, Cambridge:

About six years ago I witnessed a performance of scapulimancy in Albania [on the Black Drin].... In our honor our host the krueplak [who was a Moslem] killed a sheep and roasted it whole. We ate all of it, with the help of his henchmen. Toward the end of the feast our host tore out a scapula, covered with meat, and handed it to me, bidding me clean it. When I had done so he took it and wiped it off with his fingers, and held it up to the light. Then he examined it carefully and began uttering prophecies. In this examination he noticed the following things very carefully: smoothness or roughness of the border opposite the acromion process; thinness or thickness of the body of the scapula; and the number and pattern of blood-vessels on its body.

We may pass now to northwestern Europe. The first reference, in chronological order, to scapulimancy in northwestern Europe is that in the Itinerarium of Giraldus Cambrensis, his account of his trip through Wales made in 1188. In describing, not the Welsh themselves, but the Flemings who had come over to Wales in the early part of the twelfth century and who were settled around Rhos, he writes:

Hoc autem mihi videtur hac de gente notandum, quod in armis arietum dextris, carne nudatis, et non assis sed elixis, tam futura prospiciunt, quam praeterita et antea cognita longe respiciunt; tempore quoque praesentia, sed loco absentia, quasi prophetico quodam spiritu arte miranda cognoscunt; pacis et guerrae signa, caedes et incendia, domestica adulteria, regis statum, vitam, et obitum, rimularum quarundam et notularum indiciis certissime declarant.[29]

We may reasonably infer from Giraldus' account that scapulimancy was not a native Welsh, at least not a native southern Welsh, custom. A southern Welshman himself, he was presumably cognizant of the customs of his countrymen. What he found among the Flemings resident in Rhos in 1188 appeared to him noteworthy enough to justify a detailed account with an illustration—to which additional illustrative cases were appended by him in the second edition of his Itinerary, one of these cases from Flanders itself. From the description and cases it is fairly clear that he is referring to apyro-scapulimancy.

For four full centuries after Giraldus' Itinerary was written, no further independent mention is found, so far as I can discover, of scapulimancy in Gaelic or English sources. But from the early seventeenth century on, the records become more and more numerous, for Ireland and particularly for the Scottish Highlands and Western Islands.[30] In the early nineteenth century, the descendants of the Flemish population around Rhos (Pembrokeshire) still practiced a sort of scapulimancy,[31] but apart from this Flemish intrusion into southern Wales, neither for Wales nor for England can I find any record in older or more recent times.

In fact throughout the Gaelic and English-speaking areas there appears to be no clear evidence that the custom goes back to remote pre-Christian times, although evidence that it does may still be hidden away in Gaelic manuscripts.

To sum up the distribution for northwestern Europe: apyro-scapulimancy was practiced in Flanders at least as early as the beginning of the twelfth century A.D. and was thence introduced into Wales; the apparent silence of the earlier records on aboriginal insular Gaelic and English culture up to the seventeenth century suggest the possibility or even the probability that such scapulimancy as is found in Scotland and Ireland may be traceable to the Flemish immigration into Wales in the twelfth century or to Flemish or German traders from the continent. Twelfth-century Flemish scapulimancy may possibly have had its origin from the first Crusade.

So far as our records go, scapulimancy proper was seemingly absent from the ancient Keltic, Teutonic, Slavic, Roman, Greek, Persian, Egyptian, Hamitic, and Semitic cultures, as it was from the Indic. Apart too from the area of strong Moslem influence in northern Africa, it is not clearly recorded anywhere else on the African continent. There is, it is true, a cryptic, almost tantalizing, reference by Dornan who says of the Masarwa Bushmen: "Divination is also practised by means of the shoulder blade of a springbok, but I have not seen it done."[32]

I can find no other reference in the South African literature to anything of the kind. There is, moreover, considerable question as to whether this is really scapulimancy proper or some type of shoulder-blade divination that may have no genetic relationship to scapulimancy. Shoulder blades, like other bones, are used for divination in ways that remotely resemble or differ completely from scapulimancy: for instance, among the Northern Cree, Persians, Karens.[33] Let us hope some fieldworker among the Bushmen will soon clear up the question Dornan's statement raises.

The custom of divination by the use of the sternum of a goose[34] has much more probability, I believe, of being related genetically to scapulimancy proper than it had at the time Andree wrote. Since that time the newer data from the field have shown, I think unmistakably, that northern Canadian divination by shoulder blades and by grouse breast bones is all one.[35] This seems to render more probable the conclusion that shoulder-blade divination and divination by goose breast bone as found in southeastern, central, and northwestern Europe are genetically related. But the relationship is by no means demonstrated. Such breast-bone divination is, like apyro-scapulimancy, by color and other characters of the bone, but is usually resorted to, especially in central and northwestern Europe, for a different and specific purpose, namely, to forecast winter weather.

This ends our survey of the Old World and New World distribution of scapulimancy. We may pass on to such generalizations and interpretations as seem justified.

Summary and Interpretation

Scapulimancy is confined to a practically continuous area extending clear across northern North America, to northeastern, eastern, central, and southwestern Asia, to southeastern, central, southern, and northwestern Europe, and to northern Africa. Apart from the doubtful Bushman case, it appears to be absent from the rest of the world.

Over its area of distribution, scapulimancy occurs in two chief forms: pyro-scapulimancy, with an Oriental and American distribution; apyro-scapulimancy, with an Occidental distribution.

Detailed techniques for interpretation differ much locally between and within the two great areas. The almost exclusive interpretation by cracks in Asiatic pyro-scapulimancy contrasts somewhat with the more common but by no means exclusive interpretation by burns in North American pyro-scapulimancy.

From the historical evidence, corroborated in a measure by the ethnological, Oriental scapulimancy seems pretty clearly more ancient by many hundred years than Occidental. It goes back at least to the second millennium B.C. in China. In the Occident scapulimancy makes its first appearance, as practiced by Occidentals, only in the Middle Ages, the earliest European records dating only from the twelfth century A.D.

What light do the facts throw upon the questions of origin? The historical and corroborative ethnological evidence suggest strongly that we should look to the eastern world rather than to the Mediterranean or contiguous areas for origins; in other words, to the pyro-scapulimantic area.

The practically continuous distribution of pyro-scapulimancy from Labrador to central Asia and the absence of it from the rest of the world give us fairly good grounds for concluding that scapulimancy has spread over the Oriental and American areas from a single center—more probably from a single center *within* one of these two areas. In view of the seeming more prevalent, general culture drift from Asia to America rather than vice versa, the chances are a bit greater that scapulimancy had its origin somewhere west of Behring Strait rather than east of it.

Can we, on the evidence available, be more specific? That scapulimancy originated among a sheep-raising people or among the Chinese are hypotheses that seem at best to be only plausible. It is true that scapulimancy is very commonly by the shoulder blades of sheep in preference to other blades, and is very common among many sheep-raising peoples. But, in the form of pyro-scapulimancy at least, it is even more widespread in distribution among peoples who do not and never did raise sheep or who do or did so very little. It would be just as plausible, and perhaps in view of the ethnological evidence from eastern Asia and America, even more plausible, to infer that scapulimancy originated among hunters of the Cervidae.

As for the hypothesis of Chinese origin, it is true that in China we have the earliest dated records for the practice, but a chronology for northeastern and much of central Asia and for northern North America is lacking, and we have no means of knowing how long the custom may have existed in these parts prior to the first dated records—probably a very long time, to judge from its extremely wide diffusion and from its primary divinatory importance over so much of this area. So far as tortoise-carapace divination in particular is concerned, from the prevalence of shoulder-blade divination over the Siberian area, its exclusive use in early Japan, and its concomitant use in early China, it would look as if tortoise-shell scapulimancy is merely a specialized adaptation that developed later on Chinese soil out of earlier shoulder-blade divination.

We may ask further: Are pyro-scapulimancy and apyro-scapulimancy one in the sense that both go back to a common origin? Or had they independent origins? It is usually assumed that they go back to a common origin. But the evidence, while suggestive, is far from compelling. The criterion of form leaves the matter more or less open. Apyro-scapulimancy in itself has almost as much in common with divination by entrails and with similar practices as it has with pyro-scapulimancy. That shoulder blades, and sheep shoulder blades at that, are so commonly preferred in both the pyro-scapulimantic and apyro-scapulimantic areas looks interesting but not conclusive. For over very large sections of these areas—as, for example, in China, Japan, northeastern Asia, North America, and parts of Europe—either other bones or bony substances than shoulder blades, or other shoulder blades than those of sheep, are either exclusively or alternatively used.

The criterion of continuous distribution is slightly more weighty. The continuity in distribution of both forms of scapulimancy and the seeming absence of both forms from the rest of the world certainly seem to give tentative grounds for inferring common origin; but even so they leave much to be desired.

Perhaps the strongest ground for inferring common origin is the chronological and historical one. All our evidence points to the prior origin of pyro-scapulimancy somewhere to the east of the Occidental world. It appears significant, to say the least, that Occidental culture lacked scapulimancy up to just about the time when western Moslem and European Christian alike came, in the early and later Middle Ages, through martial and other ways, into fairly close cultural contact with the peoples of the Asiatic steppes.

All things considered, there appears to be a greater probability that Occidental apyro-scapulimancy diffused from a center or from centers of Asiatic pyro-scapulimancy, but this conclusion is very far indeed from being established. What, on this assumption, led to the shift from the pyro-scapulimantic to the apyro-scapulimantic technique can only be vaguely surmised. Possibly it was the preëxisting Occidental pattern of entrails divination.

Much of the foregoing interpretation is and has had to be tentative and hypothetical, if not at times speculative. Future more adequate information on the precise details of scapulimantic techniques may enable us to reach more confident conclusions. Perhaps, too, the archaeologist may some day come to our rescue. But, notwithstanding all our doubts, at least one clear, important point has emerged in the last decade from the newer evidence, namely, the genetic link between Asiatic and American pyro-scapulimancy.

NOTES TO "SCAPULIMANCY"

[1] R. Andree, Scapulimantia, in Boas Anniv. Vol., 143–65, New York, 1906; cf. A. L. Kroeber, Anthropology, 210–11, New York, 1923.

[2] J. M. Cooper, Northern Algonkian Scrying and Scapulimancy, in W. Schmidt Festschrift, 213–17, Moedling bei Wien, 1928.

[3] H. Faraud, Dix-huit ans chez les sauvages, 272, 1866, Paris, Fernand-Michel; C. Whitney, On Snow-shoes to the Barren Grounds, 262, New York, 1896; Paul Le Jeune, Relation 1634, JR, ed. Thwaites, 6:214; the two latter quoted in Cooper, op. cit., 216.

[4] Personal communication.

[5] Personal communication; also F. G. Speck, Spiritual Beliefs among Labrador Indians, ICA, 21:274–75 (first part), 1924; same, Culture Problems in Northeastern North America, Proc. Am. Philos. Soc. 65:281, 1926; same, forthcoming volume on Naskapi religion, Univ. of Okla. Press (Norman, Okla.), 1935.

[6] Cooper, MS field notes 1928–34; some of data gathered prior to 1928 on Montagnais, Cree, Algonkin, and Otchipwe published in Cooper, op. cit., 213–15.

[7] Personal communication. In 1927 I was informed by Cree at Moose Factory that the Cree of the Cape Henrietta barrens (James Bay) did not practice scapulimancy. I have since found that I was misinformed. They do practice it.

[8] F. G. Speck, River Desert Indians of Quebec, MAIHF-IN 4:251, July, 1927; same, Myths and Folk-Lore of the Timiskaming Algonquin and Timagami Ojibwa, Geol. Survey, Anthrop. Ser. 9:24, Ottawa, 1915; Cooper, op. cit., 214–15.

[9] F. W. Waugh, MS field notes, Div. of Anthropology, Victoria Museum, Ottawa; Cooper, op. cit., 215, and MS field notes; cf. also Sister M. Bernard, Religion and Magic among the Cass Lake Ojibwa, Primitive Man, 2:55.

[10] Drs. Hallowell and Mandelbaum, personal communications. A very obscure passage in The Kelsey Papers, 22 (ed., A. G. Doughty and C. Martin, Ottawa, 1929), may just possibly refer to scapulimancy. H. Y. Hind's reference (Explorations in the Interior of the Labrador Peninsula, 1:185, London, 1863) to it is seemingly taken from Le Jeune.

[11] R. H. Lowie, The Religion of the Crow Indians, AMNH-AP 25:434 (pt. 2), 1922. Since the present manuscript was written, Speck's data, referred to above, on Penobscot scapulimancy have been published in JAFL 48:28, 1935.

[12] C. Whitney, op. cit., 262; H. Faraud, op. cit., 272; Kaj Birket-Smith, Contributions to Chipewyan Ethnology, Rept. 5th Thule Exped. 6:82, Copenhagen, 1930.

[13] Personal communication. Since the present paper was written, I have received communications from Dr. Robert A. McKennan of Dartmouth College to the effect that among the Indians of the Upper Tanana the evidence for scapulimancy is at best very doubtful while the evidence for it among the Nedse Kutchin of the Upper Chandalar is still more vague, and from Dr. Frederica de Laguna of the University of Pennsylvania Museum to the effect that neither she nor Birket-Smith found any evidence for its existence among the Eyak.

[14] Personal communication.

[15] E. Chavannes, La divination par l'écaille de tortue dans la haute antiquité chinoise, J. Asiatique, 127–37, 1911; L. C. Hopkins, Chinese Writing in the Chou Dynasty in the Light of Recent Discoveries, JRAI, 1025–29, 1911; same, The Archives of an Oracle, ibid., 49–61, 289–303, 1915; W. P. Yetts, The Shang-Yin Dynasty and the An-yang Finds, ibid., 657–85, 1933; H. Maspero, La Chine antique, 36–37, Paris, 1927; J. M. Menzies, The Culture of the Shang Dynasty, SI-AR for 1931:549–58; C. W. Bishop, The Beginnings of North and South in China, Pacific Affairs, 7:308, 1934. I am indebted to my colleague, Dr. P. H. Furfey, of the Catholic University, for the above references, except Chavannes.

[16] W. G. Aston, Shinto, the Way of the Gods, 339–40, New York, 1905; B. H. Chamberlain, tr., The Kojiki, Trans. Asiat. Soc. Japan 10, supplement, Tokyo, repr. 1906, pp. xxix, lxxx, 24, 64; M. Revon, Divination (Japanese), in Hastings' Encyclopaedia on Religion and

Ethics. Cf. note by Laufer in Andree, *op. cit.*, 164–65, on Chinese and Japanese scapulimancy. On Ainu, see N. G. Munro, Some Origins and Survivals, Tr. Asiat. Soc. Japan, 38: 46, 1911 (pt. 3).

[17] W. W. Rockhill, The Land of the Lamas, 166, 176, 341–44, New York, 1891; A. F. Legendre, The Lolos of Kientchang, Western China, SI-AR for 1911:578.

[18] Andree, *op. cit.*, 147–51. Additional references on Kirghiz: R. Karutz, Unter Kirgisen und Turkmenen, 139–40, Leipzig, 1911; A. de Levchine, Description des hordes et des steppes des Kirghiz-Kazaks, (tr.), 333–35, Paris, 1840; J. G. Georgi, Beschreibung aller Nationen des russischen Reichs, 223, St. Petersburg, 1776; E. Schuyler, Turkistan, 2:31, New York, 1877; on Buriat: V. M. Mikhailovskii, Shamanism in Siberia and European Russia, (tr.), JRAI, 24:99, 126 (cf. 69, 158), 1895; on Chukchi: W. Bogoras, The Chukchee, AMNH-MJ 7:487–90, Leiden-New York, 1907.

[19] O. Lattimore, The Gold Tribe, "Fishskin Tatars" of the Lower Sungari, AAA-M 40:66, 1933; W. Bogoras, *op. cit.*, 489–90.

[20] William of Rubruck, Journal, in Purchas his pilgrimes, 11:88–89, Glasgow, 1906. Cf. M. Sprengling, Scapulimantia and the Mongols, AA 35:134–37, 1933.

[21] Michael Psellus, περὶ ὠμοπλατοσκοπίας καὶ οἰωνοσκοπίας, ed. R. Hercher, Philologus, 1853, 8:166–67; Andree, *op. cit.*, 156–157. I am indebted to my colleague, Dr. Martin R. W. McGuire, of the Department of Greek and Latin of The Catholic University, for the data upon the manuscript and for the translation of Psellus given above.

[22] J. R. Wellsted, Travels in Arabia, 1:344–45, London, 1838.

[23] Jordanes, De origine actibusque Getarum, ed. T. Mommsen, in Mon. Germ. histor., Auctorum antiquiss., tomi V, pars prior, Berlin, 1882, cap. 37, p. 108.

[24] D. S. Margoliouth, Divination (Muslim), in Hastings' Encyclopaedia of Religion and Ethics, 4:817; cf. s. v. Djāḥiẓ, in Encycl. de l'Islam, 1:1028–29.

[25] C. H. Haskins, Studies in the History of Mediaeval Science, 79, cf. 286, 1927 (2d ed., Cambridge, Mass.); Thomas Aquinas, De sortibus ad dominum Jacobum de Tolongo, in Opuscula omnia, ed. P. Mandonnet, iii, Paris, 1927, c. iii, p. 149. My attention was called to these passages respectively by my colleague, Dr. Aloysius K. Ziegler of the Catholic University, and by Rev. George Q. Friel, O.P., one of my graduate students. Since the present manuscript was sent in, I have recently received from the Bodleian photostat copies of these two treatises by Hugh of Santalla and of a third anonymous one dealing in detail with scapulimancy. Dr. Ziegler, after a cursory reading of them, informs me that there is no mention in them of the use of fire. They are evidently of Spanish provenance, and seemingly from Arabic originals. We hope later to publish these three treatises.

[26] R. F. Burton, Sindh, and the Races that Inhabit the Valley of the Indus, 189–92, London, 1851; C. Masson, Narrative of Various Journeys in Balochistan, Afghanistan, the Panjab, and Kalât, 3:334, London, 1884, on Hazarahs; Andree, *op. cit.*, 154–55, on Cherkess.

[27] In addition to references in Andree, *op. cit.*, 155, see: L. Dames, Balōčistān, in Encycl. de l'Islam, 1:648, on Balochistan; E. Doutté, Magie et religion dans l'Afrique du nord, 371, Alger, 1909, on Zenatah of Algeria; M. W. Hilton-Simpson, Some Algerian Superstitions, FL 26:242–43, 1915, on Shawia Berbers of Algeria; E. Westermarck, The Popular Ritual of the Great Feast in Morocco, FL 22:154–55, 1911, or, same, Ritual and Belief in Morocco, 2:128–29, London, 1926, on Arabic-speaking tribes and Berbers of Morocco.

[28] Andree, *op. cit.*, 157–60; see also: E. Durham, Albanian and Montenegrin Folklore, FL 23:225, 1912; G. F. Abbott, Macedonian Folklore, 96–97, Cambridge, 1903; Brigandage in Macedonia, Cornhill Mag. 44:358, 1881; W. R. Halliday, Cretan Folklore Notes, FL 24:358, 1913; W. J. Thoms, Divination by the Blade-bone, FL Record, pt. 1, Publ. FL Soc. 1:178, 1878. The pertinent passage on Corsica is found in N. Tommaseo, Canti popolari, 2:71–72, Venice, 1841–42; on Germany, in Hans Vintler, Die Pluemen der Tugent, (ed. Zingerle, Innbruck, 1874), lines 7845–46, p. 263, with reading differing from one cited by Andree, as follows: "die sehen an dem schulterpain was dem menschen soll geschehen." See also Hartlieb, Buch aller verboten Kunst, Ungelaubens, und der Zauberei, MS, 1455, quoted

in extenso in J. Grimm, Deutsche Mythologie (4th ed.), 3:433, Berlin, 1875, for Germany ca. 1455.

[29] Giraldi Cambrensis Opera, v. 6, Itinerarium Kambriae et descriptio Kambriae, ed. J. F. Dimock (Rolls ser.), London, 1868, lib. i, cap. xi, pp. 87–89; ditto, in W. Camden, Anglica, normannica, hibernica, cambrica, a veteribus scripta, Francofurti, 1603, 849–50; passage condensed in Ranulf Higden (d. 1364), Polychronicon (1st ed. 1327), ed. C. Babington (Rolls Ser.), 2:164, lib. i, c. lx, 1869; Engl. tr. Hoare, in T. Wright, ed., The Historical Works of Giraldus Cambrensis, 402–4, London, 1894. The much-cited passage from Drayton's Poly-Olbion, song v (in Works, ed. J. W. Hebel, Oxford, 4:104, 1933), is ultimately based solely on Giraldus; so too are the passages from Caxton and Selden quoted by W. C. Hazlitt, Popular Antiquities of Great Britain (enl. ed. of John Brand's work), 3:292, London, 1870 (in J. Brand, same, 1849 ed., 3:339–40).

[30] For Ireland: 1607, Wm. Camden, Brittania, tr., ed. E. Gibson, London, 1695, 1046 (Gibson's 3d ed., 1753, 1419, cf. 1418); 1895, Jeremiah Curtin, Tales of the Fairies and of the Ghost World collected from Oral Tradition in Southwest Munster, London, 1895, 84–85; J. A. MacCulloch, The Religion of the Ancient Celts, 250, Edinburgh, 1911. For Scotland and the Western Islands: 1691, Robert Kirk, An Essay of the Nature and Actions of the Subterranean ... among the Low-country Scots (1691), Edinburgh, 1815, 17 (repr., Secret commonwealth, ed. A. Lang, London, 1893, 31–32); 1763, (M'Leod), Theophilus Insulanus, Treatises on the Second Sight (1763), Glasgow, 1819, 73–74; Thomas Pennant, A Tour in Scotland, in 1769, in J. Pinkerton, Gen. coll. ... voyages, 3:88, Phila., 1811; same, Tour to the Hebrides, cited in Hazlitt-Brand, op. cit., 3:291; 1802, James Sibbald, Chronicle of Scottish poetry, v. 4, s.v. Spald in Glossary, Edinburgh, 1802; 1878, D. McPherson, MS, quoted in Thoms, op. cit., 177–78; 1900, John G. Campbell, Superstitions of the Highlands and Islands of Scotland collected entirely from oral sources, Glasgow, 1900, 263–66, cf. case cited as of ca. 1400 A.D.; MacCulloch, op. cit., 250. Cf. Geo. Henderson, Survivals in Belief Among the Celts, 230–31, Glasgow, 1911, shoulder blade of bear and fox, as well as of sheep, used; and (Daniel Defoe), The Life and Adventures of Mr. Duncan Campbell [1720], 241, Oxford, 1841.

[31] Wright's 1894 ed., op. cit., of Hoare's 1806 tr. with notes, of Giraldus' Itinerarium, 403, footnote 1.

[32] S. S. Dornan, Pygmies and Bushmen of the Kalahari Desert, 158, London, 1925; cf. same, Divination and Divining Bones, So. African Journ. Sci., 20:507, 1923.

[33] N. Cree, Cooper, field notes; J. Hanway, An Historical Account of the British Trade Over the Caspian Sea, 1:239, London, 1753 (2 v., 2nd ed., 1754; 1:162); A. R. McMahon, The Karens of the Golden Chersonese, 138–46, London, 1876, cf. Karen tradition of origin (p. 143) with Buriat (Mikhailovskii, op. cit., 99); cf. "M.E.F.," in Notes and Queries, June 8, 1850, 1st ser., 2:20, on Denbighshire case; A. Jenkinson, Voyage, in Purchas his pilgrimes, 12:18, Glasgow, 1906, on Tartars.

[34] The evidence for Germany, beginning with Hartlieb, 1455, has been assembled by Grimm, op. cit., (4th ed.), 2:932–33, 3:433–34, 445; cf. B. Thorpe, Northern Mythology, 3 v., London, 1851–52, 3:183. For Danish data, see Thiele, in Grimm, op. cit., 3:484, and in Thorpe, op. cit., 2:276. For Lincolnshire, England, see "St. Swithin," in Notes and Queries, Dec. 14, 1867, 3rd ser., 12:478; for Philadelphia region, "Bar-Point," ibid., March 7, 1868, 4th ser., 1:234; for Maryland, M. Whitney, Weather Sayings from Maryland, JAFL 48: 195, 1935. Cf., for Macedonia, G. F. Abbott, op. cit., 97.

[35] Cf. G. F. Abbott, op. cit., 97; E. Durham, op. cit., 225.

THE CATHOLIC UNIVERSITY OF AMERICA,
WASHINGTON, D. C.

PAPAGO NICKNAMES

By Juan Dolores

(Edited by J. Alden Mason)

The following notes on Papago nicknames or characteristic descriptive terms are copied practically verbatim from one of the grammatical notebooks written by Juan Dolores that have been in my possession far too many years for the purpose of preparing a grammar of this language, a work still far from completion. They are hardly pertinent to a grammatical sketch, yet of considerable interest for their bearing upon Papago psychology and as showing the relatively close resemblance between Papago and English usages in some instances, the differences in others. I therefore seize the opportunity of presenting them herewith without further comment.

J. Alden Mason

There are many words in this language which have more than one meaning; these words can only be understood in a sentence. Some of these words are the names of animals or birds, and when used as personal nouns or nicknames they mean that those people to whom these words are applied have the characteristics, manners, or habits of the animals, birds, or insects from which they are named.

Coyote (paN): A person who is like a coyote; he devours food and does not eat like a person. *Coyote-like* (süpaNnü·mah) (adj.): Like a coyote, eating what he can get and never getting enough. *To coyote* (paNnümaT) (verb): To lie, deceive, cheat, fool, play coyote-like tricks on another.

Woodpecker (tcühhükaM): A kind of woodpecker which, when it strikes a tree once, makes a note or two and then flits around to the other side. This bird seems to have no especial purpose in pecking at the tree, but it pretends to be doing something while it watches and hides behind the tree. The name is applied to a person who tells everything he or she hears.

Small bird (kihsuhP): A very small bird which goes to sleep at sundown. A person who goes to sleep early in the evening.

Goose (kohkǫhT): A tall, slim, long-legged person.

Water-bird (tcivihtcuhTC): A kind of bird which runs around in the water. A girl who has the bad habit of wearing short dresses.

Hawk (hauhpahLI): A kind of hawk which fights and kills his game with his claws. A woman with the bad habit of scratching.

Deer (kuvi'T): A kind of deer, big, yellowish, in open country. When this deer is frightened and starts running he is liable to run into danger because he never turns his course. A very unlucky person.

Devil (tciawuhLI) (probably from Sp. *diablo*): The Devil Cactus (*bisnaga*). This is a small cactus with long hook-like thorns. It is from this cactus that water is produced, or the juice is squeezed from it and used as water. A devilish person; one who is supposed to know something supernatural.

Dog (koKS): One who has no sense of shame; however homely he may be, he makes friends with men or women who feed him and lives at ease, not considering his appearance, as to how he looks to other people. One who growls, like a dog, at his near relations, on account of small things. When the term is applied to a woman (bitch), it means the same as in English.

Monster (ho'ohĸ) : A human being with animal-like character, supposed to have been born of a woman, a mythological character. A man or woman who is fighting all the time.

Quiver (wo'ĸscah) : A sack in which the arrows were carried on the back. A stepson or stepdaughter. A man who has a child of this kind does not especially need him, yet he has to take care of him, or carry him around on his back as it were, and perhaps some day the child will be of some use. This is the same thing as a sack of arrows carried around by someone who does not especially need the arrows at the time, until some day when he shoots away all the arrows that he carries in his hand; then he finds that he has not been working to no effect. He is well paid for carrying the sack; he is well paid for taking care of the child, though the child is not his own.

Mocking bird (cuĸ) : A person who is talking all the time.

Rat (kohsoN) : A kind of rat which lives in a house of brush and thorns where he hides his stolen booty. A person who is always stirring up hidden things.

Whirlwind (siwulihĸ) : One who is always stirring and scattering things, as a whirlwind.

Roadrunner (taṭaɪ) : A bird. A person who carries the news back and forth.

Skull (kohcüvah) : A person who seems to have nothing in his head; a blockhead.

Unbaked pot (toɪ ha'ah) : A raw olla. A person who, like a raw olla, has to be handled as a woman handles her olla, with the greatest of care. If she puts it out in the wind it will break; if she leaves it where it dries too fast it will break. So, with care, patience, and skill she makes the olla and, after all, should she happen to drop it, it will break to pieces. If she wants to have an olla of this particular size and shape she will have to begin all over again and make a new one. Some people are said to be like a raw olla; when one, with skill, patience, and care, has made a friend of one of these people, he must handle him as a woman handles her olla. Some little thing compels one to say a word or two out of place, and the friend goes all to pieces, like a raw olla.

Pet (coyikah) : A pet animal. A person who can be handled as a pet, ordered, pulled around, or punished like a pet.

Grasshopper (co'oh); ühco'ohTC : To act like a grasshopper. When such a person is spoken to, he is afraid to move or to speak; he clenches his hands like one holding on to a rope for his life. He stays in that position until he dies, like a grasshopper which seemingly clenches his hands or his feet and hangs to the grass in one position until he dies.

Salt (oN); oNnümma'T : To salt. One is said to be salting someone when he is coaxing or urging him for his personal advantage, like one who salts the food for his own use, or to suit his taste.

Flour (tcu'ɪ); tcu'ima'T : To scatter flour on something. To call a singer to sing to a sick person to make him well. This is perhaps given this term because a call of this kind is not so urgent as one to a medicine man. You call a man, leaving your words as a handful of flour scattered on something, which soon blows away.

Fingernails (hu·tc); huhkiMmuM: Breaking with the fingernails as a woman cleaning greens, preparing them for cooking. Coaxing. For instance: I am in Arizona; I meet a friend of mine and I want him to come with me to San Francisco. Here is where I tickle him or pinch him: "In San Francisco the climate is always fine and the surrounding country is beautiful; the city itself is alive day and night; amusements of all kinds are open to strangers, and one can have a better time there than here in the desert," etc.

UNIVERSITY OF CALIFORNIA,
BERKELEY, CALIFORNIA.

THE WEALTH CONCEPT AS AN INTEGRATIVE FACTOR IN TOLOWA-TUTUTNI CULTURE

By Cora Du Bois

ALONG THE PACIFIC COAST from approximately Crescent City in California to Port Orford in Oregon there existed some eighteen Athabascan-speaking settlements which are generally grouped into three tribes, the Tolowa, the Chetco, and the Tututni. These tribal divisions are arbitrary categories based on slight dialectic differences. In reality there were a series of villages located usually on river mouths and claiming well-defined territories along the coast. Inland, the boundaries between village territories were less sharply delimited. No river had inland settlements of importance except the Rogue, up which some five villages of Tututni were located. In aboriginal times there must have been a population of approximately three thousand. Today only a small remnant of Tolowa still remain in situ. Of the Tututni a handful of survivors is located on Siletz reservation to which the tribe was taken in 1856. Culturally the Tolowa-Tututni are closely related to that subarea of northwest coast culture whose focus Kroeber has placed among the Yurok of the Klamath river in northwestern California. However, the Tolowa-Tututni represent an internally marginal people whose social, ritual, and material existence was far less complex than that of either their northern or southern neighbors.

Philip Drucker, of the University of California, has studied the ethnography of these Athabascan groups for two years and his detailed report will appear later. Meanwhile he has kindly placed his notes at my disposal. These, in addition to my recent observations, form the basis of this sketch. A few illustrative cases were selected from Tolowa Notes.[1] Drucker has been consulted in drawing up these comments and his suggestions have often been followed; however, I assume full responsibility for any rashness of interpretation on the basis of material which is unavoidably fragmentary. It is not my purpose to present detailed ethnographic data but simply to excerpt such material as is applicable to my interpretations.

Not every culture integrates its social behavior to a few dominating attitudes, nor need every aspect, even of a relatively integrated culture, necessarily be aligned with major social preoccupations. It is the purpose of this paper to demonstrate that the emphasis on wealth among the Tolowa-Tututni permeates and shapes a large part of social behavior; that by such integrative emphases traits may be lent intensity and nuances which are lacking in other areas and that such emphases combine with, or produce, related attitudes which embrace the bulk of the cultural behavior recorded for these people. There are other phases of their life, however, which cannot be subsumed under the integrative attitudes of the culture. When one considers that the content of any culture is an accumulation of diverse historical factors, the surprising

---

[1] Du Bois, Cora, Tolowa Notes, AA 34:248–262, 1932.

aspect is that integration has been achieved at all. The amorphous composition of neighboring tribes in north central California indicates that even where the cultural content is not very different, integrative stresses may be absent and the resulting societies are worlds apart. The addition or subtraction of traits will not yield the differences which separate the Tolowa-Tututni from, let us say, the Wintu.

Emphasis on wealth has long been recognized as part of the northwest coast culture to which the Tolowa-Tututni belong. Like other tribes along this coast, they have a rich subsistence provided by a bountiful environment, and a relatively dense population. This point has been stressed sufficiently often to need no elaboration.

Before discussing the specific aspects of wealth emphasis among the Tolowa-Tututni, I should like to make a distinction between subsistence and prestige economy. By subsistence economy is meant the exploitation of the plentiful natural resources available to any industrious individual. Although there were privately owned fishing sites, ordinarily these were used freely by any person within the village group. The only restriction upon the use of such locations was the temporary mourner's rights. A breach of these rights led to fines, but otherwise every individual was free to pursue his subsistence activities. "Individuals who had been lazy or inefficient in gathering food . . . were forced to buy it. If they were too poor to pay for it, they were given food by others but they were looked down upon. 'Anybody could do what he liked with them.'"[2]

By prestige economy on the other hand, is meant a series of social prerogatives and status values. They included a large range of phenomena from wives to formulae for supernatural compulsion. They embraced mourners' privileges and innumerable personal dignities, the disregard of which was cause for compensation regardless of intent.

In addition to these two forms of economic activity, the Tolowa-Tututni had certain "treasures" which possessed a minimum consumption value, and which functioned as media of exchange. Primary among these were dentalia, which were the most standardized medium and which most nearly approximated the criteria of money established by economists, viz., durability, divisibility, rarity, portability, and homogeneity. Other shells, woodpecker scalps, rare pelts, obsidian blades, and certain regalia also serve to a lesser extent in transacting negotiations. The significant point in the economic life of these tribes is that their monies served as a medium of exchange primarily in the realm of prestige economy rather than subsistence economy. For example, they are not accustomed to translate the value of dried salmon or a basket into dentalia and then make exchanges whose dentalia equivalents are of equal value. In the realm of subsistence economy the Tolowa-Tututni were on a barter basis without translation into another medium—which is the essence of money economy. In their prestige economy, however, they were definitely money-minded and wealth values were associated with social status. All individuals were

---
[2] Du Bois, *op. cit.*, 255.

brought up with the social ideal of driving a hard bargain, of pushing every advantage by means of haggling, and thereby of establishing themselves socially. Since one of the means for acquiring money was the dignity-insult device, a "touchiness" developed which has been characterized as paranoid by Benedict for other regions of the northwest coast.[3]

In attempting generalizations concerning the limited sphere in which money operates, it is important not to overdraw and oversimplify the picture. Thus, a statement was made in a preceding paragraph that an improvident person might be forced to buy food if he had any money. Actually, a rich man would probably rarely, if ever, find himself without food; while a poor man could usually depend upon the bounty of a rich kinsman for reasons explained subsequently. Also there were certain phases of subsistence economy which overlapped those of prestige. For instance, a stranded whale was carefully divided on a status basis and any trespass upon the section allotted a given person was bitterly resented and even led to bloodshed. Similarly, the first sealing trip of the year was the prerogative of the person most recently bereaved. In essence, however, these overlaps between subsistence activities and prestige values are referable to sensitivity about prestige values rather than to an actual struggle for livelihood in a subsistence sense. On the whole it may be said with complete validity that the Tolowa-Tututni were on a barter basis in the realm of subsistence economy. Furthermore, the favorable environment made even barter a minor activity. In addition, food was shared by the provident with the improvident within the village group. A successful hunter was expected to be liberal with his kinsmen. The individualism and scheming parsimony of prestige economy did not extend to subsistence.

Comparisons have been made between wealth preoccupations of the northwest coast and western European society. Although there is much validity in this contention, differences are revealed upon analysis. In our culture, for instance, subsistence economy functions on a money basis, whereas among the Tolowa-Tututni the interplay between money and subsistence was shown to be at a minimum. Money was serviceable in the purchase of social protection and prestige, in sex, and in maintaining familial status, but it entered hardly at all into the subsistence equation. In Euro-American society money per se has acquired social value secondarily through the operation of that principle which Vaihinger[4] calls the "law of the preponderance of the means over the end." Today money is the essential medium through which our subsistence economy operates and secondarily it has acquired prestige values. In Tolowa-Tututni society the equation is different. Subsistence economy is divorced from prestige and money operates in the latter realm. We do not know the history of money in relation to the subsistence and prestige wealth among the Tolowa-Tututni as we do in European society, but as it functioned within the period under observation, there is no indication that their money was anything but a device for dealing in a limited set of social recognitions. There

---

[3] Benedict, Ruth, Patterns of Culture, 222, 1934.
[4] Vaihinger, H., The Philosophy of "As If," XLVI and *passim*, 1925.

is no hint that money was ever very important in determining whether a man were well or poorly fed and housed. In our society housing and food have become symbols of social rank because money has come to function in both subsistence and prestige economy. For Euro-American society the following equation might be suggested: subsistence $\leftrightarrows$ money $\rightarrow$ prestige. In Tolowa-Tututni society the equation would be: subsistence — (money $\leftrightarrows$ prestige).

This divorce between the two forms of economy not only sets apart the Tolowa-Tututni system from that of western Europe, it also distinguishes it to a lesser extent from the northwest coast culture of British Columbia. In this area the potlatch feasts were a concomitant of every rich man's social obligations. Subsistence wealth became a primary concern of every wealthy man's social activity. Prestige wealth and subsistence economy were not linked directly through the medium of a money system but they were related through the feast tradition. Among the Tolowa-Tututni, on the other hand, the feast motif was minimal and was not recognized as part of every rich man's social duties in order to maintain his status.

In addition another difference in attitude toward wealth sharply marks off the Tolowa-Tututni from the British Columbia tribes. The distribution and destruction of property for prestige purposes in British Columbia were not only unknown to the Tolowa-Tututni, but they seemed utterly preposterous when it was suggested to them. The extent to which the distribution of property was foreign to them is implied in the behavior of the following anecdote. The incident must have occurred in 1854 or 1855 immediately prior to the removal to Siletz reservation.

A Rogue River girl (Tutoten) married a man from Port Orford (Kwatami). That night the Port Orford people held a dance and the man's father broke some strings of dentalia and threw them around. Anybody could pick them up. I [the informant] was ashamed so I didn't get any. I guess I was pretty stupid.

I should judge from this account that the idea of gift distribution had percolated down from the north in recent historic times and that a Port Orford man had attempted to imitate what he had heard or seen. Obviously, however, he had no ceremonial mechanisms at his command; nor did he have any assistance from his guests in carrying out a procedure which seemed nothing short of insane to them. The informant still laughs at the procedure, considers it a ludicrous performance, and is rueful that she did not join in the general scramble which followed the scattering of the shells.

In relation to the absence of the potlatch, we encounter one of the fundamental attitudes of the Tolowa-Tututni toward wealth. They possessed a consistency and realism in this respect which differentiates them from the British Columbia peoples. Wealth is desirable as the source of all social advantages and preëminences. To destroy or distribute it with a gesture of disdain, as do the more northerly people, is to them a preposterous anomaly and quite beyond their comprehension.

Also the Tolowa-Tututni are differentiated from the British Columbia peoples by the absence of a concept of interest on loans. Although the general wealth stress is directed toward acquisition rather than display and destruction, they seem to have lacked this device for accumulating wealth. It is a peculiar omission whose history is probably irrecoverable. To a greater or lesser extent such inconsistencies are present in every social structure.

The degree to which subsistence and prestige economy are divorced, the absence of the potlatch with the attendant realistic attitude toward accumulating wealth and the absence of interest on loans serve in part to create an economic subarea in a predominantly northwest coast culture which is as different, for example, as communistic Russia and capitalistic western Europe.

Within the subarea, however, a further distinction can be drawn between the Tolowa-Tututni and the Yurok whom Kroeber considers the cultural focus of this region. The difference was adumbrated previously when it was suggested that the Tolowa were internally marginal. There is among the Tututni, in particular, a surprising paucity of ceremonialism if we define ceremonialism as group ritualism. Their only regular ceremony is the ten-night dance of the winter season. There are in addition the victory dance after a war and the more or less social gatherings for shamanistic initiations, but these two occasions are motivated by individual crises and do not represent celebrations for the social group as a unit. Even girls' adolescence dances are lacking among the Tututni. The Tolowa, however, possess them. Similarly, feasts are only occasional and on a small scale. There is a minimum of relaxation from the strained preoccupation with wealth. Esthetic outlets are as meager as the social ones. Formerly they possessed no musical instruments. The square skin drum is a recent introduction. Prior to that time the nearest approach to any instrumental accompaniment to songs was a stick for pounding roof or wall planks. The Tututni themselves admitted that their basketry was inferior to that on the Klamath river. The same held for their stone, wood, and horn work. All this reflects a certain dour paucity in esthetic and social life which presents a very different picture from that given for their southern neighbors. This must have had a distinct bearing on their wealth outlook. The Yurok had a series of localized world-renewing ceremonies whose climax lay in the elaborate displays of treasure on the last day. Comparable was the ten-night dance of the Tututni, but the quantity and the quality of displayed objects were less impressive and the whole ceremonial atmosphere far less dramatic. This subarea utilized wealth display ceremonies, as opposed to potlatches, for deriving social satisfaction and prestige-ostentation for its wealth pattern. However, the Tututni had less satisfactory expressions of this sort than the Yurok. The Tolowa seem to lie halfway between the two. This does not mean that the intensity of the wealth preoccupation was any less, but that it was more introverted.

We are now ready to consider specifically how the wealth attitudes functioned in Tolowa-Tututni society and how far their ramifications permeated and shaped social institutions.

The social unit is the exogamous village consisting primarily of paternal kin. Despite this definition of the social unit, no gens existed in Tolowa-Tututni consciousness. The same situation has been commented upon by Kroeber for the Yurok. Comparable to the absence of the gens concept was the absence of any concept of society as an abstract tertium quid regulating relationships between persons. All relationships were individualized. It is important to realize that this meant there was no political organization. Therefore there were no crimes in the strict sense of the word. All injuries, whether insult, mayhem, or murder, were torts for which compensating payments could buy atonement. In theory at least there was no infringement which a money transaction would not settle. In a society of this type, rapprochement between law and finance becomes much more intimate than we are accustomed to envisage it. In fact, the two almost reach identity. Where law and finance are so closely allied in theory, wealth and social power become identified to a marked degree in practice. Social equilibrium was the vested interest of the rich man who dominated each village. As a Tolowa informant said, "Poor people can't say anything. They haven't money to talk with. . . ." The rich man functioned as a state surrogate. He was by preference the intermediary in the settlements for injuries and it was to his own best interest to be a negotiator in disputes. This was due to the concept of referred responsibility. By referred responsibility is meant that ultimately it might be incumbent upon the rich man of the village to make payments for the torts committed by any of his village kinsmen. This attitude is consistent with Tolowa-Tututni realism concerning wealth which was brought out in relation to the potlatch. Responsibility meant payments, and responsibility therefore rested ultimately on him who could pay. For example, if a poor young man from Tutoten killed a man from Kwatami, it was the duty of the Tutoten rich man to see that the weregeld was paid. Should peaceful negotiations fail and a feud result, the life of the rich man, rather than that of the insignificant murderer, would be considered adequate compensation. The object of most Tolowa-Tututni feuds was not to kill the guilty person in our sense of the word, but the most important man, that is, the richest, of his group.

This system of referred responsibility functioned precisely and directly to produce social alignment. It was to the interest of every rich man to see that the kin under his jurisdiction should not embroil him in difficulties which would either diminish his wealth or threaten his life. It was customary for the rich man or some other responsible adult to exhort the youths in the sweat house not to quarrel with neighbors. These recommendations may not represent a system of ethical education comparable to ours, but they were probably as efficacious in achieving social good behavior because they were based directly on the paramount social emphasis of the culture, namely, wealth. We see that the widespread Indian custom in which youth is exhorted "to be good, not to quarrel," etc., was intensified in Tolowa-Tututni culture by its direct reference to the wealth value deeply embedded in everyone's social consciousness.

The problem of holding the less wealthy in control has been indicated as a function of the wealth concept accepted by all individuals within Tolowa-Tututni society. However, the question arises in how far the absolutism of the rich man can be held in check for the general welfare of the group where political organization does not exist as a tertium quid to preserve a balance of power. The answer lies in mutual interdependence between both classes of society. If the poor man depended on the rich one for payment of obligations, the rich man depended on the brawn and good will of the poor which was the underlying threat in every negotiation. Haggling over fines was basic to every settlement and the successful haggler was often the one who could muster the greatest show of force. Every time a group or an individual parted with wealth in payment for a tort it was because the threat of mayhem or death was a very possible alternative. Fundamentally, then, potential violence lubricated the social machinery. The following anecdote illustrates a number of points in connection with the checks upon the absolutism of the rich.

A Port Orford (Kwatami) man had a wife from Coquille whom he killed. About ten months after she was buried, her family asked this rich man up there to get another wife. His people were sick of him. He used to bully them into giving him hides and money. He was a mean man. When he went up to Coquille he took four of his relatives along with him. He thought they would help him fight. He went to the Coquille people and just as he stepped in the house they killed him. His relatives were glad to be rid of him and didn't help him. They just carried his body home to be buried. They didn't try to kill anyone in revenge. They felt the score was even.

It is clear from accounts of this nature that a rich man depended upon the good will of his kin group if he were to hold in check the latent violence of individual competition. He could not, therefore, function as an autocrat. His rôle was that of a successful businessman and skillful diplomat.

The institution of slavery was also tinted with the general wealth emphasis. Slaves were not taken in war but were acquired through unpaid debt. A man who became indebted to a rich man might himself enter into slavery, or, more probably, would transfer a child in lieu of payment. Debts could be incurred only in the realm of prestige economy as it has been stated previously. Therefore slaves became a source of prestige ostentation. They were symbols of money once owned and loaned. The word ostentation is used advisedly in connection with slavery since slaves were never sold and were therefore of no value in increasing a man's supply of money. A slave did assist in subsistence occupations but these were not a source of income. His status was approximately that of a poor relative. He lived in the rich man's household, was well treated as a rule and in return his loyalty and support were expected. In reality slavery was almost a form of adoption. From a Tututni informant no hint of the existence of slavery could be secured until the subject of adoption was brought up. A Tolowa informant explicitly referred to the institution as adoption. To apply the term slave to such individuals among the Tututni is in reality a misnomer. It was not unusual for a rich man to marry his female slave or to purchase a wife for his male servant. Obviously, slavery was not hereditary. Scarcely more onus seemed attached to it than to poverty, of which it was essentially a reflection. Informants when they were questioned directly said there were two social groups, the rich and the poor. Slaves, apparently, were lumped with the latter rather than forming a separate category.

Wealth not only pervades the fields of law, ethics, slavery, and the maintenance of social order; it is also basic to marriage where one of its greatest elaborations occurs. Bride prices were about equal to blood money, which means that they varied from $80 to $150. As in weregeld settlements, the wealth status of the individual served to determine the price finally agreed upon. The system of haggling held in this field also. What a man was paid for his daughter, an insult, or an infringement of his rights directly reflected his social ranking and it was to his interest to drive as sharp a bargain as possible. Whether bargaining was the direct result of the wealth emphasis is impossible to say, but that it reflected and heightened monetary engrossments is beyond doubt. Marriage settlements were interfamilial affairs. The large carefully decorated dentalia which formed the most valuable part of the bride price were displayed on shallow baskets. They were handled slowly and reverently. Dentalia were known to influential men of the community much as bibliophiles among us know the history, condition, and location of rare editions. With the bride went a dowry, the most important item of which was an elaborately decorated buckskin dancing dress presented to the groom's mother. In reality there was at marriage an exchange between families which was only slightly in favor of the woman's family when the dowry and bride price are translated into dollars and equated. Nevertheless the fiction existed that a man was enriched by marrying off his daughter. The bearing of this point will appear later. Actually the bride price was in the nature of a deposit by the groom's family with the bride's. It established a series of mutual obligations and the brother-in-law became one of the groom's most desirable allies in all litigation. Meanwhile the groom's family had various liens on the deposited bride price and for that reason families attempted to keep bride prices intact. For instance, divorce meant the return of all exchanged properties, including the dowry dress. Obviously it was to the interest of the bride's family to see that the marriage was stable. Here again we find a financial motive functioning as a social stabilizer. In how far the bride's family would permit her to be flagrantly abused before permitting her to return would depend upon the rapacity of the parents. Kroeber says that the Yurok did not permit their daughters to be ill-used. The Tututni custom of torturing a wife suspected of adultery, which will be described later, suggests that they were not always so squeamish as their southern neighbors. If the marriage contract between the two families is abrogated by death, the bride's family may and generally does offer a substitute instead of returning the bride price. We recognize in this procedure the institution of the sororate; but because the ever-present wealth emphasis is involved, it has added connotations and intensities which are lacking, for instance, in areas like north central California.

Another lien which the man has upon the bride price is concerned with the death of his children. If a child died, the wife's family was obligated to pay the husband for the value of the child. He in turn might make a return gift slightly larger in value so that ultimately the husband was the loser. Such procedure was not obligatory for the husband, however. If a woman left her husband after bearing a child, the price of the child was subtracted from the returned bride price. After a certain number of children had been born, they were considered the equivalent of the bride price and the woman was free to return to her family without submitting them to financial obligations.

The financial aspects of the marriage contract may be summarized in the following manner. The price paid for the bride was only fictitiously as large as the sums usually stated by the informants since the bride's family made a partial return in gifts. Marriage established a mutual help contract between families. It was considered desirable to hold the bride price in deposit against future contingencies. In case of divorce the contract was voided by the return of both the bride price and the dowry. In case of death the contract was continued by substituting another spouse from within the families concerned. A sufficient number of children was the equivalent of fulfilling the marriage contract and only after their birth was the wife's family free of the liens on the bride price. If children died, the woman's family made a payment which the husband might acknowledge with a comparable or larger return. We see from this situation that the bride price might be interpreted as a loan which the woman worked off for the benefit of her family by bearing children. The exchange of payments upon the death of a child might be envisaged as a pledge of good faith on the part of both parties to the contract. In the light of this system, the legal obligations, or the principle of reciprocity as Malinowski envisages it, were motivated directly by financial interests. Once more it is essentially the wealth motif which makes the social wheels turn and which places the reciprocal social obligations of the institution of marriage in the light of money interests.

The impregnation of the institution of marriage with the dominant wealth preoccupations served to color sex and familial relationships, especially in the realm of postmarital sex transgressions. Adultery was not only an offense against the highly sensitized egos of the Tolowa-Tututni; it was also an offense against vested interests and was treated as such. The following anecdote illustrates the extreme to which such cases might be carried.

> A Rogue River (Tutoten) man was jealous of his wife. One day he told her to gather a lot of wood. So she brought in a lot that day, good dry wood as he had told her. Late that afternoon he built a fire, a big blaze. She asked why he was doing that. She didn't know what he was going to do. Then another man came in. She didn't know what was the matter. Then her husband and the other man took her by the arms and held her near the fire. Her husband asked if she had stolen a man (committed adultery). She didn't answer, so they shoved her farther in the fire. They asked her again and she said no. She got all burned down her front. If a woman tells who the man is, they let her go and go after the man and kill him. Sometimes he says he will pay and they let him go.

This tale is not an isolated instance of a sadistic individual. It was a generally known device, but probably it was resorted to only in rare cases. If the male culprit were caught, he might be the victim of the force principle which underlay all Tolowa-Tututni behavior, or he could find refuge in the wealth pattern by paying the bride price plus an insult fee to the injured husband.

If the man refused, or was unable to pay, he might be seized and mutilated until his kinsmen intervened by agreeing to meet the debt. From the point of view of the rapacious husband there was a financial premium on discovering his wife in adultery. When a man conformed in entirety to the social stress upon accumulating wealth, this situation was fraught with possibilities of suspicious, antagonistic, and even brutal relationships between the spouses.

There are also instances where a certain brutal inflexibility toward marital transgressions seems to function almost of its own momentum without conscious reference to the wealth element involved. However, since this attitude is solely in connection with adultery—in other words, with an infringement involving financial transactions—it leads one to suspect that unconsciously the wealth situation may have reinforced, at least, the moralistic one. The two following anecdotes indicate that a strongly moralistic attitude existed in which no conscious wealth emphasis was reported, whatever the unconscious motivations may have been.

As a child the informant was playing on the bank of the Rogue river when she saw the corpse of a woman drift down. Her elders said to her that it must be the body of a woman killed for adultery and that no one would bury it; it would just be washed out to sea. Whether or not this was a correct interpretation, it reveals the sternness of the society toward marital transgressions.

A man from Tutoten stole a married woman from Mekwanauten. They returned to Tutoten but the people there chased them away. This might seem at first blush to be based on the desire to avoid embroilment between two villages closely related by marriage. However, the Tutoten man made an adequate payment to the injured husband which consisted of both a bride price and an insult fee. Despite this, the people of Tutoten refused to receive the couple and they went up river to live by themselves. The severity of ostracism in a society organized around the mutual financial and force obligations of the group, is far from slight.

The education of children fostered the potential attitudes toward sex transgressions which have just been described. Educational precepts stressed the suppression of sex on the one hand and on the other maximized the desirability of wealth. When a boy was about six he was admitted to the men's sweat house and his contacts with women were curtailed. In the sweat house the older men "talked to the boys, told them to make money, how to be rich, not to eat too much or they won't get rich." A boy is warned particularly "not to think about women all the time" but to concentrate instead on wealth. Then "people will think something of him, think what a big man he is." If a mother at meals showed an inclination to pamper her son, the father might cuff the boy and take him from the dwelling. A wealthy man was supposed to eat slowly and avoid evidences of hunger and greediness.[5] One means by which boys were kept partially fed was through the minor vision quest of the area. They were sent to seek wealth blessings or gambling luck, which is its partial equivalent. The

---
[5] One wonders whether in analytic terms there could have been any linkage between sex and food cravings which the educational system suppressed simultaneously.

degree to which the educational system was directed toward the acquisition of wealth is revealed in the following quotation from Tolowa Notes.

... If a poor man wanted to be rich he had to think about a lot of sad things. He would go to a lucky mountain and cry and wish hard to be rich. He would think of his father and mother and how poor they were. He just sat and cried and thought hard about beads and rich things like that.... At dawn he would come back to the village crying. It was awfully sad to hear him.... Sometimes people go crazy wishing so hard to be rich.[6]

Although boys were urged to think of wealth and not of women, yet sex and familial gratifications were associated with wealth. The intensity of that association is brought out by the following statements of a Tututni informant.

Only rich men had more than one wife. Sometimes a really poor man never gets married at all. He is just an old bachelor who goes on living with his parents. When they die he has to go live with some rich relative who will take care of him.

Since extra-marital relationships were fraught with danger and were infringements of vested interests, this meant that a very poor man might be denied direct sex outlets. Probably, however, such cases were rare.

In the education of girls the same wealth-sex antithesis was stressed although the specific instructions naturally differed. Girls had inculcated in them chastity, modesty, and industry. A Tolowa informant stated, "No girl must ever talk in front of a man or boy. If you walked in front of them, people would say you weren't brought up right. Parents had to tell girls all these things, especially how you have to act about men." The incentive parents offered to girls for proper behavior was a high bride price. This of course was a social fiction since the bride price paid for a woman was primarily determined by the financial status of her family. If one wished a girl well one said, "I hope someone buys you for a large price." Virginity was desired in marriage. If a girl was raped, her financial value was definitely lowered. A suitor would be entitled under such circumstances to offer less for her. Her family, therefore, was eager to find the guilty man and bully him into paying as large a bride price as possible. The family of a girl who was deliberately unchaste might whip her, but their attitude toward the man remained the same as in rape. The rape of a widow was a less costly matter although her affinal family would demand compensation. One informant stated that married women were even more modest than unmarried girls. "Some married women are so modest that they won't let anyone see them make string (rolled on bare thigh)." The reasons are to be sought in the preceding comments on adultery, the financial relationships between families established by marriage, and the fact that village exogamy and patrilocal residence placed the woman in a community of strangers who were not necessarily friendly. The hostility to which woman may on occasion be exposed in a strange community is revealed in the following anecdote. That she was posthumously avenged was probably very little consolation.

A rich man from Port Orford (Kwatami) married a Coquille woman. She said she was going to have a child. The husband was glad. The woman was just lying. Her mother-in-law

---
[6] Du Bois, *op. cit.*, 255.

told her son that his wife was still having her monthlies. So he got his wife to gather wood. He made a big fire. He hired another man to help him. They took the woman and shoved her in the fire. Then the man asked if she was going to have a baby. He said she was still having her monthlies. She wouldn't answer so they shoved her still farther in the fire. Still she wouldn't talk. They pushed her so far in that she died of her burns.[7]

It is conceivable that this instance would not have occurred had the woman's family been closer and able to protect her. Nevertheless protection must have been frequently remote since wives from distant villages were felt to have more prestige value than those from neighboring communities.

So far, during the discussion of education as a formative force in woman's social attitudes, the wealth concept has acted passively and simply as a reward for acceptable behavior. In shamanism, women had a more active outlet for wealth ideals. The degree to which this incentive might motivate a girl in acquiring supernatural power is illustrated by the following excerpts from the statement of a Tolowa informant.

There was a young woman who must have been poor because she felt sorry for herself. One day she was eating dried fish eggs and a woman took them away from her because they were too good for a poor person. The girl felt sorry for herself and kept thinking all the time about the fish eggs. "Some day I hope I get everything I want," she said. She used to cry all the time. When she went to sleep she dreamed she would be a doctor . . . and money would come to her.

To summarize: The education of both sexes stressed the desirability of wealth. Boys were taught to suppress sexual preoccupations although their ultimate gratification was a correlate of money. Girls could express their wealth ideals actively by becoming shamans. A high bride price and the concomitant social status was an inducement to passive social conformity. Once a marriage was made, one has the impression that the stress and strain of sex relations was intensified rather than relaxed as they are in our society. The brittle monogamy and casual philanderings of north central California were out of the question in Tolowa-Tututni society. Women responded to this strain by an increasingly modest attitude probably for the reasons given above.

The stress and strain of the marital situation is evinced further by outbursts of jealousy between spouses. A jealous husband, who might not be driven by suspicions of adultery to torturing a confession from his wife, might nevertheless slash her with a knife in rage. A jealous wife would maltreat and scratch her husband until he withdrew in ostentatious sulkiness to the men's sweat house. Cowives were also intractable if the husband showed any preferences. The following anecdote reveals the stress which might develop in a polygynous household and the method of dealing with it. One wonders if the purely architectural problem of having cowives occupy the same dwelling did not intensify the situation? The heavy plank houses represented much labor and a man possessed only one. The easily built and semipermanent bark or skin houses of some areas would have permitted wives to live separately and

---

[7] Drucker states that the moral connected with this anecdote in the minds of the Tolowa-Tututni was the contamination to which a menstruant woman exposed the group.

would have eased the strain in a society which simultaneously permitted polygyny and fostered jealousy.

A Tolowa man from Smith River had five wives. Each one cooks for herself [customary procedure perhaps indicative that coöperation was not assumed?]. The man slept with each wife in turn during the course of one night. If he didn't stay long enough with one woman, that woman got jealous. In the morning the man goes back to the sweat house and sweats, then he goes back to the house for breakfast. Then the fight starts. The jealous wife throws hot coals at his crotch. He is all naked and jumps around. Then the women fight with each other, scratch, pull each other's hair. The man goes out and lets them fight. If he really gets mad he hits them and then goes in the sweat house for a couple of days and doesn't eat.

There is an impression of basic antagonism between the sexes. It is reflected further in the belief that a man would die within a year if a woman guessed against him correctly in a gambling game. As a result women did not participate directly in this favorite pastime, although they were allowed to watch games and place bets. In other tribes outside of the northwest coast area women were often debarred from gambling directly against men, but to my knowledge this particular explanation has not been reported as the rationalization. Similarly among the Tolowa, boys who had not known women were considered to be especially lucky in gambling games.

Despite certain implications in the foregoing paragraphs upon the inferior status of women, such was actually not the case. That wives could thoroughly discomfit a husband and drive him to ineffectual sulking in the sweat house, does not imply such a situation. It has already been stated that women derived prestige value from a high bride price, or can seek direct outlet and monetary rewards in shamanism. For infringement of sex taboos, there were penalties for both men and women. The woman's penalties took the form of brutal treatment and loss of status, but the men were subject to onerous fines. In marriage, the bride's dowry, which consisted primarily of the valuable buckskin dance dress, was a gift to the mother-in-law. She became its custodian and in case of divorce was responsible for its return. Also a girl was not entirely the pawn of her family in contracting a marriage. It will be recalled that in cases of prenuptial intercourse the woman's family usually tried to legalize the marriage by securing a bride price. Girls were therefore in a position to force a marriage in cases of romantic attachments and this was an opportunity of which they seemed to have availed themselves.

The wealth concomitants of religion can be briefly reviewed. As in other phases of society the financial emphasis was present. Shamans received payments for cures. Even the singers who assisted at séances were compensated. The custom of returning shamans' fees for unsuccessful cures was in keeping with Tolowa-Tututni realism in money matters. Formulae were also a source of income. These were secured either by purchase or by revelation. They can be envisioned as commodities which could be rented. If mourners needed purification, if luck was needed in hunting, etc., the person who possessed the requisite formula was hired to repeat it. It was usually mumbled so that chance listeners would not learn it. However, a man might definitely purchase the knowledge from the owner and thereafter use it legitimately. In death observances very little destruction of property occurred. Dwellings were left intact if relatives could use them. Canoes, regalia, and all paraphernalia of the deceased were utilized by his heirs. This attitude is quite in harmony with their inability to understand the distribution or destruction of property at potlatches. However, the Tolowa-Tututni did not minimize this crisis. Instead they characteristically translated it into a series of prestige values which were worth money. Formulists were paid for removing taboos. Mourners had to be compensated before the community could enjoy the single ceremonial festivity of the year, the ten-night dance of the winter months. Also mourners were surrounded with a whole series of insult potentialities whose breach meant substantial fines. The widely distributed name taboo on the dead was one of the strongest. Here we find another widespread cultural trait given added significance and intensity by its integration into a broader network of related attitudes. Certain first fishing privileges for mourners were also recognized. Private ownership of fishing sites, ordinarily in abeyance, was stringently resurrected in case of mourner's status. The bereaved were thrown into a frenzy of "touchiness" and other individuals were penalized for their loss.

War among the Tolowa-Tututni is a final subject to be briefly discussed in the light of financial aspects. It has been pointed out before that all settlements of torts were carried on by haggling and that the agreement reached rested ultimately on a show of force. If bloodshed were precipitated by personal feuds there might follow a series of ambuscades and murders which really constituted Tolowa-Tututni warfare. Meanwhile with each death or injury the debts for compensatory payments accumulated. This in turn eventually involved the rich men of the villages through the principle of referred responsibility previously mentioned. When the final reckoning came the two sides mustered all available men and camped opposite each other. Several go-betweens met in the neutral center ground and tried to reach a satisfactory settlement. Each side offered compensations for damages and in turn demanded compensations for their own injuries. If an agreement were reached, the side which had inflicted the more severe damages was the one liable for the larger payment. As Kroeber has stated for Yurok, "In any event the greater financial drain bore on the winner."[8] Kroeber has also pointed out in this connection that this concept of war is signally ill adapted from our point of view to a social system organized around the acquisition of wealth. War, which has economic motivation in our culture, had no such interpretation in the area under consideration. The Tolowa-Tututni and their neighbors seem to have failed to interpret this institution to their financial advantage even though the wealth concept was inevitably injected into it.

In addition to the nonacquisitive character of Tolowa-Tututni warfare it will be recalled that interest on loans and debt slavery were also singularly unexploited wealth institutions from the Euro-American point of view. Such exceptions make the picture of wealth as an integrative factor in Tolowa-Tututni society less convincingly simple and sharp, but it is essential to be

---

[8] Kroeber, A. L., Handbook of the Indians of California, BAE-B 78:49, 1925.

aware of such discrepancies in order to correctly balance a portrayal of their culture. Probably no culture is completely integrated. It is to be expected that there will always be found certain institutions and fields of behavior untouched by the dominating drives of the social group. The three institutions just mentioned are phases of Tolowa-Tututni culture in which wealth concepts were deeply rooted but which were not exploited to maximum advantage. Another case in point is the laxness with which the concept of private property in land functioned. Despite the highly personalized relationships of the culture, individual land ownership was submerged in the interest of the kin group.

There were in addition certain institutions which were not only unexploited but also largely untouched by the wealth concept. Primary among these was girls' adolescence observances. The Tolowa had at least a ceremonial dance where a certain degree of wealth display was possible, although that was not its function. The girls of the wealthy among the Tolowa had a more elaborate ceremony than those of the poor. Their explanation was "the better the care and the greater the ceremony at puberty, the larger the bride price which might be expected later."[9] The Tututni, on the other hand, lacked an adolescence dance. Their rites were purely individual and contained practically no wealth emphasis except that a purifying formula terminated observances and that the girl dressed in the best finery she could muster on the last day. Slight as this display element was, there is one case on record of an adolescent arousing such envy by her clothing, that her death a short time after was attributed to poisoning by a covetous enemy. Childbirth observances were also singularly free from wealth interpretations. Dentalia were tied on the infant's ankles almost immediately after birth. A father usually gave a feast when the child was about a year old "so no one would wish him bad luck" which might well include lack of success in wealth pursuits. Formulists who removed birth contaminations, midwives, and cradle makers were all paid for their services. Persons who pierced the children's nasal septa and ear lobes were also recompensed.

So far certain relationships have been suggested, but the manner in which they function in daily practice has not been discussed. For instance, there are two social classes, the rich and the poor distinguished by separate terms. Slaves, as a by-product of poverty, are grouped with the poor for our immediate purposes. The rich man is the state surrogate but no autocrat since he depends upon the good will of his village kinsmen to maintain the show of force in haggling which is basic to all financial transactions. Boys are drilled in the desirability of acquiring wealth. Placing all these factions together and juxtaposing them to the essential democracy so generally found among small aggregates of primitive peoples, one might suppose that there was a constant shift of individuals from one social class to the other. Actually, however, informants and case material indicate that this was not the situation. Social status was relatively stable. The reason may be discovered by balancing the

[9] Du Bois, *op. cit.*, 249.

debits and credits of an individual's negotiations. Sources of income, or the potential credit side of everyone's bookkeeping, were: (1) bride price for daughters minus her dowry, (2) blood money for a relative who had been killed, (3) payments for a large range of insults, (4) mourner's compensation before the ten-night dance, (5) shamanism or knowledge of formulae which were required to lift contaminations, especially those of the life crises. On the debit side however must be entered the reverse of every one of these items. Theoretically every man's budget was balanced. However, let us suppose an optimum situation for the accumulation of wealth. A poor man has four daughters and only one son. We should expect him to accumulate a surplus from the bride prices of his daughters. It is true that as a poor man he might receive only $80 apiece for them and only a portion of that would be in dentalia money. He would then be in possession of approximately $240 minus approximately $100 for dowry. If all four daughters remained married and liquidated the marriage contract by bearing children who survived, he might then be able to buy his son a high-priced woman. In addition he might have accumulated wealth by a knowledge of formulae or shamanism. He would then be in a position to raise the status of the second generation in his family. Actually, however, the moment that he accumulated such a surplus the rich man of the village was in a position to tax him proportionally for the settlement of blood feuds, of mourner's rights, or the bride price for the rich man's son. The rich man was in a position to force these contributions since his good will and assistance were essential in maintaining a balance in the debit-credit situation outlined above. It is of course conceivable that a poor man who had succeeded in accumulating wealth would thereby secure followers. With their assistance he might then establish a schismatic village. And it is possible that in rare cases this did occur, but not sufficiently often to disturb the stability between the social classes. The point to be made in this connection is that the educational stress placed upon the acquisition of wealth as the road to social approval, was a social fiction which could not be realized by most of the individuals in whom it was instilled. Benedict in Patterns of Culture[10] has suggested that one category of psychopaths is produced by a competitive society which instils social ideals which the individual is inadequate to realize however completely he may accept them. That the Tolowa-Tututni society produced such individuals whom it considered, in its own terms, psychopathic, is suggested by their attitude toward the very poor. Among the Tolowa-Tututni the society creates demands in the individual which it, as a social mechanism, has no devices for satisfying. This is closely connected with the familiar discrepancy between theory and practice which occurs in many cultures. Here the significant point is the discrepancy between systematically implanted social ideals and the structure for their realization. In other words, the society itself, as a superorganic structure, is dislocated. Whether such a dislocated structure is reflected in the psychology of those who participate in it, is a matter for further investigation.

[10] Benedict, *op. cit.*, 274.

In conclusion, certain speculations of a generalized nature suggest themselves. This paper has been devoted to demonstrating the extent to which wealth integrates social institutions among the Tolowa-Tututni. However, a dominating engrossment may produce the interrelationship of institutions without necessarily producing a society which will function smoothly. Such I feel to be the case among the Tolowa-Tututni. Although wealth permeated and knit together the structural interrelationships of their institutions, the underlying lubrication of the social machinery was a potential use of force, as exemplified in the pattern of haggling. The wealth emphasis gave Tolowa-Tututni society its appearance of consistency and coherence, but in reality that very coherence between social forms was the root of deep-seated conflicts. It seems possible that institutions which are rephrased in terms extraneous to their immediate function produce stress and strain in the structure as a whole, as well as in the individual. For instance, marriage is an institution whose function is to permit men and women to produce offspring with social status and to coöperate for mutual economic advantage. When that direct purpose is elaborated by a whole series of concomitant attitudes and is obscured by a variety of ramified obligations, the possibilities for that institution to function smoothly and directly become more remote. If such is the case, there are only two solutions, violent and disruptive outbreaks or an intensely repressive formalization. Thus, I feel, that the Tolowa-Tututni wealth attitude was instrumental in creating tensions which easily broke out in acts of violence. That these violences could be deflected by money atonements does not lessen the underlying conflicts.

222 East Seventeenth Street,
New York City.

ESTUDILLO AMONG THE YOKUTS: 1819

By A. H. Gayton

THE SPANISH MISSIONS situated on the California coast between San Francisco and San Diego made frequent forays into the San Joaquin valley for converts during the early years of the nineteenth century. The commandants of these little expeditions usually kept diaries or made reports, some of which contain facts of interest concerning the nature of the land and people visited. None of them are very illuminating ethnographically, but they do add bits to our knowledge of the region, so different at that time. Then, as now, it was inhabited entirely by Yokuts-speaking tribes save for a fringe of Shoshoneans along its mountainous eastern edge.

The report made in diary form by Lieutenant José María Estudillo in 1819 has somehow been overlooked. Bancroft speaks of it as "not extant" and of Estudillo's campaign as "a failure."[1] He thereby apparently misled later writers, who omitted the information contained in this diary from an otherwise thorough investigation of archive material on Yokuts village sites and populations.[2] It does not figure in Merriam's discussion of California native populations, though it is used by this author in another connection at a later date.[3] The data offered by Estudillo supplement those of Moraga and Garcés used by Kroeber in his estimate of Yokuts and California Indian populations.[4] To integrate our Spaniard's calculations with the results arrived at by Kroeber, Gifford, and Schenck, is beyond the scope of this paper, the purpose of which is merely to make the data more readily available to those interested.

Meager as are the ethnographic facts recorded by Estudillo, they coincide with the details of Yokuts culture obtained by Kroeber and other investigators a century later. The sketchy lines of Estudillo's picture are readily extended into a realistic delineation of Yokuts life by those familiar with its characteristics. The aquatic habits of the valley people contrast strongly with the hunting, seed-gathering activities of the hill dwellers. Yet it is clear that they maintained close communication and enjoyed intertribal festivities on a large scale, as we have been told by modern informants. That amicable relations between the foothill Yokuts and the Western Mono (the "bad people" of the mountains) is recent, is also corroborated.

Two copies of the diary appear to have been made by Estudillo or his amanuensis. The first, translated here, is finally dated November 16, 1819. The second, not differing sensibly from this, is finally dated November 19, and is presumably a copy of the first made after his return and perhaps polished a

---

[1] H. H. Bancroft, The Works of Hubert Howe Bancroft, Vol. 19: California, Vol. II, 1801–1824 (San Francisco: A. L. Bancroft & Company, 1885), 336.

[2] E. W. Gifford and W. Egbert Schenck, Archaeology of the Southern San Joaquin Valley, UC-PAAE 23:24, 1926.

[3] C. Hart Merriam, The Indian Population of California, AA, n.s., 7:594–606, 1905; Jedediah Smith's Route across the Sierra in 1827, California Historical Society Quarterly, 25–29, April, 1924.

[4] A. L. Kroeber, Handbook of the Indians of California, BAE-B 78:488–491, 1925.

trifle. To it is added a section entitled "Notes" which contains only a few supplementary remarks of interest. The lieutenant summarizes his observations on the nature and fertility of the land, advises that the proselytizing of the Indians be carried on in their homeland to obviate the nostalgia which caused the converts to abandon their new life at the strange coast missions, and suggests the region of Kings River outlet as a suitable location for establishing a mission and garrison. Pertinent items from these notes have been interpolated in the text given below.[5]

The translation is reasonably accurate: common sense rather than pedantry has guided the choice of renditions. Dubious words or passages are given in brackets, as are other remarks inserted by the present writer. At a few points the meanings are considerably obscured by the cryptic style of the original.

The *legua* of Estudillo's day was about equivalent to two and two-thirds (2.67) miles. The *paso doble* with which he measured the Chischa village was probably the *paso* of five feet, as this fits fairly well with his calculations as transposed into *varas*, the three-foot yard. The word *tular*, meaning a swamp or lagoon filled with tules, has been retained because of its peculiar aptness. A *roblar* is an oak-covered district. The inconsistencies in the spelling of native names are in the original.

THE DIARY

A DIARY which I, Lieutenant Don José María Estudillo, Commandant of the Presidio of Monterey, made on the campaign by order of the Governor of the Province, Colonel Don Pablo Vizente de Sola, undertaken for the reconnaissance and inspection of the rancherías situated in the tulares of the plains of the Sierra Nevada, from that day to today.

Sunday, October 17, 1819.—After having heard mass I left the Presidio referred to at 10:45 in the morning, and at 1:30 in the afternoon arrived at the Rancho de Real Hacienda. After separating 183 horses I departed. I slept at the mouth of the arroyos where I arrived at 7 P.M. [copy of Nov. 19: distant from Monterey 8 leagues].

Monday, 18.—At 5 A.M. I left the said location for Mission Soledad where I arrived at 11, and at 2 P.M., in the company of the Indians Antonio and Victor, Tulareños [Yokuts], I left, to sleep at the place Los Ositos, which I reached at 6 P.M. [copy of Nov. 19: distant from starting point 11 leagues].

From this point I dispatched a corporal to San Antonio Mission for 11 Indians, and for 30 blankets to cover the soldiers of the party, and with orders to rejoin me at Mission San Miguel on the 20th.

Tuesday, 19.—At 5:30 A.M. left Los Ositos, and arrived to sleep at the hole [*poza*] of the cañon of San Miguel at 5:30 P.M. [copy of Nov. 19: distant 10½ leagues]. At 9 P.M. the corporal Manuel Butron with the soldier who had accompanied him, rejoined me.

---

[5] Another copy, but partially done and in another handwriting, of the November 19 manuscript also exists. All three copies are in the Bancroft Library at the University of California, where Professor H. I. Priestley courteously facilitated my use of them.

Wednesday, 20.—Left the hole at daybreak and reached Mission San Miguel at 10 A.M. [copy of Nov. 19: distant from the poza 7 leagues]. At 1 P.M. Corporal Sebastian Rodriquez arrived, who brought from Mission San Antonio the 30 blankets, and 25 pairs of shoes which were divided among the sergeant, 3 corporals, and 26 soldiers who composed the troop.

Reviewed the soldiers at arms, the munitions, and mounts, and in the afternoon rationed biscuits, dried meat, and pinole for 30 days.

Thursday, 21.—After having celebrated mass for a "Godspeed," which we all heard [by] the R. P. Fr. Juan Martin, titular minister of the Mission San Miguel the Archangel, I left with the troop and 30 Indians from this mission, and 11 from San Antonio, as aids. I took the route to the east, and arrived to sleep at a place called Agua Dulce, at a distance of 7½ leagues to the east.

Friday, 22.—At 5:30 A.M. started toward the east; at 8 went due east, and at 4 P.M. reached the place called Los Alisos Ultimos [copy of Nov. 19: Los Ultimos Alamos], distant from Agua Dulce 15 leagues. The land is in hillocks, without pasture for the herd of horses, and the water a bit salty.

Saturday, 23.—The assisting Indians sent me notice that the two sloughs that there are before reaching the Ranchería of Bubal [Wowol] would be found full of water and very miry. Because of this I sent the sergeant with two soldiers and Indians on foot to investigate them, and to look for a ford, and [if] they found none to construct balsas without being noticed by the natives. I ordered one of them to return and give us information, in order for the troop to go on.

Reviewed arms and munitions, and finding the swords of the soldiers Juan Martines, Salvador Espinoza, and Santos Escamillo a bit hacked, and the reserve cartridges of Juan Amezquita in bad condition, I immediately admonished them to put them to good use, and to put them in condition.

At 4 P.M. I received information from the sergeant: that failing to find a crossing they were making balsas. After breaking camp and journeying 4 leagues to the east, I arrived at the summit of the last hill before entering the great plain of the tulares. The view from south to north is beautiful, for its end can not be seen, with its lakes, swamps, and groves of trees. And from east to west, I calculate its width, from this hill to the foot of the snowy range of mountains called Sierra Nevada, to be 28 to 30 leagues. We continued traveling eastward until 10 at night, when we reached the first slough.

This was crossed on balsas, the horses swimming, and with considerable trouble because of its stickiness and obstructions. Since it would be necessary to cross another like it in the vicinity of the Ranchería of Bubal, I dispatched four confidants ahead to sound out the situation, and to obtain some balsas which they told me the natives had. Continued traveling toward it. [Copy of Nov. 19: Followed it to the east and north until 1 A.M.]

Sunday, 24.—At 1 A.M. one of those spies I had sent to reconnoiter returned with the news that no balsas had been found, and that the natives had broken camp and withdrawn. I reached the slough at 3 A.M. to find it full as I had been told. Balsas were constructed and the troop passed. I noted the location where the natives had their huts, distant from the last site, Los Alisos [copy of Nov. 19: Los Alamos], 12 leagues. Indications showed that the inhabitants had already been elsewhere many days. I ordered the company to halt, to allow the herd of horses to eat from what little the sides of the slough and swamps offered.

Knowing that the unconverted Indian named Gabriel who belongs to this Ranchería of Bubal had always been much attached to the soldiers, and with his companions had always gone out anywhere to help them, it struck me as novel that he had absented himself with his people. He [evidently?] had decided to let some other do it, and fled from our encounter. I remained considering what I ought to do in compliance with the wishes of the Superior Governor.

At 11 that day I observed with the spyglass two Indians some distance off: I sent two soldiers to overtake them, and they brought them to me in camp. After having disposed of the fear they showed, I examined them with kindliness. They declared that several Indians from Bubal (their companions) had been at the fiesta of San Miguel at the end of September, and they returned, telling that the great captain of the soldiers (thus they referred to the Superior Governor) was this time sending troops to catch and take away in bonds all the escaped Christians and unconverted [gentiles], and would kill them if they did not like it. [These natives said] that they would offer the Christians [for return], but that they would not expose those unconverted. Because of their fears some of the Christians had retreated into the interior of the lakes and swamps, and after receiving news of our coming, the rest of them had disbanded.

[They said] that at the Ranchería of Tache there arrived on the 21st three Christians from Soledad, sent with the news that we were already on the road to fall upon them, to recapture the Christians and punish the unconverted. For this reason the captain [copy of Nov. 19: *tiya*, chief] wished to catch the renegades that they had in the Ranchería and send them off. But this had been opposed and [on] their relatives the [rest of the] natives could not prevail. [They said] that they did not know where all the Indians were to be found if we awaited them, or moved to other parts.

They, with some few others, had camped together in a creek bed about 5 leagues away, where there was a little water, which could be reached on foot. After having news of our close approach, they maintained vigils, and last night they saw us as we crossed the sloughs. And finally [they said] that having been advised of our departure by the three comers from Soledad, our route on the plain was already known to everyone.

The information of finding this part of the Ranchería of Bubal at so short a distance, although in a swampy site, obliged me to surprise it, guided by these natives, and I resolved to leave for it at night.

Monday, 25.—At 2 A.M. took a route south, following the two gentile Indians, and at a distance of 5 leagues among tulares and swamps, I arrived at the side of a lake. I found the site where I had been told I would find those whom I sought, but it was already deserted. We followed the tracks some 2 leagues, with the lower halves of our bodies naked, and the troop carrying rifles and shields, until we encountered them. They obtained 45 persons of both sexes and all ages. Some others who perceived us had fled, and could not be followed because of so much water, mud, and tules.

At 11 of the day I reached camp and the spot where [these people] were accustomed to live. On examination they told me that they had retreated because the two whom I had detained had not returned, and they were much afraid. All was like the recital that the two natives had made me before. [They said] that the Indian Gabriel had left for the Ranchería of Buenavista, invited to a fiesta being made by the natives. This Indian Gabriel, although unconverted, has always shown great friendliness toward the soldiers, accompanying them on previous expeditions. Although he is not a captain of the Ranchería of Bubal he is forceful, and is respected for his valor by the great numbers of people who inhabit the valleys and lakes of the tulares. Nevertheless, these natives informed me that he had much fear because of the ill treatment resulting from the expedition made three years ago [copy of Nov. 19: two years] from Mission San Luis [copy of Nov. 19: with the Luiseño Indians]. To put aside this fear I ordered Gabriel to be advised of my coming, and that I would wait for him until the 30th in the neighborhood of the Ranchería of Tontache [Chunut]. Also that he should bring with him such Christians as they had among them, and I would give them a paper of pardon for their return to the missions.

Among the 45 Indians taken was the Indian woman, Liberata, who, because of sickness, had had permission to return home to cure herself. She will return to San Miguel with the others that come. Thereafter they continued with me. This is the village of natives nearest to the missions and with greatest frequence has "made" Christians at San Miguel. Therefore I treated them with the greatest kindness, as I had been charged by the Superior, to the end of disposing of the fears which they had as a result of the influence of the runaway Christians. I told them to return to live at their sites, to go out to the lake where they [the others] were and advise them all to reunite [and live] as before. I sent them off at 2 P.M., but they told me that they would like to remain and not go out until morning to bring in their possessions all at one time. They asked my permission to send notice to Gabriel at once, and to the scattered Indians, to which I acceded with great pleasure, and 5 Indians went out in all directions.

At 3 P.M. the old captain of Bubal, Chape, and his wife arrived. He told me that while he was fishing in the lake the renegade [copy of Nov. 19: from San Miguel] Anastasio came, and he gave him the news of my arrival, and that he was freed from being captured for having run off into the water and hiding in the swamp. [He said] that, having returned to their homes, the old people who remained told him of the good treatment they had been given, and as he already knew me from having been at the Presidio, he [now] came to see me by virtue of the order which permitted them to come to me. He presented me with some fish which I gratefully received. The Indians asked permission to catch ducks for the soldiers, and in less than half an hour within my sight, they caught many with snares which they had in the lake.

The land over which we have come is saline and miry, without any pasture for the horses.

Soon the natives all were reunited and returned to live on their land without fear of any injury the troop might do them. I left at 6 A.M. [Tuesday, Oct. 26] from this site of the Lake of Bubal for the great plain, going toward the south to go around it, and at a distance of 6 leagues to the east went toward the arroyo of San Cayetano. This I reached and followed as far as the first foothills of the Sierra Nevada in search of water and pasture. In the cañon called by the natives Agspa [the present Alpaugh?] I found it at 6:30 P.M. Made camp, having arrived with the horses and mules considerably dejected. They had not eaten for three days including today, and from necessity had walked 16 leagues over salty, loose, soil; because of this I had left 3 exhausted horses and 1 mule in the arroyo. At 11 P.M. they were reunited with the herd.

Wednesday, 27.—At sun-up I examined the cañon that forms this arroyo, with the spyglass. It is called San Cayetano by Lieutenant Don Gabriel Moraga, and Agspa by the natives [copy of Nov. 19: whose ranchería was found farther in, and the people at the fiesta at Buenavista]. It is filled with oaks, live oaks, poplars, and willows, and sufficient wild plants. Very good water runs through it for the distance of 1 league, and [there is] pasture in abundance. Therefore it appears that the herd will recover today. Those that came on the expedition of 1806 did not say it was so wide nor so covered with trees at that time. [Copy of Nov. 19: Judging by the appearance of the ranchería, it is composed of 400 souls of both sexes and (all) ages.]

Thursday, 28.—Left at 6 A.M., taking a northerly direction, and at 9 A.M. entered the arroyo of Coyaipich [Koyeti?], at a distance of 4 leagues. It was named San Pedro by Moraga in 1806. I saw two Indians, who were followed and overtaken. They spoke to me when their fear left, and they conducted me to the ranchería of the same name. Their captain, Tuckal, told me that several days before they had received news of my coming from the Tache. The night before they had been watching us until the troop began to catch the horses and saddle them. Knowing that they had no Christians among them I put aside their fears, and informed them as I had done the refugees from the missions, that they could return. The number of people composing this ranchería must be about 200 of both sexes and all ages. [Copy of Nov. 19, Notes: The Indians are of good appearance and physiognomy, seem docile. Their dialect is the same which my interpreter Antonio, neophyte at Mission Soledad, speaks.]

I followed the same direction to the east [copy of Nov. 19: Started for the San Gabriel river with two guides from this ranchería] guided by two natives of Coyaipich, and I crossed the intervening plain to the entrance of the Gran Roblar, which is 8 leagues. I encountered the Ranchería of Choijnocko [Choinok] at the sides of an arroyo that had a little water in small pools. [Copy of Nov. 19: According to the size of it, it should show the number of 300 souls.... Their dialect is like that of Tukal.] Their captain and the greater part of the inhabitants, they told me, were at Chischa, 8 leagues away.

I continued eastward and reached a deep arroyo, where I found two huts with Indians. They came out to receive me, one of them being the captain of Chischa [Joasps]. With his brother, wife, and other relatives he had retired this afternoon to weep during the night for the death of their relatives [copy of Nov. 19: two brothers and six sisters], since on the following day they would all celebrate, and various rancherías had been invited to the fiesta. He and his relatives helped to give water to the horses, since it was already 6 P.M.

[Copy of Nov. 19, Notes: From this point (Coyaipich) to the weeping place of Joasps, Captain of Chischa, and from there to his ranchería, as to that of Telame, and as far as the edge of the Roblar, the land is admirable for its fertility, although rough because of its virginity. With its moisture, it only invites all to its cultivation to give abundant crops of wheat, grains, corn, and all the legumes, as long as it is irrigated. And the waters of San Gabriel can easily be carried in case of necessity. The pasture remains green and dry the year around. The woods are oaks of various species, willows, and poplars; there are some wild plants in the level parts, and in the arroyo and bogs. Moreover there abounds a shrub that they call wild hemp, very white and strong, of which the natives make their nets for fishing and (which) we (use) for sewing our shoes. Some of it is so fine it serves for sewing clothes.

The dialect is the same. The sustenance which they have is of acorns, very savory wild grain, and different kinds of seeds which this country naturally produces with great abundance. The river has several kinds of tasty fish, the little pools and arroyos a kind of anchovy which the Indians catch and dry in large quantities to keep for the rigorous times of winter. And they have pine nuts which they gather in the mountains.]

Having had news from the Choynocos that there was a Christian from San Miguel among them at the fiesta, and that they had two horses, I spoke to Joasps. He immediately sent to tell the captain of the Choynoca to come, and to bring the Christian and horses. He [the captain] arrived at 10 P.M. with him and with a horse, begging me in his name and those of the other captains to forgive him. [He said] that they all invited me with his people to pass tomorrow at the fiesta which the captain of Chischa, Joasps, was making. I accepted, and he returned at midnight to Chischa, 3 leagues away from Choinoco.

The two rancherías [copy of Nov. 19: three] that I have seen today all had their women and children hidden, but after they were informed that no priest accompanied me, they came out and presented themselves.

Friday, 29.—At 6 A.M. started the march to the north edges of the Sierra [along the foothills?] accompanied by the native captain, Joasps, going to his Ranchería of Chischa where the reunion for the funeral celebration was to take place. Arrived at 8 P.M. There came out to receive me 7 captains from various parts, of which 2 were Telame, he of Choynoco, and 4 from other rancherías of the Roblar in the vicinity of the mountains. They begged me to come and see them all. I made suitable precautions without letting it be known, casually dispatched my horse, and accompanied by two interpreters directed myself first within the ranchería of these Chischeses. They pressed upon me various dishes of atoles and pinoles, which I tasted in order not to offend them, and they were satisfied. I counted 437 able-bodied young men in the walk I took, and about 600 women and children all placed before this village. Across the front of the ranchería I counted 358 double paces [*pasos dobles*] which makes 624 yards [*varas*], and across its back 432 paces or 756 yards in the form of an imperfect half moon. All [the houses] are of mats and willow branches. In front of the ranchería were the guests, all separated, where I directed myself along with the captains who accompanied me. Each of them were in little groups; thus men, women, and children were presented to me, and it was not possible to count them as I had done with the Chischas. However, the number of young men was not less than 600, and some 200 young women.

When I walked behind the Ranchería of Chischa I immediately came upon the arroyo which was near by. On its banks, I found more than 100 middle-aged women washing seeds for the atoles of the guests, while other younger ones were grinding these seeds on stones as is their custom [copy of Nov. 19: with large baskets of thick acorn mush].

[Copy of Nov. 19, Notes: Of the Ranchería of Chischa nothing was known until now. Its people, and those of their neighboring friends who were found assembled, presented in number some 2400 persons, all of comely appearance. Their number should be greater, judging by the scarcity (*cortedad*) of people seen, not counting the young people who were no doubt hiding in the willows which encircle the neighborhood of the river. This was proved when the sergeant of the rear-guard party saw more than 200, women, lads, little girls and boys, come out from the river edge beside it to look at us, and told me of it in a moment.

Of the population of natives who inhabit the Roblar, and from there along the Sierra to the Ranchería of Apalame, there are, or there ought to be more inhabitants in it. The number of people which I calculate could be Christianized is from 5 to 6 thousand, little more. This is from the rancherías of the lakes and rivers.]

After finishing my walk with the captains, I made known to them all the objects and ends of my coming. They assured me that they had among them no more Christians than that one from Choinoco who had been brought to me, nor had any come to Chischa. Thus neither their captain Joasps nor his people had ever seen troops, this being the first time that they had reached them. Though long ago some passed below [this was Don Gabriel Moraga in his reconnaissance made in 1806], they only heard of it through their friends from Telame. Joasps and the other captains wished to trade with us, save that we lived very far from them, and that they could not cross [the valley] to come to the mission or Presidio as they had enemies of their own in the intervening territory. But after disposing of their fears and [telling them?] that they could come when they liked, Joasps promised me that he would come to Monterey next spring. For which, and for his protection among the outposts where he would cross, I gave him a pass, which was greatly appreciated.

They presented to me as gifts various baskets [*coras*], flour [*pinole*], and grain [*arroz*], but having nothing with which to return their kindness, I did not accept them, saying that I had no means of carrying the things. I only took three measures [*almudes*] of grain and gave them some corn flour. As they asked that the soldiers be allowed to go about I permitted it. They went in parties in charge of the sergeant and corporals, and with orders to take no more than a taste of the foods and that which was given them. Thus it was done, and they were well satisfied.

At 12 that day a captain from the Ranchería of Notontos [Nutunutu] arrived, who was presented to me by the others at the gathering, and then retired with them.

At 1 P.M. there came for the fiesta from the interior of the Sierra Nevadas, 4 captains from a ranchería named Apalame. Their names were Cholmuk [copy of Nov. 19: Chomulk], Gilmosts, Ogmost, and Gulstos. With them were 69 men and 42 women. Though they had never seen soldiers they made no novelty of it, for Joasps had sent word saying that they might come without fear, as we were friends. The men arrived making skirmishes with their bows and arrows, killing dogs and chickens [*gallinas*] with permission from the Chischas, and afterward paid the latter with beads. Then they commenced to eat them with great pleasure.

[Copy of Nov. 19: In the conversation which I had with the captain, Joasps, he told me that he and his people went up on the hills of the Sierra to gather pine nuts, and that in some places there were uplands of good earth where one could easily go on horseback, but it was very far. From the people of the interior I learned some particulars of the people who live on the other side, who, they told me, gather their harvest of pine nuts and seeds from both sides (?, *en ambas vandas*), but that they themselves did not go far into the mountains for the inhabitants were very bad people. There are three ranges of mountains, though not so great as these (on the west slope of the Sierra) where there are very large acorn-bearing oak trees. They had never seen people like us before.]

I was urged many times to remain with them over night, which was that of the weeping, and for the dance on the following day. [Copy of Nov. 19: Their captain Joasps, as I have said, is making the funeral celebration which was carried out (*compone*) in the following way. They gathered in little groups with faces blackened, and giving most lamentable wails with exaggerated grief, so they passed the night. On the day following they washed themselves, and painted, and formed dancing groups by rancherías. The master of the fiesta, after giving them a feast of fish caught in the river, deermeat, venison (*benados*), and antelope (? *berrendos*) that there are in abundance, flour and mush, concluded by paying them all with beads and baskets, and they left for their homes.][6]

They offered to care for the horses, and [said] that if I wished to leave some of them during our interval and return for them, they would maintain them as the Telames had done before [for Moraga?]. I excused myself in good style and turned toward the west for Telame [Telamni]. I arrived there at 6 P.M., having left at 2:30, and walked from the retreat of the captain of the Chischas 8 leagues. In this ranchería [of Telame] I found 14 old women and 9 old men who were not at the fiesta. One of them sent me a pullet [*polla*] to sup upon [copy of Nov. 19: for which I sent back some corn flour]. Telame is distant from Chischa nearly 5 leagues, to the west, and from where I slept, 9.

Saturday, 30.—At 5 A.M. left for the Ranchería of Tontache with guides which the Indians gave me. At different times we took routes to the east, northwest, and south because of the many arroyos, tule-filled lakes, and sloughs of muddy water which there are in this great Roblar. From this we got out at 2 P.M and went west as far as the San Gabriel River. We reached the place of La Cruz at 4 P.M., having gone 13 leagues. At 5 o'clock 4 Indians of Tontache came bringing fish and ducks, and invited me to go to their ranchería in the morning. For although their captain and the greater part of the people were at Buenavista [for the fiesta], the few who remained wished to receive the troop and to know me, as they had learned of us from the Indians of Soledad.

Sunday, 31.—After having told the rosary I left at 7 A.M. for Tontache, leaving the burdens in camp, and arrived at 9, at a distance 3 leagues to the west. I found it situated on the side of Lake Bubal [Tulare Lake] [copy of Nov. 19: on fairly muddy land which could not be traversed on horseback]. I entered it with only one soldier and two interpreters and counted 103 comely young men, all with bows and arrows, and some 200 souls among the old men, old women, and children. They delivered up to me two Christians from San Miguel, and they sent in search of three that had retreated to the interior of the lake among the tules. They begged me to pardon them, for they were all either their sons or brothers. I exhorted them not to detain any Christian in the future even though he were a relative. At the time I was taking my leave I had notice from an Indian who came from Buenavista that Lieutenant Moraga had arrived there four days before, and that he could do nothing as the Indians had scattered into that lake. And that the people invited [to the fiesta] had also retreated from fright, and he had come to tell the news to their relatives. At about 12 P.M. I returned to camp and reached it at 2 P.M. The ground is sticky, salty and much under water.

These Indians corroborated the fact that they had knowledge of my leaving Soledad through the Tacho Indians and that I would come through this country. But believing themselves to be without fault they had remained

---

[6] It appears that Estudillo obtained this description perhaps from an interpreter, as he was not, according to the continuing entry, an eyewitness.

quietly on their land, though many others had fled into the lake, from which they did not wish to come out. [They said] that the news had gone out in all directions through the valley, and that I would not find any Indians in their principal villages as far as the horse-killers to the north [*a los matadores de caballada del Norte*] since these were living scattered in the mountains and swamps.

Monday, November 1.—At 5 A.M. started toward the north for the Ranchería of Taches with guides from Tontache. It is distant 12 leagues. I arrived at this site or location at 4 P.M. crossing saline, miry land. With much trouble we passed four sloughs full of water and tules, and so sticky that finally Ygnacio Solo's horse could not get out, and he and his munitions got wet all over. The swamp which I crossed today is very miry, having crossed four times today a slough full of mud and water in the same swamp.

One league away from San Gabriel River [copy of Nov. 19: Kings River] five Indians of the vicinity were seen running for the swamp. Although I sent the Indian interpreter Antonio in pursuit to speak to them he could not follow. For which, and because the mire and the immense swamp where they had fled could not be crossed, I sent him off instead with his companion, and it ended [with their] bringing news that all the Indians of Tache had disappeared from fear of us because of what Augustin and Pasqual, neophytes at Soledad, had told them, saying that the troop had left to come and kill them, and catch the fleeing Christians. Because of this their two captains (whose return they await today) had set out with 9 Christians for that mission. Other natives had taken various routes [in flight?]. I ordered sent out to them a Christian named Victor, to say for my part that all was to the contrary of what they had been told; that they were not to believe said Christians, and still less if they were renegades; and that they, the natives, should come to be with me. He returned at 9 at night, bringing with him two natives who told me the same as had Antonio. I made them understand the opposite, and that it was extraordinary since this Ranchería of Tache was so obligated to the soldiers for their friendliness for many years, and that on different occasions they had fought with them against their enemies; that they had always come out to receive us [the Spaniards] but they had not done so for me. To which they replied that the reason was because of the news given by Augustin and Pasqual, as they said the Christians wanted to kill them, and they believed it. Because of this the two captains were taking back those that could be caught. They questioned why we should wish to do them injury since they had never taken nor killed a single horse when they had cared for them many times before this. I made them put aside their fear, making them understand the contrary, but that nevertheless I had to recapture all the Christian renegades and send them to their missions. And that if they wished to maintain our friendship they should not shelter anyone; and that hereafter, if any runaways from whatever mission should present themselves, as true friends of ours they should return those persons quickly. Even if they were relatives of the ranchería they should censure them and make them do the same.

They went and advised all their relatives that I wished to see them and to know them, and that if they wished to know me they could come, and go back to catch fish in the morning as they had always done.

At 10 P.M. there arrived a graceful native youth sent from the Ranchería Notonto to know if we had reached this point, as his captain [copy of Nov. 19: Toiÿya] had returned from the fiesta at Chischas which Joasps had celebrated, and told them that we had come without doing any injury (as they had been told by the envoys from Soledad Mission). [He said] that they wished to know me and were awaiting me at their ranchería where the people were intending to fish in the river for me. As they had not killed nor sold any horses nor had any fugitive Christians among them had no fear. Heretofore [?] they had come out on solid ground to receive us, and if ever they had fought with any soldiers it was because of the falsehoods they had been told. I answered that they spoke and did well, but that because of having to talk with the Tache I could not come then, but that the day after tomorrow I would be with them in passing. He replied that this was agreeable since their captain had sent to invite other captains from neighboring rancherías to meet me, and that they would all be together for my arrival. This native was so gracious and vivacious as he spoke with me, his bravery was so manifest, and his manners so refined, that I presented him with a colored kerchief and some pinole. He departed at midnight much pleased.

Tuesday, 2.—Because of the fatigue of the horses and the dirtiness of the troop I remained here this day for the first to be refreshed and the second to wash themselves.

At 9 A.M. came four Tache chiefs, Mariano Tiesar, Goolill, Cullas, and Chilaxas. The last two are those who returned from Soledad the night before. Thirty-seven young men accompanied them, all of them prepared with hand nets for catching fish in this San Gabriel River [copy of Nov. 19: Kings River]. This they did before my very eyes, with great agility, diving quickly and staying under the water so long that I prayed. Some remained under five credos [during five "Lord's prayers"], others no less than three [*cinco Credos, y el que menos tres que yo reze*]. After having caught sufficient large fish [*mojarras*], salmon, and others very palatable, I return with all to camp, to sensibly demonstrate to those who were living within the lakes and marsh (because of believing the lies of the Christian renegades) that they could all reunite and come out to live on their land without any fear. As they could not all be seen together, [I said?] that if the road was traversable, I alone would go to their ranchería or sites. At that they replied that they had already told me the cause of their separation, and that they would, by force if necessary, catch and take to San Miguel the Christians who were missing, so [they would?] reunite on firm land. They said that one could easily go on horseback until near the marsh of the lake, and that there they would carry me until they put me in a balsa to reach the ranchería. Although there were very few people there, they would be much gratified [they said]. I accepted, and they dispatched notice to prepare for my arrival.

Immediately the troop knew of my resolution they showed repugnance, and advised the sergeant to dissuade me from going alone, to obviate any attempt [at crime] from the barbarians seeing the opportunity. But having burned my hand with some powder in their sight [the natives?], I could not go on to the ranchería, and sent the Indian interpreter, Antonio, with several others to go and bring me an idea of the situation. With this I saw them off; they left saddened by my accident, but the soldiers remained satisfied, so I was told.

At 11 P.M. the interpreter returned with his companions and the captains Cullas and Chilaxas to guide us to the Notonto ranchería. The former told me that part of the Tache had fled within the waters, and were living on a huge balsa of tule without fire [copy of Nov. 19: nor warm food]. That there was much mire in the swamp as far as the outlet of the lake, where they had some little balsas, and in order to reach it they had already prepared for me a very fine large one.

Wednesday, 3.—An envoy from Tontache arrived at 5 A.M. to tell me that Lieutenant Don Gabriel Moraga had returned to Buenavista Lake and had seized the Indians in a cañon, among them 9 Christians; the others had fled. He who brought the news had left on the 30th and walked day and night to give it. From the north news was just received of fighting with the troop from San Francisco. Many natives had been killed, but they had killed a soldier and wounded several.[7] I sent this native back to tell his companions that the killing of the soldiers and the wounding of the others was false.

At 6 A.M. I left for the Ranchería of Notonto 7 leagues to the north [on the] shore of San Gabriel River [copy of Nov. 19: Kings River], so I was told. I took to the east across a plain of miry and saline land as far as Kings River where their ranchería is situated.

At a distance of 2 leagues before reaching it, there came out on the road three Notontos Indians, one of them with three cakes of meal [*tortas de pan de arroz*] with which they regaled the guides and other Indians. At a distance of 700 yards [*varas*] the village could already be seen. And there was presented to me an Indian of the same Notontos who had already known the troop, who was call Manuel Pinto. With considerable assurance he told me the names of the captains found together, which was what I wanted. I answered that the reunion would be celebrated, and that I would like to see them. He answered that he would advise them, and that I should wait. With scorn I sent him off, saying that I would arrive where they all were before he did. Charging all [the troop] with great vigilance, I presented myself before the natives whom I found lined up and without arms (any Indians who presented themselves with bows would be treated like enemies).

Accompanied by four soldiers I went into their midst and through the interpreter ordered the captains brought together. There were the following: Taija [*tiya?*] an old captain, and Chata his nephew, new captain of the No-

---

[7] This was apparently the expedition under Sergeant Jose Sanchez; cf. W. Egbert Schenck, Historic Aboriginal Groups of the California Delta Region, UC-PAAE 23:129, 1926.

tonto; Coytisa, a captain of the Gumilchi [Wimilichi]; Guchita [copy of Nov. 19: Guchaita], and Hocha, captains of Guchetema; and Guchalne, captain of Tategüi. To them it was made known that my coming was by order of the great captain, to catch all the Christians that the natives were sheltering, and to punish them if they were bad and hostile to the troop. All the Indians at once put their hands in their mouths, and the captains drew near me and replied that the Nontos would not consent to sheltering them and sent them off immediately. [Copy of Nov. 19: And they began to cry to me "Amica, Amica, Amica, noche," which is to say, "Come, come, come, friend.".] At Tategüi two from Soledad named Oton and Estevan had arrived, and as its captain already knew of my coming he ordered them to present themselves to me before I came among the Nontos. It had been done, and he [?] delivered them to the Tache captain, Mariano Tiesar, who had returned to the mission with all of the Christians together.

I reprehended the boldness of sending the Indian Manuel Pinto to me to inquire what I wished, when through their envoy to Tache I had ordered them to do otherwise[?], and much more that he should have advised me to wait an interval, and that they should do nothing to any of the troop or there would be dire results. They all answered that they desired to placate us and questioned what and how they could do it, and regretted that I should have thought otherwise. With that I showed pleasure, and they began to bring me fresh fish and other presents. These I would not take as I had nothing to return, and made the same excuse as at Chischa.

Before going into the ranchería I had taken the precaution to see that the corporal, Sebastian Rodriguez, would count the people as they were lined up, knowing that I would not be able to do it. He did so and counted 303 robust men. Of women there were only old ones, thus proving that they were hidden. Very few children were present, and these only after being with them for some time.

After being in Notonto two hours I continued to march toward the west [copy of Nov. 19: went eastward] and crossed Kings River at 4 P.M. . . . It is 4 leagues away from Notonto, and to the point of its outlet, 11 leagues. I camped for the night on its banks after making suitable precautions against Indians that might be near.

Thursday, 4.—At 5 A.M. took a route toward the west until 10, when I came out of the Roblar and entered the plains. Thence north for the tular of San Pablo, where I arrived at 4 P.M. having gone fifteen leagues from where I slept [copy of Nov. 19: from Notonto]. This site is in the middle of the plain. It is without firewood; we had to bring a load from the mouth of the marsh. The water is in great holes. On this plain a deer was caught by lasso, and the men supped on fresh meat.

Friday, 5.—I was informed by an Indian who came out as a guide from the Notontos, that although most of the Gumilchis have joined with them in the marsh and mires there have remained some old people and one Christian. I ordered that the entrance to the marsh be sounded out, but it was not possible on horseback nor on foot, because of so much mud and tule. Because of this I sent the Indian, Antonio, with other armed Indians [copy of Nov. 19: with twenty Indians armed with arrows (*de jaras*)] who returned at 8 P.M. But without doubt the people had perceived us the day before, since the site was abandoned and they did not encounter any people.

Left San Pablo, going north to the San Joaquin River over muddy, salty, and marshy ground. We crossed several deep cuts, reaching the river at 4 P.M., having gone but 10 leagues because of so many turns. This place is where Tape had his ranchería; there were indications that it had been moved elsewhere some fifteen days ago. In nearly all of today's journey there were encountered the scattered bones of horses already dead many days. Two pack horses belonging to Mission San Miguel have died, and three were left exhausted in the plain.

Saturday, 6.—Started at 5:30 A.M., following the banks of the river northward, full of meadows and swamps. At 3 P.M. I saw the fresh track of an Indian. I followed it into the middle of a bay of willows formed by the river. Settled on its banks I found five old women, an old man, a youth of about twenty, and a consumptive-looking young woman of about the same age, also a hermaphrodite whom they called Joya. All were natives belonging to the ranchería of Othos [copy of Nov. 19: who is already christianized at San Juan] and Yulavas, [under?] captain Chegice already christianized at San Juan with the name Bartolome, and Quetas [an] unconverted captain. They informed me that a very few days before Bartolome had come, sent by the priests of San Juan, and Queutas and all the people had gone to the mission with him, leaving the possessions I saw, and the old and infirm who remained there.

Several days ago they learned that the troops from San Francisco had passed lower down on the river and fought with the natives. Because of this they had scattered into the lakes and marshes. I made these old people understand that they did wrong in not going to live at the Mission San Juan, and that I could not consent to their remaining thus, as they served to shelter those already made Christians, when they came back, and that after I returned I would send from the mission to their captains for them and their possessions, and that they would be helped and cared for, and that they would be Christians if they liked.

I followed the old man as guide to another turn of the river twelve leagues distant from the point I left, having seen several bones of horses dead some time.

At 9 P.M. the sky was covered with clouds, with wind from the south. At 10 P.M. the herd stampeded but was easily caught.

Sunday, 7.—At 1 A.M. there fell a rainstorm which lasted three hours; it was not very hard, yet sufficient to wet us all thoroughly. Left at 5:30 A.M., going north by the shore of the river. At 10 o'clock found a village already abandoned some days. As it started to rain very hard I had to cross the river [copy of Nov. 19: in search of a shelter]. At 2 P.M. we halted in a bend of the river well hidden. At dawn we departed to arrive at daybreak at the place where I had been told I would find the Ranchería of Chaneches, and the captain, Sola, a Christian from Santa Cruz, with others from that mission. The journey made today has been 12 leagues through the middle of marshes, tulares, willow thickets, and sloughs. In one of these there fell and died a mule from San Miguel. The sky covered with clouds, and with a south wind. At 7 P.M. rain commenced. At 8 P.M. the herd stampeded and was recovered with difficulty. One soldier lost his horse and gun. I crossed [recrossed?] the river at 10 o'clock [that night, or following morning?].

Monday, 8.—It rained all night, with the wind south. It began to clear, with less water. I re-counted the horses; 28 were lacking, but soon recovered. Also at 11 A.M., up to which time it rained slightly, the gun was found. At once started the march as it was said to be 9 leagues to Ranchería Caneche, for the purpose of nearing it. After going 4 leagues I saw the bones of long-dead horses at a slough. I followed it and got lost because of the swamps and tules that are along the margins of the river. I wound about through various sloughs partly filled with water; others were passable. On their banks among the tules were built many huts such as the Indians sleep in; but by the signs they [the owners] were already gone many days.

In all the sloughs about the river that had water were many fish; a very savory kind of anchovy, pike [?, *mojarras*], and many shellfish, of which the troop and I ate abundantly.

As far as this spot I have observed along all the said sloughs and in some parts on the river banks on which there are trees, many burrows [*abujeros*] of beavers or nutrias in fresh water.

I sent off [men] on foot to follow the horsetracks or in case an Indian were seen on foot. Not having encountered anyone, I followed the road north for 6 leagues [copy of Nov. 19: 4 leagues]. At night we stopped at a slough where we found water and the same signs of beaver.

Tuesday, 9.—At dawn sent four Indians to take note of the many sloughs and swamps of this plain to look for fords and the road to be followed to the Chineches and the Merced River. They returned at 8 A.M. saying that they had not found a single track, and that they could not journey toward the east because of the swamps and tules. Therefore, I followed the north shore of the San Joaquin River. After going about 2 leagues I saw a lone Indian, laden with belongings, on the opposite side of the river; I followed and overtook him. Having asked him several questions to discover where the Cheneches [copy of Nov. 19: Chaneches] were located, he declared that he had been going along alone many days, that all the people had scattered for fear of the troops from San Francisco, and because they knew of my coming according to notice communicated by the natives from rancherías to the south. In reconnoitering the site only one house for one person was found. Having to threaten the man to tell and to lead me to said ranchería, he maintained ignorance and continued to insist that that was the place where he had left them, and that since that time he had seen no one. I secured the Indian, forded the river toward the east, then going about 4 leagues we turned south [copy of Nov. 19: and crossed another time] and found signs of there having been a ranchería. There were parts of dead horses there and a sweat house of considerable capacity. Going 4 leagues more, and almost in front of my halting place of the day before, he pointed out on the other shore of the river a great willow thicket and tular, saying that it [the Chaneche ranchería] was on those banks. We went there and found four old balsas which we could not use. I had to cross by swimming and maneuvering about [*bola pie*] with considerable trouble because of the obstacles, the great density of trees, willows and *zarxamora* on both sides. It was necessary to enter partly on canes [?, *entrar en parte arrodillados*] as far as the ranchería, which was found abandoned. It was composed solely of the same tules, their ends bent [?, *dobladas sus puntas*] like those I had seen on the shores of the river and sloughs, the miserable huts all scattered and without any order.

From this native I learned that at this Ranchería of Chineches all the renegade Christians from Santa Cruz, Santa Clara, San Francisco, and Soledad had gathered in a considerable number. [He said] that Pomponio, Baltazar, and a Clareño came to it frequently; that six days ago they arrived with twelve horses and a piece of cloth that they had stolen in the neighborhood of the town and mission of Santa Clara. [He said] that when he retreated he left them there, and they had not as yet seen us; that since they always rode bareback they had no halters.

All the San Joaquin River and the arroyo of Santa Rita is studded with groves of a very large species of willow. In the largest the natives knew to watch in such a way over a great distance, for so large is this plain which they call Los Tulares that anyone is seen who comes on foot, or still better, on horseback. Today we made 12 leagues with considerable trouble because of our exposure.

Wednesday, 10.—It now seemed impracticable to continue north to the Merced River in search of an Indian village, which, according to my calculations would be 12 leagues away. For as I see it, it would have been already abandoned for many days by both natives and the renegade Christians who live with them. They would be hidden in the tules and swamps whose inviolability is a complete certainty, the more so since they carry nothing with them, and get about easily with their knowledge of the country. And already having news of this and the San Francisco expedition they would take special precautions, not even making the fires which they usually make when traveling [copy of Nov. 19: with which they are accustomed to signal when our people are traveling] on the plain. Considering the time wasted, I resolved to return to the Presidio.

Started at 6 A.M. guided by the same Indian, going toward the east [?, *oriente;* copy of Nov. 19 does not give the direction] for the Santa Rita River. I reached there at 4 P.M. having gone 11 leagues through swamps, etc.

I learned from this native named Lutuays, and from the Indian interpreters whom I brought from Soledad that in that mission he had two Christian sons called Fernando and Pastor. On two occasions they had fled from it and he had returned them there, but now Pastor was [again] with the natives. He wished to catch him to return him, and to make himself a Christian also, as well as an unconverted daughter. Since he is now old he wants his son Fernando [and his brother who although unconverted is at the same mission] to come for him, who would be able [?] to recover [the Christian Pastor?] that they have. That he is old makes no difference [in his authority?] since he is a captain, as are also his sons, particularly Fernando who is the eldest. The interpreter assured me of his veracity; he promised me that meanwhile he would bring together the natives and Christians, he would know of their plans, or ideas, and that he would find out where Pomponio, Baltazar, and the Clareño were. Also that if he could manage it he would apprehend them with [by means of ?] their relatives and his sons, for he did not believe that the troop would be able to surprise them [?, *de no avisara para que los puedan sorprender la tropa*]. I promised him that after leaving the tular I would return, that I had confidence in what he said. However, I said that I knew the natives, and that we would not cease [our efforts] until we got them, if they were not apprehended and returned to the barracks at San Juan, which was in the vicinity.

At the same time this native also told me that, several days ago, three professed Christians had brought news of having fought the soldiers on Merced River, and that many Indians were killed and several soldiers wounded, one of them in the chest so that he died. This, he said, was communicated to them by Indians of Missions Santa Clara and San José.

At 10 P.M. it commenced to rain, the downpour continuing until 4 A.M. of

Thursday, 11.—At sunrise left this location of Santa Rita, after having sent off the old native Lutuaijs. Went westward across saline land and plains as far as the entrance of the cañon of San Luis Gonzaga, which was not actually reached at 3 P.M., having gone 11 leagues. At 8 P.M. a hard shower of rain fell; then it cleared.

Friday, 12.—At 5 A.M. with wind south and in pouring rain I left this spot and entered said cañon. We crossed the ridge and peak called San Luis Gonzaga and reached the outlet of Los Auxaimas. Five tired beasts were left on the hill, having gone 12 leagues over bad road to the west.

At 8 P.M. it began to rain fitfully and lasted until 4 of the morning of

Saturday, 13.—At 5 A.M. left the place of Los Auxaimas amidst rain, and at 10 reached Mission San Juan Bautista, a distance of 7 leagues, with the horses quite exhausted and the men wet. At 9 P.M. the rain returned, which lasted all night.

Sunday, 14.—It continued raining very hard, lasting all day until 9 P.M. when it cleared with the wind north.

Monday, 15.—Left Mission San Juan Bautista at 10 A.M. At La Natividad sent off the soldiers of the barracks of Soledad and San Miguel together with the Indians of these missions and of San Antonio. I reached the Rancho de Real Hacienda at 4 P.M., a distance of 7 leagues from San Juan.

Tuesday, 16.—Left said Rancho at 9 A.M. Having put the cavalry in camp, I left for the Presidio of Monterey where I arrived at 12:30 of the day. I reported with the present diary to the Governor of the Province, Colonel Don Pablo Vizente de Sola.

Monterey, 16th of November, 1819

José M. Estudillo

New Haven, Connecticut.

CALIFORNIAN BALANOPHAGY

By E. W. Gifford

BALANOPHAGY, or acorn eating, was probably the most characteristic feature of the domestic economy of the Californian Indians. In fact, the habit extended from Lower California northward through the Pacific states practically wherever oaks grew. The northern limit of abundant oaks was the Umpqua divide in Oregon.[1] Beyond that they were relatively rare and played a correspondingly small part in the native dietary. A few grew in the Willamette valley and in the Puget Sound region.

Wherever hard seeds or grains are eaten, some sort of pulverizing or grinding device is employed, in order to render the food assimilable. Acorns do not belong in this class of foods. The nuts can be masticated as readily as walnuts or almonds. The universal use of grinding or pulverizing implements on the one hand and the limited distribution of acorn pulverizing on the other hand, point to the likelihood that the former is exceedingly ancient and the latter far less so, and that the acorn industry has here and there taken over the grinding process, not because of the hardness of the food, but for the sake of reducing it to meal, or to aid in leaching it. In California this is further apparent when it is noted that the same species of acorns which were pulverized were sometimes treated by immersion or burial and eaten without pulverizing.

The crux of the Californian acorn industry is the removal of the objectionable tannic acid from the nuts. The discovery of the relatively rapid process of leaching pulverized acorns made available a vast new food supply of high nutritive value. It is likely that once this discovery was made it spread rapidly and resulted in a greatly increased consumption of acorns. It is probable that the cruder method of rendering acorns edible by immersing them in water or mud, without pulverizing, was the antecedent of leaching the pulverized nuts in a sand basin or basket. The immersion or burial method, sometimes accompanied by boiling or roasting of the nuts, was employed to some extent among the Yurok,[2] Hupa,[3] Shasta,[4] Pomo, and Yuki,[5] the last-named burying the acorns in a sandy place with grass, charcoal, and ashes, and then soaking them in water from time to time until they became sweet. Gunther mentions burial or immersion for the Klallam, Nisqually, and Snohomish,[6] and Spier and Sapir describe burial in mud by the Wishram.[7] It should be emphasized that the immersion method dispenses entirely with the mortar and pestle.

Certain species of acorns apparently have less tannic acid than others. Among the Shasta, *Quercus chrysolepis* acorns were sometimes roasted in ashes and eaten without any preliminary burying or boiling.[8] However, burial whole in mud for several weeks was the customary treatment for these acorns.

---

[1] I am indebted to Professor L. S. Cressman, University of Oregon, for information about Oregon oaks.
[2] Kroeber, 1925, 88.   [4] Dixon, 1907, 426.   [6] Gunther, 216.   [8] Dixon, 1907, 426.
[3] Goddard, 29.   [5] Chesnut, 334.   [7] Spier and Sapir, 184.

The striking thing about the acorn eating of the American Pacific coast is the well-nigh universal knowledge of leaching, attributable no doubt to diffusion rather than separate inventions. Leaching of pulverized meal had the advantage of rendering edible at once the acorns which otherwise had to undergo months of immersion in mud and water. The time necessary for the spread of the leaching process throughout the oak districts of California was probably brief. Judged by the rapidity of the spread of maize and tobacco cultivation among primitive peoples in the Old World in post-Columbian times, it seems likely that two or three centuries would be ample for the spread of so important a discovery as the leaching of acorn meal over so small an area as California. However, as to when it spread—whether 1000 years ago or 10,000 years ago—there is as yet no clue.

The uniformity of the Californian acorn-meal leaching process, either in a sand basin or in a basket, contrasts with the multiplicity of pulverizing devices and seems to indicate that leaching carried with it no special pulverizing device, but rather superimposed itself on the local varieties of pulverizing devices which had already developed. Possibly some methods of pulverizing developed after leaching was introduced, but no method is wholly limited to acorns.

Cabrillo's expedition was the first to record[9] the use of acorns in California, but the account, which refers to the Santa Barbara region in 1542, makes no mention of leaching.

Removal of tannic acid by immersion or burial of the nuts is obviously a simple process which might be arrived at through testing the qualities of accidentally immersed acorns. Pulverizing and leaching are more complicated and involved processes, and appear as inventions to improve and hasten the tannic acid removal. The overlapping distribution of the two methods seems to indicate their genetic relationship. Reason dictates that immersion was the earlier process.

However, if leaching is a process which formed part of the original stock of culture of the ancestors of the American Indians, and not an independent Californian invention, we may look upon manioc leaching in South America and acorn and buckeye leaching in California as based upon this early knowledge. But, that leaching is such an ancient invention is by no means assured. The absence of leaching for acorns in the Southeastern area of the United States makes the case dubious. However, there the interest in extracting oils and the development of agriculture may have obliterated an earlier leaching complex. With the development of agricultural products a people would hardly resort to leaching acorns, except in time of famine.

If there was no widespread fundamental concept of leaching, then California would appear to be a region in which the leaching process was independently invented. The only clue, and that uncertain, as to the part of California in which the invention might have been made, is offered by the number of plants treated by leaching. Nevertheless, this criterion is dubious,

---

[9] Ferrel, 309, 312.

as a people learning to leach acorns may have been enterprising enough to test the method for other likely foods. However, the opposite case is offered by the Yavapai of Arizona, who leach ironwood seeds by boiling,[10] but have not applied the method to acorns.

In regard to the acorn industry on the Pacific coast, California seems central, Washington marginal. At least, this view is dictated by the methods of tannin removal. For Oregon it is to be noted that the Takelma leached.[11]

Leaching in a sandy shallow depression or basin seems characteristic of the northwestern Californian culture area and most of the central Californian culture area. The Luiseño and Cahuilla[12] were the only southerners reported to employ this method, but they also employed the southern method of leaching in a basket.[13] The Costanoan[14] and Sierra Miwok[15] of central California also employed both methods. Peoples reported using the sand basin only were the Yokuts,[16] Western Mono,[17] Eastern Mono,[18] Patwin,[19] Southern Maidu,[20] Northern Maidu,[21] Pomo,[22] Chimariko,[23] Hupa,[24] and Yurok.[25] Beals[26] reports leaching on bare hard ground for the Southern Maidu, which may be a degeneration from the sand basin reported by Powers. Reported to employ only the basket leacher were the Salinan,[27] Gabrielino,[28] and Southern Diegueño.[29] The Shasta employed a device which seems to have been sort of a compromise between the sand-basin leacher and the basket leacher.[30] The Kamia[31] used a sand basin covered with a layer of foliage. Some Eastern Mono[32] lined the leaching basin with bark.

Coniferous twigs used to break the fall of the water in leaching acorn meal are recorded for the Miwok,[33] Nisenan,[34] Northern Maidu,[35] Pomo, and Yuki,[36] but probably are used by other tribes, too.

None of the Californian peoples extracted the oil of acorns, as was done in the Southeastern area,[37] where it was used in preparing food and to anoint the body. Chesnut states that the oil was extracted by boiling the nuts in water containing the ash of maple wood.[38]

As might be expected among pottery-using peoples, acorn meal was boiled in pots among some Eastern Mono,[39] the Southern Diegueño,[40] the Luiseño,[41] and the Kamia,[42] and in steatite vessels among the Gabrielino.[43] Probably other pottery-using peoples did likewise, but there is no record. Stone boiling of the meal in baskets was the customary central and northwestern practice. However, so far as the published record goes it has been mentioned

---

[10] Gifford, 1932a, 208.
[11] Sapir, 257.
[12] Barrows, 52.
[13] Sparkman, 194.
[14] Kroeber, 1925, 467.
[15] Barrett and Gifford, 146.
[16] Kroeber, 1925, 527.
[17] Gifford, 1932b, 22.
[18] Steward, 246.
[19] Kroeber, 1932, 275.
[20] Powers, 421.
[21] Dixon, 1905, 186.
[22] Holmes, 175; Powers, 188.
[23] Dixon, 1910, 299.
[24] Goddard, 28.
[25] Powers, 49; Kroeber, 1925, 88.
[26] Beals, 351.
[27] Mason, 119.
[28] Reid, 11.
[29] Spier, 1923, 335.
[30] Dixon, 1907, 425.
[31] Gifford, 1931, 23.
[32] Steward, 246.
[33] Barrett and Gifford, 145.
[34] Beals, 351.
[35] Dixon, 1905, 186, 187.
[36] Chesnut, 306, 337.
[37] Swanton, 692.
[38] Chesnut, 340.
[39] Steward, 246.
[40] Spier, 1923, 335.
[41] Sparkman, 194.
[42] Gifford, 1931, 27.
[43] Reid, 11, 26.

specifically only for the Pomo of Ukiah and the Yuki,[44] the Southwestern Pomo,[45] Patwin,[46] Southern Maidu,[47] Northern Maidu,[48] Salinan,[49] Hupa,[50] Yurok,[51] Chimariko,[52] Shasta,[53] Miwok,[54] Western Mono,[55] and some Eastern Mono.[56]

According to Powers, the Yurok slightly parched their acorns before grinding. He also records that they cooked the meal in the leaching basin,[57] which seems a most unlikely procedure.

Of additional methods of cooking we find the Shasta roasting the moistened meal,[58] and the Pomo,[59] Lake Miwok, Patwin,[60] Central Wintun, Plains and Northern Miwok,[61] and Salinan[62] baking it in the earth oven. The Pomo,[63] Lake Miwok, and Central Wintun mixed red (presumably ferruginous) earth with the meal, a custom also followed in Sardinia. The Plains and Northern Miwok sometimes mixed ashes of *Quercus douglasii* bark with the dough.

Wherever tan oak acorns (*Pasania* [formerly *Quercus*] *densiflora*) were obtainable they seem to have been preferred. This is essentially a northern coast species. Among the other species, the preference varied: *Quercus kelloggii* (*californica*) with the Southern Maidu or Nisenan,[64] Miwok,[65] Shasta,[66] Luiseño;[67] *Quercus dumosa* with the Cahuilla;[68] *Quercus gambeli* with the Southern Maidu,[69] (although Beals[70] mentions black oak, presumably *Quercus kelloggii*); *Quercus kelloggii, Quercus chrysolepis,* and *Quercus wislizenii* with the Northern Maidu;[71] and *Quercus agrifolia* with the Pomo.[72] The distribution of the various species of oaks was largely the determining factor as to the species most highly regarded by each tribe and as to the number of species used by each tribe. After *Pasania densiflora, Quercus kelloggii* seems to have been the favorite. The Klamath of southern Oregon did not eat the acorns which grow near Klamath Falls in their territory.[73] This lack of interest may be due to scarcity of oaks and to specialization in other foods, notably water-lily seeds.

The leaching out of the tannic acid after the nut meats had been reduced to meal seems to have been limited to the Pacific coast. In central Arizona only sweet acorns were eaten by the Yavapai, and the bitter ones neglected.[74] The acorns of *Quercus oblongifolia* were obtained by the Pima from the Papago by trade. After the hulls had been removed they were parched and ground into meal.[75] Consequently, in Arizona a vast supply of bitter acorns was neglected as food. In southern California, the Diegueño, close linguistic relatives of the Yavapai, were thoroughly familiar with leaching.[76] It would seem that the separation of these two groups took place before leaching of acorns was invented, or at least before it had become known to them. It is

---

[44] Chesnut, 337.
[45] Powers, 188.
[46] Kroeber, 1932, 276.
[47] Powers, 421.
[48] Dixon, 1905, 187.
[49] Mason, 119.
[50] Goddard, 29.
[51] Kroeber, 1925, 87.
[52] Dixon, 1910, 299.
[53] Dixon, 1907, 426.
[54] Barrett and Gifford, 147.
[55] Gifford, 1932b, 22.
[56] Steward, 246.
[57] Powers, 49.
[58] Dixon, 1907, 426.
[59] Holmes, 175.
[60] Kroeber, 1932, 276, 295.
[61] Barrett and Gifford, 148.
[62] Mason, 120.
[63] Laufer, 173.
[64] Beals, 351.
[65] Barrett and Gifford, 142.
[66] Dixon, 1907, 423.
[67] Sparkman, 193, 233.
[68] Barrows, 62.
[69] Powers, 421.
[70] P. 351.
[71] Dixon, 1905, 181.
[72] Holmes, 175.
[73] Spier, 1930, 165.
[74] Gifford, 1932a, 193.
[75] Russell, 78.
[76] Spier, 1923, 335.

entirely possible, of course, that the Diegueño, moving into California, came in touch with people already familiar with leaching. Between the Yavapai and Diegueño lies a 200–300-mile stretch of oakless desert country.

Thus, a more or less concentric distribution appears for the methods of acorn utilization in the western United States—a highly specialized leaching process bordered by an area in which only sweet acorns, unleached, were utilized. To the southward, in the highlands of Mexico, lies the peripheral area of complete neglect of acorns. This concentric distribution in western America seems to indicate complete separation from the acorn-boiling area of the Eastern Woodlands.

In the Old World, provided the scanty data I have gathered present a true cross section, presumably a similar distribution prevailed. Persia, centrally located, has leaching comparable to that of California, since the acorns are first pulverized. Descending the scale, we next have boiling in Japan and Sardinia. Then over the vast circum-Mediterranean region prevailed the eating of sweet acorns without leaching, as in central Arizona. Peripheral Malaysia and New Guinea, with apparently complete neglect of acorns as food, parallel the Mexican area of nonutilization.

At this point it will be well to quote Trelease[77] concerning the world distribution of oaks:

Though a widely distributed genus, Quercus is not world-wide in its occurrence. It is absent from Africa, except for a few species of the Orient which cross the Mediterranean but remain confined to the north; and from the Australian region, though Tertiary fossils have been referred to it from Australia and New Zealand. It centers in India, from which it extends far into temperate Asia and through the Orient into Europe; and in the highlands of Mexico, from which it extends through the United States, and through Central America into the Colombian Andes, reaching also in one species each the West Indies to the east and Guadalupe Island to the west.

The second extensive American area of acorn leaching lies in the Eastern Woodlands. It extends, Professor Speck writes me, "from Ontario east to western Maine (perhaps farther east if we had data) and in southern New England to the Narragansett." In addition, the Delaware now residing in Oklahoma eat acorns of two species (bur oak and pin oak) which are roasted. The boiling of acorns was the method of removing tannic acid in the Eastern Woodlands. It preceded pulverizing, whereas the Californian leaching succeeded pulverizing. Thus, Parker,[78] in part quoting Jesuit Relations, 1716–1727, etc., states that

Acorns were boiled in lye and roasted much as corn was to remove the bitterness, and after several washings pounded up in a mortar and mixed with meal or meat and made into soup or pudding. Children even now commonly eat raw acorns but their elders at present seldom use them for cooking. Their former employment remains only a memory.

Waugh,[79] in part quoting Jesuit and other early writers, says:

The acorn was used quite commonly, probably more particularly the sweet kinds, such as those of the white oak (*Quercus alba*), the chestnut oak (*Quercus prinus*), and some others.

---

[77] P. 22. I am indebted to Dr. H. L. Mason for this reference.   [78] P. 101.   [79] Pp. 122, 123.

Even the bitter acorns of the red and black oak were used in times of necessity, and also the nuts of the bitter hickory. The Hurons are said to have prepared them by "first boiling them in a lye made from ashes, in order to take from them their excessive bitterness." According to another writer "they (the Hurons) also make provisions of acorns, which they boil in several waters to remove the bitterness, and consider them very good."

From Roger Williams' Key to the Indian Language[80] (Narragansett):

Ana'uchemineash, Akornes. These Akornes also they drie, and in case of want of Corne, by much boyling they make a good dish of them: yea sometimes in plentie of Corne doe they eate these Acornes as a novelty.

The eating of sweet acorns, that is, those containing little tannin, is probably an expectable phenomenon. Such are offered for sale in the markets of Tucson, Arizona, where they are much relished by the Papago and other aborigines.[81] Farther south, however, the Mexicans neglect acorns as food, which seems strange considering their vogue in Spain. Dr. Ralph L. Beals, who has studied various western Mexican tribes, notably Mayo, Yaqui, and Mixe, could find no evidence of human consumption of acorns, even though the higher mountains of Oaxaca where the Mixe live are clothed with great oak forests. Trelease[82] enumerates 253 Mexican species of the genus *Quercus* as against only 84 in the United States.

Stretching over a vast area in the Old World from Iberia in the west to New Guinea in the east is a host of species of oaks of the genus *Quercus*. As human food, acorns seem to have had a wider vogue in the Old World than in the New.[83] Britain, Iberia, and Morocco offer the westernmost instances, Japan the easternmost. In the lofty mountainous territory of central New Guinea, Dr. Matthew W. Stirling informs me, the Nogullo Pygmies and Papuans did not utilize two fine species growing there, so far as he observed.

I would repeat that the Mexican neglect of acorns is remarkable in view of their consumption in Iberia and North Africa and the settlement of Mexico by Spaniards. Thus Hooker and Ball[84] state: "The tree was found to be the belloot oak (*Quercus ballota* of Desfontaines), a variety of the evergreen oak, which is spread through North Africa and Spain, where the sweet acorns are commonly roasted and eaten, as chestnuts are elsewhere." Further, concerning the Moorish use of acorns is the statement of Budgett Meakin:[85] "The acorns (belloot) [of the cork oak], which are of large size, are often eaten."

A casual examination of literature on Spain yields the following accounts of their use. First, Joseph Townsend,[86] who traveled in Spain in 1786 and 1787, writes concerning the road to Alba:

For the first two leagues we ascended gradually; then entered a forest of ilex, which, as my guide informed me, stretches east and west near forty leagues. The acorns here are of the kind described by Horace, as the origin of war among the rude inhabitants of an infant world, "glandem atque cubilia propter." [Poaching acorns was sometimes the cause of war in California.] Not austere, like those of the oak, or the common ilex, but sweet and palat-

---

[80] P. 90.
[81] Information from Mr. Juan Dolores, a Papago.
[82] P. 22.
[83] Cf. Bolle.
[84] P. 268.
[85] P. 36.
[86] Pp. 90, 91.

able, like the chestnut, they are food, not merely for the swine, but for the peasants, and yield considerable profit.

However, the peasants were not the only Spaniards who ate acorns. Richard Ford,[87] describing Estremadura, states:

The acorns are still called *bellota,* the Arabic *bollot*—*belot* being the Scriptural term for the tree and the gland—which, with water, formed the original diet of the aboriginal Iberian, as well as of his pig; when dry, the acorns were ground, say the classical authors, into bread, and, when fresh, they were served up as the second course. And in our time ladies of high rank at Madrid constantly ate them at the opera and elsewhere; they were the presents sent by Sancho Panza's wife to the Duchess, and formed the text on which Don Quixote preached so eloquently to the goatherds, on the joys and innocence of the golden age and pastoral happiness, in which they constituted the foundation of the kitchen.

For Sardinia, I have two references to the use of acorns: At Ogliastra, Sardinia, fat clay was mixed in a porridge of acorn meal, the compound made into cakes, baked, sprinkled with ashes or smeared with a little grease, and taken as daily food. ("In Ogliastra op Sardinië wordt deeg van eikels tot brei gemaakt en eene zekere hoeveelheid vette kleiaarde daarbij gevoegd; het mengsel vervolgens tot koeken bereid, die met asch bestrooid of wel met eenig vet besmeerd worden, is een zeer alledaagsche kost."[88])

A full account of the manufacture of acorn bread in Sardinia is given by Antonio de Cortes.[89] The acorns are boiled until soft, pulverized in a mortar, spread on a flat stone, and mixed with a ferruginous argillaceous earth in order to counteract the tannic acid. They are then baked in an oven. As Dr. Berthold Laufer[90] has pointed out, the mixing with ferruginous earth is precisely the procedure of the Pomo of California in the manufacture of acorn bread. However, the Pomo first pulverize and leach the meal in a sand basin. Probably the boiling of the acorns by the Sardinians rids them of a certain amount of tannic acid.

Pliny (H. N. XVI, 15) reports as to the use of acorn bread: "And in the absence of cereals, a flour is milled from the parched kernels and made into a paste to serve as bread."

The ancient pile dwellings of the Po plain, like those of the Swiss lakes, yielded evidence of acorns. Thus, Wolfgang Helbig[91] reported: "Da sich Eicheln in grosser Menge und bisweilen auch in Thongefässen aufbewahrt gefunden haben, so ist es wahrscheinlich, dass sie nicht nur zur Mast für die Schweine, sondern auch den Menschen zur Speise dienten." On pages 72 and 73 of the same paper Helbig discusses the probable use of acorns in early times in Italy and Greece.

North of the Mediterranean countries in Europe acorns were perhaps eaten more sparingly than in the peninsular regions. Johannes Hoops[92] has the following to say concerning the probable use of acorns by Germanic-speaking peoples:

Selbst die Eicheln, die sich in prähistorischen Stationen besonders häufig finden, wurden wohl nicht bloss wie Heer [Planzen der Pfahlbauten 40] meint, zur Schweinemast, sondern

---

[87] P. 127. [89] See Bibliography. [91] Pp. 16, 17.
[88] Altheer, 93. [90] P. 167. [92] P. 476.

auch als menschliches Nahrungsmittel benutzt. Noch im angelsächsischen Runenliede heisst es V. 77f.:

ăc byþ on eorpan elda bearnum
flǣsces fōdor,

'die Eiche ist auf Erden den Menschenkindern Nahrung des Fleisches,' und Eichelmehl wird in den nördlichen Ländern heute noch vielerwärts als Surrogat beim Brotbacken verwendet.

Now I shall turn to the Greek use, first quoting Neumann and Partsch.[93]

Die Eicheln dieser Art [Knoppereiche, *Quercus aegilops*] sind essbar und werden noch heute vom Landvolk geröstet, ja auch roh als Nahrungsmittel verwerthet. Sie stecken in dicken, schuppigen Fruchtbechern, welche wegen ihres Reichthums an Gerbstoff einen der wichtigsten Handelsartikel des heutigen Griechenlands bilden.

Ihre Eicheln [Steineiche, *Quercus ilex*] werden in Spanien auch von Menschen gegessen, in Griechenland anscheinend nicht; sie hinterlassen einen allzu herben, zusammenziehenden Nachgeschmack. Nur einer ihrer Varietäten, der Haselnusseiche (*Q. ballota*), ... wird eine etwas bessere Schmackhaftigkeit der Früchte nachgerühmt. Wir sahen, dass Griechenland mehrere Arten mit essbaren Eicheln besitzt, immer eine werthvolle Naturgabe, und zwar nicht nur für diejenigen Gegenden, in denen das Getreide knapp war. Das Eichelessen der alten Pelasger und der Arkader ist nicht schlechthin als ein Zeichen von Uncultur aufzufassen; überall in den Ländern am Mittelmeer werden die Früchte dieser Eichenarten genossen, die Arkader sind noch heutigen Tages 'Eichelverzehrer.' Nicht als ein trauriges Surrogat bei düftigen Lebensverhältnissen, sondern als Zeichen eines natürlichen Segens im Lande gerechter Männer preist es Hesiod, dass es dort an Nahrung nicht fehle, da der Wipfel der Eichen Eicheln trage und der Stamm den Bienen ein Obdach gewähre.

Pausanias[94] attributes the beginning of balanophagy to Pelasgus:

On the other hand he [Pelasgus] introduced as food the fruit of oak-trees, not of all oaks, but only the acorns of the *phegos* oak. Since his time some of the people have adhered so closely to this diet that even the Pythian priestess, in forbidding the Lacedaemonians to touch the, land of the Arcadians, spoke the following verses:

"There are many acorn-eating men in Arcadia
Who will prevent you; though I do not grudge it you."

According to Herodotus (I 66), the Pythian prophetess referred to the Arcadians as "Many there are in Arcadian land, stout men, eating acorns."

Mr. L. L. Loud, questioning in 1935 a Rhodian friend in Oakland, California, was informed that on the island of Rhodes there are three species of oaks. The acorns of one are used in tanning. A second is wholly neglected. A third is used as food, the acorns being roasted and eaten with honey to offset the taste of tannic acid.

Oaks are mentioned in the Bible, but there are no references to acorns as food. However, modern Arabs eat them. Groser[95] states: "Another abundant species is the Valonia or prickly-cupped oak (*Quercus aegilops*), well known in the Levant, where its acorns are used in tanning, but the Arabs eat them for food." Similarly Tristram[96] says: "It [*Quercus aegilops*] bears very large acorns, and these are used as food by the Arabs, while the acorn cups are employed by dyers."

---

[93] Pp. 378–383.　　[94] Frazer, 374.　　[95] P. 68.　　[96] P. 370.

In Japan: "There are two sorts of Oaks grow in the Country, both different from ours. The Acorns of the larger sort are boil'd and eat by the common People."[97] It is not clear if the boiling was to extract tannic acid, but it may well have been for that purpose.

Concerning Persian acorn-eating, Sir Arnold T. Wilson[98] writes:

The nomads of the Zagros range from Baneh and Saqqiz in Kurdistan to Shiraz, have from the earliest times supplemented their meagre stores of cereals with bread made from acorns, which are ground or rather pounded to pulp with the aid of a boulder rolled over a flat rock; the meal thus obtained is soaked in running water for several days, dried and made into flat cakes. It is not appetizing, but it keeps well, and judging from the physical condition of whole families which have lived with no other cereals and no other food except the produce of their herds, it does not lack vitamins.

The one region of the earth where balanophagy attained its richest development was aboriginal California. I say "richest," because there the methods of ridding the acorns of the objectionable tannin were most developed and moreover many species were eaten, putting to shame the balanophagous propensities of the Arcadians.

In my hasty sampling of the literature, the Persian case was the only Old World example of removing tannic acid from acorns, according to the Californian practice of pulverizing first, then leaching. Any possible community of origin between Persian and Californian leaching practices seems at first thought unlikely, especially since I have no examples to adduce from intermediate parts of Asia. As Bolle points out, however, acorn eating was doubtless once much wider spread than now. No doubt the development of cultivated cereals has largely displaced the acorn as an article of diet. It is not beyond peradventure that some of the Asiatic forefathers of American Indians were acorn eaters, and that their descendants, upon reaching the oak regions of the Pacific and Atlantic coasts of America, revived this food habit of their ancestors.

The centers for acorn leaching preceded by pulverizing were Persia and California. In New England the tannic acid was removed by boiling the whole nuts. These facts bring us face to face with the old problem of diffusion from one center versus independent invention in two or three separate areas. Obviously, the great geographic separation makes it mandatory to accept, in the present state of our knowledge, the latter alternative. Yet, we should not close our minds to the probable very extensive utilization of acorns in preagricultural Neolithic times and to the remote possibility that in those times the knowledge of tannin removal by leaching or boiling did spread from one center of origin.

It should be noted that the acorn-leaching areas (California and Eastern Woodlands) of the New World are in the northern portion of the American oak area which stretches southward to Colombia. In other words, leaching is in the oak regions nearest Asia. As between Middle American and Asiatic origins for leaching, if the possibility of independent invention could be

---

[97] Kaempfer, 181.   [98] P. 54.

eliminated, the choice would fall to an Asiatic source. The fading, concentric distribution of acorn utilization in America—leaching, eating sweet acorns only, eating no acorns—roughly parallels the distribution of sinew-backed and simple bow, paddle-and-anvil pottery and that made without paddle and anvil, tailored clothing and no tailored clothing, moccasins and no moccasins, and various other cultural features of North America which connect with the Old World rather than with Middle America.

Of interest, but of doubtful value from an ethnological standpoint, are Trelease's statements[99] concerning the Old World relationships of certain Californian oaks: "One is tempted to concur in de Candolle's opinion (Prodromus, vol. 16, pt. 2, p. 23) that the Californian white oaks are more closely comparable—possibly in derivation as well as in aspect—with those of northern Europe than with those of eastern America." He also states: "By common consent the Asiatic oaks of the type represented in the Californian region by what has been called *Q. densiflora* . . . are now segregated under the generic name Pasania."

---

[99] P. 19.

Bibliography

ALTHEER, J. J.
  1857. Eetbare Aardsoorten en Geophagie. Natuurkundig Tijdschrift voor Nederlandsch Indië, 13:83–100.
BARRETT, S. A. AND GIFFORD, E. W.
  1933. Miwok Material Culture. PMM-B 2:117–376.
BARROWS, DAVID PRESCOTT
  1900. The Ethno-botany of the Coahuilla Indians of Southern California. Univ. Chicago.
BEALS, RALPH L.
  1933. Ethnology of the Nisenan. UC-PAAE 31:335–414.
BOLLE, CARL
  1891. Die Eichenfrucht als menschliches Nahrungsmittel. Zeitsch. Vereins für Volkskunde, 1:138–148.
CHESNUT, V. K.
  1902. Plants used by the Indians of Mendocino County, California. U. S. N. Herbarium, Contr. 7:295–422.
CORTES, ANTONIO DE
  1900. Di una Strana Varietà di Pane che si Mangia in Sardegna. Rivista d'Igiene e di Sanità Pubblica, 11:76–83.
DIXON, R. B.
  1905. The Northern Maidu. AMNH-B 17:119–346.
  1907. The Shasta. AMNH-B 17:381–498.
  1910. The Chimariko Indians and Language. UC-PAAE 5:293–380.
FERREL, BARTOLOME
  1879. Translation from the Spanish of the Account by the Pilot Ferrel of the Voyage of Cabrillo along the West Coast of North America in 1542. With Introductory Notes by H. W. Henshaw. U. S. Geog. Surv. W. of 100th Meridian—R 7:293–314.
FORD, RICHARD
  1851. Gatherings from Spain. New edition. London.
FRAZER, J. G.
  1913. Pausanias's Description of Greece. Translated with a Commentary. Vol. 1. London.
GIFFORD, E. W.
  1931. The Kamia of Imperial Valley. BAE-B 97.
  1932a. The Southeastern Yavapai. UC-PAAE 29:177–252.
  1932b. The Northfork Mono. UC-PAAE 31:15–65.
GODDARD, P. E.
  1903. Life and Culture of the Hupa. UC-PAAE 1:1–88.
GROSER, W. H.
  1888. Scripture Natural History, I. The Trees and Plants mentioned in the Bible. London.
GUNTHER, ERNA
  1927. Klallam Ethnography. UW-PA 1:171–314.
HELBIG, WOLFGANG
  1879. Die Italiker in der Poebene. Leipzig.
HOLMES, WILLIAM H.
  1902. Anthropological Studies in California. USNM-Rep. for 1900:155–188.
HOOKER, J. D. and BALL, JOHN
  1878. Journal of a Tour in Marocco and the Great Atlas. London.
HOOPS, JOHANNES
  1905. Waldbäume und Kulturpflanzen im germanischen Altertum. Strassburg.

KAEMPFER, ENGELBERT
　1906. The History of Japan, together with a description of the Kingdom of Siam, 1690–1692. Vol. 1. Glasgow.
KROEBER, A. L.
　1925. Handbook of the Indians of California. BAE-B 78.
　1932. The Patwin and their Neighbors. UC-PAAE 29:253–423.
LAUFER, BERTHOLD
　1930. Geophagy. FMNH-PA S 18:99–198.
MASON, J. A.
　1912. The Ethnology of the Salinan Indians. UC-PAAE 10:97–240.
MEAKIN, BUDGETT
　1901. The Land of the Moors. London.
NEUMANN, K. J. H. AND PARTSCH, J. F. M.
　1885. Physikalische Geographie von Griechenland. Breslau.
PARKER, ARTHUR C.
　1910. Iroquois Uses of Maize and other Food Plants. N. Y. State Mus. Bull. 144.
POWERS, STEPHEN
　1877. Tribes of California. CNAE 3.
REID, HUGO
　1926. The Indians of Los Angeles County. Privately printed. Los Angeles.
RUSSELL, FRANK
　1908. The Pima Indians. BAE-R 26:3–389.
SAPIR, EDWARD
　1907. Notes on the Takelma Indians of Southwestern Oregon. AA, n.s., 9:251–275.
SPARKMAN, PHILIP STEDMAN
　1908. The Culture of the Luiseño Indians. UC-PAAE 8:187–234.
SPIER, LESLIE
　1923. Southern Diegueño Customs. UC-PAAE 20:297–358.
　1930. Klamath Ethnography. UC-PAAE 30.
SPIER, LESLIE, AND SAPIR, EDWARD
　1930. Wishram Ethnography. UW-PA 3:151–300.
STEWARD, JULIAN H.
　1933. Ethnography of the Owens Valley Paiute. UC-PAAE 33:233–350.
SWANTON, JOHN R.
　1928. Aboriginal Cultures of the Southeast. BAE-R 42:673–726.
TOWNSEND, JOSEPH
　1792. A Journey through Spain in the Years 1786 and 1787. London.
TRELEASE, WILLIAM
　1924. The American Oaks. Nat. Acad. Sci. Mem. 20.
TRISTRAM, H. B.
　1873. Natural History of the Bible. London.
WAUGH, F. W.
　1916. Iroquois Foods and Food Preparation. Geol. Surv. Canada, Mem. 86.
WILLIAMS, ROGER
　1827. A Key to the Language of America. London, 1643. Collections of the Rhode Island Historical Society, I.
WILSON, ARNOLD T.
　1932. Persia. London.

UNIVERSITY OF CALIFORNIA,
BERKELEY, CALIFORNIA.

LOOSE ENDS OF THEORY ON THE INDIVIDUAL, PATTERN, AND INVOLUTION IN PRIMITIVE SOCIETY

By Alexander A. Goldenweiser

The Primitive Individual

ANTHROPOLOGISTS are no longer surprised when new evidence is brought forth of the existence of full-fledged individuality among primitives. In the heyday of folk theory it was glibly assumed that the primitive individual was literally submerged, that no room was left for personality or self-expression in a society ridden by tradition, dominated by established habits and dogmas, shot through with inflexible patterns. No one any longer believes this. We know now that the very uniformity of primitive patterns should not be taken literally. After all, variation is not completely spirited away; in art, craft, storytelling, dancing, social behavior, there is difference between performance and performance, difference in skill, in details of form, in facility of execution. So also in religion, as Radin and others have pointed out, some lead, others follow, some originate, others imitate, some throw themselves body and soul into supernatural participation, others offer little more than lip service to the divine. Again, the prevalence of hard and fast matrimonial regulations does not preclude occasional divagations, including elopements with a "wrong" mate, or even, in some few instances, suicides over romantic frustrations.

We learn from Malinowski that the Melanesian standards of beauty differ materially from our own, but also that, within these culturally conditioned limits, individual taste will have its sway. So also with crime; it may remain true that among primitives practice agrees with legal or customary regulation a little more closely than it does with us, but this does not preclude breaches of customs and taboos, secular or sacred. In brief, cultural uniformity as a feature of primitiveness must be accepted in a relative, not an absolute, sense.

Still, it must be granted that the range of individual variation, in all matters cultural, is relatively narrow among primitives. The question remains: In how far does this fact have psychological significance? Does the primitive chafe under customary limitations? Does he feel himself a mere cog in the wheels of society? Does he recognize himself as one unit in a set of similar or identical units? Of all this there is no evidence whatsoever. Rather is the contrary true. Anthropological field records agree in representing primitives as leading a lusty, animated, exciting existence. At first blush this psychological picture contrasts strangely with the recognized objective uniformity of folk culture. Upon reflection, the contrast should not impress one as strange or contradictory.

Consider, first, this. The customary or prescribed routine does not weigh evenly over the whole expanse of the cultural scene. The sacred things and acts come first here; in this domain the past, habitual, prescribed, has full sway at the cost of the individual and variable. Next come the social things and acts, sanctified by the divine only vicariously, such as etiquette, socioeconomic relations, the coöperative aspects of industry. Here individual variation, though still limited, has freer play. Finally, we have the wide range of activities which, in their very nature, are individual, such as hunting, fishing, fighting, the technical aspects of craft and art, and certain specialized pursuits, matter of fact at least to a degree, such as medicine. It has been shown at another place that in these domains the relative objectivity of outlook forced upon the mind by the concreteness of experience and the strictly pragmatic nature of objectives, paves the way for dispassionate observation, accumulation of valid knowledge, and invention. Patently, the individual here is no longer a slave to the social. Rules, to be sure, there are in plenty here also, but here—in contrast to the socioreligious and the narrowly social realms—these rules cannot do more than set up a framework for experience and behavior within which ample opportunity is offered to think, act, and react in one's own way. But this is not all. In such matters as fighting, hunting, or craftsmanship prescriptions can at best be only regulative. What is or can be prescribed is to act in such and such a way *if* and when so and so happens. But what will happen or when, exactly, can neither be prescribed nor foreseen nor controlled; it remains conjectural. Time, place, and event are immersed in the capricious flow of history. What is involved here is the difference between knowing how a pot is made and how to make a pot, this particular pot which has not dried quite sufficiently, bulges out so and so, must be a little larger than its predecessor which has proved a bit small, and should be fashioned with especial care to show the neighboring potter where he comes off; the difference between knowing how a lion is speared and how to spear a lion, this particular fellow, yonder not so far off, wounded but full of vim, a little too distant for a sure spear thrust but too near for taking a chance at a charge, the very lion, moreover, which carried off a fair-sized youngster from camp yesterday and devoured him. In all such situations—and their name is legion—the primitive is confronted with experience in its tridimensional capacity; or shall I say four-dimensional, including time? There is a thrill in such episodes, and a uniqueness, quite beyond the reach of customary regulations.

The final point carries us fully into the psychological domain. Personal experience is nonsubstitutive, noninterchangeable. It is *one's own,* and there the matter ends. What may be the content of such experience, whether wholly conventional, or truly original, or a bit of each, is an entirely different problem. *Whatever* the content, it *is one's own,* and counts as such. However narrowly limited acts, thoughts, skills may be, however objectively similar as between one man and the next, to each one, as he acts, performs, thinks, dreams, dances, sings, or prays, each of these episodes counts as one rung in the ladder of his life, as something he identifies himself with, something his own effort has gone into, an experience to be remembered, with pride, joy, or horror. Nor is there, from this angle, any significant difference between religious, narrowly social, or mainly personal situations. Envisaged as experiences, all situations are individual, and as such, unique, personal, historical. Society apart, man, not being a robot, lives—as an individual.

Pattern, as Limit and as Model

Another check upon the notion that individuality runs thin among primitives comes from the domain of pattern itself. We are accustomed to think of pattern as a limiting or restraining agency, of folk culture as a haven of pattern, impatient of individuality and inimical to all originality. There is, of course, a good measure of truth in such allegations. But not the whole truth. We may conceive of pattern as two-faceted: one facet faces the outside, the world of other actual or potential patterns, and vetoes it. This aspect of pattern is negative, and limiting: do not go beyond this, it proclaims. Thus, in the world beyond the pattern, change, variation, originality, are all but checked. But there is the other facet: it faces the individual, and bids him follow. There is nothing negative about this aspect of pattern. It says, I am your model, use me as a guide—a wholehearted, positive program. The negative aspect of pattern establishes a taboo, the positive aspect points to a task.

Modern society teems with equivalent and competing patterns; and imagination, now relatively unleashed, expands this realm still further. So, when a pattern rises to dominance and, like a traffic policeman, checks our progress, we resent it. We are too well aware of the varied possibilities we are forced to forego, because they are beyond our means or social class, are evil or disreputable, or against the Constitution. It is the awareness of the proscribed that strengthens our reluctance to stick to the prescribed.

The scene is different among primitives. Here the pattern functions largely as a model, and only quite secondarily as a limit. The alternatives are not here to entice one, nor does the imagination, itself well regimented, readily play with them. Before one is a task: reproduce the pattern. In the absence of a sense of restriction, the pattern has nothing about it of the stern countenance of a taboo; on the contrary, it appears as an inviting and admired exemplar.

If the point just made is well taken, then the still current notion that the concept "folk culture" somehow represents a deep psychological category, is due for revision. A folk culture is more uniform in its patterns than is the case with a culture that is not "folk." Its patterns are more dominant or categorical. The responsibility, moreover, for the patterns falls more definitely upon the group than upon its component individuals: the patterns are an interindividual rather than an individual achievement. All this need not be questioned. But also: let us note that the level of discourse, so far, is purely objective, not psychological. The picture as given might be drawn and substantiated by a statistician or a behaviorist: so and so many patterns, persistence great, individual variability slight (or such and such), etc. As between a culture and the world outside (or other cultures) the picture is correct: the term "folk" is vindicated.

What appears when a culture is viewed in the context of its carriers is an entirely different story. From earliest childhood on, the primitive is surrounded by patterns, of thought, attitude, action. What can be observed, is observed—under guidance; what must be learned is learned, with the assistance of elders. When the range of performance is fixed, or nearly so, a premium is inevitably set on the excellence of performance. In another place I have emphasized the rôle of time in this context: it takes time to achieve expertness or excellence. But there is another factor: the presence of a definite pattern tends to shift emphasis from originality in variation—a feature never quite absent—to quality of execution. To us who have much to choose from, as to doing, and who do most things badly, there is something strange about a culture where each individual is confronted with a set of tasks—under the aegis of pattern—and carries them out well, or very well. But such is the nature of folk cultures. On the objective side: a set of patterns, fairly numerous, but thoroughly incrustated. When Von den Steinen spoke of primitive art as "eine gebundene Kunst," he might have said "eine gebundene Kultur"; pattern reigns. On the psychological side, a very different picture: a scramble for excellence in reproducing patterns. From this angle primitive society is like a school of the arts of life, where competition is keen, and performance, though uniform in aim, is varied in excellence. There is no drabness in such a life. It has about it all the allurements of personal experience, very much one's own, of competitive skill, of things well done. Even as an animal bends its instinctive nature to an existence full of excitement and gusto, so does the primitive, while bowing to the pattern, lead a life rich in content and animated in tempo.

INVOLUTION

The application of the pattern concept to a cultural feature in the process of development provides, I think, a way of explaining one peculiarity of primitive cultures. The primary effect of pattern, is, of course, to check development, or at least to limit it. As soon as the pattern form is reached further change is inhibited by the tenacity of the pattern. While characteristic of all things cultural, especially in primitiveness, this aspect of pattern is particularly conspicuous in rituals and the forms of religious objects, where the tenacity of pattern is enhanced by social inertia or a sacred halo. But there are also other instances where pattern merely sets a limit, a frame, as it were, within which further change is permitted if not invited. Take, for instance, the decorative art of the Maori, distinguished by its complexity, elaborateness, and the extent to which the entire decorated object is pervaded by the decoration. On analysis the unit elements of the design are found to be few in number; in some instances, in fact, the complex design is brought about through a multiplicity of spatial arrangements of one and the same unit. What we have here is a pattern plus continued development. The pattern precludes the use of another unit or of other units, but it is not inimical to play with the unit or units. The inevitable result is progressive complication, variety within uniformity, virtuosity within monotony. This is *involution*.

A parallel instance, in later periods of history, is provided by what is called ornateness in art, as in the late Gothic. The basic forms of the art have reached finality, the structural features are fixed beyond variation, inventive originality is exhausted. Still, development goes on. Being hemmed in on all sides by crystallized pattern, it takes the function of elaboration. Expansive creativeness having dried up at the source, a special kind of virtuosity takes its place, a sort of technical hairsplitting. No longer capable of genuine procreation, art here, like a seedless orange, breeds within itself, crowding its inner structure with the pale specters of unborn generations.

Anyone familiar with primitive cultures will think of similar instances in other cultural domains. For example, in ceremonial, whether that of the Toda dairies, or that of the Plains Sun Dance, or that of the Australian *intichiuma*. In detailed content these ceremonies are, of course, quite different, but in one respect there is a common feature: in each case we are overwhelmed, almost shocked, often bored, by what seems an excessive heaping up of unit elements—whether in form, rhythm, or dance-step—with a total effect of enormous, to the novice bewildering, complexity. Similarly, in ceremonial etiquette as described, for instance, by Malinowski with reference to the interminable exchanges of presents and the like which precede, accompany, and follow the conclusion of matrimonial unions. The patterns of behavior here implied are few, as Malinowski points out, yet the actual procedure is enormously complex. Does not the reason lie in the fact that what we have here is a narrow pattern of behavior plus a possibility of further change within the pattern? If the pattern were less narrow, or if there were no pattern, the change might have been an unfoldment. Within the narrow possibilities determined by pattern, the change can only be an elaboration, leading, as an ultimate limit, to seemingly insane complexity.[1]

It may be true—I think it is—that involution characterizes primitive society, on account of the dominance of pattern in primitive conditions. Still, if the principle is correctly formulated, it should apply to conditions other than primitive, in otherwise similar circumstances. This, indeed, seems to be the case. Under this heading I have already referred to ornateness in art. A good further illustration is provided by the music of Bach, his fugues particularly. We have here a deliberate limitation of invention in so far as the basic melodic elements are concerned. On the other hand, invention, development

---

[1] It must not be assumed, of course, that *all* complexity is reducible to this factor, involution. Ordered complexity has its own appeal, especially to the sophisticated; and in such things as ritual or decorative art many primitives are sophisticates. Even disordered complexity, an infinitely variegated or multicolored chaos, may have a positive appeal. Such situations, then, if desirable as consummations, may become causal in guiding development in the corresponding direction. All that the formulation of the text should be understood to imply is that pattern plus development within the pattern limits must and does lead to involution, that is, a tendency toward elaborateness or complexity, consisting of a combination, repetition, or juxtaposition of relatively uniform elements.

goes on, only it takes the form of playing with these elements, repeating, combining, and recombining. The result is a highly complex musical texture; so complex, in fact, as frequently to confuse the ear, unless unusually musical or experienced. This feature stands out in bald relief especially when compared, say, with Beethoven, where elaboration or combination of basic melodic elements is not abandoned but supplemented by continued melodic invention. The resulting effect is relative simplicity and freshness.

Psychopathology provides another example. In neurosis, so often associated with introversion, the individual's relations to outside people or things are queered, in one way or another. The possibility of a workable understanding, on an objective level, being eliminated, an adjustment, if one is reached at all, is worked out on a subjective level: the "pleasure principle" supplants the "reality principle." Being cut off from a large number of possible external accommodations, the mind of the individual turns upon itself, unceasingly it crosses and recrosses its own tracks, like a mouse in a maze, beating desperately at times against the inner wall of the frontier of the ego, beyond which it may not go. The mind of the introverted neurotic is limited but complex—it is involuted.[2]

[2] It will be observed that, from one angle, the principle of involution represents a special case of the principle of limited possibilities. The limitation here is in range, or form, or the number of basic elements. Granted that development continues, it must, under such conditions, lead to complexity. Complexity, then, elaboration or elaborateness, repetitiousness, are earmarks of involution.

REED COLLEGE,
PORTLAND, OREGON.

A PRELIMINARY REPORT ON THE ZOÖLOGICAL KNOWLEDGE OF THE MAKAH

By Erna Gunther

THIS MATERIAL is presented here as the beginning of a very fruitful study. It is now relatively seldom that one has the good fortune to find an Indian still sufficiently aware of his native environment to give extensive information on the flora and fauna. Among the Makah a most unusual couple were available. The man, Luke Markishtum, has been a seal hunter, has trapped small animals for a living, and has guided ornithologists in fieldwork. When shown the colored plates of birds and animals, he was as anxious to learn our common names for them as I was to learn the Makah. "We are really just exchanging what we know," Luke said one evening, really flattering me, for my knowledge was not nearly equivalent to his. Last summer we worked out the material presented here. This coming season I shall fill in the gaps in this, and study the fishes and insects. With his wife I have studied flowers and shells. The division of this study between husband and wife is coincident with the old division of labor in food-getting: the men dealt with the mobile, the women with the stationary.

In addition to giving the information gathered here, Luke would stop occasionally to tell a folk tale involving the animal or bird under discussion, or if the tale were too long he would ask me to make a note of it for future telling.

While the Makah were definitely a sea-conscious people, deriving the bulk of their food from its waters or its shores, they were not completely oblivious to the hinterland. Luke's familiarity with shore birds is apparent, but he also knew a fair number of the smaller perchers. The same is true of land animals.

For help in the identification of the birds and mammals in the following list I wish to thank Martha R. Flahaut, Assistant in Biology at the Washington State Museum, University of Washington. Without her painstaking help and her excellent knowledge of the literature, as well as her field experience, this paper would not have been possible.

Since various parts of these birds are used for so many diverse purposes, it has not seemed feasible to classify them according to use. They are therefore presented according to the latest order for the birds of Washington accepted by ornithologists, Kitchin's Distributional Check-list. As Luke, my informant, and I could only discuss those illustrated by colored plates in Taverner, this list is necessarily limited. Next summer in the field I am planning to supplement it with skins of the birds mentioned in Kitchin which Luke has not seen.

In the list below I am including in parentheses all the birds that were not recognized. Wherever the Makah word is used for an entire family rather than for a specific bird, the scientific name is given in one all-inclusive fashion also.

Birds

Lesser Loon   *Gavia immer elasson*   t!ut!'to'bakc

This loon passes in migration along the shores in spring and fall. It was shot with bow and arrow. The meat was eaten but restricted to old people, as were most ducks, and forbidden to pregnant women.

Loon skins were used for blankets. The feathers were sometimes used for arrows, but were not so satisfactory as shag wings, which shed water better.

Loons call pleasantly to passing canoes.

In folk tales loon occurs as a character.

(Eared Grebe   *Colymbus nigricollis californicus*)

(Pied-billed Grebe   *Podilymbus podiceps podiceps*)

(Probably the grebe listed by Swan[1] as *Podiceps occidentalis*, which is colloquially known as the hell-diver.)

White-crested Cormorant   *Phalarocorax auritus cincinatus*   k!līkłī'x'x̱ēxł, "red around the throat"

The cormorant was eaten and its wing feathers used for arrows. Swan reports only the young cormorant as food.[2] They are known to nest at Cape Flattery, according to Taverner,[3] but this was not mentioned.

Heron   any variety   q!wa''lis

According to Swan the heron was called hah-to-bad-die and the crane was kwar-less.[4] The two plates in Taverner show the Great Blue Heron and the Black-crowned Night Heron. The informant recognized the former but added that this name was applied to all herons.

The herons were seen along rivers and on rocks. They were shot and eaten by old people, but more important than their meat was the oil they rendered for medicinal purposes. Heron feathers were used to clean out the ears and then the oil was put in.

The heron's bill was burned and ground to powder to be rubbed on fishing spears. The wing bone was used for making blanket pins.

(American Bittern)

Common Canada Goose   *Branta canadensis canadensis*   xadi'kx̱

During migration in spring and fall this goose was shot by pitch torchlight. It was eaten and greatly preferred to the snow goose.

Swan records the goose as hah-dikh,[5] meaning probably this variety.

Black Brant   *Branta nigricans*   waxwa'c

These birds are seen in migration. They are very hard to get, so they are only taken when chanced upon while hunting for other birds. The meat is eaten but there is no use for the feathers.

(White-fronted Goose)

Lesser Snow Goose   *Chen hyperborea hyperborea*   k!łista'x̱

In spring and fall the snow goose visits on migration. These geese were so tame that formerly the women had to scare them away when they were digging roots, especially on the prairies. The bird was shot for eating but its feathers were not used.

Mallard   *Anas platyrhynchos platyrhynchos*   dax̱'xa't!atc

The mallards gathered on the prairies and shores near Tcito Beach, where they were gotten by means of a duck net probably similar to that used by the Klallam,[6] although it could not be recalled exactly. They were also trapped at their feeding places and shot with bow and arrow. The observation that the mallard did not breed directly at Neah Bay is probably correct, for Taverner states that they breed at considerable distance from the water.[7]

---

[1] Swan, 94.   [3] Taverner, 71.   [5] Swan, 94.   [7] Taverner, 83.
[2] Swan, 86.   [4] Swan, 94, 95.   [6] Gunther, 205.

This bird was eaten. Mallard skins were sewed together and made double for blankets. A dried mallard head was tied to the blanket for rubbing the eyes. This was especially true for old people whose eyes watered.

Swan is specific about this variety of duck, recording dah-dah-tih as the name.[8]

(Baldpate)

Pintail   *Davila acuta tzitzihoa*
This bird was seen, but no name was known for it.

Teal   No distinction of the several varieties   tsī''ētc
The plates shown were of the blue-winged teal and the green-winged teal, but only one name was given for both.

This bird was trapped and shot along the rivers and shore. It was eaten.

Shoveller   *Spatula clypeata*
This bird was seen but no name was known for it.

(Wood-duck)

Canvas-back   *Nyroca valisneria*
This is regarded as a very rare bird and therefore not named. Taverner mentions that the canvas-back is more common in the interior.[9]

Lesser Scaup Duck   *Nyroca affinis*   wawa'katapa ł
The scaup is rare but is always shot and eaten when found. It is listed by Swan as ko-ho-ash,[10] which varies so much from the name recently obtained that it is questionable if the same bird is meant.

American Golden-eye   *Glaucionetta clangula americana*   q'oq'osa'p, "anybody that talks Klallam"

As rare as the Lesser Scaup, the golden-eye is also shot and eaten whenever found. The Makah are forever poking fun at the Klallam for their speech, especially their nasalized n. "It sounds like Klallam" is a frequent expression for anything with a strange and perhaps unmelodious sound—an excellent case of the pot calling the kettle black.

(Barrow's Golden-eye)

Harlequin Duck   *Histrionicus histrionicus pacificus*   ts!uts!o'ł tcīa, "bird that lies in the surf"

Although very common in Makah territory the Harlequin was not taken, for the Makah did not like the taste of its meat.

Swan records this bird as tsat-tsowl-chak.[11]

(White-winged Scoter)

Red-breasted Merganser   *Mergus serrator*   ts!a'p!id
The red-breasted merganser, commonly known as the saw-bill or fish-duck, is hunted with bow and arrow and eaten. It was also trapped like mallards. It was known to nest along rivers.

The webbed feet of this bird were prepared as a charm to make a boy baby a swift runner. The feet were dried, burned, and powdered, and this substance was put under the child's feet in his cradle.

(Western Goshawk)

(Sharp-shinned Hawk)

Red-tailed Hawk   *Buteo borealis calurus*   q!wēq!wēdaqapaux, "slug-eating hawk"
This hen hawk, which fortunately is irregular in its visits, was shot only for its feathers. They were used by medicine men and by kło'kwali dancers as decorations on dance rattles, often combined with eagle feathers.

---

[8] Swan, 98.   [9] Taverner, 90.   [10] Swan, 94.   [11] Swan, 94.

(Ferruginous Rough-leg)

(Marsh Hawk)
  Not a common migrant in western Washington.

Osprey   *Pandion haliaetus carolinensis*   q!waq!walabu'xc
  The feathers of the osprey are used for dance costumes, but more important is the power the bird gives. Some of the members of the secret society get a power from the osprey which allows them to see far away. When the man went to Dia to kill the Nitinat chief,[12] a person with such power sat on the roof of his house and watched for him to return. He saw him from afar and began to drum on the roof to call the people together.

(Peregrine Falcon)

Eastern Sparrow Hawk   *Falco sparverius sparverius*   t!at!aq!wik, "anything that grabs with the claws," or, quak qwo'itcik, "small in quantity"
  The pretty feathers of the sparrow hawk are appreciated by the Makah, who shoot it only for its plumage.

(Blue Grouse)

(Ruffed Grouse)

(Sharp-tailed Grouse)
  Only in eastern part of State.

Little Brown Crane   *Grus canadensis canadensis*   xadtu'badi
  In April during migration these birds come to the prairie. They are got for food and can be eaten by everybody.

(Sora Rail)

American Coot   *Fulica americana*
  This bird was well known, but, never being killed or used in any way, it had no name. It is the familiar mud hen.

(Killdeer)

(Black-bellied Plover)

Wilson's Snipe   *Capella delicata*
  This is the same as the Jack Snipe, which the informant had seen but for which he had no name.

(Upland Plover)

(Spotted Sandpiper)

(Willet)

(Greater Yellow-legs)

Least Sandpiper   *Pisobia minutilla*   xux̱upx̱a'sis
  This bird was not used except as a pet for children. They captured the bird alone and broke a wing or a leg so that it could not escape. From this and other statements it is clear that kindness to animals was not a trait instilled in the young.
  Swan calls this bird huhupe-sis.[13]

(Marbled Godwit)

(Wilson's Phalarope)

Glaucous-winged Gull   *Larus glaucescens*   qwalo'l
  Around Cape Flattery, Tatoosh Island, and Sail Rock many glaucous-winged gulls nest, but the Makah neither gather their eggs nor take the young for eating.[14] The full-grown gull is hunted with bow and arrow and eaten.

---
[12] Markistun.   [13] Swan, 94.   [14] Swan contradicts this statement (p. 86).

For dances the white part of the feathers and the down was used. When people were going into the ceremonial house for a gathering, a man might roll down into a blanket and throw it up in the air. This was an invitation for the people present to come to his house for a feast. As a part of some dancing costumes, the hair was wetted and sprinkled with down, which stuck very well to the wet hair.

Swan records kwa'-lil as name word for gulls,[15] evidently including all varieties.

(Herring Gull)

Bonaparte's Gull   *Larus philadelphia*   tɬ atla'aiyatx, "anything living way out in the ocean"

This bird is seen on migration, but does not nest here.[16] The bird is only hunted with bow and arrow for pleasure. It is not eaten or put to any use.

The translation of the name for this gull shows a realization of its habits.

(Forster's Tern)

(Common Tern)

(Marbled Murrelet)

(Band-tailed Pigeon)

(Mourning Dove)
Rare in western Washington.

Screech Owl   *Otus asio kennicotti*   tc!ē ɬ săp

This very rare bird is never killed but rather greatly feared. It is associated with death. When a screech owl flies into a house, it means that someone there will die soon. The screech owl comes for the soul of a dying person. Once a screech owl flew into a smokehouse, so they closed the house and caught the owl. They talked to it and sprinkled it with red paint and eagle down before they let it go again.

When Chestoka Peterson and his son were drowned off Cape Flattery an owl was heard hooting near his place up the creek about one year after his death.

Swan also records the incident of a party being drowned when a whale demolished the canoe with his tail. The night after this accident eight owls hovered over the houses of the dead men and one wore in his beak the shell ornament that one drowned man had had in his nose.[17]

It seems as though these owls are trying to say something but cannot speak plainly enough to be understood.

If there is an owl about in the woods, a good hunter can feel it.

Not very long ago a person turned into an owl—this statement could not be substantiated, however. According to Swan, drowned people turn into owls.[18]

Snowy Owl   *Nyctea nyctea*   k! ɬ isapextuk'tuk

This bird was only discussed, not identified from a plate. The informant noted that it was not represented in the illustrations.

The Snowy Owl came down toward the bay when the weather was turning cold. In the early days it was never killed.

(Hawk Owl)

(Pygmy Owl)

(Long-eared Owl)

Nighthawk   *Chordeiles minor hesperis*   tcitcislu'k!abatc

This hawk appears with the screech owl and is never shot.

---

[15] Swan, 94.

[16] "The only nests reported have been in the far northwest and the interior of Alaska." Taverner, 60.

[17] Swan, 88.   [18] Swan, 88.

Vaux's Swift   *Chaetura vauxi*   k!ł īk! ł īdak!a'batc, "anything that brings fog"

They are very hard to get and are of no general use, though they may be a good luck charm for someone.

The translation of the name is an interesting observation. The swifts generally feed over fresh water, that near Neah Bay can be found in the creeks back or west of the village. When the fog rolls in, during the late afternoon, it comes from the west along the same path as the swifts travel. One wonders if this association is a purely local one.

Humming Bird   *Selasphorus rufus*   k!witti'k!wutc, "anything that sticks"

The informant claims that there are two varieties of humming birds in the Makah territory and their difference is recognized but they are both called by the same name. It is possible that they regard the male and female as two varieties because of their differences. Swan also has but one name for them, kwe-ta'-kootch.[19]

Humming birds' hearts were very potent love charms. In order to make a person fall in love, a humming bird's heart was put on something he or she would eat. To capture the bird hemlock twigs were stripped of their needles and bark and rubbed with the slime of a slug. Then a group of salmonberry blossoms were tied in a bunch and these slime-covered hemlock twigs were set around this cluster in the bushes. The person stayed to wait for the birds. As the birds stuck to the twigs they would be killed and the heart removed.

Humming birds' nests were taken as hunting and fishing charms.

Western Belted Kingfisher   *Megaceryle alcyon caurina*   tc!i'ckali

The kingfisher was killed only to use its beak for a charm.

It is recorded by Swan as chesh-kully.[20]

Northern Flicker   *Colaptes auratus luteus*   k! ł ēxē'b

This type of woodpecker is singled out from all the others, perhaps because of its yellow feathers, but there are equally distinctive marks on many other species. Its feathers were used on dance costumes. Swan records it as kle-harb.[21] The informant doubtless confuses the typically Northwestern with its red shafts and the northern flicker since they intermingle and hybridize freely.

All woodpeckers listed above are called by one term, klakla'ba ł xp!ī'tc, meaning "anything that pecks wood." They are grouped by Swan under the name kla-kla-bethl-patch.[22] The skins of the young are effective charms when carried in the fishing bag.

(Pileated Woodpecker)

(Lewis' Woodpecker)

(Yellow-bellied Sapsucker)

(Red-breasted Sapsucker)

(Harris' Woodpecker)

(Downy Woodpecker)

(Arctic Three-toed Woodpecker)

(Kingbird)

(Arkansas Kingbird)

(Say's Phoebe)
   Common east of the Cascades.

(Western Wood Pewee)

(Horned Lark)

Swallows   ———   a'at'lakxk! ł ī

All swallows are called by the same name, though the Makah are aware that there are several varieties. They were shot for their skins like sparrows.

---

[19] Swan, 94.   [20] Swan, 94.   [21] Swan, 94.   [22] Swan, 94.

(Purple Martin)

(Oregon Jay)

Steller's Jay   *Cyanocitta stelleri stelleri*   kwŭckwū'ci
This bird, called by Swan kirioh-kwish-ce,[23] was never killed or used in any way. It is interesting that the Makah should choose the chattering sound of the jay for their onomatopoetic name, while the Salish use his shrill call, sk!aisk!ai.

(Magpie)
Casual but regular winter resident, west of Cascades.[24]

Northern Raven   *Corvus corax principalis*   klūktcu'd
The raven was commented upon without any illustration. He is very important in the mythology. He is never used in any way and never killed.

Northwestern Crow   *Corous brachyrhynchus caurinus*   tcak!ad[u]
The crow, like the raven, plays a prominent part in the mythology. Even his origin is explained in a tale. In the Dog Husband story the girl who was deserted, after she becomes prosperous, makes a crow of whale blubber and covers him with the black skin of the whale. She sends him with a piece of blubber to her grandmother. Because of this origin the crows are regarded as the brothers and sisters of the Makah.

In impersonating the crow the actor always limps.

The crow is always referred to as female and as a medicine man.

The feathers of the crow are never used.

(Clarke's Nutcracker)

Chickadee   *Penthestes* sp.   bū bū qua' ł c'sak, "standing with one's mouth open"
Chickadees fly in flocks and are thought of as gangs of boys.

(Slender-billed Nuthatch)

(California Creeper)

Dipper or American Water Ouzel   *Cinclus mexicanus unicolor*   tsatsatcidū''a'a
This bird is seen in streams but never touched.

Wren   ———   xūpda'bit, "something small"
All wrens were called by the same name. They were shot like all small birds.
In folk tales wren is always the small, wise person, often with unexpected strength.

(Catbird)
"Summer resident from the Cascades eastward. Casual on the west side."[25]

Western Robin   *Turdus migratorius propinquus*   xīt!ū'ū or xīt!ū'
Robins were shot for their skins.

Pacific Varied Thrush   *Ixoreus naevius naevius*   dădī'sqwa
My informant called this the winter robin, for they came when the snow was on the ground. They were captured and kept as pets. A feather was threaded through their nostrils and they were tied to a string to prevent their escape. The trap used for thrushes, robins, and other small birds that were taken alive was made of narrow strips of cedar about two and one-half feet long and one and one-half feet wide. This was set at a slant with food placed under it. When the bird was underneath, a string was pulled from a hiding place and the trap fell.

(Hermit Thrush)   (Western Bluebird)   (Townsend's Solitaire)

(Russet-backed Thrush)   (Mountain Bluebird)   (Cedar Waxwing)

(California Shrike)
Probably only east of the Cascades.

---

[23] Swan, 94.   [24] Kitchin, 15.   [25] Kitchin, 16.

(Cassin's Vireo)

(Red-eyed Vireo)
"Rare on west side."[26]

(Western Warbling Vireo)

(Orange-crowned) Lutescent Warbler   *Vermivora celata lutescens*   K!wak!wa'bakapu ł,
"something yellow near the beak"
This includes also the ruby-crowned kinglet and golden-crowned kinglet. It was very clear that the Makah neither know these small land birds nor have the interest in them which they have in the larger shore birds.

(Alaska Yellow Warbler)   (Townsend's Warbler)   (Pileolated Warbler)

(Myrtle Warbler)   (Macgillivray's Warbler)   (American Redstart)

(Western Yellowthroat)

(House Sparrow or English Sparrow)   *Passer domesticus domesticus*
"Introduced species, resident in civilized parts throughout the State."[27]
(The English Sparrow came to Neah Bay about 1902. My informant was then building the local church and he recalls that the agent, Mr. Draper, told him the name of this new sparrow.)

(Bobolink)
"Now breeding as far west as Yakima county."[28]

(Meadowlark)

(Bullock's Oriole)
Not common in western Washington.

Blackbird ——— tca tcak!at'tca'dīs
The Yellow-headed and the Red-winged Blackbirds were on the two plates shown the informant. He recognized the latter and added Brewer's Blackbird, but said that they had only one name for the two varieties. According to this information the Brewer's Blackbird was often found with the crow.
They did not use this bird in any way.

(Cowbird)
"Accidental in western Washington."[29]

(Western Tanager)

(Black-headed Grosbeak)

(Lazuli Bunting)
"Rare on west side (of Washington)."

(Purple Finch)

(Pine Grosbeak)
Uncommon in Cascades of northern part of State.

(Common Redpoll)
Casual visitor in western Washington.

(Willow Goldfinch)

Oregon Towhee   *Pipilo maculatus oregonus*   dūdūtcī'ktcadx
The towhee did not come often, and, being rare, it was shot at. Most rare birds were sought in this way. A wounded towhee was often kept as a pet.

---

[26] Kitchin, 18.   [27] Kitchin, 18.   [28] Kitchin, 18.   [29] Kitchin, 18.

Savannah Sparrow ——— sī sī′quwē
 As soon as a child began using a bow and arrow he was sent out to shoot small birds like sparrows. It was practice for accuracy. Those bird skins were used for blankets.
 While this information is appended to the Savannah Sparrow, it is an open question whether the informant really recognized this variety, therefore no scientific name has been assigned.

(Vesper Sparrow)

Junco   *Junco* sp.   tūtūbă′′ᴇk, "black head"
 Juncos were killed like sparrows.

(Tree Sparrow)
 East of Cascades.

(Chipping Sparrow)

Puget Sound Sparrow   *Zonotrichia leucophrys pugetensis*   lalaxwē cok'k'
 This is shot like other sparrows.

(White-throated Sparrow)

Song Sparrow   *Melosphiza melodia morphna*   tcūkū′dabī
 This is the best known of the sparrows. Its name, tcūkū′dabī, is also used to mean sweetheart, and is generally a pet name.

(Chestnut-collared Longspur)

(Snow Bunting)
 "Casual in winter on the west side."[30]

NOT LISTED AS OCCURRING IN WASHINGTON

The following birds pictured in Taverner are not listed as occurring in Washington. They are included here because they were shown to the informant. It is important, in my estimation, that he recognized these as unfamiliar.

Franklin's Gull	Blue Jay	Black-throated Green Warbler
Spruce Partridge	Eastern Bluebird	Oven-bird
Passenger Pigeon (No authentic records for Washington)	Brown Thrasher	Rose-breasted Grosbeak (Not in western Washington)
	Grey-cheeked Thrush	
Phoebe (Only Say's Phoebe listed for Washington)	Black and White Warbler	Lark Bunting
	Blackburnian Warbler	Baltimore Oriole

MAMMALS

The mammals were listed through the colored plates in E. W. Nelson, The Wild Animals of North America, and H. E. Anthony, Field Book of North American Mammals. The order followed in presenting this list is essentially that of Anthony's Field Book, but the scientific names have been corrected for Washington species through Taylor, Provisional List of Land Mammals of the State of Washington.

Mole   *Scapanus* sp.   tūk!tū′k!c
 The specific varieties of mole in the vicinity of Neah Bay were not known to the informant, so only the family name is given.

---
[30] Kitchin, 21.

Moleskin was dried and tied to the harpoon line for whaling as a charm. The moleskin is also used to wipe the watery eyes of old people, as is the mallard skin.[31] Swan lists the mole as took-took-sh.[32]

Shrew   *Sorex* or *nesorex*   t!ulu't!'uli
The shrew is known but not used.

Hoary Bat   *Nycteris cinerea*   k! ł īk ł ikwadya'bix, "thin wings"
Like everything else that was small, children were urged to kill them. Old people said that when the bats came out the weather would be fine. Swan lists the bat as thlo-thle-kwok-e-batl.[33]

Black Bear   *Euarctos americanus*   atkLi't'qwal (Swan, art-leit-kwitl[34])
There is no feeling of reverence toward the bear, an attitude very common in northern North America. In spite of this general statement, the custom was current that when a man went fishing he caught one and threw it in the woods, saying, "Oh, Bear, here is your fish." The bear was shot and trapped for food and for its skin. The meat was used both fresh and dried.

For blankets whole skins were used. The inside was scraped clean of tissue but was not tanned. Bear blankets were especially appropriate for whalers but others could also wear them. A necklace of bear's claws was worn by shamans.

About sixty years ago Russian Jim married a Clayoquot woman, who brought the Bear Dance-Nana Dance to the Makah. The species represented in this is the Alaska Brown Bear (Ursus). This dance is not exactly part of the kło'kwali but is danced during the Winter Festival. It is danced solo and always by a descendant of the originator, furthermore by a person without children. At present the dance is in possession of Jim Hunter through his mother, who was also a Clayoquot.

Pacific Raccoon   *Procyon lotor pacifica* (Merriam)   q'wa'lac
Raccoons are caught in traps when they come down to the water. The meat is eaten.

Northwest Pine Marten   *Martes caurina caurina*   x!ē ł
The informant was not certain of any use.

Pacific Fisher   *Martes pennanti pacifica*   sīsx ł sītī'dakt ł
The fisher is very scarce and not used.

Weasel   *Mustela* sp.   k!a'd'adi
The two varieties are not recognized. The weasel skin is used as a good luck charm in the same manner as the flying squirrel, q.v.

Pacific Mink   *Mustela vison energumenos* (Bangs)   tc!a·stu'bats
The mink is not used.
Swan lists the mink as kwar-tie,[35] which is the name for Mink as a mythological character.

Land Otter (Pacific or River Otter)   *Lutra canadensis pacifica* (Rhoads)   xī'xdi^k
(Swan, kar-to-wee[36])
This otter is not used.

Northern Sea Otter   *Enhydra lutris lutris* (Linnaeus)   tī'tcak (Swan, tee-juk[37])
The sea otter, now practically exterminated, was always prized highly but its value increased greatly after its trading worth was discovered. During the period of brisk fur trading, men dropped all other work and became sea otter hunters.

The Makah themselves used the fur for hat bands and for trimming on woven cedar-bark capes.

The word ti'tcak was applied to velvet when it first became known because it means anything sleek and alive.

---

[31] See p. 107.   [33] Swan, 93.   [35] Swan, 99.   [37] Swan, 99.
[32] Swan, 99.   [34] Swan, 98.   [36] Swan, 99.

During the mating season male sea otters are frequently found floating dead on the water from fighting.

Common Skunk (Puget Sound Striped Skunk)   *Mephites occidentalis spissigrada* (Bangs)   īlaxa'yus (Swan, e-ail-ā-hai-use[38])

The skunk was clubbed, never trapped. The fur was not used but the oil and meat had medicinal value.

The oil was rubbed on the face and body to prevent scars after smallpox.

The meat was eaten to prevent catching contagious diseases.

Gray or Timber Wolf   *Canis gigas* (Townsend)   tcōtcōwaxsī'x ł (Swan, choo-choo-hu-wistł[39])

The wolf was feared but no effort was ever made to kill it. Whether this is the animal thought of in connection with the wolf ritual is a question.

In former days the wolves came close to the villages. A woman coming from Hobuck met a pack of wolves coming down the Wyacht slough. She swung a piece of kelp in the air and they stopped. Then she followed the trail to Di'a.

A girl near Alberni found a wolf pup when she went for water. She made a pet of it. Later she was captured by a pack of wolves. When two women were going up a mountain near Bamfield they saw the girl washing and heard the wolves singing. After being seen this way in several places she came home, but she died before the end of the year.

Northwestern Mountain Lion   *Feles oregonensis*   xe'i'd

This animal was neither killed nor trapped.

The mountain lion is listed as a cougar by Swan, ha'y-aed.[40]

Red Wildcat, Barred Bobcat or Bobcat   *Lynx fasciatus fasciatus*   picpic or pa'w'ic

The name given here for the bobcat is very similar to the name the Klallam have for the domestic cat, which was probably derived from the Spanish. They call the cat mismis.

The bobcat was never hunted. It was known to attack the fisher occasionally.

Steller's Sea Lion   *Eumetopia jubata* (Schreber)   xakwa'dic (Swan, a'r-kar-wad-dish[41])

The sea lions used to be plentiful around Wa'a'da Island, where they killed ling cod when they laid their eggs there. They bite the backs out of the living cod.

Many parts of the sea lion are used. The meat is eaten fresh and dried. The stomach is dried and used as a container for oil. The hide is stripped and used as rope. The intestines are used as bowstrings. They are twisted when wet and allowed to dry in position. The sinew is not used nor is the skin used for either blanket or bedding.

Alaska Fur Seal   *Callorhinus alascanus*   k!īxla'dus

Sealing was once held in high esteem, ranked just below whaling. Anyone could try sealing but only those who prayed for the right help would ever be good seal hunters.

When my informant started sealing in 1892 he had no luck, for he could never get close enough to a seal to spear it. Some people from Barclay Sound told him this story:

"Two boys had no luck at sealing so their father said, 'Why don't you boys take my advice and go out and pray for this thing?' The boys answered, 'You can't seal today yourself; in your day there were plenty.' So the father fixed up his canoe; he burned it as they used to do. He carried pieces of seal meat into the woods and with hemlock boughs he killed the flies in the meat. He got all the flies together and found some worms that have many feet and are yellow along the sides. They curl up when they are touched.[42] These are rubbed with the flies in charcoal and this is applied to the canoe. The seal curls up just as the worms did. He ties up hemlock and spruce root together and curls them up like a seal asleep. Six or seven of these are fixed beside a creek or a pond. He takes water in his mouth and spits it out, praying meanwhile for long life. Then he swims in the creek, morning and evening for four days.

---

[38] Swan, 99.   [39] Swan, 99.   [40] Swan, 95.   [41] Swan, 99.

[42] These have not been found for identification.

Then he went out sealing, taking his wife along. They loaded their canoes with seals and were the first ones back ashore. He went up to his house and said, 'Sons, go down and pack up those seals.' "

Beside having this medicine applied to them, canoes are built so they make no noise in the water as they move along. When they have this medicine on them, a hunter can come so close to the seal he can take it by hand.

Seal meat is used fresh and dried. The fat is rendered into oil. Although my informant never saw a blanket of fur seal he said that they used to be used, and were called k!ixlatwa″ak.

Formerly seals were plentiful and came into the Straits. When whaling was stopped as a leading pursuit the Makah turned to sealing until government control reduced the revenue derived from it.[43]

Pacific Harbor or Hair Seal   *Phoca richardi richardi* (Gray)   k!actc!u

Harbor seals frequent the caves at the Cape, and the courageous hunter swims into these caves and clubs them.[44] This is the theme of adventurous stories told by the Makah. Otherwise harbor seals are speared on the rocks.

The meat is used fresh and dried. The oil is extracted. The hide is turned inside out, inflated and used as floats for whaling.[45] With its many uses the harbor seal was more highly prized than the fur seal until the latter became commercially important.

Chipmunk   *Eutamias* sp.   tsūtsū′tsid, "scratches on back"

If a chipmunk or a squirrel is bothered it turns into a head. When one is killed accidentally, the tail is pulled off to prevent its growing a second head at the tail end.

Squirrel   *Sciurus* sp.   tsībī′tsa'wi (Swan, se-bi-to-wie[46])
See chipmunk.

Olympic Flying Squirrel   *Glaucomys sabrinus olympicus* (Elliot)   k! ł ē'ēdī″yu

The flying squirrel is never hunted but only taken when found by chance. Anyone who finds one is lucky.

The skin of the flying squirrel is tied to the rope of the whaling harpoon to make the whale turn toward land. The skin is also kept with fishing tackle for salmon.

Pacific Beaver   *Castor canadensis pacificus*   k!at!aw (Swan, de-hai-choo[47])

Beaver dams are found along Wyacht slough and in the creeks back of the village. Just recently some beavers have come back into those creeks. Beavers were speared in their dams.

Beaver tails were eaten fresh and also dried. Beaver skin was cut in strips and worked into the neck banding and edges of capes. Beaver teeth were used for dice in the women's gambling game.

Olympic Elk   *Cervus canadensis occidentalis*   tu'wisak (Swan, too′-suk[48])

Elk were formerly plentiful in the Tsuess valley, Ozette country, and even came out to Cape Flattery.

Men in certain families trained to be hunters. To do this a boy must wake early, go out and bathe and rub his body with branches. They ate only dried fish and grease. Like athletes they chewed gray moss and maidenhair fern to make them light-footed. Purity was necessary for the hunter so that there would be no smell about him. He did not tell when he was going hunting so the news would not travel ahead of him. Since elk and deer travel only on dark nights they are especially hunted then. Elk hunting is good in spring and fall. Hunting is usually done within packing distance from home. Strong women are taken along

---

[43] Waterman, 48.

[44] In discussing the seal Swan indicates that it is the fur seals which gather in the caves for breeding purposes. This, according to zoölogists, is possible but not probable, for they migrate out in the ocean at some distance from the shore. The harbor or hair seals, however, are the variety that are apt to breed in these caves and my assumption is that Swan was possibly careless in distinguishing the varieties.

[45] Swan, 30.   [46] Swan, 99.   [47] Swan, 99.   [48] Swan, 96.

to dress the meat and help pack it home. If the hunting was done far from home, the meat was sometimes dried before packing it home.

Elkskin was cut in strips for rope. It did not tan well, at least according to the Makah, so it was not used for clothing. Elk horn was used for barbs on harpoons, and as points for fish spears. Elk bone was used for chisels; but wedges such as those from the Puget Sound groups were not known. The tallow was filled into the intestines to be carried home and stored. Tallow was used as face grease to prevent chapping, sunburn, and for a paint base. The meat of course was used both dried and fresh. The leg bones were split and the marrow eaten.

Columbian Black-tailed Deer   *Odocoilens c. columbianus* (Richardson)
    bū'kwōtc (Swan, bo-kwitch[49])

Deer were gotten along creeks, in mountains, and along beaches. They were taken with bow and arrows and by spring traps. A hunter in the woods would drive deer toward the water by giving a wolf call. Hunters in canoes would be ready to club swimming deer.

Deermeat was used fresh and dried. The hoofs were used for dance rattles. Two groups of the horns were used in one of the kło'kwali dances. Dance aprons were made of slit deerskin, trimmed with dentalium and finished with dewclaws at the end of each strip.

Mountain Goat   *Oreamnos americanus americanus* (Blainville)   tcotcu'b

Although the mountain goat does not occur on the Olympic peninsula the informant was familiar with the animal and knew the picture. Mountain-goat wool was bought in Victoria through the Klallam. Finished blankets were bought more often than the raw wool.

Killer Whale (Blackfish)   *Globicephala scammoni*   Kawa'd, "fin" (Swan, klos-ko-kopphr[50])

Killer whales were speared just like whales, but hunters did not go out especially for them, they just went out when they saw one going by. They were killed for the pleasure of the chase, for the meat was not used.

Killer whales are dangerous for they chase canoes. Once a killer whale was towed into the mouth of a creek near Baadah Point and since then no salmon have gone up that creek.

East of the Warmhouse there is a cave where killer whales change to wolves. This belief is the basis of many dances.

The tooth of the killer whale is ground and used as medicine but the informant did not know what illness this cured.

---

[49] Swan, 95.   [50] Swan, 99.

Bibliography

Anthony, H. E., Field Book of North American Mammals (Putnam, 1928).

Gunther, Erna, Klallam Ethnography, UW-PA 1 (no. 5), 1927.

Kitchin, E. W., Distributional Check-list of the Birds of the State of Washington, Northwest Fauna Series, no. 1, 1934.

Markistun, Luke, How the Makah Obtained Possession of Cape Flattery, MAIHF-INM, no. 6, 1921.

Nelson, E. W., Wild Animals of North America, National Geographic Society (Washington, D. C.), 1918.

Swan, James G., The Indians of Cape Flattery, SI-CK no. 220, 1869.

Taverner, P. A., Birds of Western Canada, Museum Bulletin no. 41, Biological Series, no. 10 (Victoria Memorial Museum, Ottawa), 1928.

Taylor, Walter P., Provisional List of Land Mammals of the State of Washington. (Manuscript.)

Waterman, T. T., The Whaling Equipment of the Makah Indians, UW-PA 1 (no. 1), 1920.

University of Washington,
Seattle, Washington.

DREAMING IN RELATION TO SPIRIT KINDRED AND SICKNESS IN HAWAII

By E. S. Craighill Handy

THE HAWAIIAN WORD for dreaming is descriptive: moe uhane, spirit (uhane) sleep (moe). Kepelino (114–5),[1*] an early Catholic convert whose Moolelo Hawaii (Hawaiian Lore) is one of our best sources of native lore, wrote:

> Dreams (na moe uhane) were things seen by the spirit (uhane). They were called revelations (he mea ia i ike ia, "a thing seen") to the spirit and their name was "doings of the night" (na hana o ka po), or another, the "great night that provides" (ka po nui hoolakolako).[2]

In the old native culture, dreaming was a controlling and directive influence in the Hawaiian's life, particularly in fishing and planting, in house and boat building, in love and in war, in relation to birth and naming, to sickness and to death. Unpremeditated dreaming still governs the lives of present-day Hawaiians, especially those who consciously adhere to the heritage of their ancestors. Before Christianization, dreams arising out of premeditation in the form of prayer (pule) constituted for kahunas (priests, doctors, craft experts) their primary means of divining favorable and unfavorable signs. In canoe-making, for example, as described by another early native writer, Malo, in his Moolelo Hawaii (168):

> When a man found a fine koa tree he went to the kahuna kalai waa and said, "I have found a koa tree, a fine large tree." On receiving this information the kahuna went at night to the mua [men's quarters], to sleep before his shrine [kuahu], in order to obtain a revelation from his deity in a dream as to whether the tree was sound or rotten.
> And if in his sleep that night he had a vision of someone standing naked before him, a man without a malo, or a woman without a pau, and covering their shame with the hand, on awakening the kahuna knew that the koa in question was rotten (puha), and he would not go up into the woods to cut that tree.
> He sought another tree, and having found one, he slept again in the mua before the altar, and if this time he saw a handsome, well dressed man or woman, standing before him, when he awoke he felt sure that the tree would make a good canoe.

Hawaiians distinguish dreaming in deep sleep (moe uhane) when the spirit sees the "doings of the night," and the swift vision in half sleep, which is termed hihi'o. They also distinguish the unpremeditated dream (me ka noonoo mua ole, without previous reflection) and the premeditated dream (i loaa mamuli o ka mana'o, procured in consequence of thought). Kepelino (114) wrote:

> Some dreams were true dreams and some not true. In olden days dreams were taught by dream interpreters and their teachings spread everywhere even to this day.... Their meanings were memorized like a catechism learned by memory in childhood.... There were two important kinds of dreams as regards the dreamer, unpremeditated dreams and those which were the result of premeditation on the part of the dreamer. Of all dreams the most significant ones were those which came when one was startled in a very deep sleep or just as the eyelashes closed together when falling into a doze. These were true dreams.

---

* Superior figures refer to notes at the end of this essay, p. 127.

The "catechism learned by memory" spoken of by Kepelino was the system of interpretation in accordance with native symbolism, which will be discussed after the nature of dream experience, as conceived by the Hawaiian, has been considered in more detail.

In dreaming, the uhane is subject to communion with its "spirit kindred dwelling in the night" (na aumakua i ka po). To quote Kepelino (114) again:

The "doings of the night" held an important place in the thought of old Hawaii...and these things were called "the doings [*hana*, work, activities] of the *aumakua* [spirits] of the night."

The word po means literally "night." In relation to the superorganic human spirit and discarnate spirit kindred, po designates in an abstract sense the state or condition of physical invisibility, comparable to the invisibility of physical phenomena in the dark. Po as descriptive of the psychic in life and of the primordial in mythology is the "Unseen." But in relation to psychic phenomena it retains always its specific reference to "night-time," when bodies (kino) sleep and spirits work and play.

Many dreams are taken in their literal or manifest meaning. On waking, there is the recollection of some person known or unknown to the dreamer, but presumed to be a discarnate relative who has died (kupuna), or a related nature spirit (kupua) or god (akua). Words, acts, or some scene are remembered on waking and are interpreted literally—a mother is seen weeping: her child will die; some sensation suggestive of eating is experienced: hunger will be satisfied.

Other dreams are taken as symbolic, and these are interpreted in accordance with a traditional code of symbolism based upon the native culture. In the example quoted above, the canoe kahuna interpreted nudity as signifying unsoundness in the tree selected. The reason behind this interpretation, I am told, lies in the fact that nudity in dreams relating to human beings implies sickness. The same implication was inferred in relation to the tree, symbolized in the kahuna's dream by a man or a woman.

Dreams in which a canoe appeared constitute an important category in the system of symbolic interpretation in relation to sickness and to good and bad fortune to be expected. A canoe laden with food and goods coming ashore meant wealth to come. A canoe sinking presaged death or misfortune in the family. The meaning of the symbolism here is as obvious as in our own expression "when my ship comes in," referring to the coming of fortune. But to understand the full significance of canoe dreams in general in relation to sickness requires a knowledge of the native culture. We read in an account of the old dream interpretation (Fornander, 6:90), that when a doctor set himself (after the manner of the canoe-maker) to discern through dreaming the chances of recovery of a prospective patient,

...if he had a dream the night before [he planned to go to attend his patient] in which he saw a canoe, the medical man would say, "It is not proper for me to go, because there was an unfavorable dream in the night."

The canoe dream in relation to sickness was coined into a current proverbial expression, "Moe waa," meaning literally, "canoe sleep," but serving actually as a euphemism meaning impending death. The symbolism in this case becomes plain in the light of the ancient practice of using a man's canoe as his coffin.[3]

Today the aumakua concept is still a vital reality to many Hawaiians by reason of dreaming. To be comprehended, it has to be understood as a component part of native psychological heritage which Christianization has obliterated in some but affected very little in others who are by nature psychic. In other words, the concept needs to be considered in terms of experience rather than as a body of archaic beliefs. It is dreaming that endows this element of the native cultural heritage with vitality and permanence beyond that of any other. Herein lies the importance and value of studying dreams.

While taking an early morning swim one day several years ago, I noticed an elderly native gathering a certain variety of seaweed that was being washed inshore by the surf. I approached him, and after exchanging aloha (greeting), the following conversation ensued: "Is that kind of seaweed good eating?" "No. Medicine." "What for?" "Rheumatism. I come every morning early before eat, pick this kind limu [seaweed], take home, kaukau [eat]. Now rheumatism almost pau [finished]. Long time arms ache, no hanahana [work]. Now maikai [good]. You see!" [He demonstrated limberness of his arms.] "Who tell you this limu maikai?" "I dream." "Dream how?" "Dream tell me go kahuna live Kalihi. Kahuna say eat limu. Eat. Now maikai!"

In another instance, an elderly native woman who for years had suffered from a chronic organic disorder, dreamed that an ancient Hawaiian wearing the malo (loincloth), whom she took to be an ancestor (kupuna) of her family, came to her and prescribed a decoction of certain herbs and certain other measures. She did as she was told and, she assured me, she was cured. She would not give me the recipe nor describe the treatment, for when a prescription is given thus in a dream by a spirit it is, like the inoa po, or name revealed by a spirit, sacred and secret. Such dream experiences, in which a specific remedy for some chronic or critical illness of the dreamer or some relative is given, are very common. The expression quoted at the beginning of this paper, the "great night that provides, or fulfills needs" has reference to this type of dreaming.

The following example, from M. K. Pukui (see Bibliography), is an interesting specific illustration of this type of dreaming.

My aunt [a midwife and herbalist] had a dream in which she saw a woman in a white dress who said to her, "Woman of the East will come. Give her son the petals of the lehua blossom to eat, and give him also something you yourself have baked."

The next day a woman came to the house and inquired for my aunt. She gave her name as Ka-hikina-a-ka-la, which means "Woman of the East."

My aunt knew that boy's parents had promised many things on his behalf that had not been carried out. After talking to the woman [and telling her this was the cause of the illness], my aunt gave her the medicine and a package of biscuits she had baked that morning.

The boy recovered.

From a manuscript written by a medical kahuna named Ka-wai-lii-lii in the last century comes the following interesting statement, indicating the degree to which the native doctor, in some instances at least, relied upon dreams.

I was not taught to diagnose by feeling with the hands [haha, one of the traditional methods of physical diagnosis]. I received my knowledge through dreams. I was taught the recipes and the methods of treating the sick, to diagnose, and whatever else that the dreams revealed in this way. For insanity (*pupule*) : if while asleep at night I dream that I am told that *popolo* is the medicine for this disease, then I gather two handfuls of *popolo* ... [details of the treatment follow].

* * * * * * * * * * *

Only in dreams have I been given the recipes for medicines and the methods of treating all manner of diseases, from those of adults to those of children.

Pregnancy, childbearing and rearing are naturally phases of a woman's life and of family life with which dreaming is associated. An expectant mother, or a relative, will sometimes dream that the child is to be given a particular name, and that is to be consecrated to a particular kupuna (ancestor) or aumakua (spirit guardian). Because it comes in the night, out of a dream, such a name is termed an inoa po, a "night name." It marks the child as a kama akua, a god's child. It is only occasionally that a child has such a name given, only when a dream commands it, or in the old days, when a kahuna would indicate that some god had singled out a child. The inoa po, like the medicinal remedy imparted through a dream by a spirit, should be kept secret within the family. Instances are frequently recounted in which the lingering illness of a child is hopelessly combatted until it is found that the mother or a relative has failed to obey a mandate to give the child a particular name, or has been negligent with respect to some food or other kapu indicated when the name was given. Instantaneous recovery, or rapid disappearance of symptoms, are said to follow correction of the error. In cases of this sort, sickness is the direct consequence of offending the aumakua.

The following illustration comes from a native friend.

My mother dreamed that her mother (long dead) told her to write to her younger sister saying, "If you have any love for me, give the name Kiha-nui to the child in your womb." (At the time, my mother had not even heard that her sister was pregnant.) The letter was sent as commanded.

The child was born; but its father, a stubborn man, objected to the Hawaiian name, and insisted on giving it his own Christian name, Benjamin.

The child grew, but was constantly afflicted with a skin disease that made his skin look rough and shiny like a lizard's. But it was not contagious, for, despite the fact that little Benny slept with the other children, none of them got it.

When Benny was 12 years old, the parents went to a haka (spirit medium). The haka said, "This disease comes from some trouble within your family. You must have a family discussion and find out what is the matter."

My aunt came to my mother. Mother said, "You know what I wrote you. I have nothing more to do with it. You must settle the matter, you and your husband."

So the husband agreed to name the boy Kiha-nui. In about a week the boy was free of that skin eruption. He grew up, married, and had children.

Kiha-nui is the name of the great lizard in the story of Laie-i-ka-wai. The moo (lizards) are one of our aumakua.

The fact that an infant is a god's child is sometimes indicated by a birthmark (ila). Rough skin on the lower limbs indicates the aumakua moo. Moo means literally lizard or, in legends, giant lizard; but the aumakua moo include also the freshwater gobi fish of one variety, several varieties of reef fish, turtles, brindle dogs, and certain human beings. A black patch on the face is the sign of Kane-hekili (god of thunder). A dark spot at the base of the spine is the sign of Ka-uila-ma-ke-ha (god of lightning). A patch anywhere on the body that looks like a mouse or rat means the aumakua iole (rat).

Aumakua nowadays appear in dreams generally in human form, and are termed kupuna (ancestors). They used to appear, I am told, either in the form of their animal embodiments, or in human form. All aumakua may be seen in human form, for they possess the power of assuming human appearance at will. Melei, a sea-worn boulder until recently standing near the Makapuu lighthouse on Oahu, has a romantic and exciting history in the annals of the last two generations of a local part-Hawaiian family, to certain members of which she habitually appears as a beautiful young woman. In the case of some aumakua, a whole plant or animal species, or several such species, will represent the aumakua and be sacred as spirit kindred. Such is the case with the moo already mentioned. Kamapuaa, famous in legend and god of sweet-potato planters, assumes at will human form, the body of a hog, that of a small fish with a head suggestive of a pig's snout, foliage of the candlenut tree (which somewhat resembles that of the sweet potato), the wild grass called kukae puaa (hog's excrement), and the lipehu seaweed. There is nothing in the grass or seaweed suggestive of a reason for associating them with the hog-god. This akua's (god's) name means "Hog-child." He is the aumakua or spirit kin of certain families.

Most aumakua are embodied in a single species, such as the rat, mud hen, eel, taro plant, etc. The embodiment, or embodiments, are termed kino lau, which may be translated either "innumerable bodies" or "leaf bodies." The term is significant in that it indicates the conception of the multiform embodiment of a single being.

The case of Benny, subsequently named Kiha-nui, described above, illustrates the fact that sickness may arise out of failure to obey the mandate of the aumakua with respect to naming his god-child. Eating the embodiment or kino lau of one's aumakua will likewise cause sickness.

The large elekuma crab was the aumakua of a family in Kohala, on the island of Hawaii. A woman of that family, after eating this crab, broke out in great ulcerous sores that nothing could heal. They sapped all her vitality. When hope for her life had been given up, a relative came to call, and, knowing about such sickness, he recognized the cause of the trouble instantly. With prayers and medicine, the sores were gone in less than a week. (M. K. Pukui.)

The following is a prescription from an old manuscript in the library of the Bishop Museum:

For sickness caused by the displeasure of the caterpillar spirit (*aumakua peelua*). The *aumakua* causing this sickness can be identified by the rolling movement of the patient's body and in a caterpillar-like manner of walking. Take eight sweet potato leaves (*palula*) and wrap in a *ti* leaf packet. Make five of these packets. Take a whole sweet potato (*u'ala*) vine and let the patient wear it around his neck a whole day. [The treatment is completed with a feast including cooked sweet potato tubers and leaves.]

In explanation of the above treatment, it should be said that the tender foliage of the sweet potato is one of the favorite foods of the native caterpillar.

Another prescription from the same manuscript:

For sickness caused by the displeasure of the eel spirit (*aumakua puhi*). The *aumakua* causing this sickness may be recognized by the appearance of the patient. His body perspires freely, his mouth is slimy, his skin is reddened, and his general appearance suggests that of an eel. Sprinkle him five times with salt water and turmeric [an agent used to exorcise any spirit], take five tender leaves of the *manini* variety of taro, tear each of them up into small pieces and wave them before the eyes of the patient, while reciting [the proper prayer]....

The eel is fond of the manini fish, a small brightly striped reef fish, as food. The manini taro is so named because the coloring of its brightly striped stem is suggestive of the manini fish. It is the rule that in ceremonials calling for a particular fish, chicken, or hog with specified coloring or marking, taro or sugar cane resembling it in appearance and bearing the same name may be substituted. In the ceremony of house consecration, the red kūmū fish is called for. If one is not procured, the kūmū taro with bright red stem may be substituted.

The most important aumakua having animal forms in modern Hawaii are the sharks which are associated with families of fishermen. The shark aumakua are considered as a class, as is evidenced by the fact that all are subject to Ka-moho-alii, the lord of the sea. But shark aumakua differ from all others in this, that whereas in other cases a species of plants or animals are the kino lau of the spirit and all have to be respected, with the shark aumakua it is a matter of intimate personal relationship with a particular shark frequenting a given locality, recognized by color or markings, and called by its own name. These shark aumakua act as protectors in danger at sea—there are innumerable stories describing the rescue of foundered fishermen; and the shark aumakua are said to lend a hand in fishing by indicating favorable localities and driving off marauders of their own species, for which they exact tribute in a first share of the catch.[4]

Shark aumakua differ from other aumakua also in the way they originate, or are created. There are two ways. A Mano-kaku-ai-ia (Shark-created-by-offering-food) is created in the following manner: The bones of a deceased person, child or adult, are wrapped in a bundle and thrown into the sea, along with offerings including pig and awa (*Piper methisticum*), while the kahuna employed for the work prays. The bones will, I am told, "turn into" a shark aumakua. I have no direct evidence to support this opinion, but it is my belief that in ancient Hawaii the theory behind this practice was that the spirit of the deceased person was first placed under the spell, and that the remains and offerings, when eaten by some shark after they were cast into the sea, induced possession of the shark body by the discarnate spirit of the deceased relative. This interpretation is true to the theory of animal embodiment of human spirits in other parts of Polynesia.

The other way in which shark aumakua originate is closely related, except that in this case a shark spirit has chosen to be born through a woman of the family to which he belongs. A native friend writes:

> In our family there has been, and is, a shark *aumakua*. When he was born [as a stillborn foetus], he was taken to the sea, wrapped in *lipahapaha* seaweed and released. Some years later he came through a *haka* (spirit medium) and forbade any worship of himself, and also he forbade the eating of that species of seaweed, in which he was wrapped, by any member of the family, as it was used as his clothing. To this day that seaweed is referred to in our family as "ancestor's pants." The warning was that anyone breaking the *kapu* would be punished not by sickness or death, but by a catarrhal condition of the nose which would make the breath unbearable to others [like the odor of a shark]. This shark was named Pakaiea, which is also another name used for the *lipahapaha* seaweed.
>
> Once my mother, at the age of twelve, ate a piece of shark meat at someone's house. Her stomach began to swell until it was like a globe and the skin stretched until the discomfort was great. Her mother [a woman versed in the old prayers] heard of it and came. Mother was taken at about midnight to the beach and grandma used the *laau kahea* [literally "calling medicine," a form of verbal transference of pain or evil influence]. While grandma prayed, two lights were seen coming in from the sea. They came closer and closer and proved to be the eyes of a shark. As it approached, the swelling in her stomach began to subside. A sound in the sea was heard, as of bursting, and a water bag in her stomach broke and the water passed quickly out. The shark turned and swam quickly out to sea. My grandmother said to my mother, "You are forgiven! Do not do it again." Since that day she has never touched a piece of shark meat.

Another instance:

> N. P.'s mother was pregnant. While walking a long distance, she was taken with birth pains and gave birth to a premature foetus. She tore off a piece from her calico chemise and wrapped it around the foetus and buried it in the sand on the beach and walked on. In the evening she was met by her husband who was coming for her in a canoe, having heard what had happened. They looked for the buried foetus, but it had disappeared. Her husband took her home. Later, when she had regained her strength she went to the beach to bathe. A little shark, having a stripe on its body similar to that on the calico in which the foetus had been wrapped, swam up to her and nursed at the breast.... This was her first-born. Many years later a daughter who was subsequently born was in Kona, Hawaii. In a boat one day, her hat blew off and was carried away by the tide. Soon she saw it moving toward her against the tide. A shark with the same markings described above was pushing it toward her.

One of the most fertile sources of illness that is mentioned by Hawaiians today is speaking maliciously about some relative, disrespectfully about the aumakua or a god's child, or abusing such a child, or promising something and failing to fulfill the obligation. This fault (hewa or hala, meaning to make an error in work or speech) is designated by the phrases, Ua hewa ka waha or Ua lawe hala ka waha, "The mouth has committed an error." Whether the fault be committed toward living human kin or toward spirit kin, it is an offense to the aumakua of the family, and this calls for an apology. According to M. K. Pukui,

> The ancient Hawaiians believed in the good and bad effects of words of the mouth. When they gave their oath and did not fulfill it, it came back to punish the one who uttered

those words and also the one to whom the oath was made. This was called *hua olelo* [fruit of speech].

My grandmother's saying was: "Say nothing that you do not wish to come true. When you say to your child in anger, 'I wish so and so would happen to you,' and afterwards it happens so, your tears will flow because of the seed of the mouth."

What has sometimes been called, by students of Hawaiian religion, "confession," actually combines confession or admission of fault with apology to the offended aumakua. The following story, which appeared in a vernacular newspaper (see Kuokoa, under Bibliography) some forty years ago, illustrates such confession and apology.

A certain man promised not to eat any bananas of his fine, ripe bunch until his shark god has eaten of it first. While he was fishing with his companion in a canoe, his wife in the meantime had taken some of his bananas. The head of the shark appeared beside the canoe and he guessed at once that there was something wrong at home, that the bananas had been eaten. He pressed on the shark's head with his hand and whispered lest his companion hear what was being said, "I am at fault, the bananas were the cause of the trouble." The head of the shark sank out of sight and rose again, the man whispered the same words, the second time. At the third and fourth time he spoke louder and his companion heard him and asked "What is it?" He had not finished his question when the head of the shark reappeared and this time the man spoke loudly enough so that his companion heard him distinctly: "Didn't you hear me say that I am at fault and that it was caused by my promise of bananas?" at the same time, pressing on the head of the shark with his hand. The shark vanished, because the man had openly confessed his fault so that his companion heard him....

Confession, then, in Hawaii is open avowal of fault and apology to the spirit guardian.[5] Words bind (*kapu*), and words make free (*noa*).

BIBLIOGRAPHY

BECKWITH, MARTHA W., Hawaiian Shark aumakua, AA 19:503–17, 1917.

CLEMENTS, FORREST E., Primitive Concepts of Disease, UC-PAAE 32:185–252, 1932.

FORNANDER, ABRAHAM (Thomas G. Thrum, ed.), Fornander Collection of Hawaiian Antiquities and Folk-Lore, Mem. B. P. Bishop Museum, vol. 6.

HANDY, E. S. CRAIGHILL, Field notes and translations from native manuscripts.

KEPELINO, KEAUOKALANI (Martha W. Beckwith, ed.), Kepelino's Traditions of Hawaii, B. P. Bishop Museum, Bull. 95, 1932.

Kuokoa (vernacular Hawaiian newspaper), March 11, 1893.

MALO, DAVID (Nathaniel B. Emerson, ed.), Hawaiian Antiquities, Honolulu, 1903.

PUKUI, MARY KAWENA, personal communications, notes, and manuscripts.

NOTES TO "DREAMING IN RELATION TO SPIRIT KINDRED AND SICKNESS IN HAWAII"

[1] References in full are given in the Bibliography at the end of this essay.

[2] The verb lako conveys the sense of fulfilling a need.

[3] Dreams of nudity and dreams of canoes in Hawaii demonstrate the need for caution in analyzing dreams of non-European peoples in terms of any symbolism, psychoanalytic or religious, other than that derived from and implicit in the native cultural heritage and the local environment. A conventional psychoanalytic interpretation would, I believe, attribute to the dream of nudity an erotic implication. Knowing Hawaiians and Polynesians, I would say categorically that my informants are right when they say that the fundamental implication of nudity is sickness. A man seen about a house with loins ungirt, or a woman without her skirt, would be a sick person or a deranged one. To gird the loins with the malo or don the pau was, in the life of the native man and woman respectively, the antecedent of work, play, worship, etc. To be about ungirt simply meant disability. Nudity is definitely not associated with eroticism, for nakedness was commonplace in every phase of native living, whereas love-making, both physical and psychic, was associated with stimuli of sound, movement, and touch having nothing to do with the visual images of a crude sort which the educated European of the Victorian era found exciting by reason of his overdressed body and mind. Both body and mind of the Hawaiian were, in pre-Christian days, normally and conventionally undressed.

The canoe, by reason of its form, ought, according to orthodox Freudianism, to be a female symbol. In the Hawaiian mind, however, the canoe is as thoroughly dissociated with woman as is possible. Canoes were kapu to women except under exceptional circumstances when women must be carried as passengers. Essentially the canoe was associated—in the "unconscious" as well as the conscious mind of the native—with fishing (men's work, kapu to women), with transportation of food and goods (men's work), and with the disposal of the skeletal remains (of men only) after death.

As to religious symbolism, none is authentic in interpretation of native dreams except that strictly true to the traditional religion of native Hawaii. Christian Hawaiians like to term aumakua "guardian angels." But aumakua are less like "angels" than they are like totems of American Indians. Some anthropologists will term aumakua "totems." But any student of totemism who will carefully study the Hawaiian aumakua concept will conclude with me, I believe, that while it may have arisen in part out of totemism, it certainly is not now, and was not when the islands were discovered, a form of totemism.

[4] Shark aumakua along the Puna coast of the island of Hawaii are described by Beckwith (see Bibliography).

[5] Clements in his interesting study, Primitive Concepts of Disease, indicates (204–9) a rather limited distribution in the world of the theory that breach of taboo is punished by illness. He found this appearing sporadically in Africa, Asia, and the Americas, and occurring as an element of prime importance in the religions of Mexico, Colombia, and Peru, in Polynesia, and in Assyria, Babylonia, and Palestine. He concludes that the theory originated independently in the New World, in Polynesia, and in the Pacific. For the practice of confession as a means of treatment of sickness he finds an even more limited distribution: Asia Minor, Polynesia, and the advanced pre-Columbian civilizations of Middle and South America, and again he favors independent origin.

Probably the concepts in question have had independent origin in the areas mentioned. Unquestionably they have had independent evolution. But it appears likely that the localization in limited areas is largely due to conceptual limitations on the part of recorders of religious phenomena, and also to giving too much heed to the words taboo and confession as defined phenomena. In Hinduism and Buddhism, disease is a consequence of sin, through the immediate or ultimate action of karma. And certainly there are many totemic people and near-totemists like the Polynesians, who apologize to offended animal kindred and their spirits. To what extent illness may be one punishment for offense I cannot say, for I have made no study of this phase of native belief outside of Polynesia. But I do feel, in consequence of such investigations as I have made in Polynesia, which is generally believed by ethnologists to be fairly well understood, that our knowledge of these subtle intricacies of the religions of primitive and civilized folk of the world as a whole is extremely limited, too limited for any but the most cautious generalizations. Clements' generalizations are impeccably cautious. His descriptive material was suggestive in the beginnings of the particular research upon which this present paper is based.

BISHOP MUSEUM,
HONOLULU, HAWAII.

CHEMEHUEVI SHAMANISM

By Isabel T. Kelly

THE CHEMEHUEVI,[1*] the most westerly band of Southern Paiute, lived formerly in southern California, along the western shore of the Colorado. They were, by their own account, a nineteenth-century offshoot of the Las Vegas (Nevada) band of Paiute, and, as might be expected, the shamanistic beliefs and practices of the two groups remained relatively close. As a matter of fact, a Chemehuevi, in describing his own customs, often cited Las Vegas shamans as examples. One informant, here designated as the joint Vegas-Chemehuevi informant, gave information on both groups. For these reasons the account below will contain frequent mention of the Vegas; but unless explicitly stated otherwise, the material is Chemehuevi.

The Chemehuevi considered four kinds of shaman "good" : the true shaman or curing shaman, who was a general practitioner; and three specialists, whom they designated as rattlesnake, arrow, and horse shamans. "These four kinds cured and did not kill." Of the curing shamans (puaxa'nt ^{i}), the two outstanding ones were Tsakɔ'ra ^{n} kura (wild-geese-neck), of Chemehuevi valley, "the best of all"; and Tava'rï(ï)mp ^{a} (squirrel-mouth), of Pa'ruïp ^{i}, the southernmost of the Chemehuevi river settlements, upstream from Blythe.

As among all the Southern Paiute, shamanistic power came through dreaming. To reject a spirit visitation brought illness and eventually death. A person ill from such cause would be advised by a curing shaman to accept the calling. If shamanistic power did not come unsolicited, it could be acquired by visiting Gypsum cave (Pua'rïnkan, doctor-cave), in Vegas territory, or a cave on Kwi'nava mountain, across the Colorado, in Yavapai country. Neither offering nor fasting was required. The person went "alone, at night, and talked to the cave, telling it what kind of a doctor he wanted to be."[2] He stayed the night and by daybreak had received a dream, that is, a spirit visitation. He did not announce his calling until later, when his tutelary informed him he was to start curing. A shaman's very first curing effort always was successful, it is said.

Most good curing shamans had two familiars (tutu'v ^{i}); "some had more, but two were best." Such spirits usually were birds or other animals, not humans, plants, or natural phenomena. The very best was Xutsi'mamapïts (ocean-woman: "just a name; not a woman and not in the ocean"). One who derived power from this spirit could "hear 'him' grinding corn on a metate, and the grinding sounded like the beating of a heart." Tsakɔ'ra ^{n} kura, the most renowned Chemehuevi shaman, had for guardian spirits, ocean-woman, bat, and mouse. These he sometimes exhibited publicly, in the form of white balls "like an egg or a snowball."

The rôle of the tutelary is indicated by the following:

In his dreams a doctor talked with his spirit helper. It told him what to do and how to

---

* Superior figures refer to notes at the end of this essay, p. 141.

do it. It gave him a song, told him how to suck, and how to dance. And when he treated someone, it told him just what to do and whom to blame (i.e., named the sorcerer). During a treatment the spirit stayed far to the north until just at daybreak, when it came to the doctor.

If, by any odd chance, a shaman forgot his dreams, he was chased with a firebrand, or "hung up and a fire built beneath to frighten him" into recollection. A shaman might lose his curing power by accusing another unjustly of sorcery, after which "he would still dream but could not cure." This is said to be the case with Iura'ïnkov, a Vegas shaman; "he was not strict about telling."[3] But a "good" shaman rarely lost his power except in old age, when it passed to a younger member of the family. When that happened a shaman soon died, for he had "nothing to live for." Thus Billy Eddy, the present Chemehuevi shaman, whose power and songs are passing to his young niece (see below) prophesies his death in two years.

The transfer of shamanistic power, which amounts practically to inheritance within the family, is illustrated nicely by the following:

"Certain families had certain songs[4] that came to them from way back." It is said that the same curing song and the same guardian spirit might pass to a person even though he had never heard the song nor seen the relative who last possessed the power.

Billy Eddy, the present shaman, a Dutch(?)-Chemehuevi half-breed, has three guardian spirits: ocean-woman, bat, and mouse. These spirits and the accompanying songs first were possessed by his mother's father, Tuxu'ant-tɔtɔts (enemy [Halchidoma]-head), although he did not cure with them. On his death the tutelaries and songs passed to his daughter and later to her younger brother. About this time Tsakɔ'ra ⁿ kura, the famous shaman mentioned above, began dreaming of the same spirits, and after the death of the daughter and son of Tuxu'ant-tɔtɔts, the power passed to him. He was some relation to Tuxu'ant-tɔtɔts, probably his sister's son. He became a renowned shaman. Although he had six children none of them obtained shamanistic power. He told them, "I do not want to give this to you; I want you to live normally, not to suffer." And while none of his children is a shaman, one son, Ïtcïïn (ugly; Tom Painter), "knows enough to help Billy Eddy sing." In the meantime Billy Eddy, the son of Tuxu'ant-tɔtɔts' daughter, began dreaming of the same songs and spirit aides. "He got this himself; it was not exactly given him."

At the present time Julia Tobin, the half sister of Billy Eddy, either has or is acquiring shamanistic power.[5] And her daughter, Eunice, a girl of 13 or 14, also is said to be acquiring power. It came to the latter unsolicited and unannounced; "she did not know what it was. She has spells when she is out of her head and thinks the dead, especially her father, are speaking to her. Her dreams are not clear." People outside the family say that she has, in part, a ghost tutelary, probably referring to her communication with the dead. One of her songs is said to come "from way back" and at present she is acquiring her uncle's (Billy Eddy) songs. There appears to be some conflict between the two sources, but she inclines to her uncle's songs. In recent months she has been obviously abnormal, and her uncle is treating her. Some time ago he announced that she was becoming a berdache but since has altered his opinion. He may or may not be giving her his songs; of this I am not sure. But "when his songs are gone he will have nothing to live for" and he prophesies his death in two years.

In January, 1934, the girl was first treated by Billy Eddy, then was taken to the government hospital.[6] While there she seemed completely oblivious to her surroundings and was subject to laughing spells. The government physician, Dr. Nettle, believes the girl to be normal physically and is inclined to diagnose the case as dementia praecox.

We have, in short, the transfer of a shaman's songs and guardian spirits through four generations, from the original possessor to (1) his daughter and son, (2) his nephew (?), (3) his grandchildren, and (4) his great-granddaughter. The question of deliberate versus involuntary transfer remains confused. Billy Eddy is said definitely to have obtained the power of his own accord and without the formal sanction of the previous possessor; but the fact that Tsakɔ'ra ⁿ kura withheld the power from his children in order to spare them, indicates a deliberate transfer, or rather nontransfer. It may be noted in passing that this semi-inheritance of shamanistic power is a notion quite foreign to the Southern Paiute at large; it was encountered only among the two westernmost groups, the Las Vegas and the Chemehuevi.

A shaman usually treated when asked; Tsakɔ'ra ⁿ kura, for example, always kept his moccasins and cane in readiness for a call. Sometimes, however, a shaman was "lazy" and might tell the relatives to find another doctor. Or if he had once cured the patient and the latter had disregarded his directions for maintaining subsequent health, the shaman would be inclined "not to bother with that man again."

Immediately upon being summoned, the shaman proceeded to the patient. If the latter were very ill, he might give a short treatment at once, but ordinarily he waited until nightfall. Then the patient was moved to a circular brush enclosure, in which there might or might not be a fire, according to the whim of the practitioner. Some, such as Billy Eddy, insisted on absolute darkness. Treatment was preceded by a feast and by the presentation of the shaman's fee. The latter was returned if a cure were not effected.

According to the Vegas-Chemehuevi informant, a shaman initiated the treatment by sucking in order to relieve the pain. He removed blood, a small snake, or whatever disease object were involved. This was clearly visible and was taken to one side and blown to the east from between the palms. The Chemehuevi informant said that sucking culminated the treatment, and that the shaman "sucked toward morning, just before his spirit helper came." According to the same informant, the disease object was not exhibited. In sucking the usual Southern Paiute position was followed, with the shaman on the ground beneath the patient, his lips in contact with the ailing part.

The shaman sang and danced throughout the night. "In his song he traced the route of his spirit helper from the far end of the earth. It always came from the north and crossed the Colorado at a place called Pu'ayant ⁱ-turup ¹ (shaman-earth), just downstream from Boulder canyon."[7] The tutelary specified which songs were to be sung; those of the second night were a continuation, not identical with the ones sung previously. Evil shamans repeated their songs, which was considered "very bad"; and Iua'rïnkov, a sorcerer of the Vegas band, is said by the Chemehuevi sometimes to sing his first song three times.

Toward morning the guardian spirit arrived. The shaman advanced to meet it, taking it between his palms and placing it in his mouth. He returned to camp and blew it directly from his lips into the seat of the ailment. The length of time the spirit remained within the patient was a gauge of the shaman's ability. Nowadays, when none of the doctors is "any good," considerable time is required; but "with Tsakɔ'ra ⁿ kura it took no time at all." The tutelary traveled through the body of the patient, emerged of its own accord with the sickness, and departed for the north, accompanied by the disease. This seems to have been an added measure to insure recovery, for the disease object had been sucked out prior to the insertion of the familiar.

As among all the Southern Paiute, shamanistic regalia were unimpressive, in this case a simple catsclaw staff, hooked at the end. This cane is said to have "talked just like the spirit, only not very much. It told where the pain was and how to cure it." The communication was audible to the shaman alone, but he might relay the message. A really good shaman was able to tell, by means of his cane, whether the patient would recover. At the conclusion of the séance, he stuck the staff into the ground at the head of the sick person. If it would not sink its full length the patient was doomed. This is no longer done, as present-day shamans are not sufficiently able.

Naturally, the mode of treatment just outlined varied somewhat with the supposed cause of the disease. In pre-Caucasian days most illness was attributed to shamanistic sorcery or to bewitchment through contagious magic. These required the attention of a shaman. Illness which did not result from supernatural cause was treated by practical remedies[8] or by arrow, rock, or horse shamans as will be noted below. But nowadays there is much unaccountable illness:

Sometimes we think there is so much sickness now because of the food brought in by the whites. Maybe we take too much sugar in our coffee; maybe our meals are not balanced.

The commonest cause of illness was disease-object intrusion which resulted directly from shamanistic malice. In his dreams an evil shaman instructed his tutelary either to shoot the victim or to insert some malignant object. If, for example, a snake were to be inserted, the shaman dreamed of a snake; although, according to the informant, the latter was not his familiar. Certain shamans who had coyote for a guardian spirit might have the spirit bite the victim.[9]

Sometimes evil shamans were pitted one against the other:

A doctor had his own tobacco,[10] which was the same as that used by other people, but in his dreams it was different (?). Sometimes just before he started to treat, a doctor asked four men to smoke with him for luck. It did not matter whose pipe or whose tobacco they used. Each man took one puff; then the doctor held the pipe to the four directions, first to the south, then east, west, and north. The doctor himself took four puffs.[11] This was dangerous because sometimes a doctor would kill one of the men who smoked with him.

Once a doctor named Tɔsa'nawïn (white tip) from Cottonwood island (Vegas) was traveling in the northeast. He was somewhere north of the Shivwits country, where they understood his language.[12] A doctor there asked him and three others to smoke with him. The Cottonwood island man was suspicious. He went to one side and called his guardian spirit and asked it to sit in his throat. Then he smoked without difficulty. The other doctor had planned to kill him.

Before he left the Cottonwood island man decided to kill the one who had tried to murder him. He had the power of knowing where another person was and where his head lay in sleep. For a spirit helper he had a spotted cat (?) (paru'-kumumunts, water-lion) and this he sent to kill the other doctor as he slept. The cat traveled underground so it could not be seen, and clawed the man to death as he slept. The next morning the Cottonwood island doctor left very early. About midday he fell asleep on the trail. His spirit helper came to him and said, "I have killed the one who tried to kill you," and he showed him a bloody arrow.

After this the man did not dream of his spirit for a year and a half. This was because it had plenty of flesh (of the victim) on which to feed. And for a year and a half the doctor himself dreamed of feasting on the meat. It was always so when a doctor killed a person. The Cottonwood island doctor told us this when he was old and did not care if people knew.

The intrusion of a ghost, instead of a material disease object, is a common Southern Paiute belief. But the Chemehuevi pronounced it a Moapa Paiute notion, saying "we have not believed in that since the world was new (i.e., legendary times)." One informant stated that Chemehuevi ghosts were not troublesome, although to hear them presaged death. "The Mohave used to be bothered by ghosts because the souls of their dead went only to the Spirit mountains; but the Chemehuevi souls went to the far end of the earth."

Ideas on soul loss seem to have been minimal. My Chemehuevi informant first said that the soul departed at death; "then the doctor would say that the soul had left already and that he could not cure." Later the same informant said that an evil shaman could steal the soul; "then the man was as good as dead." He seemed unfamiliar with the common Paiute practice of dispatching the tutelary in pursuit of the missing soul. The joint Chemehuevi-Vegas informant gave an account somewhat at variance, perhaps reflecting his Vegas background. An evil doctor, he said, could have his familiar remove the soul (muxu'av). A curing shaman, once he had diagnosed the case, sent his guardian spirit in pursuit, while he himself awaited its return, seated and singing. He sucked, but removed nothing. Upon its return the spirit was met by the shaman, who returned to camp with both the spirit and the missing soul in his mouth. Then with his lips he transferred the two to the patient, either into the mouth or into the afflicted part. The spirit then disseminated itself throughout the body, distributing the soul as it went.

Be the illness caused by intrusion or by soul loss, the tutelary informed the curing shaman which sorcerer was responsible. The malefactor was summoned. Sometimes he would confess, sometimes not. Then the curing shaman would speak to him privately; "he kept right after him" to retract the evil influence by singing. Sometimes the sorcerer acquiesced and sang, pretending to cure, "and all the time he was killing the person." If such deceit were detected, the perpetrator would be dispatched promptly, either with a shot or a blow on the head.

In curing a person bewitched by an evil shaman a definitely complicating factor was that certain of the latter, called niti'na-puaxant [1] (follow-doctor), had the ability of following a victim in his travels and of bewitching him from afar. The exact means of injury to the victim is not clear, but presumably did not differ from the usual practices just noted. If the victim were a swift walker he might be able to travel considerable distance before the shaman located him, "but such a doctor could follow a person mentally and kill him."

Inasmuch as it was necessary that the sorcerer be present to effect a cure, such long-distance bewitchment usually terminated fatally. While most evil shamans "were able to cure sometimes, a follow-doctor had no power to cure, only to kill."

A man named Ïrïmpˤï, of Cottonwood island (Vegas band), was a follow-doctor who killed several people, including a Moapa chief. He may have had a spirit helper; I am not sure about that. Among others he killed Eliza Sackett's father. This was because the latter once killed the younger brother of Ïrïmpˤï. He traveled to Chemehuevi valley, to Yuma, and on to Barstow, where he died.[13] Ïrïmpˤï himself was killed through (contagious) magic, by means of a powder made for the purpose. After this had been given him he wanted to sleep all the time. Finally he died alone at Cottonwood island.

The northern people (Las Vegas band) are not good; they are always jealous of an older man and think that he must be a doctor. They cannot understand how he has lived so long and try to kill him. There were many doctors around Charleston peak (near Las Vegas). When one of our people visited there he always sneaked home, for if one of those doctors saw him he would kill him before he reached his own country. And our people treated Vegas visitors the same way: when they reached home they would die.

"In the old days there were many doctors, all claiming to be good. It was hard to know which one to choose, like buying medicine today, in bottles." But evil shamans usually were known and ordinarily were not asked to treat. Even they cured sometimes. Those, for example, who dreamed of coyote might cure for a short time, although not permanently. It is said that an evil shaman was not to be considered responsible for his malevolence; "it was the fault of the spirit helper. It always told him to kill."

A shaman whose guardian spirit was to the east or near by—"in his hair, or on his lip, or in his clothing"—always was malevolent. So also was one who dreamed of coyote (sïnab, the animal, not Sïna'wabi, the mythical figure), or of ghosts, or of Paruɣubˤï (a water spirit). To dream of the latter caused one's relatives to die quickly. Shamans possessed of water-spirit tutelaries sponsored the Ghost dance among the Chemehuevi.

Some doctors had dreams that were not plain; they dreamed of corn and melons growing on the mountain, where they should not grow. They might think the corn was cane, but it really was corn. A person who dreamed this way was called tuxu'antˤï-puaxantˤï (enemy-doctor); he never could see clearly: it was as though his dream was behind him. He himself did not know what he had, and he did not know what his dreams were. Sometimes he cured but not often. He lived well as long as he was killing someone (referring to a shaman's feeding, in his dreams, on the flesh of his victim). George Johnson, of Needles, is this kind of doctor.

Most informants agreed that women shamans had power, songs, and spirit helpers but invariably were sorcerers. Moapa women shamans, they said, could cure, but not their own. My chief Chemehuevi informant, however, declared that women were not always malignant. This may perhaps be attributed to a delicate consideration for my interpreter, whose mother is a shaman. By most people the mother is regarded as a sorcerer; "that is why all her children die."

A woman had stronger power than a man. It was like running a race: if you had good breath you would win (?). Not all women doctors were bad; some cured. A woman doctor always went through the motion of gathering seeds over the (prone) body of the patient. She scooped up the earth at his head, carried it away in her hands, and threw it toward the east. Four times she did that to take out the sickness.

Magic seems to be the best translation of masu'tïk [i], a concrete object possessed of supernatural potency, which might be used for success in the chase, in gambling, in love, or in disposing of an enemy. Masu'tïk [i] was not associated with dreaming, and although it was known to many, perhaps to most evil shamans, it might be obtained by anyone, either by gift or purchase from one who had the requisite knowledge. But a person who disseminated this knowledge was likely to lose his child as a consequence. Women rarely used masu'tïk [i]; "they would not give it to women." Perhaps they used only the love charm.

Masu'tïk [i] for hunting was a small cane filled with honey. A hunter using this bathed early in the morning and abstained from salt and greasy foods for four days before the hunt. The cane he carried stuck in his hair. When he sighted a deer or mountain sheep, he removed the cane and placed it on the track. "This slowed the animal and made it weak in the limbs; in summer its hoofs fell off." Masu'tïk [i] for gambling worked on the same principle: it "slowed" one's opponent. The gambling charm consisted of various dried plants—which ones the informant refused to specify.

Masu'tïk [i] for attracting members of the opposite sex proved fatal to the victim within several weeks, and "in ten or twenty years" to the one who exercised the power. The love charm seems to have been used chiefly on women, whence it was called mama'u-masu'tïk [i] (woman-magic). Its composition could not be determined, but "it was not made of plants." A sorcerer addressed his charm, then established contact with the prospective victim by acquiring some personal possession—a hair, chewing-gum, or the like.[14] Immediately the victim became infatuated, and within several weeks paid with her life. Piïŋkwiepu (caterpillar—?), a Ghost-dance singer, is said to have killed many women through masu'tïk [i], using a hair of the victim.

For outright murder, masu'tïk [i] worked on a strictly contagious magic basis. A person could make one "as good as dead" by stepping four times, twice with each foot, on the victim's tracks; or he could spit upon the track, cover it, then have the victim step on it. Or some personal possession of the victim might be sprinkled with "a powder of some kind" with the same effect. Iïïmp [i], the "follow-doctor" of Cottonwood Island, was killed this way. After the powder was administered "he wanted to sleep all the time. Finally he died alone at Cottonwood island." Another kind of masu'tïk [i] for murder was little used because "it was too much trouble to make. All kinds of strong-smelling weeds were boiled together until nearly dry." They were removed from the fire and the moisture allowed to evaporate. The mixture was put in a small container ("some kind of little sack"), together with a seed of one sort or other, usually a corn kernel. The kit was carried about, ready for use, and when the victim neared, the seed was extracted and flicked at him. It might be set on his track or on his clothing with the same effect; or the preparation could be put on the tip of a stick and the clothing or the track of the victim touched with it. This kind of sorcery was almost invariably fatal, although occasionally a shaman "was able to take it out." Ordinarily shamans "were afraid of this and could not cure it."

The joint Vegas-Chemehuevi informant claimed that masu'tïk [1] applied equally to both bands. He, as did Vegas informants, associated such devices with the "Utah people," apparently the Beaver Paiute or the Pavant Ute. But contagious magic appears to be quite unknown to the easterly Paiute bands, and its report from these two westerly groups suggests very strongly that here it results from contact with southern California, where contagious and "love magic" are well known.[15]

Among the Chemehuevi shamanistic prognostication was not very pronounced, but by virtue of communication with his guardian spirit, a shaman had certain insight into the future. He knew in advance that he was to be summoned on a case, having seen in his dreams the payment that was to be offered. He knew also when he was to die. "All good doctors dreamed of dying at a place called Tuwa'siaxant [1] (dark crevice); then shortly afterwards they died." And a shaman whose songs and familiar were passing to a younger person knew that his death was at hand, for "he would have nothing to live for." A dead shaman was without power "because his mind (muxu'av: soul)[16] had left; after death his spirit helper just wandered around."

While curing shamans had a limited power of prophecy, augury was not confined to them:

Once a Chemehuevi woman was traveling to the river. She was afraid of the Mohave. She stopped on the high hill by Needles and broke off a twig of creosote bush, where it branched from the main stem. She split the fork and looked at it. It was a clear, light color, from which she knew she could proceed safely. If the twig had showed a reddish stain, she would have been killed. This woman dreamed, but I do not think she was a doctor.

Although not prophecy, the following is somewhat related; it might be called second sight:

Sometimes a person would want to know about a friend or relative who was far away or who was missing. Then he would go to a certain man and ask him to sing and tell him if the person were alive. The singer was not a doctor but he dreamed and had a song. The latter was called kɔtɔ'tɔ-xuviïb (travel-song). A man had to be something like Coyote to have this (?); as he sang something like Coyote traveled over the country and saw what had happened.[17]

The Chemehuevi, as well as the Las Vegas, had a layman who predicted the loss of land and the general dispossession of his people. This was one Muwa'in [1] (drinks-from-spring-without-cup), of Chemehuevi valley. At present there is a layman who speaks of the future, discusses government land allotments, and predicts that "the Chemehuevi will lose what little they have left."

Specialists

All the Southern Paiute, from the Kaiparowits on the east to the Chemehuevi on the west, recognized a rattlesnake shaman apart from the curing shaman. From the Shivwits west, several other specialists enter the picture, although somewhat sporadically: a rock shaman, who had power to climb high cliffs and, among some bands, to cure injuries received in falls; an arrow shaman, who treated wounds; a horse shaman, who cured injuries inflicted by horses; and a rain shaman, who specialized in weather control. Of these specialists, the Chemehuevi had the full complement.

Snake shaman.—The snake shaman "was not very important; he was about like the arrow doctor." Three such shamans are remembered: Tuxu'antsaxwarïm (enemy-blue), of Chemehuevi valley; and Surama' a'u (meaningless) and A' a'usïpɩrïm ("pretty good man"), both of Pa'ruïp [1] (site upstream from Blythe).

A small boy who refused to bathe became a snake shaman. He began to dream in childhood but did not cure until adult. Through dreaming he obtained songs but no tutelary. To cure he sang, sucked, blew upon the patient, and applied pressure with his hands, but used neither herbs[18] nor tourniquet.

A snake doctor sang one song for a rattlesnake bite, another for a "side-winder" (grey snake, giving a small bite) bite. He sucked poison from the wound or some other part of the body but did not suck out a snake. There was no one who treated the bite of tarantulas or that of small black spiders (u'kwam), which were fatal to children. Sometimes people died from the bite of a horned toad.

Billy Eddy, the curing shaman, used to be able to treat snakebite. Once he cured his favorite dog, and after that the power left him. It may come later to one of his sons or it may be gone forever.

The last statement is interesting in its implication that snake, as well as curing shamanism tended to remain within the family.

The joint Vegas-Chemehuevi informant asserted that a snake shaman who was angry could cause snakebite. "He talked to himself (*not* to a snake) and dreamed that a snake bit the man." Such a bite was incurable; relatives, unaware of the cause of death, did not avenge themselves. However, my Chemehuevi informant denied that snake bite was caused by a shaman.

A snakebite victim should not eat produce until the yield from his neighbors' gardens is ripe. Otherwise his garden will dry, or the crops will taste flat.

One of Billy Eddy's sons was bitten by a "side-winder" (tana'kats) at Fort Mohave. They took him to the hospital and he recovered. But a year ago the Eddy melons were not good; they tasted like water. This was because the boy did not wait until the melons in other gardens were ripe.

Rock shaman (tïmpï'-buaxant [1]).—Wanaxɩr [1] (meaningless) of Chemehuevi valley, cured injuries received in falls. My informant once saw him heal a child who was "all broken." He sucked, sang, and set fractures, to which he applied splints. He had "good dreams of rocks," but no "real" guardian spirit. In addition to curing, he was able to climb to eagle nests to steal the young birds.

Arrow shaman.—An arrow shaman is said to have been "stronger" than a snake shaman and to have cured more rapidly than a regular shaman. He had no guardian spirit: "he did nòt need one for he had a cool breath and a good hand." Although he sang but two or three songs at a treatment, he dreamed many, beginning in early youth. He dreamed of arrows and guns and that the latter were as ineffectual as water. Arrow and bullet wounds, broken bones, and blows received from clubs, he treated chiefly by singing, which "braced" the patient and overcame drowsiness. He also blew upon and pressed the body of the patient; he sucked only body wounds.

I saw a man who lost three fingers from a pistol shot. The doctor told him, "That is nothing but water with which you have been shot." He sang three songs and the man was cured. Arrow wounds are worse than gunshot.

There were many arrow doctors. I remember one named Kopi'tïnïv (burned stump), at Chemehuevi valley; there was another down the river, at Pa'ruïp ï, but I have forgotten his name.

Once two Yuma were hurt in a Cocopa-Yuma battle. Two Chemehuevi arrow doctors were visiting the Yuma and were asked to treat the boys. They had the people cut down three or four willows and build a shade. In the evening one doctor attended one patient, the other, the other patient. They placed the boys with their heads to the east. Then each doctor kicked the sand at the foot of his patient, then at the head. They started to sing and to blow upon the boys. They had finished four parts of the song and were blowing, when the boys opened their eyes. Each stood up, as though he had been asleep. The Yumas gave the doctors beads and other things in payment.

Horse shaman.—A horse shaman dreamed of a horse and cured injuries inflicted by horses. No details of treatment were recorded except that broken bones were set and bound between cane splints. The Chemehuevi say that the Yuma, as well as the Vegas Paiute and themselves, had such shamans.

Weather shaman.—The Chemehuevi wanted rain, not for their gardens, but "to make the grass grow on the desert; to make the deer fat; and to provide drinking water during the fall harvest of yucca fruit and pine nuts." A weather shaman (unwadïm-buaxant ï, rain-doctor) might summon rain or mist at his pleasure: "if he saw rain in the distance he might call it or send it away." A person who solicited the services of a weather shaman offered "a buckskin or whatever he had."

Some tried, with occasional success, to bring rain by singing or by whirling a bull-roarer. The latter, thought to bring rain and cold weather, "could be tried by any man (not by a woman) even though he were not a doctor; often it did not work." Wooden bull-roarers were toys, but those of mountain sheep horn were for rainmaking. The horn was boiled until soft, then, with a stone knife, was notched its full length. The tip was perforated for the attachment of a light wand handle.

Weather shamans had no guardian spirits. They dreamed of rain, of lightning and thunder, and that rain would respond to their requests. Some dreamed of ripe fruit. As a rule weather shamans had few songs; some, presumably those using the bull-roarer, did not sing at all.

Some claimed to be rain doctors but never proved it. A certain man named Samï'kwituts (bread), of Kwie'rasïp ï (screwbean-stomach, a site on the west shore of the Colorado, opposite Parker), claimed to have this power. He dreamed of ripe fruit. One day when he was tracking a mountain sheep he stumbled and bruised his leg. It pained so that he cried. Rain and thunder came and this man thought he had caused it. Although he lived to be very old and always claimed this power, he never proved it.

It is said that rain falls when a mountain sheep is killed. Because of this some mountain-sheep dreamers (i.e., game charmers) thought they were rain doctors.[19] Once when we were short of water a mountain-sheep dreamer offered to try to bring rain, thinking that his songs would be of use. He sang and sang, "It will rain in four days," but it did not.

According to the Vegas-Chemehuevi informant, both bands had, in addition to rain shamans, wind shamans (nïar ⁱ-puaxant ⁱ, wind-doctor) who could cause wind either to blow or to subside.

People did not like the wind. There were doctors who had power to stop it. This they did secretly, so no one knows just how it was done. To bring wind a doctor gathered earth in two small piles, then kicked them. He sang only one song. He dreamed his power, and when he raised his voice in anger, a wind would spring up. He seldom brought wind, and then only for spite.

Quite a different account was given by a Chemehuevi informant, who claimed that wind shamans were war scouts who caused wind in order to erase their tracks or to lash the trees so that they might pass undetected through enemy country:

Wind doctors were brave men. They had no songs but dreamed that their tobacco smoke became wind. When scouting, they smoked, so that the wind would cover their tracks in the sand or lash the trees so the enemy would not hear them pass.

When the wind was cold, these scouts would go into the enemy's camp to sleep. They were not recognized in the dark because in those days all wore long hair and the same costume; only the footgear was different. Once a Chemehuevi scout overslept. In the morning he was still in the enemy camp. He pulled his hair over his face and escaped.[20]

Wind doctors could stop the wind too, but I don't know how that was done. I am not sure if they used a bull-roarer; it was mostly mountain-sheep dreamers who used that.

Datura (mɔmï′mpⁱ).—Among the Chemehuevi the association between shamanism and datura was weak. According to one informant a shaman did not take datura, for "it would have killed him"; according to another, datura "would give you anything, even curing power." It seems to have been used medicinally upon occasion, but chiefly for aid in locating lost objects. The latter was not a shamanistic function, and the datura was taken by the interested party himself.

Mɔmï′mp ⁱ is like liquor: if a person takes it once or twice he always wants more. In the legends this plant was the medicine of Antelope ground squirrel. Some plants have flowers and some have almost none; these are the female and male plants [respectively]. When a person wants to find a lost object he chooses a male plant with a root growing east. He may do this any time of year. He stands to the west of the plant and talks to the root, saying, "I have lost something and have come for help; take care of me." He also tells the root whether for the search he wants to walk about or lie quietly at home.

He digs up the root and bakes it in the ashes. He chews a small piece and takes three swallows. If he is to stay at home, he takes the root at night and lies down afterwards. He sleeps lightly, with open eyes. Everything is magnified. He traces his recent movements and locates the missing object. By morning he is well.

If he is to walk around, he takes the root in the morning and the effects wear off by evening. This is more dangerous. A person may die of thirst, not realizing that he wants water. Or, in hot weather his throat will be dry, so that he drinks too much and dies. Then too, mɔmïmp ⁱ may not like the person; then his hands, feet, and eyes will swell.

The Vegas-Chemehuevi informant stated that datura was administered under the supervision of an experienced individual. This was a man (not a woman) whose knowledge of the procedure was learned from another, not through dreaming. Supervision was necessary because an overdose was fatal.

> The person who knew about mɔmïmpⁱ chose a plant not in bloom—early winter was a good time. He dug a root growing east; other roots were no good. In the hole he left a little money, or anything that he had. He mixed the root with water in a clean basket cup which had eagle or hawk feathers placed (not woven in) around the edge. He told the root, "This person has lost something and wants help." Then he gave the man or woman a small quantity to drink. This was afternoon; by the next afternoon the lost object (or person, according to this informant) had been found. Anyone who had taken datura was watched closely. He seemed to be dreaming but did not sleep. He ate nothing but could drink water.

The same informant has twice taken datura as a medicine, once because he felt listless, once because of continued headache. Billy Eddy, the curing shaman, is said to have boiled and drunk datura "to see why he was sick."

Datura was not given, as among the Moapa, to mental defectives. Absence of the Jimsonweed cult is attested by the statement that "it was not given to boys; it was bad for them." But some took it on the sly to test the sensation.

Conclusion

On the whole, Chemehuevi shamanism is a simple, straightforward affair, without associations of medicine men, without involved ritual and elaborate regalia. It consists in no more than an individual communication with the supernatural, followed by an established pattern of treatment. Its nucleus, essentially Southern Paiute, may be summarized briefly as follows. Persons of either sex may become shamans. Their power is derived from dreams, in which they confer with the supernatural, a tutelary spirit usually in animal form. This familiar, which is possessed by shamans alone, gives them songs and instructions for curing. Sickness is most commonly attributed to the intrusion of a malignant object and is treated by song, by sucking, and by the insertion of the guardian spirit into the body of the patient.

While the Chemehuevi, and the Las Vegas for that matter, adhere to the fundamentals of Southern Paiute shamanistic beliefs, there is a minor grafting of divergent traits which probably reflect their intimate southern California contacts. The chief of these are the semi-inheritance of shamanistic office and the emphasis on contagious magic. And in minor details, such as the directional offering of tobacco and the diversion of wind-control to the purposes of war scouts, River Yuman influence may be apparent. The rather interesting development of the horse shaman is perhaps an importation from the same source. The weakness of soul loss among the Chemehuevi, however, is not explicable in the light of southern California contacts.

NOTES TO "CHEMEHUEVI SHAMANISM"

[1] Data for this sketch were obtained during the winter and spring of 1933–34, incidental to an ethnogeographic investigation of the Southern Paiute, made as a National Research Fellow in the Biological Sciences. Informants were obtained at Las Vegas, Nevada and at Parker, Arizona. Notes on the shamanistic practices of the remaining bands of Southern Paiute will be ready for publication soon.

[2] Probably this means that he selected his guardian spirit. It is said that only curing shamans—not sorcerers or near-shamans (i.e., special practitioners without a guardian spirit)—obtained power from caves.

[3] Further comments of the Chemehuevi upon this shaman may be of interest. "People have to be careful the way they talk to him; to quarrel with him is to wish yourself in your grave. He is no good, and if he tries to cure anyone they die. Before there were laws, we would have killed such a doctor right away."

[4] This applies not only to shamanistic songs, but to the Yuman and other song cycles which have spread to the Chemehuevi, and to the songs of deer and mountain sheep dreamers.

[5] According to her daughter, she "dreams of a spirit river all the time." The meaning is not clear; natural phenomena were said not to be tutelary spirits, and Mrs. Tobin is said, moreover, to have the three spirits originally possessed by her grandfather.

[6] This sequence always is necessary because Billy Eddy's familiar "is afraid of the smell of medicine." After the birth of her first child my interpreter was threatened with tuberculosis and did not menstruate for two years. She was treated first by her uncle, Billy Eddy, then was taken to the hospital. Within four days the situation righted itself, a cure which is attributed by her family to the shamanistic treatment.

[7] This may be since the Chemehuevi have been moved to the reservation, on the east shore of the river. In their previous location there would have been no necessity for a spirit, traveling from the north, to cross the Colorado.

[8] Practical remedies included the following. For colds: children bathed with water containing pawab (*Hymenoclea salsola* T. and G.). Sores: covered with pounded roots of awa' apip ï (species of *Dalea*?). Sore eyes: said to be caused by strong wind "which dried them." Dropped tobacco juice into eyes or washed them with tea from tops of tïvi'γeb ï (earth-neck-dirt; *Euphorbia polycarpa* Benth.). Measles, smallpox: patient placed on hot-bed of *Hymenoclea salsola* T. and G. For smallpox, wa' ap (juniper) leaves (?) ground "like talcum powder," mixed with water, and used as wash. Stomach-ache: drank tea of *Euphorbia polycarpa* Benth. Kidney disorders: drank tea of tutu'p ï (Mormon tea, *Ephedra trifurca* Torr.). Rheumatism (and "pain in the bones, muscles, or teeth"): treated with cautery. Nonshaman "with healing hands" burned the area "6, 10, or 12 times" with coal of pika'r' arïp (called also na'rawanïmp ï; same plant used by Las Vegas band). Coyote attributed with first use of this plant in cautery. "Palms, soles, and heels are hardest to burn." First application of coal painful, subsequent ones less so. Burned skin peeled off and open wound covered with charcoal. Healed quickly if administered by capable person. Informant Tom Painter has had knees burned "about 100 times" for rheumatism; claims temporary relief. When one's "legs felt tired and heavy" knees slashed with arrow point to let blood.

[9] There were no distinctive external symptoms of this affliction, which could be diagnosed only by a curing shaman. The latter sometimes was able to cure by sucking out blood and white phlegm.

[10] Women shamans are said not to have smoked.

[11] The notes suggest that the shaman's four puffs followed the directional offering. The latter is the only mention of such a procedure among the Southern Paiute; its appearance among the Chemehuevi probably may be attributed to River Yuman influence.

[12] The Chemehuevi are acquainted as far east and north as the Moapa Paiute, but beyond that they are vague as to bands and territory.

[13] According to a Vegas informant, this individual died an ordinary death "of some disease."

[14] The informant did not react to the suggestion that nail parings might be used.

[15] Luiseño (Sparkman, P. S., The Culture of the Luiseño Indians, UC-PAAE 8:215, 217, 1908); Cupeño (Strong, W. D., Aboriginal Society in Southern California, UC-PAAE 26: 253, 1929); Cahuilla (Hooper, Lucile, The Cahuilla Indians, UC-PAAE 16:338, 1920); Yuma (Forde, C. D., Ethnography of the Yuma Indians, UC-PAAE 25:196, 1931).

[16] The soul (muxu'av, muγu'an; translated, mind) is in the head; after death it travels and becomes a spirit (naγuts). A ghost is ïnïp ï; the breath is sïwïp ï; the heart, pïïmp; the pulse, unnamed.

[17] This kɔtɔ'tɔ-xuviïb is pretty doubtful. Despite the above account, my Vegas informant denied it was either a Vegas or Chemehuevi song. And although two Vegas men could sing it, she said, one at least never did so without sending for a Death valley Panamint named Tɔmɩmpï (acorn). The two sang all night and during the song (both?) became unconscious and "traveled far away." My Vegas interpreter saw a dance and song called kɔtɔ'tuviïv at Moapa, where it was purely a social diversion directed by a "Paiute"-Shoshone half-breed woman from Ash Meadows. As the Vegas claim the split-stick rattle was associated with the song, a northern or western (Californian) provenance is suggested.

[18] Some believed a tea of tïvi'kïγebï (earth-neck-dirt; *Euphorbia polycarpa* Benth.) would cure snake bite; but my informant was dubious.

[19] According to this informant, a mountain-sheep singer always dreamed of rain, a bull-roarer, and a quail-tufted cap of mountain-sheep hide.

[20] An almost identical anecdote is told by the Maricopa concerning a Halchidoma spy among the Yuma. (Spier, Leslie, Yuman Tribes of the Gila River, Univ. Chicago Press, 46, 1933).

UNIVERSITY OF CALIFORNIA,
BERKELEY, CALIFORNIA.

SPECULATIONS ON NEW WORLD PREHISTORY

By A. V. Kidder

ALL THROUGH the years that we excavated at Pecos we were bombarded with questions. Tourists visited our work in shoals, for the highway passes close by the ruin. We had people of every sort and their queries ran the entire gamut of human curiosity. But there was one that we always knew would, sooner or later, be asked by every visitor. From ranchman, movie director, hitch-hiker, plutocrat, we had the inevitable "How old?" And our modest guesses that a thousand or, in moments of exaltation, fifteen hundred years would carry back to the founding of Pecos (it must be remembered that we were then in the pre-Douglass age) lowered our ruin, and with it ourselves, very perceptibly in popular estimation. We were often told that Pompeii (we got awfully sick of Pompeii) was older than that. What our visitors would have thought of us had they known then that everybody's old friend, 1066, would probably have seen the Pecos valley still untenanted by Pueblo Indians, one hates to contemplate.

This craving for antiquity is not confined to the traveling public. Archaeologists have it too, some, of course, much worse than others. And all of us, I think, have a sneaking sense of disappointment as the pitiless progress of tree-ring dating hauls the Cliff-dwellers, and with them the Basket Makers, farther and farther away from the cherished B.C.'s.

The same thing has been going on in Mexico, where Vaillant, undismayed by the weight of lava flows, is lopping millennia from the "Archaic"; and in the Maya field, Vaillant and Thompson, those Young Turks of Central American archaeology, are almost indecently hauling the revered Old Empire upward by two-hundred-and-fifty-year jerks.

Our ideas regarding the rate of Southwestern development have been forced to undergo a thorough overhauling. The Maya, also, may well have got on much faster than has hitherto been supposed. We miss the comfortable amplitude of Old World dating. We have to stuff a tremendous lot of cultural events into an ever-shrinking chronological container. It is well, under such conditions, to back off, so to speak, for a fresh view of the whole chronological situation.

We immediately encounter a paradox, for while the upper end of our time scale is being distressingly compressed, its lower end is being vastly expanded by the recent unequivocal determination of the high antiquity of Folsom Man.

As everyone knows, the discovery of the European Palaeolithic was followed by attempts to identify, in America, the traces of an occupation equally remote. The often ill-founded and sometimes preposterous claims for the great age of man in the New World brought about the then very salutary reactions of Holmes and Hrdlička. But these gentlemen eventually swung so far to the right, they became so ultraconservative, their attacks upon any find suggesting even respectable age were so merciless, that further purposeful search for early remains was most harmfully discouraged; and palaeontologists and geologists, with whom for the past forty years archaeologists should have been working upon the problem of man's arrival in America, were actually frightened away from participating in the investigation.

The discoveries of Figgins at Folsom, New Mexico, and by Harrington in Gypsum Cave, Nevada, have, however, not only reopened the question, but have been followed by those of Howard at Clovis, New Mexico; of Shultz in Nebraska; of Roberts in Colorado and Sayles in Texas, which prove beyond possible doubt that man was present in the New World contemporaneously with many mammals now extinct. Whether these animals disappeared with the Pleistocene or whether they persisted into postglacial times has not definitely been established. The latter supposition seems the more likely. But it can no longer be questioned that human beings were here at the very least ten thousand years ago. Antevs' recent estimate of fifteen thousand appears, indeed, to be reasonably conservative. It is my personal opinion that the first migrations took place before the dawn of the Old World Neolithic.[1]* If this be true, what was going on in North America during the millennia that intervened between the time of the pre-Neolithic Folsom nomads and, say, the Basket Makers who, according to the readjustments in our chronological estimates made necessary by tree-ring dating, must now presumably be placed subsequent to the birth of Christ? And what was happening in Middle America and the Andean area between the Folsom epoch and the period of the well-developed farming, pottery-making cultures of those regions, the oldest of which, according to Vaillant and Kroeber respectively, are not earlier than the beginning of the Christian era?

In North America, hunting cultures apparently persisted. We shall, I believe, ultimately discover that there was a long, slow and, in flint-chipping at least, degenerative transition from Folsom to the cultures which were existing in North America when the maize-pottery complex spread north and inaugurated over wide areas a new era of sedentary agricultural life.[2] Strong's admirable excavation at Signal Butte, Nebraska, has already begun to fill the void. During those same millennia, somewhere in the south, there were being planted, both literally and figuratively, the seeds of aboriginal American civilization.

This last statement is made *ex cathedra*. Like most archaeologists in this country I am 100 per cent American regarding the origin of the higher cultures of the Western Hemisphere. But we do not know for certain that we are right, and this matter of New World beginnings involves some of the most fundamentally important of all anthropological problems. Were, for example, such processes as agriculture, pottery-making, metal-working, loom-weaving, the recording of thought by written characters, discovered once and once only? Were they single and unrepeatable mutations, so to speak, of the superorganic? Or do all human beings possess an innate urge to take certain definite steps toward what we call civilization; and innate ability, given proper

---

* Superior figures refer to notes at the end of this essay, p. 152.

environmental conditions, to put that urge into effect? In other words, is or is not civilization an inevitable response to a law of human conduct?

There have been reams of writing upon psychic unity, and upon diffusion as against independent invention. But the one question whose solution would do most to throw real light upon these and other anthropologically vital matters cannot yet be answered with full assurance. Why have we not progressed further in our research upon this outstanding problem of New World history?

There have been various hindrances. The study has many inherent difficulties and relatively few qualified persons have given it serious attention. But even more to blame is the fact that American archaeologists have been attracted by such spectacular remains as the cliff houses and mounds, the Maya temples, and Peruvian cemeteries. They have thus as a rule been concerned only with the latest manifestations of aboriginal culture; and in their quite natural predilection for interesting and striking finds they have been aided and abetted by the museums, which institutions have had the direction of practically all archaeological field work.

We have also been steered away from purposeful study of origins by the general trend of archaeological thought in America prior to about 1910. During several decades before that date it was the general fashion to connect all prehistoric remains with the peoples occupying, at the time of the Discovery, the regions in which such remains occurred. This was due to a healthy revolt against the still older tendency to see in "Mound Builders" and "Cliff-dwellers" and "Toltecs" mysterious races of vast antiquity. But the very commonsense attitude of our immediate predecessors resulted in a most unfortunate loss of historical perspective; speculation as to beginnings was, in fact, almost taboo. Archaeology accordingly became preponderatingly descriptive; effort was directed toward identification of ancient sites with modern tribes; research upon American prehistory, striking forward rather than back, upward rather than down, was left without foundations. And as under the prevailing dogma of our student days the Indian was considered a creature of yesterday, the problem of how he could so quickly have spread throughout these continents, attained astonishing linguistic diversity, and built up a very respectable and highly ramified civilization became so puzzling a riddle that many of us merely dodged the issue of origins and comforted ourselves by working in the satisfactorily clear atmosphere of the late periods.

But now the Folsom discoveries have given us ample chronological elbow-room, even by Old World standards. This is a great relief to me personally, as I think it must be to many other believers in the essentially autochthonous growth of the higher American cultures. I plead guilty to a strong bias in that direction, but at the same time I recognize, as result of a recent rather careful review of the history of American archaeology, how strongly fashions of thought can influence judgment. And I believe that all American archaeologists, the hundred-percenters perhaps even more than others, would agree that the question cannot be considered settled except on the basis of a great deal more factual information than is at present in our hands.

The obviously correct method is to start with what we actually know and work backward. Excellent beginnings have been made. The discoveries in the Valley of Mexico by Boas and Gamio of more ancient and simpler cultures underlying the Toltec and Aztec gave the first strong impetus to research upon the development of New World civilization. Those finds really opened the modern period of American archaeology. There followed the brilliant "Archaic" hypothesis of Spinden, the effect of which upon archaeological thought cannot be overemphasized. At about the same time recognition of the significance of the Basket Maker remains inaugurated the study of Southwestern beginnings. Vaillant's work in Mexico, Lothrop's in Salvador, the Ricketsons' at Uaxactun in Guatemala, Uhle's pioneer investigations in Peru, followed by Tello's and Kroeber's and, more recently, Bennett's in Bolivia, have all been potent factors in lengthening our historical perspective.

But our work to date has not, as a rule, been first-class. The methods of stratigraphic excavation have, it is true, been developed and refined; the surface survey, using potsherds as a criterion, has assiduously been practiced, particularly in the Southwest. But the study, classification, and published description of the artifacts and pottery, upon which our final conclusions must rest, are still, with far too few exceptions, both hasty and inadequate.[3] Important classificational and taxonomic advances have been made by Guthe and McKern in the East and by Gladwin and Roberts in the Southwest. But classifications and nomenclatures, and the statistical analysis of stratigraphic data are useless unless the specimens concerned have undergone rigid typological study. There is no quick or easy road to success in research upon material culture.

Most of us have worked, I think, too much in restricted fields; and in those fields we have perhaps devoted ourselves too exclusively to site excavation. The comparative methods of ethnography might well be given greater consideration by archaeologists. Nordenskiöld's results, achieved on the basis of the scanty South American data, show how much can be accomplished by such means. Single lines of evidence should be followed over wide areas. We have been very remiss as regards this type of research. Studies do not exist, for example, of the typology and the distribution in the New World of such outstandingly important objects as metates, stone axes, spindle whorls, anthropomorphic clay figurines.

One could go on indefinitely pointing out valuable lines of investigation. But it needs no stressing that much more work is required before we can compare, trait by trait, the prehistoric cultures of the Americas with those of Europe and Asia, and so be able to draw sound conclusions regarding their relationship. It is also necessary to keep in mind the importance of ascertaining the actual as well as the relative chronology of cultural developments, not only in America, but also as between the New and Old Worlds. In America, however, we seem to come very soon to a dead end, for such authorities as Kroeber and Vaillant believe that the oldest remains so far discovered in Peru and Mexico are not older than the time of Christ.

But, while the estimates of Kroeber and Vaillant may be approximately correct, they are, after all, no more than well-considered guesses. What we need, for a chronological starting-point, are ascertained facts. For these we must turn to southwestern United States, as there, thanks to Douglass and dendrochronology, we have the only accurate dates that have so far been made applicable to prehistoric American remains. The Maya time record must, however, also be taken into account, but with the reservation that its intrinsically reliable sequence of some seven centuries has not as yet been certainly correlated with Christian dating.

Let us take, then, the Southwest as our chronological and cultural datum. In the northern part of that area we find a succession of horizons whose relative ages have been established by stratigraphy, and which indicate a steady and seemingly almost wholly autochthonous growth from a non-pottery-making but already maize-growing stage (Basket Maker), through an early pottery-making, house-building stage (Modified Basket Maker), to increasingly higher achievements (Developmental Pueblo, Great Pueblo).[4] The actual age of all but the earliest part of this northern development has been determined by Douglass and his disciples. Basket Maker has not yet been dated, but by the latter part of the fifth century A.D. the Modified Basket Maker period was under way in the San Juan, to last, in that region, until about the beginning of the ninth century. Thereafter progress was extraordinarily rapid, the eleventh and twelfth centuries witnessing the highest achievements of the Great Pueblo period. In this we see confirmation of the generally held opinion that in the absence of outside stimulation progress of a nascent culture is slow, but that once it finds itself, so to speak, it can attain its peak in a relatively short time.

If Modified Basket Maker required four, or perhaps five, centuries to run its course and change into Developmental Pueblo, it might seem reasonable to postulate an even longer time for the preceding Basket Maker period. I once suggested, indeed, that Basket Maker beginnings might have been 1500 or even 2000 years before Christ. In the light of our present knowledge, this seems much too early a date and I now believe the San Juan Basket Maker to have been a relatively short period, extending back, perhaps, not more than a century or two before the opening of the Modified Basket Maker. I base this guess, for it is no better, to some extent upon the paucity of Basket Maker remains, but more upon a belief that the introduction of maize agriculture could not long have preceded pottery-making. In other words, it seems to me that the Basket Maker was not a true developmental stage, but rather that it represents a short phase of transition during which an essentially nomadic population (and as such doubtless of very high antiquity in the Plateau country) was assimilating, in maize, the most obviously and immediately useful trait from gradually expanding farming cultures to the south.

Until recently the actual source from which the Basket Makers derived knowledge of maize was a puzzle. No culture approaching the Basket Maker in antiquity was recognized anywhere north of the Valley of Mexico. The origin of Basket Maker pottery was also problematical. Nothing like it was known from more southerly regions. It even seemed that it might have been an independent invention, for, as Morris some years ago pointed out, all the steps in a logical growth from Basket Maker containers of unfired clay to the fired and later decorated pottery of Modified Basket Maker and Developmental Pueblo are found in the northern country. But in spite of this, and also in spite of the almost entirely self-contained evolution of Southwestern culture in the subsequent periods, the gross facts of the distribution of American civilization, with its highest and therefore theoretically its oldest manifestations in Middle and South America, and particularly the strong probability that maize was originally derived from a southern prototype, all make it appear that the Basket Maker-Pueblo development was peripheral to a southern nucleus.

The work of the Gladwins and their associates of Gila Pueblo has, of late, greatly strengthened the above hypothesis. These investigators have brought the hitherto neglected southern part of the Southwest into its own. They have established, on the firm basis of stratigraphy, the several periods of the important Hohokam culture of the Gila-Salt drainage and have linked those periods, through cross-finds of traded pottery, with the various stages of the Basket Maker-Pueblo series.[5] The results of their remarkable excavations of 1935 at Snaketown have not as yet been published, but I have the permission of Gila Pueblo to state that below the previously known Colonial Hohokam, which equates chronologically with late Modified Basket Maker and early Developmental Pueblo, they have discovered some five older phases. Although these have not been dated by dendrochronology, I would suppose that the first of them must run back to the time of Christ.

The finding of these pre-Colonial remains in Hohokam territory renders Anasazi development much more comprehensible by locating, on the road from Mexico, a culture probably as early as, or perhaps even earlier than, Basket Maker. It also strengthens the belief that Modified Basket Maker pottery was inspired by or perhaps actually copied from that of the pre-Colonials. Decision as to this point must await study and publication of the Snaketown ceramic material.

To sum up: We have a pottery-making culture (the Modified Basket Maker) in northern Arizona by at least 500 A.D. In the southern part of the state pottery-making may well go back to the dawn of the Christian era.

From Arizona we are forced to jump clear to the Valley of Mexico before encountering known remains of even respectable antiquity. The vast intervening area is, from that point of view, a blank, and, as Mark Twain said of the weather, everybody complains but nobody does anything about it, save the Ibero-Americana group at the University of California. However, it seems certain that important early materials will eventually be found along the slopes of the Sierra Madre.

Vaillant, as has been said, believes that nothing he has yet found in the Valley is older than 1 A.D. If this be so, and if the earliest pre-Colonial is of approximately the same age, the pre-Colonial must derive from still older, sub-"Archaic" cultures which still await discovery. And such cultures must have existed, for Vaillant's Arbolillo I is, as he has pointed out, very far from primitive. The question is whether they existed in Mexico.

Central Mexico, because it is within the range of *teocentli,* the supposed ancestor of corn; and also because "Archaic" remains are there found underlying volcanic deposits, was believed by Spinden to have been the breeding-ground of American civilization. But Lothrop and Vaillant have shown that Spinden's "Archaic" is by no means the simple and fundamental sort of culture required by his hypothesis. We must have something more primitive, more uniform, and presumably much older. How much older should it be?

This brings us to consideration of our second New World chronology, that of the Maya. The Maya calendar was in full working order and monuments bearing Initial Series dates were being erected in 8.14.10.13.15 (Stela 9, Uaxactun), which corresponds to about 50 A.D. according to the Spinden correlation, to about 300 A.D. by the Goodman-Thompson-Martinez correlation, and to about 550 A.D. by a third correlation tentatively suggested by Thompson.

According to the hypothesis held by most students of Middle American history, Maya culture was derived from an antecedent highland culture akin to the "Archaic" of the Valley of Mexico. Traces, indeed, of such a culture have come to light in the Guatemala highlands at Arrevalo-Miraflores; and the theory is strengthened by the fact that these remains in some respects resemble materials from deposits of the pre-stela period at Uaxactun, itself the oldest dated Maya city. Were the Maya dates accurately correlatable with the Julian count we should have an exceedingly valuable datum for Middle American chronology. But while exact correlation is of the most vital importance for study of Maya history as well as for research upon the relations between the developed Maya and other advanced peoples of Middle and South America, it is of less significance for the present discussion of the ancient periods. The spread between the correlations amounts, after all, to only five centuries; and as the Goodman-Thompson reckoning splits the difference, and as it seems, at the moment, to be the one most acceptable to a majority of students, one may perhaps take it as a working basis.

Under the Goodman-Thompson correlation the Maya calendar was in full operation at 300 A.D., and Maya architecture and the other arts were apparently in full bloom. Cultural efflorescence can, it is true, be an almost explosively rapid phenomenon, as is proved by fifth- and sixth-century Greece and by what, on a more humble plane, happened in the Southwest between 900 and 1050 A.D. But such flowerings always seem to have required long periods of rooting, and in the very nature of the Maya calendar we have a strong indication of antiquity. Thompson believes that the time count must have reached its perfected form some four centuries before the erection of the earliest Uaxactun monument, namely, at about 100 B.C. And it is certain that no system so complex could have been devised save on the basis of astronomical data recorded over a long period, approximately how long, it may be remarked, calendrists should probably be able to calculate. Whether the necessary extent of such records was one or five centuries, the mere fact that they were kept implies a stability of residence and a freedom from turmoil which in turn argues for a relatively sedentary life and a secure, almost certainly agricultural, economy. We must accordingly postulate for the Maya, or for their cultural ancestors, a settled existence of, say, three centuries. This runs them back to 400 B.C., and, while we are speculating, it seems reasonable to allow several hundred years for the theoretically slow transition, in Middle America or elsewhere, from hunting to agriculture. So we now arrive, for the beginnings of American civilization, at a date somewhere around 1000 B.C., or approximately 2500 years before the Discovery. This seems to me an irreducible minimum. In the Old World a considerably longer time was apparently required to reach a comparable stage of advancement.

But where are the remains of the postulated cultural ancestors? Nothing that can be recognized as such has yet been found. Everything more primitive than the "Archaic" that has come to light is most reasonably to be interpreted as peripheral, as, for example, is the case with the Hohokam and Anasazi. One would suppose that traces of the basic culture should occur in the highlands of Middle America. Exploration has, of course, been very superficial, and there is a strong possibility that volcanic deposits, which cover so much of those regions, have buried the remains under lavas and tuffs, but if there was even a scanty agricultural, pottery-making population there during the postulated period of several centuries before the "Archaic" one would think that some sites or at least artifacts would have turned up. Intensive search, at any rate, is needed before we turn to other fields.

In the above guesses as to the time and location of basic New World culture first consideration has been given to the Middle American highlands: because agriculture seems to be a prerequisite necessity for the development of such a culture; because maize was the New World staple; and because *teocentli*, currently believed to have played a part in the origin of maize, is apparently only to be found in those regions. Furthermore, the Maya was in many ways the most advanced of all American civilizations and on theoretical grounds one expects to find, as Nelson has pointed out, the early stages of a culture at or near the point where it reached its highest development.

The supposed rôle of Middle American *teocentli* in the ancestry of maize may, however, have confused us. Other possibilities must be considered. *Teocentli* may not have fathered maize; it may yet be found in South America. Some other plant ancestor, as yet undiscovered, perhaps even extinct as result of maize culture in the lands favorable to its growth, may exist, or have existed, in South America. These very problems, so crucial for New World history, are at present being attacked by Collins and Kempton as a joint project of the Bureau of Plant Industry and Carnegie Institution of Washington.

If maize should prove to derive from South America, the whole setup would in some respects be more comprehensible. According to Kempton, the great number of this plant's Andean varieties would indicate to a botanist, who knew nothing of *teocentli*, that maize originated in that area. And the number, size, richness, and diversity of the cultural remains in Bolivia and Peru give one the impression that they must root back to high antiquity. In later times South America seems to have contributed to the north the important trait of metal-working. The agricultural complex might similarly have spread north in the pre-"Archaic" period. The "Q-culture" of Lothrop and Vaillant has a southern tinge. Even if maize is of Middle American ancestry there is the possibilitiy that sedentary life, with its attendant art of pottery-making, might have been developed in South America on the basis of some other plant, and maize have been brought into cultivation in Middle America by northward-migrating people already familiar with horticultural processes. This, I admit, is clutching at a straw, but if no remains more primitive than the "Archaic" are ever found in Middle America we can only look to the southern continent for the foundations of New World civilization.

It will have become obvious that I am not a polygenist as regards American culture. I believe that it had a single point of origin, though this tenet, I grant, is illogical in view of my strong feeling that civilization sprang up independently in the Old and New Worlds. It is possible that there were both North and South American nuclei. But I nevertheless hold to Spinden's conception of an outflowing from one center; I merely feel that he mistook a latish branch for the root. And it may need a lot of digging to uncover it.

Gladwin, who has the invaluable habit of questioning everything which smacks of unproved dogma, and who, incidentally, is nowadays administering much-needed doses of intellectual salts to Southwestern archaeologists, has accused me, during our many discussions of the origin problem, of backing southward as successive failures to find really early remains first in Mexico and then in Guatemala, knock away one northern prop after another. He says that eventually I shall probably be pushed off the tip of Tierra del Fuego, and that it is a long jump to Antarctica. I shall come to a halt, however, in Central Chile. But not before all possibilities above that latitude have been exhausted, shall I begin looking overseas.

NOTES TO "SPECULATIONS ON NEW WORLD PREHISTORY"

[1] I disagree with Spinden's belief that American cultures rest on a world-wide polished-stone "peneplane."

[2] It seems to me certain that the Folsom culture, in the western plains at least, must have lasted relatively unchanged for a very long time. Only by such a supposition, or on the much less probable theory of a dense population, can we account for the great numbers of Folsom points which have come to light since 1927. These now number many hundreds and if it be taken into account that they have been found by a few individuals collecting more or less casually and intermittently, and if it be remembered that they have come from the relatively few places where wind or water have chanced to lay bare the artifact-bearing strata, it can be realized how many scores of thousands of them must still remain undiscovered.

[3] The reports of Strong, Roberts, and Haury, to quote only from the literature with which I am most familiar, are models of accuracy and completeness.

[4] I follow the terminology recently suggested by F. H. H. Roberts, Jr.

[5] I here rather hesitatingly launch a trial balloon. It is now evident, because of the segregation of the Hohokam, that the term Pueblo can no longer properly be applied to all the sedentary, agricultural, pottery-making peoples of southwestern United States and northern Mexico. We must speak of Hohokam and Basket Maker-Pueblo. But the latter is an unwieldy designation which also causes confusion when we wish to refer to either of these two sequent elements separately. Might we therefore not use the word Anasazi, which has the same meaning ("Old People") in Navaho that Hohokam bears in Pima? It would apply to the northern or San Juan Basket Maker and Developmental Basket Maker; and to those Pueblo groups which can be shown to have derived the basic framework of their culture from the Basket Maker.

CARNEGIE INSTITUTION OF WASHINGTON,
WASHINGTON, D. C.

THE DISTRIBUTION AND FUNCTION OF MONEY IN EARLY SOCIETIES

By E. M. Loeb

ETHNOLOGISTS have long been under pressure to trace the so-called "evolution" or development of some trait or social complex from the earliest condition of mankind to the present day. Naturally, ethnology assumes the greatest interest when it deals not only with institutions prior to our own, but also with those from which our own may be shown to have developed by some natural and inevitable historical process. Unfortunately, most of the attempts made by the so-called evolutionists have foundered on the rocks of well-merited criticism. It is now well enough established that private property did not necessarily evolve from tribal communism, monogamous marriage from sexual promiscuity, nor monotheism from savage animism. Foreign cultures, no matter how alien to our own, have an equally long history, and foreign patterns of behavior, while often different from ours, are not by necessity prior or inferior to Caucasian standards.

Yet, at least in material culture, certain artifacts are obviously superior both in form and function to earlier artifacts which they have supplanted. Thus, as Professor Thurnwald has pointed out on a recent visit to the University of California, the plow is an obvious improvement on the digging stick. Likewise, the automobile is superior to the early chariot and the steamboat to both the sailboat and the hand-propelled canoe.

In the present paper I propose to outline the history of money[1]* from the earliest times onward, attempting to equate the form and function of prevailing geographical media of exchange with commonly accepted epochs of culture history and showing how monetary forms increased their complexity and utility under stress of added requirements. This evolution of monetary forms took place as a natural adaptation to commercial requirements, and not as specific inventions. Finally, I will sketch the economic lives of certain more advanced communities which endeavored, either through chance or design, to transact exchange operation without the use of money. These sketches will demonstrate the importance of the function of money in civilized societies.

Professor Lowie[2] has presented a commonly accepted timetable of culture. According to this, history may be divided into the Old Stone Age, New Stone Age, and the Metal Ages, these last being in turn subordinated into the Copper, Bronze, and Iron Age. The culture of the Old Stone Age is still preserved in approximate form by savage hunters and fishers without pottery. Most of the present-day primitive peoples, however, are in the Late Neolithic, and have hoe farming and domesticated animals. True civilization started in the Old World with the Bronze Age, at the beginning of the third millennium B.C. This period likewise introduced the extensive use of metallic currency.

---
* Superior figures refer to notes at the end of this essay, p. 167.

Stone Age money.—Money is not known to have been in existence during the Old Stone Age of western Europe. Elliot Smith writes that sea shells are to be found in the Upper Palaeolithic burials of southern Europe.[3] Regling likewise records the occurrence of mussel shells and animal teeth in Palaeolithic finds. But he believes that these objects were used as decorations, not as money.[4] That modern hunters and fishers do not, as a rule, use decorations as money appears to confirm the absence of currency in the Old Stone Age.

The origin of money probably is to be sought among primitive peoples of the New Stone Age, who utilized decorations and domestic animals as media of exchange and standards of value. Thilenius defined this early variety of money as *Nutzgeld* (use money), writing, "It is the peculiarity of use money that it can functionally serve now as consumer's goods, and again as money."[5]

Naturally, the first use of money was not in any sense of the word an invention induced by the hardships of barter;[6] rather, specific decorations, foods, or animals became highly prized in different geographical regions, and gradually assumed the rôle of money. The mere fact that a tribe made use of money differentiated it very little economically from other tribes of the same cultural level who did not. Processes of exchange continued even among currency-using peoples on a purely barter basis, with money as one of the objects of barter. Thurnwald deserves special praise for his observation that primitive money and trade are essentially of social rather than economic significance.

Primitive exchange has, primarily, no economic meaning at all, but a social one, as when women are given for cows in Africa, or boars' tusks for pigs (in New Guinea) or the Kula trade (in the Trobriands).[7]

To these examples illustrating the social significance of exchange I might add the Burning Ceremony of the Hill Maidu. Among the Maidu, at the time of a death, property and beads are given away to friends and relatives, return gifts of equal value being expected at a later ceremony.[8]

Money among primitive people is prized primarily for the prestige which it bestows rather than for its economic worth. For this reason, it is often difficult to draw a clear-cut line between primitive currencies and other treasures. Thus a rich man gains power by the accumulation of wealth, while a poor man may not be able to enter a secret society or obtain a legal wife. However, the most indigent member of a primitive community need not starve. He can always depend on his clan mates for food and shelter, and certain women are to be had without the proper formalities of marriage.

Although not actually money in our sense of the word, primitive currency nevertheless fulfills all the requirements of civilized coinage. Thus the Pomo clamshells not only served as media of exchange and stores of value, but also as standards of deferred payments. Owing, however, to the wide variety of currencies used even in such a small region as California, a standard in one community had quite a different value, or no value at all, in another.

I will now outline the geographical usage of money among primitive people, usually tribes without metals, giving briefly the function of the currency used in each culture area.

Primitive hunters and fishers the world over are nonusers of money. Thus the Australians, the Pygmies, the Veddoids of Asia and Indonesia, the Great Basin Shoshoneans, the Plains tribes, and the Eskimo are all moneyless and conduct their trade by barter alone. The Indians of the west coast of North America, however, are exceptions to this general rule.

The origin of the wealth complex on our Pacific coast is unknown, but the trait is at its peak in the Northwest. While still a strong factor among the northwest Indians of California, it is modified in north-central California, and disappears on the Colorado. Thus Kroeber writes:

> On the whole, the Mohave appear to have used shells as jewelry rather than money; in which they resembled the southwesterners.[9]

Ridgeway has suggested that the Northwest coppers (and hence perhaps the entire Northwest monetary system) is of Asiatic origin.[10] The coppers are imported from north of the Sitka river, and are tested, like a gong, by the sound they produce when struck with the hand. Since metallic gongs are unknown in Siberia, the coppers therefore appear to be indigenous to America.[11] This is the only known use of metallic money among Stone Age people.

The Northwest Indians furnish a splendid example of the social rather than economic importance of money in primitive civilization. These tribes had dentalia shell and probably the etched coppers as their original currency; later they obtained woolen blankets from the Hudson's Bay Company, which they likewise made units of value.

Owing to the abundant supply of fish, the institution of the potlatch, and the custom of lending at interest, no Kwakiutl ever ran the least risk of going hungry. The potlatch provided for the frequent distribution of goods among the tribal members. If an individual ever became needy he merely had to borrow at the customary rate of 100 per cent interest. Then when the principal fell due, he reborrowed. Debts were allowed to accumulate until payment became hopeless.[12]

The entire subject of Kwakiutl economic life needs further investigation. Curtis states that potlatch gifts had to be returned at a subsequent potlatch, but never with interest. Yet Boas makes the interest-bearing feature of the potlatch the kernel of the entire economic system—the method by which a chief ruined his rivals. Benedict explains that 100 per cent interest was not any great amount to pay with dentalia as counters, since an indefinite amount of such currency could be obtained from the sea.[13]

It may readily be demonstrated that the possession of a supply of shells by a fishing people will not of itself produce a monetary system unless the idea of money arises independently or is diffused from outside sources. In fact, as has been shown, the only true fishers who make use of money are the Indians along our western coast. Dentalium is a shell of wide occurrence, and is to be found in almost identical form in northwest America, California, and the east coast.[14] The shells are readily collected from a boat, and then strung by squaws with dried sinew, no great labor necessarily being involved. Yet dentalium was not used as money at all in the East, and the Yurok and Karok of California received their entire supply from the north, unaware of the presence of the shell along their own shores.[15]

The tribes of central and southern California used clamshell money in place of dentalium. There were two sources of supply: in the North Bodega bay, the home of the Coast Miwok; the coastal stretch extending from Morro bay near San Luis Obispo to San Diego, in the south.[16] The value of clamshells depends on the work put into the beads, and not upon the scarcity of the shells themselves. Special craftsmen broke the pieces, shaped them roughly, bored, strung, and then rounded and polished them on a sandstone slab. Upon the introduction of the modern pump drill, the Indians were able to manufacture money so readily that they had a currency inflation and clamshells finally became worthless.

The users of clamshells never placed a high prestige value on their wealth, as did the Indians of the Northwest and the Melanesians. Still those tribes near the source of supply, namely, the Pomo, Wintun, and Maidu, were the most particular in their use of money, and either counted the beads or accurately measured the strings.[17] Yet money was seldom if ever lent at interest in central California; it played the same rôle as any other commodity in trade transactions, and was customarily destroyed with its deceased owner.[18]

While abalone was much prized for the making of ornaments in California, it was never used as money, the same rule probably holding true for the small univalve *Olivella biplicata* and other species of the same genus. This univalve is far more common in graves than clam disks.[19] It is probable that both the Olivella and the clam disks found in shell mounds were used as ornaments rather than money, and that currency is of no great antiquity in California.

Primitive people usually have more than one kind of currency and establish a fixed ratio of exchange between the different varieties. Thus wampum was utilized by the horticultural peoples of the eastern coast from Maine to Florida, and along the Gulf as far as Central America. The beads used in wampum were either white or black, and the black beads were usually worth two of the white.[20] Likewise in California, cylindrical magnesite in the north and cylindrical shells in the south were associated with the clamshell money and rated as of much greater value.[21]

Among horticulturists, the distribution of money is extremely sporadic, depending as it usually does on historical diffusion. Thus money is entirely unknown in South America, even among the semicivilized Incas. On the other hand, Africa is noted for its wide varieties of money, the nonhorticultural Pygmies and Bushmen alone being known to depend entirely on barter. The Polynesians are moneyless, while the Melanesians, with the exception of the natives of New Caledonia and the Loyalty islands, have well-defined currency systems.[22] The primitive Indonesians likewise are without currency.[23]

While stone and mussel-shell money or more probably decorations were introduced into Indonesia in pre-Hindu times,[24] and the use of Chinese gongs as a medium of exchange is widespread in the islands,[25] the original Indonesians had no currency. In Mentawei, for example, the villages are practically self-supporting units with but a minimum of trade carried on with the Malays. The indigenous word "saki" means indeed "to buy," but it signifies favors bought from the spirits by prayer and sacrifice.[26]

The Polynesians likewise acquired their first money from the whites. While residing in Niue I had my native house well decorated with strings of snail shells, which the people called "kaloa," wealth. These shells, however, were never used as money. The natives traded by barter with foreigners, but among themselves exchange is even today based on a system of reciprocal gifts, or "fakalofa" (something done out of love). Polynesian exchange is never performed for the sake of profit, a man always seeking to return a better gift than the one he has received.[27]

According to Thurnwald,[28] the characteristic feature of primitive economics is the absence of any desire to make profits either from production or exchange. The validity of this theory (now modified by Thurnwald himself), however true it may be for such peoples as the Polynesians or the Eskimo, appears more doubtful for the black-skinned natives of Oceania, the Melanesians. To these we now turn our attention.

Money is of unquestionable importance in most of Melanesia. In New Britain, for example, there is not a custom connected with life or death in which the local shell currency does not play a great and leading part.[29] One very common name of money in Melanesia (tambu, i.e., taboo) indicates a sacred origin. In these islands, as elsewhere, currency may be used either for consumption or decoration. Pigs, a form of wealth, are eaten at feasts, and other forms of money—including mats, feathers, mother-of-pearl, snail shells, dog teeth, dolphin teeth, sperm-whale teeth, beads, turtle shells, and even fruit disks—may be used or worn as decorations.[30] Whale teeth money occurred in Fiji, boar tusks and dog incisors in New Guinea.[31]

An important aspect of money in Melanesia is its use in connection with secret societies. In the Banks islands, for example, a man who is able to accumulate sufficient wealth passes through all the grades of the secret ghost society and emerges with powers greater than that of any chief. He then is in position to levy toll on members of lesser grades as they in turn seek advancement.[32]

Among the many forms of African money may be listed: iron bars, or iron in the shape of spears, knives, and hoes; cakes of salt, ivory disks, slaves, and cattle.[33] While it would be possible to arrange the forms of African money cartographically, the sequence of the varieties would remain uncertain. Thus it is not certain that ivory was considered valuable before the days of the slave trade. Likewise, while bar iron is in use throughout the continent, and preceded the utilization of copper and bronze, no date can be designated for the beginning of African iron-smelting.

Contrary to popular impression, the cowry shell is but a modern form of African currency. While the use of both the true money cowry (*Cypraea moneta*) and the ring cowry (*Cypraea annulus*) are mentioned for the Bantu and the West Africans,[34] the shells are not native to the continent. Cowry was imported from the Maldive islands in the seventeenth century by the Dutch and Portuguese, who used it as ballast.[35]

Cowry, however, was long used in Asia as an adornment,[36] and is mentioned in the Ya-King, the oldest Chinese book. One hundred thousand cowry shells were an equivalent for riches.[37] Elliot Smith has indeed broached a fascinating but entirely unproved theory, claiming that gold was first utilized by mankind in imitation of the cowry, for the purpose of assimilating the life-giving qualities of these shells.[38] While it is true that small gold cowry imitations circulated in China between 613 and 590 B.C.,[39] that the earliest gold ornaments found at Troy were imitation cowry,[40] and that the earliest Egyptian hieroglyphic sign for gold was a necklace of shell amulets,[41] we should not overlook the Aztec use of gold as currency although cowries are unknown in the New World.

The stone money of the island of Yap (in the Carolines) is mentioned in every article on primitive economics. This island not only furnishes a splendid example of New Stone Age money, but again illustrates the social rather than economic importance of primitive currencies. The women use shells in exchange transactions, but the men take great pride in their huge stone money, which consists of large limestone wheels, perforated in the center for the sake of portage, and measuring from 25 to 75 inches in diameter. Although used in buying and selling, these curious bank notes exist mainly for show and for payments in connection with the men's clubhouses. The stones must be quarried and carried by boat from the source of supply 240 miles to the south.[42]

Values here are purely fictitious and the wealthiest family on the island has never even set eyes on its treasure. Two or three generations ago, its huge stone counter slipped off ship in transport and now lies secure at the bottom of the sea, where it is still considered of value.[43] In Yap, at any rate, the banker's definition of wealth as "confidence" seems fully confirmed.

Metallic currency.—The entire question of the origin of metallic currency and its relationship to cattle currency is confusing, and has proved a rich field for controversy. Unfortunately, most of the writers on the subject have paid too great attention to Old World archaeology and classical writings, and too little to ethnography, especially that of the New World. Therefore, when Ridgeway proposes the theory that the Mediterranean talent of gold originally represented the value of an ox,[44] the scheme, even if valid, is of but local application. The same objection must be applied to the work of Laum, which is based on the results obtained by Ridgeway. Laum suggests that cattle became valuable not, as commonly assumed, because they were sought as objects of trade, but as the chief articles of religious sacrifice.[45]

It appears certain that cattle were utilized as money among the Indo-Germanic peoples, the Mediterranean civilizations, and the Asiatic cattle and reindeer herders, before the use of metallic currencies. Our language still retains survivals of this stage in such words as capital (Latin, *caput*), pecuniary (Latin, *pecus*), and fee (German, *Vieh*). On the other hand, cattle were a comparatively late introduction into East and South Africa and of course they never penetrated into the farther islands of the Pacific nor into the New World until introduced by the whites.

In the Old World, gold appears to have been used in ornaments (although not as currency) before the Copper or Bronze Age. This is but natural, since gold was obtainable in the natural state, and copper required smelting. Thus, MacCurdy believes that gold was probably the first metal known to man.[46] For example, a gold bead was found in the Neolithic Grotte du Castellet in Brittany.[47] Likewise gold ornaments were found among the Neolithic Lake Dwellers of Lake Neuchatel.[48]

In the New World, however, while raw copper was utilized before the days of the whites in some Arctic regions, in the neighborhood of the Great Lakes, and in the Northwest both for utensils and (according to Boas) money,[49] gold, although plentiful, was entirely neglected north of Mexico.

In the Old World, silver remained unknown until after the beginning of the Bronze Age,[50] and in Egypt until middle Predynastic times.[51] This metal, however, is early in the New World for it often occurs native in Mexico and South America, and it is used alongside copper and gold in early Chimu ornamentation.[52]

Gold and silver as a rule were too precious to be used as currency until scales were in common use. The Chinese, however, of the Chow dynasty (1100 B.C.) circulated gold in square-inch cubes,[53] while the Aztecs not only utilized the Mayan currency of cacao beans, but likewise measured out gold dust in goose quills and passed it as money.[54] The Incas not only had small balances, as mentioned by Prescott and later writers,[55] but they even had the Roman scale or steelyard for weighing gold and silver prior to white contact.[56] However, these Indians had no system of currency.

The use of the simple scale is very ancient in the Old World, in fact it may well be one of our oldest mechanical inventions. The earliest weights known are small blocks of limestone found in the Amratian Age of predynastic Egypt.[57] The balances might have been designed for weighing gold, for both copper and gold were known in Egypt after the close of the Badarian Neolithic culture.

It is impossible to state at the present time whether the scale and systems of weights were first invented in Egypt or Babylonia.[58] However, according to Flinders Petrie, as far back as the Old Kingdom of Egypt there extended a uniform system of weights covering Egypt, Babylonia, Assyria, Syria, and Persia. In this system the talent was divided by 60×60. Early India and China had a different talent, divisible by $10 \times 10 \times 16$. This latter system was carried into Europe from Asia by the Etruscans.[59] According to Nordenskiöld,[60] the Incas used gold and silver weights having probably a pure decimal system, and hence different from any found in the Old World prior to the French Revolution.

Egyptian mural paintings of the Old Kingdom show the weighing of rings of the precious metals,[61] and the idea of psychostasy (the symbolical weighing of souls) dates back in Egypt to at least 2000 B.C.[62] In the laws of Hammurabi of Babylon at the end of the third millennium B.C. grains of wheat are referred to as units for weighing shekels of silver, and the Aryans upon entering India in Rig Veda times (ca. 1500 B.C.) used the balance and seed weights for measuring their gold.[63] The convenient manner of referring to the precious metals in terms of "grains" persists to the present day.[64]

Although the use of the simple balance thus extends as far back as that of the metals themselves, the measurement of metals, as described below, indicates that their diffusion preceded the diffusion of the scales among barbaric peoples. Therefore, where gold and silver rings circulated among the prehistoric natives of Mycenae, the Celts, and the Teutons, the objects probably were classed as treasure and ornaments and not as currency. The bronze double axes of Gaul and Central Europe likewise were of an ornamental nature.[65]

When, indeed, early bronze began to pass as currency it had to be cast into such form as to insure ready measurement. Thus, the bronze of the early Italians at the beginning of the second millennium B.C. was traded by measurement,[66] and the first Italian *as* money was a bronze bar probably one foot long and half a foot in diameter. The bar was divided by transverse strokes into twelve parts (*unciae*, inches), each of which could again be divided into twenty-four parts, each called a *scripulum* (scratch).[67]

With the rise of international trade, metals were substituted for cattle, since commerce could scarcely take place with cows as media of exchange. The metals in this way became the money of all advanced nations, and the Bronze Age ushered in civilization to the peoples of the Mediterranean, Northern Africa, Persia, India, and China.

Coinage.—While coinage has eliminated the necessity of weighing the metals, our language still retains vestiges of the former stage. Thus, the verb "expend" is derived from the Latin *pendere,* to weigh. In fact all the first coins derived their names from the custom of weighing or weight standards, including the shekel, stater, drachm, obol, libra, and litra. This method of nomenclature appears in French livre, Italian lira, and English pound.[68] Owing to legal convention, weighing of amorphous bronze (*aes rude*) persisted in Rome long after the introduction of large block bronze currency (*as signatum*) and the round bronze coins (*as grave*). The Roman conveyance of the Twelve Tables (450 B.C.) called for a sale *per aes et libram* (through bronze and the scales),[69] and hence raw bronze was weighed out for some centuries following 450 B.C. and the introduction of actual coinage.

Coinage is commonly classified as an "invention" made by the kings of Lydia about 700 B.C.[70] Yet the custom of marking ingots of monetary metals had developed in India, Assyria, Crete, and Mycenaean Greece before the beginning of the last millennium B.C. In Mohenjo Daro, in fact, bars of copper were punch-marked in the third millennium B.C.[71] Then, again, the Ancient World had fairly good substitutes for coinage, such as the Babylonian clay-tablet letters of credit, and the leather letters of credit of ancient Carthage.[72]

The Lydians, therefore, followed an ancient established custom when they stamped their electrum blocks. This was done with the idea of facilitating the export of the mineral by guaranteeing its weight and fineness, and not for domestic exchange. The time proved ripe, however, for actual coinage, and presently the precious metals commenced to move by tale and not by weight.

From Lydia the practice of coinage spread to Asia Minor and the Greek mainland. Finally, by the beginning of the Christian era, the new Lydian medium of exchange, consisting of a metallic ingot bearing a hallmark, had spread through the greater part of Europe and Asia.[73] Even the Chinese "cash" currency is indirectly ascribed to Lydian influence, for about 670 B.C. sea traders of the Indian Ocean established a colony south of Shantung, and introduced the custom of inscribing the large Chinese bronze knives (of regular weight) with a distinctive mark or emblem. In 235 B.C. the coins were rounded, with square holes punched in their centers, and they became the "cash" of today.[74]

Certain historians believe that the introduction of coinage revolutionized ancient life, and destroyed the aristocracies of the day. Thus Wade-Gery writes that "more than one thing, coinage destroyed the old aristocracies."[75] Likewise Burns believes that coinage encouraged the rise of commerce and gave rise to a moneyed class which broke up the aristocratic basis of contemporary political organization.[76] Breasted similarly attributes the rise of middle-class power in Greece to the newly discovered art of coinage.[77]

Two factors support the contention that coinage changed the social and political life of the peoples of the Mediterranean. In the first place all the backward nations of antiquity had clung to weight transactions. Thus, the great empires of Egypt, Crete, Babylon, and Assyria had transacted their affairs without coins, and the Phoenicians had no coins prior to Persian rule. Secondly, coinage was introduced into Athens and Rome at the period of great reforms. The first coins of Athens, the silver drachma, were introduced at the time of the reforms of Solon (600 B.C.), and Rome coined her first bronze at about the time of the Twelve Tables (450 B.C.).[78]

Coinage probably did not actually cause the social changes in Greece and Rome, but rather aided certain movements long under way. The ancient power of the clans (called by Engels the "gentile constitution") was on the wane in Athens before the reforms of Solon, and the old social order of blood kinship was destroyed in Rome even before the end of monarchy.[79] Yet Rome did not really begin to enjoy the commercial benefits of coined money until she issued her first silver in 268 B.C.[80] It must be granted, however, that coinage, both in Greece and Rome, aided in the rise of the rights of individual testament, as opposed to ancient clan inheritance. Limited power of testament was recognized both by Solon and the Twelve Tables,[81] and coined money was a convenient object for division among heirs.

Moneyless civilizations.—The best way to gauge the function of money in human society is to study social organizations which, whether by chance or design, operated without a currency system. We have seen that money is not essential for hunting and fishing people, nor for those practicing horticulture.

Norman Angell has shown that moneyless societies were able to prosper on a small scale in medieval manors, monasteries, feudal estates, and early frontier farms.[82] It also can be demonstrated that certain societies endeavored to function without money (and without inheritance of property) on a national scale. In two of these societies, Ancient Sparta and Inca Peru, conditions were primitive enough to make the experiments economically successful. However, from the humanistic viewpoint, these early attempts of state socialism were of dubious merit. "If an elaborate civilization is to exist without money," writes Angell, "it must be by rigid rules which rob the individual of freedom."[83] Both Inca Peru and Ancient Sparta were regimented, beehive communities, where individuals were allotted their tasks and forced to work at them.

The economy of the Inca state was based upon horticulture, foreign trade being unknown. Hence state socialism was successful for the four hundred years of early Peruvian history, and only ceased functioning at the time of the Spanish Conquest (1541 A.D.). Money was entirely unknown in Peru; the vast amounts of gold and silver gathered for the Incas were designed for the temples and had no purchasing value. Gold was devoted entirely to the services of the sun, and silver to the worship of the moon.[84] The land was owned by the ruling Incas and the church, and was allotted to the commoners for cultivation. Taxes were gathered in kind, worked up by trained artisans, and then redistributed. Under the beneficent tyranny of the ruling race, methods of agriculture and communication were improved, and the people were freed from economic suffering.[85] On the other hand, but small advances were made in the arts and sciences[86] and certain of the arts, including weaving, pottery, and metal work, positively retrograded.[87]

While the Inca civilization was based on Bronze Age horticulture, the early Spartans had Iron Age agriculture. The Incas made no use of money, for currency was unknown in South America. The Spartans, however, of about 700 B.C. purposely prohibited the introduction of gold, silver, and even copper for commercial circulation. The rulers desired to prevent inequality of wealth, and for this reason (according to Plutarch) they made the people use iron bars which were too heavy to lift.[88]

The central feature of the so-called Lycurgan reform was the abolition of the Dorian tribes and the substitution of five new tribes, with membership based on locality rather than descent; thus Sparta anticipated by a century a similar reform at Athens. The object of the reform was military, for soldiers could best be recruited by locality; social, for each free man in the state was bound to supervise his private section of land, which was inalienable; and political, for the gerousia, or ruling body, was now territorially elected.[89]

While these reforms were of a progressive nature, other Spartan customs of the period (said perhaps to have been imported from Crete) were reactionary. Thus foreign trade and strangers were tabooed, and the Apella, or free male citizens, were forced to show their equal status by eating in common dining rooms. Certain Spartan customs actually verged on the primitive, as, for example, the strict separation of the sexes, the nocturnal visits of the husbands to their wives, the initiation of boys at puberty, and the merging of the youths in age classes for the purpose of military training.[90]

Wade-Gery, writing of socialistic Sparta, comments, "Whether the 'reform' was fetched from Crete or not, the discipline meant, for Sparta, saying goodbye to much of her own civilization. The city, which had been as beautiful as any in Greece, became a barracks. There were no more great poets or artists. The discipline impoverished their spirits. Finally, after 550 B.C. even the art of pottery declined."[91]

Soviet Russia, strictly speaking, is not an early society and hence does not belong to the scope of ethnology. Yet her example is illustrative, for here also an attempt was made to run a socialistic state without the use of money. Actually money never passed out of circulation, for before 1921 prewar rubles still had nominal value, and since the introduction in 1921 of the N.E.P. (New Economic Policy) a new variety of rubles (the *chervonets*) came into general use for settling internal economic transactions. At the time of the Revolution, however, the Soviets attempted to abolish money altogether and collect taxes in kind. Partly because the peasants were accustomed to think in terms of money, and partly because Russia was becoming industrialized at this period, the whole scheme failed. While the Soviets before the inauguration of the N.E.P. seriously considered introducing a Marxian system of money based on labor-time, the idea was never given a trial.[92] Although some such scheme, that is, erg currency, has likewise been advocated by the technocrats of this country,[93] it is perhaps the only conceivable monetary plan which had never been in use by any people, savage or civilized.

Conclusion

The progress of man from the Old Stone Age to the classical civilizations of Greece and Rome called for an increasing complexity in the forms and functions of media of exchange. The forms such media assumed were limited by the products of the periods in question. While shell and stone money were adequate for the early Neolithic, and cattle for many of the agriculturalists, the age of metals soon produced metallic currencies. With this improved medium of exchange commerce and international trade became possible.

Metals were first measured, then weighed, and finally coined. Private stamping in one form or another was an actuality long before it became generally applied in Lydia at the beginning of the eighth century B.C. Yet this "invention," like so many others, was neglected until the need for it arose, this being created by the rise of individualism in the liberated states of Greece and Rome.

While primitive hunters and fishers have no need for a money system, and horticulturists who have currency usually prize it simply for its prestige value, true civilizations are built upon the economic valuation of wealth measured in terms of money.

Passing judgment upon the basis of the so-called moneyless civilizations, it becomes apparent that a destruction of the customary forms of evaluating individual wealth creates a retrogression in the status of the society as a whole. Whether such a retrogression, as say from a commercial community to a farming community, is desirable or not, naturally depends upon the point of view of the individual theorist.

Bibliography

Angell, Norman
    1929. The Story of Money. New York.

Benedict, Ruth
    1934. Patterns of Culture. New York.

Boas, Franz
    1897. The Social Organization and the Secret Societies of the Kwakiutl Indians. USNM-R for 1895.

Breasted, H.
    1914. Ancient Times. New York.

Burns, A. R.
    1927. Money and Monetary Policy in Early Times. London.

Childe, V. Gordon
    1934. New Light on the Most Ancient East. New York.

Codrington, R. H.
    1891. The Melanesians. Oxford.

Curtis, E. S.
    1915. The North American Indian. Vol. 10. The Kwakiutl. Norwood, Mass.

Danks, B.
    1888. Shell-Money of New Britain. JRAI.

Engels, F.
    1902. The Origin of the Family. Chicago.

Firth, R. W.
    1929. Primitive Economics of the New Zealand Maori. New York.

Furness, W. H.
    1910. The Island of Stone Money. London.

Keller, F.
    1878. The Lake Dwellers. Vol. 1. London.

Kroeber, A. L.
    1925. Handbook of the Indians of California. BAE-B 78. Cited as Handbook.
    1928. Peoples of the Philippines. AMNH-Handbook 8. New York.

Laum, B.
    1924. Heiliges Geld. Tübingen.

Lee, G. C.
    1922. Historical Jurisprudence. New York.

Loeb, E. M.
    1933. The Eastern Kuksu Cult. UC-PAAE 33:139–232.
    1935. Sumatra. Its History and People. Wiener Beiträge zur Kulturgeschichte und Linguistik. Vol. III. University of Vienna.

Loeb, H.
    1933. Life in a Technocracy. New York.

Lowie, R. H.
    1934. Cultural Anthropology. New York.

MacCurdy, G. G.
    1933. Human Origins. Vol. 2. New York.

Maine, H.
    1931. Ancient Law. New York.

Matsumura, Akira
    Contributions to the Ethnography of Mikronesia. Jour. College of Science, Tokyo University, vol. 40, article 7.
Mead, C. W.
  1924. Old Civilizations of Inca Land. AMNH-Handbook 11.
Means, P. A.
  1931. Ancient Civilization of the Andes. New York.
Moret, A.
  1912. Kings and Gods of Egypt. London.
Munroe, K.
  1890. Lake-Dwellings. London.
Nordenskiöld, E.
  1921. Emploi de la balance romaine en Amérique du sud avant la Conquête. SAP-J. Paris.
Petrie, Flinders
  1926. Ancient Weights and Measures. London.
Petri, H.
  MS. Melanesian Money.
Powers, Stephen
  1877. Tribes of California. CNAE 3. Washington.
Prescott, W.
  1847. The Conquest of Peru. Vol. 1. New York.
Radin, Paul
  1934. The Story of the American Indian. New York.
Regling, K.
  1925. Geld. Reallexikon der Vorgeschichte. Berlin.
Ridgeway, William
  1892. The Origin of Metallic Currency and Weight Standards. Cambridge.
Rivers, W. H. R.
  1914. The History of Melanesian Society. Vol. 1. Cambridge.
Smith, G. Elliot
  1919. The Evolution of the Dragon. London.
  1929. Human History. New York.
Sokolnikov, G., and associates
  1931. Soviet Policy in Public Finance. Stanford, California. Note by Plehn.
Stearns, R. E. C.
  1887. Ethno-Conchology. USNM-R.
Thilenius, G.
  1920. Primitives Geld. Archiv für Anthropologie.
Thompson, J. E.
  1933. Mexico before Cortez. New York.
Thurnwald, R.
  1932. Economics in Primitive Communities. London.
Torday, E.
  1930. African Races. *In* Herbert Spencer, Descriptive Sociology. Vol. 4. London.
Unger, E.
    Gewicht. Reallexikon der Vorgeschichte.
Wade-Gery, H. T.
    The Dorians. *In* Cambridge Ancient History, vol. 3.
Wells, H. G.
  1931. Outline of History. New York.

NOTES TO "THE DISTRIBUTION AND FUNCTION OF MONEY IN EARLY SOCIETIES"

[1] Our word "money" is derived from the issue of the first *denarius* coined in Rome on the Capitoline Hill in the temple of Juno Moneta in 268 B.C. The coins were referred to as *moneta,* whence comes the English word money. (Burns, 65.) I am not confining this discussion, however, to coined money, but I am including all such media of exchange as likewise functioned as a standard of value.

[2] Lowie, 11.
[3] Smith, 1929, 299.
[4] Regling, 204.
[5] "Es ist die Besonderheit des Nutzgeldes, dass es funktionell bald Gut, bald Geld sein kann." (Thilenius, 12.)
[6] Thus Regling (206) claims that the difficulties of barter led primitive man to designate certain wares as media of exchange. This old view of the classical economists runs counter to ethnological investigations.
[7] Thurnwald, 105.
[8] E. Loeb, 1933, 152 f.
[9] Kroeber, Handbook, 739.
[10] Ridgeway, 18.
[11] Curtis, 145, writes that the Kwakiutl purchased their first coppers from northern tribes, notably the Haida. This investigator "supposes[!] that these northern tribes received their sheet copper from the Russians and the idea of engraving them from Russian icons." Boas, 341 ff., however, states that the coppers were originally made from native Alaska copper but are now fashioned from imported metal.
[12] Curtis, 141.
[13] Benedict, 184.
[14] Stearns, 315.
[15] Kroeber, Handbook, 22.
[16] Kroeber, Handbook, 824.
[17] Kroeber, Handbook, 824.
[18] Powers, 67, writes that a Tolowa accumulates great stores of shell money, and on his deathbed makes a will disposing of it. However, the accumulation of shell money is foreign to California custom, and wills were unknown to primitive man.
[19] Kroeber, Handbook, 826.
[20] Stearns, 306.
[21] Kroeber, Handbook, 825.
[22] Petri, Melanesian Money (MS).
[23] Loeb, 1935, 169.
[24] Loeb, 1935, 17.
[25] Kroeber, 1928, 120.
[26] E. Loeb, 1935, 169. In English the original meaning of the verb "to buy" is unknown, but the verb "to sell" corresponds in various ancient Teutonic languages to words meaning to give, to deliver up, to offer, to sacrifice. (Murry, New English Dictionary, verb, sell.)
[27] Firth, 13 f.
[28] Thurnwald, xiii.
[29] Danks, 315 f.
[30] Petri, MS.
[31] Regling, 208.
[32] Codrington, 80; Rivers, 61 f.
[33] Torday, 300 f.
[34] Stearns, 302.
[35] Thurnwald, 257.
[36] Ridgeway, 13.
[37] Ridgeway, 21.
[38] Smith, 1929, 292.
[39] Burns, 23.
[40] Smith, 1919, 222.
[41] Smith, 1929, 297.
[42] Akira Matsumura, 161 f.
[43] Furness, 97.
[44] Ridgeway, 2 ff.
[45] Laum, 17 f.
[46] MacCurdy, 175.
[47] MacCurdy, 120.

[48] Keller, 459; Munroe, 53.
[49] Thurnwald, 23.
[50] MacCurdy, 180.
[51] Childe, 98.
[52] Means, 85.
[53] Ridgeway, 22.
[54] Thompson, 84.
[55] Prescott, 127.
[56] Nordenskiöld, 12 f.
[57] Flinders Petrie, 4.
[58] Unger, 309.
[59] Flinders Petrie, 28. This generalization included the ancient Aryan Hindus, but not the people of Mohenjo Daro and Harappā, who had a binary system in the small weights, and then a decimal system. (J. Marshall, Mohenjo-daro and the Indus Civilization, 2:596, 1931, London.)
[60] Nordenskiöld, 170, 171.
[61] Ridgeway, 128.
[62] Moret, 121.
[63] Burns, 186.
[64] Our carat weight used by goldsmiths is based on the Egyptian carob or locust seed. (Murry, New English Dictionary, noun, carat).
[65] Ridgway, 35.
[66] Burns, 16.
[67] Burns, 30.
[68] Burns, 196.
[69] Maine, 188.
[70] Herodotus (l. 94) writes that the Lydians were the first nation to introduce the use of gold and silver coin.
[71] Burns, 39.
[72] Wells, 195.
[73] Burns, 53.
[74] Burns, 50 f.
[75] Wade-Gery, 542.
[76] Burns, 52.
[77] Breasted, 301.
[78] Burns, 44.
[79] Engels, 138, 157.
[80] Breasted, 523.
[81] Lee, 170 f, 203 f.
[82] Angell, 22.
[83] Angell, 15.
[84] Prescott, 89.
[85] A succinct summary of Inca economics is given by Mead, 59. Means, 284 ff., presents a more complete survey of the subject with complete source material.
[86] The decimal *quipu* may be cited as such an advance. Prescott, 109, however, points out that the Incas were ignorant of even such elementary knowledge of astronomy as possessed by the neighboring Muysca and still divided their year into lunar months.
[87] Radin, 142, 144, writes: "In all forms of art the Incas were borrowers and at best only imperfect imitators." "In sculpture, in the working of gold, of copper, and of bronze, in the molding of pottery, in the manufacture of fabrics and textiles, the glory had departed before the Incas came upon the scene." And yet (p. 121) Radin calls Inca rule "one of the most interesting experiments in civilization."
[88] Plutarch's Lives. Lycurgus. Plutarch follows Herodotus (l. 65) in ascribing the Spartan constitution to the mythical Lycurgus. The iron money mentioned in Plutarch (and as found in excavations) were bars weighing about 1¾ lbs. each. The Dorians had brought iron with them in the twelfth century upon entering Greece, and iron at one time was the common medium of exchange of all Greece. Iron nails or obols were superseded by silver coins at the beginning of the seventh century in all the countries of Greece with the exception of conservative Sparta, which stuck to iron until about 300 B.C. (Burns, 22, 26, 142).
[89] Wade-Gery, 560.
[90] Plutarch's Lives. Lycurgus.
[91] Wade-Gery, 564.
[92] Sokolnikov and associates, 75 ff.
[93] H. Loeb, 1933, 34.

181 BROOKSIDE AVENUE,
BERKELEY, CALIFORNIA.

LEWIS H. MORGAN IN HISTORICAL PERSPECTIVE

By ROBERT H. LOWIE

ON THE FIFTIETH anniversary of Lewis H. Morgan's death Russian anthropologists held a meeting in his honor; and The Academy of Sciences of the U. S. S. R. is publishing Ancient Society in its "Classics of Scientific Thought." Morgan's work is officially proclaimed as "of paramount importance for the materialistic analysis of primitive communism," while his critics are taunted with their bourgeois prejudices. But naturally his results "could not fail to fill with anxiety the hearts of those who connected their fate with the preservation of such relations and conceptions as were congenial to them."[1]

Attempts to rehabilitate Morgan, however, are not restricted to Soviet philosophers. A Hindu writer dubs him "the Tylor of American anthropology," and a *greater* Tylor at that. Morgan, who found all primitive religions "grotesque," is quaintly credited with a deeper insight into religious phenomena; and still more oddly, Tylor's method of "putting together disjoined scraps of things pertaining to man in one basket" is contrasted with Morgan's quest of "the grand harmony" in otherwise meaningless facts.[2]

Morgan evidently remains more than a merely historic figure. It is worth while, then, to reassess his contribution and his influence in historical perspective. The task is difficult, but it is lightened by Dr. Stern's labors,[3] which make it appreciably easier to relive the intellectual situation of Morgan's epoch.

Morgan is profitably considered under three heads: as a gatherer of facts, as a philosopher of culture history, and as a contributor to the field of social organization.

As an ethnographer, Morgan takes high rank. One naturally thinks first of his League of the Ho-de-no-sau-nee or Iroquois (1851), but the results of his very brief visits to more remote tribes are likewise most creditable. He discovered the matrilineal exogamous clan organization of the Crow, an observation once doubted but wholly confirmed by later research; and he registered sororal polygyny as a Crow usage. Exactly as I did some decades later, he noted that men and women chopped off a finger joint in mourning or as a religious sacrifice. What is more, his description of the Crow kinship system is vastly superior to my original attempt in this direction, for he recognized that cross-cousins were put into different generations from the speaker's. As

---

[1] N. Matorin, Soviet Ethnography, 6; E. Kagarov, The Ethnography of Foreign Countries in Soviet Science, 89 (both in Ethnography, Folklore and Archaeology in the USSR, vol. 4, 1933).

[2] Panchanan Mitra, A History of American Anthropology, 109–120 (Calcutta, 1933). The phrase from Morgan is in Ancient Society, pt. 1, chap. 1.

[3] Bernhard J. Stern, Lewis H. Morgan, Social Evolutionist (Chicago, 1931). *Id.*, Selections from the Letters of Lorimer Fison and A. W. Howitt to Lewis Henry Morgan, AA 32:257–279, 419–453, 1930.

I subsequently wrote: "My error seems the less pardonable because the essential facts had already been grasped by Morgan."[4]

Morgan's honesty as a field worker is no less conspicuous than his acuity. According to his theoretical scheme, the Dakota ought to have been organized into clans ("gentes" in his terminology); yet, we learn in the early 'sixties he himself "could find no satisfactory traces of gentes among them." Again, he registers similar failure among the Athabaskans of Hudson's Bay territory, and the inability of another investigator to discover them for Morgan in the Slave Lake area.

It must be admitted that Morgan was not uniformly interested in the whole of culture. Like most recent investigators, he devoted himself intensively to particular aspects of native life and skimmed over others. As Stern remarks, his League tells a great deal about Iroquois social organization, but, *pace* Mr. Mitra, little about religion, and economic life is treated inadequately. However, Morgan did not neglect technology, and altogether his account remains an outstanding achievement, both for its fullness and the sympathy evinced toward his subjects.

As a culture historian, Morgan was handicapped by lack of essential facts. Not, however, in the light of recent discoveries but as a contemporaneous verdict we must uphold Lubbock's stricture in 1878 that "Morgan's knowledge is anything but exhaustive." He was indeed incomparably ahead of his times along special lines, yet even there his neglect of accessible sources distorted the picture he gave of ancient society. Though he had himself noted the Iroquois fraternities, he never considered the relationship of clubs, military organizations, or religious corporations to the social structure of American natives, let alone of Melanesians or Africans. Yet Maximilian's account of the Mandan warrior societies was available in English and German; and their police activities certainly had some bearing on that "Idea of Government" to which Morgan dedicated fifteen chapters of Ancient Society.

Equally astonishing is Morgan's neglect of aristocracy and monarchy among ruder peoples. He laid it down as an axiom that monarchy was incompatible with clans, that it appeared only in "civilization," that is, in the period of literacy. Aristocracy, he argued, did not develop before the "Later Period of Barbarism," that is, not before the Iron Age.[5] This dogmatism happened to yield a valuable by-product—the critical scrutiny of the Spanish chronicles with their extravagance about a feudal Aztec empire. But the general propositions were wide of the mark. Had Morgan never heard of the African courts described by early travelers? Was he ignorant of Chaka's spectacular conquests in the early nineteenth century? Had he ever peeped into Captain Cook's Travels? But it was not even necessary to go so far afield. Caste distinctions and slavery were well-established phenomena among the natives of British Columbia. Since Morgan's honesty is beyond reproach, failure to note

---

[4] Ancient Society, pt. 2, chap. 6. Swanton, The Social Organization of American Tribes, AA 7:663–673, 1905. R. H. Lowie, Notes on the Social Organization and Customs of the Mandan, Hidatsa, and Crow Indians, AMNH-AP 21:21–26 f., 56, 1917.

[5] Ancient Society, pt. 2, chap. 5; pt. 4, chap. 2.

such facts can be imputed only to sheer ignorance. Evidently indefatigable in ferreting out what was relevant to clan systems and relationship terms, sparing no pains to acquire the kinship terminology among Hawaiians and Rotumans, Maori and Samoans, he seems to have had no inkling of the class distinctions that prevailed in Polynesia. How did he interpret Tylor's statement that in eastern Asia and Polynesia the names of kings and chiefs were held sacred?[6] Probably few men were further than Morgan from a "functional" view of different cultures as so many living wholes.

From this deficiency springs one of Morgan's worst errors of classification, the inclusion of the Australians and "the greater part of the Polynesians" in the "Middle Status of Savagery." To be sure, the Australians "rank below the Polynesians," but because they lack bow and arrow, Maori and Kurnai are both placed below the Northern Athabaskans.

Psychologically, a flair for individual cultures and historical-mindedness naturally go together. Morgan lacked both; his conclusions had a bearing on time sequences, but his chronology did not rest on archaeological stratification or written records, but on an abstract scheme. The peoples of the world are classified "according to the degree of their relative progress" into three periods, Savagery, Barbarism, and Civilization, the last being characterized by literacy. The two earlier periods are each subdivided into a Lower, Middle, and Upper Status. The Lower Status of Savagery was avowedly hypothetical, ending with the use of fire and the acquisition of a fish subsistence. The Middle Status terminated with the invention of bow and arrow; Australians and most Polynesians thus fall into this rubric. The Upper Status of Savagery ended with the manufacture of pottery, thus embracing the Indians of northern North America. Barbarism begins with pottery, and its Upper Status coincides with a preliterate Iron Age.

In the abstract, Morgan admitted his tests only with qualification. But in dealing with concrete material he acted precisely as if they were absolute. Specifically, he has sufficient confidence in them to deduce unknowable history from the scheme. This appears precisely where up to a point Morgan did avail himself of written documents. So far as a general ethnologist can judge, he studied the sources on Greek and Roman society with painstaking zeal. But while setting forth the records for the historical period, he goes far beyond ascertainable facts. According to him exogamy was characteristic of the Greek genos and the Roman gens, "a novel doctrine," as Tylor remarked in 1878, "which his evidence fails to establish."[7] What is more, Morgan admits "the absence of direct proof of ancient descent in the female line in the Grecian and Latin gentes," but follows Bachofen in assuming that it once existed. "It is impossible to conceive of the gens as appearing, for the first time, in any other than its archaic [i.e., matrilineal] form; consequently the Grecian gens must have been originally in this form." That is to say, granted a universal

---

[6] E. B. Tylor, Researches into the Early History of Mankind and the Development of Civilisation, 142, 1865.

[7] Quoted in Stern, op. cit., 141.

law of progression, that law necessarily applies to Greek and Roman, as well as to other cultures. If, however, laws give us the essence of history, why trouble at all about a piecemeal study of the detailed course of events in particular societies? Here lies the inevitable conflict of the "unilinear evolutionist" and the culture historian. To the evolutionist it is obvious that progress has been "substantially the same in kind in tribes and nations inhabiting different and even disconnected continents, while in the same status." Hence the conclusion that the archaic structure of Greek and Roman society "must even now be sought in the corresponding institutions of the American aborigines." The historian's approach is radically different. Dealing with observed sequences, he is quite prepared to find diverse trends among diverse peoples. When Laufer discusses the development of art in India, he explicitly points out that it is wholly different from that of the Chinese; while Chinese painting evolved from calligraphy, the lack of ornamental penmanship precluded parallelism in India, where the science of physiognomics played a corresponding part.[8]

Of course, all the eminent evolutionists knew that deviations from a norm of progress were inevitable; and Tylor expressly stated that most of human culture had "grown into shape out of such a complication of events, that the laborious piecing together of their previous history is the only safe way of studying them." Far from always asserting independent development, he anticipates many diffusionist conclusions that are now generally accepted. He derives the Malagasy bellows, the Andamanese outrigger canoe, from Malaysia; he envisages a single origin for the bow and arrow; he supports the view that North American pottery "spread from a single source."[9] Tylor did not, as has been erroneously alleged, abandon this view in later years, but maintained it in discussing the patolli game in the anniversary essays in honor of Bastian. Indeed, that paper discusses the methodology of diffusionism; and the only reasonable criticism of Tylor is that he did not uniformly balance the contradictory principles of explanation. Notably, his famous statistical discussion fails to consider the effect of transmission on the course of organic development.

To turn back to Morgan, he was not wholly content with the patter of the day. At least sporadically he asks himself what may be meant by similar causes: "The phrase 'similar conditions of society,' which has become technical, is at least extremely vague. It is by no means easy to conceive of two peoples in disconnected areas, living in conditions precisely similar."[10] He was, indeed, fond of mentioning "the unequal endowments of the two hemispheres" as explaining the cultural differences in the same period, namely, the possession of domesticable animals that could furnish meat and milk to Old World

---

[8] B. Laufer, Dokumente der indischen Kunst; erstes Heft: Malerei; das Citralakshana, nach dem tibetischen Tanjur herausgegeben und übersetzt., 32, 1913. Morgan, Ancient Society, pt. 1, chap. 1.

[9] Tylor, Researches, 4, 167, 366.

[10] Systems of Consanguinity and Affinity, 472 f., 1871. Ancient Society, pt. 1, chaps. 1 and 2.

peoples. Here, once more Morgan was hampered by ignorance. It was no secret in 1877 that the same domesticated animals were quite differently used by the Chinese and the Egyptians or the pastoral nomads; in other words, that "equal endowments" did not automatically evoke similar cultural responses. In any case, whatever transitory qualms may have arisen in Morgan's mind about the improbability of frequently similar conditions, they did not impress his philosophy of progress. The very sentence that points out the difference of the Old and the New World terminates with the clause: "but the condition of society in the corresponding status must have been, in the main, substantially similar."

As to diffusion, Morgan's position was strange. In his system the Upper Status of Barbarism begins with the Iron Age. Yet he puts the ancient Britons, "although familiar with the use of iron," into the *Middle* Status. "The vicinity of more advanced continental tribes had advanced the arts of life among them far beyond the state of development of their domestic institutions." As Stern remarks, this exposes the weakness of the entire scheme. It rests avowedly on "such ... inventions or discoveries as will afford sufficient tests of progress," that is, on the arts of life. Now we suddenly learn that arts of life can spread by borrowing without affecting cultural status. But the very same principle applied to ancient Britons can be logically applied to an indefinite number of other cases. The vicinity of bow-using peoples might explain the archery of the Northern Athabaskans, who on other grounds might well be degraded to the Middle Status of Savagery, the level of Australians *and* Polynesians (*sic*); and so forth.

In short, Morgan never considers what remains of a scheme of development if warped by incessant borrowing. Since every human group has been exposed to unique outside influences from time immemorial, how can we maintain that "the experience of mankind has run in nearly uniform channels?" Some manner of evolutionary parallelism might still be rescued from the débris, but surely its limitations should be recognized.

It is no reproach to Morgan that he failed where Tylor fell short of complete clarity, where we of today are still floundering. But the special ways in which Morgan invoked diffusion are objects of legitimate wonder. He regarded the clan ("gentile") organization as nearly universal; and from an archevolutionist convinced of a "logical progress" in human institutions we should expect that this would serve as a sample of what "the natural logic of the human mind" would everywhere produce in similar circumstances. Yet Morgan takes precisely the opposite position: the clan is treated as so "abstruse" a conception that a single origin is postulated. The biological advantages of exogamy were such, it seems, that this type of organization "would propagate itself over immense areas."[11] I am aware that the multiple origin of clan systems remains a moot problem; but nowadays the theory of a single historical source is linked with a general diffusionist bias, not with a belief in evolutionary laws.

---

[11] Ancient Society, pt. 2, chap. 15.

Odd as such rank diffusionism appears in its evolutionist setting, it is almost mild compared with Morgan's intransigence in dealing with his favorite kinship data. Mere diffusion is not deemed sufficient here; borrowing, Morgan argues, would have involved the taking over of the very terms themselves. Hence, racial affinity alone can explain resemblances in the classification of relatives. Because the Hawaiian and Zulu nomenclatures share certain features, the Polynesians and the Kaffir must have sprung from the same stock; because the Tamil of India and the Seneca in New York state have similar systems of relationship, the affinity assumed in the name American *Indian* stands ultimately justified.[12]

This extraordinary intrusion of a biological factor to explain linguistic and sociological data cannot be treated as in any way due to contemporary currents of thought. Lubbock, for instance, at once demolished Morgan's conclusions. The Seneca resemble not merely the Tamil but also the Fijians and Australians in regard to relationship systems; are they, then, specifically related to all these races? Still more decisively the critic points out that on this basis the Two-Mountain Iroquois would have to be considered racially closer to the Polynesians than to the other Iroquois tribes.[13]

This case is especially illuminating. Morgan was here dealing with material he mastered incomparably better than any of his contemporaries. Yet the historical conclusions he arrives at are manifestly absurd on the basis of the data he had himself presented. No better proof can be required of his deficiency in historical tact. Again, the contrast with Tylor is startling. The numerous instances of transmission Tylor adduces, especially in the Researches, are not all valid; but none of them is plainly absurd, many remain suggestive, if not convincing.

Turning now to Morgan's specifically sociological work, we cannot divorce his interpretations from either his raw material or his philosophy of progress. As noted, his picture of society was inevitably imperfect from neglect of associational phenomena, a gap not filled until H. Schurtz's Altersklassen und Männerbünde (1902). It was further marred by the biographical accident that Morgan's contacts with aborigines began where they did—among the democratic clan-organized Iroquois. I have often wondered what his scheme might have been like if chance had first thrown him among the clanless Paiute, the wealth-craving Yurok, the pedigree-mad Polynesians, or the monarchical Baganda. Proceeding from the Seneca and encountering for hundreds of miles nothing but broadly comparable social structures, Morgan prematurely generalized what primitive society was like, even though on an apparently wide inductive basis. And when he had once formulated the generalization, he could dismiss contradictory evidence about the Columbia River tribes with the cheap auxiliary hypothesis that their clan organization had fallen into decay. I say "cheap" advisedly, because the proper procedure—

---

[12] Systems, 500–508.

[13] Lord Avebury, The Origin of Civilisation and the Primitive Condition of Man; 6th edition, 179, 1911.

whether definitive or not—on Morgan's own principles would have been to examine the kinship systems, which he believed always embodied evidence of preëxisting social conditions.

On the positive side we note, first, that Morgan personally secured much of the North American material, either directly or by correspondence; and that his outline of North American social organization remained for decades the only comprehensive summary. Indeed, imperfect as it is, no adequate substitute in the light of present knowledge has yet been provided. Secondly, Morgan was not indeed the first to conceive the distinction between territorial and kinship organization, but he grasped Maine's important conceptualization (1861) and made it underlie his own treatment of social development. In my judgment, Maine and Morgan err in completely denying local ties among primitive groups, but doubtless these bonds are comparatively weak; and whatever the ultimate verdict may be, Morgan deserves credit for recognizing the enormous importance of this luminous distinction.

A genuine contribution was the clearing up of the concept "exogamy." Contrary to his wishes, Morgan did not, indeed, succeed in banishing the term from scientific nomenclature, but his critique of J. F. McLennan in Ancient Society made it possible to use it intelligently with reference to observed facts. McLennan confused the issue by speaking of tribes as endogamous or exogamous, respectively. Morgan explained that the clan, a subdivision of the tribe, was the exogamous unit; and that marriage enforced outside this unit normally took place *within* the tribe, so that "both practices exist side by side."

Another valid stricture advanced against McLennan related to his representation of polyandry as a general phenomenon at a certain stage, while Morgan rightly regarded it as exceptional—a view shared with Lubbock.[14]

Various views popularly associated with Morgan need not be discussed in detail, because they were not in any sense peculiarly his. Thus, the priority of maternal over paternal descent had already been postulated by J. J. Bachofen and become part of the scientific credo of the period. Lubbock, Tylor, and Lang were only a few of the scholars who supported this view. Again, the notion that individual marriage was inconceivable among rude savages and must have been achieved by gradual progressive stages beginning with sexual communism was merely contemporary doctrine.[15]

For the same reason I can see nothing remarkable in Morgan's ideas on property. According to Professor Matorin, to be sure, Morgan's investigations "have proved the communistic character of the primitive community and have filled with mortal fear the hearts of all obscurants, all those who are guarding the foundations and pillars of traditional morality."[16] If, however, the Russian scholar had looked into Lubbock, he would have found much the same position as in Morgan—a firm conviction that individual land ownership was always preceded by a period in which the land was common."[17] Morgan, of course, attempted to fit specific ideas on this topic into his general

---

[14] Avebury, *op. cit.*, 151. [15] Avebury, *op. cit.*, 103. [16] *Loc. cit.* [17] Avebury, *op. cit.*, 478.

scheme. Thus, we learn that savages owned nothing but rude chattels, hence had not yet developed a passion for their possession; that at first children inherited only from their mother; that slavery—a well-established institution on the Canadian West coast—only sprang into being in the Upper Status of Barbarism, that is, in the Iron Age. At best commonplace, the section of Ancient Society devoted to the "Growth of the Idea of Property" is at its worst vitiated by the complete neglect of aboriginal slavery, aristocracy, and monarchy.

On the other hand, Morgan, though not ahead of his time in this respect, cannot fairly be criticized for ignoring the innumerable instances of incorporeal property that at once nullify the theory of primitive communism, since the relevant facts failed to arouse interest until a much later date. However, for his servile followers of today the excuse will not hold. It has, indeed, been asserted that primitive "copyrights" are economically insignificant, having merely sentimental value for their holders. But this allegation is demonstrably false. A Plains Indian who purchases a sacred bundle can readily transmute it into the most material of economic goods; he is making the safest of investments for the future. Similarly, the Eskimo, communistic as they are in the distribution of food, are rabid individualists when it comes to magic formulae. "Those who possess the words will not part with them, or if they do, it is at a price which would soon ruin an expedition." Rasmussen found an old woman who had taught a fellow tribesman her spell; in return he provided her "with food and clothing for the rest of her life."[18] In modern parlance, she had bought herself an annuity.

If Morgan deserves no more credit than a dozen other writers for being stimulated by biological evolutionism, he achieved unique distinction by his treatment of kinship; his fame rests securely and primarily on the Systems of Consanguinity and Affinity. In order to visualize the greatness of his achievement, we must first picture to ourselves the status of relevant problems before Morgan. Missionaries and others had, of course, noted that primitive peoples classify relatives according to non-European norms. But prior to Morgan no one had seen a problem in such exotic usage; no one had systematically garnered the several nomenclatures, compared them with one another, attempted a typology or interpretation. Morgan, evincing that "eye for essential fact" which even Lubbock was willing to concede, devoted twenty years to assembling the pertinent facts, partly by personal field studies, partly through the services of numerous correspondents. The result is a mass of raw material incomparably fuller than anything yet brought together by any of his successors. The work represented the terminologies of 139 distinct tribes or peoples and presented them, on the whole, in the greatest detail. Anyone who has worked out a single system in the field knows what is implied in this statement. Morgan was inevitably limited by the state of ethnographic knowledge. Africa was still the Dark Continent, South American information was scant or buried in inaccessible sources, from which it is only now being disen-

---

[18] Knud Rasmussen, Intellectual Culture of the Iglulik Eskimos, 165, 1929.

gaged by men like Kirchhoff. Having regard to the contemporary situation, Morgan must be credited with sparing no pains to achieve a world survey, in which he included Indo-European and Semitic as well as native peoples.

The case is illuminating as to Morgan's psychology. Nothing is less apt than Mr. Mitra's rhetorical flourish that "like a colossus he strode in every field of anthropology." The truth is that in most fields he did not stride at all. His contemporaries—say, Lubbock—dealt with art, language, and religion; on none of these topics can we find any enlightening general ideas in Morgan's writings. His interests were narrowly focused, but when he dug, he dug deep. And the result is clear. Lubbock's versatile mind, outside of prehistory, has left little mark on his successors; while in the one subject to which he devoted himself—social organization and especially kinship terms—Morgan remains a towering figure. His work has been revised and amplified, but it cannot be ignored.

Naturally, the mere assemblage of raw data would never confer the title of greatness; nor, may we add, would Morgan ever have collected them on so vast a scale unless goaded by the search of general principles. It is here, in the appraisal of Morgan's interpretations, that discrimination is imperative. For, as we have already seen, the assumption of racial affinities because of terminological resemblances was not merely wrong, but absurd in the light of Morgan's own data.

Intermediate, however, between ultimate explanation and the accumulation of mere data comes the process of classification and conceptualization. The qualities Morgan displayed here were those characteristic of him in general—not subtlety, but painstaking industry and rugged intelligence. In contrast to most of his successors he saturated himself with the chaotic mass of fact, and thus, quite apart from his main purposes, was able to foreshadow much of the subsequent typology. He noted the aberrant features of the Crow-Hidatsa nomenclature and its parallels elsewhere; he personally discovered the "Omaha" type of system among the Kansas and indicated its distribution; imperfectly informed as he was about our Western tribes, he detected such anomalies (from the Iroquois angle) as the distinction of paternal and maternal grandparents and the use of reciprocal terms.[19] Incidentally Morgan thus provided a solid basis for distributional studies and discoveries of historical connection, even though of an order less pretentious than that he consciously envisaged.

In the conceptualization of types of relationship terminology Morgan was not wholly successful. He was hampered by defective knowledge of those very tribes whose systems had a crucial bearing on the problem of classification. The data from Eastern and Central North American tribes, eked out by Oceanian and Australian reports, inevitably encouraged the inference that all aboriginal tribes grouped relatives into large classes. Hence, Morgan's main category of Classificatory Systems, to which he opposed that of Descriptive Systems as supposedly characteristic of the Indo-European family.

---

[19] Systems, 179, 188, 211, 245, 247, 252 f., 262.

Rivers pointed out that "descriptive" was not an apt term since most English terms, for instance, are denotative rather than descriptive. To be sure, Morgan's contention was rather that the *original* "Aryan" system was descriptive; that, like Erse, it had denoted a few primary relationships by specific nouns and described all others, that is, "son of brother," "son of son of brother." But obviously even on that assumption Rivers was right in objecting that modern Indo-European languages for the most part failed to fall into Morgan's rubric. From the opposite side Kroeber has urged that English and related tongues are not devoid of classificatory terms, such as "cousin." To me, however, there seems to be a still more vital objection. "Descriptive" designates a *technique* for defining relationship, "classificatory" a mode of grouping. The two concepts are thus not mutually complementary but relate to different subjects of discourse. Hence, a descriptive phrase, say, father's brother's son, might quite conceivably be applied to an indefinite number of individuals.

At present we are, indeed, still far from a satisfactory grouping of nomenclatures, but certain conclusions seem definitive. A nomenclature of relationship is not usually one system, but the result of several crisscross currents: as Kroeber phrases it, there are a number of diverse categories.[20] Morgan fully realized the significance of *one* category, that of grouping collateral with lineal kindred, but he rather naïvely assumed that features which merely chanced to appear with this fundamental trait were organically bound with it. Thus, the separation of junior from senior siblings constantly figures as a criterion of "classificatory" systems. Yet obviously the aborigines in question are not thereby making classes larger than ours, but on the contrary are introducing distinctions foreign to us. If the term has any significance at all in such a context, it is we who are classificatory; and, however that be, the segregation of senior from junior siblings is not possibly related—except by historic accident—to the inclusion of parallel cousins with siblings or of paternal uncles with the father.

Morgan's strength and weakness appear clearly in his treatment of the Eskimo "system." With exemplary candor he points out that eight of the ten features indicative of the North American Indian terminologies are lacking. Nevertheless, he defines it as classificatory. "It is... a classificatory as distinguished from a descriptive system. But in the greater and most important fundamental characteristic of this system it is wanting. The Eskimo form not only fails in the necessary requisites for the admission of this people, upon the basis of their system of relationship, into the Ganowanian family, but furnishes positive elements to justify their exclusion." There may possibly be, he argues, an ultimate, there is certainly not an immediate relation of the systems; indeed, the Eskimo nomenclature approaches the Aryan and Uralian more closely than it does that of the American Indians.[21]

Comparing this statement with Frazer's glib reference to the Eskimo ter-

---
[20] A. L. Kroeber, Classificatory Systems of Relationship, JRAI 39:81, 1909.
[21] Systems, 277, 470, 510.

minology as "classificatory," we at once recognize Morgan's immeasurable superiority. There is all the difference in the world between a bowing acquaintance and a serious grappling with refractory kinship data. Morgan has not achieved conceptual clarity, but he knows that here is something different from the Seneca norm, something so different that it verges on the exact opposite of a classificatory system, even if he cannot quite muster up courage to call it "descriptive."

Apart from his blind spot as to racial affinities, Morgan by concentration on his schedules was preserved from errors to which more casual investigators have fallen prey. His rebuttal of McLennan, for example, refutes the quaint notion that kinship through females implies ignoring of patrilineal kin, a conclusion apparently not yet universally accepted.

The distinction of Morgan, then, is not simply that he heaped up vast stores of information on a subject of theoretical import, but that he immersed himself in this welter of fact, came to grips with it, *thought* about it. The specific quality of his thinking shows to advantage in the discussion of the clan organization as a possible cause of the Seneca type of classificatory system. He examines the implications of such an organization and conclusively demonstrates that, while it would account for the identification of sisters' children with siblings under maternal descent, the similar identification of brothers' children would remain unexplained.[22] So, of course, it does except in the specialized case of exogamous moieties.

Of Morgan's scheme for the evolution of the family, little need be said because, as already suggested, it contained little that distinguished him from the other evolutionists. Promiscuity naturally came first, but avowedly not as anything but a theoretical deduction; the monogamous family came last; and there were intermediate stages bridging the gap. Morgan's originality lay in bringing this scheme of stages into correlation with forms of kinship terminology. That he committed a number of grave errors in this connection is pretty generally admitted. In harmony with the spirit of the times he took it for granted that what was simpler must be older, hence inferred that the Polynesian nomenclatures are more archaic than their American equivalents. He made a really fatal error in supposing that when a Polynesian addressed his father and, say, his mother's brother by a single term this implied conceiving the uncle as a possible procreator. Objectively formulated, the fact simply is that one common term applies to the begetter and other male relatives, that the Polynesians lack a term denoting paternity in our sense. Hence, Morgan's conclusion that the maternal uncle once mated with his sister (the speaker's mother) is fallacious: that custom would indeed logically produce the observed classification, but it is not the only possible usage that can lead to this result. Members of the same sex and generation may simply be grouped together under a blanket status term. Morgan's mistake, then, lies in misinterpreting the import of the aboriginal facts by reading a modern meaning into the translated kinship terms and in ignoring alternative determinants.

---

[22] Systems, 476.

When, however, we discount a pioneer's pitfalls and the warping due to contemporary bias, a magnificent and valid conception remains. Lists of relationship terms are lexical elements devoid of interest except to a linguist unless they are brought into contact with the elements of reality to which they refer. What is more, the linguistic approach culminates not in an explanation of the phenomena, but in a negation of the possibility of explanation. Kinship nomenclatures are certainly amenable to the changes which affect words, and since these changes are capricious we can never hope to reduce all features of relationship terminology to social antecedents. However, insofar as they are explicable at all they must be explained on sociological lines. The Southern Siouans and the Miwok of central California belong to diverse linguistic families, are separated by a distance of well over a thousand miles, are not known ever to have lived in close proximity. Their nomenclatures share the "Omaha" features of classing a mother's brother's son with the maternal uncle—a feature lacking in all the intervening tribes. Do the Southern Siouans resemble the Miwok more than their fellow Siouans of Montana and Dakota because of a miracle, or is it because both Southern Siouans and Miwok demonstrably share forms of marriage and linked social customs not found among the Crow and Teton? The choice lies between a sociological interpretation and the abandonment of interpretation.

We thus find Morgan's major postulate vindicated that kinship terminologies in some measure correspond to social facts, among which matrimonial rules are prominent. However, Morgan also asserted that social custom advanced while its lexical equivalents remained stationary; the use of a kinship term thus may point to the prior existence of an obsolete usage. Some who accept the correlation of social custom with nomenclature balk at this application of the principle of survivals.

Trained to view "survival" arguments with suspicion, I have become convinced that the avowed skepticism on this point harbors as much cant as the evolutionary zeal of our predecessors. Indubitably cultural changes proceed with uneven velocity, hence certain elements lag while others spurt ahead; further, linguistic phenomena are markedly conservative. These accepted facts warrant the assumption that a terminological feature in harmony with a certain custom may survive that custom. The only question is whether the social factor is the only possible determinant, whether the really vital factor is not rather one of its correlates, whether the same result may not be effected by a different cause. But when due allowance is made for this, Morgan's principle of survivals remains a valuable procedure.

In accepting the independent repetition of terminological features where social concomitants are repeated, we avowedly admit "evolution." However, it is a strictly empirical parallelism, which does not pretend to sketch culture history as a whole, but merely to account for specific resemblances. It is, indeed, very difficult to deal with cultural phenomena and fail to recognize certain organic bonds between phenomena. As Father Schmidt has recently explained, aprioristic evolutionism must be eschewed, but it is quite proper to make a "quite logical deduction from the very nature of things and men, to arrange them [cultural measures] in a certain series of phases of development."[23] Morgan certainly believed in the logical character of his deductions, and we therefore criticise him mainly for his deficient knowledge of the "nature of things and men."

Ultrascientific critics like to remind us that cultural phenomena are very complex, that we are consequently not warranted in assuming more than a functional relationship between distinct traits. There is great merit in the contention, but like everything else it can be overdone. If South African natives and North American Indians respond to the impact of white civilization by quite similar Messianic cults, shall we not admit that the contact is a temporally antecedent cause? Or do the methodological wiseacres contend that the cults could bring about the invasion of the white race?

Morgan thus figures as a typical exponent of a contemporary philosophy of civilization. That philosophy was bedecked with the follies of fashion, but part of its core was sound and a discriminating analysis will try to preserve it. As an individual, Morgan was only moderately cultivated and indifferently familiar with culture history. Most emphatically, he was not, as he has been called, a man of "brilliant delusions." He had delusions, which he set forth with schoolmasterly pedantry; but he brilliantly illuminated the subject of kinship terminologies by immersing himself in the facts, persistently arranging them, seeking and rejecting specific solutions of the problems they presented. His was not a flashy intellect, but one of unusual honesty, depth, and tenacity; and his prolonged concentration achieved the triumph of glimpses of real insight in a virgin field of scholarship. There is no better example of Darwin's saying, "It's *dogged* does it."

[23] W. Schmidt, The Position of Women with Regard to Property in Primitive Society, AA 37:244–256, 1935.

UNIVERSITY OF CALIFORNIA,
BERKELEY, CALIFORNIA.

THE CLASSIFICATION OF THE SONORAN LANGUAGES

By J. Alden Mason

[THE FOLLOWING MONOGRAPH, just as published below, was written in 1923 and submitted for presentation to the Pan-American Scientific Congress held in Lima, Peru, in 1924. The Proceedings of this Congress have never been published. Ten years later Dr. Kroeber published his Uto-Aztecan Languages of Mexico (Ibero-Americana:8) in which he arrived at the same major conclusions as I. To a great extent, therefore, the following monograph has been anticipated and superseded; its greatest present value lies in the corroboration of Kroeber's conclusions by independent research. Naturally certain data are considered which were not touched upon by Kroeber (and vice versa), and the presentation of these data, supplementing Kroeber, may constitute sufficient apology for publication.

Had this paper been written ten years later it would have been somewhat altered and made more up-to-date, but I deem it best to present it here exactly as originally written. I now notice some points that should have been altered even then, and these, together with other remarks, will be appended to the original article.—J. A. M.]

MORE THAN SIXTY YEARS have passed since Buschmann[1]* published the comparative linguistic studies on the basis of which Brinton[2] established his "Uto-Aztecan" group. Into this group Brinton gathered the Indian languages of Mexico and the western United States, which he divided into the three branches—Shoshonean, Sonoran, and Nahuatlan. This division was ignored by Powell[3] in his classification of Indian languages, but later Brinton's grouping was approved by Kroeber[4] and accepted by Thomas and Swanton[5] under the name "Nahuatlan" in their classification of the Mexican and Central American languages. Recently Sapir[6] has published a most thorough and scientific comparison of Paiute and Nahuatl, mainly on phonetic grounds, which may be considered as the final word regarding the validity of Brinton's classification.

Under the division "Sonoran Branch," Brinton names the following tribes:

Acaxees (?), in the Sierra de Topia.
Cahitas, south of the Rio Yaqui.
Coras, in the Sierra de Nayarit.
Eudeves, a subtribe of Opatas.
Guaymas, on Rio de Guaymas.
Mayos, on Rio Mayo, subtribe of Cahitas.
Nevomes, see Pimas.
Opatas, head-waters of Rio Yaqui.
Papayos, or Papagos, subtribe of Pimas.

Pimas, from Rio Yaqui to Rio Gila.
Sabaguis, subtribe of Pimas.
Tarahumaras, in the Sierra of Chihuahua.
Tehuecos, on R. del Fuerte, dialect of Cahita.
Tecoripas, speak dialect of Pima.
Tepehuanas, in Durango.
Tubares, in Upper Sinaloa.
Yaquis, on Rio Yaqui.

To these should be added the following:

Cazcan, in Zacatecas.
Concho, in Chihuahua.
Huichol (Guachichil), in Sierra de Nayarit.
Jova, in Sonora.

Nio, in Sinaloa.
Tepahue, in Sonora.
Tepecano, in Jalisco.
Zacateco, in Zacatecas.
Zoe, in Sinaloa.

Also a few languages of less importance, now extinct.

---

* Superior figures refer to notes at the end of this essay, p. 196.

All of these, with the exception of the Pima in Arizona and the Papago on both sides of the border, are found in northern Mexico. The Acaxee, Cahita, Cazcan, Concho, Eudeve, Guayma, Jova, Mayo, Nio, Sabagui or Sobaipuri, Tecoripa, Tehueco, Tepahue, Zacateco, and Zoe are probably entirely extinct and the languages long since forgotten, and the Opata, Tepecano, and Tubar are on the verge of extinction.

It will be my purpose to show that these languages, classified from a phonetic basis, fall into three—possibly four—principal groups which may provisionally be termed Western, Southern, and Central.

WESTERN GROUP

Tarahumaran	*Cahitan-Opatan*	
	Cahitan	*Opatan*
Tarahumare	Yaqui	Opata
Tubar	Cahita	Eudeve
(Concho)	Mayo	Jova
	Tehueco	
	(Nio, Zoe, Tepahue)	

SOUTHERN GROUP

Cora	Huichol
	(Guachichil)

CENTRAL GROUP

Piman[8]	*Tepehuanan*
Upper Pima, Sobaipuri	Northern Tepehuane
Lower Pima, Nevome (Tecoripa, Guayma)	Southern Tepehuane
Papago	Tepecano
	(Acaxee, Cazcan, Zacateco)

It is possible that Tarahumare should be placed alone in a fourth group; lexically it appears to be quite variant from the Cahita-Opata group.

The mutual affiliations of these three or four groups is likewise a matter of considerable interest since it will be found that, particularly from a phonetic point of view, but also from a lexical standpoint, the Central group is sharply differentiated, the others falling into one class as opposed to it. The Central languages are furthermore the most divergent from Nahua and probably, therefore, from the original Uto-Aztekan. Conversely the other groups are relatively closely related to Nahua and to primitive Uto-Aztekan, particularly, I may say, the Yaqui-Opata group and the Tarahumare. Another point of ethnological interest, doubtless of importance from an historical point of view, is the relatively slight variation and the widespread distribution of the Central group, which comprises the northernmost and the southernmost members of the Sonoran Division, the Pima of Arizona and the Tepecano of Jalisco, separated by some nine hundred miles, which increases to over a thousand when the related extinct Cazcan to the south is considered.

It is a matter for the greatest regret that so pitiably little is known of these languages. But the same remark is applicable to practically every Mexican Indian language. There is not even a modern scientific exposition of Aztec itself. So far as I am aware the writer's recently published grammar of Tepecano[9] is the first attempt at a modern scientific exposition of any Uto-Aztekan language. Dr. K. T. Preuss promises a thorough grammar of Cora, and the writer and Juan Dolores[10] have much material on Papago. A brief sketch of Yaqui has recently been published by the writer.[11] Outside of the Sonoran family we look forward to Sapir's coming grammar of Paiute. But for the rest we still must rely on grammars several centuries old, compiled by missionary priests devoted and interested enough, but untrained in phonetics, and basing their grammars on analogy with the Latin. And we are grateful enough for even these, when we consider the many languages which have perished utterly without leaving so much as a vocabulary to aid in their identification. Yet it requires some temerity to base any conclusions on phonetics culled from these.

Even these old sources are generally so rare as to be inaccessible to the average student, and the writer has, in many cases, been compelled to have recourse to the digest of them given by Pimentel.[12] From this work, from Sapir's comparative papers, and from the writer's personal notes has come the bulk of the material used in the present study.

Let us now consider the phonetics of each of these languages in comparison with original Uto-Aztekan and note the sound-shifts in each case.

Sapir[13] posits twelve, possibly fourteen, original consonants for Uto-Aztekan: *p, t, tl, ts* with its variant *tc, k, kw, s* with its variant *c, m, n*, possibly *ñ (ng), l, w, y*, and possibly *h*; and five vowels: *a, e, i*, open *o* and close *o-u*. I am unconvinced as regards the originality of *tl*. It is, as he says, found solely in certain dialects of Nahua, and in every other Uto-Aztekan language its place is taken by *t*. While as yet no rule for the development of *tl* from *t* in Aztec has been proposed, this would seem the more likely explanation. There is likewise some doubt of the originality of the nasal *ñ (ng)* inasmuch as it is not found in Nahua and the Sonoran languages. At any rate, they may be left out of the present discussion since both are regularly missing in Sonoran languages. I quite agree with Sapir, however, that *h* must be included, inasmuch as it occurs regularly in the Sonoran and certain of the Shoshonean languages, irrespective of the fact that it is found neither in Nahua nor Southern Paiute. I shall later present suggestions concerning the possibility of other sounds being assigned to Uto-Aztekan.

Of all the Uto-Aztekan languages, Tarahumare seems to be the least differentiated, every phonetic element of Uto-Aztekan apparently retaining its original value. The author of the standard Tarahumare grammar, Tellechea,[14] however, uses furthermore certain characters of doubtful yet significant value: *b*, which partakes of the quality of *p*; *r*, which is varied with *l*; *g*, which is confused with *k*; and finally *v*.

The Cahitan-Opatan languages of the Western group, taking Yaqui as typical, follow Tarahumare very closely and may belong to the same group. But one radical sound-shift is to be noted—that of U-A *kw* to Yaqui *bw*. Examples show this most plainly, all of them taken from Velasco.[15]

    Nah.: qua, "eat"
                                     Yaq.: buaie, "comer"
                                             buabua, "comer muchas veces"
                                            buacai, "comilón"
                                            buaieie, "comida"

    Nah.: quăuh-tli, "eagle"   buañe, "águila grande"
    Nah.: cui, "take"   buise, "coger"
    Nah.: cuitla-tl, "excrement"   buita, "mierda"
    Cora: kwasí, "tail"   buasia, "cola de animal"

I judge by the Opata and Eudeve words for "eagle," quoted by Pimentel: *paue* and *puaue*, respectively, that the Opatan languages follow the Cahitan languages in this respect.[16] Tarahumare, Cora and Huichol certainly retain *kw*.

Yaqui, however, also uses sounds other than the original Uto-Aztekan sounds and their reflexes. Such are, in particular, *r* and *v*. It is quite certain that Yaqui possesses both *l* and *r*. Velasco states that in some words *l* and *r* are interchangeable—probably thus denoting an intermediate sound—while in other instances the sounds must be distinguished, as *alanoca*, "speak well," and *aranoca*, "be able to speak." In my Yaqui notes I recorded both *r* and *l* without confusion, and my recordings agreed in every case with Velasco's.

Mason	*Velasco*
yo·rim, "Mexicans"	Iori, "Español, fiera, valiente"
tevaure, "be hungry"	tebaure, "tener hambre"
ili, "small"	ilit, "chica cosa"
xulen, "thus"	hulen, "así"
wepul, "only one"	uepulai, "1 solo"

I have not had the opportunity of comparing the reflexes of Yaqui *l* and *r* in other languages, and particularly in Nahua, but imagine that such a comparison would yield interesting results. Undoubtedly also both *v* and *p* are to be found in Yaqui. Whether both of these are reflexes of Nahua *p* I have not yet been able to determine; *v* appears to be the usual reflex in the Piman group. There are, however, *p-p* correspondences, as *pusi*, "eyes," in both Yaqui and Tarahumare. I recorded both *p* and *v* in my few Yaqui notes.

In the Southern group, consisting of Cora and Huichol, also very few phonetic divergences from the original Uto-Aztekan are found. There is little exact published information on Huichol, but it probably follows Cora closely in phonetic type, although apparently differing considerably lexically. The sole shift which can be designated with any degree of certainty is that of certain U-A *p*'s to *h*, others remaining as *p*.

Nahua: poçaua, "swell up"	Cora: husa, "be filled"
Paiute:[17] potqua, "be round"	Cora: hure, "make a ball"
Paiute: paqa, "kill one"	Cora: heika, "kill one"
Nahua: pil-li, "son, child"	Cora: peri, pari, "child"

r seems to be the normal reflex of U-A l, but in some cases l seems to be retained:

Nahua: pil-li, "son, child"   Cora: peri, pari, "child"
Nahua: coloa, "turn, return"   Cora: kureyi, "random flight of birds"

Sapir states that v is the Cora reflex of Nahua w, but his examples show also some instances of w.

Nahua: uei, "big"   Cora: ve, "great"
Nahua: uetzi, "fall"   Cora: ve, "fall"
Paiute: puñwi, "peep"   Cora: hiwe, "clamor"

The two sounds are so close that the difference may be ascribed to untrained ears.

It is evident, then, as before stated, that, from a phonetic point of view, there is very slight difference between Tarahumare, Yaqui-Opata, and Cora-Huichol, not above one radical sound-shift being found in any language.

As against these languages, the Central group (Piman-Tepehuanan) is strongly differentiated, no less than eight radical sound-shifts being effected. These are in detail:

U-A e to P-T $ö$[18]

Nahua: uei, "big"   Tepecano: gö, "big"
Nahua: ez-tli, "blood"   Tepecano: ö'ör, "blood"
Nahua: ten-tli, "mouth"   Tepecano: tön, "mouth"

U-A p to P-T v

Nahua: pia, pie, "remain"   Tepecano: via', "remain"
Cora: ki-poa, "hair"   Tepecano: vo, "hair"

U-A ts, tc to P-T s, c

Nahua: metz-tli, "moon"   Tepecano: masad, "moon"
Nahua: uetzi, "fall"   Tepecano: göc, "fall"
Nahua: cochi, "sleep"   Tepecano: koc, "sleep"

U-A l to P-T r

Nahua: tonal, "sun"   Tepecano: tonor, "sun"
Nahua: çali-ui, "fasten"   Tepecano: harsap, "fasten"

In most, if not all of these languages, an l is found in addition to an r, both apparently referring back to U-A l.

U-A s to P-T h

Nahua: çali-ui, "fasten"   Tepecano: harsap, "fasten"
Nahua: ce(n), "one"   Tepecano: hömad, "one"
Nahua: ce-tl, "ice"   Tepecano: höp, "cold"
Nahua: a-xix-tli, "urine"   Tepecano: hi', "urine"

These five shifts, while definite, are not very radical, the sounds shifting within only one category, generally keeping their original tongue position.

The striking fact about this group of languages is that they have developed a complete series of sonant stops from original voiced spirants. These are:

U-A *kw* to P-T *b*

This is evidently a further development of the *kw* to *bw* shift found in Yaqui. Let us review the examples given in that case:

Nah.: qua, "eat"
Yaq.: buabua, "comer muchas veces"
Pap.: pah, "swallow" (probably ba)

Nah.: cuitla-tl, "excrement"
Yaq.: buita, "mierda"
Tep.: bi·t, "excrement"

Nah.: quãuh-tli, "eagle"
Yaq.: buaûe, "águila grande"
Tep.: ba'a·G, "eagle"

Cora: kwasi', "tail"
Yaq.: buasia, "cola de animal"
Tep.: bai, "tail"

Nah.: cui, "take"
Yaq.: buise, "coger"
Tep.: bö(i), "take"

U-A *y* to P-T *d*

Nah.: yaca-tl, "nose"
Yaq.: yena, "smoke tobacco"
Yaq.: iaha, "llegar muchos"
Yaq.: iuco, "lluvia"

Tep.: da·k, "nose"
Tep.: dön, "smoke"
Tep.: da-da, "arrive many"
Tep.: du·k, "rain"

(It is an interesting and significant fact that Velasco gives Yaqui *iurasno* with initial *i* for Spanish *durazno*, "peach.")

U-A *w* to P-T *g*

Nah.: uei, "big"
Nah.: uetzi, "fall"
Nah.: uitz-tli, "spine"

Tep.: gö, "great"
Tep.: göc, "fall"
Tep.: gisu·r, "cactus"

The results of this phonetic comparison of the Sonoran languages may be formulated then as indicating beyond doubt that the Central group, Pima-Papago-Tepehuane-Tepecano, is sharply differentiated from all the others. A dual division of the family might therefore be made. As concerns the others, the phonetic differentiation is so slight that they might be placed in one group as opposed to the Central group. Nevertheless, the lexical differentiation is so great that, mainly on this basis, they have been separated into two groups.

On this latter point of lexical resemblances a little digression may not be amiss. In 1911 I had the opportunity of studying a series of vocabularies made during a census in Mexico about 1885 and of copying the seventy-five commonest words in the Sonoran vocabularies. These, of course, were made by Mexicans untrained in phonetics or linguistic work, and I also compared them rather uncritically, noting merely every obvious resemblance. Nevertheless the comparison elucidated interesting results. The vocabularies compared were three termed Yaqui, from Guaymas, Mocoriba, and Fuerte (two of them being probably Mayo and Tehueco); two termed Opata, from Arivechi and

Huepac; Papago, Huichol and Cora. To these I added for comparative purposes the Aztec and Tepecano vocabularies collected by myself.

Naturally the closest resemblances were found between dialects of the same languages, 77 per cent of the words of the Yaqui dialects, and 52 per cent of the words of the Opata dialects being evidently closely related. The next closest resemblances were, naturally, between languages in the same groups, 46 per cent of the Yaqui and Opata words being obviously related, 54 per cent of the Tepecano and Papago words, and 42 per cent of the Cora and Huichol words.

The affinities between these three groups were naturally considerably less but rather variant. The Yaqui-Opata showed about equal affinities to the Cora-Huichol and to the Papago-Tepecano group, 22–25 per cent; and the Papago-Tepecano group a little less resemblance to Cora-Huichol, 20 per cent.

Finally these three groups were compared with the Aztec with even more variable results. The relationship with Papago-Tepecano was very slight, only 12 per cent, that to Cora-Huichol slightly greater, about 20 per cent, while the Yaqui-Opata group showed 27 per cent of resemblances. Thus the conclusions reached on phonetic grounds are substantiated also, roughly, on lexical grounds—that the Yaqui-Opata group is the least, the Pima-Tepehuane group the most, variable. Unfortunately, I have not been able to obtain a good Tarahumare vocabulary which, as we have seen, from a phonetic point of view, is even closer to Aztec than is Yaqui.

It is possible that the list of original Uto-Aztekan consonants suggested by Sapir should be enlarged. First, we may have to posit an original U-A r as well as an l. Both r and l certainly exist in Yaqui. While the writer recorded only one in Tepecano, yet this one has two very different reflexes in the closely-related Papago, an intermediate r-l and a cerebral or dorsal t. Moreover, recorders of the majority of the other Sonoran languages make similar distinctions, sometimes between r and rh and sometimes between r and l.

A second suggestion is that another bilabial, possibly v, must be posited. All the Sonoran languages which I have investigated possess both v and p, the latter being in the minority. v seems to be the normal reflex of original U-A p, but the p remains unexplained. In addition to Yaqui, Papago, and Tepecano, of which I have personal knowledge, both p and v have been written by other recorders in Opata, Eudeve, Nevome, Tepehuane, Tarahumare, Cora, in fact every important Sonoran language.

CORRIGENDA

Without considering any more than the data contained in the foregoing article, it may be charged with numerous faults, such as:

No reference was made to the appearance of Sapir's second article in AA, n.s., 17 (1), 1915, as well as later in the SAP-J. Certain languages of some importance, as well as some not extinct, such as Varohio, were not mentioned in the list of languages. Mayo is still spoken and should not have been mentioned as extinct; possibly some of the others may not yet be extinct.

The table of classification of the languages is not at all good. The geographical terminology of "Western," "Southern," and "Central" for the main divisions is highly incorrect. If more concise terms than "Tarahumaran-Cahitan-Opatan," "Cora-Huichol," and "Piman-Tepehuanan" are eventually proposed, they will probably have a linguistic basis, like that of the *langued'oc* and the *langued'oil*. As a suggestion, they might be distinguished by their words for "water," as the *ba* group (Western), the *a* group (Southern) and the *sudig* group (Central).

Although their respective relations are explained in the text, the table does not give a true picture of Sonoran relationships, suggesting as it does three main groups of equal degree of consanguinity, each divided into two equally related groups. A table in the form of a genealogical tree would have presented a better picture, but, in view of our relatively slight knowledge of Uto-Aztecan philology, it would probably have been incorrect at many points. A dual division of Piman-Tepehuanan as against the other two should first have been made, and the division between Piman and Tepehuanan indicated as less important than, say, between Cora and Huichol.

The few minor and extinct languages which were assigned to one group or another and placed in parentheses had much better have been omitted entirely. Most of them were placed, on grounds of geographical propinquity, with the nearest group, and probably, in many cases, the guess was a poor one.

REVISION

Any up-to-date classification of the Sonoran languages must critically consider the work of Kroeber,[19] Sauer,[20] and Whorf.[21]

The most certain fact, admitted by all, is the specialization and relative homogeneity of the languages of the Pima-Tepehuan group. As against them, all the others apparently fall into one group, making a dual division of the family. On the other hand, as compared with the differentiation among the languages of the other groups, it might almost be considered as a single language with dialectic differences. A Papago might conceivably catch the general tenor of a conversation in Tepecano. Though Pima-Papago and Tepehuan are the best known tribes of the group and might be taken as typical of the subgroups, yet the affiliations of the various languages and dialects are very uncertain. Northern Tepehuan may be closer to Lower Pima than to Southern Tepehuan. There may be approximately equal variation between any two languages of the group, and in the present state of our knowledge no subdivision of this group should be attempted. In this I agree with Kroeber. Which of the extinct languages such as Tecoripa, Guayma, Acaxee, Teul, Colotlan, Cazcan, Zacateco, Jumano, Suma, Lagunero-Irritila, Coca, and Tecuexe should be included in this group will probably never be known. Probably Tecoripa, Guayma, Teul, and Colotlan should.

Thomas and Swanton considered Acaxee as probably akin to Tepehuan, but Sauer and Kroeber believe it more probably related to Cahita-Opata-Tarahumar. Sauer's reasons for believing the Acaxee not closely related to

Tepehuan are very cogent and must be preferred to Thomas and Swanton's unsupported hypothesis. Very few Acaxee words have been preserved. The few words and phrases quoted by Kroeber, as he says, "do not lend themselves to definitive analysis." The frequent use of the vowel *e*, which is changed to *ï* in Pima-Tepehuan, supports Sauer's hypothesis, though the symbol *e* may very well have been employed for this sound foreign to Spanish ears. The initial syllable of *veuincame*, "almighty," may very well be the C-O-T (and Nahua) stem *we*, "great," which would be *gï* in P-T. On the other hand, the most analyzable word appears much more P-T than C-O-T: *tocaca*, "our father." This almost certainly contains the P-T stem *og*, "father" with the common first person plural pronominal possessive prefix *t-*; the C-O-T words seem to be variations of the stems *atsai* and *no*.

As regards Cora and Huichol, my "Southern group," a resurvey of the material gives me no cause to separate them. They have always been bracketed, linguistically as well as ethnologically and geographically, and I believe with Whorf that Kroeber was unduly cautious in separating them. I have hastily compared Ortega's[22] Cora and Diguet's[23] Huichol vocabularies, and find a large number of words evidently closely related to each other and more differentiated from the cognate words in other groups.

The sibilant *s* seems to be lacking in Cora and Huichol, its place apparently taken by *c* (*š*) or *j*. Ortega specifically notes it as lacking in Cora, and Diguet's Huichol vocabulary shows only a couple of examples (for instance, one example in over one hundred long words in his "chant"). Lumholtz[24] writes only *sh* in both Cora and Huichol (together with *tsh* in Cora), but writes *s* in combinations such as *st* and *sj* in Cora, and *ts* in Huichol. However, Preuss distinguishes both *s* and *š* in Cora.

As in many other Sonoran languages, *r* and *l* seem to be intermediate in Cora and Huichol. This is noted by Diguet who writes only *r* while Lumholtz uses both in Huichol. Ortega states that *l* is missing in Cora, with which Preuss concurs, but Lumholtz writes *l* almost exclusively in Cora. Despite Sapir's decision that U-A **p* > Huichol *h*, Cora *p* or *h*, in my Diguet-Ortega comparative list, out of thirty-four evidently related words, the only three instances of words containing *p* in Huichol have Cora forms with *p*, and vice versa.

The extant Huichol linguistic material is still so scanty and so unphonetically recorded that little can be said with any certainty regarding soundshifts from Uto-Aztecan or within the group.[25] These seem to be relatively few and slight. Cora may be a little the more variant. Nevertheless neither gives the impression of being especially close to original Uto-Aztecan or to Nahua.

Ever since the earliest Spanish days the Huichol have been regarded as connected with the extinct Guachichil far to the east of present Huichol territory, and the fact that the latter make long journeys into former Guachichil territory to gather *peyote* that does not grow in their present habitat affords ethnological corroboration of the close relationship.

In my "Western group," Kroeber's Cahita-Opata-Tarahumar group, I was almost certainly at fault in my suggestion that possibly Tarahumar should be placed in a fourth group by itself; there is little question that it falls in general with Cahita and Opata. Kroeber makes no attempt to subdivide the group, but his triple name suggests the three apparent main divisions.

Tubar, which I classed with Tarahumar, following Thomas and Swanton, Kroeber places in the general C-O-T group with the qualification "perhaps," but refuses to classify it further. Comparing Lumholtz's short Tubar vocabulary (apparently the only one extant, in spite of the fact that the Tubar language is probably not yet extinct) with Kroeber's vocabularies, Thomas and Swanton seem to have been wrong, for Tubar seems to display on the whole more resemblances to Yaqui and Mayo than to Tarahumar, Opata, and Varohio. Many of the stems seem to be unique, but the list below gives all that seem to show resemblances with the other languages, with their nearest congeners, except in those cases where the same stem is common to all the languages:

English	*Tubar* (Lumholtz)	*Nearest congener* (Kroeber)
Mouth	tini′r	Tar. rini′
Tongue	nini′r	Yaq. nî′ni
Foot	njo′ki′r	May. go′k·i
Bone	hotara′t	Y-M. o′ta
House	ner-kita′ (my)	Opa. kīt‘
Bow	wicoli′t	May. wi′kori
Arrow	waca′t	Tar. wa′ca
Tobacco	wiha′t	Tar. wipa′; Opa. bī′vat‘
Moon	matsa′t	Opa. mêtšat
Fire	tahame′t	Yaq. *ta*′hi
Water	bata′	Y-M. bā′a
Earth, land	kvira′t	Y-M. bwi′ya, wi′y·a
Stone, rock	teta′t	Y-M. *te*′ta
Dog	tjutju	Var. tšu‘ tšu′lî

The foregoing list gives the closest correspondences, but a study of all of Lumholtz's list gives the same general impression: that Tubar shows close affiliation with no particular subgroup of the Cahita-Opata-Tarahumar group, but bears on the whole the most resemblance to the Cahita subgroup (Yaqui-Mayo), with Tarahumar, Opata, and Varohio following in this order. It probably forms a subgroup of its own, possibly together with other less important extinct languages of which even less is known than of Tubar itself. That it belongs in this larger group is almost certain; a comparison with Cora and Huichol words in Lumholtz's vocabularies shows much fewer resemblances, and with Pima-Tepehuan almost none. The Tubar list is too short, and Lumholtz's phonetics leave too much to be desired, to attempt to designate any phonetic shifts. Two apparent ones may be pointed out, however. Tubar *kvira′t*, Yaqui *b^wui′ya*, "land," shows retention of U-A *kw*. In this respect it seems to agree most closely, according to Whorf's unpublished table, with Cora and Huichol, Nahua and Shoshonean. Tubar *wiha′t*, Opata *bī′vat‘*, Tarahumar *wipa'*, "tobacco," suggests that U-A *p* has shifted to Tubar *h*, as in Cora and Huichol. Other apparent characteristics of Tubar, if we may credit Lumholtz's vocabulary, is the prevalence of consonantal endings (35 out of 46), and the great number of endings in *r* (17) and in *t* (13), these two comprising 30 of the 35 consonantal endings. As all the words given are nouns, it is possible that these are nominal suffixes (or more likely one nominal suffix, an intermediate *t-r*, possibly like Papago dorsal *ṭ*), possibly genetically related to the Aztec nominal ending *-tl*. The accent is predominantly on the ultima; out of the 46 examples, where the accent is noted, as it is in the great majority of cases, in only five instances is it otherwise than on the ultima.

The Concho should not have been included by me, even provisionally, with the Tarahumar. Kroeber's conclusions that it "was a distinct language within the C-O-T group, most closely related to Opata, and perhaps most different from Tarahumar" are probably sound.

The principal difference between Kroeber's classification and mine is that he refuses to subdivide his Cahita-Opata-Tarahumar group, though by implication apparently considering the three principal exponents are equidistant, while I made a dual subdivision, bracketing Cahita and Opata as opposed to Tarahumar. I have studied various extant vocabularies to consider whether Cahita and Opata are more cognate than either is to Tarahumar.

There are available for comparison rather large Cahita and Tarahumar vocabularies, Velasco's Cahita,[26] with cognates of about 2500 Spanish words, and Ferrero's Tarahumar[27] with even more. Both are Spanish-Indian, arranged alphabetically and therefore easy to compare.

A comparison of these two vocabularies indicates that the languages are rather closely related, both lexically and phonetically. As might be expected, in the majority of cases the same Spanish word is translated by a different root in the two languages so that the percentage of cognate words is not great, but where related at all the resemblance is quite close, often amounting to apparent identity. About 160 such cases were found. A comparison of these indicates that there are few sound-shifts between the two languages. In the great majority of cases every consonant and vowel in Tarahumar has a very similar reflex in Cahita. Unfortunately, in the cases where sound-shifts have been claimed, in certain labial and labialized consonants, Spanish phonetic idiosyncrasies predispose to confusion untrained recorders accustomed to that language. The average Latin-American finds it difficult to distinguish between *ba, βa, wa, bwa,* and *gwa*.

I must retract my statement that Tarahumar certainly retains U-A *kw*; it is probable that the shift U-A *kw* > Tarahumar *w*, Cahita *bw* is correct. Kroeber suggests that *kw* may also sometimes be retained in Tarahumar, but I am now inclined to think it unlikely; in my list of 160 Tarahumar words I find no instance of *kw*, nor of *bw*. Of 41 reflexes of Tarahumar *w*, Cahita shows, according to Velasco, 25 examples of *w*, 11 of *bw*, and 5 of *b*. It is probable that several different sounds are here thrown together, as Ferrero does not differentiate between certain sounds, remarking that *hua, hue, hui* (*wa, we, wi*), and *gua, güe, güi* (*gwa, gwe, gwi*) are equivalent, as are also in some cases *hua* (*wa*) and *ba*. Examples of this shift that seem almost certain are:

English	Nahua	Tarahumar	Yaqui	Tepecano
Excrement	cuitla-tl	huitaca	buita	bi't
Tail		huasira	buasia	bai

That U-A *t* is often or generally shifted to Tarahumar *r* seems to be almost certain. In my comparisons of Tarahumar and Cahita, from Ferrero and Velasco, the majority of the Cahita reflexes of Tarahumar *r* are *t*, some *r*, and a few *l*. Of course *t* is common in Tarahumar also, and the Cahita reflex of this is always *t*. Ferrero says that in certain words *t* and *r* are interchangeable, that is, probably of an intermediate nature.

It is pitiful that we still have to refer to uncritical vocabularies for these data on still living languages, and all conclusions based on these are liable to future revision. But on the data available it appears that Tarahumar has at least two sound-shifts in divergence from Uto-Aztecan, is lexically not very variant from Yaqui, for instance, and merits classification with the latter and not in a separate group. I must therefore retract certain statements in my original paper.

As regards the relations of Opata to Tarahumar, Cahita, and the other languages, I have been unable to secure an Opata vocabulary, but have made a brief and hasty comparison with a vocabulary of the kindred Heve language.[28] This suggests that Heve is both phonetically and lexically slightly removed from these two, though possibly closer to Cahita. A comparison of Heve with Lumholtz's short Tubar vocabulary suggests that these two are almost certainly more closely related. The proportion of words ending in *t* (16 in 37 compared) should be compared with that of Tubar words ending in *r* or *t*, and again suggests a nominal ending. This was noted in the case of Opata by Kroeber, as was also the sound-shift U-A *y* > Opata *d* (or fricative δ) as probably the first step to Pima-Tepehuan *d*. It is possible that the P-T shift of U-A *kw* > *b* is also functional in Heve, as indicated in the following examples:

English	Heve (Smith)	Cahita (Velasco)
Tail	basit	buasia
Pheasant	pura'va	buerutaru
Thief	etzbaan	eet buame

Whorf, in his unpublished chart of Uto-Aztecan sound-shifts, grants the *kw* > *b* shift in Eudeve-Heve, but believes that *kw* or *gw* is retained in Opata. Kroeber evidently has insufficient data on this point, as he leaves the Opata reflex of *kw* blank in his chart. As given in my original article, Pimentel quotes Opata *paue*, Eudeve-Heve *puaue*, "eagle" (Nahua *quauh-tli*). If this were certain it would look as though Opata follows Heve in the *kw* > *b* shift. However Pimentel has certainly misquoted, since Buckingham Smith gives *paue* for "eagle" in Heve. I have been unable to check up the Opata form; if Pimentel reversed the two forms and if Opata *puaue* is correct, the shift may hold, but one cannot base any conclusions on a single example possibly misquoted.

As a result of these hasty comparisons I retract my bracketing of Cahita-Opata as opposed to Tarahumar, and agree with Kroeber that the three should be grouped, and that studies upon them are not yet far enough advanced to warrant any further subdivision of this group. When such is made it is most likely that Opata and Tubar will be found to be those most entitled to a subheading.

However, there is apparently no disagreement that certain languages or dialects fall with Cahita and others with Opata, and that these, together with others that I did not note, are approximately as given in my list. Yaqui, Mayo, and Tehueco are generally agreed to be the prominent members of the Cahita subgroup, while Heve or Eudeve falls with Opata. Kroeber is not certain of the relationship of Jova to Opata but thinks it likely. Nio, Zoe, and Tepahue, which I classed as doubtfully Cahitan, are not well enough known to warrant further classification than that that Kroeber has given them, as "presumably" or "perhaps" in the C-O-T group.

Whorf's tables do not grant Yaqui an r. Inasmuch as Velasco insists that in some cases r and l must be differentiated, and sometimes form the criterion for distinguishing words otherwise homonymous, and as my recordings of l and r agreed in every case with Velasco's, I am still inclined to believe that they are separate phonemes.

As regards the original Uto-Aztecan sounds proposed by Sapir, both Kroeber and Whorf have published critiques of these and further comment by me is unnecessary. Whorf agrees with my "hunch" that U-A tl is not an original sound, but disagrees with a similar surmise regarding palatal $ñ$; he likewise agrees that an original r should be posited as well as an l.

Since my original article was written, two grammars of Uto-Aztecan languages, there noted as looked forward to with expectancy, have appeared, Preuss's Cora,[29] and Sapir's Paiute.[30]

THE UNIVERSITY MUSEUM,
PHILADELPHIA, PENNSYLVANIA.

NOTES TO "THE CLASSIFICATION OF THE SONORAN LANGUAGES"

[1] J. C. E. Buschmann, Die Spuren der Aztekischen Sprache (Berlin, 1859); Grammatik der Sonorischen Sprachen (Berlin, 1864).

[2] D. G. Brinton, The American Race (New York, 1891).

[3] J. W. Powell, Indian Linguistic Families of America North of Mexico, BAE-R 8, 1893.

[4] A. L. Kroeber, Shoshonean Dialects of California, UC-PAAE 4, 1907.

[5] Cyrus Thomas and J. R. Swanton, Indian Languages of Mexico and Central America, BAE-B 44, 1911.

[6] Edward Sapir, Southern Paiute and Nahuatl, SAP-J 10 and 11, 1913 and 1919.

[7] *Op. cit.*, 134.

[8] The term *Piman* was employed by Powell to denote the linguistic family of which the Pima is the principal representative in the United States, and is thus synonymous with the term *Sonoran* used here. It should not be confused with the term as used here for the smaller division.

[9] J. Alden Mason, Tepecano, A Piman Language of Western Mexico, Annals of the New York Academy of Sciences, 25 (New York, 1917).

[10] Juan Dolores, Papago Verb Stems, UC-PAAE 10, 1913; Papago Nominal Stems, Phoebe Apperson Hearst Memorial volume, *ibid.*, 20, 1923.

[11] J. Alden Mason, A Preliminary Sketch of the Yaqui Language, UC-PAAE 20, 1923.

[12] Francisco Pimentel, Cuadro Descriptivo y Comparativo de las Lenguas Indígenas de México (Mexico, 1862).

[13] Sapir, *op. cit.*

[14] Miguel Tellechea, Compendio Grammatical (México, 1826).

[15] J. B. de Velasco, Arte de la Lengua Cahita (México, 1737). Edited and reprinted by Eustaquio Buelna (Mexico, 1890).

[16] I quote Pimentel correctly, but he probably has these two reversed. Buckingham Smith gives *páue* for "eagle" in Heve or Eudeve; I have not been able to check up the Opata form.

[17] Paiute and Tepecano phonetic renderings have been slightly simplified.

[18] Probably identical with Sapir's *ï*.

[19] A. L. Kroeber, Uto-Aztecan Languages of Mexico, IA 8, 1934.

[20] Carl Sauer, The Distribution of Aboriginal Tribes and Languages in Northwestern Mexico, *ibid.*, 5, 1934; Aboriginal Population of Northwestern Mexico, *ibid.*, 10, 1935.

[21] B. L. Whorf, *Review of* Kroeber's Uto-Aztecan Languages of Mexico, AA, n.s., 37: 343–345, 1935. Also unpublished chart of Uto-Aztecan sound-shifts.

[22] P. Joseph de Ortega, Vocabulario en Lengua Castellano y Cora (Mexico, 1732).

[23] Leon Diguet, Idiome Huichol, SAP-J, n.s., 8:23–54, 1911.

[24] Carl Lumholtz, Unknown Mexico (New York, 1902); brief vocabularies of Tarahumare, Tubar, Cora, Huichol, Northern and Southern Tepehuane and Tepecano, 2:486, 487.

[25] As Dr. Robert M. Zingg and Mr. Charles Wisdom have just returned from a long period of work among the Huichol, we may now look forward to accurate ethnological and linguistic data on this interesting and neglected tribe.

[26] Juan B. Velasco, Arte de la Lengua Cahita (edited by Eustaquio Buelna, Mexico, 1890).

[27] H. José Ferrero, Pequeña Gramática y Diccionario de la Lengua Tarahumara (Mexico, 1920). We may hope that before long Bennett and Zingg will provide us with Tarahumar linguistic data recorded with more phonetic accuracy.

[28] Buckingham Smith, A Grammatical Sketch of the Heve Language, Translated from an Unpublished Spanish Manuscript, J. G. Shea's Library of American Linguistics, III (New York, 1861).

[29] K. Th. Preuss, Grammatik der Cora-Sprache, IJAL 7:1–84, 1932; Wörterbuch Deutsch-Cora, *ibid.*, 8:81–102, 1934.

[30] Edward Sapir, Southern Paiute, A Shoshonean Language; Texts of the Kaibab Paiutes and Uintah Utes; Southern Paiute Dictionary; Proceedings of the American Academy of Arts and Sciences, 65, 1–3, 1930–1931.

APPENDIX

By B. L. Whorf

Mason's classification as finally corrected and revised by him in the foregoing paper presents notable differences from the table included in his early paper (see page 184). It might be well to glance at the result in the form of a new table, into which I will take the liberty of injecting some few ideas of my own in terminology and grouping, although the table still remains essentially Mason's.

Group 1. "TARACAHITIAN"

Tarahumaran	*Cahitan*	*Opatan*
Tarahumar	Cahita	Opata
	dialects:	Eudeve (or Heve)
	Yaqui	Tubar
	Mayo	Concho
	Varohio (?)	Jova
	Tehueco	
	Acaxee, Cazcan, Zacateco	
	Nio, Zoe, Tepahue (perhaps)	

Group 2. "CORAN"

Cora   Huichol
       Guachichil

Group 3. "NAHUATLAN"

(see comment below)

Group 4. "PIMAN"

Type A	*Type B*
Tepecano	Upper Pima, Sobaipuri
Southern Tepehuan	Lower Pima, Nevome (Tecoripa?
Northern Tepehuan	Guayma?)
	Papago

It would be well to reject the name "Sonoran" entirely, even as a term for Group 1 above, because it is apt to lead to misconceptions born of its earlier usage. For this reason I have used the made-up composite word "Taracahitian" to designate Group 1, which is to all appearances a definite natural family or substock of the whole Uto-Aztecan stock. Coran and Piman are in the same way natural families, and Piman is notable among the three groups in the close mutual resemblance between all its languages. They are in fact litttle more than dialects of a single language, probably mutually intelligible as Mason supposes. Hence one must realize that the table undergoes a sudden change of scale in its bottom group. This whole Group 4, in spite of the number of names in it, if represented on the same scale as the rest of the table, should probably be allotted no more space than the Cahita language with its dialects Yaqui and Mayo receives therein.

It may be asked: Why have I added a fourth group, "Nahuatlan," one which Mason does not assume to treat at all, and inserted it withal into the very middle of the table, wedged between Coran and Piman? I have done this to emphasize that the three groups which Mason in 1923 separated out of a larger linguistic mass do not together constitute any tripartite unity; that there really is no "Sonoran" group in the older or Brintonian sense. The collection of languages with which Mason started was delimited in a purely accidental manner by Brinton's premature division of the stock into Shoshonean, Sonoran, and Nahuatlan. Of these only Nahuatlan is a natural group and that is because it is practically a group of dialects of one language. And Sonoran was the poorest of Brinton's divisions because it included Piman, a group which is poles apart from the other Uto-Aztecan languages of Mexico. I have inserted Nahuatlan between Piman and Coran to emphasize that Taracahitian and Coran are more like Nahuatlan than they are like Piman. Even with Piman dropped out, it would be impossible to draw a circle around the other three groups and consider that it enclosed a unity or a grouping that should have a separate name. After Group 3, Nahuatlan, should come in succession several of the as yet imperfectly classified groups in the United States (I except the "Plateau" or Ute-Chemehuevi-Kawaiisu group from the term "imperfectly"), and only toward the end of the list should we place Piman, as being one of the groups most unlike the groups with which we began the classification; an opposite pole, as it were, to such languages as Tarahumar, Cahita, Cora, and Huichol. Piman is such an opposite extreme in spite of the fact that at first glance Opata, Yaqui, and other "Taracahitian" languages might seem to have a quasi-resemblance to Piman in that they show in a limited way some of the consonantal shifts that Piman shows in an extreme way.

In Piman there is an extensive set of shifts applying to the U-A consonants in all positions and under all conditions: $*p > v, *w > g, *y > d, *kw > b, *ts > s, *s > h$. No Uto-Aztecan language, however, preserves the original consonant-scheme absolutely intact. If they do not make some of the above shifts, they make other shifts under certain special conditions, as in Tarahumar $*t > r$, or in Nahuatl $*p >$ zero. A great many of them shift $*p > v$ under special conditions too complicated to be here detailed. Yaqui shows $*kw > bw$ but the Tuxtla dialect of Nahuatl goes so far as to show $*kw > b$ like Piman; Tarahumar (Bennett's unpublished material) has $*kw > w$ and so has Tübatulabal in California. Opata (Pimentel's vocabulary) has $*y > d$ or g (*deguat* "la madre" $< *ye$—"mother"; *da* "irse muchos" $< *ya$ "go"), and $*w > gw$, with *gwo* either becoming secondarily *go* or else heard as *go* by the recorder (*gue* "grande" $< *we$ "great," *gue* "estar en pie uno" $< *wene$ "stand," *goko* "pino" $< *woko$, "pine," *gode* "dos" $< *woye, *wo$—"two"). In Opata $*kw$ apparently gives *gw* ("*gu*"), unless "*gu*" indeed really means *kw*, undistinguished by the recorder from *gw* (*guaka* "comida" $< *kwa$ "eat"). The word *paue* "eagle" is evidently a loan-word in Opata, for I believe it is the only instance of its kind. These likenesses in certain shifts to the set of Piman shifts do not make these languages closely related to Piman; in fact they have not much to say on the question of relationships. Piman shows a markedly different grammatical apparatus, a different kind of verb treatment, with its verb preceded by numerous prefixes; its whole set-up is distinct from that of the other groups shown in the table.

I see no objection to setting up Group 1 into three subgroups as Mason has done instead of lumping all its languages, like Kroeber, if one is making a finely graded classification, and provided one does not carry the distinctions too far. After all, there is a closer likeness between, say, Opata and Heve than between either and Yaqui, and Tarahumar is just a little bit off by itself, though such fine distinctions are no doubt less important than recognition of the common similarity that justifies our setting up the main group.

WETHERSFIELD, CONNECTICUT.

NOTES ON THE SANTA BARBARA CULTURE

By N. C. Nelson

Introduction

ARCHAEOLOGICALLY CONSIDERED, the strip of southern California coast from Point Conception to San Pedro, taken together with the adjacent Channel Island groups, constitutes one of the most unique and even somewhat puzzling culture provinces in North America. For one thing, it is geographically isolated—almost insulated; for another, it is not conspicuously favored—except perhaps climatically—by environmental conditions; and, for a third, it was inhabited by a hunting, fishing, and vegetable-gathering people of two distinct linguistic stocks. Nevertheless, a combination of more or less highly specialized material traits was here developed that has no exact parallel anywhere, though it reminds one of the Eskimo complex and in a limited sense of the North Pacific Coast culture.

The region in question abounds with easily discernible habitation sites—partly of the nature of shell heaps—as a rule more than ordinarily rich in artifact materials of a markedly varied nature and of a high order of workmanship. As a natural consequence numerous locations on both the islands and the mainland have been exploited and explored, so far as can be determined, since about 1870; although knowledge of the region's archaeological wealth did not become general until after the Wheeler Survey investigations in 1875, for when Stephen Powers wrote his Tribes of California in 1874 he obviously knew nothing about the area. At first it would seem to have been a Frenchman, Count de Cessac, who excavated and took away to Europe a considerable collection. Next, after the Wheeler Survey, it was chiefly local enthusiasts who dug to supply the market furnished by private collectors and the newly opened American museums. Finally, during the last two or three decades the field has been entered also by professional archaeologists and real investigation begun. The general result has been that rich Santa Barbara collections of one sort or another have by this time found their way into most—perhaps all—of our larger American museums and some material is to be seen also in several of the sister institutions of Europe.

Professor Kroeber has himself been concerned with the Santa Barbara culture area and its problems for more than twenty-five years and has in that time published at least two brief summaries of its outstanding traits, first in the Putnam Anniversary Volume in 1909 and later in his Handbook of the Indians of California, BAE-B 78, 1925. In the interval he has also accumulated for his Anthropology Museum at the University of California a vast amount of material data, the latest acquisition being made in proper fashion by his pupil and colleague, Ronald Olson, whose final report on the chronological development of the Santa Barbara or Channel Island culture is still awaiting publication. In the meantime the National Museum, the Museum of the American Indian (Heye Foundation), the Southwest Museum, and the Santa Barbara Museum of Natural History have also been active and have for the most part made their published contributions.

Another and for the time not unimportant contribution to the study of Channel Island prehistory might also have been made by the American Museum of Natural History at least as long ago as 1891. In that year there passed into this museum's permanent possession, as part of a large private collection, some 15,000 (not counting quantities of beads, chips, etc.) southern California archaeological specimens, derived mostly from the Channel Islands and the immediately adjacent mainland counties. This collection was accumulated by Mr. James Terry, of Hartford, Connecticut, who functioned as the American Museum's first Curator of Anthropology between the years 1891 and 1894, when his place was taken by Professor F. W. Putnam. The collection itself was made long previously, ranging over an interval of time between the years 1875 and 1887. The first portion of the material reached the Museum in 1880 and was exhibited as a loan, at least up to 1891. Since its purchase in that year it has been an on and off exhibit as conditions permitted, though it was mostly in storage when the writer took charge in 1912, since when it has again been liberally displayed as something out of the ordinary.

The Terry Collection is still practically intact, but its special importance and value have naturally decreased little by little as new and properly excavated data have been accumulated and published by other institutions. Mr. Terry furnished a fairly complete and satisfactory catalogue so far as description and general provenience go; but the specimens, being for the most part purchased from local exploiters, such as A. W. Barnard, Cyrus Barnard, and Stephen Bowers, are naturally not accompanied by field notes of any particular significance. The collector's diaries and some of his private correspondence covering the years in question have recently been made available to the writer, but unfortunately neither reveals anything of scientific importance. The present value of the collection inheres, therefore, largely in its exhibition qualifications, until such time as someone thoroughly familiar with the culture chooses to give it an adequate examination.

To that end I have long considered the advisability of bringing the Terry Collection to the attention of interested students and the present opportunity seems as good as any. Little by little in the interval some of the rarer type specimens in the collection have been reported upon and illustrated by others, but there are still a few which seem to merit attention. Aside from these few items it is not the purpose here to describe or illustrate the collection in detail. This has been done sufficiently well by F. W. Putnam and his coworkers in the Wheeler Survey report, vol. 7 (1879), by Geo. G. Heye, in Indian Notes and Monographs, vol. 7 (1921), and by others in a more limited way; while the first attempt at a chronological presentation of the culture was supplied by Ronald Olson, UC-PAAE 28, 1930.

The Terry Collection has been handled in whole or in part in a curatorial way a number of times during the past twenty-three years and its contents are therefore tolerably well known to the writer. Circumstances nevertheless make it impractical to check it completely for present purposes and thus give a first-hand descriptive account. In order, therefore, to present in brief form all the more essential features of the large body of material, I have simply gone over the collector's catalogue, accepted his descriptions as to identification of the objects, and separated them according to the given general localities and also the nature of the basic raw materials employed. The results appear in the table on pages 202–204.

GENERAL COMMENTS ON COLLECTION

European objects.—In addition to the nearly exhaustive inventory given in the foregoing table, the Terry Collection contains a number of foreign objects. Among these are mentioned several European items, including some 60,000 glass beads, mostly globular and of plain blue, green, red, and white colors, as well as a small series of larger specimens of the polychrome or mosaic type. There is also a bottle of green glass, a glazed pitcher, a porcelain plate, and portions of a leather sword sheath. Of bronze or some similar metallic alloy there are 2 knives, 1 plate, 2 bowls, 1 spindle, 2 pointed rods, and 1 sword—for the most part in broken or incomplete condition. Finally, there are some partly fragmentary iron objects, including a chisel and several axe blades. All of these items, incidentally, are credited to the mainland.

Eskimo objects.—Special mention must be made also of two or more objects seemingly of Eskimo origin. One is the harpoon foreshaft illustrated in figure 3e. It is made of semiporous or coarse-grained bone and comes from San Nicholas island. The other is a wooden spear thrower, also from San Nicholas island. It is of the general type illustrated by Mason as number 8 on plate 6 of the Smithsonian Report for 1884, and by Krause as number 23 on plate 2 in the same Report for 1904, except that it is less carefully made and its bone(?) "hook" is lost. A steatite object closely resembling a lip plug may be of the same origin, as may also the slate lance blade illustrated as figure 3a, though this seems less certain as there are no less than five specimens of the general type in the collection. The occurrence of these foreign aboriginal items I will not attempt to explain; but I have some recollection of having been told long ago by the late Hector Alliot of the Southwest Museum that he possessed several similar objects and had found some historical references indicating that a body of Alaskan natives were once brought to the Santa Barbara region for the purposes of hunting sea mammals.

Number and distribution of specimens.—Turning to the tabulated data of supposedly local origin, it must be said first of all that the indicated distribution in one sense probably means very little, inasmuch as we have no proof of systematic or exhaustive excavation anywhere. The majority of the mainland specimens, or some 6000 in all, came from Santa Barbara county. About 365 items are derived mostly from four specified sites in San Luis Obispo county, and Ventura county is represented by 450 specimens. All the rest are from the islands, as indicated.

TYPE AND LOCATION ANALYSIS OF SANTA BARBARA COLLECTION

	Mainland	S. Miguel Island	Sta. Rosa Island	Sta. Cruz Island	S. Nicholas Island	Sta. Catalina Island
Chipped stone						
Animal forms (fetiches)...	1	69	...	...	9	4
Arrow points.............	154	190	...	...	68	11
Blanks..................	3	...	...	...	...	...
Bunts...................	2	1	...	...	1	...
Cores...................	2	...	...	...	...	...
Drills or flake scarifiers...	48	2409	...	...	16	2
Fishhook (?).............	1	...	...	...	...	...
Knives..................	459	935	...	...	476	29
Knives hafted in wood....	...	...	...	...	13	...
Picks, triangular cross-section..................	4	6	...	...	3	...
Scrapers................	1	...	...	...	2	...
Spear points.............	523	236	...	...	45	6
Ground stone						
Arrow straighteners......	27	...	...	...	5	...
Balls...................	5	...	...	...	4	...
Beads...................	346	689	2	...	97	2
Bowls, steatite and sandstone..................	100	...	...	4	7	...
Carvings................	1	1	...	...	3	...
Charm stones or plummet shapes..................	127	...	3	...	89	...
Chisels.................	1	1	...	...	...	...
Club heads, subspherical and disk shaped........	100	45	1	1	410	4
Cups....................	53	1	...	1	52	4
Dishes..................	23	...	...	...	11	...
Drill (?) mounted in redwood shaft (see fig. 3b).	...	...	...	...	1	...
Drill points, plummet shaped..................	42	...	...	...	185	...
Figurines: whale, bird, etc.	24	8	...	1	19	9
Fishhooks...............	...	...	...	...	3	...
Game stones.............	2	...	...	...	...	...
Hammerstones............	118	...	...	...	1	...
Implements..............	2	...	...	...	...	1
Ladles..................	2	...	...	...	4	...
Lance points of slate (fig. 3a)...................	4	...	...	...	1	...
Manos..................	70	...	...	...	1	...
Metates.................	3	...	...	...	...	...
Mauls...................	2	...	...	...	...	...
Mortars.................	230	4	...	...	54	5
Ollas of steatite.........	102	1	...	...	1	...
Ornaments...............	...	...	...	...	4	...
Pendants................	33	...	2	...	48	...
Pestles..................	643	1	...	...	3	...
Pins or spikes...........	10	1	...	...	3	...
Pipes, straight and bent..	97	1	...	1	24	3
Rings...................	...	...	...	...	4	...
Saws or polishers........	19	1	...	...	23	...
Spoons..................	2	1	...	...	7	...
Spindle whorls...........	5	...	...	...	...	...
Tools, mostly pointed....	10	...	...	...	3	...
Tortilla plates...........	49	...	...	...	1	...
Tubes, plain and ornamented..................	2	...	...	...	1	1
Vessels, boat shaped......	...	...	...	...	4	1

TYPE AND LOCATION ANALYSIS OF SANTA BARBARA COLLECTION—*Continued*

	Mainland	S. Miguel Island	Sta. Rosa Island	Sta. Cruz Island	S. Nicholas Island	Sta. Catalina Island
Bone						
Awls of bird bone	42	48	...	...	70	...
Awls of fishbone	4	2	...	...	1	...
Awls of mammal bone	196	44	...	7	47	...
Barbs for hook or spear	35	7	...	...	180	...
Beads	8	25	...	...	1	...
Charm (fossil bone)	1	...	...	...	...	...
Chisels	23	26	...	...	173	...
Cups	1	1	...	...	...	...
Daggers	4	...	...	...	...	...
Dishes from whale vertebrae	10	...	...	...	2	...
Disks with central perforation	5	...	...	...	8	...
Epiphyses of vertebrae with central perforation	1	...	...	...	5	...
Fishhooks and other hooks	13	1	...	1	2	...
Fish vertebrae ornamented with shell beads	7	...	...	...	...	...
Harpoon points with barbs	3	...	...	...	13	...
Implements, mostly pointed	476	115	1	33	117	...
Insignia of power (fig. 3c)	...	2	...	...	7	...
Knives, with and without handles	14	...	...	...	1	...
Knife hafts covered with asphalt and shell beads	2	...	...	...	...	...
Lance heads and points	12	...	...	...	16	...
Needles	3	...	...	...	10	...
Ornaments (eagle claws covered with shells)	7	...	...	...	3	...
Pendants of bear and sealion claws	15	2	...	...	7	...
Pointed implements of penis bones	35	4	...	1	15	...
Spoons	1	...	...	1	...	...
Tubes, some ornamented with shell beads	281	77	...	...	8	1
Whistles, bird and mammal bones	42	13	...	...	40	1
Worked and ornamented horn	2	...	...	...	...	...
Shell						
Beads	5954 (20 lots)	36,492 (9 lots)	...	...	39,909 (23 lots)	3000 (1 lot)
Crescents (abalone)	41	24	...	...	6	...
Cups	1	...	...	...	...	...
Dentalium shells	...	...	...	...	...	46 (lot)
Disks, perforated	96	14	...	...	24	...
Earrings	...	...	...	...	2	...
Fishhooks	159	16	...	1	316	...
Ornaments, irregular	94	90	...	1	996	...
Paint dishes	3	...	...	...	...	...
Pendants	169	83	...	...	68	3
Rings	8	7	...	...	16	...
Squares, perforated	26	84	...	...	...	...
Strips, perforated	47	3	...	...	...	...
Worked limpet shells	311	265	...	...	20	...

Type and Location Analysis of Santa Barbara Collection—*Concluded*

	Mainland	S. Miguel Island	Sta. Rosa Island	Sta. Cruz Island	S. Nicholas Island	Sta. Catalina Island
Wood						
Board or plank fragment..	1	...	...	...	...	...
Knife handles............	...	1	...	...	11	...
Ladle....................	...	...	...	...	1	...
Arrow shaft..............	...	...	...	...	1	...
Dart foreshafts with bone barbs (fig. 3d)..........	...	...	...	...	1	...
Miscellaneous						
Awl handle of asphaltum..	1	...	...	...	...	...
Basket impression on asphaltum..............	...	1	...	...	...	...
Bottle of basketry covered with asphaltum........	...	1	...	...	...	...
Brushes (soaproot?)......	2	...	...	...	...	...
Clay head, burnt.........	...	...	...	...	1	...
Cup of black adobe.......	1	...	...	...	...	...
Grass rope and fragment of weaving..............	1	...	...	...	...	...
Gypsum spalls, mostly unworked...............	4	...	...	...	...	...
Jars of red clay...........	5	...	...	...	1	...
Ornamented stones.......	6	...	...	...	23	...
Pebbles with asphaltum..	30	...	...	...	127	...
Potsherds................	2	...	...	...	...	...
Quartz crystals with asphaltum..............	23	...	...	...	2	...
Red and black paint......	+	+	+	+	+	+
Seeds....................	+	+	+	+	+	+
Skin pouch with black paint...................	1	...	...	...	...	...
Whistle of baked adobe...	1	...	...	...	...	...

EXPLANATION OF FIGURE ON PAGE 205.

Fig. 3. Unique or rare implements and ornaments from the Santa Barbara culture area. *a*, lance point of slate with serrated margins, thin and delicate, probably ceremonial, from Santa Barbara county. *b*, supposed drill made of redwood shaft set with plummet-shaped point of coquina, from San Nicholas island. *c*, spatulate implement of bone with concave base and transverse curvature, from San Nicholas island. *d*, dart foreshaft of wood with bone point-and-barb, cemented with asphaltum, from San Nicholas island. *e*, harpoon foreshaft with slit for point, forked barbs, perforated for hafting and for cord, from San Nicholas island. *f*, animal figurine (?) chipped from flint, from San Miguel island. *g*, ornament of worked limpet shell in the form of a ring set in asphaltum and decorated with shell beads, from San Miguel island. *h*, button or bead of clamshell, with perforations meeting at a wide angle, from San Miguel island. *i*, tubular bead of clamshell with incised ornamentation, from San Nicholas island. Scale: one-half natural size.

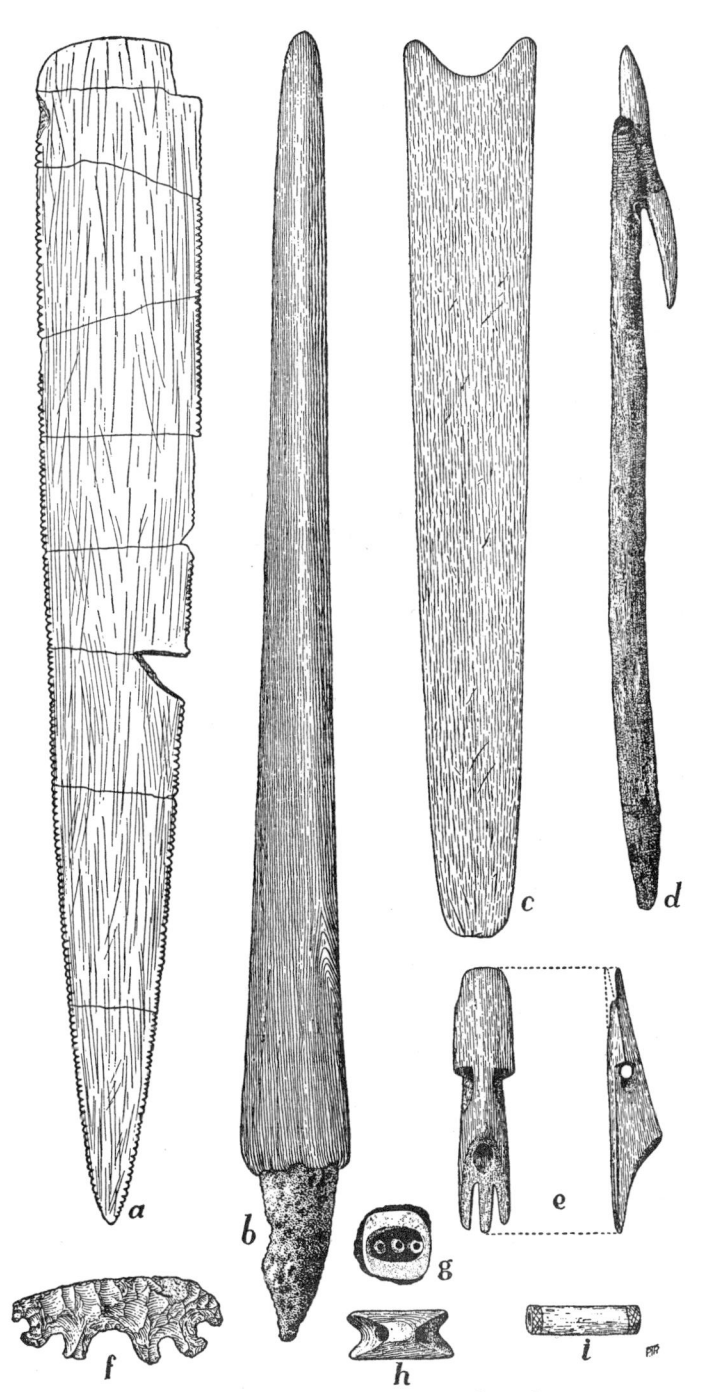

Fig. 3. Implements and ornaments from the
Santa Barbara culture area.

Validity of collector's identifications.—As to the recorded type series, it is again to be admitted that the collector's identifications are not always precise or even faintly indicative of what the designations stand for. Under "chipped stone," for example, there are many more cores, blanks, and scrapers than appear in the list. Likewise there is a large number of flakes, in particular a variety of minute prismatic forms of brown-colored chert, mostly sharp pointed, which may have served for incising or scarifying, but which Mr. Terry has called "drills." Again, under "ground stone" the collector has often used such expressions as "tools," "implements," "ornaments," "balls," "carvings," "game stones," "saws," etc., without clearly indicating what is meant. Incidentally, the well-known "hooked stones," of which there are several from Santa Cruz, San Nicholas, and Santa Catalina islands, as well as from the mainland, have been hidden away under the designation "bird stone fetiches" and therefore appear in the table under "figurines." In like manner, from among the varied forms of bone implements the collector has singled out a thin, oblong, subtriangular blade with a concave base and sometimes transversely curved (see fig. 3c) and called it "insignia of power," though more than likely it served a practical purpose.

By way of final comment, it may be worth while to add a few explanatory remarks on each of the tabulated major artifact groups.

Chipped stone items.—The chipped stone series is of a relatively high order of workmanship both as to outline and general finish. Chert, chalcedony, and obsidian (including the mottled red and black variety) have served as the chief sources of raw material. Some of the larger and heavier blades, neatly symmetrical examples of which measure up to 3.5×7.5 inches, which may have served either as knives or spear points (probably the former), still retain asphaltum on the base end, showing that they were once firmly hafted. Certain other blades are extra long and slender but thick dorsoventrally, as may be seen on plate 1 of the Wheeler Survey report. A number of knives of different sizes still remain hafted in well preserved wooden handles. The arrow points and some of the moderate-size spear points (perhaps knives) exhibit a variety of basal modifications, such as pointed, convex, concave, and stemmed. Barbs, often extra long and delicate, are common. The side-notched form is very rare, and the notches occur near the middle of the blade and not at the base as is usual elsewhere. The several picks of triangular cross-section, presumably for working steatite, are remarkably like the picks of the early European neolithic, and the same may be said for certain of the drill points, also of triangular cross-section, almost identical with the otherwise unique triangular file-shaped arrow points of the Baltic region. The so-called "animal forms" (see fig. 3f) may be saws or surgical instruments, as has been suggested, but at least some of them are remarkably realistic animal representations.

Ground stone objects.—The ground and polished stone inventory is notably rich and varied and by far the bulkiest of the lots. Steatite and sandstone predominate but other rocks of a more nearly granitic character are also represented. Most conspicuous is a large series of well-worked mortars and pestles of considerable range in size and shape. The mortars appear both in hemispherical and in truncated cone shapes and the pestles come with and without flanges. Both are occasionally decorated with inlaid shell disk beads. Ollas or jar-shaped cooking pots of steatite are next in bulk and after these comes a considerable series of shapely hemispherical bowls with either round or flat bottoms, partly of sandstone but mostly of steatite. The latter are as a rule highly polished; several are decorated by incised straight-line geometric patterns, while a few are inlaid with round and angular bits of shell. A small number of the steatite vessels are of oval, boat-shaped, and scoop-shaped outlines and at least a few are in the form of truncated cones. The tobacco pipes are mostly of the straight tubular variety, but a few elbow and other aberrant forms are present and at least a few of them bear incised ornamentation. One specimen is provided with two longitudinal partly detached prongs on opposite sides of the pipe body and rising to the top level of the bowl. Under the designation "club heads" appears a large number of perforated stones of considerable range in size and shape, some being subspherical and others more nearly disk-shaped and difficult to distinguish from what might be spindle whorls. The larger ones are often highly polished on one side and were presumably weights for digging sticks. The charm stones also show considerable range in size and shape as well as to manner of suspension. A series of similarly plummet-shaped objects made of a finely broken and cemented shell formation—coquina—have been called "drill points" and may conceivably have served for drilling pipes and for perforating the numerous club-head items. One such imperfect specimen occurs, still cemented in a tapering wooden shaft, and is illustrated, though not now for the first time, by figure 3b. Under "figurines," it may be repeated, are placed a series of the characteristic "hooked stones," the collector's impression being that they resemble bird heads; but most of the "figurines" are effigies, partly of the killer whale and partly no doubt of fishes. Grooved and notched sinkers—perhaps in some cases anchor stones—are present in the collection, though not indicated as such in the table. Pendants occur in considerable variety: disk-shaped, oblong with round or flat cross-section, and either knobbed or perforated for suspension. Several are incised with crisscross patterns and a few are inlaid in the usual fashion with small shell disk beads. Beads, finally, appear in a variety of forms, such as globular, compressed globular, barrel shaped, lozenge- or plummet-shaped, cylindrical (with and without deep transverse grooves) and ordinary disk-shaped. All the remaining items in the table speak largely for themselves and need no further description.

Bone implements.—The large series of artifacts derived from bird, mammal, and fish bones contains a few groups in need of special comment. The comprehensive designation "implements," for example, covers a variety of forms, mostly of uncertain purpose. Among these are many stout, straight, or curved whale ribs, up to two feet in length, bluntly pointed at one or both ends and doubtless serviceable for a variety of purposes, such as root digging, prying abalones off the rock, and so on. There are also numerous shorter single- and double-pointed implements of flat, curved mammal ribs. A few rather short mammal ribs of roundish cross-section are bluntly pointed at one end and may have served as pressure chippers. Under the same designation falls also a large series of extra long, slender, tubular bird bones pointed at one end and which conceivably may have served as hairpins. Very much like these are also a considerable number provided with a slantwise point at both ends, the purpose of which is hard to guess, though they might conceivably have been used for splaying fish while drying. Finally, the term "implement" covers a large series of small, straight, or slightly curved and double-pointed objects of rounded cross-section, 1 to 4 inches long. These are sometimes called "gorge hooks" but may also have served merely as barbs for fishhooks or prongs for harpoons by having been lashed to a shaft or stem after the manner illustrated in figure 3d.

The rest of the tabulated inventory speaks largely for itself, but a few explanatory remarks may not be amiss. The collection contains a number of neatly worked, symmetrical, stemmed knife or dagger blades; but the wooden handles into which the stems are fitted look suspiciously modern. The harpoon points are all of the simple pointed base variety with one to six barbs along one side. Several plain round-sectioned lance foreshafts and arrow foreshafts are present and one of the latter terminates in a flat, double-barbed point. The oblong, triangular round-pointed blades with concave base, illustrated in figure 3c, have already been mentioned, and closely related to them are also a number of more simple spatulate forms, suggestively chisel-like. One interesting specimen is a stout, oblong, rectangular, cross-sectioned bone with a hole through the middle, suggestive of the Eskimo arrow straightener. The tubular bones completely covered with an inlay of small shell disk beads set in asphaltum range in length up to fully 6 inches and can scarcely have served other than ceremonial or decorative purposes. The whistle comes in two varieties or sizes, one of bird bone and the other of deer bone. Lastly, the collection contains one single flute with four vents, very similar to those typical of the Southwest Pueblo ruins.

Shell objects.—As would be expected, numerous shells and shell artifacts are found in the collection. The shell species used include abalone, clam, pecten, limpet, cowrie, dentalium, olivella, and other univalves of uncertain identities. Some few of the bivalve forms have served as natural containers for paint, asphaltum, etc. In the same manner a number of univalve shells (olivella, etc.) have been used in practically unaltered form as beads or pendants by merely having the tip of the whorl rubbed off or a hole pricked through the side for facilitating stringing or suspension. The artificially designed items—largely of abalone shell—are for the most part ornaments of endless variety of forms, chiefly beads, pendants, and rings; but fishhooks or hooklike objects will be seen to be fairly numerous. Among the decorative objects are first of all some washer-like rings, a few oval pendants, and a number of rather large, oval, longitudinally perforated beads—all of clamshell and all ornamented with punctate designs in the form of triangles, as well as straight and meandering lines. Of special interest is a button-like object illustrated, I believe, for the first time as figure 3*h*, of which there are several specimens from San Miguel island. The indicated perforations meet at a wide angle. Figure 3*g* is a limpet shell ring set in asphaltum and decorated within the central area by an inlay of three shell disk beads. It is a type which has been previously figured in the Museum of the American Indian report, also from San Miguel island. There are several of these specimens in the Terry Collection, but whether they are complete in themselves or are merely fragmentary parts of something else does not appear. Figure 3*i* is merely a sample of tubular beads of clamshell, the extremities of which are ornamented with crosshatchings. For the rest the numerous beads are mostly of the round disk variety, either flat or concave.

Wooden objects.—Naturally enough, the collection contains but few items of such perishable material as wood. Nevertheless they are present, but all may of course be of relatively late date. The tabulated identifications are sufficiently explicit, except perhaps for the last item, the dart foreshafts, of which one of two examples is illustrated by figure 3*d*. The foreshaft only is of wood and is pointed at the base for insertion in the shaft proper, while the front portion is provided with a lateral groove into which a bone point-and-prong piece is fitted. This bone element is not one of the ordinary straight "gorge hooks," because the prong portion diverges noticeably from the axis of the point-end portion. Both extremities of the foreshaft retain portions of the asphaltum used in fastening the three parts of the weapon together, and traces of string windings are plainly visible. Both of the available specimens are from San Nicholas island, as is also the basal portion of a delicate wooden arrow, evidently picked up on the surface.

Miscellaneous items.—Little more can be said about the Terry Collection in such a brief compass. The indicated miscellaneous items speak for themselves, with the exception perhaps of the pottery, and these items unfortunately are not now, it seems, present in the collection. The exception is a small seemingly burnt clay bowl or dish and some broken pipes, the real ceramic character of which is doubtful.

In conclusion it can only be regretted that the large and it seems fairly representative Santa Barbara collection has been lying so long undescribed and that the task could not even now be more adequately done. It is the writer's hope, nevertheless, that this brief delineation may result in bringing it to the attention of those specifically concerned about this interesting seacoast culture.

AMERICAN MUSEUM OF NATURAL HISTORY,
NEW YORK CITY.

SOME TRADING CUSTOMS OF THE CHILKAT TLINGIT

By Ronald L. Olson

THE FOLLOWING is a description of the trading which was regularly carried on between the Chilkat villages and the bands (or tribes) of Athapascans who occupied the territory across the coastal range in the extreme northwest corner of British Columbia and southern Yukon Territory.[1] It is based on information obtained from Joe Wright ("Skookum Joe") of the Chilkat village of Yandestá'kyah, and refers primarily to the decades before the Klondike gold rush. The Tlingit tribes of the coast certainly knew of the existence of the interior tribes centuries before the voyages of discovery by whites, and, according to tradition, carried on an intermittent trade with them, exchanging mainly dried fish and eulachon oil for furs and dressed skins. The coming of the fur traders stimulated this trade to a marked degree and at the same time brought about a change in the type of goods moving inland, European wares displacing fish and oil.

The Tlingit refer to the Athapascans as Gunána' (people of the interior) but distinguish the various bands or tribes. Culturally, the Tlingit were decidedly superior to the tribes of the hinterland and quite naturally regarded them as inferiors who were easy dupes in what was a skin game in more ways than one. According to Tlingit tradition the various Athapascan bands had been discovered by certain clan ancestors who thereby gained the right to trade with the band in question and the right to the trade route. These rights were passed from uncle to nephews (or other kin) so that the rights came to be the property of the maternal clan. Thus at the village of Klàkwan the Ganaxtedi'h, a Raven moiety clan, and the Dàklàwedi'h, an Eagle moiety clan, "owned" the trail leading over Chilkat pass to Kusawa (kusawa'a') lake. The Klokwaha'dih, a Raven clan of Yandestá'kyah and Chilkoot villages, "owned" the trail leading from Dyea (daiye'h, bay) over the Chilkoot pass to Lake Bennett and Tagish lake. In theory, members of other clans did not share in these rights. In practice there were few restrictions on trade. Those who belonged to the clans mentioned inevitably had blood relatives and relatives by marriage in the other clans and their requests to participate in the trading could not well be refused. The leader of an expedition, however, was invariably a chief of one of the "owning" clans, and most of the participants were of these clans.

It was customary to make one or two trips to the interior per year, usually in the middle of winter when the deep snow of the passes was packed hard by high winds. Each of the house chiefs (or elders) of the Dàklàwedi'h and Ganaxtedi'h clans usually mustered five to ten younger men of the household

---

[1] The data presented here were gathered during the summers of 1933 and 1934, incidental to research on the social structures of the Tlingit tribes, financed in part by a Grant-in-Aid from the Social Science Research Council.

[211]

to serve as packers for his goods. Often these were his sister's sons who had taken up residence at the uncle's house, or at any rate were his clansmen. The trading expedition commonly numbered upward of one hundred men. (Women seldom or never made the trip.) About three out of five men carried ordinary trade goods; one in five was detailed to carry food, while the house chiefs carried packs of special trade goods and luxuries. Usually the bulk of the freight consisted of firearms, powder, shot, dress goods, blankets, iron tools, etc.

The party traveled by canoe a few miles up the Chilkat river, then took to the foot trail over Chilkat pass. Heavily loaded as they were, it took upward of twenty days to reach Kusawa lake. The Athapascans knew the approximate time of arrival (arrangements having been agreed upon at the conclusion of the previous year's trading) and concentrated at their permanent village for this, the greatest event of their year.

It is necessary to explain at this point that each leader or house-chief in the Tlingit party had a "trading partner" (akyàk! a'wuh, lit., "my own man") among the Athapascans.

Partners were always of the same clan (or at any rate of the same moiety).[2] The Tlingit, upon arrival, ranged themselves in a line at the edge of the village. The men of the village formed a line facing them a few paces distant so that each elder stood opposite his trading partner. The villagers then did a dance accompanied by a song, music being furnished by a drum. The local chief then made a speech, given to me as, "I am glad you have come. My people have been getting ready [etc.]." The Tlingit ranking chief (his partner) answered, "Yes, we are here. I remembered that we promised to come this month." The Tlingit chief then asked for the drum and his party sang a song and danced.

Each householder of the village then escorted his partner and his partner's men to his house. As soon as they were inside, the Tlingit took all the packs except his own and the food pack and gave them to his partner, saying, "Here, my partner, these are for you." The head of the house took them and, without examining them, placed them in a small storage room in a corner of the log house.

The two chiefs then took the seats of honor at the rear of the house, with the host's wife at his right. The others ranged themselves on either side. The Tlingit chief then went to his own pack, took out a bundle of leaf tobacco, and, after carefully closing the bag, gave the tobacco to his host. The host and his wife smoked while the others of the household prepared food for the guests. After they had eaten, the guest chief ordered one of his men to open the food pack. This usually contained such exotic items as rice, sugar, tea, and coffee. The Tlingit men then cooked a meal for their hosts.

After a time the entire village and the guests assembled for such games as

---

[2] My informant stated that the people of Kusawa lake had two clans or moieties, the Dàklawedi'h (Eagle side) and Ganaxtedi'h (Raven moiety). These are names of Tlingit clans, and I was unable to learn whether these were the actual names or merely equivalents of the respective Tlingit groups.

blanket-tossing in a moose skin and broad-jump contests in which both men and women joined. (The chiefs, however, never participated.) During and after these games the Tlingit men paired off with the females of the village and "took them into the woods." It was said that neither husbands nor parents ever objected to this. Perhaps it may be regarded as a variant of the "Arctic hospitality" of the Eskimo and some of the more northerly Athapascan tribes.

Two or three days usually elapsed before actual trading was begun. During this time the travelers rested, renewed acquaintances, and so on. The host and wife secretly inspected the contents of the gift packs during this interval. The host's son or nephew was then told, "Tomorrow you go." This was an order to go to the hidden cache of furs (usually in an elevated storehouse) some miles distant and bring in the catch for the year. Most of the furs were piled in a corner of the house but some of the finer ones were hidden away in the storeroom. The chiefs again took the seats of honor and a son or nephew of the host started piling furs in front of the guest chief. "It used to make us glad," said my informant, "when we saw that half the pile of furs was worth ten times the value of what we had brought." When the host thought enough furs had been given, he said, "What do you say, partner?" If there was no answer he piled on more furs.

This was the crucial phase of the trading. On the one hand the host did not wish to offend his partner by appearing stingy and on the other the guest was careful not to seem greedy. When reluctance to give more furs became evident the guest chief went to his pack and took out such gifts as cloth shirts and dresses, bundles of leaf tobacco, vermilion, and so on, but carefully left other things in the pack. These gifts he distributed to various members of the household. The host thereupon ordered that more furs be added to the trade pile, and at last gave the word to throw all the remaining skins on the heap. He then asked, "What is that which you have left in your pack, partner?" When shown the remaining gifts he said, "Put it on my side." He then went to the corner storeroom, where he had concealed some exceptionally fine furs. These he gave to his guest. His wife would produce moccasin boots and a caribou-skin shirt, which she gave to the guest to put on. Finally she usually gave him a robe of ermine skins for his wife. It is noteworthy that the final exchanges involved a pseudo giving back and forth, each party knowing full well that he would receive more.

During the time that trading was in progress the younger men of both parties were careful to take no part in the proceedings. At best the young Tlingit were permitted to take along only a few articles of their own. These they might trade with the young men of the village, but this was done semi-secretly at meetings out-of-doors. Such unofficial exchangings often led to the formation of "partnerships" in later life.

When the trading which had been going on in each house was completed, everyone feasted. After the feasting, as many as could get in assembled in the largest house in the village—that of the chief. There the Tlingit ranged themselves on one side of the room, the villagers on the other. Speeches were made and the hosts were requested by the guests to teach them several songs. These the Tlingit later sang at festivals in their own villages, it being considered a great thing among them to be able to sing a "new" song or perform a "new" dance. After a day or two spent mastering the new songs the Tlingit party made ready for the return. Each host was expected to supply his house guests with food for the trip, and his wife often presented them with a quantity of spruce gum for chewing. Arrangements for a subsequent trading expedition were completed and the party set out for home.

* * * * * * * * * * *

The people of Yandestà'kyah and Chilkoot villages traveled to the interior by the easier Dyea (Chilkoot pass) route. The trip to the head of Lake Bennett took about four days. A fleet of umiak-like boats was kept there and in them they voyaged to the foot of the lake where lived the Tagish. (These boats consisted of a frame covered over with sewed walrus hides. The hides were secured in trade with the Tlingit of Yakutat. I know of no other reference to the use of skin boats by the Tlingit.) Some members of the expedition often proceeded (by means of rafts) to the village of the Tŭtkenkwa'n (King Salmon People), a day's journey farther on. Occasionally they went on to the Xlek! kakwa'n (Paint People) or even to the country of the Ayan in the vicinity of Dawson.

* * * * * * * * * * *

In the trade between Tlingit and Athapascans the former held a decided advantage. As middlemen they knew the value of the goods they exchanged in terms of the value of the goods they received. They gave, that is, only a small measure of powder for a red-fox pelt, or a single leaf of tobacco for a marten skin. For the latter they would receive a blanket from European traders. The Athapascans seldom ventured down to the Coast and then usually made the trip merely out of curiosity. The docility or downright humility of the Athapascans in the face of the Tlingit sense of superiority made them poor bargainers. Furthermore, the potlatch system of the Tlingit made them greedy for gain, and trade with the interior tribes offered a quick road to wealth. Tlingit men often married women of the interior tribes for the sole purpose of securing greater trade advantages. Such women usually remained with their kinsmen and saw their husbands only once or twice a year. These men usually had a wife and family in their home villages but "only a foolish woman would object to her husband's having another wife in the interior country. It meant that he would be able to bring home more furs."

Trade between the various Tlingit tribes and villages involved few formalities, perhaps precisely because it was domestic rather than foreign. "Trading partners" and other institutionalized features of Tlingit-Athapascan trade were unknown in intervillage or intertribal trading among the Tlingit themselves.

UNIVERSITY OF CALIFORNIA,
BERKELEY, CALIFORNIA.

WIDE-LOOM FABRICS OF THE EARLY NAZCA PERIOD

By Lila M. O'Neale

IT HAS BEEN ASSUMED, because there appears to be no direct evidence to the contrary, that a large-size loom was unknown in Peru before Spanish times. "The looms found and described are all of the type attached to the weaver's belt, or small setups for special purposes. The indirect evidence of the fabrics indicates the same. These almost always fall below 30 in. or 75 cm. in width. Of the 650 pieces examined, only 15 were woven wider than this in a single setup; these measure 32½ in. to 47½ in."[1] Two methods were used to form garments of greater breadth: sewing together narrow pieces, and loom-joining strips by weft manipulation, or by interlocking with an extra length of yarn[2]—"a procedure that would certainly not have been followed by anyone acquainted with a large frame loom. This simplicity of the basic machinery for weaving would be expectable in an early period."[3]

It is now certain that we must recast our opinions to take into account a garment of the mantle type which even by the standards of the modern power loom merits recognition as a wide-loom fabric. The specimen consists of five fragments listed under three catalogue numbers in the Cahuachi Nazca collection excavated in 1926 by A. L. Kroeber for the Field Museum of Natural History. Textile finds from the Cahuachi site are definitely assignable to the Early Nazca period by the associated pottery. These five fragments, four of which are corners showing loomstring ends and side selvages, fit together to form a rectangle at least 6 ft. 8 in. long by 5 ft. 5 in. wide (fig. 4). If more evidence than the reconstructed rectangle were needed to prove that the fragments were originally one web, the similar yarn counts per inch, the identical designs, and the colors of the decorative yarns could be cited. The overall dimensions warpwise by weftwise are as follows:

Specimen number	Length in inches	Width in inches
Aj-10 171218a	38	48½
Aj-10 171219a[1]	30½	40
Aj-10 171219a[2]	12	18
Aj-10 171219a[3]	3½	7
Aj-10 171220	26	33

The mantle is referred to throughout this paper by one number, 171220.

The original breadth of the garment, 5 ft. 5 in., gives it a notable place among Peruvian fabrics so far published upon, but it shares honors with two specimens of much less artistic pretension, mummy wrappings from the Paracas Necropolis. Before proceeding to a detailed analysis of the Cahuachi Nazca mantle, it is desirable to present what is known of the Paracas specimens.

---

[1] Lila M. O'Neale and A. L. Kroeber, Textile Periods in Ancient Peru, UC-PAAE 28:29, fn. 14, 1930. Cited as: UC-PAAE 28.

[2] *Idem.*, fn. 15.   [3] *Idem.*, 30.

216   *Lila M. O'Neale*

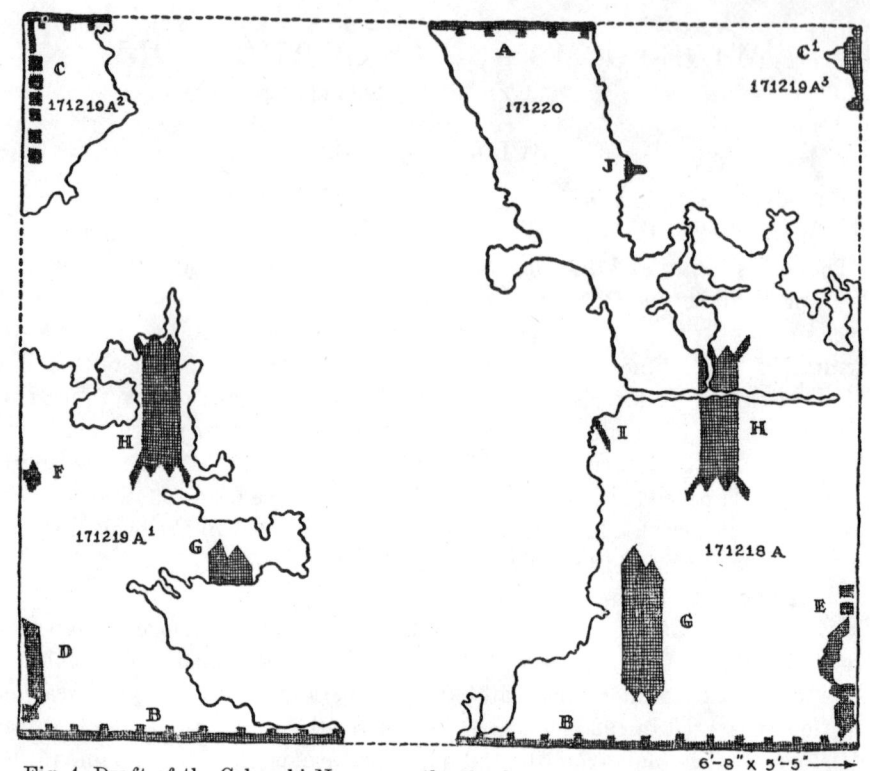

Fig. 4. Draft of the Cahuachi Nazca mantle, the fragments of which are catalogued as numbers 171218, 171219, and 171220. The draft shows the placement of border and main design units. The letters indicate the motives found in the garment.

In August, 1932, a large mummy bundle in the Museo Nacional in Lima was opened, and its garments and artifacts singly removed. Each step in the process was recorded by two scientifically minded members of the Museum staff who have recently made their data available.[4] Among the larger cloths from Paracas Mummy 217 is a specimen described as follows:

15 (12–8806). Wrapping (*envoltura*) completely carbonized; the fragments not pulverized are dark brown and indicate that the width of the piece was 230 cm. (7 ft. 7 in.). The length cannot be determined owing to the bad condition; nevertheless, it was more than 4 m. inasmuch as the cloth takes more than two turns around the bundle. Plain weave, coarse; 29–31 warps, 11 wefts per inch; the wefts are combined in pairs, at times in threes, and are double yarns of soft twist. Also some of the warps appear grouped in pairs.[5]

The writers continue: "It was possible to follow the yarns of the weft the whole distance of the width of the weaving (230 cm.), and to establish that they bent (*doblaban*) at the edges to return in the ordinary manner. It was evident, then, that in the present case no extra yarns had been introduced. In order to clinch this observation, we have also examined a similar cloth (specimen 17 from Mummy 382: 690 cm. long by 250 cm. wide [8 ft. 3 in.]; 30

[4] E. Yacovleff and J. C. Muelle, Un fardo funerario de Paracas, Revista del Museo Nacional, 3:63–153, 1934.
[5] *Idem*, 77; pl. 1e, f.

warps, 12–17 wefts per inch), but well-preserved, arriving at the same conclusion."[6]

There is no more doubt that Kroeber's Cahuachi Nazca specimen is a single-web fabric than there is doubt concerning the Paracas wrappings. Fragment 171218a together with fragment 171220 form the complete breadth. The pieces are irregular, as shown by the draft of the reconstructed garment (fig. 4), but not an inch of the original width is missing. A straight tear warpwise of the web beginning at a point about 22 in. from the end and extending to within 2½ in. of the loomstrings divides one rectangular embroidered motive into two unequal portions. A second tear weftwise through the smaller portion divides specimen 171220 from 171218a, leaving on the former a bit of the embroidery which exactly completes the rectangle. To add to the certainty that the two fragments were once one in spite of the difference in their side borders, there are similar dark stains and generous splotches of yellow paint (?) on either side of the lengthwise tear. Careful scrutiny under a microscope has failed to arouse the slightest suspicion of a join of any type.

The two Paracas mummy wrappings, remarkable from the technological standpoint if from no other, together with the mantle 171220 are the most startling representatives of a group of Early-period fabrics exceeding the average breadth of weavings made, presumably, on belt looms. Others of the group referred to in the quotation above are given in the order of their widths:[7]

Site	Specimen number	Complete length (inches)	Complete width (inches)
Cahuachi, Nazca	171305b	?	36
Cahuachi, Nazca	171306	124	36½–38½
Majoro, Nazca	170465a	?	37
Cahuachi, Nazca	171265	48	38
Cahuachi, Nazca	171222	48	41½
Cahuachi, Nazca	171216	57	47½
Cahuachi, Nazca	171182a	56	48

The construction of pieces with such dimensions demonstrates that we have, indeed, only begun to discover the range of skills and accomplishments evidenced by the work of the Early-period weavers. How did they manage set-ups of the lengths and widths found at Paracas and Cahuachi? A loom attached to the weaver's belt in itself imposes certain definite restrictions on the width of the finished web. Because the weaver sits at the center of the lower loom bar, assuming she works alone, the woven fabric can be no wider than the greatest distance between her outstretched finger tips. In actual manipulation of the loom the added reach gained by swaying from side to side is little advantage. Regardless of the shuttle device, or the manner in which the weft yarn is carried, it must be started by hand from alternate sides through the opened space between the odd and even warps.

Theoretically, a weaver can manage a warp setup as broad as her longest

---

[6] *Idem.*, 79–80.   [7] UC-PAAE 28: fn. 14.

reach. Practically, it seems unlikely that she would attempt it. Length of reach does not solve all the problems. There is shedding, picking, and battening; in other words, separating the warps; passing the weft yarn through them, and finally, beating it down to the growing web of material. The heddle device makes the open space, or shed, and Peruvian types so far found are similar to those used by the Navaho weavers, among many others. The heddle stick from which cord loops drop to encircle alternate warp yarns in the set-up is at least as long as the web is wide. The weaver sitting at the center of her loom bar manipulates the warp yarns so encircled by pulling up the heddle at its center point. It is incomprehensible to a modern craftsman how a heddle stick long enough for a 5 ft.-5 in. web, sufficiently heavy so as not to bend under the strain, and with the attached warps offering resistance could be pulled up by one hand. Granted, however, it could be raised, the space between the controlled warps and those left down must be secured by inserting a sword or batten device. The sword, like the heddle for the narrower fabrics, is at least as long as the breadth of the web. Granted also that a sword of the length and weight necessary for successful battening could be inserted by a weaver whose free hand (one holds up the heddle stick until the batten is in place) barely touches the edge of her weaving, there is still the problem of keeping even side selvages, a notable feature of any Peruvian fabric.

After putting across a weft strand a weaver usually holds with right or left hand whichever edge the weft entered, in order to maintain an even selvage by preventing that side from drawing in. The other hand pulls the weft through, allowing for the necessary amount of slack or take-up. To place her right and left hands in the position required for these steps would force a belt loom weaver 5 ft. 6 in. tall to bend over a 65-in. breadth almost parallel to her work. The belt loom manipulated by one person is an improbable explanation of the method by which Kroeber's Cahuachi Nazca mantle could have been woven, but it is a wholly inadequate explanation of the method used for weaving the 7–8-foot wide Paracas mummy wrappings.

If the loom upon which breadths over 5 ft., 7 ft., and 8 ft. were woven was related to the belt loom, several weavers must have been seated side by side, possibly in separate belt contrivances to maintain the necessary tautness of the whole warp setup. By this arrangement each could take the responsibility for her third or fourth of the width, could raise the alternate warps by pulling up on the section of the heddle directly in front of her, could guide the sword between them to make an opening for the weft, pass the weft yarn through her portion of the web, and finally beat it down to the already woven fabric. The idea is not new. Cashmere shawls were woven by two workers at stationary horizontal looms, and many of today's Oriental rugs are woven by rows of children or women sitting on benches before vertical looms. The huge pictorial tapestries of the seventeenth and eighteenth centuries were made on looms with heddle devices in sections since the process of building up a design motive required the separation of the warps in only one small area at a time. Hence, the continual raising and lowering of uninvolved warps the whole width of the web was needless if not impossible. There may have been some such division of the Early Nazca heddle into short lengths so that each of the several weavers could manipulate her own length.

Suppose, for the sake of argument, that one pictures a single sword long enough to keep open the shed for the passage of the weft yarn from side to side in fabrics like Kroeber's Cahuachi mantle and the two Paracas wrappings. Swords are usually made of heavy, fine-grained woods, smoothed and pointed at the ends. Those in use today among primitive weavers are from 8 in. to 10 in. longer than necessary to reach across the warp setup. It seems unlikely that pieces of wood of the type and shape used the world over for battens could have been overlooked by archaeologists in a region where wood of any quality is scarce.

The Navaho weaver uses a short sword because she, like the tapestry weaver of any time, builds up separate motives to complete the whole design, and requires a shed through only a fraction of the warp setup. The problem is a different one in plain weaving. The weft yarn in a standard plain weave passes from one side edge to the opposite one, crossing either over or under every warp yarn in the setup. But perhaps for these very wide pieces from the Early Nazca period, weavers used the ordinary short swords which, as the warps were raised in front of them by means of a long heddle, or several sectional ones, were passed along to make a shed for the weft yarn. In addition to the heavy wooden swords, the modern Peruvian weaver uses a llama leg bone. She first beats her weft yarn into place with the sword, and then more vigorously presses each strand down to the finished cloth with the bone tool. This double battening is suitable for tightly woven materials like tapestries and warp-face mantos, but the additional battening with so small an instrument as a bone tool could not be successful on open-texture fabrics like the Cahuachi Nazca piece, nor could small instruments alone be used. The wefts lie in straight lines, such as can be explained only by a wide batten. There might have been tools among the loom accessories of the Early Nazca weavers to supplement the work of the sword when wide-loom fabrics were under construction, but they must have been of appreciable width.

If the idea of an oversize belt loom worked upon by several weavers seems fantastic, one can always fall back upon either of the two accepted explanations of wide-loom fabrics: that they must have been products of stationary horizontal looms held firmly by pegs driven into the ground similar to the type used by the Upper Nile Bedawin peoples; or that the cloths must have been woven on vertical frames similar to those in use today among the Navaho and the Araucanians.[8] The ancient Egyptians according to their wall paintings had both horizontal and vertical looms. Some paintings show two weavers seated in front of the vertical web. Others show two weavers passing the weft yarn between them from one side to the other of the warp stretched on a horizontal loom.[9] The Lima authors quoted above suggest that the two Paracas

[8] H. Ling Roth, Studies in Primitive Looms, fig. 89a, Halifax, 1918.
[9] H. Ling Roth, Ancient Egyptian and Greek Looms, figs. 1–11, 13, 14, 16, Halifax, 1913.

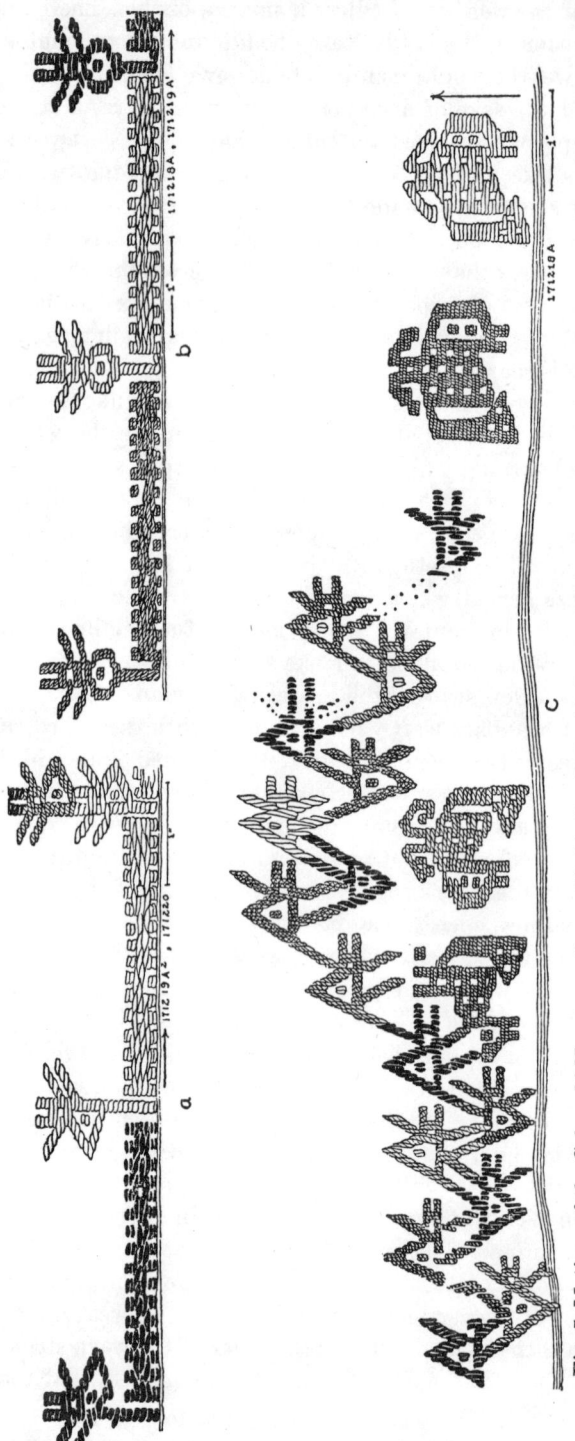

Fig. 5. Motives of the Cahuachi Nazca mantle. *a*, side border A. *b*, side border B. *c*, end border E. Arrows denote direction of warp.

wrappings were made on some type of large loom whose models have not come down to us because it was impossible to place them in the tombs.[10]

An analysis of the length measurement of Kroeber's Cahuachi Nazca mantle and the reason behind the assumption that 6 ft. 8 in. is the minimum also involves uncertainty. Specimens 171218a and 171219a[1] are opposite corner pieces on the same side, and although the embroidered motives bordering the ends are different, the side borders are identical (fig. 5b). The same sequence of four colors in the two halves of the design unit, (1) Blue, Green, Yellow-Orange; (2) Blue, Green, Red, is maintained through two complete repetitions, or four half-units, from the corner of specimen 171219a[1]. The cloth has disintegrated from under the last two motives, leaving long loops of the Green yarn still interlocked at the change from Green to Red (fig. 8b). The few remaining Red loops are only a fraction of their original length. On the other side of the break the sequence picks up at Blue and continues: Blue, Green, Red,—the second half-unit of the repetition,—and then unbrokenly to the corner of specimen 171218a where the sequence ends on Blue. In numerals, to represent Blue, Green, Yellow-Orange, Red, the sequence is as follows:

123–124; 123–124; cloth missing–124; 123–124; 123–1.

A determination of the original length of this mantle depends upon two factors in the analysis: the approximate length which seems in reasonable proportion to a mantle width of 5 ft. 5 in., and the clues furnished by the measurements of the border motives. These last are perhaps more tangible and may be considered first.

Peruvian color sequences are in many cases consistently maintained. There is no reason to suppose that the destroyed portion of the original mantle between what is now represented by specimens 171218a and 171219a[1] was any exception to that rule. There is no reason, either, to suppose that the lengths of the three embroidered elements in each half-unit, totaling approximately 8½ in., should have varied in the missing portion. The mantle's total length should, then, have been equal to the fragmentary border lengths, 33½ in. (which includes the length of the fragmentary Red element, 3 in.) and 38 in. plus the first half-unit of the sequence, the missing Blue, Green, Yellow-Orange motives, approximately 8½ in., total 80 in. This is the minimum length. Of course, there is no arbitrary limit to the length, but if the original mantle was longer than 6 ft. 8 in., then the amount must almost certainly have been governed by the combined lengths of the two half-units in the border, approximately 17 in.–18 in. In other words, adding 11½ in. to the lengths of the two intact borders provides for completion of the fragmentary Red motive and for the missing half-unit, Blue, Green, Yellow-Orange. If this seems an insufficient amount, then whole units each measuring 17 in.–18 in. must be considered in addition to the 11½ in. which fills the gap in an otherwise perfect color sequence.

From the standpoint of proportions, there is, unfortunately, less material

---

[10] Yacovleff and Muelle, *op. cit.*, 80.

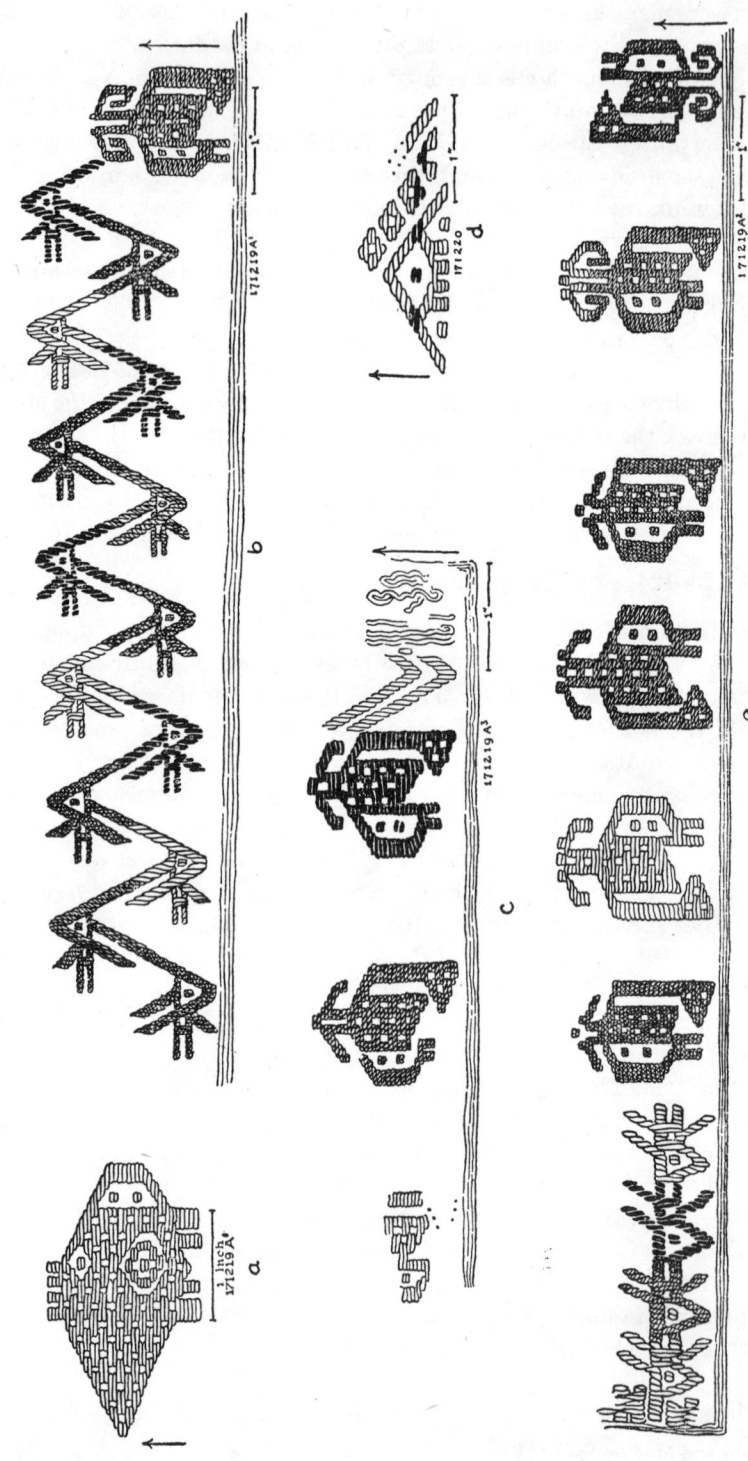

Fig. 6. Motives of the Cahuachi Nazca mantle. *a*, free standing end border motive F. *b*, end border D. *c*, end border C[1]. *d*, fragmentary motive J in main body of web. *e*, end border C. Arrows denote direction of warp. (Artist: Miss Octavie Page.)

upon which to base estimates concerning the length of the original mantle. The Field Collection from Early Nazca sites contains ten mantles furnishing complete dimensions. Their lengths range from 40 in. through 68 in. and their widths, whether composed of one or two webs, from 38 in. through 52 in. The following tabulation, omitting the mantle under analysis, presents the proportions of widths to lengths.

Specimen no.	Length (inches)	Width (inches)	Proportion W-L
1. 171305a	68	52	0.764
2. 171265	48	38	0.791
3. 171214	55	45	0.818
4. 171222	50	41.5	0.830
5. 171216	57	47.5	0.833
6. 171182a	56	48	0.857
7. 171262	60	52	0.866
8. 171223a	52	50[11]	0.961
9. 171224	50	50[11]	1.0
10. 171119	40	40	1.0

If we assume the original dimensions of mantle 171220 to have been 6 ft. 8 in. (33½ in. + 38 in. + missing half-unit, 8½ in.) by 5 ft. 5 in., the proportion of width to length is .812, placing the mantle third in the group. If, however, we assume the original dimensions to have been about 8 ft. (33½ in. + 38 in. + missing half-unit, 8½ in. + a complete unit, 17 in. +) by 5 ft. 5 in., the proportion of width to length is .67 first on the list. There is, in reality, no more foundation for one than the other assumption except that the available mantles show lesser rather than greater differences between their two dimensions. It may be of interest at this point to note that Kroeber's Cahuachi Nazca mantle seems to have conformed to a local style which dictated proportions. The celebrated embroidered mantles from the Paracas Necropolis representing a period approximately coeval in time[12] are not only unlike the Early Nazca mantles in the Field Collection in general appearance and decoration, but also in dimensions. A summary of three basic tables is here presented:[13]

Range in lengths of 67 Paracas Necropolis mantles.......... 83 in.–144 in.
Range in widths of 53 Paracas Necropolis mantles.......... 31 in.– 64 in.
Range in proportions of widths to lengths of 53 Paracas mantles... .242–.605

Even assuming a length measurement for mantle 171220 which would place its width-to-length proportion first in its group does not alter the fact the Paracas mantles radically differ in shape from the available Early Nazca examples.

Technologically, Cahuachi mantle 171220 presents few unusual details. The basic weave is plain, and the texture has something in common with modern scrim except that the more tightly twisted yarns of the mantle account for a slightly crêped surface. The warp-weft counts per inch vary sufficiently to

---
[11] Full width inferred from measurement of one breadth. As a general rule, the widths of two separately woven webs forming a garment are approximately equal.
[12] UC-PAAE 28:25, table 1. [13] Unpublished MS.

224   Lila M. O'Neale

Fig. 7. Motives of the Cahuachi Nazca mantle. *a, b*, motives H and G in main body of web. Arrows denote direction of warp. (Artist: Miss Octavie Page.)

indicate that hand weavers are pretty much alike in all times. The warps were set up 26, 28, and 30 per inch. Wefts count 24 and 26 per inch. The yarn is 2-ply white cotton, spun medium to hard twist.

This Cahuachi Nazca mantle, like so many other textiles in Peruvian collections, brings up the ever-recurring question of whether a certain technique shall be classified as brocade or embroidery. The answer is made no easier by references to older writings in which are described brocades worked with the needle and embroideries accomplished in the loom. Either description confuses by reason of the fact that brocading has been more or less firmly established as a weaving process, and that the term embroidery has for ages been restricted to a method of patterning a fabric already woven. With the best intentions two English writers seek to clarify the situation in the following paragraph:

> Many of the Peruvian patterns are woven by the method of brocading. This closely resembles a simple form of embroidery, and it is sometimes difficult to determine the one from the other, brocading being really a form of embroidery applied to weaving. In brocade weaving, the threads forming the pattern are inserted as an addition to the weft threads and in a line with them during the course of weaving, and this is done with a needle or some form of bobbin, the warp threads being so regulated in their use as to secure the brocading threads somewhat slackly at certain defined points in the pattern without themselves being evident: there may be a special warp for this purpose. The brocading is therefore part of the process of weaving, but it has not the structural element of tapestry. The same process carried out by the needle on the woven fabric is true embroidery.[14]

The description is accurate; also adequate, if two details be added: first, that the weft threads forming the brocade pattern regularly alternate, wherever used, with the weft threads of the basic material; and, second, that the warp threads appearing at "certain defined points" often in themselves make a secondary pattern on the brocading weft threads as well as "secure" them.[15]

In analyzing these same Early Nazca specimens for the preliminary report[16] the borders and rectangular motives were termed brocades. The basic fabric is a fairly coarse, open-mesh material, and counting its threads in order to embroider the geometric elements in the patterns implies no such skill as do other Peruvian techniques of this Early period, the needle-knitted bird and flower fringes, for example. But, if one inclined to interpret mantle 171220 as a brocade, one might argue that the straight-line work of the pattern rectangles could be put in more easily with a shuttle weaving over and under stretched bare warps than with an embroidery needle subsequent to the weaving. This reasoning assumes a knowledge of what the Cahuachi weaver considered easy, or convenient. And, too, if one of the heavier pattern yarns was never found to cross a basic weft which parallels it on either side, the brocade interpretation could stand against any argument for embroidery. Perfectly done, embroidery in the brocade manner cannot be distinguished from brocade. The smaller motives which form the lower borders, the finial

---

[14] Mary Symonds and Louisa Preece, Needlework Through the Ages, 108, London, 1928.
[15] UC-PAAE 28, pl. 23b shows warp shedding for secondary design.
[16] *Idem*, fn. 16.

motives out from the corners of the rectangles, and the side borders with their interlocking yarns at color changes do not bear the stamp of the brocade technique although it is conceivable that they might have been made by that method.

The patterning of Cahuachi mantle 171220 is not the least interesting of its features. There are seemingly illogical differences in the four borders, inconsistencies in the arrangement of design forms, and unanswerable questions as to the original size of several fragmentary motives. Added to these aspects—and largely because of them—is the regrettable lack of actual evidence for the patterning of the missing center third of the mantle.

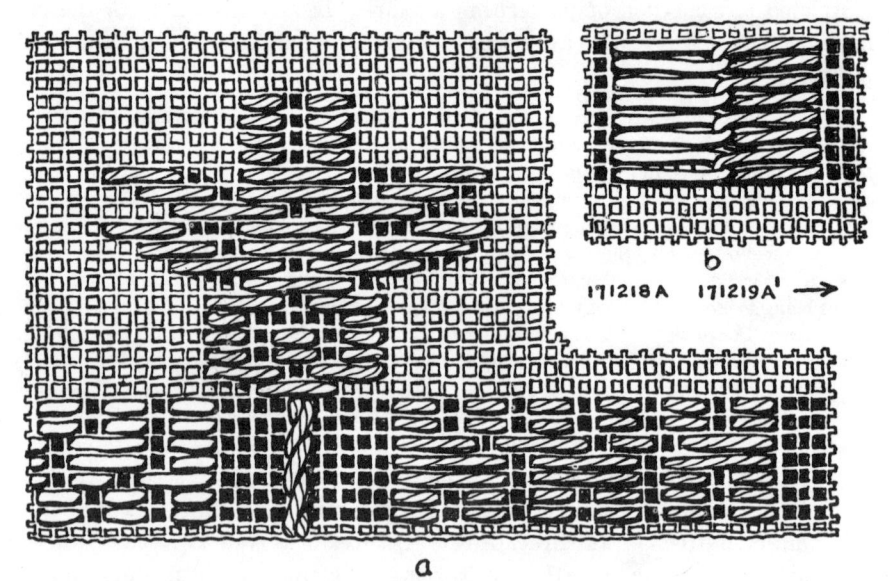

Fig. 8. Details of the Cahuachi Nazca mantle. *a*, detail of side border B at the point of color change. *b*, detail of interlocking yarns on the reverse side at the point of color change. Arrow denotes direction of warp.

Figure 4 shows schematically the proportions of the reconstructed garment, and the placing of its various design areas. Each area is a composite of elements more or less similar in appearance, but not identical. The characteristic simple and elaborated elements forming the motives are the following:

1. Lozenge shapes: plain 4-sided diamonds of various sizes, with and without embroidered center dots (fig. 7*b*); angular figure-8 forms composed of two lozenge shapes (fig. 7*a*); elaborate lozenge shapes with wide framing lines and hexagonal center dots (fig. 7*a*).

2. Triangles: isosceles and equilateral, both with and without embroidered center dots (fig. 7*b*).

3. Chevrons, small simple forms as well as elaborated ones (fig. 7*b*).

4. Bird forms: in flight, profile view (figs. 5*a*, *c*; 6*b*, *e*); in flight, top view (fig. 5*b*); six heads (?) radiating from a central point (fig. 7*a*); two heads (?) in profile, bodies forming sides of the chevron (fig. 7*a*); bird (?) form with short tail feathers and very long tail feather (?) turned back under body (figs. 5*c*; 6*b*, *c*, *e*).

5. Serpent forms, the bodies a composite of lozenges and triangles (fig. 7*b*); highly conventionalized form, possibly a serpent (fig. 5*a*, *b*).

These design elements are variously combined in forming eleven different border and basic web motives, each of which requires a separate description. The letters correspond to those on figure 4.

A. A border on one long edge (specimens 171219a[2] and 171220) composed of 2½ in. to 3 in. units with half-inch space between them. Each space is broken by the bill of a bird in profile; alternate birds face in the same direction, a method of countering which seems never to have been practiced to any appreciable extent in the Peruvian periods so far determined (fig. 5a). Colors in repeated sequence, as given above are: Blue, Green, Yellow-Orange; Blue, Green, Red. There is little doubt that the rectangular unit as well as the bird form is in embroidery technique. The mantle edge is thickened where several strands of wool yarns have been crowded in between the basic warp threads. The motives are all more or less alike, but what they were meant to represent is not clear. Perhaps a double-headed serpent, a form to be seen in two of the large rectangles in the center of the web (fig. 7b). Wherever the color change takes place, the individual embroidery yarns of the two involved sets interlock underneath the space occupied by the bird form, as shown in detail drawing figure 8b.

B. A border on opposite long edge formed by specimens 171218a and 171219a[1]. In color sequence and other respects this border is identical with border A except that the bird figures which fill the spaces between the rectangles are represented full top view instead of in profile (fig. 5b).

C and C[1]. The end borders on fragments 171219a[2] and a[3]. Figures 6c and 6e show the form and arrangement of design elements which may or may not be birds. The apparent lack of system is to be noted both in the arrangement of the motives in relation to each other, and in their relation to the border as a whole as evidenced by the sizes, spacing, and countering of the design parts.

D. An end border on fragment 171219a[1]. Profile bird forms in zigzag arrangement, the bill of the upper bird forming the leg of the lower bird, and vice versa. At the corner of the border, and for no obvious reason based upon spacing, there is a single element identical to the motives in end border C (fig. 6b).

E. An end border on fragment 171218a. A second arrangement of the bird motives of border D in a double zigzag drifts off without reason into a pair of the same motives used alone in border C (fig. 5c).

F. A free-standing motive, animal (?) or fish (?) on the end of fragment 171219a[1] (fig. 6a). In solid color, Blue.

G. Rectangular motives in the main web, complete in specimen 171218a and partially complete in 171219a[1]. The individual elements of this design are lozenges, triangles, and chevrons so arranged as to form double-headed serpent forms. The stitchery in all the rectangular motives is parallel to the weft yarns giving the effect of woven brocade (fig. 7b). The colors, Red, Green, Yellow-Orange repeated 1232–1232–123, appear as lengthwise stripes on the Blue ground of the motive.

H. Rectangular motives, portions of which appear in specimens 171218a, 171219a[1], and 171220. The rectangles are approximately the same size as those described under G, but the basic elements are differently combined. In addition, each corner is extended by a zigzag line terminating in a bird form (fig. 7a). The same stripes of Red, Green, and Yellow-Orange yarns run lengthwise through these motives as in the G type. Birds are in Red and Green on opposite diagonal corners; in Blue and Yellow-Orange, on the remaining two.

I. A finial in the form of a bird extending out from the corner of a missing design motive. The original shape of the motive cannot be determined. The distance between the finial and the basic web of fragment 171220 is too short to allow a rectangle as large as those lettered G and H. There is no clue to the main design motive except that the bird is embroidered in Red and Green as in type H.

J. A motive of unknown size and shape on fragment 171220. Here there is space for a form similar to the rectangles lettered G and H, but the bit of intact embroidery is unlike either, although apparently composed of some of the common elements (fig. 6d).

The one constant factor in the patterning is the limited range of colors used. If mantle 171220 showed fewer signs of fading, the number of hues might be analyzed with greater certainty. The yarns matched to the printed samples in Maerz and Paul's Dictionary of Color yielded the following results: Bronze Green (16L12),[17] two Yellow-Orange hues similar to Raw Siena (12J9 and 13L9), two dark Blues (39H3 and 40H10), a Brown similar to Chestnut (7H9), the familiar Brickdust (5L11), and perhaps several other Reds, which at this time look like faded yarns. Upon analysis it has been found that the Peruvians had dyes to produce a wide range of Reds,[18] but in this particular case it seems wise to stop with the one Red which is certainly present. Many of the yarns in mantle 171220 show strands differing in color, and it is doubtful whether matching an assortment of swatches would mean very much. The impression given by the whole mantle is of embroidered motives in Red, Blue, Green, and Yellow-Orange, with occasional small areas in dark Purplish Brown. The repetition of a series of these colors is nowhere insistent except in the two side borders, A and B, but it does make itself felt as a deliberate repetition.

Kroeber's Cahuachi Nazca mantle 171220 presents a number of features common to the Early-period fabrics as we know them: the cotton basic web with a pattern in wool; the bold designs, no doubt conventionalized and affected by local tastes, but not rendered meaningless through slovenly handling; the strong rich colors of the dyed yarns, the whole general effect of a garment woven and embroidered by craftsmen who were aware of involved techniques but who had them under perfect control. This is evident in the evenly spun yarns, and the uniform surface texture of the material.

The mantle also presents in its 5 ft.-5 in.-breadth a feature which makes impossible the further acceptance of a narrow weaving device as the single prehistoric Peruvian type. At the same time that the narrow looms were turning out turban bands, ribbons, and materials of average width, there must have been either an ingenious adaptation which allowed several persons to weave simultaneously on the same warp setup, or a large frame type. So far we have no knowledge of the latter, and it is one of the important problems confronting the textile analyst. The finding of identifiable loom parts or a partly finished web still in position on the frame would carry us many steps beyond speculation.

[17] A. Maerz and M. Rea Paul, A Dictionary of Color, New York, 1930. Each printed color sample is cited by plate, column letter, and row number.

[18] Unpublished MS.

UNIVERSITY OF CALIFORNIA,
BERKELEY, CALIFORNIA.

THE HOUSE-CLAN COMPLEX OF THE PUEBLOS

By Elsie Clews Parsons

A RECENT HOUSE CENSUS of Taos shows 125 houses belonging to men as against 48 houses belonging to women. Taos reckons descent bilaterally and its exogamous rules are bilateral, it is without clan organization. At the other end of the Pueblo territory are the Hopi, among whom the matrilineal clan is the outstanding principle of social organization and no men own houses. In the other tribes there is a consistent relationship between house proprietorship by sex, and clanship: with the increase of male proprietorship, there is a decrease in the social importance of the clan. In towns with male as well as female house owners, the Keresan towns, the ceremonial life is unrelated to clanship. Among the northern Tewa where clanship does not even control marriage choices there are more men house owners than women. The importance of women in the ceremonial life follows the same curve: women are most important ceremonially among the Hopi, decreasingly important among the Keres and Tewa, and least important at Taos.

Consideration of these relationships has led me to the hypothesis that house ownership by women was a prime factor in the development of the matrilineal clan, a hypothesis advanced independently by William Duncan Strong in his Analysis of Southwestern Society.[1] It is an opportune moment for the discussion of this hypothesis, since Kroeber made the first coherent and significant study of clanship among the Pueblos and at Zuñi the first study of the relations between housing and clanship.

From the point of view of distribution the occurrence of the matrilineal clan among the Pueblos has been an enigma. The Pueblos have not been in contact with any culture similarly characterized, with one exception, the Navaho.[2] The Navaho have matrilineal, matrilocal clans and they may have passed on these principles to the Hopi, but it looks as if it were the other way around. Clanship is such an integral part of Hopi life that it would seem to antedate comparatively recent contacts with the Navaho. Navaho clanship is disassociated with Navaho ceremonialism, in the way of the eastern Pueblos; inferably among them all, Navaho and eastern Pueblos, clanship may be taken as a marginal or borrowed trait.

Dr. Strong came to his hypothesis by way of analysis of the house-fetish-chieftaincy complex. "The heart of the clan organization being the fetish, and the lineage which possesses it, it would seem that in these two fundamental concepts, house-owning and fetish custodianship, we may have the cause for male or female lineage differentiation. If the woman owns the house and is custodian of the fetish, as occurs among the Hopi and at Zuñi, it seems logical that maternal reckoning of descent might follow."

Hopi women coöperate in the ceremonial life in a variety of ritual particu-

---
[1] AA 29:1–61, 1927.
[2] With the Navaho I am including the western Apache, who are more removed from the Pueblos.

lars and there are three women's societies with women chiefs, but most of the chieftaincies are in men's hands, even the women chiefs are assisted considerably, in singing and in setting altars, by men members, and on the whole the ceremonial organization is run by the men. Why then did the custody of fetishes, a very important matter, fall to the women? Because the fetishes have to be fed and feeding the household is a function of its women,[3] and because, given the great reluctance to remove or even touch a fetish, once house ownership was associated with women, fetish trusteeship or custody would be similarly associated.

The origin of house ownership or trusteeship by women is and ever will be a speculative matter. There is a general feeling among the Pueblos that land belongs to the user and this feeling more or less attaches to house lots and houses. Even in the towns where male proprietorship in houses preponderates, a widow would never be dispossessed of her deceased husband's house if she wished to continue in it. As women stay at home and use the houses more than men, it would be quite compatible to think of women as house owners. For obvious reasons women could become house owners, systematically, only if a man lived in his wife's house. House ownership by women and matrilocal residence are complemental. Whether original or derivative, the unwillingness of the women to leave home and the desire of the family to add to its male providers, are other factors in matrilocal residence observable today.

Still observable also are certain conditions indicating how the matrilocal family or lineage blossomed into the matrilineal clan. In several towns, house clusters of relatives are referred to by the name of a household head or by a topographic name. Some of the lineages with ceremonies at Zuñi, the rain chieftaincies, are referred to topographically, Onakwe, Road People, Paɫtokwe (paɫtok refers to a certain part of town), the Red-door rain chieftaincy. In the recent clan and house census made by White and Titiev at Oraibi, informants proved far more reliable and consistent about clan affiliations as associated with houses than as given genealogically. The ordinary Hopi is not genealogically minded enough to keep track of lineages at all systematically, so that he will ascribe a person now to one lineage now to another *within the same clan*, to the utter confusion of the ethnologist. The house where the fetish is kept and the lineage associated with this house are of course known, for the ceremony is of communal interest and concern; but there is no call to keep track of other lineages, the clan is a catch-all.

From topographic necessity a lineage tends to scatter away from an original house cluster, but ritual associated with the original maternal house and many of the economic ties may still be kept up. Some name for such a scattered group would be of considerable convenience, both for outsiders and for group members. A sense of genealogy is acquired with difficulty; where the sense of relationship carries over beyond common residence people tend to

---

[3] As among the paternally organized Cahuilla groups of southern California (Strong *op. cit.*, 35). Incidentally, note some striking parallels between the mat-wrapped fetish bundles of the Cupeño, the ma'swut bundles, and those of the Hopi Marau or Mamzrautü woman's society, even to the name.

be confused about their degree of relationship. Classificatory kinship terms and a group name are a godsend. Clanship nomenclature is a lazy way out of genealogical confusion.

Unfortunately for the ethnologist, the Hopi stick to names for lineages as well as for clans. Out of a clan's stock of names a woman may give her family a lineage name, according to Stephen,[4] and recently Titiev has noted one or two similar instances at Oraibi. At Zuñi, where a large part of the ceremonial organization is independent of clan or lineage trusteeship, lineages have no names; only one clan, the Pikchikwe or Dogwood, has two names. The lineage-clan system either began to lapse at Zuñi when its ceremonialism was enriched by the Keresan medicine societies which are unrelated to clanship or, more probably, the lineage-clan system developed first among the Hopi and was only partially borrowed by Zuñi, that is, the clanship idea was borrowed full-fledged with the lineage idea dropped out or almost dropped out.

Why are the "clan mothers," whether old women or young, important figures in Hopi society? They are important not because they perpetuate the clan or tribe, but because in their houses they look after the fetishes of the ceremonies. Why are there no authentic totems in Pueblo clanship? Because the Spirits are primarily associated with the ceremony and only derivatively with the clan. There is no clan ancestor whom clanspeople must respect (taboo) or especially venerate. Masauwu, god of death and fire, or the kachina Chakwaina is in charge of the Kokop clan or the Mustard clan, but Masauwu and Chakwaina are not clan ancestors. Chakwaina is called grandmother, to be sure, but as a courtesy, because of long-standing association, not because the Mustard clan or even the Chakwaina lineage are her descendants. Chakwaina and other masks live in certain houses only because there they are well entertained, well fed, "that is why they chose those houses to live in."

All these considerations indicate that the clan instead of being an early trait or development among the Pueblos is an end product, just as Hopi-Zuñi tradition has it, the clans getting their names not before the Emergence but after it, and the early migrations taking place not by clans but by ceremonial groups. Myth or legend aside, it would appear that Pueblo ceremonial preceded Pueblo clan. The clan was a convenience, the ceremony was a necessity.

The clan proved to be a verbal convenience, a convenience in mating, in hospitality, and in safeguarding or perpetuating ceremonial. The ceremony was indispensable to weather and crops, against disease or enemies, a vital necessity, "what we live by." The Pueblos could get along without clans, some of them do, but destroy their ceremonies and you destroy the culture. In the western pueblos men are beginning to own houses. If men come to preponderate as house owners the clans may become patrilineal or even disappear. There will still be a Pueblo culture. But let the ceremonies become obsolescent because, let us say, the young are schooled away from them, and few distinctions between pueblo and American town will be preserved.

[4] A. M. Stephen, Hopi Journal, App. 2, CU-CA 23, 1936.

RYE, NEW YORK.

OJIBWA AND OTTAWA PUBERTY DREAMS
By Paul Radin

Introduction

THE FOLLOWING PAPER speaks for itself. It is an attempt to show the various stages through which the fasting-dream pattern of the Ojibwa and Ottawa passed, as Ojibwa and Ottawa culture disintegrated and lost its original basis. The salient fact in that disintegration was the manner in which the actual dream experience was gradually freed from its specific cultural trappings and was remembered and told as a personal dream. I do not think it is too much to say that during the full functioning of the culture, no dream was ever *retold* except in a definite pattern, one that had been rigorously fixed by the puberty fasting experience. As the puberty fasting experience lost its social implications, dreams, in general, lost theirs and relapsed into their true significance, that of being more or less symbolical disguises and distortions of personal problems. Undoubtedly this original meaning must have, from the very beginning, attempted to reassert itself and must have, at all times, played havoc with the pattern itself. Among the Ojibwa and Ottawa, as is well known, a rigorous supervision was exercised over the fasters and the form in which their dreams were cast. In fact, the form and not a little of its content were specifically given to the young and impressionable child. Dreams which did not lend themselves to this mold were simply rejected. Naturally this did not prevent individuals from dreaming them, a fact that we must constantly remember, for it constituted at all times a covert threat to the whole pattern. The pattern depended upon the proper social and economic functioning of the culture and was always more or less vulnerable. The moment the economic conditions disintegrated, then, the purely personal content of the dream seized the opportunity afforded and easily regained its old ascendancy.

Such, in its main outlines, is the historical transformation which the dreams here presented portray. In the first section I give two dreams collected by Kohl at La Pointe, Wisconsin, from the Ojibwa, at the beginning of the nineteenth century. Ojibwa culture had, it is true, been subjected to many far-reaching transformations by that time, but the puberty dream pattern had survived, if not entirely in its true functioning, at least as something in the nature of a spiritual oasis for the die-hards. For the third dream collected by Schoolcraft a generation later, presumably from the Ojibwa of Michigan, the same holds true. In all three cases the old puberty dream formula has been retained in all its formal completeness. In fact, I suspect, it is redundantly complete, and that by the beginning of the nineteenth century, with the whole social and economic structure of the culture so irretrievably shattered and broken up, it had become merely a static and unchanging ritual utterly divorced from reality. This static ritualistic aspect becomes even more pronounced as we approach the third set of puberty dreams, those collected by myself in the second decade of the twentieth century from the Ottawa of Michigan, and the Ojibwa of Michigan and Ontario. By that time fasting had apparently become something to which unpopular grandparents drove their unwilling grandchildren. Ojibwa and Ottawa culture had ceased to function even in a remotely significant manner. The old formulae are beginning to show definite indications of wear and tear and the purely personal content of the dream is everywhere apparent.

In the final section, on the personal dreams of two individuals, J. Sh. and J. P., both of them Ottawa, collected by myself in Michigan in 1926, the puberty dream pattern is completely gone. So completely has it been forgotten that a purely personal dream like that, for instance, of J. Sh. (dream 10) which does not possess the remotest resemblance to the older puberty experience is nevertheless identified as one by an older member of the tribe. Strangely enough, the interpretation this old man actually gave is an excellent example of the ancient Ottawa mode of thought, but it has no applicability to the particular dream of J. Sh. The disassociation is complete. There are some faint survivals. It is, for instance, possible that the flying motif in dream 7 of J. Sh. is not simply the well-known dream theme, but the last vestige of a mythological motif quite common in Ottawa and Ojibwa folklore and which actually reappeared in one of J. P.'s dreams.

From the point of view of dream interpretation the dreams of J. Sh. and J. P. merit careful attention and I shall devote the rest of this necessarily short introduction to discussing them. The former was about 48 years old when I met him. He was a tall, well-built man, married to an Indian woman older than himself who completely dominated him. In his conversations with me he frequently indulged in daydreams of when he would be free of her. I saw no attempt on his part, however, to make love to other women although he had ample opportunity to do so while working for me. When in her presence he was the most obedient and cowed of husbands. From what he told me he had been strongly attached to his mother, who had died only a few years before I met him. He spoke of her frequently and she appeared repeatedly in his dreams. He was as markedly inarticulate in his waking life as he apparently was articulate in his dream life. His adjustment to the hybrid civilization in which he lived—the immediate neighborhood of Petoskey, Michigan—was fair and no more. He had spent a few years, when a child, in a Catholic school, but Catholicism had left very little impress upon him.

J. P., in contrast to J. Sh., was an old man between 70 and 75, with definite indications of senility. He was a widower living in an isolated section of north-central Michigan not very far from Lake Houghton. Quite a number of his children and grandchildren lived with him. He knew no English at all although he claimed to have been brought up as a Protestant in an English-speaking community. His most pronounced character trait was his marked feeling of inferiority, which was but one phase of his utter lack of adjustment to the world around him. Apparently he had never made a success of anything and had always been poor and dependent upon charity. He was highly introverted and egocentric. He proved to be an excellent informant because he took every question asked him as a special indication of his importance.

None of the dreams of J. Sh. and J. P. were dreamt during my association with them except the last one of J. P. J. Sh. acceded to my request to tell me his dreams immediately. He told all of them at one sitting and in no way indicated that any one of them was more important than another. J. P., on the other hand, could only with difficulty be persuaded to tell any of his dreams. When he finally consented he gave them piecemeal and over a period of at least a month. He gave no reason for his resistance except that he could not remember them easily, which may have been true. He insisted that he had dreamt the first dream he told me repeatedly throughout his life, but he resolutely refused to make any comment upon it for a long time, until he finally broke down under conditions to which I shall refer presently. As the first dream dealt with sex inversion I was naturally anxious to get his reaction.

The comments of J. Sh. and J. P. upon their dreams were given without much pressure on my part. I told them they could say anything they wanted to about them, but that I particularly wished to know whether a given dream was a good or a bad one, and whether it meant anything specifically. Both of them understood what I wanted almost immediately. J. Sh. seemed to enjoy the comments; J. P. tried to limit them to a bare minimum.

With regard to the nature of my contact with the two men, it is somewhat difficult for me to make any definite statement. My impression is that J. Sh. regarded his relation to me as part of a business undertaking for which he was being unusually well paid. He was slightly flattered by the fact that I had selected him as an informant and probably was, unconsciously, grateful for the opportunity afforded him, in the comments upon his dreams and in his conversations with me, of expressing himself freely about his real sentiments toward his wife. There certainly was no transference.

J. P. had established a far closer contact, which showed itself in frequent alternations of mild anger and mild affection. He was prodigiously flattered by my having engaged him as my informant and by my having traveled 200 miles to get him. This seemed to fit in definitely with certain dreams of grandeur in which he was in the habit of indulging. A somewhat new personality developed which was further reinforced when I told him that I had often read about a famous chief who had borne his name. The certainty that he was descended from this chief increased with amazing rapidity during his stay with me. The new ego which he thus created for himself very soon became reflected in the details of some of the dreams he told me although the dreams themselves antedated my coming, by a number of years.

J. P.'s irritation toward me increased whenever J. Sh. was around. He was profoundly jealous of him, personally and professionally, and it was in an attempt on my part to appease him that I finally stimulated him into having a dream which he remembered and which he was willing to tell me, and that I succeeded in getting an explanation of his first and, according to him, his most important dream.

The specific conditions were these. I am giving them in some detail because of their importance for what followed. I asked him to accompany me to Mackinaw island and visit the famous Indian battlefield there, as well as to get me some information from some Indians living on the island. We arrived in due time and J. P. visited the battlefield. He was in the best of spirits. In the evening he went out to get me the information and came back about 9 o'clock unsuccessful, saying in excuse that some young women there had been so anxious to make advances to him that he had not been able to get anything. I presume I made no comment upon this, but apparently J. P. had a bad conscience and this, plus his jealousy of J. Sh., who had been with us just before we started, led to a violent outbreak of temper in which he accused me of slighting the work he had done for me and always preferring that which J. Sh. secured. I tried my best to reassure him and insisted that it really did not matter whether he had brought back any information or not. Nothing would appease him, however. He ended by insisting that he be paid and be allowed to leave immediately. Fortunately, the last ferry between the island and the mainland had already left. So we had to stay. But he refused to talk to me any further and went to bed without saying good night.

I had not the slightest idea how he would behave the following morning. When, however, I entered the breakfast room there he was waiting for me, all smiles as if nothing had happened. Before I could say anything he exclaimed gleefully that he had a dream for me and thereupon told me his dream (dream 32). I do not doubt for a moment that in this dream I am the game warden; that the otter J. P. killed, out of season, were symbolized by the sexual advances which he made toward the young women he accused of making advances to him, and that the action of the game warden who suddenly relented and let him go, represented my first reaction to his lack of success and my subsequent willingness to forget the whole matter.

During the pleasant and happy interval that then followed I again asked him what his first dream meant. I had asked him this so frequently and had been so consistently repulsed that I did not really anticipate any success. But, much to my surprise, he immediately answered and said, "You know that ever since childhood I have had this dream over and over again." Thereupon I seized my opportunity and said, "Tell me, Jim, if you had a chance to be born again, what would you like to be?" Since the Ottawa believe in metempsychosis I thought he would simply say, "As J. P.," but his immediate and direct answer was this: "If I could be born again I would like to be a woman, and marry a man with a large penis."

The quest was over. Had Ottawa culture been functioning I doubt whether J. P. would have admitted to those guarding his puberty fasting that he had ever had such a dream. Had he admitted it, his fasting would have terminated immediately and he would probably have been forced to put on a woman's dress and become a berdache. From this the breakdown of his culture saved him.

THE OLDER SOURCES

AGABEGIJIK'S FASTING EXPERIENCE[1]

1

We went up to our old man, and sat down as quickly as possible on his mat, while laying a couple of packets of tobacco in his lap as greeting. According to Indian habits, it is not proper or polite to remain standing any length of time in their lodges. If you do not sit down soon, or if you walk about, the squaws will soon make some sharp remarks, or you will hear from all sides the exclamation: "Sit down; pray sit down." Indian guests, when they enter a hut—even that of a stranger—hence sit down at once. If he be a perfect stranger, or has some favor to ask, he will take a seat very modestly near the door, and remain silent, till the head of the family asked the cause of his visit. If, however, he has business with any person in the lodge, he walks straight up to his mat, and places himself at once under his protection by squatting down by his side. . . .

"Well, then, Agabegijik, thou rememberest thy promise to us, yesterday, to tell us thy dream of life and thy great youth fast, with all the accompanying incidents. Wilt thou now keep thy promise?" So we spoke at once to our host, with whom we were as good as alone, for the rest of the company took no notice of us, but went on with their little amusements, as if living in so many different rooms.

"Ah!" the Cloud said, after a long silence and rumination, "when God cleaned and arranged His great wigwam, I was swept out like a useless grain of dust, cast into a corner like a patch of dirt. As the whole room was prepared for the great festival, I lay, my whole life, in the corner, poor and forgotten, while the others were dancing. I grew old in a night. What great story can a man like me tell?"

After the old man had thus spoken, he was again silent. What he had said was a modest introduction to his story—a *captatio benevolentiae*, after the Indian fashion.

"Thou speakest truly," we replied. "We men are all so. Nature is a great banqueting-hall, in which man appears forced to suffer more than all the other creatures. And especially when we grow older it seems to us as if the human beings around entirely forget us. But we Christians say of the Great Spirit that He even counts the hairs on our heads, and we are all numbered by him. Speak! Didst thou obtain in thy dream of youth a lesson of life—a revelation? Tell us what thou didst see in thy great fast."

"Kitchi-Manitou," the old man went on, after another pause, "sent us our *mides* from the east, and his prophets laid it down as a law that we should lead our children into the forest so soon as they approach man's estate, and show them how they must fast, and direct their thoughts to higher things; and in return it is promised us that a dream shall be then sent them as a revelation of their fate—a confirmation of their vocation—a consecration and devotion to Deity, and an eternal remembrance and good omen for their path of life.

"I remember that my grandfather, when I was a half-grown lad, frequently said to my father, in the course of the winter, 'Next spring it will be time for us to lead the lad into the forest and leave him to fast.' But nothing came of it that spring, but when the next spring arrived, my grandfather took me on one side, and said to me, 'It is now high time that I should lead thee to the forest, and that thou shouldst fast, that thy mind may be confirmed, something be done for thy health, and that thou mayst learn thy future and thy calling.'

"The grandfather then took me by the hand, and led me deep into the forest. Here he selected a lofty tree, a red pine, and prepared a bed for me in the branches, on which I should lie down to fast. We cut down the bushes, and twined them through the pine branches. Then I plucked moss, with which I covered the trellis-work, threw a mat my

---

[1] Kohl, J. G., Kitchi-Gami, Wanderings round Lake Superior, 228 ff.

mother had made for the occasion over it, and myself on top of it. I was also permitted to fasten a few branches together over my head, as a sort of protection from wind and rain.

"Then my grandfather said to me that I must on no account take nourishment, neither eat nor drink, pluck no berries, nor even swallow the rain-water that might fall. Nor must I rise from my bed, but lie quite still day and night, keep by myself strictly, and await patiently the things that would then happen.

"I promised my grandfather this, but, unfortunately, I did not keep my promise. For three days I bore the lying, and hunger, and thirst; but when I descended from the tree into the grass on the fourth day I saw the refreshing leaves of a little herb growing near the tree. I could not resist it, but plucked the leaves and ate them. And when I had eaten them my craving grew so great that I walked about the forest, sought all the edible sprigs, plants, mosses, and herbs I could find, and ate my fill. Then I crept home, and confessed all to my grandfather and father."

"Wert thou not severely punished?" I interposed.

"Not further than that they reproved me, and told me I had done wrong, at which I felt ashamed; and, as I had broken my fast, it was all over with my dream, and I must try again next spring. I might now have been a man, but would remain for another year a useless fellow, which was a disgrace at my age."

I. "I pray thee stop a moment, and permit me to ask some questions here, as we have a year before us. Why did thy grandfather manage all this, and not thy father?"

The Cloud. "My father was still young. My grandfather was old. For all such affairs old men have the most experience and knowledge. And they also pay greater attention that the children shall be instructed, and that all shall be done according to old customs."

I. "Further tell me how high do you make your dream-beds in the trees?"

The Cloud. "Generally from ten to twelve feet above the ground. Sometimes, though, they are more than twenty feet. The tallest and finest trees are selected."

I. "Why do you make this bed in the trees? Why do you not build a hut on the ground?"

The Cloud. "On account of the Evil Spirit."

The Cloud gave me no further explanation of this laconic reply, and left it to me to imagine that, in all probability, according to the Indian theory, the good spirits and salutary dream genii reside high in the air, while the Matchi-Manitou wanders about on the ground and annoys people. At any rate, the latter has his snakes, toads, and other animals, against which the dreamer, who is not prepared for hunting and defense, cannot protect himself.

I may here add another parenthetical remark, that if the entire operation of the dreaming is interrupted by a nightmare, or any bad dream, it is rendered impossible during that spring. The Ojibbeways have divided the dreams into various classes, and give each a special name. The excellent Bishop Baraga, in his lexicon of that language, has collected the Indian names for a bad dream, an impure dream, an ominous dream, as well as for a good or a happy dream....

The boys are warned, so soon as a nightmare or a bad dream oppresses them, to give up the affair at once, come down from the tree, and return home, and try again and again till the right dream comes.

But to continue:

The Cloud. "When the spring of the next year was approaching, my grandfather told me, although a great deal of ice and snow still lay in the forest, that it was time for me to go out again to fast, and try my dream. As, however, I was ashamed of my defeat in the last year, and had determined on carrying out the affair now, I begged him to let me go alone, as I knew what I had to do, and would not return till my right dream had come to me. I had already selected a place in the forest I knew, where I intended to make my bed. It was on a little island covered with trees, in the centre of a forest lake. I described the place to my friends, that they might come in search of me if anything happened to me, and set out."

I. "Why didst thou select that precise spot?"

The Cloud. "Because I knew that one of my relations and friends was lying on his dream-bed in the same locality."

I. "Didst thou intend, then, to communicate with thy friend during the period of dreaming and fasting?"

The Cloud. "Not so; for he was some distance from me—two or three miles. But though I could not see or hear my friend, nor be allowed to speak with him, there seemed to me some consolation in knowing him near me and engaged in the same things to which I was going to devote myself.

"There was ice still on the little lake, and I reached my island across it. I prepared my bed, as on the first time, in a tall, red pine, and laid myself on the branches and moss.

"The first three or four fast-days were as terrible to me as the first time, and I could not sleep at nights for hunger and thirst. But I overcame it, and on the fifth day I felt no more annoyance. I fell into a dreamy and half paralysed state, and went to sleep. But only my body slept, my soul was free and awake.

"In the first nights nothing appeared to me; all was quiet: but on the eighth night I heard a rustling and waving in the branches. It was like a heavy bear or elk breaking through the shrubs and forest. I was greatly afraid. I thought there were too many of them, and I made preparations for flight. But the man who approached me, whoever he may be, read my thoughts and saw my fear at a distance; so he came towards me more and more gently, and rested, quite noiselessly, on the branches over my head. Then he began to speak to me, and asked me, 'Art thou afraid, my son?' 'No,' I replied; 'I no longer fear.' 'Why art thou here in this tree?' 'To fast.' 'Why dost thou fast?' 'To gain strength, and know my life.' 'That is good; for it agrees excellently with what is now being done for thee elsewhere, and with the message I bring thee. This very night a consultation has been held about thee and thy welfare; and I have come to tell thee that the decision was most favourable. I am ordered to invite thee to see and hear this for thyself. Follow me.'"

I. "Did the spirit say this aloud?"

The Cloud. "No: it was no common conversation: nor do I believe that I spoke aloud. We looked into each other's hearts, and guessed and gazed on our mutual thoughts and sensations. When he ordered me to follow him, I rose from my bed easily and of my own accord, like a spirit rising from the grave, and followed him through the air. The spirit floated through the air. I stepped as firmly as if I were on the ground, and it seemed to me as if we were ascending a lofty mountain, ever higher and higher, eastward.

"When we reached the summit, after a long time, I found a wigwam built there, into which we entered. I at first saw nothing but a large white stone, that lay in the middle of the hut; but, on looking around more sharply, I saw four men sitting round the stone. They invited me to take a seat on the white stone in the midst of them. But I had hardly sat down than the stone began sinking into the earth. 'Stay!' one of the men said; 'wait a minute; we have forgotten the foundation.' Thus speaking, he fetched a white tanned deerskin, and covered the stone with it; and when I sat down on it again, it was as firm as a tree, and I sat comfortably."

I. "What is the meaning of this deerskin: who was it that gave it to thee?"

The Cloud. "On that point I have remained in uncertainty. A man does not learn everything in these dreams. As I sat there and looked round me again, I noticed a multitude of other faces. The wigwam was very large, and filled with persons. It was an extraordinary council assembly. One of the four took the word, and ordered me to look down. When I did so, I saw the whole earth beneath me, spread out deep, deep, and wide, wide, before me."

I. "Did it appear to thee round?"

The Cloud. "No; it had four corners. Immediately another of the four took the word, and bade me look up. I looked up, and saw the whole sky over me quite near. I gazed a long, long time, and almost forgot where I was, for it was a glorious sight. Then a third took the word, and spoke: 'Thou hast gazed. Now say; whither wilt thou now—down below, whence thou camest, or up above? The choice is left thee.' 'Yes, yes,' I replied, 'I will go up; for that I have fasted.'

"The four men seemed pleased at my answer, and the fourth said to me, 'Ascend!' He pointed to the back of my stone seat, and I saw that it had grown, and went up to an extraordinary height. There were holes cut in it, and I could climb up as if on a ladder. I climbed and clambered higher and higher, and at length came to a place where four white-haired old men were sitting, in the open air, around the pillar. A dazzling cupola was arched above them. I felt so light that I wished to go higher, but the four old men shouted 'Stop!' all at once. 'Thou must not go higher. We have not permission to allow thee to pass. But enough that is good and great is already decreed for thee. Look around thee. Thou seest here around us all the good gifts of God—health, and strength, and long life, and all the creatures of nature. Look on our white hair: thine shall become the same. And that thou mayst avoid illness, receive this box with medicine. Use it in case of need; and whenever thou art in difficulty, think of us, and all thou seest with us. When thou prayest to us, we will help thee, and intercede for thee with the Master of Life. Look around thee once more! Look, and forget it not! We give thee all the birds, and eagles, and wild beasts, and all the other animals thou seest fluttering and running in our wigwam. Thou shalt become a famous hunter, and shoot them all!'

"I gazed in amazement on the boundless abundance of game and birds which flocked together in this hall, and was quite lost at the sight. Then the four old men spoke to me. 'Thy time has expired, thou canst go no higher; so return.'

"I then quickly descended my long stone ladder. I was obliged to be careful, for I noticed it was beginning to disappear beneath my feet, and melt away like an icicle near the fire. When I got back to my white stone it returned to its former dimensions. The great council was still assembled, and the four men round the stone welcomed me, and said, 'It is good, Agabegijik. Thou hast done a brave deed, and hast gazed on what is beautiful and great. We will all testify for thee that thou didst perform the deed. Forget nothing of all that has been said to thee. And all who sit round here will remember thee, and pray for thee as thy guardian spirits.'

"After this I took my leave, and let myself down to my bed in the red pine. I found that three more days had passed away. During this time my body had lain there motionless as a corpse; only my soul had wandered so freely in the air. Then I breathed, sighed, and moved about like one waking from a deep sleep. When I opened my eyes and looked around me, I found the green branches of the tree gnawed and sucked, and guessed that my craving body during my absence had bitten off the bark and licked the sap of the pine-shoots. This was a sign to me of the wretched condition into which my body had fallen. I also felt myself so weak that I could not stir.

"All at once I heard a voice, a whistle, and my name called. It was my grandfather, who had come on the tenth day to seek me. 'Come down, my son,' he said, 'and join us here.' I could only reply to him in a weak voice that I was unable to stir, and that I could not return over the lake. I had walked across the ice ten days before, but the warm weather had melted it all, and I was cut off on my island. My grandfather ran home quickly, and returned with my uncle. They brought a canoe, took me down from the tree, and carried me across the lake. From there we were obliged to go on foot. At first I could hardly move, but by degrees I grew better.

"On the road home a bear met us. My uncle wished to shoot it, but both grandfather and myself said, 'Stay! that must not be! On his return from his dream and his great fasting, a man must not shed the blood of any creature, or even shoot any animal for three days after.' I then walked up to the bear, and said to it, 'Bear, my cousin, I have great strength. I have a powerful medicine. I come from the spirits. I could kill thee on the spot, but will not do so. Go thy way!' The bear listened to me, and ran away into the forest. Perhaps my miserable appearance terrified it, for I was thin, pale, and exhausted.

"At home they prepared for me a soft bed of moss, on which I lay down like a patient. It was not till the following day that I took any food, but three days later I was quite recovered, and strong. And from that time I was, and remained, a perfect man!"

LITTLE RAVEN'S DREAM[2]

2

I was a boy so tall, that when I was standing, and my father was seated on the mat, we were both of one height. It was harvest time. We had gone to gather the wild rice.

One day when we were hard at work, and all busy husking the grain and filling our canoes, I heard gunshots in the distance. These shots came from our village, and were replied to from the neighbouring village. They were mourning shots, which are heard from village to village when any one is dead.

When I heard these shots, I quickly left off working, and became solemn and very mournful, for the thought at once crossed my head that my mother was dead. Soon, too, the messengers of sorrow came, hurrying to the lake where we were collecting our harvest, and brought us the sorrowful intelligence that my mother was dead. We buried her with many sighs. I wished, however, to weep out my heavy grief all alone, and I longed to go out into the forest. But my father, uncle, and sisters would not let me go, and watched me closely when they noticed my melancholy and disturbed manner.

Once, however, my father and uncle were invited to a *fumerie*. Then I sprang away from my sisters, and ran into the forest so far and so quickly as I could. When I was far enough from the village, I began weeping and calling loudly on my mother. At last I climbed a tall tree, where I wept myself out, and being quite exhausted by pain and weariness, I remained hanging in the branches of the tree.

All at once I heard a voice near me, and perceived a black form hovering over me. "Who art thou?—why dost thou weep?" the form asked me.

"I am an Indian lad," I replied, "and I weep for my mother."

"Come, follow me," the black figure said, and took me by the hand. It walked with me through the air with one step to the next tree. It was an *epinette blanche*. When we stepped on the top of this shaking tree it trembled and bent, and I feared it would give way under us. "Fear not," the stranger said, "but tread firmly. The tree will bear us." Then she put out the other foot, and we reached with the second step the top of a tall young birch. This tree also shook greatly, and bent down, and I feared that it would let us fall to the ground. "Fear not," my black companion said again, "step firmly. The tree will bear." And thus we stepped out again, and with the third step came to the foot of a tall mountain. But what appeared to me three steps were, in reality, three days' journeys: during the nights we had rested on the tops of the trees, and many forests and prairies already lay behind us.

When we stood on the top of the mountain, she said to me, "Knowest thou the mountain?" and when I said I did not, she replied, "It is the Mountain of the Stag's Heart." She waved her hand. Then the mountain opened, and we saw, through a long narrow ravine, the sunlight shining brightly at the other end. We went through the rift in the rock. My black conductress glided along before me. At the other end we walked out into the light and sunshine. In the centre of the brilliancy there was a house.

"Go in there," said the black woman.

The door opened and I walked in, but my companion remained outside. I found a supernatural light inside, and covered my eyes with my robe. I trembled from fear and expectation. At length a person who sat in the back of the room began speaking, and said:

"Kagagengs, as I saw that thou wert sorrowful for the death of thy mother, I sent for thee. Thou art welcome. Come nearer. Look around thee. Thou art welcome. Come nearer. Look around thee. Thou canst now see how I live, and how things are with me."

---

[2] Kohl, *op. cit.*

After growing a little accustomed to the light, I looked around. I saw nothing at first but a lamp hanging in the middle of the hut, which gave a tremendous light. It was the lamp of the Sun. The Sun itself was sitting behind, and spoke further to me:

"Look down!" Then I looked down through an opening in the floor, and saw the earth far beneath us, the trees and forests, the mountains, the big sea water, and the whole round of the world. "Now look up!" said the voice. I looked upwards through an opening in the roof, and saw the whole vault of heaven above me, and the stars so close that I could grasp them.

Then again, after I had looked at all this above and below me, the voice of the Sun said, "Now look straight forward. What seest thou? Knowest thou him?"

I was terrified, for I saw my own image. "See," the Sun said, "thou art ever near me. I see thee every day, and watch over thee. I gaze on thee and know what thou doest, and whether thou art ill or well. Hence be of good cheer. Now look out to thy right and thy left. Dost thou know the four persons that surround thee? They are a present which I, the great source of life, make thee. These four are in thee. They will come from thee. They are thy four sons. Thy family shall be increased. But thou, thyself, shalt live long, and thy hair shall become like to mine in colour. Look at it." I then gazed on the white locks of the Sun Spirit. They shone like silver, and a feeling of joy came over me, that I should have so long and happy a life.

"In remembrance of thy visit to me," the Sun continued, "and for a good omen, I give thee this bird, which soars high above us, and this white bear with the brass collar."

Then the Sun dismissed me, after saying to me that the woman he had sent to me with this invitation was awaiting me, and would lead me back. The two presents, though, I received—the white bear and the eagle—have ever since been my protecting spirits.

"Didst thou really bring such presents home with thee from heaven, or from the forest?" I asked Raven.

"Not so," he replied.

"In Indian dreams," my interpreter explained to me, "it is not necessary that the presents which spirits make them should be really led away. The gift is rather a spiritual present. The idea or image of the thing is given them, and they then have permission afterwards to make the best use of it they can. Thus, Kagagengs in his late years caught a number of young eagles, which he brought up, and in memory of his dream let them free again. He also took the image of the white bear with the brass collar as his token, and has scratched it a hundred times on his pipes, or sewn it into his blankets, or carved it out of a piece of wood, which he carries about in his medicine-sack."

A GIRL'S FASTING EXPERIENCE[3]

3

When I was a girl of about twelve or thirteen years of age, my mother told me to look out for something that would happen to me [presumably her first menstrual flow]. Accordingly, one morning early, in the middle of winter, I found an unusual sign and ran off, as far from the lodge as I could, and remained there until my mother came and found me out. She knew what was the matter and brought me nearer to the family lodge and bade me help her in making a small lodge of branches of the spruce tree. She told me to remain there and keep away from everyone, and as a diversion, to keep myself employed in chopping wood, and that she would bring me plenty of prepared bass-wood bark to twist into twine. She told me she would come to see me in two days, and that in the meantime I must not even taste snow.

I did as directed. At the end of two days she came to see me. I thought she would surely bring me something to eat, but to my disappointment, she brought nothing. I suffered more from thirst than hunger, though I felt my stomach gnawing. My mother sat quietly down and said (after ascertaining that I had not tasted anything as she

---

[3] H. R. Schoolcraft, Oneota, 430–432.

directed), "My child, you are the youngest of your sisters, and none are now left me of all my sons and children but you four." (Alluding to her two elder sisters, herself and a little son, still a mere lad.) "Who," she continued, "will take care of us poor women? Now, my daughter, listen to me and try to obey. Blacken your face and fast really that the Master of Life may have pity on you and me, and on us all. Do not, in the least, deviate from my counsels, and in two days more, I will come to you. He will help you, if you are determined to do what is right. Tell me whether you are favored or not by the true Great Spirit; and if your visions are not good, reject them." So saying, she departed.

I took my little hatchet and cut plenty of wood, and twisted the cord that was to be used in sewing up mats for the use of the family. Gradually, I began to feel less appetite, but my thirst continued; still I was fearful of touching the snow to allay it, by sucking it, as my mother had told me that if I did so, though secretly, the Great Spirit would see me, and the lesser spirits also, and that my fasting would be of no use. So I continued to fast till the fourth day, when my mother came with a little tin dish, and filling it with snow, she came to my lodge, and was well pleased to find that I had followed her injunctions. She melted the snow and told me to drink it. I did so and felt refreshed, but had a desire for more, which she told me would not do, and I contented myself with what she had given me. She again told me to get and follow a good vision— a vision that might not only do us good, but also benefit mankind, if I could. She then left me, and for two days she did not come near me, nor did any human being, and I was left to my own reflections. The night of the sixth day, I fancied a voice called to me, and said: "Poor child! I pity your condition. Come, you are invited this way," and I thought the voice proceeded from a certain distance from my lodge. I obeyed the summons, and going to the spot from which the voice came, found a thin shining path, like a silver cord, which I followed. It led straight forward, and, it seemed, upward. After going a short distance I stood still and saw on my right hand the new moon with a flame rising from the top like a candle, which threw around a broad light. On the left appeared the sun, near the point of its setting. I went on and I beheld on my right the face of Kaugegagbekwa, The-Everlasting-Woman, who told me her name, and said to me, "I give you my name, and you may give it to another. I also give you that which I have, life everlasting. I give you long life on the earth and skill in saving life in others. Go, you are called on high."

I went on, and saw a man standing with a large circular body and rays from his head, like horns. He said, "Fear not, my name is The Little Man Spirit. I give this name to your first son. It is my life. Go to the place you are called to visit." I followed the path till I could see that it led up to an opening in the sky, when I heard a voice and, standing still, saw the figure of a man standing near the path whose head was surrounded with a brilliant halo and whose breast was covered with squares. He said to me: "Look at me, my name is O-Shau-wau-e-geeghick, The Bright Blue Sky. I am the veil that covers the opening into the sky. Stand and listen to me. Do not be afraid. I am going to endow you with the gifts of life, and put you in array that you may withstand and endure." Immediately I saw myself encircled with bright points which rested against me like needles, but gave me no pain, and they fell at my feet. This was repeated several times and at each time they fell to the ground. He said, "Wait and do not fear, till I have said and done all I am about to do." I then felt different instruments, first like awls, and then like nails stuck into my flesh, but neither did they give me pain, but like the needles, fell at my feet as often as they appeared. He then said, "That is good," meaning my trial by these points. "You will see length of days. Advance a little farther," said he. I did so, and stood at the commencement of the opening. "You have arrived," said he, "at the limit you cannot pass. I give you my name, you can give it to another. Now, return! Look around you. There is a conveyance for you. Do not be afraid to get on its back, and when you get to your lodge, you must take that which sustains the human body." I turned, and saw a kind of fish swimming in the air, and getting upon it as directed, I was carried back with celerity, my hair floating behind me in the air. As soon as I got back, my vision ceased.

In the morning, being the sixth day of my fast, my mother came with a little bit of dried trout. But such was my sensitiveness to all sounds and my increased power of scent produced by fasting, that before she came in sight I heard her, while a great way off, and when she came in I could not bear the smell of the fish or herself either. She said, "I have brought something for you to eat, only a mouthful, to prevent your dying." She prepared to cook it, but I said, "Mother, forbear, I do not wish to eat it—the smell is offensive to me." She accordingly left off preparing to cook the fish and again encouraged me to persevere and try to become a comfort to her in her old age and bereaved state, and left me.

I attempted to cut wood, as usual, but in the effort I fell back on the snow, from weariness, and lay some time. At last I made an effort and rose, and went into my lodge and lay down. I again saw the vision, and each person who had before spoken to me, and heard the promises of different kinds made to me, and the songs. I went the same path which I had pursued before and met with the same reception. I also had another vision. My mother came again on the seventh day, and brought me some pounded corn boiled in snow water for she said I must not drink water from lake or river. After taking it I related my vision to her. She said it was good and spoke to me to continue my fast three days longer. I did so; at the end of which she took me home and made a feast in honor of my success and invited a great may guests. I was told to eat sparingly, and to take nothing too hearty or substantial; but this was unnecessary, for my abstinence had made my senses so acute that all animal food had a gross and disagreeable odor.

CONTEMPORARY SOURCES

OTTAWA FASTING EXPERIENCES

4

At the end of ten days the boy was always asked what he had fasted about. If it was the water-spirit, the sea-lion, the thunder-bird, or any other ferocious animal, this meant that he was to be a warrior.

If during his first fast he did not dream of any spirits at all, he was passed up until he did. A successful faster bears in mind all his dreams and uses them whenever called upon.

If he has dreamt of ants, then in wartime the enemy would feel that the faster and his party were like ants and hard to hit.

If he has dreamt of the water-spirit, this spirit will come to him in his waking state and from him he can obtain some slime, etc., from which to make medicines to be used in time of crises or disease.

If he has dreamt of the sea-lion with the bobbed copper tail, that animal will come to him and permit him to have some of the copper, etc.

5

When parents want their children to be bright they tell them to fast. Once a boy was sent out to fast and the very first night he had a dream. He dreamt that a woman came to him and then when she turned her back to him, she looked like a water-spirit. "I think," said the boy, "that she must live in a lake near here." When the boy's father heard of this dream he told his son, "No, I don't want you to accept that dream, because if you do, afterwards, when you get married, all your children will die. You must stay another night and try again."

The next night another being appeared to the boy. It looked like a man. "I will help you in war," it told the boy. It was a water lynx. "No," said the father when the boy told him about it, "I don't want you to accept the blessing of a water lynx." "But, father," said the boy, "I'm getting very hungry." "My son, try again."

The third night he dreamt of a pagak, but his father objected to this one too.

The boy was getting very hungry indeed.

The fourth night he dreamt of a robin. The robin said, "Boy, I'm going to give you my color. Now, rub your chest and you will become a robin."

When the father came the next morning to see his son, he had become a robin. He tried to free him, and begged him to come back and stay with them as a human being, but it was all of no avail.

The Indians regard robins as transformed human beings and believe that they can speak Ottawa. For example, they say that the robins when chirping are really chanting: "I have a presentiment that thunder is coming."

6

Once a young boy went to the woods and fasted ten days. On the morning of the tenth day, he had a dream, and that was the dream he went by all his life. In this dream a snake appeared to him and said, "If you accept my blessing I will help you whenever you are on the warpath, whenever you are in danger. All you will have to do is to think of me and you'll immediately become a snake."

Many years after that the boy, then grown up, went on a warpath. He was almost killed, but managed to get away. Behind him, however, he saw his pursuers. Then suddenly he recollected his dream and changed himself into a snake and the enemy were deceived.

7

Once there was a boy who never believed in fasting. He thought he could get along in life without it, that he could be good and do everything right without it. He lived near the Masabe river.

On one occasion, he was camping near a lake not far from their place and began thinking of the spirit called mckodac. He wanted badly to hear this spirit bellow. The mckodac knew immediately what the young man was thinking of.

The boy built his fasting wigwam and on the very night when it was finished he heard the mckodac bellow. He did not know what animal it was for he had forgotten completely all that he had ever thought of in connection with the mckodac. Unquestionably it was the mckodac who was bellowing. When the mckodac came near him he got so frightened that he became unconscious. The next morning when he woke up just at dawn, he saw his canoe hanging on a tree and he himself was entirely naked. His buckskin clothes and his bow and arrow were all hanging on the tree. After he had collected them together he went home.

That same night he dreamt of the mckodac and the mckodac said to him, "Do not think of me any more. I could easily have killed you if I had wanted to but I really didn't want to hurt you. I just wanted to show you how strong I was."

8

At Cut-Head point there lived an Indian with his son. Both started one day for Grand Haven because it was at that place that the father had decided his son should fast.

The son began his fast and on the eleventh morning he dreamt of the bebikwakizine, that is, the mckodac spirit. The boy at first refused. Whereupon the mckodac spirit told him, "I will meet you again tomorrow and then you will see how strong I am." The next day, he met him in the woods. The boy had an axe along with him and tried to kill him, but when he struck him, the head of his axe fell off. Then he tried to shoot him, but his bowstring would not rebound. Then he tried to stab him with his knife, but the knife broke to pieces. Then the boy got frightened and fainted. When he came to, he didn't see the mckodac any more. He now felt sorry that he hadn't accepted him.

The next night he dreamt of the same spirit. This time the spirit looked like a man and not like an animal. He spoke to the boy and said "Did you see how great was my power? I would have given you all that, but you didn't want me to. Now I will never help you."

The next day the boy dreamt of a spirit who told him, "I'm coming here to see you. If you take me, I'll give you all the powers I possess. I can see eight tiers below the ground and eight tiers above the clouds." The boy accepted him. This spirit was a bird called kackimontigon.

This boy's cousin was very bright and he thought that he was much brighter than this young boy. The cousin told the young boy that if he dived into the water he would not know where he had gone. "All right," said the young boy, "dive in." So the cousin dived in at a point called Cat-Head's point. From this place there was a large underground hole to Cadillac and the exit of the hole was in the middle of the lake near Cadillac. There the young boy waited for his cousin, and when he emerged, he grabbed him and held him by both cheeks. The cousin said, "Don't do that, you will hurt me."

Before they returned home the cousin died. He died at a place called Sigenakna. When the young boy grabbed him by the cheeks he hurt him more than he wanted to because he didn't know how great his power was.

This boy was named Kingfisher.

9

Once a young boy went out fasting. He was to fast ten days. During this time his grandfather came to see him every morning to ask him how he was getting along and whether any spirit had appeared to him. On the morning of the tenth day, the old man appeared and asked, "What have you seen?" The young boy answered: "Grandfather, an old man appeared to me and said, 'I have come to you to help us (spirits) out. A certain evil spirit is attacking us. I want you to come to our aid and shoot him.' Then this old man turned around and went away. As he left I heard a thunder-clap. Hardly had he left when another man came and said, 'I want you to help us. We are in trouble. We are being attacked by an evil spirit. He wants to carry us up and we want to carry him down.' Then he turned around and went out.

"Then when the blue morning appeared I went to the lake where they told me to come, taking with me my bow and arrows. When I got there the water looked like syrup. Then I saw a cloud come down to the lake and heard a thunder-clap above and saw an animal just below the place where it had thundered. As I looked more closely, I saw two beings entangled, the one in the other. I spoke to both and said, 'I am here.' Then the first man spoke. 'Shoot this man down who is below me.' But the other man said, 'Don't shoot me; shoot the other man above!' 'Well,' said I, 'whom am I to help? Both of you came to me!' The first one, who was the thunder-bird, said, 'If you shoot the other person, then when you are in trouble, when you are on the warpath, I'll give you all my great power. All you have to do is to think of me.' When I heard this I held my bow ready to shoot, but before I had shot, the other man spoke again, 'Don't shoot me. I have just as much power as the one above me. If you shoot this person above me, I'll make you rich and let you have everything you desire.' Thereupon, I lowered my bow.

"Indeed, grandfather, I was puzzled. I thought to myself, 'Now this second person's blessing won't help me much, but the first person's promise to aid me on the warpath, that's worth while.' I therefore decided to accept the thunder-bird's blessing. I took my bow and arrow, raised it and shot the person below. The water seethed and I saw the thunder-bird carry an animal up with him. Then I returned to my fasting wigwam full of thought. That is all."

Not long after he had finished telling his grandfather of his experience, the boy's father came. "What did you dream of?" he asked him. The boy repeated the story to his father. "That's all right," said the old man, "I'll let him break his fast now." The old man went home to bring him some food. He only gave him a little at a time because otherwise a faster is likely to get very sick.

Now this boy in later life was a famous warrior. The thunder-bird really helped him. He used to wander a good deal, too, and on one of his travels came to Osage Indians. He told one of the Osage about his early fasting experience and this Osage said, "I dreamt of the same thing, but I shot the man above, the thunder-bird. . . .

Informant's interpretation of dream 9.—All this is quite true. In the early days we Indians didn't know anything. Now, we do. We didn't know what was good for us. We thought that we would always be able to live our own kind of life. We didn't know that the white people were going to come here.

Today, we Indians of Michigan haven't anything. We are good fighters. We were good fighters in the Civil War. That was because the thunder-birds had blessed us. If you look up the records you will find that very few of us were killed either in the Civil War or the World War. The Indians of Oklahoma, however, are very rich. They accepted the blessing of the water spirit.

10

Once a boy fasted for ten days. On the eighth night, he dreamt that someone came to him and said, "I've come to see you and to help you. I will always protect you against your enemies, even if they are close upon you."

On the ninth night, another person appeared. It was a snake spirit. This spirit promised him all the power he possessed. He offered to give him the power of being invisible in battle, the power of being able to transform himself into a snake. He told the boy not to accept the blessing of the previous spirit.

On the tenth morning, the first person came back. He was a mckodac. He said to the boy, "This is my last offer. If you accept it, I'll give you all my powers. If you don't, you will lose out."

On the eleventh morning, the boy dreamt about the snake spirit again. This time the snake spirit looked like an Indian. The boy accepted the blessing of the snake.

Not long after that the boy, while alone, saw some animal coming toward him. It was rushing against him fast. As the animal came nearer he looked at it. It resembled a little dog. Rushing for his canoe, he jumped into it, taking his bow and arrows. The animal—it was a mckodac—came nearer and nearer. Then the boy tried to shoot the mckodac, but the arrow, as it left the bow, just swung around and fell into the water. He was unable to discharge an arrow from his bow. He tried arrow after arrow, but he was unable to get anyone of them to reach the ground where the mckodac was standing. Finally, the mckodac ran off into the woods.

That night, the mckodac appeared to the boy in a dream and said, "I merely wanted to show you how great was the power that I would have bestowed upon you had you accepted me. If then, in later years, you would have been fighting against your enemies, the arrows aimed against you would have dropped half way just as yours did. Since you didn't take my advice, you will be defeated. Your enemies will exterminate you and yours."

11

A young boy once fasted for more than ten days. He almost starved to death. On the tenth morning, the boy's father came and asked him of what he had dreamt. The boy told him, but it was not what the father wanted him to get, so he told him to go right on fasting. The father always said that it would be for just one night more and in this way the boy had to fast so long that he almost died. It was then that he had a dream. He dreamt that he had received a blessing from the spirits of the Four Cardinal Points. He saw eight round djiski lodges. The power he received was very strong, just like the wind. In after life, he possessed the ability of going from one place to another with great speed. He could get whatever he wanted. If he wanted huckleberries in winter, he could transport himself to a place where it was summer, collect them, and be back in a short time.

OJIBWA FASTING EXPERIENCES[4]

12

In olden days Indians used to fast for the purpose of revealing their future. When a young Indian began fasting he was given very little to eat in the morning and at night, with nothing at all at noon, for two days. Then the older people would build him a scaffold on top of a hill near some big tree, an iron-wood preferred. There he would stay both day and night. His father and mother would come in the morning to inquire about his dreams. If he had dreamt of a snake or some kind of serpent, he would have to give up fasting entirely; but if he dreamt of other animals, he received a blessing. If he was blessed by land animals, he became a hunter, and if he dreamt of birds, he became a great man among his people.

When a faster starts to dream, a man or woman appears to him with a blessing. If he accepts the blessing offered, the spirits will take him away and show him what is the nature of the blessing that he is to use in years to come. After this, the spirits take him back to his fasting place. Here he sees the spirit disappear and he can then tell what is the identity of the spirit who has blessed him.

13

When I was a boy of eleven my mother told me that it was time for me to find out about my future. I was told to fast. First, I was told not to eat or drink anything except at suppertime. This I kept up for five days. On the sixth day, a wigwam was built on the bank of a little creek, running through the woods. There I was left on the evening of the sixth day and there my mother came to see me the next morning to find out if I had had a dream. But I had not slept that night, for I went to a creek for a drink of water. It was early in the fall of the year and the nights were quite warm. My people saw the tracks along the creek the next morning and immediately realized that I must have left my sleeping place. They asked me where I had been and I told them that I had gone to the creek for water. Then I was told to go home.

After about two weeks I had to start all over again. This time I was placed together with another lad. On the fourth day, they changed my wigwam to another part of the woods far away from the creek. On the evening of the fourth day, I went to the place they had built for me. That night, the other boy had a bad dream, and when our mothers came the next morning he told his mother that he had dreamt. He had had a vision in which a snake appeared to him and made him sick and that he finally died. He was told to go home. After that I was all alone in the wigwam. My people visited me quite often, about three or four times a day. I stayed there five days, and on the fifth night I had a dream.

I dreamt that I was alongside a lake and had not had anything to eat for some time. I was wandering in search of food for quite a time when I saw a big bird. This bird came over where I was staying and spoke to me, telling me that I was lost and that a party was out searching for me and that they really intended to shoot me instead of rescuing me. Then the bird flew out into the lake and brought me a fish to eat and told me that I would have good luck in hunting and fishing; that I would live to a good old age; and that I would never be wounded by a shotgun or rifle. This bird who had blessed me was the kind that one rarely has a chance of shooting. From that time on the loon was my guardian spirit.

14

When a boy gets to be ten years old, his grandmother always wishes him to fast so that he may know what blessing he is going to receive. Such a boy will start to fast in the autumn, getting very little to eat in the beginning either for breakfast or supper. Of course, not everyone is very strict about eating in the daytime.

---

[4] Experiences 12–23 inclusive were obtained in text.

In the spring a little scaffold is made and on it is built a little wigwam for the fasting boy. Here he is to stay for ten days and nights, getting a little to eat twice a day. He is warned by his grandmother not to believe every spirit that comes to bless him, for some like to deceive people. She tells him to accept only that spirit who comes with a great noise and with mighty force.[5]

On the first and second nights, I didn't dream of anything, but on the third night a very rich man came to me and told me to go with him and that I would become rich. I went with him but I refused to accept his gift. Then I returned to my wigwam and looked around, for the man had told me that I would be able to recognize his identity when he went away. He was an owl and the big house was a hollow tree with holes all around it.

The next night, another rich man came, dressed in red. He offered me the same thing as the first one and, in addition, he told me that I would be able to buy two suits of clothes a year. Then he told me to turn around. I did so and saw nothing but oak trees with dry and green leaves.

The next night, another man came and offered me boxes of sugar, but although I went with him, I refused his gift. I went with all of them, even after I decided to refuse. The last man, like the others, told me to turn around to see who he was, and when I turned I saw a big maple tree.

Twice a day my grandmother came to feed me and to ask what I had dreamt of. I told her of what I had already dreamt. She then warned me not to accept any spirit until one with noise and strength came, and that before the tenth night was up I would surely be blessed if I had observed carefully all that I had been told. Sure enough, on the night of the tenth day, I heard a gust of wind above me and when I looked up I saw a very stout man. I went with him toward the north and came to a place where nine old men were sitting in a circle, with a very old man in the center. The man in the center was the one who had blessed me. He told me that he had just been sent from above.

Then the one who had been sent after me took me back to my wigwam and told me to turn around as soon as he had gone some distance. I did so and saw ten big white stones in a circle and another one in the middle.

In the morning, when my grandmother came to feed me and inquire about my dreams, I told her of what had happened. That was the end of my fasting.

Some fasters are fooled by a bird called the chickadee. This bird also comes with a gust of wind.

15

When I was a boy of ten years, my father told me to fast, so that I might know in what manner I was to be blessed. My father told me to blacken my face with charcoal in the morning and to leave it on all day till evening. Then I could wash it off. During the day I did not eat much. The next day I again blackened my face, and I kept this up for four days. On the fifth day, when I got up, my father told me not to blacken my face any more and that I was to eat. However, I was to eat only my breakfast and to drink a little water at night. For two days I kept this up. On the eighth day, my father built me a little hut on top of four poles, in which I was to live and in which my maneto was to visit me.

The first night I spent there I did not sleep a wink. I was up all the next day. In the evening my father brought me something to eat and inquired if I had dreamt of anything or if anyone had come to bless me. I told him that I hadn't slept a wink. In this fashion a few days passed and I became very hungry. On the night of the ninth day, I lay down with the hope that I would dream of something. The next morning, my father came to bring me some food and inquired again whether I had dreamt of anything, and when I told him that I hadn't dreamt of anything, he got angry and told me that I had better give up. However, I told him that I would try once again and if then I had not dreamt of anything, I would stop.

---

[5] Here the narrator suddenly changes from an impersonal to a personal description.

On the tenth night, I went to sleep early and, after a while, I dreamt that I heard a great noise. Then I jumped up and ran to the north until I came over to a river. There was no way in which I could get across and there a man caught me and took me back to my wigwam. From there he took me to a place where another man waited for me.

This is my fasting experience, but I won't tell the exact details of how I was blessed for I would never tell that to anyone.

16

When I fasted I was about ten years old, that being the age at which grandparents generally desire their grandchildren to fast. My parents never bothered me at all about fasting, and I don't suppose I should have fasted at all if I hadn't had a grandparent at that time.

About the middle of the little bear month, that is, February, my grandmother came to our house to fetch me. I did not know what she wanted of me. After two days she told me why she had come. So the next morning I received very little to eat and drink. At noon I didn't get anything to eat at all, and at night I only got a bit of bread and water.

There were about seven of us fasting at the same time. All day we would play together, watching each other lest anyone eat during the day. We were to keep this up for ten days. However, at the end of the fifth day, I became so hungry that, after my grandmother had gone to sleep, I got up and had a good meal. In the morning, she found out that I had eaten in the night, and I had to start all over again. This time I was very careful to keep the fast, for I didn't want to begin another ten days.

After a while, they built me a little wigwam. It was standing on four poles and about three to four feet from the ground. This was my sleeping place. My little wigwam was built quite a distance from the house, under an oak tree. I don't know whether it was the custom to have the young boy fast under a particular tree or not. I believe that the wigwam was built in the most convenient place for the old folks to watch it during the day.

The first morning, my grandmother told me not to accept the first one who came, for there are many spirits who will try to deceive you, and if you accept their blessings you will surely be led on to destruction.

The first four nights, I slept very soundly and did not dream of anything. On the fifth night, however, I dreamt that a large bird came to me. It was very beautiful and promised me many things. However, I made up my mind not to accept the gift of the first one who appeared. So I refused, and when it disappeared from view I saw that it was only a chickadee.

The next morning, when my grandmother came to visit me, I told her that a chickadee had appeared in my dream and that it had offered me many things. She assured me that the chickadee had deceived many people who had been led to accept its offerings.

Then a few nights passed and I did not dream of anything. On the eighth night, another big bird appeared to me. I determined to accept its gift, for I was tired of waiting and of being confined in my little fasting wigwam. In my dream of this bird, he took me far to the north where everything was covered with ice. There I saw many of the same kind of bird. Some were very old. They offered me long life and immunity from disease. It was quite a different blessing from that which the chickadee had offered, so I accepted. Then the bird who had come after me brought me to my fasting wigwam again. When he left me, he told me to watch him before he was out of sight. I did so and I saw that he was a white loon.

In the morning, when my grandmother came to me, I told her of my experience with the white loons and she was very happy about it, for the white loons are supposed to bless very few people. Since then I have been called White Loon.

17

When an Indian is about to fast, he gets up very early in the morning and prepares the charcoal. Then he blackens his face with it. In the evening he washes his face for the first time. For two days he eats very little. Then he rests for two days, that is, he breaks his fast for two days. Then, at the place where he commenced his fast, he remains six days. There he paints himself. After he has commenced to fast for five or six days, he repeats the same. Thus he does in the earlier part of his fasting. After a while his fasting-place is changed. About forty rods from his house they built a lodge for him. Ten days he is to stay there. There he will find out who is to bless him. He will see the animal, his mineto.

After a while the people select one who can run fast, not one who can run only a little. On the night of the ninth day, ten days after the fasting-lodge has been built for him, he prepares a fire. Early in the morning he is to be let out. As soon as the faster is let out, that is, on the next morning, he starts to run; though he is very thin. The mineto gets wild, that is, he is in a state of frenzy. The fast runner immediately pursues him; he catches him and asks him what spirit has blessed him. Then he is given a little soup to drink.

The faster had outdistanced the one who was running after him. He, the one who had fasted, had been blessed by a pagak. It is said that this spirit rose up into the air. Even now they are the ones who make a noise up above as they fly around.[6]

18

When I fasted for two days, as soon as I woke up in the morning, I would paint myself. I ate nothing either in the morning or at noon. It is not until the evening, after one has washed oneself, that a very little soup is eaten.[7]

Then you break the fast for two days and it is during this time that the faster is tested. A piece of broadcloth is spread upon the ground and little thin splints are laid upon it. These suddenly turn into snakes and crawl around, just as a real snake crawls. After this, pieces of wood cut out into the shape of human beings are placed upon the broadcloth. They are made to dance and they do dance, just like human beings. When they are taken up, they change into splints again, lying on the broadcloth. Thus, the faster will really believe that the one who has been exhibiting was blessed; and that he will be able to do the same as he was shown.

After the faster has rested two days he starts to fast again. Now he starts to fast for five days and then he does what he did before and breaks his fast for two days. After a while, he again breaks his fast for three days and is given some deer soup to drink. Then he is to begin his ten days' fast. When it is time, a person who can run very fast, not merely one who is a normal runner, is selected to pursue the faster when he starts to run after being let out. He is very thin then. Even if he is a *mide*, the fast runner overtakes him.

Then he starts to fast again. For ten days he is to fast now, and then finish. He is taken to a house specially made for him, where he is to stay for ten days. There is a fire in the center. Every evening, the people come to ask him of what he has dreamt. If he has dreamt of anything he does not speak. Thus, by his silence, they know that the faster is dreaming and they leave him alone when they come to see him in the evening. On the evening of the ninth day, they come again. On the following morning he is to be let out. Then he is asked by whom he had been blessed and he tells them. Then they know how long he is to live, what is going to kill him, and when he is to die. It was in this way that the old people used to get their power. By fasting the faster finds out all about his future life. It was by reason of this that Tecumseh was so wise.

19

In the early times the Ojibwa used to believe that the one who is about to fast should think only of his fasting and be careful about it. He was not to eat in secret or do anything in secret. The same applies to those who are Christians; they should not drink in secret.

---

[6] Pagak are thin airy spirits. They lived once on the earth, but they got so thin that they rose into the air. It is believed that if anyone hears them shout, he will die.

[7] The change from direct to indirect discourse follows the text.

One who fasted tried to dream of some spirit. It is at night that he enters the place where he is to fast. If he thinks the fast is going to be successful, then he starts. Ten days more or less does he fast, if he wishes to be blessed. He will be seventeen years old at the age of fasting and verily he will be benefited by his blessing.

Once there was a man named Minisne who had fasted very much and who had used his blessings well. His daughter had married and was living at a place far away. He had not seen her for many years, him whom they called Minisne. He had been blessed by a ghost, so he used to be asked to conjure. He conjured in order to find out how his daughter was getting along and whether she was still living. He made a djiski lodge and entered. One always tries to find out these things at midnight. That is the time he conjured and got possession of the soul of his daughter in the djiski lodge. She said that she would come to the place he was staying at in the summer. And truly they, that is, daughter and husband, arrived. He told those who conjure not to ask the absent person to stay in their lodge for a long time. If they do stay, if the soul leaves the body for too long a time, it will be killed.

The daughter arrived in the summer. That is how the Ojibwa used to benefit when they fasted, before they had become Christians.

20

When an Indian used to fast he would give away all that he possessed. He was blessed to become a warrior. He always fought whenever there was a battle. Never would he be killed, he was told by the chief. When he was going to fast, someone told him that no one would take him, that is, no spirit would take him to his home. Just when he had about finished fasting, after fifteen days, a boat came for him and he was taken to a floating island. That is where he was found.

When anyone fasts too long his family becomes lonesome for him. When he returns, he tells all those who ask about his blessing. If he can't conjure, he isn't much of a shaman. When they had the smallpox last, that is when he died.[8]

21

Formerly the Indians used to fast, but they never fasted in summer. Only in the wintertime did they fast. When an Indian fasts he does not eat in the morning. He goes and lives in a special place that has been purified for ten days. Not for ten days does he eat. An old man, a mide shaman, will help him who fasts. Every morning he will go and ask what he has dreamt of. He is told all that they dream. If it is bad they do not accept it, but if it is good they accept it. One dreams of many things—birds, and animals, and snakes. When he is finished with fasting, that means the spirits have blessed him—animals, birds, snakes, and insects. In this case they told him that he was to become a *mide* shaman—one who knows everything.

The *mide* shamans know in advance everything that is going to happen to them. That is why they become *mide*. If anything untoward happens to them in life, then they think of what they were blessed by when they fasted and the spirit helps them. In a fight one uses the spirit who bestowed the blessing during fasting.

If a person fasts, then, when another individual is sick, he is asked to djiski and build a djiski lodge. When the shaman goes in, the djiski lodge will shake. Sometimes there are two djiski lodges. Then the shaman will go into one of the lodges and take off his clothes and both will shake, so much power he will have.

If someone has been blowing upon another person, that is, trying evil magic upon him, then they call upon one who is a *mide* shaman. He catches the offender and takes him to the lodge of the *mide* shaman where he tells all he knows and why he is trying to do this, that is, practice evil magic. If he promises to stop, then he, the one who is making the other one sick, is allowed to live. Sometimes they kill the person they go after. They place a turtle at the door of the person they are seeking until he had been let out.[9] That

---

[8] This account is quite confused and incomplete.   [9] This passage is very obscure.

is what they used their supernatural powers for. They were terrible in their use of power, those who had fasted. No matter what they attempted, they succeeded in accomplishing it.

22

In olden times the Indians fasted. When a boy was about ten years old his people built a lodge for him and there he had to stay ten days, sleeping all the time. He does not eat till the setting of the sun. If he eats when the sun is up, it will not be good for his blessing. Nor is it good to have the sun look at him when he is eating.

I, myself, when I was a boy of about twelve years, was told by my father to blacken my face. In the morning, when I began, I was given nothing to eat. At sunset I was given a very small piece of bread and water to drink. Every three days, in the morning, I blackened my face before the sun rose. When it set I washed my face. This is what was laid out for me. There, where I stayed all alone in the little wigwam, I was told to sleep all the time. In the evening they would come to see me and ask me whether any one spirit had come. I was also brought something to eat. I had been told, when I started out to fast, not to accept the first spirit of whom I dreamt, but to wait for the one who came with great noise. There are many spirits, I was told, who fool the fasters. Three nights after I stayed there, a man came to me and said, "I am coming after you, to take you; if you believe me, you will be blessed." I didn't go. Then another man came and said, "We saw you in a pitiable condition and, if you go with us, nobody will be able to kill you. Before you are killed, you will get blind, that is, you will live to be an old man. You will be as solid as my back; that is how strong your body will be." So I went with him and I saw a number of men of whom one was the leader, and he said to me, "This is how I am going to bless you. You will live for a long time; you will have many children and their bodies will be as strong as my back. Now, you are to be taken back to your home. Turn as you go and you will know who we are." I turned back and saw that turtle had blessed me.

23

When I was a boy, the Indians used to fast so that the young people should not be poor and that they might be blessed by the various spirits with the power of knowing what was to happen to them later in life. A person is blessed with the knowledge of what he is to do in life, in order to help his brothers.

When I was a boy I fasted. There were many of us, when we fasted, and some were fooled by the spirits who blessed them. They are already dead. There were only two when a fasting lodge was made for us to which I was taken. Ten days I was told to stay there and to sleep all the time. I had stayed there four days and had not dreamt of anything. I was told, "You should not come home until someone has blessed you." After I had stayed there seven days, a bird came and blessed me and told me that as long as I should live I would be superior to the other people, that I would live long, and they—that is, the other people—would all be afraid of me. I was named after the one who blessed me. Only lately my sons changed my name.

24

When children wished to fast, they were told to blacken their faces with charcoal every morning. They were not given anything to eat all day except what was given them when they began in the morning. This was kept up all winter. Early in the spring a little house near by was made for the faster where he was to stay for ten days, during which time he was not to eat anything. His parents always told him what they wished him to dream, and he was told not to accept anything until a spirit came with a strong gust of wind. Some people are blessed by trees. When a tree comes to one who is fasting, he shows him a big house filled with merchandise, and what he discards is on the floor, and so when the faster looks back, after accepting the tree, he sees that the leaves are the food and the dead leaves are the goods discarded. Some people are blessed by stones. Those who are blessed by stones are generally given great strength and long life.

The people who look after boys when they fast are careful as to what the boys dream of. I used to hear that there were only a few things that they could be blessed by. The wolf always stands for war, stones for health and strength, and the others I don't remember just now.

25

Thomas' fasting experiences.—He told me that when he was a boy he always used to see people who fasted and always wished to be like those he saw in the dances. One day he asked his parents to let him fast, but they told him that he was too disobedient, and would not do what he was told and would be only making himself hungry if he tried to fast.

One morning, however, his parents woke him up early and told him to go to the creek and have a bath. He did not feel like getting up, but he was told that if he wished to fast he would have to go. He knew that it was very hard when the people fasted but he did as he was told. From that morning on he was not to eat anything for ten days. He was given a house, where he was to stay during his fasting. He did everything he was told except that he swallowed the lead that was given him to keep his throat moist. After he had stayed there nine days, a big man came and took him to his home, where he blessed this boy. Afterward he brought him back. As the big man was leaving he told the boy to look and see who it was that had blessed him. When the boy looked, he saw a giant leaving. In the morning, the boy told his father that a large man had come after him that night, and that when he had arrived at the large man's house the giant told him he was to be like him. Then the father said, "Accept him; that is the giant who blessed you."

Examples.—Once, when Thomas was traveling around, he came across ten Americans who wanted to fight. Although he was not afraid of them he did not wish to fight unless he had to. He told them that his right arm was made of steel and his left arm of brass. The ten men rushed at him, but he only struck them a blow apiece and they were all knocked down and lay on the ground for some time.

Another time, he was traveling with a man who had a family with him. One day Thomas heard the man say that he wasn't killing anything and was not going to give him any meat. When the children ran over to where Thomas was living he told them what he had overheard their father saying. Soon the father came over and apologized for what he had said, for he was afraid of Thomas.

Another time, a man's horses left in the night and Thomas told him where to find them. This was another blessing he received from the giant—that he would know and hear things for long distances and that he would know everything that was going on around him wherever he was staying.

Another time, he was going down to visit at Walpole island, and before he left he told his wife a witch was going to pass by his house that night, and, sure enough, they saw a fire coming towards the house, and it passed by the house. This was the power he was given by the giant when he fasted.

THE PERSONAL DREAMS OF J. SH. AND J. P.

DREAMS OF J. SH.

1

I dreamt that I was married to a half-breed colored girl. She was prettier than Indian girls. After marriage we owned a home. We had a big, nice house. After we got to the house we gave a wedding feast. There were lots of girls there—also Indian girls. Soon many colored people came, dark as a stove. I felt very bad at seeing them. Indeed, I didn't like them at all although they were nice and happy. In the house I saw many tables lavishly decorated with silver. Outside of the hall I saw my nice big car. I knew I had everything nice. We didn't eat at all and I woke up.

Comment.—A man told me that this means that my son is going to marry a rich girl.

2

When I was a child and before my father died, I dreamt that my father and myself went to a certain place together. We entered a funny-looking house. The floor was very shiny. We walked through the house and in the second room we saw that the floor was slightly curved and this curved trough was covered with nice sheepskins. Both of us knelt down and as we looked up we saw a place like a Catholic church in front of us. God sat at one side. He had long whiskers. Jesus sat on the other side, and there was a little white bird in the middle. Jesus held a ball in his palm. God, Jesus, and the bird sat on something raised high from the floor. Christ made the sign of the cross to us and we did the same.

Comment.—This is my life. I am very good-natured.

3

Afterward, I got married. I was then nineteen years old. I dreamt that my wife and I were living on a farm. We had crops planted on this farm—corn, beans, etc. I was hoeing corn when my wife came over to me. Suddenly I seemed to see my home and I started to dig graves there. I dug them in such a fashion that one grave cut across the other at right angles. I didn't know who was going to be buried there. Everything was ripe at the time. Then I woke up.

Comment.—This is a bad dream. By next summer both my wife and child were dead; they died when everything was ripe.

4

I dreamt that I saw a great big snake lying in the road. It was about a quarter of a mile long. I had to go in the direction the snake was lying and so I started running on its back. Its head was sticking up. When I reached the head of the snake I saw another snake 20 inches in diameter lying there. It was 150 feet long and bloody and cut to pieces. I was so scared that I jumped off the bank of the road on which I was standing. Then I woke up.

Comment.—Bad dream. About Christmas time a cousin, my stepbrother, and myself had a fight with another Indian. We were going away from him but we again came across him unexpectedly. He grabbed hold of my stepbrother and threw him on the ground. I got mad, turned on him, and struck him till he was quite bloody. I didn't know I could fight like that.

5

I dreamt, early in the spring, of my mother-in-law, after she was dead. My wife said, "Let's go and see my mother's grave." "All right, let's go." As we entered the cemetery it looked like a house. We went inside the house and I saw many coffins lined up. My mother-in-law's coffin was in the center. We looked at it and saw that the lid was slightly opened. My mother-in-law's eyes were open too and seemed to be looking at us. I told my wife, "Your mother's eyes are open." We didn't go near but turned around and went back home. A few days after, my wife said, "Let's go to my mother's grave. Let's go nearer this time." We went again. Everything was as before. I stood at the door and stopped. I saw my mother-in-law's arm moving and I said to my wife, "Your mother's arm is moving. Can you see it?" "Yes." "Well, I'll go nearer and look at it." I went closer with my wife near me and I saw my mother-in-law move. I lifted up the cover and talked to her, "What's the matter?" said she. "Why, you've come back to life. You've been dead." "Am I dead?" "Yes, indeed, you've been dead for quite a while." "I didn't know I was dead; I thought I just woke up." "Oh my, you've been dead for quite a while." "Well," said she, "I'm going to get up. Bring my clothes." I looked around and saw all her clothes. She put them on and I helped her get out of the coffin. She said, "I'm in a hurry to get home." "Good, we'll go right away."

We walked out and I held her by the arm, afraid she might fall down. My wife said, "You go ahead. I can't walk so fast." When we started out, there were streets just as in a town. We went around the corner and I looked back and saw my wife quite some distance back. We went one block and turned again. Then we came to a place with woods on all sides. We walked one and a half blocks farther and found our home. It looked different from our home, however.

I went toward the house and saw my horses on fresh ground recently dragged. I said to my mother-in-law, "I'm going to take care of these horses. You go into the house." Then I started toward the horses. They ran toward the corner of the field. I looked around and saw potatoes, corn, beans, etc., all of different sizes from the ground. Everything looked poor. I started to chase the horses and caught them. Just before I got there I saw a man running toward me yelling, "Leave my horses alone." "These horses belong to me," I said. I licked him. I took the horses toward home but before I got there I woke up.

Comment.—In dreams, one, of course, always whips the other fellow. You never get licked yourself. I don't know what this dream means. My brother told me that it meant that crops would be good for the coming year and that I had better plant them. "Perhaps the spirit told you to plant these things. Perhaps the coming winter will be hard." My brother-in-law, said, "I think that it means that it isn't time to plant crops this year. I guess it will be a pretty poor crop. When the corn is a foot high you may die." (Long dreams always mean something.)

6

I dreamt that I saw my mother coming. I knew that she was dead. I was very glad to see her coming. As she passed she didn't look at me at all, but she spoke and said to me, "So you are going to leave today. Be careful, take good care of yourself and don't be foolish. I don't want you to get hurt or get into jail." Then I went away toward the woods, where I found some camps. I entered one hut and saw a lot of groceries piled on the table. I also saw a woman there who asked me, "Are you looking for work?" "Yes," I answered. "Well, I think you can get a job right here," she said. I didn't see anybody else and I started to walk away from the camp. I hadn't gone very far when I woke up.

Comment.—Every time I dream of my mother I have a quarrel with my wife. The groceries mean that I was going away. Indeed, I did go away. I went to Indianapolis and I left my wife for a long time.

7

I dreamt that I was standing on top of a high rock. I jumped down and as I was jumping I had the feeling that I was really flying down. I saw the world just as a bird does. Then I fell into some deep blue water and almost got drowned. There was no place to save myself, for the rock from which I had jumped was very steep and the water was very close to it. Then I thought I would save myself by hollering and someone woke me up.

Comment.—I don't know the meaning of this dream.

8

I dreamt that I was in a room and that I had to get to this room by passing through a number of rooms in which there were many women and men. Then I dreamt that I left my pants on the other side of the house and that I had to go through all these rooms to get them. I walked through just with my shirt on. I felt very much ashamed but I had to do it. As I crossed through one of these rooms somebody stopped to talk to me. I didn't like it at all, because I felt that somebody was looking at me. Finally, I got away, and just as I had put on my clothes I woke up.

Comment.—I don't know what this dream means.

9

I dreamt that I was walking in the woods and came upon a lake that had no outlet. Logs were lying all over this lake and there were trees standing in it, too. There were just a few clear places where a person could take a boat and paddle around. Then I saw a boat and I got into it and paddled off. Suddenly I hit a log without seeing it. I pushed back because I didn't want to get stuck. Then I saw a snake killed against the log. I had killed it as I hit the log. I got so frightened that I went back.

Comment.—This is a bad dream.

10

I dreamt when I was a child that two boys about eight to fourteen years old, one of them four feet high and the other five feet high, coaxed me to play with them. I consented and they took me toward a big hill. Then one of them said, "Let's go into my home." I went in. There was very little room. Whenever these boys laughed, they laughed in a very funny way. I stayed inside with them for quite a while and then I decided to come out. I came out and they said to me, "Now, remember, whenever you want to go and play somewhere just let us know and we'll go with you." I went out of the hole inside of the hill. Then as I looked back I saw that the places I had left were really graves. These people were dead people.

Comment.—An old man told me that this dream of mine was an old-time dream. He said, "Spirits have come to you, you will be a scout and will have the power of being invisible. If you think of these spirits, no one will be able to see you when you are on the warpath." And you know, Paul, he was right. I really have this power and I have frequently thought of my dream.

11

I dreamt that I saw a road, first going down the hill and then going up. The ground on top of the hill was level and from the top of it one could see another hill in the distance. In the center of the road I saw a rope. I walked along the road until I came up to the rope, and I saw that it was all knotted up. Along the road I also saw a number of boxes. As I stood on top of the hill, I saw many of these boxes, many knotted-up ropes, and a number of other things. After I had ascended the first hill and got to the top I looked behind and I saw my wife coming behind me with a little boy. I waited for her at the top of this hill, but she never came. The road as it wound up and down the various hills took on a bluish look in the distance.

Comment.—An old man told me that this dream was my life. I dreamt this before I had married. This old man told me, "One of these days you are going to be married and you will lose both your wife and your child. The knotted-up rope means sickness. When you come to the box, that will mean that you have a good job and that you own property. The hills mean that you will live many years and the blue means long life. You are going to live to be an old man. Whenever you are sick, you must think of this dream and it will help you."

12

I dreamt that a bull ran after me. I ran but I didn't make much progress, just when the bull was about to catch me, I woke up.

Comment.—The bull means sickness. Something is going to happen to me.

13

I dreamt that I went across a lake in the sailboat. We had started from a place called Harbor Springs. We sailed nicely around the point, but we didn't go very fast. Then I woke up.

Comment.—It is dangerous to dream of water. To leave for somewhere means that you are going to get sick.

14

I dreamt that I was going across the ice and that suddenly I saw a railroad track on the ice. I decided to wait till the train came, for I knew that my mother was coming on that train. I waited and soon I saw the train coming very fast. I stepped back in order to see my mother because I knew that the train would not stop. Then the train passed and I saw my mother in the train and I waved to her and she waved back to me. The train was going in a straight line toward the east. Then I woke up.

Comment.—This was the train of the dead and it meant that somebody was going to die.

15

I dreamt that I went across the ice and saw the railroad track on the ice. I knew that a train was coming and that my mother would come on this train. Soon the train came and this time it stopped. A number of people got on, I too was to go on, but somehow I got left. I didn't see my mother, although I knew she was on the train. Then I saw the train leave.

Comment.—Same as *14*.

16

I dreamt that my body was in a coffin and that I walked around and saw my body in the coffin in the house. I tried to talk to my people but they wouldn't talk to me. I didn't know that I was dead. Then I woke up.

Comment.—When I woke up I found myself pressed in somewhere and for a moment I really thought I was dead. I kicked and yelled and putting out my hand I felt something that was real hard. Then I knew that I was under the bed. Apparently in my dream I had got out of my bed and crept under it.

17

I dreamt that I went to war. I was pretty close to the battlefield and I could hear the guns. Then I had to go across the place where they were shooting. I told someone, "I have come here to go across." Then I took my gun with me and walked across on knees and hands. I was terribly scared, and I could hear the bullets whistling past me all the time. I didn't know where the American soldiers were. When I got across, I ran into the bush thinking that the Americans were there, but they were Germans. As soon as I found this out I rushed into the raspberry bushes and walked on my knees and hands. My purpose was to go back to where I had come from, but by a roundabout way. The German soldiers did not see me. Finally, I returned and told the general that there were Germans on that side. The Americans then brought their big cannon around and shot them. The jar of the shot woke me up. It was thundering terribly when I woke up.

Comment.—A man told me that this dream means that I was never to go to the war and that I never would smell powder.

18

I dreamt that I was in a small boat all alone. Near me was a steep rock against which the spray was dashing continually. I was pretty close to the rock when the waves rushed back. I was frightened and thought that the boat would surely tip over. Finally, I landed at some place or other and found a woman there. She said, "I have been waiting for you to come. I'll give you something to eat." She gave me a very small dish full of meat and some other food in small plates. I thought it was a pretty small meal for me. She said, "Don't think so." I had not said a word, as a matter of fact, but she knew my thoughts. She said, "You can't eat all that. You'll never get hungry if you taste it." Then I began eating it and I couldn't finish it. I got up from the table and I saw her. She looked like an Indian half-breed. She took me into the house to look around. I saw many horses there in what looked like a barn. After I had eaten she came back and she saw the food I had left on the table. There were many big plates and lots of food. She said, "Your table will always be like this." Then I woke up.

Comment.—The work that I do is of such a kind that I never find myself hungry.

I often dream of this woman. She looks very much like my wife. The Indians believe that if a man dreams of such a woman he will get power from her and that she will help him. I did not tell these dreams to my wife because she wouldn't like it.

19

I dreamt that a man told me, "You take this road." Then I followed along that road. It was pretty wide. I could see tracks where I was going, but none were coming back. When I got to my destination a man stopped me. He had a big sword and he said, "Now you have to pick out which road you wish to take. There is one to the left, one in the center, and one to the right. Here is the box from which you must pick out a number; the number will tell you in which direction you are to go." I picked out a number and got the road to the left.

Then I started. Before I got to the place, I saw a wall of rock, but I could see right through it. There were no windows, yet everything inside was very clear to me. I saw a man. He said, "Wait a minute, here is your name-card with all the particulars as to where you have to go." Then he handed me the card. He turned around and told me, "Pick out a place where you wish to sit until something comes." I went over there and found a number of seats. They looked like pews in a church. I sat there but I saw nobody. Then I tried to get up but I couldn't and someone said to me, "You can't get up. That is your seat." Soon I heard a wind coming. The wind came like a fire and I felt myself to be burning. I couldn't see; I couldn't move as it passed through me. I looked at myself and saw that I wasn't in the least burned. I tried again to get up but I couldn't. Then another gust of fire came. Again I tried to get up. This time I felt as though I were burning a little bit longer. Then from above I heard the voice of the man whom I couldn't see saying, "You come on; I'll show you something." So I got up, turned around, and saw some steps. I went up a little way and there I saw the man. He was dressed like a priest, in garments of gold. He opened the door and said, "Look down there." I looked and there I saw some people who were still living. What I saw was something like burning syrup and people in it. Then he shut up the door and opened another. I looked and I saw a nice green field full of flowers. Then the man said, "You are not ready to come here yet; I am just showing you this. Tell your father and mother. Now step over here and I'll show you something else." I stepped over and I saw my father sitting there playing an organ. There were people looking like women standing near him singing. I couldn't make out who they were. Then the man said, "Which one of these three do you like best?" I said, "This last one." Then I turned around and came back. On the road a man stopped me and asked, "Did you see all the things down there? Did you see your father? Your father used to do that work in this world and he has taken the same position there." Then I woke up.

Comment.—An old man told me, "You will have two burnings. This dream means that your heart is going to burn twice before you die." And indeed, my heart did get two burnings.

20

I dreamt that I was walking along a road and finally got to a hill which I ascended. I saw my uncle ahead of me, and behind me I saw my stepfather coming. I didn't know what to do, wait for my stepfather or catch up with my uncle. Finally, I waved my hat to tell my stepfather to come faster, and I went over the hill. My uncle had preceded me over the hill, and when I was going down the hill I saw my stepfather coming up and walking fast. I motioned to him to come still faster. When I got to the top of the next hill, my uncle had already crossed it. There I suddenly saw my mother standing and she asked me, "Where are you going?" "I don't know. I am trying to catch my uncle and wait for my stepfather." Then she said, "You had better go home with me." She was sick in bed at the time. I turned around to go with her and woke up.

Comment.—Before I told my mother this story, she told me, "I dreamt of you last night. I dreamt that your uncle passed over this road. I saw you pass too and I tried to grab hold of you but missed you. I also saw your stepfather coming behind you." My mother had had a bad boil that night. She motioned to me to come, saying, "Jo, come here." I told her that I had had the same dream. The boil burst then and she became well. This is the way my mother interpreted the dream: she said that my uncle would die first, then I would die, and then my stepfather. However, my stepfather died first, my uncle afterwards, and I am still alive.

DREAMS OF J. P.

1

I dreamt I was a woman and had a little girl. I was laughing as I woke up.

Comment.—This is a good dream. I was very much amused at this dream.

2

I dreamt that somebody was chasing me. He never caught me. I have dreamt this often.

Comment.—This is a good dream. (J. Sh., another Indian, who was present, volunteered the following interpretation: "J. P., this is a good dream. What was pursuing you was disease. Disease can never catch your life. You will live to be an old man.")

3

I dreamt that a small black bear ran after me. I tried to climb a tree to escape him, but the bark was slippery and, furthermore, would always come off as soon as I attempted to climb. When I woke up I had an erect penis.

Comment.—None given.

4

I dreamt I was very rich. I saw a large round hotel, and in it I saw many large sacks full of money, all of which belonged to me.

Comment.—This is a bad dream. I got sick soon after dreaming it.

5

I dreamt I was lousy. When I walked I could see myself covered with lice. Then I went to the bush to get rid of these lice.

Comment.—This is a lucky dream. The year in which I dreamt it I was very lucky. I made $500.

6

I dreamt of honeybees.

Comment.—This is a lucky dream.

7

I dreamt that I ran away from three people. I ran toward the southeast. These three people, however, ran after me in order to kill me. I was alone and there were three of the others. I finally came to a lake about a half a mile from where I lived. I intended to swim across this lake and thus get away from them. As I reached the lake there was one man in front of me and two behind. I jumped into the water and turned around immediately to watch the man. When I was about halfway across I saw two of the men in the water following me. One fellow was pretty close to me. I had nothing in my hand with which to defend myself. This fellow soon got so close that I could almost reach him. Then I struck him and knocked out one of his eyes. The second man behind me then came along, but I got to the other side before he reached me. I thought then that I had got away from all three. I walked toward the west, toward a river, but when I had walked about half a mile I found two of the men in front of me again. One of them said, "This is the man who almost killed my brother." He was a very big fellow. Then he spoke again to his partner and said, "If you can kill him, do so!" Then I thought to myself, "I'm going to fight him and the best man will live." We all walked a little farther together along the shore. I felt as mad as the devil, and thought to myself, "I'm going to kill him (the man who had spoken), if I can." Then this one stopped and went back. He told his partner that he wouldn't fight. "This Indian is going to kill us," he said. "We had better run away."

Then I went to the river to see what kind of boat these people had had. As they paddled back I saw the occupants. They were the muskrat, mink, and otter.

Comment.—This is the finest dream I have ever had. Everything was going along nicely when I dreamt it. That winter I made $200.

8

I dreamt that a person I had known very well, in fact, a girl who had been my sweetheart, and who had been dead about ten years, came to me. Smiling, she put her hand on my chest and gradually brought it down lower and lower. I knew she was going to touch my penis. Just before she got there I shrieked out and awoke.

Comment.—None.

9

I dreamt that I saw two logs and between them a naked girl who wanted to cohabit with me. I got on top of the logs and tried to get into a position for copulation, but couldn't succeed.

Comment.—None given.

10

Some time after my mother's death I dreamt I was at home. I saw my mother's footprints and although I knew she wasn't there, yet I looked for her everywhere. (On another occasion I dreamt that she was at home.)

Comment.—This is a bad dream.

11

I dreamt I saw a well and that there were two women living in it. They were then outside of the well. They were my sweethearts and they were called Women-living-in-water. They spoke to me and wanted to take me down into the well with them, but I told them that I couldn't go down. Then they said, "Don't be afraid; you won't die for we will help you to get out afterwards. Do come with us for we have a nice home." I at first refused because I was afraid that if I went with them I would die. So I played with them on the outside of the well. They urged me to go with them and tried to entice me to live with them in the well. I again said, "No, I don't want to go there, for if I do I'll die." Finally, however, I did go with them. I entered the well and felt nothing in particular, nor did I die. They had a very nice home in the water. However, I knew I was a prisoner and that I wouldn't be able to get away again. Indeed, I tried to get out, but there was a high fence around me. I felt as you feel toward people whom you don't like yet who are very good to you. Finally, I got out just as I woke up.

Comment.—This is a good dream. I felt unhappy when I woke up for I wanted, in my dream, to get out of the well and yet I also wanted to stay, because these women were so good to me.

I asked an old man what the dream meant and he said that it meant life for me; that I would overcome every sickness that came to me and that I would live long. He said that if I hadn't succeeded in getting out of the well, I would have died.

12

I was sleeping with my wife. At that time we had two children, and this is the dream I had. I stood on top of a platform and as I looked around I saw lots and lots of people. Everyone was looking at me. Some of these people motioned to me with their hands. Everyone was laughing and feeling good. Then I left the platform. All the people present—white, red, black—wanted to see me. After that I went to another place, to a big church. On this journey a woman went along with me. I wore a long coat. Just before I got to the place, I saw a large number of people standing around the church. I knew some of them. I had nothing in my hand. As I began to walk up the steps of the entrance I suddenly felt that I had a black book in my hand. A man standing at the door—the bell-ringer—began to toll the bell, and as I entered they all bowed their heads and didn't look at me. I tried to smile and look at them, but no one would look at me. I was still holding the big black book. I knew that I was to be the preacher in the church. I went up to the pulpit, and just as I was to open the book my wife woke me up and asked me what was the matter. Apparently, I had been talking in my sleep.

Comment.—I asked an Indian about this dream (this was twenty-five years ago) and he said, "Soon every white man will look at you and help you out. So this is true, for white people have helped me out and now you have come to ask me all these things."

This is a good dream.

13

I dreamt I was standing near a lake, and there in the water I saw my brother drowning. I tried as hard as I could to drag him out of the water before he drowned. I could see him moving under the water. However, I couldn't reach him in any way. When I woke up I left him still drowning in the water.

Comment.—I was told that this was a good dream, and that my brother was going to live long. He is still living and is ninety-two years old.

14

I dreamt that my wife was going to leave me and that a white woman was going to help me out with my children. I didn't want her to go and I didn't want the white woman to come. I thought to myself, "I can help myself out." My wife was already in the train ready to leave. I was outside. My wife was going away alone and I didn't know where. Then my wife left and the white woman came to take care of the children. I didn't want her. She was very good to the children. Then I woke up.

Comment.—I was told that when a man dreams that he is dreaming, it means that he has almost died.

My wife told me that this dream meant that I was going to get another wife after she died. She died shortly after.

15

I dreamt, after my wife's death, that I was with my wife and that she was still sick. She didn't speak much to me. We were living together in the house and taking care of the children. Soon after, the huckleberry season began and we went away to pick huckleberries. There I dreamt that I saw an old friend of mine who was also picking huckleberries. My wife was sick all the time. Then she left me and I didn't know what became of her. I looked everywhere but I couldn't find her. Then I woke up.

Comment.—I have dreamt this dream very often. It is always the same; my wife is always sick.

16

I dreamt that the end of the world had come and that a few Indians were standing around me. As I stood on the ground I could almost hear the fire burning under the ground. West of this place there was a hill. There also I found a road and at the end of it, a large house, low on one side and high on the east side. Everyone was supposed to enter the house and get a yellow permit. Then, when the end of the world came, the possessor of a permit would not have to go to hell. I didn't have one of these yellow slips and I asked a man, "Can't you go in and get this permit for me?" "No, you have to get it yourself." So I didn't get it. I was ready to go in and was quite frightened, but I woke up before I went in.

Comment.—This is not a good dream.

17

I dreamt that there were many people around me and they were all looking at me. All of them—white, red, black—were good to me and talked to me kindly. Some of them really wanted to hurt me, but yet they spoke to me kindly. Some of them wanted to hurt me, but I got away. They were drunk. I ran away and got into some mud and hid myself there, with just my nose sticking out.

Comment.—I have dreamt this dream repeatedly during the last two years.

18

I dreamt that as I was walking alongside of a river I saw all kinds of snakes lying around on the ground. They were all quiet. I killed most of them and then walked on.

Comment.—This is a bad dream.

19

I dreamt that I saw two big snakes of greenlike color like an apple snake. These snakes were going to fight me, but I killed them all.

Comment.—This is a bad dream. Snake dreams mean you have an enemy. If you kill the snake it means good luck.

20

I dreamt I was naked and in an empty house in a city. I hid myself there. Then I asked for clothes from some of the people who were passing and they were just about to give them to me when I woke up.

Comment.—Some people say this is a good dream.

21

I dreamt that I saw two suns shining in the sky together and that the world was going to end. That was what all the people were saying. Everybody was looking at the sun, hollering and crying. I saw many goats running toward the west telling everyone that the world was going to end.

Comment.—This dream is neither good nor bad.

22

I dreamt of Pharaoh's little wood idols.[10] They came after me and began jumping on the pit of my stomach, tickling me. I laughed and cried out and my wife woke me up.

Comment.—This dream is neither good nor bad.

23

I dreamt that I was walking along and came to a river. There, along the bank, I saw lots of people. They were all washing and talking, laughing, and feeling good, at the same time. As soon as they finished washing their clothes they all jumped into the water. I looked at them and they all turned into muskrats. Then I dreamt that I was going to set the trap for them and kill them. I fixed my traps and was preparing to go after the muskrats. When I was finished blackening the traps I woke up.

Comment.—This is a good dream.

24

I dreamt that my dead uncle was alive and was talking to me. He wanted to show me how to hunt and to help me out as much as he could.

Comment.—None.

25

I dreamt that I was still a schoolboy at Carlisle, that I was just beginning to go to school again. I had a number of books in my hand. I knew that I was going to study for another five years and it seemed a very long time to me. I was very lonesome and I wanted to go home. However, I had to stay there for another five years. Then I came home again.

Comment.—This is a good dream.

26

I dreamt of seeing an old abandoned log road. On this road as I walked along, I met a young boy smaller than myself. He was kind of Negro-like. This boy, three feet high, was not a human being, I felt, but really the devil. He had a tail. He was very good-natured, but nevertheless he was the devil. He laughed at me and tried to push me as a joke. He didn't really want to hurt me very much. However, he got me mad so I thought I was going to knock him down. But I couldn't lick him; he was too quick for me. During all this time, he kept on laughing and was very good-natured. We fought for a long time. Neither of us got licked. He kept right on laughing. Then I woke up.

Comment.—This is a good dream. J. P. thought the boy was a devil because he had a tail.

---

[10] He had seen illustrations of the Tutankhamen discoveries.

27

My wife dreamt of a woman who was wearing a white dress and who was in our house. She was an old woman and my wife dreamt that she was going to have a race with her. She dreamt that the old woman said, "The one who wins this race is going to live." My wife looked at the woman and saw that she was very smart and that she could jump well. So the two started. But my wife, in spite of her illness, beat the old woman. And the old woman said, "Well, you have beaten me. Now you can go."

Comment.—My wife lived for another two years. She asked an old woman what the dream meant, and this old woman said that the person with whom she had raced was Death, that if the old woman had beaten her she would have died.

28

I dreamt that I saw a road about two feet wide. It was straight. I dreamt this last April before my boy died. Under the road was water. The road was four feet high. If you fell in the water you would die. I had to cross this road. The water was about as large as Lake Michigan. I went across without trouble and then came to a high hill on the other side of the lake, covered with snow. I went on top of the hill to look around. I could see far in the distance. I don't know what I was doing there; I was just walking and looking around. Then I went back to the place I had started from. I did not go the same way back.

Then I was to cross again in the same way, so I went across and I saw a lot of Indians who were not able to cross. No one could go more than fifty rods and then he would fall into the water and die. I looked at them and I couldn't help them in any way. I could only look after myself. I didn't cross again, for I was waiting for them to get ready and to gain strength. Then I awoke.

Comment.—This is a good dream. This is life. I guess I am going to be an old man.

29

I dreamt that I was going to take a ride with a crow. I sat on its back just below its neck. The crow flew up with me on him. It got to the top of a tree and took a rest there. I held on to him tightly. The tree was a beech and there were many other crows there. My crow could talk Indian and said to me, "Let's go over there." "All right," I said. "Well, hang on." The other tree was lower and he flew in a big curve and left me there. Then I thought to myself, "How am I going to get down?" Then I awoke.

Comment.—None.

30

Twenty years ago I dreamt that I was going to get married. The woman was young and very rich. Her hair almost reached to her feet. She didn't talk much but liked me all the same. Before I was to be married, I saw everything, food and presents on a table. One of the presents was a small table made of diamonds. Then the woman and myself walked and got ready to meet the preacher. My mother-in-law to be was there and she liked me too. I felt fine. Then I got married. My sister was there and helped me out. Then I woke up.

Comment.—Bad dream. My wife left me that fall for two months. She got angry at me.

31

I dreamt that I killed a man. I was going to be arrested and so I ran away. Then the "murdered" man came to life again and I was excused.

Comment.—None.

32

I dreamt that I had killed an otter and that the game warden was chasing me. I ran with the otter strapped to my shoulder. I had really killed the otter merely out of deviltry. I ran into the bush but the game warden followed my tracks. Finally, he caught me, talked to me and then let me go.

Comment.—This dream means good luck for the winter's hunting.

BERKELEY, CALIFORNIA.

ATTITUDES TOWARD AVOIDANCE: A SUGGESTION

By Gladys A. Reichard

INTEREST HAS RECENTLY been shifted in some quarters from the study of theoretical reconstruction of culture and problems of diffusion to a study of the attitudes which primitive people have toward their customs at the present time regardless of the way in which these customs originated. This interest has, in my opinion, pointed to a desire for the understanding of man as a human being as compared with using him as a laboratory animal. It is necessary and proper that observation of attitudes should follow studies of the formal structure of cultures because without a knowledge of prevailing customs it is impossible to detect or realize the significance of individual attitudes toward them.

A comprehension of present-day attitudes may not bring us to a determination of ultimate origins, but it seems to me it will broaden the possibilities for speculation regarding them, and of course will show up interrelationships between the customs themselves. Such an understanding must necessarily make a difference in the approach an investigator uses in his research, especially when he is in the field.

Observations of the attitude toward mother-in-law avoidance among the Navaho have prompted me to send forth the suggestions in this paper. Lowie[1] has discussed the avoidance in a logical and reasonable manner, reviewing the literature and weighing the evidence. At an earlier time Parsons,[2] prompted by Rivers, discussed the question. I have no intention of repeating their arguments here, or of trying to controvert them. I wish merely to present some new material, not so much to point out in how far their conclusions are valid or invalid in specific cases, as to suggest that their leads may be subject to slightly different interpretations and may be followed out to confirm or to modify their general inferences.

In comparing these two writers I find the arguments of both sound. It has been shown repeatedly that the psychological reactions of primitive people are different from our own only in their cultural conditioning, and some of us accept this fact. It seems to me, however, that we do not *use* it, for we seek origins and understanding of alien customs in large comprehensive ideas which imply consciousness of universal effects. Yet we know that many of the most powerful influences in our own society are due to individual prejudices, sporadic flashes of emotion, and unreason with its accompanying rationalization. For this reason I find Parsons more satisfactory than Lowie in her suggestions about avoidance, for she considers human foibles.

For example, the present Navaho attitude toward mother-in-law avoidance is better explained on grounds other than that of preventing incest, although I do not mean by this that the incest motive never did enter in. I think we have no proof either that it did or did not. The dominating attitude

---
[1] Primitive Society, 80–109, Boni and Liveright, New York, 1925.
[2] Avoidance in Melanesia, JAFL 29:282–292, 1916.

is that of mutual helpfulness. There are constant demonstrations that avoidance means just that, but the best examples I can give are rationalizations. When in 1923 I first went into the Navaho country I found no case of the breakdown of the mother-in-law taboo. That does not mean there was none but it does mean that occurrences were few and far between. During the period 1923–1925 I met a great many Navaho and talked with them about this very matter, and even though the young educated men wanted to treat the mother-in-law "like a mother" they were forced to accede to her wishes that she be avoided so as not to hurt her feelings.

In 1930 I went to the Navaho again and have stayed with them for five successive summers. During this period, however, I have not come in contact with nearly as many people as in the preceding period nor was I specifically seeking material on social organization. In one summer I came quite accidentally upon half a dozen cases of nonavoidance. I discovered that this is due to rationalization on the part of the young made convincing to the old, although inwardly they never entirely cease to demur, even the young having their qualms. "It seems," say some of the educated, who by this time may be in the parent-in-law class themselves, "that a woman never feels as good (has as good health) if she sees her son-in-law."

At any rate the movement, under the encroachment of white culture, away from the formality of avoidance is making rapid progress. Let John, one of my informants who is middle-aged and brought up in white ways, give his opinion. He is a good orator and is often called upon to make speeches. At a wedding I attended, and even at his own wedding, he made speeches the burden of which is as follows:

"There always comes a time when a woman needs help and her son-in-law is always ready to give her that help. But I feel that he can do this better if he can 'see' her than he can if he has to hide every time she comes in sight."

This is John's constantly repeated rationalization and on the basis of it he has been instrumental in making various parties agree at the time of the wedding that they will not observe avoidance. If the agreement is not made at that time the individuals concerned must "forever hold their peace."

That John's attitude is really one of expediency is demonstrated by his own experience. For years he had been a widower but finally he acceded to the requests of his relatives to marry, and, having submitted, he promised to marry the old-fashioned way, that is, a woman selected by his relatives who had the qualities generally required—dignity, virtue (she should not have gone to dances, meaning the "Squaw Dance"), capability. To these requirements John added another, "And her mother must not mind if I see her. I will help her all I can but I will not hide every time she comes near me." In explaining this John added, "I couldn't do this, I would be too embarrassed because I am not used to it."

The woman chosen for him belongs to the most conservative and uninfluenced of Navaho families, which does not live near the one I know best. Although the mother-in-law accepted John's dictum, it would interest me to know how "embarrassed" *she* might be at "seeing" her son-in-law. On this matter I have no information.

If the idea of hostility between mother- and son-in-law had ever had much weight, there has long been plenty of material from America to show it is not valid. Lowie rightly points out that avoidance means respect and Parsons that it preserves status of family and especially of seniority. Those interpretations are interrelated and both may be abundantly demonstrated. Parsons in refuting Rivers' group hostility thesis goes on to emphasize the fact that mutual helpfulness is characteristic of Melanesian avoidance. It is this feature which I feel comes out most strongly not only in Navaho avoidance but also among those tribes to which they are most closely related. My material demonstrates, I feel, a further statement of Parsons':[3] "We are apt to like those we help or those who help us." It shows an extension of the idea of mutual helpfulness which goes so far that it may be called affection although it is *in absentia*.

Avoidance was rigidly kept in the family with which I lived. As is usual, especially with matrilocal residence, it was frequently inconvenient. Attention to keeping the formality was about equally divided between the younger and the older members observing it. However, the sons-in-law seemed to have first choice at being present at a ceremony or in going on an excursion. I believe this phase was exaggerated in this case because the sons-in-law assisted the father-in-law, who chanted the ceremonies, and Maria Antonia, the mother-in-law, was naturally self-effacing. "She would rather stay home."

Maria Antonia was always greatly concerned for her sons-in-law and favored them whenever possible. She sent them tidbits when she cooked and gave them presents. She called them "my sons" in speaking of them and they called her "mother" although her daughter added, "She ought to call them 'son-in-law' and they ought to call her 'the-one-I-do-not-see.' But she likes them too much to do that and she thinks of them as her sons."

One reason for this additional remark is the fact that, although the observance of avoidance is serious and punctilious, both custom and terms are frequent causes for joking. The word for "son-in-law" has so long been subject to banter that it has a derogatory meaning.

The culmination of the attitude of fondness came when Maria Antonia was on her deathbed. After submitting to numerous "sings" she was finally taken to the hospital. Her family visited her yearningly and attentively, but she became worse and worse. Finally when her end seemed near, her three sons-in-law, one of whom had been called back from a distance by her illness, dressed up in their best costumes and went to *see* her. She had intermittent moments of consciousness and during one she opened her eyes and saw her three "sons." This was a surprise and a pleasure to her. They could have done no more to show not only their respect, but even their regard for her.

This attitude is not by any means restricted to the Navaho. Miss Ella Deloria tells me the Dakota have it in much the same way, the mother-in-law depends upon the son-in-law for small favors and voluntary thoughtfulness

---

[3] *Op. cit.*, 285.

for her welfare; it happens that she may sometime do him a major favor. She not only seizes the opportunity to do so but sometimes even makes one. The Apache have the same attitude.[4] Of the Cheyenne, Grinnell[5] says:

> Among people of good family, indirect courtesies often passed between a wife's mother and her son-in-law. It was not uncommon for a woman to make a lodge for her son-in-law, ornamenting it with quilled, pointed, or beaded linings, pillows, bed-covering, and other furniture. Often a newly married woman had little to do, her mother looking after everything, even to making moccasins for her son-in-law.
>
> ...a young man sometimes presented—but always through another—a horse to his mother-in-law. This was a creditable thing to do, and was an honor to the woman. It happened only among well-to-do people.

And in the naïve account of a Cheyenne woman[6] we read,

> My mother did all the cooking, but my husband's meals were always taken to our own tipi. This was for me to do.... My mother took especial care that my husband received the best portions of food,

showing that there was favoritism even in the details of daily life as among the Navaho.

For the Blackfoot, Wissler recounts:[7]

> However, as usual with such taboos, there are ways of adjusting this restriction (mother-in-law avoidance) when necessary. If the son-in-law is ill, she (mother-in-law) may, in case of need, care for him and speak to him; upon his recovery the taboo is considered as permanently removed. Each may call on the other when in great danger, after which they need not be ashamed to meet. Sometimes when a man went out to war or was missing, his mother-in-law would register a vow that if he returned alive, she would shake hands with him and give him a horse and feel no more shame at meeting. The son-in-law may remove the taboo by presenting a few captured guns or horses.

These are by no means the only examples in the Plains region which indicate the attitude, but they are typical and the ones which give the greatest detail. They take us back to Dr. Parsons' remark that we like those whom we help or who help us. That statement has limitations which the Indians, good psychologists that they are, realize. Helpfulness to be satisfactory must be reciprocal, large one-sided favors are dangerous to social relationships. However, an individual helped in a big way may reciprocate by an accumulation of little deeds which show his gratitude in thoughtfulness rather than in the recognized medium of exchange. Consequently, helpfulness, becoming mutual, may conceivably become competition. If this is not exaggerated too much, I at least can conceive how it may pass over to affection or fondness, which though formal, may be very real. This may or may not be related to sexual privilege or restriction.

The formality of the relationship is definitely related to distance. In the Navaho case, distance is always preserved; I know of nothing short of the

---

[4] Personal information from Dr. Ruth Benedict.
[5] Grinnell, G. B., The Cheyenne Indians, 1:146–147, Yale University Press, New Haven, 1923.
[6] Michelson, Truman, The Narrative of a Southern Cheyenne Woman, SI–MC 87:8 (no. 5).
[7] Wissler, Clark, Blackfoot Social Life, AMNH–AP 7:13, 1911.

deathbed example I have cited which can break it down once it has been established. It is, however, a crisis phenomenon, and the Plains illustrations given above demonstrate the fact that a crisis may allow a let-down of the taboo. The illness of the Blackfoot son-in-law, his return from indefinite and worrisome danger, or the presentation to his mother-in-law by a Mandan brave of the scalp of a slain enemy and his gun,[8] these are crisis phenomena.

The crisis must, however, be formalized; an ordinary crisis, no matter what dangers it brings on or averts, cannot automatically remove the taboo. Distance as it preserves respect may be lessened, therefore, and not only by an occasion of desperation. The Cheyenne "woman might face her son-in-law if she chose formally to present him with an ornamental robe."[9] This she did in ceremonial fashion, after which the taboo ceased to operate. The Crow[10] taboo may be removed by a presentation of a substantial gift by the son to his parents-in-law, and Lowie thinks there is an exchange of gifts. Death among the Crow may shorten the distance, for upon the death of her daughter a woman may address her daughter's husband as "son," from which time there is a mother-son relationship, one of respect but not of avoidance. Among the Navaho, who avoid only one woman, the wife's biological mother, and among the Apache, who avoid the entire group of "mother's sisters," the death of the intermediate relative makes no difference, avoidance continues until one or the other observing it dies.

From these illustrations, illuminating but sketchy, it is apparent that the "shame" of avoidance between affinal relatives among the Athabascans of the Southwest is like a curse or a blessing. Once it is established, it can only with the greatest difficulty be removed, if at all. There is a choice, however, as to whether or not it will be taken on, in the agreement at marriage between the relatives concerned—among the Navaho certainly a recent development, among the Apache older, but perhaps not *very* old.

The Plains Indians treat parent-in-law avoidance more like a garment. Marriage leaves no choice about putting it on, but there are ways of removing it subject to formal approval. Those means are the customary Plains solutions to any quandary—an exhibition of bravery, an exchange of gifts, or both.

These considerations should lead us to a definition of respect which would lengthen the discussion unduly at this point. Besides, our information on specific attitudes which doubtless differ in every tribe, following only basic patterns for large areas, is still too inadequate to be more than suggestive. That which we have implies, however, that it may be as difficult to differentiate between respect and deeper feelings which we may call affection, as it is to draw a line between religion and magic.

One manifestation of it is hesitancy, which is nearly the same as keeping at a distance. The Navaho word for "to respect" means literally "to hesitate." The Navaho shows respect for the inmates of a house by "hesitating," that is,

---

[8] Maximilian, Prince of Wied, Early Western Travels, 23:283, 1748–1846. Edited by Reuben Gold Thwaites, Cleveland, 1906.

[9] Grinnell *op. cit.*, 147.   [10] Lowie, AMNH–AP 9:213.

by stopping at a distance and remaining silent for some minutes before entering or calling attention to his own arrival. The hosts reciprocate by ignoring him for the same length of time or longer. A Navaho entering a house in which there is a "sing" may wait an hour before he shakes hands with his friends. The distance which he keeps between himself and his mother-in-law is an exaggerated hesitancy, one which is permanent. Distance as applied to respect is a matter of degree, literally illustrated by citations of Dr. Parsons[11] that in Tikopia brothers-in-law may converse *at a distance,* and that a Torres Islander may speak to his mother-in-law if the two keep a distance of five or six yards between them.

Respect is a category which includes many manifestations which have by no means been differentiated and named. In keeping off persons it involves such taboos as "not seeing," "not touching," "not naming." When honor is paid to an animal and its distance is psychologically measured it may be in terms of "not killing," "not eating," "not naming." It seems to me that the mother-in-law taboo, to which may be added avoidance between other relatives, belongs in the same class. Respect may lead to affection, different perhaps in a way from the affection, let us say, between joking relatives, but nevertheless real and possibly deeper.

We have the same reactions in our own society; we name and interpret them differently. Students put off appointments with professors they admire and respect because they are "afraid"—"afraid" to talk over the work they are doing. When the appointment is inevitable they stutter and stammer over the most elementary matter. This behavior cannot be explained by anything "real" on the side of the professor—he is usually kind and encouraging—or that of the student. The student knows this but he "hesitates" in spite of his reason. He may later, in spite of his "fear," endow a chair at his University because of admiration and even a "distant affection" for his professor.

Behavior of this sort obtains also between men and women. Admiration does not always lead to familiarity; it may lengthen rather than shorten the psychological distance between two people. All this, by way of brief illustration, may take mother-in-law avoidance out of an incest-preventing category and put it into one far more inclusive, one which may include religious as well as social phenomena. It suggests furthermore a possible explanation of avoidances other than those across sexes and between in-laws. Where there is a conscious dichotomy of attitudes based upon kinship, as among the Dakota, one can understand how certain peculiar avoidance (or joking) relationships came about. A Dakota, before he can even converse satisfactorily, must determine whether he has an avoidance or a joking relationship with the stranger he is meeting. He determines which it is through genealogy; someone through someone else, etc., etc., etc., must be related, if not biologically then through band, to someone through someone else on the other side.

Attitudes are extended: I, a male, have a respect relationship to my sister and therefore to many other individuals who trace their relationship to me

---

[11] *Op. cit.,* 289–290.

through her. I, a man, respect my father's sister because my father respects her; I joke with my father's brother because my father jokes with him. This is merely a bit taken from the rich material furnished by Miss Ella Deloria, but I cannot refrain from mentioning it here because of the many explanations it suggests.

The Navaho family with which I have lived used kinship terms with me. These terms are not very consistent because, since the patriarch of the family is old, the respectful term was "maternal grandfather." His daughters are sisters to me and the parental generation is missing. But his daughters' husbands should by all logic be "brothers-in-law" to me. Here, as among the Sioux, but not at all obviously, the brother-, sister-in-law relationship is a joking one. It was only after several summers and with the clue furnished by the Dakota material that I realized why I was "sister" to the young men of the family: the only son does not live at the same place. The delicacy of this solution to an intruding problem I credit to Red Point, the family head, who doubtless discussed the matter, as he did others, with his sons-in-law so as to preserve the dignity of his household.

This clue will account for a number of peculiar occurrences of avoidance and joking which are otherwise difficult to understand. For instance, it seems to me a possible explanation for a man's avoiding his wife's brother's wife among the Crow. Siblings of opposite sex are in the avoidance category; a wife avoids her brother; because she does, her husband, out of respect to her, avoids the person of the opposite sex most closely related to him, namely, his wife. The same explanation holds for the relationship of a man to his brother-in-law, which is one of deep friendship allowing limited joking but not obscene personal references. A woman would not speak lightly to or of her brother, and her husband, who is of the same sex, is allowed a degree of familiarity with the brother but it is strictly limited so as to preserve the respect accorded by a man to his sister and hence through her to her husband.

The definition of these attitudes which are general will, I believe, do much to make for an understanding of various relationships at least within the Plains area. The Assiniboin have the notion. In many of their social interpretations the Navaho belong with the Plains Indians. It is to be expected of course that each tribe will make different analogies and therefore reinterpret the categories even if the ultimate basis is as described. Where the basic interpretation prevails, the reasoning of the Indian mind through his genealogy will clear up some of the otherwise obscure adhesions of the avoidance or joking principles.

A consideration of the material on attitudes, sketchy as it is, seems to me to strike nearer to the core of the questions of avoidance and joking than we have come for a long time. It does not explain why one or the other attached itself to certain individuals rather than to others, although light is shed even on this problem, but it does suggest that a deeper knowledge of the attitudes now obtaining among primitive tribes may gradually, or even suddenly, unlock one door of understanding after another. We should have more facts from the Indian point of view to determine more definitely what we shall ultimately mean by such too-subjective terms as I have used, "respect," "affection," "psychological distance." I suspect these will have to be defined quantitatively as well as qualitatively and that, as is the case with other social and psychological phenomena, there will be no sharp dividing line between some of them.

BARNARD COLLEGE,
COLUMBIA UNIVERSITY,
NEW YORK CITY.

HUPA TATTOOING

By Edward Sapir

CHIN TATTOOING FOR WOMEN, as is well known, is characteristic of the tribes of northwestern and central California and northward into Oregon. The custom is described for the Hupa by P. E. Goddard in his Life and Culture of the Hupa (UC-PAAE 1:20):

> All mature women have marks tattooed on their chins. These marks are vertical and vary in number and width. Sometimes curved marks are added at the corners of the mouth. Delicate marks were placed on the chins of quite young girls. These were added to in size and number later in life. The Hupa deny that they mark age or social status, declaring that they are for ornament only. The tattooing was done by pricking in soot with a sharp flint or a splinter of bone.

An equivalent statement for the Yurok is made by Kroeber in his Handbook of the Indians of California (BAE-B 78:77–78). Figures 45 and 46 of this work give a convenient summary of Californian skin-tattoo designing.

In the summer of 1927, in the course of linguistic and ethnological work among the Hupa, I secured from Sam Brown, a very intelligent half-blood Hupa Indian, a brief text on tattooing. It follows in as literal translation as is consonant with easy intelligibility.[1] Notes, which explain or amplify various passages, follow the text.

Long ago, when the Jumping Dance[2] was held at Ta'k'imiłdiŋ,[3] I saw it, how in the fall girls raised their little burden baskets in the morning and went off after fir pitch. They all went across the river. And then Water-flows-past-him-place,[4] now dead, came across with them in order to interpret for them with the Yurok Indian who understood chin tattooing. Widow-he-has-been-made,[5] he used to be called.

He said to the girls, "Now! go to get pitch!" And then when they had gone up the hill to In-the-big-flat-place,[6] each of them carried out pitch in her burden basket to where that Yurok Indian was staying across from Ta'k'imiłdiŋ on the gravel. And then he built two roofed structures circle-wise with rocks, and in them he dumped the pitch. And then he built

---

[1] The field work was undertaken for the Department of Anthropology of the University of Chicago, to which thanks are due for permission to use the material in this place.

[2] This is the fall -č'idilye', popularly known as "Jumping Dance." For an account of the ceremony see Goddard, op. cit., 85–87.

[3] The main village, ceremonially, of the Hupa as a whole. It belongs to the lower, or northern, geographical moiety of the Hupa. See Goddard, op. cit., 12, 13, and map opposite p. 88. A plan of the village is given, op. cit., 129. The name, while very likely referring to the acorn feast held here, literally means "where one prepares acorn mush"; cf. Goddard, op. cit., 80.

[4] This name, to·xode·ldiŋ, is the name of a house in the village of Me'dildiŋ. The owner of the house, Captain John, was named after it. The wealthy men or "chiefs" of the Hupa and Yurok were generally called after the houses they occupied rather than by their proper personal names. Cf. Kroeber, op. cit., 12.

[5] The Hupa form of the name is 'isdiya·nĕwiŋ xowilĕwe·n. The "widow" refers literally to a woman and the name is equivalent to Shaved-head. This Yurok was from Johnson's (Hupa name, ni'nidahsa'andiŋ, "where earth round-sits above, knoll-place") on the Klamath river, above the Yurok village of Requa. He was visiting among the Hupa for the dance.

[6] Hupa xonte·lkohme', up on a bench back of Oscar Brown's place.

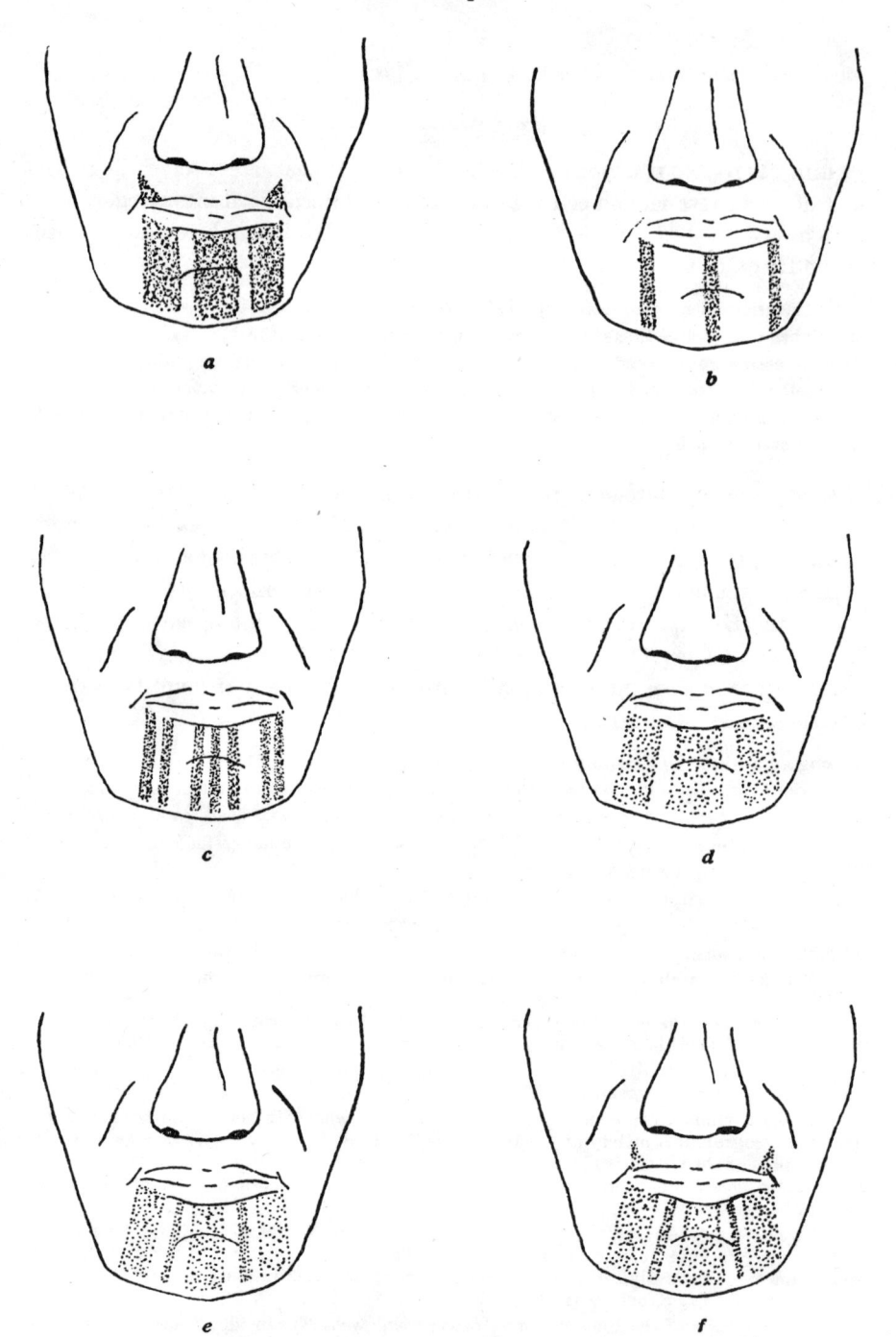

Fig. 9. Chin tattoo designs of the Hupa and neighboring tribes.
See text for interpretations of varieties *a-f*.

in the rocks all around until they met on top of the structure.[7] Then with fire he poked the pitch,[8] did this to the pitch in both places. And then, after a while, when it burned up, after he had taken the rocks off from the fire,[9] he scraped from them all the fine particles of black which had been thrown on by the fire.[10] When he had done this to all the rocks, every one of the girls sat down.

With soot mixed with marrow[11] they were already marked[12] down their chins in whatever way they wanted it. And then of one of them first he tattooed the chin, with a quartz sliver[13] he keeps cutting it, he keeps cutting at it in short dabs. With a stick he scraped off the blood. And then he keeps putting in that pitch soot. Finally, when he has tattooed the chins of one or two girls, night falls.[14]

And then, when he has tattooed the chins of all of them, they do not eat, anything white they do not eat—only seaweed and anything blue, such as salal berries, so that their chin tattoo marks may turn blue. But if she eats anything white, her chin cannot turn blue.

Just that much do I know of this tattooing of their chins.

They used to say, if a girl's chin was not tattooed, "You, are you going to look like a man? Lizards run into your mouth, your chin is not tattooed. Your ears are not punched through."[15]

Men used to be tattooed only inside their arms, some on their chest; some used to make signs of measuring where dentalia are measured. As soon as they stop growing, they tattoo for that purpose.[16]

The ten chin-tattoo designs illustrated in figures 9 and 10 were drawn by Sam Brown.[17] The interpretations are also his.

Figure 9a, characterized by three broad bands on the chin and two triangles at the upper corners of the mouth, is a combination of two distinctly

---

[7] In other words, he built two circles of boulders and then put other rocks on top of each in ever-lessening circles until they met in the center, which stood a foot or a foot and a half from the ground. The ground within the circle of boulders was somewhat scooped out to hold the pitch. The inner faces of the rocks were to catch the soot. It is of some interest to note that the Hupa verb for "building a roofed structure," -ɫ-miŋ' (-me'n), Mattole -ɫ-biŋ' [-be'n] "to build a house," is also found in Navaho, -ɫ-bį' "to build a (new) hogan." This verb is based on an old Athapascan noun, "roof, roofed structure," which appears dialectically as "roof" (Carrier, bən, Kaska [Jenness], bə'n) or "house" (Chasta Costa, mən), in Hupa as a diminutive, min'-ž, "menstrual hut."

[8] "To poke the pitch with fire" is the technical term for "to light the pitch."

[9] Carefully, so as not to shake off the soot. He collects it for the "ink," as Sam Brown put it.

[10] Hupa has a technical term for these particles, dahc'isde'.

[11] This fatty stencil soot is called miɫ-xo'a'diɫ'e'n in Hupa.

[12] The Hupa verb for "tattooing," -ɫ-tač', really means "to mark" and is used in this passage as well as in those referring to tattooing.

[13] This tattooing instrument is called cehlgay, literally "white stone." A boulder of quartz is broken up and the sharpest bit, which is quite small, is taken for the knife.

[14] In other words, he cannot expect to tattoo more than two girls at most during the day, the work is so slow. Tears drop down their cheeks as he cuts. He has to wait quite often. They had to be careful with the tattoo marks. They generally kept them covered until they healed, which took about five or six days.

[15] An incidental reference to another required bodily mutilation. The ears were punctured with a porcupine quill. It was pricked in lightly in the evening, and by morning it had worked its way through. The Yurok did not, it seems, perforate the ear; see Kroeber, op. cit., 77.

[16] For these measuring tattoo marks, see Goddard, op. cit., 48, 49. "Signs of measuring where dentalia are measured" correspond to Goddard's "creases on the left hand." Sam Brown's marks "inside their arms" are doubtless also for measuring. Goddard states: "He also had a set of lines tattooed on the inside of the left forearm. These lines indicated the length of five shells of the several standards."

[17] My thanks are due Mr. John Crowley, a Yale student, for redrawing the originals for reproduction.

named designs. The band design is called nite·l-wiltač', "wide-marked"; the triangular one, me·siwidlay, "several carried up along it."

Figure 9b, three narrow bands, is called 'ist'ik'iʒi-wiltač', "slender-marked."

Figure 9c, a developed form of b, is called 'ist'ik'iʒi-k'ine·lno', "slender-several are stood up."

Figure 9d illustrates the banded design of a, without the triangles.

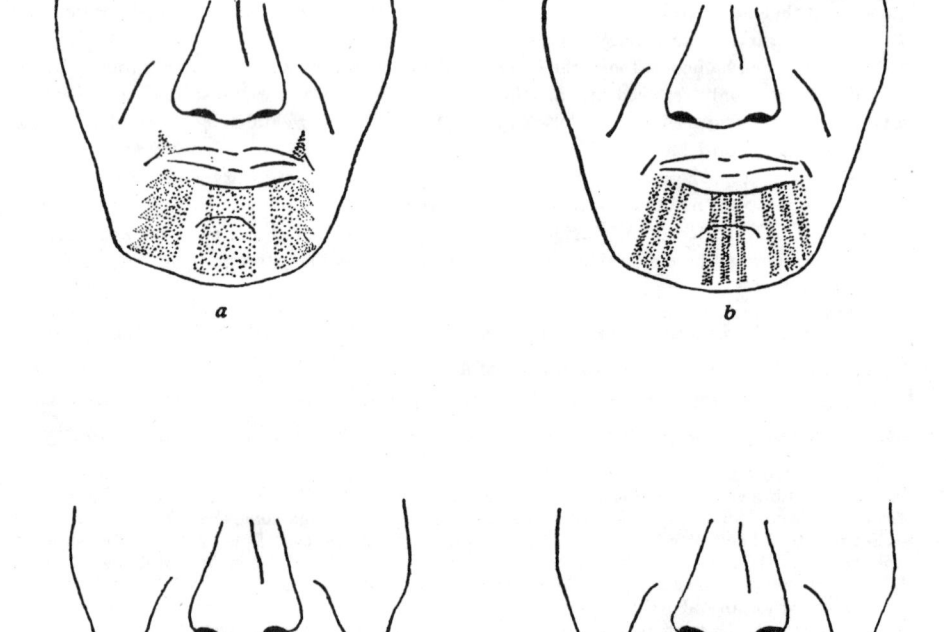

Fig. 10. Chin tattoo designs of the Hupa and neighboring tribes.
See text for interpretation of varieties a-d.

Figure 9e is developed from a by the insertion of a narrow white streak between the center band and each of the two outer ones. The design is called nite·l-wiltač' milgai' wilčwe·n, "wide-marked + made with white thereto."

Figure 9f is a combination of e and the triangular design in a. The design name of the whole is compounded of the two names, the "wide-marked" being omitted: milgai' wilčwe·n me·siwidlay, "made with white thereto + several carried up along it."

Figure 10a is developed from figure 9a by the addition of a row of triangular spurs to the two outer bands. Its name combines the three features: nite·l-wiltač' me·siwidlay č'ah-č'e·η'eλ'-wilcwe·n, "wide-marked + several carried up along it + made with 'caps' in a row coming out." This design was said to be Yurok and Wiyot, not Hupa. The element č'ah- was entirely obscure to Sam Brown. It is almost certainly the Hupa reflex of the Athapascan noun *č'a'x, "cap, headgear" (cf. Navaho č'a'h, "cap," Mattole č'ah, "hat," Ingalik c'əx, "cap of beaver fur," Kutchin c'e'h, "cap," Kaska [Jenness] c'a'h, "cap," Chipewyan c'a', "hat, cap"). The word had become obsolete in Hupa, not being applied to the woman's basket cap, but lingers on in a disguised form in a design name. Perhaps its proper meaning was originally "peaked fur cap" rather than "headgear" in general.

Figure 10b differs from figure 9c in having all three of the units of figure 9b triplicated instead of only the center one. This design is named ta·q'i na·ya·ḳida'ay, "several with three standing up straight."

Figure 10c is merely a slight variant of figure 9b.

Figure 10d differs from figure 9a in substituting forked figures for the simple triangles of the latter. The compound design name is nite·l-wiltač' łigiw me·siwidlay, "wide-marked + with forks carried up along it." This tattoo design, like figure 10a, was said not to be Hupa, but to belong to the Athapascan tribe of Van Duzen creek (No·ŋgahł in Hupa).

It is worth noting that all the names of tattoo designs recorded are strictly geometrical in character. This is in accordance with the general character of Northwest Californian basket design names. The Hupa basket designs described by Goddard (op. cit., 44–48) are named partly geometrically ("sharp and slanting," "set on top of one another," "points sticking up," "it encircles," "they come together," "one-on-the-other its scratches"), partly after fancied resemblances which have no true symbolic significance ("rattlesnake's nose," "grizzly bear his hand," "frog his hand," "swallow's tail," "sturgeon's back," "worm goes round").[18] Interestingly enough, at least one of the tattoo design names is identical with the name of a basket design. This emphasizes the purely technical, geometrical nature of design nomenclature among the Hupa. The identity in question is č'ah-č'e·ŋ'eλ' (fig. 10a), which I have rendered "with 'caps' in a row coming out," and Goddard's tcaxtceûñeL, rendered "points sticking up." According to Goddard this design "is applied indiscriminately to series of projecting angles" (op. cit., 47). Kroeber obtained the name also for an isolated triangle,[19] but it is probable that the triangle was thought of, in this case, as merely abstracted out of a projecting row of triangles. Furthermore, the simple "tca" or "tcax-hultcwe" (read probably č'ah and č'ah-wilčwe·n, "cap" and "cap-made, made into a cap" respectively) was obtained by Kroeber for the basketry design called "waxpoo" in Yurok and "apxankoikoi" in Karok.[20] In this too the projecting triangle seems to be the fundamental feature.

---

[18] See, further, Kroeber, Basket Designs of the Indians of Northwestern California, UC-PAAE 2:133–139. See pp. 159–162 for pseudo-symbolism in Californian basketry design.

[19] Basket Designs, 136.   [20] Basket Designs, 137.

YALE UNIVERSITY,
NEW HAVEN, CONNECTICUT.

AMERICAN AGRICULTURAL ORIGINS: A CONSIDERATION OF NATURE AND CULTURE

By Carl Sauer

ON THE SOUND descriptive principle that archaeology is where you find it, the science of prehistory is being pieced together from the evidence produced by digging. It cannot however depend exclusively on the limited testimony provided by the enduring materials of ruins, graves, and refuse heaps, but seeks other inductive approaches by tracing culture survivals, be they words, institutions, forms of settlement, tools, crops, or other culture traits. Such data, contributed from diverse sources, may provide also new leads for the field archaeologist in his explorations. Culture history moreover may set up working hypotheses that use partially deductive approaches, as by postulating from sufficient experience certain probable relationships between environmental advantage or disadvantage on the one hand and the origin and development of culture on the other. As in all other fields of culture history, there is permanent need of interdisciplinary synthesis and hypothesis. In these pages probability of original development of American agriculture in certain hearths is considered in the light of certain fundamental characteristics of native crop plants and farming practices, which point to specific natural environments and hence would limit the number of eligible localities in which such cultural beginnings may have been made.

Origin of American agriculture in desert or steppe?—The most widely known thesis of the origin of agriculture in America is the one formulated by Spinden, who has regarded "irrigation as an invention which accounts for the very origin of agriculture itself," and who therefore would place the beginnings of farming and sedentary village life, as well as the sites of most rapid cultural advance, in arid and semiarid parts of the New World.[1] His position is very much like the familiar "potamic" theory that Old World civilization originated in the river oases of the Near East by irrigation—a theory elaborated especially by Kropotkin and Metchnikov. The arguments which have been advanced by Spinden are in particular: (1) that the earliest records of cultivated plants, pottery, and weaving come from areas where irrigation was practiced, these areas in the New World including specifically Peru and Mexico, (2) that pressure of population made itself felt early in such areas and acted as an incentive to cultural advance, (3) that "in the desert the clearing of the field is less laborious than in the jungle," and (4) that the comparative food value of plants originating under desert conditions is perhaps higher than that of plants which belong originally in climates exacting less extreme physiologic qualities.

The archaeologic evidence that agriculture originated in association with irrigation is by no means convincing, as the supporters of this thesis conclude.

---

[1] ICA 19:269–276. I have taken exception to his view elsewhere (Ibero-Americana, 1: 58–60).

The case is far better for the Old World than the New, but even there it is weak. The great stratigraphic records of early culture in the Old World are in the great river oases, or their margins, it is true, but what warrant is there for associating irrigation with the oldest or older of these horizons? Nor is it safe to assume, because the longest-known stratigraphic series are established in the river oases, that still earlier records will not be discovered elsewhere. The archaeologic knowledge of Mesopotamia and Egypt is enormously superior to that available for other areas, because their great ruins of ancient historic civilizations first attracted scientific curiosity. We are just beginning to see attention directed to the archaeology of Iran, Asia Minor, and India, any or all of which may possibly precede the rivers of the deserts in development of agriculture and sedentary life. For the New World the assertion that agricultural beginnings in Mexico were associated with irrigation appears to be unwarranted. I am unaware of any such evidence for early Mexico or Central America, or even of the major importance of irrigation at any time in their aboriginal history. Where there were large populations on the Gulf or Caribbean coasts and in the interior plateaus, irrigation generally was not needed. For that part of the west coast with which I am acquainted, the evidence is that irrigation was not employed, but that farming depended on rainfall supplemented by the natural seasonal flooding of streams.

If American agriculture arose in desert or semidesert regions, whether by irrigation or by dependence on natural flooding, three areas, chiefly, would come under consideration: (1) The Sonoran desert, which lies near the Gulf of California, and the steppe lands marginal thereto. Perhaps no other area in the New World comes as close to the physical conditions of the Old World Fertile Crescent as does this one. The lower Colorado, Sonora, Yaqui, Mayo, and Fuerte valleys are large, superbly good areas for flood farming or for irrigation, suitable for growing many crops, and in part capable of raising two major crops a season. All of them, with the exception of the Colorado river, are very favorably situated with regard to possible routes of migration between north and south. Yet, without exception, these great flood plains have yielded no evidence of important archaeology. On the contrary, the headwaters of these northwestern Mexican rivers, in more humid and mountainous country, have significant archaeologic remains, though not, so far as known, of great age. The Gila and Salt rivers, tributary to the Colorado, hold remains of the Hohokam culture, which produced the most extensive irrigation of aboriginal North America. Though the elaboration of this culture developed strikingly autochthonous characteristics, it is not doubted that the beginnings of it were introduced from the south. (2) The Pueblo culture area of our Southwest, with its major axis running from the upper San Juan river along the Rio Grande into central Chihuahua. Here, in more numerous but smaller bodies of land than those of the Hohokam, irrigation was practiced. Its Basket Maker beginnings of agriculture however are also based on southern introductions. In neither of these arid areas of North America, and they are the only notable ones that come into consideration for this continent, is agriculture considered otherwise than as a diffusion from the south. In both, moreover, many of the small early sites depended on farming without irrigation, with or without natural flooding of the fields.[2] Perhaps for both areas the interpretation may be permitted therefore that irrigation is subsequent to the establishment of agricultural settlement and that it is especially characteristic of the period of maximum expansion and greatest vigor of the cultures. We may consider as most probable that crops and farming methods were brought in from the south but that irrigation was a local invention.

(3) There remains therefore as a likely source of agriculture under arid conditions only the coast of Peru. It has against it first of all a strongly marginal location in its relation to the higher cultures of the New World, but also increasingly the evidence that its cultivated crops are not native to that area. Like the other arid-land cultures it appears to be a colonial area, though perhaps early, with rapid and high local elaboration under the stimulus of gregarious oasis habitation.

Against the desert thesis, the following arguments also weigh heavily: (1) The evidence of the domesticated plants of the New World overwhelmingly points not to desert or steppe but to several humid climates for their origin. With minor exceptions they have physiologic qualities that do not fit into dry-climate habitats. These qualities, critical for the consideration of culture origins, have been overlooked and will be considered in the following sections. (2) Finally, desert lands, unless they be forested flood plains and hence non-desert in vegetation, are not easy, but difficult to clear for cultivation. The dry areas of North America which would come under consideration abound in brush and scrub, deeply rooted, tenacious of life, and difficult to eradicate even under modern methods. The preparation even of the bare surface usually demands much labor in leveling for the effective distribution of water. The engineering problems of diversion and delayed discharge of water, in their simplest terms, are rather formidable. The irrigation works of the Hohokam of Arizona involved a very considerable amount of engineering skill, as well as a great deal of collective labor.

Site qualities favorable to the origin of culture hearths.—Having found desert and steppe unfavorable sites for the origin of American agriculture, we may examine other situations and criteria in the search for hearth areas. Without denying the existence of irrational or "prerational" attitudes in the satisfaction of subsistence needs by primitive groups, it is nevertheless obvious that of all culture forms, the business of getting food, clothing, and shelter depends most largely on rational use of the natural environment. A consideration of rational solutions of the problems which such a group may have encountered in making a living from a particular environment is therefore not to be dismissed as rationalization.

(1) Ratzel has emphasized the importance of "forcing-bed" conditions in

---

[2] I have discussed the question of the natural conditions involved in agriculture in the arid Hohokam country, including the desert Papagueria, in Prehistoric Settlements of Sonora, with Special Reference to Cerros de Trincheras, Univ. Calif. Publ. Geog., vol. 5, esp. pp. 119–124.

the origin of cultures. In this concept is involved the availability of a limited, valuable subsistence area which rewards intensive use by sufficiently increased returns, and which has somewhat inelastic limits, so that improved use rather than expansion of used area tends to result. A further consideration is a bounding zone which fends off easy incursions by other groups, but which is not a barrier so effective as to isolate the group from contacts with others. Under such conditions, it is argued, social advance is encouraged and increasing pressure of population hastens the advance from gathering to planting. The view of course may be construed as favoring a multiple origin of cultivation.

(2) Another stimulus to cultural advance is seen in the availability of diversified raw materials, each in moderate amount, rather than in the great abundance of one or a few staples. Each primitive group needs, as the pioneer farmers did, a varied supply of raw materials for a well-balanced economy. If it is to continue to improve or even to maintain its standards, either these resources must be maintained so as to provide a certain quota per capita or else there must be discovery or creation of at least equivalent substitutes which continue to be available in like amount to each individual. A varied sustenance basis and the possibility of maintenance or enlargement of this sustenance basis would therefore be necessary material prerequisites for cultural advance.

(3) Vavilov has developed the thesis of the mountain-valley origin of agriculture: "Mountainous districts supply an optimum of conditions for the manifestation of the varietal diversity (of plants), for the differentiation of the varieties and races, for the preservation of all possible physiological types.... It is very probable therefore that mountainous districts, being the centres of varietal diversity, were also the home of primeval agriculture."[3] Under such varied physical conditions the best opportunities were given for the occurrence of numerous kinds and types of useful plants, the primitive plant breeder had the richest material with which to experiment by selection and crossing, and hence there may be postulated the best prospect of producing new and more useful forms.

(4) For primitive agriculture a soil is required which is amenable to few and weak tools and which rewards tillage by yields sufficient to encourage continued planting.

(5) Similarly the native vegetation must be such that it can be displaced by simple means and without excessive effort. The theme is developed later that forest lands yield most readily to the primitive cultivator.

(6) Climatic conditions are indicated which provide a definite growing and resting season. A well-defined tapering off of the growing period into a period of vegetative rest stimulates the production of seeds and tubers, the primary objects of gathering plant food and of planting. Also, under such conditions maturity takes place *en masse* in a short period; in other words,

---

[3] Vavilov, N. I., Studies on the Origin of Cultivated Plants, Bull. Applied Botany and Plant Breeding, 16:218–219, 1926.

there is a definite harvest season. The necessity of providing against a recurring period of no production places a premium on thrift and industry which is lacking in lands of weak or no seasonal contrast.

(7) The early significant advances of the human race, by which the level of sedentary, agricultural life was attained, appear to have taken place in lands of genial climate. The theory that man progresses only by being continually driven by the lash of nature has been overworked, as in Spinden's statement that "theoretically, agriculture would be more likely to originate under conditions that were hard than under those that were easy." On the contrary, it appears that in the earlier stages of his cultural advance man fared better under a nature that was benign, varied, but not too opulent in any particular respect, and that offered a sufficient and ready reward to the industrious, the skillful, and the provident. How great a part of the major early advance of the human race, both before and after the development of cultivation, is to be found in the truly temperate (mesothermal) climates, away from tropical exuberance, from desert extremes, and lands of heavy winters!

Indicated centers of American agricultural origins.—Under these terms, then, we should seek for the cradles of higher culture in humid lands of mesothermal climate, especially such as have a marked dry season (Cw or Cs of Köppen), which were moderately forested, had loose, and preferably rich, soils, a considerable variety of raw materials such as might be provided by a sufficient range in elevation, possessed a limited but good subsistence area, and were protected by partial barriers such as coasts or mountain ranges. Vavilov has objected to the great river plains of the Near East as the cradles of Old World agriculture and has sought to place its origins in the mountain valleys of Iran, Turan, India, and Abyssinia. Similarly in the New World we would suggest that the most promising trail for discovery skirts the humid flanks of low-latitude highlands at intermediate elevations.

(1) The basal flanks of the great volcanic chain that stretches across Mexico from Tepic to central Vera Cruz have highly eligible sites with plentiful summer rain and rich, friable soils. Of least promise are the central portions, which on the north open up widely to the Gran Chichimeca, the great steppe and desert country that reaches across the international border, whence raiding tribes exerted pressure against the settled lands to the south. The southern slope of the central volcanic area also is disadvantageous, for it falls off for the most part steeply into the rain-shadow basin of the Balsas or Mexcala valley. Both the eastern and western ends, however, are suitable as culture hearths. (a) At the west, the country west of Guadalajara is well sheltered against the north by difficult barrancas. Tepic in particular has rich land, genial climate, varied relief, a rich flora, and a well-protected location which nevertheless is sufficiently convenient for the intrusion and diffusion of cultural impulses. Of its archaeology only the curious Ixtlán figurines are known. (b) At the east, the Valley of Mexico is a great, snug bight of most attractive land, limited in early attractiveness chiefly by its elevation and restricted

flora. The basins of Puebla, mountain-rimmed and extremely well protected against the turbulent north, might be considered superior to the Valley of Mexico. They are also more diversified in relief and flora. No reconstruction of the original vegetation of these volcanic uplands has been made, but the indication is that it was a country of deciduous hardwoods, among which oaks are prominent.

(2) To the south of the Mexico-Puebla area an easy corridor leads to the temperate upland of Oaxaca, a sheltered site as well as a passageway, possessing mellow soils and a highly favorable diversity of relief, climate, and flora.

(3) The volcanic slopes of Central America repeat on a smaller scale the favorable conditions of the Mexican volcanic belt. Thus in a loose cluster the northern continent offers four superior areas as possible hearths.

(4) The southern continent suggests only one area of equal eligibility, the temperate inter-Andean structural valleys of Colombia and Venezuela.

(5) However, the Brazilian Highland in its more elevated, eastern parts, and probably especially toward the south, has conditions generally favorable, except for off-side location and a terrain that is perhaps too open.

Such an inspection of the New World may be discounted as resting on the suitability of present-day climates, whereas the time here involved lies thousands of years in the past. There are some, and they rely especially on Ellsworth Huntington, who would argue that the distribution of climatic areas in the prehistoric past of the New World was markedly different from that of the present. Climatic change involving the progressive displacement of climatic limits requires, however, either an important alteration of relief and of the distribution of land and sea or else significant change in the general atmospheric circulation. The former operates slowly. The latter type of change did take place during the Ice Age. Then and immediately thereafter the range of paleolithic man in the Old World suffered considerable displacement. So far as we know, postglacial climates settled down to their present form in the New World before agriculture got under way. The burden of proof rests on those who think otherwise. In our present knowledge of climatology we can point to no competent postglacial disturbing force. The appeal to a climatic change in order to get around some apparently inconvenient cultural distribution is too often an easy and careless way out of a perplexing situation. It has been improperly applied to our Southwest, where the entire archaeologic distribution is fully intelligible in terms of present climates. It has been postulated for the ancient Maya because of supposed present climatic unsuitability. In both of these applications the wish is father to the thought and more knowledge of the culture and the country makes such hypotheses entirely unnecessary.

Climatic and edaphic adaptations of New World crops.—The crops of the Old World perhaps may be grouped roughly under two sets of centers of origin, one in the Near East and the other in the monsoon lands of southeastern Asia. Climatically the former is a mosaic of dry lowlands and of humid highlands, which are mesothermal with preponderance of cool-season rains and dry summers (*Cs* of Köppen). This climatic type recurs in detached areas as far east as Afghanistan. The lands of lengthy winter rainy season border most of the Mediterranean, including at its eastern end Syria and Palestine, and reappear beyond on mountain flanks eastward to the borders of India. In these eastern mountain "islands" Vavilov and his associates place the original home of many of the most important Old World crops. In this habitat the crops are fall-sown, make a large part of their growth of stalk and leaf in cool weather, and complete their maturity during the long summer days in the season of warmest weather. These climatic adaptations made easy the diffusion of such crops into northwestern Europe, even into latitudes where the planting shifted to spring. In the European lands there still was the same condition of a cool, moist starting period, though the start was shifted to spring, and maturity still took place during the long days of midsummer. It is not without significance that Europe has midsummer harvest festivals.

In the New World we encounter a strikingly different situation. Most of the New World domesticated plants, the potato being the principal exception, like or require a warm start, summer rains, and a dry fall with lowered temperature. They are late in starting, and late in maturing, and if they can be brought under one seasonal definition, they may be said to be planted at the beginning of summer and harvested at the end of fall. This seasonal characterization is admittedly very rough, but it does bring out a contrast to the crops of western Asia and of Europe. The most widely spread and most important American crop, maize, typifies the dominant climatic adaptations of American domesticated plants. Planting is delayed generally until the ground is well warmed and cold nights are past. Under such conditions maize germinates well even if the soil be only slightly moist. In north Mexico and among the Indians of our Southwest, for instance, deep planting is practiced a month or so before the exceptionally delayed summer rains of those sections begin. After the corn is well sprouted, the more rain and warmth the better the growth. The yield of the commercial corn crop in the United States is almost directly proportionate to the rainfall and temperature of the two months after the first leaves are formed. The inhabitant of the Mississippi valley calls the muggy summer thunderstorm periods "corn weather." Then a combination of high temperature, high humidity, warm rain, and warm nights brings the luxuriant vegetative growth necessary for a good yield. Thereafter a tapering off of rainfall is beneficial and maturity is aided either by dry weather or by gradual lowering of temperature. The most active vegetative period of New World crops tends to extend through the period of maximum warmth and long days. Comparable conditions in the Old World are found in the summer monsoon lands of southeastern Asia. It may be noted that the European area which has been most successful in the cultivation both of maize and of monsoon climate crops is the Po valley, which has a marked period of rain during the heat of midsummer. In terms of the Köppen classification of climates the optimum habitat of American cultivated plants is in the *Cw* climates, and for the more tropical varieties, such as manioc and sweet potato, the *Aw* climates. The potato and its cultural associates, however, are excluded from these generalizations because of their intolerance of hot weather.

The American crop plants are in general poorly adapted to withstand drought while making their growth, upland cotton of Mexican origin being a partial exception. The leaf surfaces of the common American crops lack the devices that even slightly xerophytic plants have for economizing transpiration. In size and abundance of leaves most American domesticated plants are far more luxuriant than the nontropical Old World crop plants. Those which are of exceptionally rapid maturity, for instance, the tepari bean (*Phaseolus acutifolius*), may grow where the total rainfall is low. Even though water is needed only for a brief season, the plants require a dependable water supply while making their growth and suffer damage quickly if water is lacking at such time. Others, such as manioc, potato, and sweet potato make use of a short rain season to develop tubers or root-stocks for underground storage, some of them being adapted to a double annual rain period, others to a biennial growth period. Apparently none of these plants, however, has any provision for withstanding low, uncertain, and irregular rainfall. Although a considerable number of such native crops can get along on a short rainy season, it is hardly proper to call them drought-resistant. In the savanna climates (*Aw*) and their boreal borders, the rainy season may be shortened to two months, but during that time rainfall is quite dependable, and may come in daily thunderstorms. It has been this condition, perhaps, that has misled some observers with respect to the climatic adaptations of American crops. A climate may be dry during the greater part of the year, but it is not therefore a semiarid climate any more than is a land of long winter. Both are simply climates with long resting periods and with brief growth periods. The growth period however is not a time of drought at all and the vegetation is not drought-resistant, but either matures rapidly or passes into a resting state until the next rain season. The most general remark that can be made in this connection is that American crops vary greatly in the length of rain period required, but that generally they have no provision for the conservation of moisture during their vegetative period and that they suffer quickly if the moisture supply is seriously interrupted within the limits of this time. The Mexican cotton, which can stand drought remarkably well, is perhaps therefore especially notable among American crops. In general our New World domesticates do not have the deeply developed root systems which are common to dry land vegetation and to some of the Old World crops. Many are shallow feeders.

Another significant contrast to the crops of western Asiatic origin is the markedly low tolerance of American crops for alkaline soil conditions. Our beans are notoriously sensitive to alkali in soil. Corn fares little better. Upland cotton is rather tolerant in this respect and one strain, the Acala, brought from Chiapas by O. F. Cook, is fairly alkali-resistant. The source of this particular variety is one of the especially dry interior areas of southern Mexico. It represents perhaps an old selection from a plant which originally favored the drier margins of a summer-rain mesothermal climate. The experience of farming practice in the United States would appear to indicate that the New World crop plants belong pretty well on the neutral border between alkaline and acid soils, with cotton showing a leaning to the alkaline side, though also a large tolerance in the other direction, whereas the potato, sweet potato, peanut, and tomato are quite tolerant of fairly acid conditions, and the corn-beans-squash complex thrives best approximately on the neutral border line. These nutritive habits again point toward a moderately humid climate with upland cotton displaced toward the dry margin, and the sweet potato, peanut, and tomato toward the wetter side.

The remarks have been kept in general terms chiefly because there is little quantitative information on the optimum and limiting climatic conditions for the individual crops. The field of agricultural climatography has remained sadly neglected and is virtually a blank for the climates of Latin America, which are of the greatest importance for the present problem. In summary therefore we can only say at the present time that the cultivated plant assemblage of New World origin is dominantly mesophytic, that with the exception of the potato complex their growth begins with warm weather and rain and continues through the period of maximum warmth and moisture, that some require for their vegetative growth a rainy season of as little as two months whereas others require four or five months, and that maturity takes place under a dry season following. The natural plant association most nearly representative of these conditions is to be found in summer-green forest lands of deciduous habit.

Place of origin of individual crop plants.—The latest and most comprehensive evidence on place of domestication comes from the Russian Institute of Applied Botany and Plant Breeding. It is principally this material that is basic to the following discussion.[4]

The Russian Institute has added a great deal to our knowledge of native crop plants as to kind, range, habit, and kinship. For the first time the entire assemblage of American cultivated plants has been made the object of collection and study. In each area the Russian botanists have regarded the whole agricultural complex and have attempted to get specimens and data not only for each species cultivated, but also on as many varietal forms thereof as possible. A good beginning has been made in charting geographic range of cultivated plant forms and of characterizing habitat, including elevational and phototropic limits. A generous collection of seeds and tubers made possible further study of growth habit by the planting of these materials in Russian experimental gardens, thus making possible the comparison of original habitat with new environments. Many varieties have been further subjected to genetic analysis, by chromosome counts and by an elaborate systematic

---

[4] Bukasov, S. M., The Cultivated Plants of Mexico, Guatemala, and Colombia, 47th Supplement to the Bulletin of Applied Botany, Genetics, and Plant-Breeding (Leningrad), 1930; includes articles by Kuleshov, N. N., on maize, and Mauer, F. M., on cottons. Kuleshov, N. N., Distribution of the Varietal Diversity of Maize, Bull. Applied Bot., vol. 20: 506–509 (Leningrad), 1929; Rybin, A. V., Karyological Investigations on Potatoes of America, *ibid.*, 711–718; Zaitzev, G. S., Contribution to Classification of Gossypium, *ibid.*, 18:1–66 (no. 1); Ivanov, N. R., Origin of Forms of Phaseolus, *ibid.*, 19:209–212 (no. 2).

determination of dominant and recessive characteristics. Thus these geneticists have undertaken a classification *de novo* of varieties and have referred these to ancestral forms. The collecting was done, it is true, by rapid but energetic sampling, mostly along main-traveled routes and hence under somewhat unfavorable conditions for finding the more primitive plant materials, preserved in the remoter byways. Nevertheless, the collectors came out of the New World with the most varied and remarkable body of cultivated plant materials that has ever been assembled and subjected to genetic analyses.

The Russian inquiry is not only of great interest for its facts; further, it has used methodically the familiar procedure of culture history in an approach to a neglected line of culture historical evidence. In the manner in which cultivated plants have been dealt with these are in effect aboriginal culture traits, which are considered with respect to their geographic distribution, centers of origin, directions of diffusion, and changes in the process of diffusion. Presence or absence of a particular plant form, that is, culture trait, has been noted throughout the area of observation. In the determination of the identity of the form or trait the geneticist should be able to operate with greater precision than the culture historian can do ordinarily, since the qualities dealt with can be classified with respect to primitiveness. If the elements of culture in general could be arranged with reference to dominance or recessiveness the whole problem of cultural diffusion perhaps could be resolved by distributional analysis. Having determined specific identity tentatively, the Russian Institute personnel proceeds first to establish within a species the genetic relationships of varieties to each other and thereby to place them as differentiated from ancestral plants; secondly, to chart the occurrence of each variety, and thus find the area of maximum varietal diversity of a species. If such diversity agrees also with the maximum development of dominant traits, it is concluded that the center of origin of the plant has been located. The procedure is obviously in close agreement with the general ethnologic method of determining origin and diffusion of culture traits. The Russian geneticists may have hit upon a means of recognizing relative age and manner of migration of culture that should rank next in definitiveness to the stratigraphic results of the archaeologist, and that may provide knowledge that is irrecoverable by archaeologic means. Here, at the least, is an approach to culture beginnings which culture history cannot disregard. Either it must be disproved as concealing an as yet undiscovered error or it should be used as a major aid in the reconstruction of cultural origins.

The Russian botanists have proposed eight centers of plant domestication for the New World, unspecified with respect to independence or interdependence. The evidence submitted does not exclude explicitly, and perhaps not implicitly, the possibility of a primary center from which the others may have developed by supplementary and alternative domestications. Whereas the investigators have not committed themselves on the ultimate question of single or plural origin, their evidence may be interpreted in favor of multiple independent beginnings of New World agriculture.

Colombia, as in the work of DeCandolle, is moved into a major position in the history of domestication, and indeed into one where possibly it may have priority. If one may propose that the first step in domestication was the obtaining of an adequate supply of starchy food, Colombia is especially noteworthy (1) in having an important local crop in the Arracacha (*Arracacia xanthorhiza*), which the Russians consider as possibly more ancient than either maize or potato, and which occupies the altitudinal zone between manioc and potato, or roughly that of maize; (2) in having at least two primitive kinds of potato (24 chromosomes), indigenous to Colombia; and (3) in the possibility that the most ancient form of maize originated here, which is held to be flour corn (*Zea mais amylacea*). The argument for the great age of flour corn rests (1) on its distribution, by far the widest of all the maize groups, (2) on its greatest richness in morphologic and biologic diversity, and (3) on the dominant character of the starchy endosperm. Few varietal forms of this group were noted by the Russians in Colombia in spite of its abundant production in that country, and hence the reasons for considering that its origin may have been in that country are not apparent. For New World cotton they reduce the ancestral species to two, bringing *Gossypium peruvianum* under *G. barbadense* and making this group South American in origin. The original qualities which they have determined for this group as markedly mesophytic perennials—relative intolerance of hot weather, and marked adaptation to a short summer day—would indicate that its origin must be sought in low latitudes at moderate elevation. The intermediate humid mountain valleys of Colombia or Venezuela, where also the varietal diversity is extraordinarily high, would then be the most probable centers.

Central America, in particular Guatemala, to which may be added the adjacent Mexican state of Chiapas, yielded handsome returns to the Russian explorers. Here they found for flint corn (*Z. mais indurata*) "a varietal diversity not known in other parts of the world." Southward this group is found to continue predominant through the coast of northern Peru and eastward through the West Indies. The flint group they consider as having originated by a crossing of the more ancient starchy form with a Guatemalan Euchlaena. Central America is indicated also as a major center in the domestication of *Phaseolus*, the kidney bean (*P. vulgaris*) being referred either to Mexico or Central America, the ayecote (*P. multiflorus*), next widest in distribution after the kidney bean, being identified as of Central American origin, and the lima bean (*P. lunatus*) as belonging originally to moist lowlands in Guatemala and southern Mexico. They even found the tepari bean (*P. acutifolius*) important in Chiapas, in hot areas of brief rain period. This bean, almost unique among native crops in the shortness of its required rain period, in its tolerance of heat, and in its quickness of maturity, is widely distributed all along the west coast of Mexico as well as in the American Southwest. Its range and problem of origin are perhaps parallel to that of chia (*Salvia chia*). Both conceivably may have spread into the American Southwest from the south, out of one of the drier spots in west Mexico in which agriculture was established fairly early. This possibility gains some support from the apparent archaeologic appearance of the tepari bean in the Southwest well after the introduction of the kidney bean. A careful study of the tepari bean may possibly therefore be of especial interest in reconstructing cultural diffusion between West Coast Mexico or even Central America and our Southwest.

As Central Mexico's great contribution the Russian group labels confidently dent corn (*Z. mais indentata*), which shows "no such variety of forms and types elsewhere in the globe." Popcorn of the rice grain type is also credited by them to Central Mexico, whereas the pearl popcorn is held to be a Colombian variant of flint corn. Huautli, which is a cultivated amaranth, and the mescal type of agave are other starchy foods which are more or less restricted to the areas that came under Mexican influence. "All upland cottons spread in cultivation have originated from Mexican cotton" (*G. hirsutum*), for which the Russians assert a perennial original form. Its resistance to a long dry period and to high temperatures is markedly greater than that of *G. barbadense*, and it is closely related to one or more wild forms of the west coast. The indicated place of origin therefore is at low elevations in lands of markedly shortened rain period such as characterize various areas on or near the Mexican west coast.

For South America the Russian synoptic report has not been received. The meager statements available outline a culture hearth in Brazil from which manioc and peanut originated, another in winter-rain Chile, where they find the original home of the Irish potato (*Solanum tuberosum sensu strictu*), and a third in the Andes, where they assert the existence of no less than a dozen species of potatoes, none of which is ancestral to the potato of commerce. The famous old archaeologic coast of Peru virtually disappears in their analysis as a center of domestication and becomes rather an area of colonization from the east and north.

Until much more material has been gathered and the genetic relationships have been made definite, the results of the Russian investigators may continue to be regarded as tentative. They are, however, a serious challenge to many customary notions of cultural origins and they may force a large revision of American prehistory. These findings fit remarkably well with the other lines of evidence and theoretical considerations previously set forth in this paper. The rainy tropics, the semiarid steppes, and the deserts are alike strikingly missing from the picture of crop origins as presented by the Russian botanists. Mesophytism is indicated as dominant, with individual adaptations to various seasonal rhythms of rain and dryness. The limited latitudinal diffusion of many American domesticates may be connected with narrow phototropic range, maize however showing an extraordinary elasticity in this respect.

The question of competitive or alternative domestication and of the single or plural origin of agriculture.—One of the outstanding characteristics of native American agriculture is the large variety of plants that have been domesticated for the production of starch foods. Just as carbohydrate foods are far and away the most important element in modern agriculture, accounting for the use of much more land and labor than any other form of farm production, so we may postulate the need of a more adequate supply of starches as the most urgent and earliest objective of primitive agriculture and hence as indicating the first plants that were brought under domestication. We may consider that the most ancient plants cultivated were starch staples, unless agriculture had a noneconomic origin. In the gathering stage these were the substances normally needed in largest amount, the ones requiring the largest area for their collection, and those most likely to become depleted. Such plants therefore would first suggest the advantages of propagation and would hence be the first subject to selective improvement, the oldest members of the agricultural complexes.

What then is the meaning of the multiplicity of starch staples in the aboriginal American scene? Almost all of these crop plants as we know them are far removed from wild ancestral forms and involve a very long process of domestication. A question to which we should like to know the answer is whether in the same area more than one such plant is likely to have been carried through the tedious business of its improvement? Would generation after generation of cultivators in one locality have given their attention to the breeding, let us say, of a grass, a nightshade, and a morning glory in order to have a multiple source of starch food? The sustained, parallel effort seems far too great to be reasonable, when we consider that the end is identical. At the beginning of agriculture a variety of plants may well have been used for similar ends, but if one showed an inherent advantage over the others in productiveness, nutritiousness, or keeping quality, attention would become concentrated on its propagation and improvement and the rest would soon disappear. The competitive domestication of plants in the same area may be considered improbable.

From Old World parallels two exceptions suggest themselves, but neither appears to have much significance in New World agriculture. The one is the development of an off-season, secondary crop that can make its growth when the weather is too dry or too cold for the major staple. The American starches, however, are generally grown at the same season. The other is that some of the plants in question may have been voluntary associates, originally weeds or ruderal plants, that gradually came to be appreciated and developed. The growth habits of the several American starch plants are, however, in major part unsuited for such ecologic association, the general American practice of "hill" cultivation was not favorable thereto, and the thesis explains more readily the introduction of supplementary crops, that is, plants of different utility, than the introduction into cultivation of a competitive crop. If one successful starch food was already at hand, it is unlikely that effort would be expended on the improvement of a wild plant serving the same ends.

Such evidence as we have on the origin of the basic, or starch-food, domestications indicates that each has a center of origin distinct from the others, in other words, that there may be as many American centers of plant domestication as there are domesticated starch plants. These appear to arrange themselves in some sort of climatic series. The sweet potato points to origin under conditions of greater humidity and warmth than any other of the starches unless it be the bitter manioc. Both perhaps came from different moist margins of a savanna climate. The sweet manioc appears to belong to the dry margins of savanna conditions. Maize and arracacha belong to similar mesothermal conditions, found at intermediate elevations in low latitudes. The cultivated amaranths and the Jerusalem artichoke also come from mesothermal climates. The several Andean tubers, such as the potatoes and oca, come from high altitudes of cool to cold climates. The Chilean potato, if distinct, as determined by the Russian geneticists, is assignable to a mesothermal land which provided a winter growth period, simulating the conditions of summer growth on the Andean plateau. The basic starches thus by and large may be interpreted as alternative domestications, coming from various, climatically differentiated centers.

The cultivation side by side of two starch crops, one local, the other of wide range, suggests the priority in time of the local crop for that area. In Colombia, for instance, maize and arracacha are widely grown in the same area, and in part manioc is also cultivated in the same agricultural complex. Under such circumstances the introduced plant needs some quality of superiority over the local plant in order to invade the new area successfully. The survival of the local domesticate is aided by the inertia of habit, such as its traditional rôle in accustomed dishes. Qualities that are insufficient to cause the development side by side of two similar foodstuffs from different wild ancestors may be sufficient to keep one in use if a more valuable crop is brought in from another area.

The case of maize is especially significant. It is of all American starches the most widely distributed and the most useful, partly because of its ease of storage and keeping qualities, partly because it contains also fat and protein and is a more nearly complete food than the others. Maize in the northern part of its range tends to be the exclusive starch food. In South America prevalently it is grown in areas in which other starch plants are also produced. These more localized crops, then, may have been domesticated forms available prior to the introduction of maize. Such may be the explanation for the Colombian arracacha, but also perhaps for the Mexican huautli, perhaps even for the Jerusalem artichoke of our Southeast. All these are distinctly less useful than maize and therefore difficult to explain if maize was available to these areas when the plants under discussion were taken under cultivation. The diffusion of corn, however, undoubtedly required a long time. The older forms of maize may be considered as having required a long, warm, moist season, more rapidly maturing forms developing by slow selection on the successive boreal fringes of its cultivation and in part also on the drier margins. Slow ecologic selection was demanded of all crops that diffused through a wide latitudinal and altitudinal range, the diffusive energy of such a crop being probably a complex expression of its desirability and of inherent ecologic plasticity. It is doubtful, however, whether safe inferences can be made from breadth of diffusion to comparative age of domestication of plants.

Maize is also grown as the one staple starch where there are eligible wild sources of starch that have not been taken under cultivation. An illustrative example is the excellent, hardy wild potato of Arizona and New Mexico, perhaps as good raw material as were the wild potatoes of the Andes. The fact that such a foodstuff was not domesticated in our Southwest indicates that agriculture was brought in with maize and that the forms of maize available were well enough adapted to local climatic conditions so that there was no necessity of experimenting with local wild starch foods. The availability in any area, when farming began, of an adequate set of crops is undoubtedly the reason for many unutilized possibilities in the local wild vegetation.

Having ventured thus far into a highly speculative problem, we may look at the final and most inaccessible question, that of the single or multiple origin of agriculture in America. The basic elements of native agriculture, aside from the crops, are very simple and not highly formalized. There appears, for instance, to be great irregularity from one part of the New World to another in the agricultural work as performed by each sex. The tools were similarly simple and informal for the most part, and no progressive areal variation of form has been established. The business of punching a hole and dropping a seed or tuber is an extremely rudimentary process on which to base an assertion that it must have diffused from one center to all agricultural areas of the New World. Is it reasonable to assume that agriculture spread *per se* or that it spread by the transmission of a desirable staple? In the latter assumption, however, we are confronted by the diversity of the fundamental staples, which we consider to be the starches. Would one people, seeing that another had acquired a crop such as maize, turn to the domestication of an alternative starch or would it introduce maize when it borrowed agriculture from its neighbors?

Obviously, alternative domestication would be carried out, if agriculture spread from a common center, only if the crop could not succeed in the borrowing area. The potato complex may well have been such an alternative domestication because the cold climate of the Andean highlands barred introduction of the lowland starch crops. Perhaps there is some connection here with the veritable rash of domestication that broke out in this area, most conspicuously unsuited to the other starch plants, if the determination of the Russian Institute of Applied Botany is confirmed that at least a dozen distinct species of potatoes were domesticated in Andean lands.

Interdependence of American agriculture by alternative, imitative domestication is in general, however, by no means apparent. Though the remaining starch staples show somewhat different climatic adaptations and limitations, these are by no means so emphatic that they indicate original climatic restrictions by which it became easier to domesticate a new form than to introduce one already cultivated. Except for the higher altitudes the interpenetration of the native starch crops is notably free. The single origin of American agriculture in the view of such facts as we possess would appear to be a far more difficult thesis to vindicate than that of a plural origin, by which, in favorable sites, where amenable plants were available, various social groups independently of each other passed from gathering to planting and selective plant-breeding. Under this view the diffusion of the superior crops, such as maize, cotton, kidney bean, and manioc, came later but may have been more rapid because of the prior wide development of planting practices. This suggestion of the origin and spread of agriculture is made with considerable diffidence, with the hope however that the proponent may not be regarded as antidiffusionist because he does not see the basis for unitary origin in American agriculture.

Conditions adverse to primitive farming.—In latitudinal and altitudinal range Indian farming was almost as widely distributed as is modern agriculture. Crops and methods from the Old World have made possible certain notable extensions however. The areal discrepancies between aboriginal and modern agriculture are principally:

(1) Lands requiring drainage and irrigation. The former were excluded from agricultural penetration (an exception is the floating gardens), whereas irrigation was possible where diversion did not involve a major problem of raising the water level. All irrigated lands however may be considered as late in the development of agriculture. Irrigation was of greatest extent and development in the coast of Peru and in the American Southwest, both areas rather marginal in position and probably in time to the general spread of American agriculture and both, in terms of plant conquests, indicated as areas of colonization by agriculturists rather than as areas of origin of plant domestication.

(2) Areas of low rainfall, without a well-defined rainy period. The European small grains have invaded subhumid intermediate latitude areas with insufficient summer rain and in part with a length of growing season insufficient for our native crops. Thus on the Great Plains and their margins climatic conditions were in large part unsuited to Indian agriculture. The Old World grains have been able to occupy additional areas in our western states and in the prairie provinces of Canada either because they can be fall-sown or because they can use winter moisture in early spring planting and get an early start that is impossible for the American plants.

(3) Areas with rain during the cool season, and dry weather during the warm period (Cs climates). The largest winter-rain region of the New World is the Pacific coast of the United States. Although the old agricultural lands of the Southwest included the lower Colorado River valley, agriculture did not establish itself farther west, on the immediately adjacent coast of California, nor to the north thereof. The absence of cultivation in this large region of genial climate is sometimes referred to the adequacy of wild food supplies and to the cultural inertia of the population. Lack of contact with agricultural peoples can hardly account for the absence of agriculture on the Pacific coast of the United States. The Indians of southern California were in com-

munication with agricultural peoples along the Colorado. It is not likely that California Indians refrained from experimenting with the crops grown on the Colorado river. The resistance to the westward diffusion of agriculture was probably environmental rather than cultural. The crops which were available had little prospect of success in winter-rain lands. Maize and squash especially were ruled out by the rain regime, but the conditions also are predominantly unfavorable for beans. The Pacific coast of the United States, as a land of Mediterranean climate, had to wait on the introduction of crops from the European Mediterranean.

The other winter-rain area, central and southern Chile, had an agricultural opportunity because it had the potato, which was not available at the north. The Russian botanists indicate that our commercial potato is a native of Chile. By the more prevalent view it has been held to be an immigrant from the cool Andean plateau, where climatic conditions during the growing period of summer simulate the temperature and moisture conditions found in Chile in winter.

(4) Heavy soils could not be used by the aboriginal cultivator. Digging and planting-stick, even the primitive mattock of bone or stone, are of little use except for light soils. I have no knowledge that Indian agriculture occupied anything but sandy and light loam soils. Even the early European colonist could do little with the heavier lands until he had adequate draft animals and tools. One of the reasons for the Pilgrim settlement at Plymouth was the availability of sandy Indian fields which the Pilgrims could work with their meager and weak tools. The Pilgrim chronicles leave no doubt that this quality of soil which determined the location of fields by the Indians was equally appreciated by the colonists. In northern Mexico an extension of agriculture onto heavy soils has taken place only in late years and is still continuing by reason of the introduction of American plows, farming methods, and heavier draft stock. In that area the Tarahumar and Tepehuan tribes had a territory with large bodies of rich clay and clay loam lands which were not used agriculturally by them, their settlements being restricted mainly to flood plains and to rough mountain lands which they were able to plant. A wooden stick cannot be pushed successfully into heavy soil. Soil texture indeed was of much more importance than productivity. Poor, sandy lands were farmed where rich, heavier lands were not, as any survey of Indian field distributions in our glaciated areas will show.

California had a second drawback in soil conditions, the coastal belt being prevalently a land of very heavy soils, even in the valley floors. In availability of soil to aboriginal agriculture the Pacific coast and large parts of the interior plains of the United States ranked especially low. Creek bottoms were most attractive to pioneer white and aborigine alike. Here the soil was likely to be mellow and productive. Outwash trains and loess areas were preferred for cultivation in and near the glaciated regions. The distribution of Mound Builder sites is closely related to loess and alluvial light loam areas. In our Southeast, there are important bodies of moderately sandy residual soils, most notably the granitic Cecil soils and their derivatives, predominant in the southern part of the Piedmont. The Carolinas and Georgia uplands for this reason and because of their long growing season were a region of superior attractiveness. The southeastern tribes, especially the Cherokee, held an especially favored country for extensive agriculture.

(5) Partial or complete exclusion of agriculture from grass- and brushlands. Perhaps most important of all was the association of Indian agriculture with forest lands. Sod was an almost impossible obstacle to such tools as they had. The white pioneer was balked for years by the grasslands. Indeed, the chief reason why the prairies were avoided by the early settlers was that they were unable to break the heavy sod until special sod-breaking plows had been developed. To grow crops in grassland the grass must be eradicated, else it will promptly choke out the crop. Planting-stick cultivation of grasslands is almost an impossibility.

The thesis may be advanced that not only in the New World, but generally, the beginnings of agriculture are to be sought in forest lands. The removal of trees from competition with the crop requires only the breaking of the cambium layer, for which no sharp tools are needed. As the trees die, full light is admitted to the forest floor, which is free from weeds and has a litter which provides food and mulch for the crop. Dead tree trunks and stumps are no handicap to planting-stick or to hoe agriculture. Under climates in which fungi and bacteria attack dead wood actively the forest deadening soon becomes an open clearing. The Indian mode of girdling trees was adopted by the American frontiersman. Our westward movement was through forest country by an advancing fringe of "deadenings."

Brushland is difficult to clear under primitive conditions. Brush cannot well be girdled and left to die but must be cut or pulled to make room for planting. Brushy growth also commonly has a tendency to sprout and often to sprout more heavily if it is cut back. Sprout reproduction may be discouraged by vigorous burning, but the ability to burn successfully presupposes the ability to cut brush freely. Stone Age man was pretty helpless before either grass or brush, but not so in the presence of forest. Vegetational limits may be subject to displacement for various reasons, so that it is unsafe to envision always a similar natural vegetation for prehistoric and present time. The fact that grasslands in many parts of the world extend beyond grassland (steppe) climates into adjacent (forest) climates raises the question whether this general anomaly of forest-grass limits may have been affected by early man (e.g., repeated burning) and whether areas which we know as grassy may not have been forest. Thus the North American prairies and the South American pampas cannot as yet certainly be assumed to have been grasslands *ab origine*. Whatever their origin, as grasslands they pretty well excluded the possibility of primitive agriculture except in the forest lands along the valleys.[5]

---

[5] The loess areas of central Europe, rich in neolithic sites, have been interpreted as grasslands in a forest country and hence as available to settlement by farming peoples, who

did not invade the forests. The evidence for the loess areas as relict steppes rests on the existence within them of elements of a steppe flora. These occurrences however do not prove the original steppe character of the loess, any more than would the appearance of a specialized flora along a railroad embankment. If the loess area became deforested, members of a steppe flora would readily enter and establish themselves in the artificial openings. The only question would be whether steppe plants were available sufficiently close at hand. The evidence of floristic elements is entirely insufficient for postulating original grassy conditions. We should say rather that such plants were archaeologic weeds, primordial ruderal plants about the loess areas, which escaped into these earliest of European clearings.

Loess is most unlikely material to preserve a xerophytic plant assemblage into a moister climatic period, as is implied in this thesis of steppe survival. On the contrary, a climax mesophytic forest develops more readily on loess than on almost any other soil type, except, in part, alluvial lands. Absorbing moisture from rains to an extraordinary degree and providing in dry weather capillary water to the roots beyond the capacity of most soils, loess is notably drought resistant and with us (e.g., Missouri valley) supported a luxuriant and varied forest growth where other upland soils held only a limited and scanty tree growth. Of all soils associated with continental glaciation it is the one which would be most likely to receive first the advancing forest and to lose the steppe flora that had spread north with the retreat of the ice. Were not the events therefore in this order? (1) Mesophytic, deciduous, climax forests became established on the loess lands. (2) The variety of the forest vegetation, the ease of killing and removing the deciduous as against the ecologically less advanced conifers, and the mellowness and fertility of the loess lands continued to make these by a large margin the preferred tracts of earlier settlement. It is difficult to see why American primitives should have found forest lands preferable for farming and Old World primitive planters should have found grasslands preferable. The problem of tillage was similar. Even if the European cereals originated beyond the forest edge, that is, were of grassland origin, they would still be far more readily cultivable by digging-stick and hoe in a forest clearing than in a grassland. Leaving breaking of sod aside, a grass association exerts a powerful pressure against weak cultivation that is wanting in a mesophytic temperate climate forest. (3) The superiority of texture and fertility of the loess lands then retained such areas under continued agricultural occupation and thereby developed in them the longest archaeologic record for Central Europe.

UNIVERSITY OF CALIFORNIA,
BERKELEY, CALIFORNIA.

DONNER UND REGENBOGEN BEIM HÖCHSTEN WESEN DER YUKI

By W. Schmidt

Einführung

Zu den Stämmen Kaliforniens, um deren Erforschung Professor Kroeber sich so unvergängliche Verdienste erworben hat, gehören nicht an letzter Stelle die verschiedenen Yuki-Stämme; zu der Aufhellung ihres Zusammenhanges untereinander und ihrer verwickelten Geschichte hat er nicht nur selbst wertvolles Material beigesteuert, sondern auch wichtige Klarstellungen herausgearbeitet. Dazu gehört an erster Stelle die Tatsache, dass diese Stammesgruppe nach Sprache, Physis, und Kultur unter all den anderen ethnologisch alten Gruppen und Stämmen Nordzentralkaliforniens als die älteste erscheinen muss. Wenn es dann feststeht, dass diese nordzentralkalifornischen Stämme in ihrer Gesamtheit die ethnologisch ältesten von ganz Nordamerika sind, so mag man ermessen, zu welcher Wichtigkeit sich die Yuki-Gruppe erhebt. In meinen eigenen Untersuchungen[1] konnte ich mich von der absoluten Richtigkeit dieser Aufstellungen nur selbst überzeugen und sie meinerseits noch etwas schärfer herausarbeiten.

Das höchste ethnologische Alter der Yuki-Gruppe gilt aber nicht nur hinsichtlich Nordamerikas, sondern geht beträchtlich weiter, wodurch natürlich die Bedeutung dieser Gruppe noch um so mehr steigt. Das möchte ich im Folgenden für zwei Punkte etwas näher darlegen, die ich bereits in der Ueberschrift bezeichnet habe: die Beziehungen des Höchsten Wesens der Yuki zum Donner und zum Regenbogen.

Ich bemerke noch, dass jedesmal, wenn ich von Yuki schlechthin spreche, ich die gesamte Yuki-Gruppe im Sinne habe, oder vielmehr das alte Yuki, wie es vor der Zersplitterung in die einzelnen Stämme und deren verschiedenartiger Mischung mit den benachbarten Stämmen bestand, und wie ich es einigermassen zu rekonstruiren versucht habe.[2]

I. Der Donner

1. DIE BEZIEHUNG DES DONNERS ZUM HÖCHSTEN WESEN DER YUKI

a. Im Gebiet der heutigen Yuki-Gruppe

In der ganzen Yuki-Gruppe ist das Höchste Wesen aufs Engste mit dem Donner verbunden, ja man könnte es schlechthin "Donner" oder "Donnerer" nennen. Bei den Kato ist *Tšenes* "Donner" sein einziger Name; bei den Küsten-Yuki scheint *Ehlaumel* die gleiche Bedeutung zu haben; die Süd-Yuki (Huchnom) nennen ihn *Onamel Nun* "Donnerhaupt," die Sherwood-Pomo *Makila*

---

[1] *Ursprung der Gottesidee*, 2:57 f., 297 ff.; 5:323 ff., 365 ff.; 6:97 ff., 198 ff. Im Folgenden immer unter der Sigle *UdG* zitiert.
[2] UdG 5:69 ff.

"Donnermann," und auch die Inland-Yuki, bei denen es ganz mit dem Stammvater Taikomol zusammengeflossen zu sein schien, kennen ihn noch unter dem Namen "Donner."[3]

Genauer gesprochen scheint der Donner die Stimme des Höchsten Wesens zu sein, und diese wird äusserlich dargestellt durch das *grosse* Schwirrholz, zum Unterschied von dem kleinen Schwirrholz, das für die Frauen die Stimme der (Natur-) Geister darstellt, die in der Knabenweihe erscheinen. Die Art und Weise wie dieses grosse Schwirrholz verwendet wird, ist bei den einzelnen Stämmen verschieden.

Bei den Küsten-Yuki, wo es keine Stammvatergestalt gibt, kennt man kein kleines Schwirrholz, sondern nur das grosse, das *tinem* "Donner" genannt wird und öffentlich von Knaben geschwungen wird um ein Gewitter zu stillen, so dass also der Donner als Stimme Gottes das Gewitter zum Weichen bringt.[4] Bei den Kato stellt das grosse Schwirrholz (*telbut*) den Donner dar. Es wird von einem "Doktor" geschwungen, der in rot und weiss, den Regenbogenfarben, bemalt ist und durch das Schwingen eine Furchtkrankheit (Psychose) heilen soll, die durch ein Traumgesicht, in welchem *Tšenes* der Donner dem Patienten erschien, bewirkt wurde.[5] Aehnliches geschah bei den Sherwood-Pomo, wo das ((grosse ?) Schwirrholz *medim* heisst.[6] Bei den Inland-Yuki wird das grosse Schwirrholz, das den bezeichnenden Namen *a lamo 'otom* "Donners Atem" trägt, am ersten Tag der allgemeinen Knabenweihe und später immer dann geschwungen, wenn der unterrichtende Häuptling vom Höchsten Wesen Donner spricht.[7] Fraglich bleibt es, ob das grosse Schwirrholz als Darstellung des Donners sich findet bei den Süd-Yuki (Huchnom).[8]

Der Gebrauch des Schwirrholzes, schon an sich etwas recht altertümliches, wird es hier noch mehr durch seine Besonderheiten. Da ist zunächst der Unterschied zwischen grossem und kleinem Schwirrholz. Dieser findet sich auch in Südostaustralien, aber dort werden beide nur zur Bezeichnung des Stammelternpaares verwendet, und zwar das grössere zur Bezeichnung des Stammvaters, das kleinere zur Bezeichnung der Stammmutter. Der einzige Fall, dass in Südostaustralien das grosse Schwirrholz zur Bezeichnung des Höchsten Wesens gebraucht wird, ist der des Daramulun bei den Yuin, aber nur deshalb, weil dort der Stammvater mit dem Höchsten Wesen zusammengeflossen ist. Freilich wird dann auch hier das Schwirrholz als die Stimme des Höchsten Wesens, der Donner, angegeben, der den Regenbogen herbeiruft; aber das ist nur eine spätere "Volksetymologie."[9] In der Yuki-Gruppe aber findet sich das grosse Schwirrholz als Bezeichnung des Donners, der Stimme des Höchsten Wesens, *ohne* das kleine Schwirrholz als Stimme der Geister, gerade bei dem ältesten Stamme, den Küsten-Yuki. Ein zweiter Unterschied der Yuki-Gruppe von den Südostaustraliern liegt darin, dass bei den letzteren die Schwirrhölzer nur bei der Knabenweihe gebraucht werden und um die Frauen

---

[3] UdG 5:3, 13, 38, 45 f., 50, 57.
[4] E. M. Loeb, The Western Kuksu Cult, UC-PAAE 33:216, 1932; W. Schmidt, UdG 5:38 f.
[5] UdG 5:31 f.
[6] Loeb, a. a. O., 11; Schmidt, a. a. O., 51.
[7] Loeb, 66 f.; Schmidt, 57.
[8] Loeb, 60; Schmidt, 46.
[9] Schmidt, UdG 3:1021 ff., 1058 f.; 6:352.

zu schrecken; bei den Yuki wird nur das kleine Schwirrholz zu diesem Zwecke gebraucht, nicht das grosse, das bei den Küsten-Yuki ganz öffentlich und von (nichtinitiirten) Knaben geschwungen wird. Vielleicht liegen die Verhältnisse etwas ähnlicher bei den Ituri-Pygmäen, wo nur ein Schwirrholz gebraucht wird und zwar nur in der Knabenweihe. Aber es bleibt zweifelhaft, ob es die Stimme des Stammvaters oder die des Höchsten Wesens und des Donners darstellt;[10] wir müssen also die genaueren Berichte P. Schebestas von seiner soeben vollendeten zweiten Ituri-Expedition abwarten.

Es verdient hervorgehoben zu werden, dass in der Yuki-Gruppe, auch in den Stämmen in welchen der Stammvater entweder das Höchste Wesen in den Hintergrund gedrängt hat oder ganz mit ihm verschmolzen ist, weder der Name des Donnerers, noch die Funktion des Donnerns, noch auch, wie es scheint das grosse Schwirrholz je auf den Stammvater (Taikomol, Nagaičo, Dasan) übergegangen ist.[11] Nur bei den Inland-Yuki wird das grosse Schwirrholz, das bei der Initiation immer dann geschwungen wird wenn der Name des Donners genannt wird, auch dann gebraucht wenn von Donner und Taikomol die Rede ist.[12] Bei den Kato hat der Stammvater zwar ein besonderes Schwirrholz (*telbut*), verfertigt aus den Schulterblättern zweier Hirsche, aber es wird nicht gesagt, ob es an Grösse dem grossen Schwirrholz des Donnerers gleichkommt;[13] der Name ist identisch (vgl. oben).

b. Im früheren Gebiet der Yuki-Gruppe

Wie ich anderwärts dargetan zu haben glaube,[14] war das ganze jetzige Gebiet der Pomo- und Miwok-Stämme bis an die Bay von San Francisco früher Gebiet der Yuki-Gruppe, die dort verschiedene Spuren hinterlassen hat, darunter auch die Beziehungen ihres alten Höchsten Wesens zum Donner. Auch diese Fälle müssen wir uns kurz vorführen.

In dem Gebiet der Pomo (und Miwok) ist freilich der Donner nicht mehr das Höchste Wesen; es ist dort verdrängt durch andere Gestalten. Bei den Ost-, Nordost, und Südost-Pomo ist mehr oder minder *Marumda* das Höchste Wesen, dem sein "Bruder" *Kuksu* zur Seite steht; beide kommen aus dem Maidu-Patwin-Gebiet.[15] Bei den übrigen Pomo- und den Miwok-Stämmen dieses Gebietes nimmt mehr oder minder Coyote die Stelle dieses Höchsten Wesens ein, das mit einer neuen, mutterrechtlichen Strömung von Südwesten gekommen ist.[16] Der Donner ist in diesem ganzen Gebiet eine untergeordnete Persönlichkeit geworden und um so stärker verblasst, je weiter es nach Süden geht. Diese Zurücksetzung beginnt schon bei den Süd-Yuki, wo der Donner in den Kraftproben von dem Stammvater besiegt wird, während das Umgekehrte ursprünglich war.

Bei den Ost-Pomo führt es den Namen *Kalima-toto*, das mit *Kalibatautau* der Zentral-Pomo identisch ist. Das grosse Schwirrholz ist überall bei den Pomo der Donner und wird bei den Ost-Pomo als solches in bestimmten

---

[10] Schmidt, UdG 4:247 f., 260 f., 285 f.
[11] Schmidt, 74.
[12] Loeb, 66; Schmidt, 57.
[13] Loeb, 120; Schmidt, 25.
[14] Schmidt, 268, 282, 290, 325, 351 ff.
[15] Schmidt, 5:266 ff.
[16] Schmidt, 5:289, 295.

Zeremonien verwendet.[17] Von dort ist es auch in das Gebiet der Patwin zu den Hügel-Patwin und den Cache-Creek-Patwin gelangt.[18] Wir finden eine Donnerzeremonie mit dem Schwirrholz schliesslich auch noch in die Pololo-Zeremonie der Küsten-Miwok eingefügt.[19]

So ziemlich überall im Yuki-Pomo-Gebiet wurden die kleinen Schwirrhölzer bei der, unzutreffenderweise "ghost ceremony" genannten Feier, die in Wirklichkeit eine Stammes- Knabeninitiation ist, als Stimmen der niederen (Natur-) Geister verwendet, die dabei erscheinen.[20]

Bei zwei Pomo-Stämmen finden wir nun die Gestalt des Donners ausser mit dem grossen Schwirrholz auch noch mit einem anderen Ausdruck des Donners verbunden. Bei den Nord- wie bei den Ost-Pomo trägt Donner ein Gewand von Abalonemuscheln und hat auch Abalonemuschel-Augen; er trägt ein Haarnetz und Tanzfedern auf dem Haupte. Das Rollen des Donners wird durch Schütteln der Augen bewirkt; das Zwinkern mit den Augen bewirkt den Blitz.[21] Hier ist weiter ausgemalt, was wir auch schon bei dem nach Norden angrenzenden südlichsten Yuki-Stamme, den Huchnom, finden. Dort heisst das Donnerwesen *Onamel Nun* "Donnerhaupt," dessen Körper, wenn es mit dem Stammvater Taikomol in der zweiten Jugendweihe auftrat, in all den Farben bemalt war, welche die Indianer anzuwenden verstehen, und es glänzt "wie das Innere einer Abalonemuschel."[22]

2. DIE DONNER-WESEN DES ÜBRIGEN NORDAMERIKA UND DER ARKTIS

Diese enge Verbindung des Donners mit dem Höchsten Wesen, wie wir es hier bei der Yuki-Gruppe als eines der ältesten Elemente ihrer Religion angetroffen haben, ist sicherlich etwas sehr altertümliches. Wir treffen sie bei zwei asiatischen Pygmäenstämmen, den Semang und den Andamanesen, an, sowie bei einem afrikanischen Pygmäen- und einem Pygmoiden-Stamm, den Nduye-Efe und den Equateur-Batwa; aber nur bei dem Efe-Stamm kommt auch das Schwirrholz hinzu.[23] Eine andere Gruppe von Stämmen mit der gleichen engen Beziehung zum Donner finden wir bei den südostaustralischen Stämmen der Kulin, Wiradyuri, Kamilaroi, Yuin; aber bei keinem von ihnen ist der Name des Höchsten Wesens vom Donner hergenommen, und das Schwirrholz ist nur bei den Yuin die Donnerstimme des Höchsten Wesens geworden, indes nur auf dem oben (S. 300) angegebenen Wege.

Aber in ganz Nordamerika und bei allen arktischen Stämmen steht die Yuki-Gruppe mit dieser Beziehung des Höchsten Wesens zum Donner allein da. Diese Beziehung findet sich schon nicht mehr weder in Nordzentralkalifornien bei der Maidu-Patwin-Gruppe noch auch in Südzentralkalifornien. Im ganzen übrigen Nordamerika und bei allen arktischen Völkern ist die Funktion des Donners nicht mehr bei dem Höchsten Wesen zu finden, sondern

---

[17] E. M. Loeb, Pomo Folkways, UC-PAAE 19:301 f., 1926; Schmidt, a. a. O. 2:228, 237 f.
[18] Schmidt, 5:177, 193.
[19] Loeb, Pomo Folkways, 301 f.; *idem*, Western Kuksu Cult, 116 f.; Schmidt, 5:258.
[20] Schmidt, 353 f.
[21] Schmidt, 267.
[22] Loeb, Western Kuksu Cult, 60; Schmidt, 46.
[23] Schmidt, a. a. O., 6:251.

ist anderen Wesen übertragen, und zwar entweder einem einzelnen (menschenartigen) Wesen oder vier Vögeln, deren Standort sich an den vier Himmelsgegenden befindet.

Eine ausführliche Bibliographie über das Vorkommen dieser Wesen in Nordamerika bringt Truman Michelson in seiner Studie, A Sketch of the Buffalo Dance of the Bear Gens of the Fox Indians.[24] Es zeigt sich, dass die eigentlichen Träger dieses Glaubens die Algonkin und die unter ihrem Einfluss stehenden Sioux- und Caddo-Stämme sind: Bungi, Ojibwa, Sauk, Foxes, Kickapoo, Menomini, Prairie-Potawatomi, Cree (?), Lenape (?), Atsina (?), Blackfeet, Assiniboin, Winnebago, Dakota, Iowa, Arikara, Wichita; von dort ging er auf die Irokesen, Cheroki, und Creek über. Die am weitesten verbreitete Form ist die der vier Donnervögel an den Enden der Welt, die mit den gehörnten Schlangen oder Panthern, bösen Wassergeistern, in beständigem Kampf stehen. Im äussersten Osten und Westen des Gebietes, bei den Nordost-Algonkin, den Lenape (?), den Cheyenne, den Atsina, erscheint dafür ein einziger Donnergeist, der dann gewöhnlich als Schützer des warmen Südens mit der Kälte des Nordens kämpft. Das Vorkommen von Donnerwesen bei Nordwest-Selish- und Dene-Stämmen entbehrt dieses Gegensatzes zu den Wassergeistern oder dem Nordwesen und erweist sich damit als atypische Randerscheinung.

Ganz die gleichen Donnerwesen finden sich aber auch unter den arktischen Völkern bei den Samoyeden und zwar sowohl in menschen- als in vogelähnlicher Form. Bald sind es einäugige, einarmige, einfüssige Wesen, die mit dem Wärme bringenden Südlandstier gegen dem Kälte bringenden Nordlandstier kämpfen, bald Donnervögel, deren Rede der Donner ist und aus deren Mund die Blitze züngeln, Gehilfen des guten Höchsten Wesens und erbitterte Feinde des bösen Wassergeistes, der dem Höchsten Wesen feindlich ist.[25]

3. DIE BEZIEHUNG DES DONNERS ZUM HÖCHSTEN WESEN DER SAMOYEDEN

So durchgängig nun in der Arktis und in Nordamerika das Höchste Wesen der Funktion des Donnerns entkleidet, und diese anderen Wesen übertragen worden ist, ausgenommen eben das Höchste Wesen der Yuki-Gruppe, so haben wir doch am äussersten Westrande des arktischen Gebietes, bei den Samoyeden, eine Spur ganz beweiskräftiger Art, dass auch dort das Höchste Wesen einmal die Funktion des Donnerns selbst innehatte.

Dass gewisse Funktionen des Höchsten Wesens bei den Samoyeden—wie auch bei anderen arktischen und nordamerikanischen Völkern—abgesplittert und zu selbstständigen höheren Wesen umgeformt wurden, ist dort nichts Seltenes,[26] und so brauchen wir uns nicht sonderlich wundern wenn auch die selbstständigen Donnerwesen auf diesem Wege entstanden sind. Dass das in der Tat der Fall ist, lassen sie mit aller Deutlichkeit erkennen in einem ganz charakteristischen Zug des Höchsten Wesens, den sie mitübernommen haben.

[24] Contributions to Fox Ethnology. II, BAE-B 95:51 ff., 1930; vgl. Schmidt, a. a. O., 6:59 ff., 87.
[25] Schmidt, a. a. O., 3:361, 371 f.; 5:813 ff.; 6:58 ff.
[26] Schmidt, UdG 3:545, 552 ff.; 6:58 ff.

Bei den Samoyeden ist nämlich der Regenbogen der Saum des Mantels des Höchsten Wesens: diesen schönen Schmuck haben auch die Donnerwesen, und nur sie, für ihren Mantel mitbekommen.[27]

Damit bekommt die Yuki-Gruppe in ihrer weiten Einsamkeit innerhalb des nordamerikanisch-arktischen Gebietes in den Samoyeden einen Gefährten: *bei beiden ist das Höchste Wesen auch der Donnerer.*

Die Brücke zu dieser Erkenntnis war für uns bei den Samoyeden der Regenbogen. Wir werden sehen, dass auch bei den Yuki Donner und Regenbogen beim Höchsten Wesen vereint sind.

II. Der Regenbogen

1. Die Beziehung des Regenbogens zum Höchsten Wesen der Yuki

In der ganzen Yuki-Gruppe steht der Regenbogen in engster Beziehung zum Höchsten Wesen. Es hat den Anschein, dass der Grundgedanke dabei der ist, dass er das Kleid des Höchsten Wesens sei.

Die Farben, in denen der Regenbogen dargestellt wird, sind rotweiss. Mit diesen Farben ist bei den Kato der (unbekleidete) Mann bemalt, der das Höchste Wesen darstellt in der Zeremonie, die eine Angstpsychose von dem Menschen wegnehmen soll, der im Traum es gesehen; der Mann trägt auch ein grosses Schwirrholz in seiner Hand.[28] Aber es kam bei den Yuki-Stämmen im Ganzen selten und im Anfang vielleicht überhaupt nicht vor, dass das Höchste Wesen durch einen Menschen dargestellt wurde. Bei den Inland-Yuki und den Sherwood-Pomo geschieht es noch jetzt überhaupt nicht, und so wissen wir nicht, ob und wie bei dem dortigen Donner-Höchsten Wesen die Beziehung zum Regenbogen sich äussert. Bei den Süd-Yuki (Huchnom) wird es dagegen oft dargestellt, und hier trägt der Darsteller, der überdies in allen Farben bemalt ist und wie das Innere einer Abalonemuschel glänzt,[29] einen mit roten und weissen Streifen bemalten Stab.[30] Bei den Inland-Yuki ist es der Stammvater Taikomol, der auf einem Regenbogen zum Himmel emporsteigt;[31] aber das kann er wohl nur deshalb weil er hier das Höchste Wesen fast verdrängt hat, bzw. in ihm aufgegangen ist; bei den Sherwood steigt das alte Donnerwesen *Makila* zum Himmel auf.

Die rot-weisse Farbe ist im ganzen Yuki-Gebiet nur dem Regenbogen und damit dem Höchsten Wesen reserviert. Sie kommt weder dem Stammvater noch den übrigen höheren Wesen zu. Der erstere hat bei den Küsten-Yuki als Farbe schwarz-weiss, bei den Sherwood-Pomo rot-weiss-schwarz; von den Kato, Süd-, und Inland-Yuki kennen wir seine Farben nicht. Die übrigen Geister haben bei den Süd- und den Inland-Yuki weiss-schwarz, bei den Kato, Küsten-Yuki, Sherwood-Pomo rot-weiss-schwarz.[32] Es ist klar, das der Stammvater hier in denselben Farben erscheint wie die übrigen Geister, also als einer von ihnen.

---

[27] Schmidt, UdG 3:344, 361.
[28] Loeb, Western Kuksu Cult, 31; Schmidt, 5:16, 31; Loeb, 3; Schmidt, 51.
[29] Vgl. oben S. 302.
[30] Loeb, 60; Schmidt, 46.
[31] Schmidt, UdG 2:61.
[32] Schmidt, 5:72.

Diese beiden Farben erscheinen auch bei den Geistern der jetzigen Pomo- aber ehemaligen Yuki-Gebiete: weiss-schwarz Südost- und Süd-Pomo, See-Miwok, Hügel-Patwin; rot-weiss-schwarz Nordost-Pomo, Ost-Pomo, Zentral-Pomo, Küsten-Miwok. Nur Cache-Creek-Patwin fällt ganz aus dieser Reihe heraus mit seinen Farben rot-weiss, die im eigentlichen Yuki-Gebiet dem Donnerwesen vorbehalten sind.[33]

Welche Farben der Stammvater hat, ist in diesem Gebiete nicht mehr zu sehen, da hier nicht mehr er, sondern der aus der Maidu-Mythologie stammende Kuksu erscheint, der, wie der Kuksu der Maidu, schwarz ist und einen schwarzen Stab trägt; nur bei den Hügel-Patwin erscheint er weiss.[34]

Während wir nun in dem ehemaligen Yuki- und jetzigen Pomo- (-Miwok)-Gebiet die Beziehungen des Donners zu dem alten Höchsten Wesen in Spuren noch wieder finden, ist bis jetzt hier von seinen Beziehungen zum Regenbogen eine Spur noch nicht aufgefunden. Das kann allerdings auch daher kommen, dass bisher nach solchen Spuren nicht gesucht worden ist, oder dass sie, wenn gefunden, nicht als solche erkannt worden sind. Es würde sich besonders darum handeln, zu erfahren, ob der Darsteller des Donners oder sein Stab besondere Farben getragen und welche.

2. DIE BEZIEHUNG DES REGENBOGENS ZUM HÖCHSTEN WESEN DER SAMOYEDEN

In welcher Beziehung der Regenbogen bei den Samoyeden zum Höchsten Wesen steht, haben wir bereits gehört (oben S. 303 f.). Er ist der Saum seines Mantels, und diesen Mantelsaum haben auch die Donnerwesen mit sich genommen, als sie sich vom Höchsten Wesen absplitterten.

Dass wir in dieser Gleichheit der Beziehungen des Höchsten Wesens zum Regenbogen einen historischen Zusammenhang der beiden Gruppen vor uns haben, der durch dieses ausserordentlich charakteristische Qualitätskriterium sichergestellt ist, wird auch wie in einem Quantitätskriterium durch die zweite Gleichheit der Beziehungen des Höchsten Wesens zum Donner bekräftigt, die wir im ersten Teil unserer Untersuchung uns vorgeführt. Dieses Quantitätskriterium wird noch viel mehr verstärkt durch eine ganze Reihe anderer Beziehungen der beiden Gruppen, an denen vielfach von der einen Seite noch andere arktische, von der anderen weitere nordamerikanische Stämme teilnehmen und dadurch noch ein drittes verstärkendes Kriterium, das Kontinuitätskriterium, schaffen, welches ich schon ausführlich dargelegt habe.[35]

Was aber die Beziehungen des Höchsten Wesens zum Regenbogen bei den Yuki und Samoyeden betrifft, so gleichen sie auch darin seinen Beziehungen zum Donner, dass sie in dieser Eigenart und Stärke sich nur bei den Yuki und den Samoyeden finden und bei keinem anderen Stamme der arktischen und der nordamerikanischen Urkultur. Die Beziehungen des Höchsten Wesens zum Regenbogen, die sich bei einigen anderen Stämmen der nordamerikanischen Urkultur (Maidu, Lenape, Mascoutens, Cheyenne) finden, sind ganz anderer Art und Stärke, als dass sie direkt hieher gezogen werden könnten.[36]

---

[33] Schmidt, 193, 247, 352 f. Bei den Südost-Pomo sind einige Geister weiss.
[34] Schmidt, 343. [35] Schmidt, UdG 6:21–102. [36] Schmidt, 6:54 f., 86.

Auch was bei einigen Pygmäen-Stämmen (Andamanesen, Gabun-Pygmäen, Ituri-Pygmäen (?)) an Beziehungen des Höchsten Wesens zum Regenbogen bekannt geworden ist, ist anderer Art und kann nicht direkt hierhergezogen werden.[37] Eher ist das der Fall bei dem alten Höchsten Wesen der (Nord-) Kulin Binbeal, das den Namen "Regenbogen" trägt und Beziehungen auch zum Donner hat.[38]

EPILOG: DER CLEAR LAKE

Es war eine grosse Freude für mich, als ich im Frühling dieses Jahres, auf meiner Reise nach Ostasien die Vereinigten Staaten durchquerend, dort eine Reihe von wissenschaftlichen Freunden, deren Werke mir die gesicherten Grundlagen für meine Forschungen über die Religionen der Urvölker Nordamerikas geliefert, und die mich ausserdem mehrfach in zuvorkommender Weise durch Uebersendung ihrer Manuskripte oder Korrekturabzüge unterstützt hatten, besuchen und in einem, zumeist leider nur zu kurzem Zusammensein gemeinsam interessierende Probleme besprechen und daraus neuen bedeutenden Nutzen ziehen konnte. Es waren Professor Fr. G. Speck in Philadelphia, der verdienstvolle Erforscher der Lenape-Delawaren und der Nordost-Algonkin; Dr. Truman Michelson in Washington, der gründliche Erforscher der Foxes; Professor J. M. Cooper in Washington, der erfolgreiche Erforscher der Nord-Algonkin; und dann in Berkeley drei hervorragende Erforscher der Stämme von Kalifornien und des Great Basin—Kustos E. W. Gifford, Professor R. H. Lowie, and last, but truly not least, unseren sehr verehrten Jubilar Professor A. L. Kroeber.

Wir hatten nun in diesen Tagen ein hübsches Erlebnis, das uns glauben lassen könnte, die alten mythischen Zeiten des Hochgottes, von dem hier die Rede war, lebten wieder auf, und er begünstigte mit seinen Hulderweisen noch immer diejenigen, denen er gewogen ist. Es lag mir bei meinem Aufenthalt in Kalifornien sehr daran, zu dem Clear Lake zu kommen, der ja für die Kulturgeschichte, besonders aber für die Religionsgeschichte von Nordzentralkalifornien von überragender Bedeutung ist. Denn an seinen Ufern wohnen nicht nur verschiedene Pomo-Stämme (Ost-, Südost-, Nord-Pomo), ein Vertreter der Yuki-Gruppe, die Wappo, und der Miwok-Gruppe, die See-Miwok, sondern hier hat sich bei den Ost-Pomo mit ihrem Höchsten Wesen Marumda und seinem Bruder Kuksu jene eigentümliche Vermischung der vom Osten kommenden Maidu-Patwin-Gruppe mit der dort ansässigen Yuki-Gruppe vollzogen, die dann ihrerseits ihre Wirkungen in die Gebiete der Patwin, der Yuki, und der Pomo ausstrahlte, bis von den letzteren her eine neue Bewegung ausging, die ebenfalls bis an die Ufer des Clear Lake gelangte.[39]

Diese hohe Bedeutung des Clear Lake-Beckens hat ja auch schon Kroeber vortrefflich dargestellt in seinem Vergleich desselben mit dem Gebiet des Sacramento-Tales.[40] Die direkt religiöse Bedeutung des Sees scheint noch herauszuklingen aus den ernsten Worten des Häuptlings, mit welchen er die Kinder, mit denen Marumda das Höchste Wesen in Gestalt eines alten Mannes gespielt

---

[37] Schmidt, 290.   [38] Schmidt, 3:674 ff.; 6:326 ff.   [39] Schmidt, UdG 5:326 ff., 331 ff.
[40] Kroeber, The Patwin and their Neighbors, UC-PAAE 29:402, 1932.

hatte, aufklärt: "Der alte Mann, der daher kam uns zu lehren, ist der Eine, der uns gemacht hat. Er lehrte uns Dinge, die wir nicht kannten.... Das war kein alter Mann. Er machte sich selbst zu einem alten Manne. Und dann wuchs er sich Flügel an. Sein Name ist Marumda. Er ist der Eine, der die Welt machte. Er machte den See. Er machte alles, was ihr seht.... Er machte diesen grossen See, und er kann ihn wieder austrocknen. Er machte auch uns Menschen. Er machte alles hier auf Erden. Bedenkt das wohl, ihr Knaben!"[41]

Mein Interesse war, in einem Autoausflug wenigstens einen kurzen Blick zu tun in die Landschaft und ihre Kommunikationsmöglichkeiten, die einen so lebhaften und bedeutungsvollen Austausch von Kulturen und Religionen an den Ufern dieses Sees herbeigeführt hatten. Den Tag und die Nacht aber, die dem für diesen Ausflug bestimmten Tag vorausgingen regnete es in Strömen bis in die Morgenstunden hinein, so dass die Möglichkeit des Ausfahrens sehr zweifelhaft erschien. Da heiterte es sich gegen sieben Uhr teilweise auf, und ein prachtvoller Regenbogen spannte sich über die Bay von San Francisco. "Der alte Yuki-Hochgott ruft uns und versichert uns seiner Huld," rief ich im Scherz aus, "wir folgen ihm!" Aber am Nordufer der Bay angelangt, wurden wir wieder von prasselndem Regen empfangen, der auch auf der Weiterfahrt fast eine Stunde anhielt. Dann aber heiterte sich der Himmel immer mehr auf, und immer schöner entfaltete sich um uns die kalifornische Landschaft. Das erreichte seinen Höhepunkt, als wir gegen Mittag am Ostufer des Clear Lake anlangten, und nun die träumerische Schönheit und fast religiöse Stille und Einsamkeit des weithin zwischen Waldbergen wechselnder Höhen sich ausbreitenden Sees uns umfing. Diese Stunden, die wir dort verweilen konnten, werde ich nicht leicht wieder vergessen. Wir umfuhren dann den See und machten einige Vorstösse nach Norden und Westen, wobei wir auch einige Pomo-Gruppen sehen und sprechen konnten. Spät nachts langten wir wieder jenseits der Bay von San Francisco in Oakland an, wo ich mein Quartier hatte.

Als ich bald darauf Professor Kroeber von unserer Fahrt berichtete und besonders von dem Regenbogen, der uns den Mut dazu gegeben hatte, frug er verwundert: "Und haben Sie nicht auch den Donner gehört, der um dieselbe Stunde rollte, und der um diese Jahreszeit (15. oder 16. April) hier selten genug ist?" Ich musste es verneinen. Aber jedenfalls ist es durch einen so zuverlässigen und autoritativen Zeugen, wie unser Jubilar es ist, festgestellt, dass an jenem Morgen die "Einladung" des alten Hochgottes nicht nur durch seinen Regenbogen, sondern auch durch seinen Donner erfolgte, eben jene beiden Charakteristika, die, wie ich in dieser kleinen Arbeit gezeigt, ihm in einer für ganz Nordamerika einzig dastehenden Weise zu eigen waren, und die, wie er Wert darauf zu legen scheint es zu bezeugen, noch heute in seinem lebendigen Besitze sind.

So möge er, und mit ihm all die anderen kalifornischen Hochgötter, deren "Entdeckung" und vorurteilslose Herausarbeitung nicht zu den geringsten

---

[41] J. de Angulo, The Creation Myth of the Indians, A 27:261–274, 1932; zitiert bei Schmidt, UdG 5:225, 227, 274.

Verdiensten unseres Jubilars gehören, ihm hold sein, dass er, neben vielen anderen Arbeiten, sein klassisches "Handbook of the Indians of California," das, begreiflicherweise, schon geraume Zeit vergriffen ist, noch in neuer Auflage veröffentlichen könne, um durch die Hinzufügung seiner und seiner Freunde späteren Materialien und Forschungen dieses Werk zu seinem eigentlichen und besten *monumentum aere perennius* zu machen.

St. Gabriel-Mödling bei Wien,
Austria.

THE MAN PETROGLYPH NEAR PRINCE RUPERT

OR

THE MAN WHO FELL FROM HEAVEN

By Harlan I. Smith

ONE OF THE MOST remarkable of Canadian antiquities is the man petroglyph near Prince Rupert, on the northern coast of British Columbia (see plates 3 and 4). It is unusually large, and instead of the common grooved outline, the entire figure is deeply hollowed out. Because of its rare character, scientific value, artistic interest, and accessibility to tourists to the Pacific coast of Canada, its preservation should be encouraged.

This unique Indian sculpture, about five feet, eight inches long, lies on nearly horizontal rock off the western of the two rocky tips of Roberson point on the Metlakatla Indian reservation not over three and a third miles west of Prince Rupert, or one and a half miles nearly southeast of Metlakatla, on the north side of the channel from Prince Rupert to Metlakatla and in sight of Metlakatla. The rock is part of the peninsula at low tide, an island at part tide, and probably awash at extreme high tide. Around the rock of this petroglyph are halophytic or salt-loving seed plants.

The great man petroglyph lies with its head about south, the arms straight down at the sides and the legs straight down with the feet pointing outward. No fingers or toes are indicated. The figure was no doubt made in the common way by pecking, but all traces of the process seem to have weathered away.

The origin of this petroglyph is explained by some of the Tsimshian Indians in the following story. An important Indian man, to astonish the people, said he was going up to the sky. He disappeared, but came back home some days later as he could not stay hid very long for lack of food. He explained to the people that he had fallen through the sky and struck the earth. To prove this he took the Indians to this rock sculpture and said that it was the dent he had made when he fell from heaven. He really sculptured it himself while hiding.

According to another story this sculpture was made where the body of a drowned Indian was found.

Photographs, a tracing, and a plaster of Paris mould have been taken of this man petroglyph for the National Museum of Canada. From the mould, casts may be taken for exhibition in various museums. If made of concrete, the casts may be placed out of doors as in public parks. They should withstand the weather and last fully as long as concrete sidewalks. Outside, they will not take up valuable space within museum buildings. The casts, especially if placed in the ground surrounded by vegetation, will hardly be distinguishable from the original. In museums and parks they would make this remarkable petroglyph known to the many people unable to view the original.

The visitor to Prince Rupert, however, may readily visit this unique Canadian petroglyph by rowboat in calm weather or by motorboat. The return trip of only about five miles is perhaps one of the best ways to fill in the time between train and steamer, especially since it gives inland people a chance to prove to themselves by actual tasting the saltiness of the sea of which they have learned in school days, to see starfish, anemones, and other sea life on wharf piling, perhaps to observe tens of thousands of jellyfish, to turn over a few beach stones and watch probably as many as twenty crabs sidle away, to observe the grotesque wind-deformed trees and luxuriant shore vegetation on acid soil, including acres of moss such as was used for surgical dressing during the Great War, and to examine the archaeological remains of ancient villages, as well as to visit one of Canada's unique antiquities.

The visitor may enjoy finding for himself some of the other near-by antiquities. Of these there are a few small, simple, and inconspicuous petroglyphs scattered on the rock on the same little point. Others may be seen at about the high-tide line on both sides of the cove in the south side of Wilgiapabi island immediately adjacent. There is a large shell heap on the west side of this island. Among the many other sites of this neighborhood there are also a few markings on the rock at about the high-tide line in the wave-cut base of a shell heap at Metlakatla which may be seen from the beach of the point east of the mission.

Along the top of the bluff or terrace immediately to the north of the man petroglyph is a shell heap, the refuse of a former Indian village and probably the home of the native who made the figure. The shell and refuse are easily seen where the land is under cultivation in the potato patches of the Indians who have a house near by. The extent of this heap is obscured by vegetation, but, judging by the lay of the land, it may extend in length an eighth of a mile eastward. It is probably 100 feet wide, shell-heap material being found at the base of the low sea cliff and 100 feet back from the edge of the terrace. The depth, although unknown, appears to be at least 4 feet. Such a great accumulation of village refuse would seem to indicate a very long period of occupation, a large population, or both. Judging by what has been found by comparatively small excavations in similar shell heaps near Prince Rupert, Vancouver, Victoria, and other places on this coast, a careful search of this vast accumulation of refuse would yield many objects such as points, both chipped and ground from stone and made of polished fragments of bone, for use on arrows and spears, adzes made of stone, weapons and tools, and art carvings made of stone, all left by the ancient Indians who inhabited this old village site near the man petroglyph. Even the bones of the people have been found in the shell heaps near Prince Rupert and in those near Vancouver, where some of the skulls showed that the ancient Indian understood the art of the difficult and dangerous operation of trephining and performed it successfully.

This petroglyph, like Canada's few other monumental Indian rock carvings, should be prized. The petroglyphs of Canada are threatened by at least eight different kinds of danger of mutilation and complete destruction. Some have already been injured, but all could be cast in cement so that the casts would serve not only for study, photographing, sketching, painting, and exhibition out of doors in Dominion parks and other public places, but also as a scientific record exactly like the original in cases where it becomes damaged or destroyed. The casts can be placed where people can easily see them, as in the parks of Banff or Jasper, while many of the originals are in far out-of-the-way spots and some in almost inaccessible places.

The dangers threatening the petroglyphs are as follows:

(1) People carve initials, pictures, and obscene marks among and on the petroglyphs in at least one place. There is a Provincial law punishing this action. But in out-of-the-way places the perpetrators are seldom if ever caught.

(2) A log boom was fastened to an iron stake placed in the rock within two feet of one petroglyph, subjecting it to chafing by the logs and log chains.

(3) A horse trail crosses petroglyphs at least at one locality.

(4) The tide and waves lave them in twelve localities.

(5) A stream now flows over them in at least two localities.

(6) Boulders are rolled over them by the surf in at least six localities.

(7) Driftwood is rolled over them by the sea in at least seven localities.

(8) A logging railroad will probably be built over the largest petroglyph known in Canada, since to log the valley above, the road would have to be built in the narrow pass occupied by the carvings between a 70-foot canyon and a steep mountain.

(9) A water pipe has been laid on one of the most romantic groups of petroglyphs on a narrow shelf above a fall, obscuring at least part of it.

(10) Camp fires are built on petroglyphs because local people, who seldom regard the carvings as more valuable than bare rock, have been taught to build campfires where the fires cannot spread and to put them out on leaving. They throw water on the fire, cracking the hot stone of the petroglyphs, and the petroglyphs will soon be ruined.

Canada has few antiquities such as monuments, castles, or ruins, compared, for instance, with Scotland, England, Ireland, Italy, Spain, Greece, and Egypt. Those she has are not only of artistic and scientific value to all the world, but are also useful as tourist attractions.

THE NATIONAL MUSEUM OF CANADA,
OTTAWA.

EXPLANATION OF PLATES

Plate 3. Near view of man petroglyph near Prince Rupert, B. C.
Plate 4. Bird's-eye view of man petroglyph near Prince Rupert, B. C.

NEAR VIEW OF MAN PETROGLYPH

BIRD'S-EYE VIEW OF MAN PETROGLYPH

INLAND ESKIMO BANDS OF LABRADOR

By Frank G. Speck

NOTE: Timed with the completion of several articles[1]* on the distribution and identities of the Montagnais-Naskapi bands of the Labrador peninsula, and a treatise dealing with their religious beliefs and philosophy,[2] a systematic survey of the Labrador Eskimo was realized as the next necessary step in the direction of solving problems of early history of the two racial groups involved. Accordingly, in the spring of 1934 and again in the spring of 1935 grants (nos. 238 and 286) were awarded by the Faculty Research Fund of the University of Pennsylvania for the purpose of carrying out the project, and a trip was undertaken in July and August with the following results briefly summarized.

Existing accounts of the Labrador Eskimo have been found inadequate for the study of comparative traits of the two groups, especially in the proportions with which the Indian bands of Labrador have been investigated by the writer. To bring knowledge of the two types of native culture more upon a similar level, the idea was conceived to make systematic inquiries in the topics of native life that would show the amount of prehistoric as well as later borrowing between the two peoples. An analysis of traits would be expected to lead to possible conclusions relative to the nature of very early civilization of the circumpolar tribes. Drs. Birket-Smith and Mathiassen (National Museum of Denmark) have brought out material of different meaning in reference to the make-up of Eskimo culture, raising the question of type of the economic habits and utensils of the people who first settled in the far north. The question, drastically abbreviated, centers around the greater antiquity of the Indian cultures of the interior highlands as contrasted with those of the Eskimo who have remained attached to the coasts. The fact that some of the Eskimo in northwestern Canada (Caribou Eskimo) exhibit a type of the interior culture has induced Dr. Birket-Smith to assume that the Eskimo at some early stage of their history, like Indian caribou hunters, followed an inland mode of life, and changed in the course of time to their present littoral manner of living. This brings us to two objectives of the recent trip of investigation; one, to gather evidence of supposed Indian-like traits of certain bands of Eskimo on the Atlantic coast of Labrador, the other, to scrutinize tendencies of Labrador Eskimo culture which seem to suggest affinity with Indian modes of life in dependence upon the caribou of the interior barrens, by contrast with dependence upon the economy of sea mammals, especially the seal. Bearing upon this point information was gained during the trip to show that one band in Labrador, on lower George river, possess an economy in which the use of seals, and seafaring habits in general, are noteworthily weak or absent. The beginning of a series of notes on the non-Eskimo particulars of this band was obtained and may later develop to form the leg of a new angle of interpretation of Labrador Eskimo history. Another objective was the point-by-point comparison of essentials of Indian and Eskimo ethnology, focusing attention upon those of importance as factors in the growth of culture among primitive people.

The topics investigated in some detail, as time and opportunity permitted, were the following: conceptions as to the nature of the soul and its agency in issues of life, both internal and external, the spiritual overlords or "owners" of animals, the means of satisfying the animal "owners" to secure the release of the animals for the purpose of food and clothing, the use of masks in dramatic pantomime to placate malevolent local demons (results published in article Labrador Eskimo Mask and Clown, General Magazine, Univ. Penn., 37:159–73 (no. 2), 1934, the psychotherapic function of amusement in the form of games and contests of skill and strength as antidotes to the affliction of melancholy induced in man by the desolation of environment in the far northern regions,[3] economic properties of the Eskimo which reflect a deviation from usual and typical Eskimo practices due to possible Indian borrowing, in respect to housing, clothing, tanning, hunting and winter travel

---

* Superior figures refer to notes at the end of this essay, p. 329.

in the forests, the acquisition of herbal remedies for disease treatment derived from Indian sources as a nontypical trait of Eskimo culture, the existence of territorial rights inherited in the family, covering the caribou hunting grounds of the Eskimo when they leave the coast for the interior, refined phonetic recording of texts and classified glossary of Labrador Eskimo terms for comparison with material of Greenland, Baffinland, Simpson and Melville peninsula and Alaskan Eskimo dialects recorded by Dr. Birket-Smith and Dr. Jenness leading to a further check-up on relationship, testing for linguistic liaisons between Naskapi (Algonkian) Indian and Labrador Eskimo, a survey of archaeological sites in districts bordering the Straits of Belle Isle and southern Labrador (the regions depopulated by the Eskimo through the attacks of the French and Indians in the nineteenth century) with a view to ascertaining early zones of Eskimo distribution, and sifting evidence of transient residence of Eskimo in the Straits advanced by Gosling, resumption of effort to determine something of the cultural status of the Beothuk Indians of Newfoundland, exterminated about 1830 by the settlers before any information had been salvaged to betray their identity of language and civilization. In 1914 Beothuk and Indian relationships were investigated in the field, and published.[4] On the last occasion, elements of Beothuk and Eskimo culture were a center of attention, the ecology of the two fundamentally different cultures of the Labradorean aborigines, Eskimo and Indian, was borne in mind as a problem for detailed future research. The two racial types with their cultural divergences have been segregated, in their development, to the two physical zones, the coast (Eskimo) and the interior plateau (Indian), implying certain historical or organic factors as operating in human migrations, culture shifts, and biotic adjustments. This area is admirably suited for the examination of phenomena still actively in operation. A pretentious, perhaps even pert, program if judged by the modest results achieved in the first period of work instead of being regarded as no more than a step in organization of plan.

Contact with Sir Wilfred Grenfell was made at the field headquarters of the Grenfell Labrador Association Mission and plans discussed for the research outlined above, yet with no definite results or proposals considered.

The expedition, supported in part by Grant no. 238, was carried out with Frank G. Speck, five focal points on the Labrador and adjacent coasts of northern Newfoundland being visited for the purposes delineated in the outline of the project. In 1935 the time was spent among the Naskapi of the St. Augustin band and with the mixed Eskimo families about Eskimo river and bay.

INVESTIGATION in the summer of 1934 of the alleged inland life and residence of Eskimo in northeastern Labrador led to the disclosure of the following facts relative to a small band of the people living inland from Nachvak westward to the drainage area of Whale river. This group habitually occupies the hinterland and possesses a type of culture determined by the inland environment, not the coast. The facts in general so far summarized, chiefly from data furnished by Mr. Richard White of Nain, and members of the Nain band whom I encountered at St. Anthony, are given as follows. Some published observations made on this group by other writers are appended. The question of historical relationship of the groups in mind with the otherwise typically coastal Eskimo of Labrador is an important one. It raises a point bearing upon the theory of Dr. Birket-Smith in explanation of the supposedly earlier more archaic type of Eskimo culture portrayed in the inland life of the noteworthy Caribou Eskimo.

The band in question is known by the name Kaŋi'lualucua'miut, Big Bay people, the term referring to their location in Ungava bay, in proximity to "Keglo bay," at the portion of its east side where, halfway between Whale river and Cape Chidley, the mouth of George river makes out through a deep fiord running about twenty miles inland. It is this fiord which gives the band its name and which Hawkes (1916) has listed as Kani'lualucu'a'miu't, Long Narrow Bay people, of George river.[5] He indicates them on his map of Labrador as inhabiting north of latitude 58° on the mainland to about Eclipse bay. Hawkes has nothing in particular to say of the inland peculiarities of the band beyond their having written their name across the interior region between the Atlantic and Ungava Bay coasts, which tells a definite story in itself. L. M. Turner (1884) has a few observations on the band, from which I quote. He calls the band by its usual name, spelled somewhat at variance, Kangukȼlualuksoagmyut, without translation, and George river as Kangukȼlua'luksoak. He states that the population of the division from George river to Whale river is about fifty individuals.[6] Boas also mentions them in his list of Central Eskimo tribes as Kangivamiut on George river, northern Labrador.[7] Packard, who explored the coast in 1860–1864, publishing his account in 1891,[8] marks on his chart Kangerdwaluksoak just west of the George river fiord, and Kangiva northeast of it.

Again a few notes by Dillon Wallace, 1907, who marked on his map of George river, near the coast at the embouchure of the river, the name Kangerlualuksoak, very big bay, and gave some observations on the Kangerlualuksoakmiut, people of Kangerlualuksoak. He noted some personal names besides that of Potokomik, "Hole cut in edge of skin to stretch it by," who was chief and conjuror of the band. Besides citing a case of anthropophagy he gives passing notice of tent life and furnishings and a few native terms.[9]

The keynote of interest concerning this group lies in the summary statements of Mr. White, who has observed them personally on frequent occasions.

> They hunt all the year and dwell in the interior. They do not bother with seals or hunt on the coast. They dress like the Indians in caribou skins and dwell in tents of the same. Their tools, utensils, their methods of hunting largely correspond to those of the Naskapi. Moreover, they resemble Indians in their looks.

This band occupies the northeastern district of the peninsula where one of the three great herds of caribou is found;[10] the herd that determines their economic position supplying their needs of life as completely as does the caribou supply the requirements of the Naskapi. Not to discount too firmly the possibility that this band of Eskimo may have been at some former time a typical littoral group which changed its economic habits from sealing and a coastal residence to caribou-hunting and an interior domicile, is something to be kept in mind. Such has been the history of at least one division of the Central Eskimo, namely the Utkuhigjalingmiut, "who formerly lived at the mouth of Back River, have now, through the influence of the Hudson's Bay Company's trading station at Baker Lake, become a perfect inland tribe hunting caribou and trapping in the lower reaches of Back River south of Lake Franklin." Nevertheless there are some remnants of the Haningajormiut and Uardliardlit, "who from of old are inland tribes, now only consist of a few families round the great lakes at the middle course of the same river."[11]

The question of Eskimo residence of the two types discussed by Doctors Birket-Smith and Mathiassen, as it relates to the groups west of Hudson bay, has been reviewed and evaluated by Jenness in a recent publication.[12]

As for seasonal or perennial inland residence of Eskimo in eastern and southern Labrador, the following, quoted from a previously published article, may be added to the observations just made.[13]

That they may have even dwelt in part of the interior, as an inland type of Eskimo, next remains to be considered, as appears from the testimony of several cartographic sources, one dated 1660, the other 1695. The latter exists in a map of S. Sanson (1695) by H. Iaillot. The region of the interior, east of the headwaters of Ste. Marguerite river, is marked as occupied by Eskimo. On a still earlier map attributed to Creuxius (the Jesuit du Creux) (1660) Tabula Novae Franciae is marked in the same general location as the name natio Esquimauxiorum....

The name Nitchikirinouets appears on maps of the eighteenth century (Laurie and Thwaites, 1794) in slightly variant forms, but not in documents of the preceding century. The people bearing the name are indicated in the area about Lake Nichikun, where a band of the same name has, until recently, had its residence. The name itself has had a continuous existence, its modern form being interpreted by the members of the group as "otter hunting people." We shall, however, have to account for the designation of these people as a "tribe of Eskimo" on the Laurie and Whittle's map (1794), which might be dismissed as an error were it not for the suspicion from other sources that Eskimo may have entered the interior as far as this district, as will be discussed shortly. The name itself is clearly Montagnais-Naskapi, yet it also happens that the first two syllables denote "seal" in Eskimo.

In considering the names on the maps in question, to be sure, one has to take into account the lack of distinction between Indians and Eskimo in the designation of native groups, a fault of which Cartwright for instance was guilty by frequently inscribing the Eskimo as Indians. In the case of the Senex map, however, the distinction was specifically made between the names of groups known to be Indians through the evidence of name and location, and those accompanied by the designation "tribe of Eskimo," even though they bear names in the Indian language.

Furthermore, on the map of John Senex (1710) is written "Little Eskimaux" across the stretch of country adjacent to the coast and inland south of Lake Nichikun between Hamilton inlet and St. John river on the gulf coast. The other Indian tribal names mentioned in the preceding paragraph are all there in the usual locations while two more appear of which we know also something, namely, Ouchestigoueks (Ouchestigoutec) and Nikikiriniouek (Nichikun) north and northeast of Lake Nichikun. On the Laurie and Thwaites map (1794) is the designation "Little Eskimaux" repeated in the same general location as on the earlier Senex map, with the addition Netchikirinouets marked as a tribe of Eskimo, and the same (tribe of Eskimo) written after the name Nitchikirinuets (Nichikun) and also after the name Attikirinuets, which is clearly "caribou people" in Montagnais-Naskapi, as being located southeast of Lake Attikonipi on the chart in Laurie and Whittle's atlas (1794). Unless we ignore these hints of Eskimo mixed populations in the eastern interior of the peninsula we are at a loss to explain them away as indications of what they profess.

The meeting of another early writer on the region with occasional errant Eskimo in the interior of the peninsula indicates that in the seventeenth century their presence cannot be denied in the forests northeast of the Saguenay, now exclusively inhabited by Indians.

The priest, Francis de Crespieul (1671), is one who establishes this. On a trip up the Saguenay, begun November 6th, 1671, his party was joined by a family of Christian Eskimo. They told the priest that they had fled from the other Eskimo to escape being strangled for having become converts. It is not possible to locate with accuracy where this took place from the terms of the narrative, but by March the priest had reached the "Lake of the Cross," so named from its shape. On May 17th, 1672, the voyagers again reached Tadousac.

While it is perhaps of no great significance in our present query, it is true that Eskimo family founders have joined the Indian bands in the interior in historic times as is recorded of the Mistassini and the Indians about Seven islands.

The question again arises of the southern Labrador Eskimo penetrating the interior of the southern peninsula, the region held by the Montagnais-Naskapi since the first mention of these people. Eskimo occupancy is indicated for the territory in question on the chart alluded to. If the ground be taken that the historic Eskimo confine themselves to the coasts and do not penetrate the interior at all, cognizance must be given to a definite exception to the rule as concerns northwest Labrador. In this instance we have a recent condition to consider. The northern Labrador Eskimo penetrate the inland steppes when hunting caribou, the Indians in consequence of its preëmption by the Eskimo have continued to avoid it. (Low, Explorations in the Labrador Peninsula, 1890, Geological Survey of Canada, 1891, pp. 44–45 L, and in particular R. J. and F. H. Flaherty, My Eskimo Friends, New York, 1924. Low [44 L] refers to the Eskimo hunting caribou inland north of Stillwater river and keeping north of the Indian boundaries when so engaged.)[14]

CARIBOU-HUNTING ACTIVITIES OF THE LABRADOR ESKIMO

Since the publication of the article just referred to,[15] in 1931, in which I opened discussion of the contact between Labrador Eskimo and the Montagnais-Naskapi Indians in the last two centuries, the accumulation of certain evidence has progressed to show that there has always been some activity among the Eskimo of Labrador in the line of caribou hunting in the interior plateau, and even of continual residence back of the coasts of the St. Lawrence and inland from Hamilton inlet and Lake Melville. To what extent the early references to inland Eskimo occupancy of the interior here may be taken as indication of an inland cultural type, like that of the caribou Eskimo northwest of Hudson bay studied by Dr. Birket-Smith, is as yet a point calling for cautious handling by the unprejudiced ethnologist. The data concerning the Eskimo of southern Labrador, especially the extinct groups south of Lake Melville and west to Seven Islands bay, are exceedingly fragmentary and difficult to use. There is evidence, however, not to be cast aside lightly, to point out that a more extensive dependence upon the caribou formerly characterized these bands than is usually the case among the coastal people. There are correspondences in a number of features between the arts and crafts of the interior Indians and the southern Labrador Eskimo, some of which are to be noted.

Some few of the listed objects are known to the bands of Eskimo possessing typical coastal culture farther north, and the whole series may possibly link up to form a chain of evidence indicating a cultural rapprochement between Indians and Eskimo in the Labradorean area. If, on the other hand, it is not cultural rapprochement, then we may consider the other alternative, that of there having been an ancient inland and coastal culture of mixed composition, retaining, however, strong inland traits as the form of culture possessed by the Labrador Eskimo at the time of their migration into the country.

The indispensability of the caribou to the Eskimo here, if not to the same extent elsewhere, is shown in the following notes relevant to the present hunting life of the Eskimo from Hopedale to Nain.

In recent years the coast Eskimo ascended the rivers leading to the interior about the end of July or early in August and remained until September, when caribou skins cease to be fit to be made into clothing. After the early part of September the hair of the skins begins to get long and comes out easily, since the animals are getting their winter coats. These prime skins are called "fast hair skins" by the traders. The Eskimo in the strip of country mentioned stayed in the caribou country long enough to get skins sufficient for winter clothing and to dry the meat. This required from two to three weeks. Occasionally they stayed in until the latter part of September. Their return to the coast was hastened at this time by the necessity of being at the coast to meet the early run of harp seals appearing from the north. It took as many as thirty sealskins to supply the family with materials each winter for boots, dog-sled traces and sealskin-hooded coats. Some of the hunters working on shares in the last few years have taken 300 to 500 annually in nets. Ordinarily the hunters from the Nain band, to cite one case, went up Fraser river some 20 or 30 miles to Ixalivik lake; others go up 50 miles to Nepatutuk by kayak and hunt inland from these points to secure their caribou meat and skins and to trap. From the other coast settlements of the Eskimo the same distance inland is approximately traveled. So Mr. White informs us.

The time of the inland hunt has been changed somewhat in the last few years through the influence of the traders. They go inland just after Christmas and remain there until about the first of May.

The account of Dr. S. K. Hutton, an eyewitness to the event among the natives of the village of Okkak (between 1908–1912), is too vivid and intimate to overlook in view of our greed for details, hence is quoted generously.

The men stood chattering in groups; the women indoors were sewing and mending from dawn to sunset and sometimes far into the night; "Tuktu, tuktu, tuktu," (Caribou) was in everybody's mouth—the reindeer hunt was coming. Presently the word went round that the Nautsertortut (scouts) were out, and the excitement became intense. This was early in March, and all day long the people were going in twos and threes to the top of the nearest hill, to watch the sledge track for the home-coming of the scouts.... The scouts seldom bring home any venison; they have done their part if they bring home a report, such as "I saw no reindeer yet," or "I have seen tracks, kannitomekorput" (they seem to be near); or, best of all, "I saw three deer in the distance, sivorliojut (the leaders) probably." Then the excitement bubbles over into energy. Men stand grouped round sledges on the snow, planing and smoothing and polishing the runners, binding up slack joints and patching weak places with iron plates; harpoons are shoved among the rafters of the roof, and kajaks are hoisted on poles, out of reach of the prowling dogs; women are stitching as if for dear life, getting the boots and clothing ready for the great occasion; there is stir and bustle all day long.

All this is a prelude to the reindeer hunt and at last the great day comes, and with shouting and cracking of whips the sledges are away in the dark of the morning, and the hunters have started. I have watched them off in the gathering light, stern-faced and eager, each man to his own sledge, and mostly alone. A boy of thirteen is handy with a gun, and useful to take care of the dogs; but smaller folk must stay at home, beseech they never so prettily. The reindeer hunt is no time for useless weight upon the sledge: I knew a man who took his wife with him, but the lady had to walk the seventy or eighty miles home, trailing laboriously beside the sledge, because there was such a load of meat and skins that the dogs could pull no more.

On Easter Tuesday[16] morning the sledges make their start, and track westward up the frozen rivers and through the winding valleys to the moss-covered wilderness where the reindeer find their food. The hunters have no luggage on their sledges; no tent, no sleeping gear, only a scrap of dried seal meat or fish for themselves and the dogs, and a gun, an axe, a knife, a packet of sticking plaster for the inevitable cuts, and a tin of grease for their sunburnt lips and cheeks—that is their whole equipment, with the occasional addition of a kettle for the making of a cup of Eskimo tea, weak as water, and flavoured with a mouthful of molasses out of a bottle.

They start together, but after a while they get separated and travel in ones and twos, or alone. This man's dogs are slow and lag behind; the other man wants to try such and such a valley instead of the beaten trail; and so they separate.

When night comes they build snow huts for shelter, and sleep on a bed of dogs' harness spread on the hard snow floor—not for any great comfort there is in it, but because if they left it outside the dogs would devour it in the night. In the morning each man boils his own tea and munches his own solitary feed or dried meat or ship's biscuit, harnesses his team, and drives on alone. Alone he travels where his fancy leads him; he will find the deer. Solitude has no terrors for the Eskimo; it wakens his best instincts; it matters not that he meets nobody, sees nobody; alone he finds his way to the hunt and back again, trusting to his marvellous memory for landmarks, and guided by the stars and the sunrise.

Year by year the same scenes come: the start on Easter Tuesday, the daily tramp of the women to the top of the look-out hill, the daily chatter over the work. Three days have passed. "Ah," say the women, "our men have found reindeer; if they had not they would have come home before this, for they have only three days' food. Nakomek, soon we shall be tasting tuktuvinemik" (reindeer flesh). And the men; it is the time of their lives! How graphically they tell of the keen moment when they first see the deer. Cunning fellows, away they circle so as to come upon them from the lee side, and if they cannot see the herd, but only find tracks, they know how far away they are by the freshness of the spoor. They turn their sledges upside down before they get within range, and make the team lie down; then the dogs are safe, for they cannot drag an upturned sledge. Woe betide the luckless hunter who lets his dogs get too close; away they go—no power can stop them—they are as keen as wolves to do a little hunting for themselves, and for the nonce they have become wolves again.

My neighbors liked to talk about the reindeer hunt. "Ah," they said, "It is fine to see the herd upon the hillsides, all grey and white like the snow upon the rocks. Yes, there are many tuktu; you may watch them all day, marching along the hills, more and more and always more, a great, great number. Ah, it is fine to watch them—but only Eskimo eyes can see them, because our eyes are made for hunting. There they graze, digging through the snow with their forefeet to get at the moss underneath. Often they dig through much snow, more than the height of a man, but they always find the moss, because they can smell it with their feet. It is fine to see them—and all the cows have their little calves beside them, and the old bull is keeping watch. When we shoot the cow, the little calf will not go away; it stays close to its dead mother and noses her and cries. We 'shoo' it away, and make it run after the herd but sometimes it will not go, and we must kill it too. That is no good; it has fine meat, and its skin is soft for clothes for the baby, but it is better to let it live and grow big for next year."

However much the seals may mean to the Eskimos, it always seemed to me that the reindeer hunt was the big event of the hunter's year. There never was such excitement as when the sledges were sighted—such roars of welcome, such a stampede over the ice, such a willing crowd to help with the groaning sledge.[17]

We have a few facts in regard to the equipment of the Eskimo when inland to show the carrying over of their usual cultural traits in this environment. They entrain for this journey provided with sealskin tents of the conical form as made by the Indians, about fifteen feet in diameter at the base. The poles for these skin tents are made, kept, and carried with them during their moves. It has been mentioned that they journey to the hunting, trapping, and inland fishing grounds by means of their usual kayaks. Of especial importance, furthermore, is the observation that they carried with them, until about fifteen years ago, their stone lamps and the necessities for lamp cooking instead of resorting to wood for fuel. Now, however, they often burn wood, the material being gathered in favorable spots and conveyed with them in the kayaks. It is in the winter hunt in the interior that the coast Eskimo employ snowshoes, following the necessity of travel in deep snow which the Indians of the interior undergo. The Eskimo at various coast villages make snowshoes after the Naskapi style, yet indeed they prefer to obtain them by trade with the Indians. The Eskimo-made snowshoe is netted with caribou rawhide (babiche) if this is available, but the middle or foot section is apt to be netted with sealskin rawhide strings. The Eskimo at Nain like to buy the wooden snowshoe frames from Indians and fill them by their own labor.

Hunting Territory Adaptations

At the time of the annual caribou hunts and upon their shorter excursions from the coast to the head of the rivers, even when, as is customary with some, they only proceed four or five miles up, the hunters with their families preempt a section of country which they trap over, fish for trout and salmon, and dwell in without interference by others. This is determined by choice and by common recognition. Other hunters refrain from trespassing upon the occupied tracts. There is room for all, as the family groups are not so numerous as to require definite boundaries to protect their interests. Hawkes notes that the "vast interior where the Eskimo hunt for deer in autumn and spring" is free to everyone.[18]

The boundary divisions of the inland-hunting Eskimo and the Indians permanently inhabiting the interior require some discussion, since a question of conflict arises from consideration of occupancy claims by both groups. The Eskimo ascend and hunt the drainage valleys of those rivers which rise on the eastern slopes of the height of land running in a generally north-and-south direction situated from twenty to fifty miles back from the coast. Some of the rivers are the discharges from lakes lying upon these slopes. Several such have been mentioned in the preceding paragraph, and they bear Eskimo names. The Eskimo when inland range over this area and not west of the dividing ridge. For beyond lie the territories of the Naskapi bands, who for their part do not hunt or live east of the same ridge.

The Indians do not even cross eastward or linger there except during their annual or seasonal excursions from their haunts for the purpose of trade with the establishments of the Hudson's Bay Company or the independent traders located on the various bays of the coast. On this point of contact between the two peoples we have the testimony of Mr. White to show that within the term of his residence as trader at Nain the relationships of the Naskapi and the Eskimo have become more friendly in nature. When he first came into the country the Eskimo avoided the Indians when the latter came out to trade, and retired to the islands offshore, never visiting the Indian bivouacs. Little by little the tension has waned and now he finds them visiting each other's camps and even hunting seals at the mouths of the rivers in mixed companies. Having a definite bearing upon this important situation, I may note that one of the Eskimo informants from Nain, much to my surprise, proved his ability to use the Naskapi trading vernacular with some familiarity. His name was Ike'tciak. Intermarriages are, however, not recorded as yet except in one instance which did not endure for long.

One may surmise from the above remarks that before the Naskapi had pushed their hunting territories as far to the northeast as they are at present, the Eskimo had been free to penetrate farther into the hinterland. It would coincide with the indications of Eskimo occupancy of the southern interior on the old French maps. This makes the Indians the aggressors, as the facts of history of the two races of the peninsula palpably indicate. In the southern portion of the peninsula, south of Lake Melville and Hamilton inlet, the circumstances seem to point to an even more extensive inland residence of the Eskimo and a more violent period of conflict over the question of inland tenure. The succession of retreats of the Eskimo from within the Gulf of St. Lawrence, in their abandonment of locations, began definitely, according to tradition in history,[19] with the massacre of the Eskimo at Esquimaux point (longitude 64°) near the western end of Anticosti island (about the middle of the seventeenth century), and continued for a century, ending in their withdrawal to the Straits of Belle Isle.[20] Here at the western end of the Straits they remained until the close of the eighteenth century (about 1760), when again the Montagnais, now aided by the French, fell upon them viciously in retaliation for continued acts of piracy upon the fisherman fleets, driving them from Eskimo river[21] and Old Fort bay out of the Straits onto the Atlantic coast. Massacre again at Battle harbor (about 1750) and the southern coast of the peninsula was cleared of Inuit. Those around Battle harbor survived late enough as a mixed-blood band to have earned a name in the tongues of the bands farther north, namely, Patla'vamiut, a corruption of the English place name Battle harbor pronounced in Eskimo vocables (Patla'va, Battle harbor).[22] The "native" Labradorean families of this section of the coast are of noticeable Eskimo extraction, as Dr. Michelson also observed. Persons are known to have lived until within a generation ago on the north shore of the Straits who still retained conversational knowledge of the Straits of Belle Isle or Battle Harbor dialect. Such was an old man named Gibbons (?) known to Mr. White, who lived near Bonne Espérance or at Belles Amours and at whose shack he stopped. Several Eskimo seen by Packard, in 1860, near the mouth of Eskimo river and at Caribou island, fifteen miles west of Bradore, might have been "stragglers from the north," yet he was convinced that they had a more or less permanent foothold on the northern shores of the Gulf. Packard quotes a Mr. Carpenter as authority for an estimate of several hundred Eskimo at Chateau bay opposite Belle Isle in 1765. One of the family names (1860) at Salmon bay was Dukes. Members of this family left descendants of the name of Goddard. Others survived at St. Augustin, among them "Louis the Esquimau," one of whose family was living in 1880.[23] Other families conceded to be of Eskimo extraction are named Shettler, Belvin, Welman, and Leon, besides the Goddards, all between St. Augustin and Salmon bay in summer, a branch also of the Fequet family. At Middle bay a few miles east is another of Eskimo descent named Drudge.

Besides the blood strain, the economic tradition of the Gulf and Straits Eskimo furthermore survives in the winter life of the native "Livyeres" (Live Heres),[24] in such devices as winter transportation by dog sled, dog harness, and dog signals, the use of Eskimo sealskin boots, some forms of winter clothing, the log-and-sod shelters and meat scaffolds, the hooded "dickey," or white cloth outer coat, and the retention of a number of Eskimo terms for hunting and travel equipment as well as for some forms of animal life.

After the massacre of Eskimo at Battle harbor the retreat to Sandwich bay around Cartwright left them in their last stronghold. Here the Netcetu'miut were located, the term translated as "People of the Valley," and also by an alternative, "Seal Hunting People." Mixed-blood survivors still dwell in these environs, and Hawkes reported, in 1914, still two old women there who spoke Eskimo among others who showed physical characteristics of the race.

The inland habits of these groups must still remain a subject of conjecture. Their descendants[25] are given to the fall hunting and trapping excursions into the interior below Lake Melville and Hamilton inlet and the list of articles made and used by them in their "forest" life shows patent evidence of adaptation to inland forest conditions or, as it may well be, the acquisition of Indian ideas along such lines.[26] In either case it is the inland forest cultural determination that strikes attention along with the Eskimoid configuration. Interblending of blood with the Montagnais-Naskapi is also asserted in Indian tradition.

While the easternmost of the Indians, the St. Augustin band of ten families (1935), show practically no evidence of Eskimo mixture, they are definitely conscious of the prior rights of the Eskimo on the lower and upper courses of Eskimo river east of them. They also point out the sites of traditional Eskimo residence on the islands in Eskimo bay at the western entrance of the Straits of Belle Isle, where the mixed-bloods of this race still survive, and in the drainage of Eskimo river almost 100 miles inland where Eskimo penetrated in pursuit of seals which here live in the inland waters and breed in the lakes between the Straits and Hamilton inlet. Again Eskimo hunting preëmptions in the southeastern hinterland! The Indians this far to the east are relatively recent immigrants, it would seem, from latitudes to the west; perhaps descendants from the group imported by Courtemanche two centuries ago (see fn. 20). I shall discuss the ethnology of this interesting band in a later paper.

The next step is to chart the caribou hunting and trapping grounds of the northern inland Eskimo hunters, band by band, and Mr. White has already been requested to start the task.

ESKIMO OCCUPATION SOUTH OF HAMILTON INLET

Some discussion has been provoked over the question raised by the historian of Newfoundland and Labrador, W. G. Gosling, in regard to the nonpermanency or transiency of the Eskimo in southern Labrador and the Straits of Belle Isle and northern Newfoundland. Gosling formed his opinion as being that the regions in question were occupied only seasonally, or by Eskimo raiders and adventurers whose permanent homes were north of Hamilton inlet. Hawkes summarizes the opinion as follows.

> Some authorities are of the opinion that the Labrador Eskimo never settled permanently farther south than Hamilton inlet, and that the large bands encountered by early French and English explorers were summer voyagers from the north. It is true that after this date the Eskimo descended into the strait from their strongholds in the north, but it would appear that the presence of fortified settlements, camps, and burying grounds south of Hamilton inlet, as well as *archaeological material extending as far south as the state of New York* [sic!], were evidence of at least a scattered population.[27]

The first part of the quotation possesses reason, the second does not as viewed by standards of scientific methodology. Hawkes goes on.

> There is also a tradition in this region that the Eskimo were accustomed to visit the northern coast of Newfoundland yearly. [Quoting an edict of Governor Palliser forbidding Eskimo from crossing to Newfoundland in their customary search for a "certain wood" for their harpoon shafts.] It is improbable that they would make the trip to Newfoundland from the country north of Hamilton inlet in their skin boats under the ice and weather conditions which prevail on the Atlantic coast of Labrador, but in favorable weather it would have been quite easy to have crossed the Straits of Belle Isle from the southern camps.[28]

It should also be recalled, as proof definite of Eskimo presence in northern Newfoundland within historic times, that in 1765 Eskimo were met by the Moravian missionary Drachart. They accosted him with a few words of French at Quirpont (Quirpon of today). And a similar encounter was held at Chateau bay. Packard subscribed to the theory of Eskimo from Labrador hunting caribou in the forests and seals on the coasts of Newfoundland, and also that the Labrador Eskimo "were an older people than those who migrated into Greenland" (as also did Crantz).[29]

Hawkes, however, was apparently not familiar with the fact, which should make us cautious, at least, that Eskimo migrants have wandered the entire coastal lanes of the Labrador Atlantic shore since the dispersion of the bands of "Southerners" a century ago, even as they had been doing earlier, to the dismay of the Moravian missionaries (1783). A hitherto unrecorded notice regarding the identity of Eskimo families on the northern coast shows that the descendants of the Eskimo woman Mikak, and her husband Tuglavinia, from Cape St. Charles at the entrance of the Straits of Belle Isle, the former taken to England (about 1767) and immortalized in a biography of this interesting character,[30] constitute family groups among the Nain Eskimo. Family tradition corroborates the transmission of the name. Legends of early encounters with the whites far away to the south are also reported among the Nain families. They perpetuate the names of Caubvick among other Eskimo of South

Sandwich bay, staged in the scenes so vividly portrayed (1773) in Cartwright's journal.[31] Among the legends attached to these personages it is related of Tuglavinia, apostrophized as a "fiend" by his modern tribesmen descendants, that he and his confrere pirates ate some children, Eskimo forthwith, and became the terror of the less violent and valorous kayak rovers; how they stole aboard a British frigate, surprising the deck watch by disguising their kayaks with a covering of duck skins, slipping through the fog upon the decks, killing some men and officers and making off with their red uniforms and swords. These souvenirs are reported to have been treasured as heirlooms in the families of their posterity until later years when the Moravian missionaries induced them to relinquish such criminal trophies of rapine.

Archaeological proof of Eskimo residence in northwestern Newfoundland is furnished by the recent findings of W. J. Wintemberg, of the National Museum of Canada (1929) on the cultural affinities of the finds at Fleur-de-Lys, Newfoundland, and Bradore on the Labrador coast opposite. They include cylindrical hammer stones, semilunar knives, adze blades of nephrite and slate, sandstone lamp, bone needle case with perforated bone needles, soapstone pots, triangular chert, chalcedony and quartz arrowheads with one face convex, the other flat, and soapstone plummet. Jenness defines the series as being of the Dorset type, which he points out most suggestively as representing a phase of Eskimo history of the twelfth to fifteenth century, the Dorset of the eastern Arctic, raising the "presumption that the Dorset people *subsisted more on fish and land-game animals than on sea-mammals, resembling, in this respect, the Indians to the south and west.*"[32] How this estimate of economic content of the southeastern Labrador Eskimo coincides with certain implications beneath the historical references just gone over is apparent. In having to arrange new adjustments for the handling of archaeological and ethnological data concerning Eskimo and Indian life in this area, and perhaps in lessening the distinctions between the two, we discover, in going back through time, that in the eastern Arctic prevailed "an intermediate stage, as it were, between a predominantly inland people, like the Caribou Eskimo, and a predominantly maritime people like the Thule" (Jenness, *op. cit.*, 395). And as we proceed the obstacles encountered serve to place more fuel on the flame of our purpose.

Having now briefly capitalized the data at our disposal concerning some points of importance in Labrador Eskimo and Indian relationship, in the extent of Eskimo territorial occupation, its stability in the southern area of the peninsula, and some aspects of ethnology, it is appropriate to revert to statements which I cautiously proposed as convictions several years ago as leads for future work in the area with the aim of reducing the unknown quantities in Labrador Eskimo history to a minimum. I deduced from various sources of evidence that the original Eskimo population of the Labrador peninsula might be ranked as one possessing certain features of culture indicative of that period of eastern Eskimo history when inland caribou-hunting traits were still strong; that certain groups of the people had preserved the inland traits with some distinctiveness down to historic times in two localities of the peninsula, the northwestern between Ungava and Hudson bay and the southeastern from the Straits of Belle Isle west to about Seven Islands bay in the Gulf of St. Lawrence and south of Hamilton inlet, where true Eskimo have been extinct during the last century; that cultural parallels are apparent in the life of Eskimo and Montagnais-Naskapi Indians of the peninsula to a sufficient extent to require attention and explanation, if possible at this late date, as common properties of the two subarctic races dating from the time of their first incursions into the peninsula, or that through several centuries of contact in the southeast they had transferred the traits in question to each other. I did not then, nor do I now, pretend to define the Labrador evidences of inland Eskimo life as being strong enough to print them as comparable in their historic significance to the claim of being rated with the Caribou Eskimo as a precursive type of culture of the Eskimo race, or, on the other hand, as being fairly recently Indianized Eskimo, as professed in the conflicting theories of sequence of Drs. Birket-Smith and Mathiassen.

The implications as reviewed were given in the articles which I produced in 1926 and in 1931.[33] I see no reason as yet after continued study of the whole question and its approachable field among the living groups and through documents, to retreat from the position taken then or to modify it radically. For certain of its details naturally someone will have to become the executor of the ideas proposed.

As a result of recent findings I would now accept the following assumptions.

(1) That Eskimo were, until their extirpation by the Montagnais-Naskapi Indians in the seventeenth and eighteenth centuries, permanent residents of the southern and southeastern interior and coasts of the Labrador peninsula, within the Gulf of St. Lawrence as far west as the 65th latitude, and of northern Newfoundland, dividing their time as limited nomads between the interior and the coast according to season, as do the still existing bands on the northeastern coast.

(2) That a blending of Eskimo and Indian blood and culture had started to develop among the southern Labrador representatives of the groups, despite the contrary evidence of cranial features, as reported by Hallowell.[34]

(3) That the deductions of dialectic relationship of the Labrador Eskimo and those of Baffin island as pointed out by Dr. Birket-Smith are sound, and that the Labrador groups are the offshoot of the Baffinlanders by a southward migration.

(4) That the Eskimo preceded the Montagnais-Naskapi in the peopling of the peninsula.

(5) That the Indians in question had experienced an earlier period of contact with Eskimo in the adjacency of southern Hudson bay, meaning that they had previously left Eskimo contemporaries at an earlier age farther west and reëncountered them in the Labrador peninsula as they moved into it from the southwestern portions, drifting eastward during the fifteenth and through the seventeenth centuries.

The ethnologist who aims to leave a good reputation behind should not hasten to approve theories of cultural history too firmly while so many nuances of judgment remain before us, but a venture in speculation always has its fascinations; even may possess value. The dispute over inland residence of any group in the north shows a focal point of interest.

My own view would be that an archaic arctic culture existed somewhere in the Labradorean area where either the Dorset or Thule types, or both as variations according to Mathiassen, are found located by exploration (one not precisely definable in linguistic classification as to its being Eskimo or Indian), in which the life cycle, *possibly even the annual cycle,* was divided between inland pursuits and coastal hunting as seasonal abundance or other circumstances necessitated, the two inclinations possibly alternating as they do still among both Eskimo and Indians, with a not too sharply defined place of residence—inland or coastal, finally resulting in different cases to cause some groups to adhere to the coast, others to the inland environment, and some to a more fluid cultural state between the two. The three semblances are preserved in outline as preferences among various bands of both peoples of the Labrador peninsula. The preceding pages have been planned to disclose some essentials of those among whom the inland preference has been strong.

COMPARATIVE LIST OF MONTAGNAIS-NASKAPI AND LABRADOR ESKIMO TRAITS[35]

The Eskimo bands with which we are concerned in the lists are in particular the Patlava'miut, "Battle Harbor people," the Netcetu'miut, "Sealing Place people," the Aivitu'miut, "Walrus Hunting people" (Hamilton Inlet band), and the Nuneηu'miut, "Nain people."

The numbering at the left in parentheses in the Indian column refers to the list of Eskimo traits of material culture enumerated by Dr. Birket-Smith in his comparative and analytical study found in the Report of the Fifth Thule Expedition, 1921–24, 5:234–94 (pt. 2), 1929.

Occasional references are made, for the purpose of check-up, to occurrences in other bands of Labrador where traits are not specifically recorded for those of the east coast.

The Indian traits listed, with few exceptions, are those peculiar to the Montagnais-Naskapi and not recorded of other Algonkian groups. The series is expanded from treatment given in a previous article.[36]

MONTAGNAIS-NASKAPI	LABRADOR ESKIMO
1. Clothing and Personal Adornment	
Woman's hair ties over ears[37]	Same
(A 63) Men's "calotte" bob	Same
Men's trousers, tanned caribou skin, knee-length, short-waisted	Similar men's trousers, sealskin[38]
Hooded coat, closed front, caribou skin, for men	Same in sealskin
Woman's hooded coat same as men's	Same in sealskin
Unborn-caribou skin for baby coat	Same[39]

MONTAGNAIS-NASKAPI	LABRADOR ESKIMO

Boot moccasins
  dog skin (Natasquan)
  sealskin (Ste. Marguerite, St. Augustin)
  caribou skin (Barren Ground)
	Boot moccasin, sealskin, caribou skin (Hamilton inlet)

Low sealskin moccasin	Same (Hamilton inlet)
Low caribou-skin moccasin	Same[40] (Hamilton inlet)
Fine vamp puckering (over 50 creases)	Same (Hamilton inlet)
(A 53) Fur caps for men	Same (Hamilton inlet)
Hood caps for children	Same (Hamilton inlet)
(A 55) Mits with one-piece thumb, caribou, moose, tied with shoulder string	Same in sealskin
(A 67) Snow goggles (Barren Ground)	Same
(A 64) Needle-and-thread, and pricking tattoo	Pricking tattoo

2. Tools and Household Articles

(A 3) Tent, ridge pole type when formed by two tents joined, caribou-skin	Same, caribou-skin[41]
Pack dogs (Barren Ground)	Same
Dog pack-line	Same
Snowshoes, round type	Same (often obtained from Indians)
Open deck skin canoes	Skin "umiak"
Compartment, or "roll-up" skin bag, caribou, bird skin, etc.[42]	Same, sealskin, bird skin
Caribou leg-skin hunter's bag	Same[43]
Baby sack (no board) (cloth, formerly sealskin)	Baby bag
(A 45) Dog-trace toggle (Barren Ground)	Same
(A 44) Fan dog harness (east of Seven Isles)	Same
(A 77) Seal scapula scraper	Same
(A 79) Ice chisel of bone, now of iron	Ice chisel, iron
(A 75) Ulu[44]	Same
Toggle-head harpoon, wood and bone or iron	Same (ivory and iron)
(A 26) Caribou spear	Same
(A 77) Chisel-like scraper for caribou skins	Same
(A 17) Wooden spoon for eating fish	Fish spoon
(A 22) Flat-notched two-feather arrow	Same
(A 20) Simple staff bow (no sinew backing)	Same
(A 23) Mediterranean arrow release	Same
(A 20) Caribou lance with fixed head	Same
(A 19) Sling	Same
(A 87) Snow shovel	Same
Bow with bone end for beaver call (tapping on ice) at end for composite tools for ice work	Harpoon with bone ice pick at butt Composite wood-bone tools for ice-work
(A 32) Fish decoy of wood and bone	Same, ivory or stone
Crooked knife	Same[45]
Tambourine drum and beater	Same
Wooden toggle-cup	Same[46]
Deep-bowl slate pipe, wood stem, bone cleaner	Same

Montagnais-Naskapi	Labrador Eskimo
3. Art	
No fringe in decoration	Same
Nonuse of feathers in decoration	Same
4. Social Customs and Religion	
Athletic dances	Same
No ritual dances	Same
Game owner concept	Same
Dual self (soul)	Same
Herb remedies	Same[47]
Boiling with hot stones (Barren Ground)	Same (Ungava)
Taboo for dogs to eat caribou meat	Same[48]
Sucking noses	Same
Abandoning aged with little food	Abandoning aged with no food
Smoking stone pipe by a chief or "great man"	Same
Cloth, "məntû (supernatural) skin"	Cloth, "magic skin"
Wind spirits at four corners of earth	Wind spirits at six corners of earth[49]

NOTES TO "INLAND ESKIMO BANDS OF LABRADOR"

[1] Montagnais-Naskapi Bands and Early Eskimo Distribution in the Labrador Peninsula, AA 33 (no. 4), 1931. Ethical Attributes of the Labrador Indians, *ibid.*, 35 (no. 4), 1933.

[2] Naskapi, Savage Hunters of the North, Univ. of Oklahoma Press (Norman, Okla.), 1935.

[3] Topic investigated in consultation with Sir Wilfred Grenfell for its bearing upon the question of welfare, health, and racial adjustment of populations on the Labrador coast.

[4] F. G. Speck, Beothuk and Micmac, MAIHF-INM, 1922.

[5] E. W. Hawkes, The Labrador Eskimo, Geological Survey of Canada, 23, 1916.

[6] L. M. Turner, Ethnology of the Ungava District, SI-AR 1889–90:169, 176.

[7] F. Boas, Central Eskimo, BAE-R 6:470, 1884–5.

[8] A. S. Packard, The Labrador Coast, opp. p. 232 (New York, 1891).

[9] Dillon Wallace, The Long Labrador Trail, 175, 217 (New York, 1907).

[10] Located, according to recent reports from Mr. White, on the plateau of 1000 to 2000 ft. north of Nachvak where the Torgnak mountains rise, by estimate, to over 5000 ft. at points, in whose inwards both Eskimo and Indians believe the overlord of the caribou herd to dwell.

[11] Kaj Birket-Smith, Five Hundred Eskimo Words, Report of the Fifth Thule Expedition, 1921–24, 3:26 (no. 3), 1928.

[12] Diamond Jenness, The Problem of the Eskimo, *in* The American Aborigines, Their Origin and Antiquity, edited by D. Jenness, University of Toronto Press, 1933, pp. 381–3, 388–90. See also D. Jenness, A New Eskimo Culture in Hudson Bay, Geographical Review, 15:428–37 (no. 3), 1925.

[13] F. G. Speck, Montagnais-Naskapi Bands and Early Eskimo Distribution in the Labrador Peninsula, AA 33:566, 567–568, 571, 1931.

[14] *Ibid.*, 571.

[15] F. G. Speck, *ibid.*, 557, 564 *et seq.*

[16] The author explains that the caribou hunt is now postponed until after Easter through the pressure of the Moravian missionaries, restraining the natives at home to enable them to participate in the mission rites of the season.

[17] S. K. Hutton, Among the Eskimos of Labrador (London, 1912), pp. 231–40.

[18] Hawkes, *op. cit.*, 25.

[19] Reviewed by W. G. Gosling, Labrador, etc., N. Y. (1911), pp. 160–70.

[20] In the paper referred to on Montagnais distribution I did not give sufficient emphasis, I fear, to the definite record we have of 30 or 40 families of Montagnais being brought, sometime after 1704, by Sieur de Courtemanche to reside near his newly established Fort Pontchartrain, now Bradore, near Eskimo river at the western entrance to the Straits of Belle Isle (Gosling, *op. cit.*, p. 150; also Memoir Concerning Labrador, 1716–17, author unknown, quoted by Gosling, pp. 137–8).

The successor of Courtemanche referred to the presence of the same Indians at the place as hunting, fishing, and trapping retainers. We learn subsequently of conflicts between the French and the Eskimo in which these "Montagnais" allies were also involved in accordance with their old animus of hostility.

[21] In 1843, remains of turf embankments and stone tent rings were noted about a mile from the house of a Mr. N. Lloyd of St. Pauls, in circuit more than half a mile (H. Robinson, Notes on the Coast of Labrador, Transactions of the Literary and Historical Society of Quebec, 4:45–0, 1843 [quoted by A. S. Packard, *op. cit.*, 60]).

[22] Hawkes, *op. cit.*, 24, gives the form as "Puʼtlaʼʼvaʼmiut, Battle Harbor," without further comment.

[23] Packard, *op. cit.*, 67, 251, 256. Mr. H. Haynes, Hudson's Bay Company factor at St. Augustin, has traced this identity to a Louie Youngs, supposed to have been a full-blood Eskimo, who died about 1895.

[24] Sir Wilfred Grenfell, The Romance of Labrador, N. Y., 1934, p. 121.

[25] W. A. Stearns (Labrador, Boston, 1884, pp. 294–5) has some particulars of this mixed but interesting partly Indianized group, living at Karawalla.

[26] Hawkes, *op. cit.*, pls. 3, 4, 7, 8, 10, 21, 29, 30, 31, show artifacts of this genus. Attention is also called to a pair of dressed dolls from Cartwright, illustrating the modified Eskimo garb of these southerners, in soft *smoke-tanned*, unhaired caribou skin "dickeys" of the usual Eskimo pattern for both sexes, and Indian style moccasins with knee-length canvas tops.

[27] Hawkes, *op. cit.*, 17. I underline this portion of his quotation as another challenge to the extreme view held by Parker, here supported by Hawkes, that the *ulu*-like scrapers and several other types of slate implements found in New York state, and even farther south in fact, are to be held as indication of postglacial signs of Eskimo occupation. I have discussed this far-fetched conclusion in another paper, The Ethnic Position of the Southeastern Algonkians, AA 26:195.

[28] Professor Tylor inclined to the opinion that man dwelt amid glacial conditions of life farther south in eastern United States, but to designate people of such an age as "Eskimo" upon the sole evidence of several types of utensils, which includes the oil lamp, is just cause for censure.

[29] Packard, *op. cit.*, 245–7, 250–1.

[30] Gosling, *op. cit.*, 267–9, 273.

[31] Caubvik incidentally means "wolverine," xábvik (*Gulo luscus*).

[32] D. Jenness, *op. cit.*, 390–391, 393–395. The italics in the above quotation are mine.

[33] F. G. Speck, Culture Problems in Northeastern North America, Proceedings American Philosophical Society, 65:288–90, 293; and Montagnais-Naskapi Bands and Early Eskimo Distribution in the Labrador Peninsula, AA 33:566, 568, 569, fn. 28, 571, *passim*, 1931.

[34] A. I. Hallowell, The Physical Characteristics of the Indians of Labrador, SAP–J 21: 357–71, 1929.

[35] For aid in the completion of the list I am indebted to Mr. Richard A. Faust. See also Speck, Indian and Eskimo Backgrounds in Southern Labrador, The General Magazine, Univ. of Penna., 38:1–17, 1935.

[36] F. G. Speck, Culture Problems in Northeastern America, *op. cit.*, 293–5.

[37] Illustrations, plate photograph, Hutton, *op. cit.*, 294, Canadian Field Naturalist, 42:54 (no. 13).

[38] Turner, *op. cit.*, 213.

[39] Peter Freuchen, Eskimo, N. Y., 1931, p. 342.

[40] Hawkes, *op. cit.*, 147, 179, f.

[41] Turner, *op. cit.*, 226; Hawkes, *op. cit.*, 63, 187, pls. 11, 12.

[42] Stearns, *op. cit.*, 170, gives this article the local name "hossac" among the mixed Labradoreans of the Straits of Belle Isle, a derivation of east coast Eskimo ip'iasuk, the name for the bag of the leg-skin construction (see fn. 43).

[43] Hawkes, pl. 9a.

[44] Among St. Augustin band called "oodloo" (Stearns, *op. cit.*, 179). The present Indians of this band do not know this term. It is used by the white-Eskimo mixed-bloods of this district.

[45] Not in Baffinland, but in Alaska and Labrador.

[46] Also Boas, *op. cit.*, 100–101 (Baffin land). See also Grenfell, *op. cit.*, pl. opp. p. 323.

[47] Hutton, *op. cit.*, 289; H. Carson, MS notes.

[48] Also Turner, *op. cit.*, 201.

[49] Turner, *op cit.*, 267.

UNIVERSITY OF PENNSYLVANIA,
PHILADELPHIA, PENNSYLVANIA.

THE ECONOMIC AND SOCIAL BASIS OF PRIMITIVE BANDS

By Julian H. Steward

MOST ANTHROPOLOGISTS have rejected Morgan's theory that matrilineal societies were the most ancient human institutions. Instead, they have postulated chronological priority for the bilateral family, that is, the biological family consisting of father, mother, and children.[1*] Clans are usually considered to be later, particularistic developments from such families.

Although the bilateral family is no doubt as ancient as the various social forms of which it is a part, there is no evidence to indicate that it was ever the sole human institution nor that it was the direct progenitor of the clan. In all modern societies it is an integral part of some larger aggregate of individuals. The simplest of these aggregates have variously and often loosely been called lineages, hordes, bands, or tribes. I shall use the term band. Empirically and logically, bands fall into three types, the characteristics of which are as follows:

(1) Patrilineal band: politically autonomous, communally land owning, exogamous, patrilocal, patrilineal in land inheritance, and consisting theoretically or actually of a single lineage, which, however, comprises several households or elemental bilateral families.

(2) Composite band: similar to (1), but nonexogamous, bilateral in descent, lacking in rule of residence and consisting of several independent families.

(3) Matrilineal band: like (1), but matrilineal and matrilocal.

Because unilineal bands resemble clans so greatly that they have often been classed with them, it is obvious that they cannot be subsumed with composite bands in a category which is characterized merely by possession of the bilateral family. It would be equally artificial and misleading to class unilineal bands and clans in one category based purely on unilateral descent.[2]

This paper is concerned with the band types which occur among certain hunting and gathering peoples. I shall show that the patrilineal band is most common because it is produced by recurring ecological and social factors which may be formulated into something akin to cultural law, and that the composite band occurs where there are special factors, which may readily be ascertained in each instance. The method will be to analyze functional or necessary relationships. It will not undertake statistics or correlations.

The ethnic groups selected for this treatment have a purely hunting and gathering economy superimposed upon an environment which is so unproductive that the population density is extremely sparse. Because population seldom exceeds one person per five square miles, the social aggregates are necessarily small. Similar conditions may obtain among ethnic groups not

---

* Superior figures refer to notes at the end of this essay, p. 348.

included here. Also, patrilineal and composite bands are known among peoples having an ecology which permits greater population density. These are omitted, with the exception of a few examples, for they involve certain special relationships which are beyond the scope of this paper.

The broad problem is to formulate the ecological and other factors which produce the primitive band.[3] This is resolved into a series of more specific problems which shall be treated successively. Why are human beings the only animals having land-owning groups? Why is the bilateral family never the independent social, economic, and land-owning group? And finally, what factors determine the size and characteristics of the primitive band?

The first task is to ascertain the causes of the distinctively human fact of territory ownership, that is, exclusive land utilization by some definite group of individuals. The more important causes are: (1) Any animal may secure food and water more efficiently in terrain which it habitually utilizes and therefore intimately knows, especially in an arid region.[4] (2) All human groups practice some food storage. (3) People may conserve food resources in their territory.[5] (4) A certain amount of paraphernalia hinders extensive migration. (5) Greater human intelligence eliminates the strife of unrestricted competition for food by developing property concepts. Because of these facts, human groups will reach an equilibrium in which land is parceled among definite social groups. Warfare, migration, and other disturbing factors may, of course, prevent such adjustment.

The next query is what the land-owning group must be. Now the bilateral family everywhere constitutes the molecule of the larger social structure. As it is apparently lacking among apes, it must be regarded as the product of factors which are at least in part distinctively human. Its more important causes appear to be: (1) A chronic, rather than seasonal, sex excitability, which in human beings as in other primates constitutes a constant stimulus of attraction between members of a group.[6] (2) The peculiarly human fact of greater need for child care, due to prolonged infancy and the requirements of education. (3) The sexual division of labor which, among peoples considered here, requires the economic union of a man and a woman to support existence.

For these reasons, the minimum human social and economic institution cannot be less than the family. Actually, however, although the family is often the seasonal independent subsistence unit, additional social and economic factors require the unity and territorial autonomy of an aggregate of several such families, that is, the band. The most important factors which produce the band are: (1) Among the apes[7] and most other mammals, the "social" aggregate is usually greater than the biological family. Therefore, primates provide no reason to suppose that human beings ever were divided into family groups. (2) In practically all human groups several families cooperate in some economic activity and frequently share game and even vegetable foods communally. This provides a kind of subsistence insurance or greater security than individual families could achieve. (3) It is rare that land, if subdivided into family tracts, would provide sufficient variety of foods, unless the economy were highly specialized, as among the modern beaver-trapping Algonkians, or, in arid regions, that there would be a sufficient number of water holes.[8] (4) Realignment of family tract boundaries each generation, especially as some families grow while others shrink, would entail serious practical difficulties. (5) Social activities, such as games, dances, and ceremonies tend to unite several families. (6) A large group provides greater security in warfare or feuds.

Among all known people, therefore, the autonomous, land-owning sociopolitical group is greater than the bilateral family. But whether this group is a band, and, if so, what type of band, depends upon ecological factors.

With a given population density, the size of the territory and of the band owning it are direct variables. If the group be enlarged the territory must also be increased in order to support it. Among the ethnic groups in question, however, the population is sparse, ranging from a maximum which seldom exceeds one person per 5 square miles to one person per 50 or more square miles. This prevents indefinite enlargement of the band because means of transporting the food to the people or the people to food are limited. The area which the band can conveniently forage averages some 100 square miles and seldom exceeds 500 square miles, a tract roughly 20 miles to a side. Consequently, the band averages 50 individuals and seldom exceeds 100.[9] Only in regions of unusual conditions—for example, where there are herds of migratory game—does the tract utilized, and therefore the group size, surpass these figures.

We now have to consider why these small bands are ordinarily patrilineal. First, it is characteristic of hunters and gatherers in regions of sparse population that postmarital residence is patrilocal. This has several causes. If human beings could be conceived stripped of culture, it is not unreasonable to suppose that innate male dominance would give men a commanding position.[10] If, in addition to native dominance, however, the position of the male is strengthened by his greater economic importance, as in a hunting culture,[11] or even if women are not given greater economic importance than men, it is extremely probable that postmarital residence will be patrilocal.

But in these small bands patrilocal residence will produce the fact or fiction that all members of the band are patrilineally related[12] and hence matrimonially taboo. Band exogamy—that is, local exogamy—is therefore required. Probably at one time or another such bands have actually consisted of relatives with traceable connection. Genealogical data on the tribes of southern California, for example, show that more often than not the band comprises a true patrilineal lineage. Because life is so precarious that population expansion is impossible and budding collateral lineages often become extinct, the possibility is small that several independent families which have no traceable connection will develop in any band. Such families will occur only if the band is extraordinarily large. And even in this event, the fiction of relationship may be perpetuated after the connection is forgotten if group unity is reinforced by patrynymy, myths, and other factors.[13]

For these reasons, the band, among hunters and gatherers who live in sparsely populated areas, must ordinarily be patrilineal. But special factors may make it composite. Thus, if unrelated and hence intermarriageable families exist within a band, local exogamy and patrilocal residence with respect to the band are unnecessary. This will occur when parallel-cousin marriage is permitted or where bands have, for various reasons, become unusually large and lack any factor that would create or perpetuate a fiction of relationship between its members. Occasional matrilocal residence will introduce into one band families which are not related patrilineally. This will prevent strictly patrilineal inheritance of band territory and tend to weaken the fiction of relationship between band members. I shall particularize the causes of the composite band in treating concrete cases below.

Political unity in all bands is very similar. Centralized control exists only for hunting, for rituals, and for the few other affairs that are communal. Consequently, the leader has temporary and slight authority. In patrilineal bands, he is usually the head of the lineage. In bilateral bands, he is a person of prestige. There is rarely an institution of chief. Frequently the shaman is more influential than the leader. Bands which are ordinarily autonomous may temporarily unite for special occasions, such as Australian and Fuegian initiation ceremonies.

The remaining sections of this paper will discuss the patrilineal and bilateral bands among ethnic groups in areas of low population. Attention will be paid only to the characteristics of the bands specified above. The occurrence of clans among Australians, Ojibway, and others, of moieties in Australia and southern California, and of other social forms in no way affects the cause and effect relationships with which we are concerned. Such institutions may obviously be introduced by diffusion and coexist with bands.

Tribes With the Patrilineal Band

This section will treat of the functional relations of the various characteristics of the patrilineal band among tribes in a sparsely settled environment. The important characteristics are: land ownership, political autonomy, patrilocal residence, band or local exogamy, and patrilineal land inheritance. Reasons for departures from the patrilineal pattern will also be indicated.

The Bushmen.[14]—A hunting and gathering culture imposed upon an arid and unproductive native environment has produced a sparse population among the Bushmen. Population aggregates are therefore necessarily small,[15] and each group that coöperates on various occasions is politically autonomous and unified. Although the band splits seasonally into smaller, probably family groups, it owns and communally utilizes a definite territory. Some hunting requires joint effort of all band members and game is often shared by all.

The bands of the Northwestern Bushmen, including the Heikum, are ordinarily patrilineal owing to patrilocal residence and local or band exogamy. The Naron bands, however, are sometimes composite because matrilocal residence, which is said to be practiced occasionally in order that the wife's mother might help the wife with her children, introduces families which are unrelated patrilineally into the same band. This weakens patrilineal inheritance of the estate and tends to obviate the necessity of band exogamy, which, however, is preferred.[16] The Cape, Namib, and !Okung bands also tend to be composite because, although band exogamy is preferred, matrilocal residence, for a reason which has not been revealed, is sometimes practiced. Band endogamy, moreover, is facilitated by cousin marriage, parallel or cross, which is barred among the Northwestern groups.[17]

Central African Negritos.—Although the Central African Negritos are surrounded by Bantu tribes, with whom some bands live in a kind of symbiotic relationship, their existence is based largely upon hunting and gathering, and their subsistence level is extremely low. Fragments of information now available indicate that the band is patrilineal. It seemingly owns its territory and is independent except when dominated by the Bantu. Band members live and hunt together and sometimes share game and vegetable foods communally. Schebesta[18] reports that the Bambuti, Éfé, Bac'wa, and Batwa have exogamous, totemic clans, which are subdivided into exogamous, patrilocal, and generally autonomous sibs ("sippe") or families of male relatives numbering 60 to 65 persons each. The relationship of the latter, which is the true band, to the "totemic clan" is not clear.

These bands sometimes tend to be composite for two reasons. First, it is customary at marriage for the husband's band to furnish a woman who marries a member of his wife's band. When no woman is available, he lives with his wife's people. Second, band endogamy, that is, marriage even of related members of the band, which is felt to be a breach of incest laws, is often practiced when other bands are remote and inaccessible.[19]

The Negritos of Gabon in French Equatorial Africa are grouped in some 100 or 150 villages, each of which usually comprises one family "rangée sous l'autorité d'un seul chef, le père du clan, généralement de 30 à 35 individus mâles." These seem to be independent, patrilocal, and exogamous, and therefore true patrilineal bands. But they belong to some kind of larger, patrilineal totemic clans, which are preferably, but not always, exogamous.[20]

Semang.—The more or less inadequate information now available indicates that many of the Negritos of the Malay peninsula possess the patrilineal band. Largely hunters and gatherers and more or less isolated in the sparsely settled mountain forests, their groups are small, ranging, according to fragments of evidence recorded by Schebesta,[21] from individual families which are probably temporary subdivisions to groups of 50 or more persons. These seem to be politically autonomous, land-owning bands. Skeat and Blagden[22] say that the Kedah Semang band often amounts to an enlarged family and, somewhat obscurely, that the chief is practically "the head of a family, which in this case is represented by a larger family, the tribe." It may be, however, that band territory is sometimes further subdivided among bilateral families so that each owns an area for its durian trees. Schebesta says[23] that "the individual groups wander within the tribal boundaries but always return to their family territory, especially at the time of the durian crop" and that the trees are owned by men as family heads. These family tracts are, perhaps, comparable to the Algonkian and Athabaskan beaver-trapping territory.

That these bands are truly patrilineal is indicated by Schebesta's statement[24] that the unit of society is the "sib" like that of the Congo Negritos, but he does not particularize its characteristics. Elsewhere he observes[25] that there is considerable band exogamy and patrilocal residence, although he records one band that is composite. One reason for the occurrence of the latter among the Kenta Semang is that durian trees are sometimes inherited matrilineally. This would, of course, favor matrilocal residence and tend to set up a composite band.

Philippine Negritos.—The predominantly hunting and gathering Philippine Negritos live in comparative isolation from the Malay. They are clustered in bands which Vanoverberg[26] says comprise "a certain group of families." These remain in the same portion of the forest and seasonally exploit different parts of an area which has a radius of not over 20 square miles. Trespass on the land of neighboring bands is not forbidden but is avoided. The land is hunted communally by its owners, but cultivated trees and honey nests are privately owned. It is not recorded, however, how trees are inherited. Bands seem to be politically autonomous, but the lack of an institutionalized band chief is implied by the somewhat vague statement that authority rests in the father of the family.

There is some indication that Philippine Negrito bands have recently changed from patrilineal to composite. Schmidt,[27] quoting Blumentritt on the Zambales-Bataam, says that the bands are now endogamous but at the end of the eighteenth century were exogamous. Present-day endogamy is further shown by the presence of unrelated families in the same band.[28] Nevertheless patrilocal residence is recorded, although it is not clear whether it is with respect to the band or family.

There is, therefore, some doubt as to the frequency of the two types of bands and the customs concerning residence and other matters which would produce them. It appears, however, that some factor has tended to produce a change from patrilineal to composite bands during the past century. At least one important cause of composite bands today is the practice of marrying cousins. Although marriage was preferably between cross-cousins, parallel-cousins were eligible.[29]

Australia.[30]—The relatively low productivity of Australia has permitted but a sparse population which averages only one person per 12 square miles for the entire continent.[31] The population is gathered into relatively small, autonomous bands which Radcliffe-Brown calls hordes. Each band comprises 20 to 50 individuals and owns 100 to 150 square miles of land. The male members of the band inherit and communally hunt[32] their tract, which is definitely bounded and protected from trespass.

These bands are truly patrilineal and approximate male lineages. They are almost universally exogamous and patrilocal. The idea of relationship between band members is further reinforced by kinship terminology. Even those ethnic groups which have moieties, sections (formerly called "marriage classes"), and matrilineal clans and totems, have not, except in a portion of western Australia, lost the patrilineal band.[33]

Tasmania.—Information on the Tasmanians, though incomplete, indicates the presence of the patrilineal band. The scant population[34] was divided into autonomous bands of 30 to 40 persons each. Each band owned a tract of land on which it wandered seasonally in search of food. It protected its hunting rights against trespass, which was a common cause of war.[35]

The Tasmanian band must have been patrilineal, for evidence assembled by Roth indicates, although it does not prove beyond question, that the band was exogamous and marriage patrilocal.

Tierra del Fuego.—The Ona of Tierra del Fuego fall strictly into the patrilineal band pattern. The low subsistence level, based largely upon guanaco hunting, produced a population of only one individual to 4.5 or 5 square miles. This was grouped in politically independent bands of 40 to 120 persons, each owning an average of 410 square miles. Gusinde[36] believes that the manner of life would not have supported larger aggregates. Each territory was named, band rights to it were sanctioned by myths, and hunting privileges were protected against trespass. Although each band was politically autonomous, there was no institution of chief.

The band was patrilineal because it was exogamous and patrilocal. Local exogamy was required even among the large bands in which relationship between members was not traceable, for native theory held that each band was a male lineage.

Patagonia.—The Tehuelche of Patagonia, although very incompletely known, are instructive when compared with the Ona. Also dependent largely upon herds of guanaco, their economic life appears formerly to have resembled that of the Fuegians. There is evidence that they were divided into bands, each having some degree of localization[37] and led in its travels, etc., by a patrilineal chief[38] who was called "father."[39] The band chief, however, acknowledged a general cacique, who, according to Musters, had very little authority. The institution of general or tribal cacique may easily have developed subsequent to the arrival of the European.

The introduction of the horse about a century and a half ago completely altered ecological conditions in Patagonia. It enabled people to move widely in pursuit of guanaco herds and to transport foods considerable distances. This would, of course, tend to eliminate band ownership of small parcels of territory, had it even existed. It also permitted enlargement of population aggregates far beyond the size of the usual lineage. Further motivation for amalgamation of formerly separate bands was provided by internecine strife, which was stimulated by competition for foods and war against the white man. The political unit consequently increased in size and had a single, although not absolute, chief. Thus, in 1871, bands numbered as many as 400 or 500 persons, although they occasionally split into smaller groups.[40] As there is no mention of exogamy of any form, it must be assumed that these bands were composite. This is common in bands of such size.

Southern California.—The Shoshonean-speaking Serrano, Cahuilla, and Luiseño, and some of the Yuman-speaking Diegueño of southern California are divided into patrilineal bands. This region is exceptional in that abundance of acorns and other wild seeds permits the unusually dense population of 1 person per square mile. But this great density is accompanied by small territory size rather than large band size, probably because the very few and small sources of water prevent greater concentration of people. Therefore, bands average only 50 individuals and the territory only 50 square miles.

The other factors producing the patrilineal bands are those which operate elsewhere. Patrilocal residence coupled with the small size of the bands makes most of them actual patrilineal lineages, so that local exogamy is required. In addition, a band chief, priest, ceremonies, ceremonial house and bundle, and myths contribute to group cohesion.[41] This strongly fortified patrilineal pattern may also serve to maintain the band at lineage size.

The culturally similar neighboring Cupeño provide an illuminating contrast to these groups. Because the local abundance of food and water permits greater concentration, they are able to live in two permanent towns, each numbering some 250 persons. Each village contains several lineages and has a chief. Bands are therefore composite.[42]

A further contrast is afforded by the Shoshonean-speaking Paiute of Owens valley in eastern California. Although the population is sparser than in southern California, being 1 person per 2 square miles for the region, the band-owned tracts are of greater size. This may be explained by the distribution of foods, which requires the utilization of a wide territory to secure all the necessary products. Bands consequently comprise 150 to 300 or 400 members. This produces unrelated families within each band, so that band endogamy is possible and the bands are composite.[43] Apparently like conditions prevail among the culturally similar Surprise Valley Paiute in northeastern California.[44]

TRIBES WITH THE COMPOSITE BAND

The composite band is, like the patrilineal band, politically autonomous and land-owning, but does not have band exogamy, patrilocal residence, or land inheritance by patrilineal relatives. It occurs among peoples having an economy similar to those already described, but among whom special factors have prevented consistent patrilocal residence, allowed cousin marriage, or greatly increased band size. Any of these will prevent the band from consisting of patrilineal relatives, and will therefore prohibit patrilineal land succession and usually obviate the necessity of band exogamy.

The Northern Algonkians.—The relatively unproductive environment of the nomadic hunting and gathering Algonkian-speaking tribes of Canada has limited population to 1 person per 5.3 square miles north of the Great Lakes and to 1 person per 34.6 or more square miles in the eastern sub-Arctic region.[45] The political unit is the band, which generally numbers several hundred individuals. Each band has a patrilineal chief, usually seasonal festivals, and often slight dialectical distinctiveness.[46] Land, however, is owned by the family, which, according to Speck,[47] consists of the "individuals of one family connection, primarily through blood but also through marriage relationship, who hunt together as a herd within the confines of a certain tract of country." The family tract is inherited patrilineally.

The unusual feature of family land ownership bears an intimate functional relationship to the highly specialized economy introduced by the fur trade. Fur-bearing animals, especially the beaver, may be husbanded in relatively small areas.[48] Barter of pelts with the white man for other goods enables a group to subsist on an area which is smaller than would otherwise be possible. Jenness suggests that title to land originally rested in the band and that the family subdivision is a post-European development. He records, for example, that partition occurred among the Athabaskan-speaking Sekanni on the headwaters of the Peace river during the last hundred years, "after the necessities of the fur trade compelled the families to disperse among the different creeks and rivers." In view of this, it is understandable that Montagnais families were apportioned their land in the time of the Jesuit missionaries,[49] and that Micmac family territories should be "less permanent, less hereditary . . . and the judicial power of the chief in the reassignment of territory . . . rather more definite" than elsewhere.[50] Among the Canadian Algonkians, therefore, the subsistence and land-owning unit is usually the bilateral family but the political unit is the band, which was probably formerly also the land-owning and in part subsistence and social unit.

These bands are composite rather than patrilineal for several reasons. First, the segregation of family units, each of which is preferably patrilocal, prevents the band as such from being patrilocal. Second, each band is so large that the relationship of individuals and families to one another would be forgotten, even if it had once existed, unless special factors, which did not exist, had been present to preserve the fiction.

The larger of the land-owning families[51] may become patrilineal bands, for patrilocal residence, if consistently practiced, would mold each into a male lineage. No doubt many are patrilineal bands, but supporting conditions are too unstable to make this very frequent. Speck states that patrilocal and matrilocal residence depend "upon the number of sons and daughters in the family group, the conditions of physical ability of its members, whether the father is living, and the circumstances of the uncles, the conditions of the game . . . the conditions of the hunting districts . . . upon temporary climatic conditions, and even upon personal circumstances." Therefore, although residence is preferably patrilocal and it is common for the oldest son to inherit the paternal hunting tract, his brothers often join their wives' families.[52]

The Canadian Athabaskans.—The habitat of the Athabaskan-speaking tribes of the Canadian far north is so unfavorable that the population varies from only one person per 50 square miles to one person per 80 or more square miles, some regions being virtually uninhabited. The population was nevertheless grouped in politically independent bands[53] which seem to have been definitely localized.

Speck[54] quotes various sources to demonstrate that "segregated family hunting, trapping and fishing grounds exist among many of the tribes," especially in the west. Jenness, as already noted, believes that this is the result of the fur trade and that the entire band formerly utilized the land communally. Morice's observations bear the same implication. He says that "sedentary" game, chiefly the beaver, is regarded "as the object of as strict proprietorship as the domestic animals or personal chattels," whereas "nomadic" game, the larger animals which are taken primarily for their meat, is usually shared within the band when killed.[55] Osgood says that the individual beaver-hunting territory among the Satudene and Slave exists now, though not formerly.[56] Birket-Smith believes[57] that the collective nature of caribou-hunting among the Chipewyan would preclude family hunting territory.

The Athabaskan band seems usually to be composite, for Jenness observes[58] that marriage in general "depended on blood relationship only, and often occurred within the bands; but many were so small that they were practically exogamous units." Causes of composite band require separate treatment of the eastern and western Athabaskans.

The bands of the eastern or mainly Mackenzie basin Athabaskans are extraordinarily large in view of the sparse population, numbering several hundred persons each.[59] This surprising size must be explained by the local economy. There are large herds of migratory musk ox and often caribou in much of the area. These are hunted more or less seasonally and collectively by large groups of people. Population, which otherwise has to be distributed over an enormous area, may concentrate during these hunts in a group having some temporary centralized control and thus constituting a political unit. The bands are generally so large that they comprise unrelated families. Local or band exogamy is unnecessary and consanguinity is the only bar to marriage.

The Western or Cordillera Athabaskans have a much denser population and more settled life, due to the presence of excellent fishing streams.[60] The band here is profoundly affected by influence emanating from the Northwest Coast. Diffusion has been so great that not only much material culture, but caste systems, potlatching, and matrilineal clans and moieties have been introduced to many groups. Now, while a patrilineal band by no means inevitably succumbs when clans are introduced, if matrilocal residence and matrilineal property rights are also implanted, society will be completely revamped. Accordingly, we find that the Carrier have five matrilineal, landowning phratries, each of which apportions tracts to its component clans.[61] The neighboring Babine have matrilineal clans and matrilocal residence.[62] The Chilcotin have a somewhat obscure system of clans with the addition of social stratification.[63] The Tsetsaut have matrilineal moieties. The Tahltan have moieties, each subdivided into three clans, which are said formerly to have claimed distinctive territory but now share land communally.[64] The

	Number of persons per square mile	Average size of band	Average square miles in band territory	Permanent residence patrilocal with respect to band	Exogamy of band, i.e., of locality, required	Band politically autonomous, weak chief	References and remarks
Patrilineal bands							
N. W. Bushmen...	?	50-60	?	×	×	×	Schapera, 1926, 1930; Dornan, 1925:85; Stow, 33, 229-230; Dunn, 1931:7, 22.
Congo Negritos— Bambuti, Éfé, Bac'wa, Batwa..	?	60-65	?	×	×	×	Schebesta, 1931; Schmidt, 1910
Negritos—Gabon	?	20-70	?	×	×	×	Trilles
Semang..........	1/2-1/8	35?	?	×(0)	(×)	×	Schebesta; Skeat and Blagden
Australia—W.....	1/5	30	150	×	×	×	Brown, 1930:688
—S.............	?	40–	?	×	×	×	Brown, 1930:690
Victoria........	1/15	50+	750	×	×	×	Brown, 1930:691
Queensland.....	3/10	30	100	×	×	×	Brown, 1930:694
Herbert R.......	1/5	20-25	100	×	×	×	Brown, 1930:696
Average........	1/12	35	420	×	×	×	
Tasmania........	1/8-1/13	30-40	350	×	×	×	Brown, 1930:695; Roth
Ona.............	1/4-1/5	40-120	410	×	×	×	Gusinde
California: Miwok, Luiseño, Serrano, Cahuilla, Cupeño.	1	50	50	×	×	×	Gifford: 1926 Kroeber, 1925:883, 58; Strong, 1927, 1929; Gifford, 1926
Diegueño (N&S)..	1/2	50?	50?	×	×	×	Gifford, 1926
Composite bands							
S. Bushmen.......	?	100-150	?	0	0	×	Schapera, 1930
Andaman.........	3	50	16	0	0	×	Brown, 1922:22-87; Man
Algonkian........	1/3-1/5	25?	?	0	0	×	Patrilineal family territory. Speck, 1915:9-10
Ojibway..........	1/5	95-240	100-1000?	0	0	×	Patrilineal family territory. Speck, 1910:11-30; 1915a: 298-9; 1917:89
Montagnais.......	1/5-1/35	44-700	250-10,000	0	0	×	Patrilineal family territory. Speck, 1927

	Number of persons per square mile	Average size of band	Average square miles in band territory	Permanent residence patrilocal with respect to band	Exogamy of band, i.e., of locality, required	Band politically autonomous, weak chief	References and remarks
Penobscot........	1/17	400	10,000	0	0	×	Patrilineal family territory. Speck, 1915a:299-302; 1917:95-96
Micmac (Newfoundland)......	1/86	300	26,000	0	0	×	Patrilineal family territories. Band chief. Speck, 1917:89
Slave.............	1/50	220	4,000-20,000	0	0	×	Morice, 1906; Jenness; Osgood, 1933
Satudene.........	1/50	?	32,000	0	0	×	Osgood, 1933
Dog Rib..........	1/50	287	15,000	0	0	×	Morice; Osgood, 1933

Nahani[65] and Kutchin or Loucheux[66] have, in addition to independent bands, matrilineal moieties, the relationship of which to the economic system is not clear. Thus, ecological conditions favor patrilineal or composite bands, but Northwest Coast influence seems to have destroyed them among most of the Western Athabaskans.

The Andamanese.—The Andamanese are instructive by way of illustrating several special conditions. The unusual productivity of the natural environment permits the relatively dense population of 3 persons per square mile in spite of the hunting and gathering culture. Although the people undoubtedly could, as far as ecology is concerned, live in fairly large bands, each band actually averages only 50 individuals and the territory it owns only 16 square miles. The reason for this is not clear, but it may be noted that each band tract affords an ample variety of foods, so that a motive for ranging over a wider territory is lacking. The bands are politically independent but have no definite chiefs.[67]

Some tendency of the bands to be patrilineal is indicated by Radcliffe-Brown's statement that probably a "majority of marriages, or at any rate a large proportion, were between persons belonging to different local groups."[68] Otherwise, the bands are composite despite their small size. The reason for this is apparently the great frequency of child adoption, which Radcliffe-Brown says is usually between bands. Even though marriages between foster brothers and sisters were forbidden,[69] it is evident that several unrelated and hence intermarriageable families would be established in such bands. Consequently, even if consistent patrilocal residence should tend to convert these small bands into patrilineal lineages, adoption would constantly offset its effect and obviate the necessity of local exogamy.

Summary

The primitive band.—All peoples in an area of low population density have some form of politically autonomous, land-owning band, which is greater than the bilateral family. The size of the band and the extent of the territory it utilizes are determined by the number of persons who, due largely to ecological factors, habitually coöperate at least during part of the annual round of economic and social activity. Band unity is expressed in a consciousness of common interest and submission to some degree of central control during community enterprises, although such control may be lacking during parts of the year. The authority of the leader is consequently small and temporary and his position is seldom a fixed institution.

The patrilineal band.—The band will be patrilineal when it is in fact or native theory a patrilineal lineage and therefore locally exogamous. It is produced by the following factors:

(1) Culture and/or environment which delimits the ecologically possible social aggregate to an average of some 50 or 60 members and seldom more than 100, or

(2) where a larger band is ecologically possible, due to greater population density, some social factor which nevertheless has brought about occupation of small parcels of territory by correspondingly small groups. Thus, the southern California and Andaman bands are probably smaller than was ecologically necessary. Even some horticultural peoples in regions of relatively dense population have small bands which own extraordinarily small tracts.

(3) Patrilocal residence, practiced because of innate male dominance and/or the male's greater importance in a hunting and gathering economy, and

(4) incest taboos which prevent marriage with blood relatives and therefore with fellow band members who are known to be related. The requirement of band exogamy may persist, however, after knowledge of relationship is forgotten if the patrilineal complex is reinforced by other features such as names, kinship terminology, myths, ceremonies, totems, etc. Thus, the bands of Australia, southern California, and Tierra del Fuego are less variable than elsewhere because they possess such supports. Among the Bushmen, Negritos, and others, patrilineal bands frequently become composite when special conditions exist.

The importance of these findings for theories of clan origin is now clear. Patrilineal bands easily develop among hunters and gatherers. Matrilineal bands may arise if women are economically of sufficient importance, as, for example, in many horticultural societies. If the unilineal pattern of either type becomes so rigid because of fortifying features that the band retains its unity, affiliation of members, and exogamy, after being dislocated from its territory, it is *ipso facto* a clan. Such dislocations may occur especially when a changed economy permits greater population concentration.[70]

The composite band.—The composite band will be produced, even in groups which are ordinarily patrilineal, when certain special factors are present. It fails to be unilineal in group composition and land inheritance and may be endogamous when it consists of unrelated families. Band endogamy has been found to be made possible by:

(1) Unusual band size, produced by: greater population density (Cupeño and many tribes who are on a higher subsistence level than those considered here); or unusual ecology, such as reliance on migratory herds (Eastern Athabaskans).

(2) Adoption of children between bands (Andamanese).

(3) Legitimacy of parallel as well as cross-cousin marriage (Cape, Namib, and !Okung Bushmen and Philippine Negritos).

(4) Remoteness of bands into which to marry (Central African Negritos, Philippine Negritos).

(5) Subdivision of band territory into family tracts for special economic reasons (Algonkian and Athabaskan fur trapping; possibly Semang fruit orchards; possibly some Australian wild seed plots).

It also fails to be patrilineal in composition and land inheritance although it may, if small, continue to be exogamous when the rule of postmarital residence is not consistently patrilocal. Matrilocal residence has been found to occur for the following reasons:

(1) A shortage of men in the wife's family or more favorable conditions in the territory of the wife's family (Algonkian).

(2) Desire to secure the assistance of the wife's mother in child rearing (Naron Bushmen).

(3) Lack of a woman to exchange with the wife's band in marriage (Congo Negritos).

(4) Sufficient strength of borrowed matrilineal institutions. The last may tend to produce matrilineal bands or even societies which are not classifiable as bands.

Underlying this paper is the assumption that every cultural phenomenon is the product of some definite cause or causes. This is a necessary presupposition if anthropology is considered a science. The method of this paper has been first to ascertain the causes of primitive bands through analysis of the inner functional or organic connection of the components of a culture and their environmental basis. Next, through comparisons, it endeavored to discover what degree of generalization is possible. It is not assumed, of course, that generalizations may be made concerning all culture traits. On the contrary, it is entirely possible that the very multiplicity of antecedents of many traits or complexes will preclude satisfactory generalization and that the conclusion with respect to some things will be that "history never repeats itself." The extent, however, to which generalizations can be made may be ascertained by further application of the methods followed here.

This paper, therefore, is but the first of a series which I shall devote to this general objective. Other problems concerning these hunters and gatherers with a low subsistence level which I shall treat in the future are the relation of primitive bands to kinship systems, to law and property concepts, to comparative linguistic and cultural unity in larger ethnic units or groups of contiguous bands, etc. The same method, of course, may be used to analyze peoples on a higher subsistence level.

Bibliography

BEERBOHN, JULIUS
    1881. Wanderings in Patagonia or Life Among the Ostrich-Hunters. London.

BINGHAM, HAROLD C.
    1932. Gorillas in a Native Habitat. Rept. joint expedition of 1929–1932 by Yale University and Carnegie Inst. of Wash. for psychobiological study of mountain gorillas (*Gorilla berengei*) in Parc National Albert, Belgian Congo, Africa. iv + 66 pls., 5 figs.

BIRKET-SMITH, KAJ
    1930. Contributions to Chipewyan Ethnology. Report of the 5th Thule Exped., 1921–4, vol. 4 (3), Copenhagen.

BROWN, A. R. (see RADCLIFFE-BROWN, A.)

DAVIDSON, D. SUTHERLAND
    1928. The Family Hunting Territory in Australia. AA, n.s., 30:614–632.

DORNAN, S. S.
    1925. Pygmies and Bushmen of the Kalahari. London.

DUNN, E. J.
    1931. The Bushman. London.

DIXIE, LADY FLORENCE
    1880. Across Patagonia. London.

GIFFORD, E. W.
    1918. Clans and Moieties in Southern California. UC-PAAE 14:155–219.
    1926. Miwok Lineages and the Political Unit in Aboriginal California. AA, n.s., 28: 389–401.
    1931. The Kamia of the Imperial Valley. BAE-B 97.

GUSINDE, MARTIN
    1931. Die Feuerland Indianer. Band I. Die Selk'nam. Verlag der Internationalen Zeitschrift, Anthropos, Vienna.

JENNESS, DIAMOND
    1932. The Indians of Canada. Canada Dept. Mines, Natl. Mus., Bull. 65.

KELLY, ISABEL
    1932. Ethnography of the Surprise Valley Paiute. UC-PAAE 31:67–210.

KOPPERS, WILHELM
    1921. Die Anfänge des menschlichen Gemeinschaftslebens. Vienna.

KROEBER, A. L.
    1925. Handbook of the Indians of California. BAE-B 78.
    1934. Native American Population. AA, n.s., 36:1–25.

LOTHROP, S. K.
    1921. The Indians of Tierra del Fuego. MAIHF-C 10:1–244.

LOWIE, R. H.
    1920. Primitive Society. New York.

MACLEOD, W. C.
    1922. The Family Hunting Territory and Lenape Political Organization. AA, n.s., 24: 448–463.

MAN, H. R.
    1882. On the Aboriginal Inhabitants of the Andaman Islands. JRAI 12.

MORICE, A. G.
    1906. The Great Dene Race. A 1:229–278, 483–509, 695–730.
    1907. The Great Dene Race. A 2:1–34, 181–196.
    1909. The Great Dene Race. A 4:582–606.
    1910. The Great Dene Race. A 5:113–142, 419–443, 643–653, 969–990.

MUSTERS, GEORGE C.
    1873. At Home with the Patagonians. A Year's Wandering over Untrodden Ground from the Straits of Magellan to the Rio Negro. London.

NISSEN, H. W.
    1931. A Field Study of the Chimpanzee. Comp. Psych. Monog., vol. 8, ser. no. 36.

OSGOOD, CORNELIUS B.
    1933. The Ethnography of the Great Bear Lake Indians. Natl. Mus. Canada, Ann. Rept. 1931:31–92.
    1934. Kutchin Tribal Distribution and Synonymy. AA, n.s., 36:168–179.

OUTES, FELIX F. and BRUCH, CARLOS
    1910. Los Aborigines de la Republica Argentina. Buenos Aires.

PASSARGE, S.
    1907. Die Buschmänner der Kalahari. Berlin.

PORTMAN, M. V.
    1899. A History of Our Relations with the Andamanese. 2 vs. Calcutta.

QUATREFAGES, A. DE
    1895. The Pygmies. New York.

RADCLIFFE-BROWN, A.
    1922. The Andaman Islanders. Cambridge Univ. Press.
    1930. Former Numbers and Distribution of the Australian Aborigines. Official Year Book of the Commonwealth of Australia, no. 23:671–696.
    1930a. The Social Organization of Australian Tribes I. Oceania, 1:34–63.
    1930b. The Social Organization of Australian Tribes II. Oceania, 1:204–246.
    1931. The Social Organization of Australian Tribes III. Oceania, 1:426–456.
    1935. Patrilineal and Matrilineal Succession. The Iowa Law Review, 20:286–303.

ROTH, H. LING
    1899. The Aborigines of Tasmania. London.

SCHAPERA, I.
    1926. A Preliminary Consideration of the Relationship between the Hottentots and the Bushmen. South African Journ. Sci., 23:833–866.
    1930. The Khoisan Peoples of South Africa. London.

SCHEBESTA, PAUL
    1929. Among the Forest Dwarfs of Malaya. London.
    1931. Erste Mitteilungen über die Ergebnisse meiner Forschungsreise bei den Pygmäen in Belgisch-Kongo. A 26:1–17.

SCHMIDT, P. W.
    1910. Die Stellung der Pygmäenvölker in der Entwicklungsgeschichte des Menschen. Studien u. Forschungen zur Menschen- u. Völkerkunde, 6, 7, Stuttgart, 315 pp.

SERRANO, ANTONIO
    1930. Los Primitivos Habitantes del Territorio Argentino. Buenos Aires.

SKEAT, W. W. and BLAGDEN, C. O.
    1906. Pagan Races of the Malay Peninsula. London.

SPECK, FRANK G.
    1915. Family Hunting Territories and Social Life of Various Algonkian Bands of the Ottawa River Valley. Canada Geol. Surv., Mem. 70.
    1915a. The Family Hunting Band as the Basis of the Social Organization of the Algonkian. AA, n.s., 17:289–305.
    1917. The Social Structure of the Northern Algonkian. Publ. Amer. Sociol. Soc., 12: 82–100.
    1917a. Game Totems Among the Northeastern Algonkians. AA, n.s., 19:9–18.
    1922. Beothuk and Micmac. MAIHF-INM no. 22.
    1923. Mistissini Hunting Territories in the Labrador Peninsula. AA, n.s., 25:452–471.
    1927. Family Hunting Territories of the Lake St. John Montagnais and Neighboring Bands. A 22:387–403.
    1928. Land Ownership Among Hunting Peoples in Primitive America and the World's Marginal Areas. ICA, 22nd, 2:323–332 (Rome).

STEWARD, J. H.
    1933. Ethnography of the Owens Valley Paiute. UC-PAAE 33:233–350.
    1935. Ecological Aspects of Southwestern Society. In MS.

STRONG, W. D.
    1927. An Analysis of Southwestern Society. AA, n.s., 29:1–61.
    1929. Aboriginal Society in Southern California. UC-PAAE 26:1–358.

STOW, GEORGE W.
    1905. The Native Races of South Africa. New York.

TRILLES, R. P.
    1932. Les Pygmées de la Forêt Équatorial. A, 3:1–530.

VANOVERBERGH, MORICE
    1925. Negritos of Northern Luzon. A 20:148–199, 399–443.
    1929. Negritos of Northern Luzon. A 24:3–75, 897–911.
    1930. Negritos of Northern Luzon. A 25:25–71, 527–565.
    1933. Philippine Negrito Culture: Independent or Borrowed? Primitive Man, 6:25–35, 1933.

YERKES, A. W. and R. M.
    1929. The Great Apes. Yale Univ. Press, New Haven.

ZUCKERMAN, S.
    1932. The Social Life of Monkeys and Apes. New York.

NOTES TO "THE ECONOMIC AND SOCIAL BASIS OF PRIMITIVE BANDS"

[1] E.g., Speck, 1928. For full citations, see Bibliography, pp. 345–347 above.

[2] The important differences between the unilineal band and clan have been amplified elsewhere (Steward, Ecological Aspects of Southwestern Society). The main difference between these bands and the small, localized, autonomous groups in California called by Kroeber, 1925, "tribes" or "tribelets" is that the former are nomadic within their territory whereas the latter have permanent villages.

[3] The extraordinary frequency of patrilineal bands has been noted particularly by the German "culture historical" school and explained by them in terms of diffusion of "kulturkreise." Schmidt's "exogam-monogamistischer kulturkreis," the earliest phase of his "urkultur," found now among pygmy and pygmoid peoples and characterized by band land ownership, local exogamy, and patrilocal residence is presumed to have originated during man's earliest culture stage. See especially Koppers, 1921:88–89. Radcliffe-Brown, in a recent paper, 1935, has clarified the legal concepts involved in patrilineal and matrilineal succession.

[4] Radcliffe-Brown has stressed the importance of this factor in Australian land ownership.

[5] Speck, 1928, emphasizes this point.

[6] See Zuckerman.

[7] This statement is based on Bingham's field study of gorillas, Missen's of chimpanzees, and Zuckerman's of baboons, which are among the few reliable records of primates in a state of nature. Yerkes has collected a small amount of evidence to indicate a more hermit-like existence among orangs.

[8] Schebesta, 1931:12, believes that isolated families could not survive among Congo Negritos.

[9] Koppers, 1921:72, observes that 15 to 20 individuals is common and about 100 the probable limit.

[10] Bingham observed gorillas in a state of nature in groups of 8 to 22 individuals, each group under a dominant male; chimpanzees are said to be similar; and it is probable that the males among the baboons observed in nature by Zuckerman had a comparable dominance.

[11] E.g., the extraordinarily low status of women in the arduous hunting area of northern Canada. Radcliffe-Brown has observed that Australian hunters would be much less successful in territory which was not known to them from childhood.

[12] Relationship is seldom traced beyond three generations among these people.

[13] I make no effort to solve the very difficult problem of why there are incest laws at all. Marriage with relatives to the third generation, i.e., cousins, is taboo in most of these cases, although cross-cousin and even parallel-cousin marriage is permitted among several.

[14] Based on Schapera, 1926, 1930; Dornan; Dunn; Stow; Passarge.

[15] Schapera, 1930:67–81, has gleaned a few figures on band size from various sources: Cape Bushmen, who were seriously affected by foreign contacts, 100 to 150, according to one estimate, and 3 to 4 families each, according to a more recent figure; Heichware, 20; Kalahari, 30; !Okung, not exceeding 30; Northwestern Bushmen, ranging from 20 to 150 and probably averaging 50 to 60 each.

[16] Schapera, 1930:81–85.

[17] Schapera, 1930:82–83, 102–107.

[18] Schebesta, 1931.

[19] Schmidt, 1910:173.

[20] Trilles, pp. 20–23, 409–419, 143–151.

[21] 1929.

[22] Pp. 495–497.

[23] 1929:83; also pp. 234, 279.

[24] 1931.

[25] 1929:70–75.

[26] 1925:430–433.

[27] 1910:72–73.

[28] Vanoverberg, 1930:538–539, found that some bands contained related males and also that related males occurred in different bands.

[29] Vanoverberg, 1925:425–428.

[30] This material is largely from Radcliffe-Brown, 1930, 1930a, 1930b, 1931, esp. pp. 455, 436–439.

[31] Radcliffe-Brown, 1930:696. The population range is 1 person per 2 square miles in the most fertile section to 1 per 38 square miles in the more arid regions.

[32] Davidson, 1928, has collected evidence that in some localities the land-owning group is the bilateral family. It is the opinion of Radcliffe-Brown, 1931:438, however, that "the particularism of the family whereby it might tend to become an isolated unit is neutralized by the horde (i.e., band) solidarity."

[33] Radcliffe-Brown, 1931:438.

[34] Radcliffe-Brown, 1930:695, gives the aboriginal total as probably 2000 or 3000, which is one person to 8 or 13 square miles.

[35] Roth, pp. 58–59, 104–107.

[36] Pp. 302–306.

[37] Nuñez, quoted by Serrano, p. 157, says that among the Northern Tehuelche the head chief owned the land and that the lesser chiefs could not change their land without giving notice to him.

[38] Outes and Bruch, p. 126. Beerbohn, p. 93.

[39] Musters, p. 194.

[40] Musters, pp. 64, 70, 96–97, 117, 188.

[41] Strong, 1927, 1929; Gifford, 1918, 1926, 1931; Kroeber, 1925, 1934.

[42] Gifford, 1926:394–396; Strong, 1929:188–190, 233.

[43] Steward, 1933.

[44] Kelly, 1932.

[45] Kroeber, 1934:3–4.

[46] Speck, in an excellent series of papers, has recorded such bands and the land-owning families into which they are divided, among the Mistassini, Dumoine River and Kipawa Algonquins, the Timiskaming, Timagami, and White Earth Lake (Minnesota) Ojibway, the Montagnais, Abnaki, Penobscot, Micmac, Naskapi, Narragansett, Northern Salteaux, Passamaquoddy, Malecite, some Cree, and even the Pamunkey of Virginia. McLeod also attributes band organization to the Lenape of Delaware.

[47] 1917:85.

[48] Speck, 1915a:293–295.

[49] Jenness, 1932:124, quoting the Jesuit Relations.

[50] Speck, 1922:85–86.

[51] The families are variable in size. Among the Mistassini they average 6 individuals, owning 15 square miles each (a greater per mile density than is given by Kroeber, probably owing to unusual local productivity); among the Toudasac and Escoumains Montagnais, 5 individuals owning 141 square miles; among the Penobscot, 18 individuals owning 500 to 2000 square miles; among the Timiskaming, 34.4 individuals. Micmac family territory ranges up to 2000 square miles.

[52] 1917:97–98.

[53] There were no chiefs. Prestige, skill, and other qualities gave temporary authority when leadership was required. See, e.g., Osgood, 1933:73–75.

[54] 1928:326.

[55] 1910:130–131. Among the Western Déné, however, the hunter has greater freedom in disposing of his game.

[56] 1933:41, 71.

[57] 1930:69.

[58] 1932:123, 380, 381–384.

[59] The Slave had 5 bands, averaging 220 individuals each; the Hare had 5, numbering 120 or more each; the Dog Ribs, 3, numbering 380 persons each (Osgood gives 4 bands); a Yellow Knife band is stated to have numbered 190 persons. These figures are based largely on Morice, 1906:265; also Jenness, 1932:390–391; Osgood, 1933:3.

[60] Morice, 1909:583.

[61] Jenness, 1932:365–367. Morice, 1910:135, speaks of fishing places among the Carrier and Babine which are owned by "families or groups of related families."

[62] Morice, 1910.
[63] Jenness, 1932:362.
[64] *Ibid.*, pp. 369–370, 372–373.
[65] *Ibid.*, pp. 396–399.
[66] *Ibid.*, pp. 399–404; also, Osgood, 1934.
[67] Radcliffe-Brown disagrees with Man's assertion that each group of bands forming a "tribe" had a superior chief and states that the bands were entirely independent, authority being vested in elders. If sufficiently persuasive, a man or woman might exercise some influence over neighboring bands. Radcliffe-Brown, 1922:22–25, 43–48. Man, pp. 108–109.
[68] Radcliffe-Brown, 1922:73. Schmidt, 1910:172–173, deduced from Portman's and Man's data that marriage was formerly locally exogamous, but Man, pp. 135–141, states that band endogamy was permitted.
[69] Radcliffe-Brown, 1922:72, and Man, p. 127, disagree on this point.
[70] Lowie, 1920, postulated clan origins in these terms. The origin of Yuman patrilineal clans and Pueblo matrilineal clans from such unilineal bands has been discussed elsewhere.

BUREAU OF AMERICAN ETHNOLOGY,
WASHINGTON, D. C.

FLORIDA CULTURAL AFFILIATIONS IN RELATION TO ADJACENT AREAS

By M. W. Stirling

THE NATIVE CULTURES of Florida, being essentially marginal to the Southeastern area, should be properly discussed in relation to Southeast centers. Unfortunately, the chronology and prehistoric focal areas of this region are not as yet clearly defined. However, considerable progress has been made in recent years by a small group of workers. In the lower Mississippi region early historical sites of the Natchez, Choctaw, Caddo, and Tunica[1] have been identified, and their cultural remains found in stratigraphic relationship to prehistoric materials. Farther east, early Cherokee material has been identified and demonstrated to be closely related to that from some of the large mound groups. The unusually extensive excavations conducted in the vicinity of Macon, Georgia, under the direction of Kelly, and the fine work recently accomplished in the Tennessee valley by Webb and Lewis have done much to shed light on this problem.

It is perhaps too early to make close estimates as to the antiquity of the prehistoric cultures of the Southeast, but indications are that the mound-building ceramic culture of the region is a relatively recent development. Despite the great size of certain individual mound groups and shell heaps the cultural deposit is a thin one. It is likely that all of the great mounds from the Ohio to the lower Mississippi were built during a comparatively brief "golden age" with no considerable chronological gaps separating them, just as it can now be demonstrated that the great building period in the Southwest extended over not more than two centuries. Differences in material culture appear to be more regional than temporal.

Despite the fact that large sedentary settlements were necessary in order that these great mound sites be developed, nevertheless the tribes of the Southeast have been restless as compared with those of the Southwest, with the result that highly specialized local developments did not have the same chance to appear as they did in the pueblo area. When the sites giving evidence of a ceramic culture are eliminated from consideration, but little remains to indicate earlier occupations.

The peninsula of Florida juts out from the southeastern corner of the United States as a huge *cul de sac* which has received and blended a variety of impulses from the north. At the beginning of the sixteenth century Florida was occupied by two principal Indian groups, the Calusa and the Timucua. Unfortunately information is very scant concerning the Calusa, who occupied the southern part of Florida, but Swanton has produced evidence indicating that they were related to the Hitchiti and Choctaw.[2] It is probable that their ancestors represented the first important cultural invasion of the peninsula.

[1] J. A. Ford, Outline of Louisiana and Mississippi Pottery Horizons, Louisiana Conservation Review, April, 1935.

[2] John R. Swanton, Early History of the Creek Indians and their Neighbors, BAE–B 73, 1922.

The Timucua, who were later arrivals, occupy the northern half of the peninsula and as might be expected are rather closely related to the Muskhogeans. The final migration was that of the Seminole, who touched practically all of the present state of Florida. The movements of the Seminole fall entirely within relatively late historic times, so that their history is well known.

Archaeological remains identifiable with each of these groups have been found in various sections of the state. It is a significant fact that none of the remains found in prehistoric sites differ materially from those definitely attributable to the Calusa and Timucua. If an earlier people occupied the peninsula, they must have constituted a sparse population without the art of pottery making.

Until more is known of culture centers in the North it does not seem advisable to attempt to tie up the recognizable culture thrusts in Florida to other than their general geographic points of origin. Florida ceramics show, however, a demonstrable tie-up with the North.

Pottery occurs in all sections of the state. The ware is characteristically untempered excepting in the extreme north where both shell and grit tempering occur. The manufacture of pottery from muck composed largely of disintegrated vegetable matter appears to be a Florida contribution to the potter's art. This ware is extremely light in weight and is smooth to the touch. It burns to a brick-red color, the surface of which fades to buff on weathering. Usually the interspace is black as a result of incomplete firing.

Decorated sherds other than stamped ware are very scarce in village site refuse, which contains primarily a rather inferior grade of cooking ware. Most of the decorated specimens are mortuary offerings. Burial mounds are frequently erected on top of a layer of village site material, which accounts for frequently reported cases of undecorated crude pottery stratigraphically preceding the decorated ware. Typically, mortuary ware is "killed" by means of a small circular hole in the bottom of the vessel.

While variations in decoration, texture, and form have a distributional value in Florida, they do not appear to have much chronological significance. It seems possible to identify most of these varieties with the Indians occupying the peninsula in early historic times, or their immediate ancestors.

Pottery forms are so varied as to almost defy classification, but certain of the more characteristic have distributional significance. Footed ware, vessels with three or four basal supports, extends across the northern part of the state in a narrow belt from the Gulf coast to the St. Johns river. Compartment vessels with from two to five sections have approximately the same distribution. In this area also are found certain deeply incised vessels with duck bills in appliqué depending from the rim on two sides.

In the northeast Florida coast and St. Johns River areas, a peculiar crude effigy ware was developed, which has been called by Holmes extemporaneous ware.[3] In addition, shallow bowls and deep vases with rounded bottoms are

---

[3] W. H. Holmes, Earthenware of Florida: Collections of Clarence B. Moore, Journal of the Academy of Natural Sciences of Philadelphia, second series, volume 10, part 1, 1894.

common. On the Gulf coast practically every known type or form may be seen, including effigy vessels, deep jars, flat plates, bowls with both incurving and flaring rims and either flat or round bottoms. In the area lying between the Manatee river and the Caloosahatchee are found a great many bottlenecked jars. In southern Florida, generally, simple hemispheric bowls are the prevailing form.

From the standpoint of surface decoration, Florida pottery may be classified as punctate, incised, stamped, appliqué, and painted. Sometimes vessels occur having various combinations of these techniques. The most characteristic decoration is found on the negative design ware which extends from the north along the Gulf coast as far south as the Caloosahatchee river. It spreads eastward from the coast in gradually diminishing quantities to the St. Johns. Although rectilinear designs are not infrequent, the characteristic elements of this decorative technique consist of incised curvilinear negative designs set off by punctate areas or areas filled with closely placed horizontal parallel incised lines or crosshatched areas. The negative design areas are broken here and there with single lines terminating in small circles or triangles. In the north this ware is characterized by deep and boldly executed incised lines set off with coarse heavy punctate areas. Toward the west-central Gulf coast, where the technique reaches its highest development, the designs become much more refined and are applied with a lighter touch. This is the typical Weeden Island ware.[4] Here the negative designs are frequently outlined with dotted lines. In Florida this ware is prehistoric. In early historic times a somewhat degenerate ware, exhibiting the same techniques less skillfully handled, makes its appearance in the same region, but extends also farther south to the Caloosahatchee river. This I have called Safety Harbor[5] ware. An additional form of decoration characteristic of this ware is the use of appliqué figures on rims. A special area between the Manatee and Caloosahatchee rivers produces a distinct aspect of this technique, here frequently applied to bottlenecked jars. This has been termed Arcadia ware. In the southern peninsula south of Lake Okeechobee and including the Florida keys, the pottery is poorly fabricated. Except for frequent notched lips and a few crudely incised rim designs, it is practically free from decoration. This I have termed Glades ware. It is accompanied to some extent by the omnipresent check-stamped ware.

The origin of the punctate negative design area appears to be in the Louisiana-Arkansas region. At Marksville[6] and Jonesville[7] in Louisiana, the Hopewell negative-design rouletted ware underlies the punctate ware, which seems to have evolved out of it. From here the punctate ware spread eastward and along the Gulf coast.

[4] J. W. Fewkes, Preliminary Archeological Explorations at Weeden Island, Florida, SI–MC 76 (no. 13), 1924.

[5] C. B. Moore, Certain Aboriginal Mounds of the Central Florida West Coast, Journal of the Academy of Natural Sciences of Philadelphia, volume 12, 1903. See figure 88.

[6] F. M. Setzler, Pottery of the Hopewell Type from Louisiana, USNM–P 82 (art. 22), 1933.

[7] W. M. Walker, Trailing the Moundbuilders of the Mississippi Valley, Explorations and Field Work of the Smithsonian Institution in 1932, Publication 3213, 1933.

At more or less the same time another center seems to have developed in the Tennessee-northern Mississippi area, characterized by bottlenecked vessels, red painted ware on buff slip, and effigy forms. This development moved southward until it reached northwestern peninsular Florida, where it joined the punctate ware.

The original home of stamped ware seems to have been Georgia. Evidently, if we may judge by its wide distribution, the simple rectangular check-stamped ware developed first, and finally the complicated stamp with its variety of rectilinear and curvilinear geometric patterns appeared. The check-stamped ware invaded Florida and spread over the entire peninsula to be followed by the complicated stamp, which extended only a short distance up the St. Johns but spread across the northern part of the state and down the west coast to the Caloosahatchee river, where it is found associated with all other west coast forms of pottery decoration. Here the stamped ware went through the same transformation as the punctate ware, that is, the figures become smaller and more refined than is the case in the north.

Bowls with a heavily incised decorative panel around the rims and vessels with loop and strap handles moved down from the northern Alabama-Georgia area and spread into northwestern Florida. The scroll design incised around the rims of bowls was used almost to the Caloosahatchee but is much more characteristic of northwestern Florida.

The ware which is identified by Ford as Tunica in Mississippi and which is related to the Fort Ancient ware of the north, extends eastward into southwestern Georgia and down the west coast of Florida to the Caloosahatchee, where it is associated with the Safety Harbor ware. The forms in Florida are quite similar to those in the north, but the vessels are frequently embellished with incised and punctate decoration.

The great majority of the painted pottery has a fugitive red decoration usually applied to the entire surface of the vessel. It is not abundant at any site but has a universal distribution throughout the peninsula. On the west-central Gulf coast red painted vessels of fine quality are found in which the pigment is fired.

This brief ceramic survey suggests the existence of four archaeological areas within the peninsula, one of which falls completely within the area of two others. For sake of convenience these may be designated as the Gulf Coast, the Northern Highlands, the St. Johns, and the Glades areas.

The Gulf Coast area includes the area of Florida draining into the Gulf of Mexico, as far south as the Caloosahatchee river. The pottery of this area is characterized by the diversity of its form and decoration; negative designs, incised scrolls, human and bird effigies, and a refined stamping technique being most typical. Stone and shell plummets are particularly abundant.

The St. Johns area, which includes the drainage of the St. Johns river and the adjacent northeast Atlantic coast, exhibits a degenerated culture reminiscent of Etowah and some of the large mound groups of Georgia. This region is typified by large fresh-water shell mounds, extemporaneous ware, square elbow pipes, large polished celts, stone spuds, embossed copper plaques, shell gorgets, mica, bannerstones, and massive shell beads.

The Highlands area overlaps the northern part of the Gulf Coast and St. Johns areas and is characterized by footed pottery, compartment vessels, heavy incised decoration, red and buff painted ware, and occasional shell tempering. Stone celts and plummets are associated with this ware.

The Glades area includes the region between the Kissimmee and Indian rivers and all of the peninsula from Lake Okeechobee to the Florida keys, inclusive. This area is characterized by the use of an inferior grade of pottery, perforated shell hoes, shell plummets, antler adze sockets, and bone projectile points. Because of the frequent preservation of wooden specimens in muck, we know much more of the art of this area than of any other in the Southeast. The bird appears to have been the favorite art motive.

The question of Antillean influence in Florida and in the Southeast generally has been the subject of considerable discussion in the past.[8] Certain chronological evidence which has developed in the Southeast would seem to call for a revision of most generally accepted ideas on its significance. In spite of the geographic proximity of Cuba and the Bahamas to the Florida peninsula and the known fact that early canoe voyages were made between them, the amount of culture exchange appears to have been negligible.

Whether the postulated culture sequences in the West Indies will stand up under further systematic archaeological investigation remains to be seen. The three generally recognized horizons, the primitive cave-dwelling Ciboney, the sedentary agricultural Arawak, and the marauding nomadic Carib, are supposed to have graded into each other in the order named. We know, however, that all three of these cultures were active when Columbus reached the West Indies. There is no real proof that the Ciboney were not rural Arawaks.

The South American origin of the Antillean cultures is obvious enough to require no discussion here. The significant point is that practically all of the traits which appear to resemble Floridian items may be as easily traced to a South American source. Very little attempt has been made in the past to credit such resemblances to a northern origin; rather, the culture flow has been considered to have passed from south to north.

Comparative trait lists are very apt to be deceiving unless one is closely familiar with the materials of the two regions. Many of the traits which have been compared, such as pile dwellings, rectangular or circular houses, shell heaps, and the like, are of such a generalized nature as to have little significance. Other traits, such as the occurrence of the blow gun, poisoned arrows, and the spear thrower in the West Indies, are substantiated by such dubious references as not to be acceptable with any confidence. Still other resemblances can be traced to the availability of common materials. In this class of objects are conch-shell bowls and shell axes or adzes.

---

[8] Charlotte D. Gower, The Northern and Southern Affiliations of Antillean Culture, AAA–M 35, 1927. (This work contains an excellent bibliography.) H. W. Krieger, Aboriginal Indian Pottery of the Dominican Republic, USNM–B 156, 1931.

The writer tried experimentally a chart comparing the culture traits of Florida with those in New Guinea and obtained as successful results as when making the comparison with northern South America. It is particularly significant that the most basic and characteristic items do not occur in both regions. In Florida among the typical archaeological features may be mentioned burial mounds, perforated shell hoes, plummet-shaped ornaments of stone and shell, check-stamped pottery, and smoking-pipes.

For the West Indies such a list would include stone and shell "zemis," three pointed stones, the use of grotesque appliqué on pottery, and petaloid celts. Despite assertions to the contrary, the stone celts from the St. Johns region of Florida do not resemble those from the West Indies.

Manioc, the great staple food plant of the West Indies, did not reach Florida, although in modern times it has been introduced and successfully grown in the southern part of the peninsula.

Holmes, Fewkes, Krieger, and others have called attention to more specific resemblances in the decorative art and ceramics of the two regions. Holmes compared certain carved designs in wood from the West Indies to stamped pottery designs of the Southeast. The highest centers of development of this type of pottery decoration, however, are located in southwestern Georgia, where this style of adornment appears to be older than it is along the eastern coast. It does not seem likely that it could have been derived from the Bahamas, where the examples of wood carving are evidently comparatively recent.

The method of decorating blank areas on pottery with incised lines terminating in enlargements occurs in the Greater Antilles and is absent in Jamaica and the Lesser Antilles from St. Thomas to Trinidad. It also occurs on the northwest Florida coast and as far as northern Louisiana, where it appears to have evolved out of the earlier Hopewell ware. Here again knowledge of the chronology in the two regions would seem to force the conclusion that if a connection exists for this type of decoration in the two areas the movement must have been from north to south since this type of ware is comparatively recent in the Antilles. The only specific class of objects occurring in southern Florida which the writer believes to be of definite Antillean origin is the four-legged wooden stools which occur in the Glades area.

The matter of linguistic and ethnologic evidence has been discussed by Swanton, Gower, and others. We know from the memoir of Fontaneda that an Arawak colony settled in the Florida Keys early in the sixteenth century. They did not succeed, however, in impressing their language or culture on the Calusa. Swanton has made a good case for the relationship between the word for potato in the Southeast and the word for sweet potato in the West Indies. It appears to the writer, however, that the interesting comparisons are so few that they do not exceed the number of fortuitous resemblances normally to be found under the circumstances.

In brief, although from the standpoint of geographic proximity there should be every reason to expect evidence of Antillean influence in Florida, the fact remains that convincing archaeological evidence indicating even sporadic contacts is almost completely lacking. West Indian impulses made practically no headway against the tide from the north. Similarities which exist seem more likely to be due to an early common Middle American impulse which spread in opposite directions around the Gulf of Mexico and the Caribbean, the extremities of which are to be found in Florida and the Greater Antilles.

BUREAU OF AMERICAN ETHNOLOGY,
SMITHSONIAN INSTITUTION,
WASHINGTON, D. C.

ANTHROPOLOGICAL THEORY AND ARCHAEOLOGICAL FACT

By William Duncan Strong

IT IS NO NEW IDEA that many anthropological hypotheses based on ethnological data may be objectively checked against an adequate archaeological record. In practice, however, the findings of archaeology have usually been employed for supplementary and confirmatory rather than critical purposes. Wissler's wholesale transposition of culture areas and archaeological provinces like Kroeber's diagrammatic representation of the accumulation and diffusion of culture traits in native America, are well-known examples of this generalizing tendency. It appears in its most imaginative and undocumented form in Radin's The Story of the American Indian, and the same author has more seriously employed the method in bolstering his ethnological findings among the Winnebago.[1*]

Attempting to apply this procedure to a definite cultural province, Kroeber some years ago checked the results of an analysis of ethnological data pertaining to native society in the American Southwest against the remarkably full archaeological sequence in that area.[2] The two records, the one inferential, the other objective, seemed to him to correspond in an historically significant manner, and he cites the case as illustrating "the possibility of coöperative relation between the archaeological and ethnological approaches." He continues, "In the field of intangibles, there is no reason why the archaeologist should refrain from using the distributional inductions of ethnology; nor why the ethnologist should hesitate to buttress his findings as to the history of culture forms and organization by converting, as well as may be, the tangibles actually established by the excavator, into their corresponding intangibles." Radin's reaction to these conclusions lacks detail but not strength: "Surely no comment is necessary here, except to indicate that the analytical distributional method, in the hands of a naturalist of culture, must inexorably lead precisely to this debacle, and that none of the older evolutionists or the most uncritical of the German and English diffusionists have ever indulged in more unjustified speculations."[3]

Now it happens that the original culprit in this particular case was not Kroeber, who was merely guilty of citing and somewhat enlarging upon the "unjustified speculations" in question, but the present writer who, albeit in somewhat obscure form, had brought them forth.[4] Since the problem in the earlier of these papers involved both the ethnological and the archaeological approaches, it may be briefly reconsidered here and perhaps more clearly stated.

In skeleton outline the ethnological picture was as follows. Recent field work had indicated that the basic political and ceremonial unit in southern

---

* Superior figures refer to notes at the end of this essay, p. 369.

California, from the Colorado desert to the Pacific, was the male lineage. While single lineages prevailed over most of the area, in exceptionally favorable situations certain of these had increased without splitting off from the parent body. As a result, the actual relationship between the different lines became obscure. Such a larger grouping was technically called a gens but it differed from the smaller lineage only in degree. Each lineage (or gens) consisted of a small land-owning unit, with a patriarchal and priestly head who derived his power through custodianship of a fetish bundle containing the most important ceremonial paraphernalia of the group. This bundle, kept in the ceremonial house where the priest-chief lived, formed the sacred nucleus from which all group socioreligious activities radiated. The priest, ceremonial house, and fetish complex was intimately associated with a definite series of ceremonials and ritualistic observances.[5] In addition, there existed among all these groups either the concept of dichotomy or traces indicating that such a ceremonial division had formerly been in vogue.

Among the Pueblo peoples of Arizona and New Mexico it appeared that within the clans of the west, and probably among the clans or patrilineal moieties of the east, similar small female lineages occurred. These lineages were active and closely knit units within the larger social aggregations. They were also intimately associated with the fetish bundles and objects that motivated all ceremonial activity. The Pueblo ceremonials radiating from this priest, ceremonial house, and fetish complex likewise involved all the peculiar rites noted as characteristic of the southern California Shoshoneans. In the intervening regions between these two groups, with the possible exception of the as yet obscure Pima and Papago, this closely integrated system of socioceremonial features was lacking.

An analysis of these data indicated that the lineage was basic among both the coastal Shoshoneans and the majority of the Pueblo groups. In southern California this was a male lineage, among the Hopi and at Zuñi a female lineage, and among the less well-known eastern Pueblos probably either female lineages or the bilateral family at different towns.[6] In southern California, and among many of the Pueblos, the lineage was apparently associated with the important house, priest, and fetish complex, with the same definite associated rituals, and with an idea of dichotomy. Such complex and integrated socioceremonial similarities (or identities) could hardly be fortuitous, hence an early cultural connection between the two areas was indicated. Since the intervening Athabaskan, Yuman, and Shoshonean tribes lacked this complex, either *in toto* or in large part, it appeared that they had derived their social and ceremonial patterns from other sources. The fact that both the Pueblos and southern California Shoshoneans had developed different types of cult organizations based on the same nuclear complex, indicated a subsequent period of cultural isolation and separate development. In southern California the simple, localized male lineage with the fetish complex and associated rituals had persisted into historic times. In the Pueblo area larger towns occurred but, on the basis of the analysis given above, it was suggested that the historic

Pueblos had arisen through the fusion of female lineages into sibs and the sibs into towns. Such a process would likewise account for the great elaboration of Pueblo ritual organization and the development of the various cult societies. It was therefore suggested that Pueblo society had grown out of a status approximately represented by the modern Shoshonean tribes of southern California.

Without objective verification such a hypothesis, however logical (or unjustified, according to the viewpoint), remained purely speculative. In this case, however, the inductions drawn from horizontal distribution could be checked against an exceptionally complete vertical or archaeological record.[7] The latter indicated that, even in the most advanced centers, cultural development in southern California has been so slow as to seem almost static. The survival of relatively ancient features in this society would therefore be expectable. Second, there occurred in the intermediate region historically occupied by Pima, Papago, and certain Yuman tribes, a unique prehistoric culture sequence (the Hohokam) which differed materially from the prehistoric horizons in both Pueblo and Californian areas. It was also clear that at an early period (Pueblo I and II or Developmental Pueblo) the ancestral Pueblo culture had extended north and west around the Hohokam province almost to the borders of California. By historic times the Pueblo culture province had contracted to a few towns in New Mexico and Arizona. Thus, both the earlier continuities and the later breaks postulated by ethnology received objective proof from archaeology. Finally, the theory that the present complexity of Pueblo social organization had in considerable part resulted from the fusion of originally autonomous lineages into sibs and the sibs into towns found strong support in the archaeological record. This indicated that the modern Pueblo town of terraced houses was preceded by the large communal house of the Pueblo III period. This type had arisen through the merging together of earlier (Pueblo II) unit dwellings. These in turn had been preceded by the widely distributed small villages of Pueblo I and Basket Maker times. Each of these small habitation sites was characterized by the occurrence of a single ceremonial chamber. The associated fetish complex was also present in Pueblo I and late Basket Maker periods as indicated by the discovery of fetish bundles and associated objects in these horizons. Thus, the earliest known Pueblo unit was a localized group, comparable in size to the modern lineage, and similarly possessed of the ceremonial house and fetish complex. It is apparent, therefore, that the early derivation of Pueblo society from a status closely comparable to the historic lineage of southern California is actually demonstrable.

The foregoing hypotheses, supported by at least two converging lines of evidence, cannot be lightly dismissed as merely "unjustified speculations." By themselves they are limited and may have only transitory value, yet they rest on the same general principles as more complete hypotheses derived from distributional and sequential facts in other historical sciences. Radin's conception of "history" as a tight little body of written personal records is inconceivable to any truly historically minded person. One may be far from denying the unique value and distinct quality of written history and yet refuse to isolate it categorically from direct relationship to that demonstrable body of sequential human history of which it forms a brief and specialized part. Scientific archaeology, for example, yields a demonstrable record that is as truly historical as many complications of fragmentary documents dignified by the title of written history. Such broad human history may lack the particularity which Radin regards as the essence of written history, but it also lacks the bias that, consciously or unconsciously, pervades the written record. It is a truism that all hypotheses are subject to revision and amplification as new data become available. The eternal verities are distant and difficult of attainment and "crying for the moon," as Radin says, brings them a little closer.

Pursuing the matter of method still further, another major cultural province of North America may profitably be considered. In the Great Plains we find a different type of problem. This is an area whose native peoples have received more intensive ethnological study than any comparable group in the New World. As a result, the accepted characteristics of the "Plains Culture area," based entirely on distributional or horizontal studies, are too well known to merit more than the briefest recapitulation. With the exception of a narrow strip along the Missouri river occupied by semihorticultural tribes, the area generally has been characterized as a barren region influenced on all sides by adjacent cultures, in other words, "a series of vanishing peripheries around a vacuum." Typical inhabitants of the aboriginal Plains were believed to be nomadic and militaristic hunters that, in historic times, had taken over the horse complex, thus increasing the range but not the nature of their peregrinations. Typical tribes included such peoples as the western Dakota, Blackfoot, and Crow, whose primary activities embraced the buffalo hunt, war cult, sun dance, and vision quest. Tribes like the Pawnee, whose elaborate ceremonials and cult societies were closely integrated by a complex and highly philosophical religious system, were regarded as atypical. Likewise, their permanent earth-lodge villages and their economy based in considerable part on horticulture, were thought to be marginal to the true Plains. This has become the accepted picture as presented by the ethnologist and enlarged upon by historian and geographer.

In the light of objective time perspective, revealed by recent scientific excavations, the late nomadic and hunting life of the central Plains appears merely as a thin overlay associated with the acquisition of the horse.[8] It was preceded by a period of considerable but as yet undetermined duration characterized by small, undefended villages of earth lodges, whose occupants derived a considerable portion of their subsistence from horticulture. Ceramic remains are abundant at such prehistoric sites and they extend far to the west of the historic range of the semihorticultural tribes. Analysis of the prehistoric, protohistoric, and early historic horizons tends to connect these prehistoric sedentary peoples with the historic agricultural tribes of the eastern border. Thus it appears demonstrable that the semihorticultural ancestors of the Pawnee, for example, preceded the historic hunting tribes in the central Plains and that their settled mode of life was typical of the area in late prehistoric times. This fact throws new light on such problems as the highly accretionary nature of the sun dance and other historic Plains ceremonials and helps to explain the differential rate of survival of the late nomadic tribes as compared to the earlier sedentary peoples. However, these matters, like the still earlier sequence of true hunting cultures in the region, do not concern us here. The example is introduced primarily to indicate the fact that archaeological research can correct as well as confirm concepts derived from historical and ethnological data. In the Southwest, reference to a relatively full archaeological record tended to confirm the results of ethnological analysis. In the Great Plains, on the other hand, the application of archaeological technique seems destined to overturn one of the most strongly held ethnographic concepts in the area. It is already apparent that, critically applied, the combined ethnological and archaeological approach has possibilities that have as yet hardly been touched upon. When such an attack is combined with adequate historical studies of the physical anthropologist the method of approach will be complete.[9] The synthesis of these three techniques is, I believe, the historical science of anthropology as conceived by the majority of American anthropologists. This brings us from the realm of limited and specific problems to more fundamental definitions.

Anthropology, so defined, stands midway between the biological and social sciences. Unlike sociology and other branches of "the science of culture," anthropology is concerned not with one, but with two definitely historical processes, biological evolution and cultural development. Since man, the subject of study, is a self-domesticated animal, his natural history can be fully understood only in the light of these two interrelated trends. With three tools at his disposal, the anthropologist seeks to unravel and measure, as fully as his developing techniques permit, the rôle played by each of these factors in the life history of a unique species. Fundamental to any understanding of this essential problem is the arrangement of human biological and cultural data according to time sequence. This vast and extremely difficult task must be faced. Anthropology cannot evade this issue nor does it wish to do so. With these three tools in order it can proceed with patience toward its ultimate aims, which are the same sort of generalizations as may be attained by any other historical science. These generalizations can never be more penetrating nor exact than the data on which they are based, hence above all the anthropologist seeks objective and complete information. He is attacking a problem, involving over a million years in time, whose spatial extent covers the globe. He will not arrive at his goal tomorrow.

This basic and inevitably recurring problem, the interrelationship in time and space of biological and cultural development, forms the background of all anthropological research. Anthropology as a science is not concerned with the study of culture as an isolated phenomenon, but always in relation to the carriers of culture, living or extinct. This does not imply that culture and its processes cannot or should not be studied independently of biological factors. The assumption "that culture, a uniquely human phenomenon independent of the laws of biology and psychology, constitutes the proper subject of the social sciences"[10] is to a considerable extent based on the results of anthropological research. Yet it is, and remains, an assumption which must be further demonstrated, refined, and amplified in the light of all obtainable data regarding man and his relation to culture. Certain sociologists and others believe that "general laws" underlie cultural phenomena. The anthropologist as yet neither affirms nor denies this belief, which of course is a corollary to the first assumption. Viewing the relationship between man and culture in space and, as completely as may be possible, through time, he must test every such "law" in the laboratory of human experience. This is his rôle as an anthropologist, not the formulation of laws.

Concerned as he is with a vast yet necessarily unified task, the anthropologist has taken as his particular fields the study of the languages and cultures of nonliterate peoples (ethnology), of prehistoric cultures (archaeology), and of human evolution (physical anthropology). In regard to more fully recorded and literate civilizations, he derives the data which he needs from documentary history, classical archaeology, philology, sociology, and all other sciences. The specific data yielded by his particular fields of research and the generalizations based thereon are equally available to all other sciences. As Haeberlin pointed out, "fields of investigation cannot be 'surveyed and fenced' in the true sense of the word," but it is essential that a science worthy of the name clearly indicate what its primary objectives are. Three generations of anthropologists in America have both objectively and theoretically defined their science as a historical discipline concerned with the interrelationship between man and culture. To this end they have accumulated a mass of exact knowledge. The inductive generalizations based thereon have already cleared the intellectual field of many demonstrably erroneous anthropological and sociological hypotheses arrived at by a less broadly conceived methodology.

Since the anthropologist derives his immediate data from several fundamentally related but technically differentiated fields, specialization of attack is essential. It is further desirable since it brings to bear on the central problem three lines of independent evidence. The synthetic value of the whole increases in proportion to the objectivity of the parts. I do not believe any American anthropologist would quarrel with Radin's definition of ethnology as, "a description of a specific period, and as much of the past and as much of the contacts with other cultures as is necessary for the elucidation of the particular period. No more." Good ethnology is purely descriptive. Only when the results are used for generalizing or historical purposes are sociology or anthropology involved. The cardinal sin against ethnology is to curtail in any way or obscure its concrete facts. "Historical reconstructions," "elucidations of meaning," or "functional interpretations" should be made separately. The facts themselves are sacred. As such they may be employed as desired by the administrator, sociologist, anthropologist, psychologist, and others. When the anthropologist uses such distributional data for inferring historic and temporal relationships he must do so, as fully as possible, in conjunction with the results of the allied anthropological techniques. Considered by itself, archaeology is also a descriptive science. It assumes historicity through proved connection with documentary history and as a part of anthropology. Its prehistoric aspects can never be fully perceptible to one not thoroughly familiar with the major results and techniques of ethnology and physical anthropology. The latter, a highly specialized branch of human biology, is concerned with the evolution of the human species and the correlation of human physical types with past and present cultures. In its earliest phases it is dependent on geology for period determination and in later cultural periods on archaeology. The fact that many physical anthropologists have lacked both archaeological and ethnological training, as well as such field experience, accounts in considerable part for the unnecessarily limited physical and cultural correlations so far available. Equally potent is the fact that even today few adequate opportunities are available for such men to carry on their essential work. The problem with which anthropology is fundamentally concerned can never be solved without their aid.

Two facts in regard to anthropology are becoming increasingly apparent: first, that the three techniques on which it is based furnish definite contributions to many other sciences besides the synthetic study of which they are primarily a part; and second, that the specialist achieves success in proportion to the thoroughness of his training in, and the degree of his understanding of all three branches of the mother science. Only in comparatively recent years has the opportunity for such complete training become available. This fact makes it all the more remarkable that the threefold attack has consistently been the recognized aim of the leaders of American anthropology. Present-day anthropological training in America has been established on a broad and firm basis through the combined efforts of such scholars. Unlike the majority of their European colleagues, anthropologists in this country have thus broadly conceived their science since its inception. As a result, narrow and dominant schools have never developed and there has been no rapid overturn of one method of approach by its direct opposite. The same period in England has seen the vogue of the evolutionary, diffusionist, and functional approaches, each being conceived in the minds of its extreme adherents as exclusive of all the others. It seems highly improbable that any narrow or artificially limited method of attack can solve the major problem with which anthropology is concerned.

In a recent paper, writing as president of the anthropological section of the British Association for the Advancement of Sciences, Radcliffe-Brown takes a position widely at variance with the foregoing conclusion.[11] Of the thirty-odd pages in this report less than eight are devoted to what I have designated above as anthropology, the remainder being concerned with a study which the author calls comparative sociology. If Radcliffe-Brown's interpretation of the disintegration of British anthropology is sound, and it seems only fair that his British colleagues should be heard from in this regard, we are here presented with the utterly unique phenomenon of a more recent science, anthropology, giving birth to an older relative, sociology!

It is impossible to do full justice here to the methods and aims of comparative sociology. A condensed sketch, however, will indicate its salient outlines as indicated by its founder. The primary aim of comparative sociology is the determination of universal cultural laws. These are to be determined, entirely on the historic level, by the methods of ethnology (as the term is used in America), plus the elucidation of "meaning" of culture elements by each investigator, and the comparison of whole cultural systems with one another. An adequate sociological understanding or interpretation of any culture can only be attained by relating its characteristics to known sociological laws. The "new anthropology," i.e., comparative sociology, is "functional, generalizing and sociological." At the present time, Radcliffe-Brown says, the field worker in this subject, who should be thoroughly cognizant of all partially verified "sociological hypotheses" and "equipped with a thorough knowledge of all the latest developments of theoretical sociology," must obtain these not from books but by personal contact with those who are working in the subject. The same personal supervision is apparently indicated for the applied aspects of the new study which, it is believed, should replace anthropology in the training of colonial administrators. Radcliffe-Brown believes that knowledge of race (physical anthropology), prehistoric archaeology, and theoretical anthropology (what he calls ethnology) are of no use in such training. Indeed, they may be harmful in some cases. Instead, a year's course covering the entire field of comparative sociology, followed by a functional sociological study of the culture with which the student is to be concerned, when combined with a comparative sociological study of methods and policies of colonial administration and native education, will "provide a scientific basis for the control of education of native peoples."[12] In other words, I would interpret what Radcliffe-Brown has called the "new anthropology" as being not only sociological, functional, and generalizing, but also messianic, imperialistic, and nonanthropological.

A comparison of the theoretical positions of Radcliffe-Brown and Paul Radin is illuminating. Both are brilliant ethnologists, but where the former is a sociologist believing in universal laws of culture independent of those of psychology, the latter is primarily an ethnologist who sees the individual as the essential factor in culture change. Neither has been personally very much interested, nor active, in either archaeology or physical anthropology, and each seeks the explanation of culture change, sociologically or psychologically, on the sole basis of ethnological data. Of the two, Radin is perhaps the less consistent since he has from time to time attempted intuitive reconstructions of culture history, yet shies away from the actual synthesis of ethnological, archaeological, and human biological data which alone can give corroboration to such hypotheses. The extreme theoretical position of Radcliffe-Brown remains to be demonstrated. As Lowie has pointed out, the general "laws" so far formulated by comparative sociology differ in no regard from anthropological truisms or generalizations.[13] In my opinion, comparative sociology, although a narrow technique, may add content and perhaps more understanding to ethnology and sociology. But as long as its extreme adherents refuse to face the fundamental problem of culture change during the major portion of human history their technique may be simplified but their results, even in the cultural field, will remain limited.

Anthropology, however, is neither the dead parent of comparative sociology, nor a purely cultural discipline. It is a broad, historical science concerned with the relationship of cultural and biological factors through time and space. Its students must be thoroughly trained in all three of its techniques so that the results of their special interests and aptitudes may most effectively become part of the synthetic whole. In a world where nations can be dominated by such tragic nonsense as an "Aryan theory," or intellectually restricted by the outworn formulation of Morgan's evolutionary theory of culture, there is a great and growing need for such broad research and teaching. The maintenance of sane and scientific attitudes in regard to the innumerable problems of race and culture contact is the greatest contribution which anthropology, as a pure or as an applied science, can make to world civilization. In this regard its position is unique.

It is, moreover, a youthful science whose primary concern is still the accumulation of essential data which in many cases are disappearing with alarming rapidity. All over the world native peoples are rapidly assimilating European culture. In many cases they are being merged with other groups or are threatened with extinction. Sound ethnological field work is a primary requisite. In regions of great population, all-important archaeological materials are being vandalized with equal rapidity. In most of the world, however, scientific archaeology has not as yet scratched the surface. In this regard, Middle America, the cradle of New World civilization, is at present a dark jungle of ignorance lit up at long intervals by tiny match-flares of scientific knowledge. Asia and Africa have yielded the tiniest fraction of their archaeological potentialities, and knowledge of their ethnology is still utterly inadequate. Australia, the home of innumerable sociological and anthropological theories, is likewise rich in archaeological remains. Despite the fact that the natives of northern Australia still manufacture, employ, and trade in artifacts elsewhere regarded as prehistoric, no combined ethnological, archaeological, and physical anthropological research on any adequate scale has been accomplished. The accumulation of data, the broad and thorough training of anthropologists (not narrow specialists), and the creation of essential syntheses will go hand in hand. As Laufer, prime demonstrator of the combined anthropological method in Asia, has indicated for the New World,

> Chronology is at the root of the matter, being the nerve electrifying the dead body of history. When archaeology and ethnology have drawn up each its own chronology, then the two systems may be pieced together and collated, and the result cannot fail to appear....

We should all be more enthusiastic about new facts than about methods; for the constant brooding over the applicability of methods and the questioning of their correctness may lead one to a Hamletic state of mind not wholesome in pushing on active research work. In this sense allow me to conclude with the words of Carlyle: "Produce! Produce! Were it but the pitifullest infinitesimal fraction of a product, produce it in God's name! 'Tis the utmost thou hast in thee: out with it, then!"[14]

NOTES TO "ANTHROPOLOGICAL THEORY AND ARCHAEOLOGICAL FACT"

[1] The Winnebago Tribe, BAE-R 37:76–103, 1923. McKern has since demonstrated by direct archaeological research that certain of Radin's correlations in this regard are in error (Wisconsin Pottery, AA, n.s., 33:386, 1931). What is of particular interest here, however, is the fact that the method, or at least its affirmative side, has been employed by many ethnologists including that most stimulating of writers and methodological critics, Radin himself.

[2] Native Culture of the Southwest, UC-PAAE 23:383–386, 1928.

[3] The Method and Theory of Ethnology, 156, 1933.

[4] W. D. Strong, An Analysis of Southwest Society, AA, n.s., 29:1–66, 1927, and Aboriginal Society in Southern California, UC-PAAE 26, 1929.

[5] Among these may be listed, the "retreat" of the priest-chief prior to rites involving the use of the fetish bundle, blowing smoke and praying over sacred objects in the bundle, "feeding" the fetish bundle, and, when a lineage or gens verged on extinction, the careful burial of the bundle in a distant cave indicating that the group's ceremonial life was at an end. These ceremonials also involved the use of altars and ground paintings, prayers for rain, the asperging of water brought from sacred springs, the placing of plume offerings in certain shrines, initiation and torture of boys, personification of the gods, ceremonial pole climbing, eagle and whirling dances, and lineage ownership of eagles.

[6] Kroeber (op. cit., 384, 385) suggested that in the course of their development the people of the western Pueblos changed from a patrilineal to a matrilineal system of reckoning descent. I indicated this as a possibility (AA, 50, 51 and chart 2) but pointed out that the historic relationship of these groups to the Shoshonean peoples of southern California was most strongly indicated by their common possession of a lineage organization based on the priest, ceremonial house, and fetish complex with its associated ritual and social implications. These integrated and highly complex identities in basic pattern, plus the concept of dichotomy shared by both, appeared to me as being more significant evidences of relationship than the particular line of descent stressed in either of the two regions. The acceptance of such an important socioceremonial factor as the full fetish complex by any group, especially if there were already present tendencies toward either male or female house ownership and (or) patrilocal or matrilocal residence, might lead the borrowing group into either patrilineal or matrilineal reckoning of descent in accord with their own preëxistent patterns. It seems highly probable that problems arising from the inheritance of property, either tangible or intangible, may exert a definite influence in changing a bilateral type of social organization to a unilateral form. That such a development may proceed along either line of descent is indicated by the distribution of the two systems in native America. I believe that the simple lineage (and its logical development the sib) has developed independently many times, hence I cannot agree with Olson (Clan and Moiety in Native America, UC-PAAE 33, 1933) that all systems of unilateral descent in America were diffused from one source. That particular types of sibs are historically related is certain, but proof of such relationship must rest on more complex and fundamentally conditioning factors than mere unilateral reckoning of descent. Beals's recent conclusion (Preliminary Report on the Ethnography of the Southwest, U. S. Dept. Int., Nat'l Park Serv., Field Divis. of Educ., Berkeley, Calif., pp. 37, 43, 1935) that the so-called "vestigial clans" of the eastern Tewa are recent importations of little functional significance, whereas the older form of the bilateral family is still dominant, strengthens the case based on distributional grounds that this type of organization preceded the lineage or sib throughout the area. Even more significant is his conclusion that the moiety in the Southwest is ceremonial in origin and predominantly so in function. His conclusion in this regard is strengthened and extended by the fact that nowhere in the greater Southwest has dichotomy made any significant impress on kinship terminology. If full publication of the data supports these important conclusions it will eliminate the moiety from consideration as a basic or primary social pattern among the Southwestern and perhaps other New World groups. Briefly stated, then, it is the writer's belief that either male or female lineages may arise from a preëxistent bilateral family organization whenever changing conditions make such alignment of kin desirable; that whether the male or female line is accentuated will be determined by local patterns in each case; that the majority of Southwestern sib groupings are merely expanded male or female lineages; and, finally, that in the greater Southwest the moiety is ceremonial in origin and can probably be eliminated in any consideration of primary social patterns.

[7] See A. V. Kidder, An Introduction to the Study of Southwestern Archaeology, New Haven, 1924. For the most recent summary of this field, see F. H. H. Roberts, Jr., A Survey of Southwestern Archaeology, AA, n.s., 37:1–35, 1935. California archaeological research is

as yet less adequately developed. For a summary of the field see A. L. Kroeber, Handbook of the Indians of California, BAE-B 78, chap. 60, also R. L. Olson, Chumash Prehistory, UC-PAAE 28:1–21, 1930. Olson records evidence of the fetish bundle in prehistoric times in southwestern California.

[8] This evidence is discussed at considerable length in two previous reports (W. D. Strong, The Plains Culture Area in the Light of Archeology, AA, n.s., 35:271–287, 1933, and, An Introduction to Nebraska Archeology, SI-MC 93, no. 10, 1935). Also see W. R. Wedel, Reports on Field Work by the Archaeological Survey of the Nebraska State Historical Society, May 1–July 23, 1934, Neb. Hist. Mag., vol. 15, no. 3, 1935.

[9] Hooton's The Indians of Pecos Pueblo, New Haven, 1930, is an outstanding example of such a study in the Southwest. There is as yet nothing comparable for the Great Plains. This type of report is only possible where up-to-date, objective, archaeological technique is combined with the same kind of anthropometric analysis and synthesis.

[10] G. P. Murdoch, The Science of Culture, AA, n.s., 34:200, 1932.

[11] The Present Position of Anthropological Studies, BAAS, London, 1932, pp. 141–171. According to this writer, anthropology (in Great Britain, I presume) formerly consisted of three major divisions, human biology (including human palaeontology and physical anthropology), prehistoric archaeology, and social anthropology (including ethnology, a historical science concerned with the relations of peoples and hypothetical reconstructions regarding their past). By itself, however, social anthropology combined both the historical and the generalizing methods in an attempt to construct either hypothetical histories or psychological explanations of the origins and development of social institutions. This compromise in method, according to Radcliffe-Brown, proved to be an impossible one and two movements developed in the last decade, one toward ethnology, the other toward sociology. The adherents of both criticized social anthropology, and as a result, he says, there developed a "new anthropology" called "comparative sociology"! From the mélange that was once British anthropology, physical anthropology and human palaeontology will presumably return to human biology; ethnology, as defined by Radcliffe-Brown, remains isolated and to a great extent dependent on the new arrival; and prehistoric archaeology, unless sporadically combined with ethnology (as above defined), likewise continues in isolation. Such an interpretation implies, either that the majority of British anthropologists have a totally different conception of anthropology than that held in America, which I doubt, or that Radcliffe-Brown is confused as to the aims and methods of two interdependent but totally distinct sciences, anthropology and sociology.

[12] Radcliffe-Brown, *op. cit.*, 154–171, 1932. Also see, by the same author, The Methods of Ethnology and Social Anthropology, South African Journal of Science, 20:124–147, 1932. In the earlier of these papers he uses the term "social anthropology" in preference to sociology due to custom, and, "because a good deal of what is commonly called sociology in English-speaking countries is a somewhat formless study, of whose votaries Steinmetz says, 'On désire des vérités larges, éternelles, valables pour toute l'humanité, comme prix de quelques heures de spéculation somnolente'" (1922, p. 127). The later paper, with its completely changed viewpoint in this regard, reminds one of Nordau's statement made a quarter of a century ago, "In der Enzyklopädie der Wissenschaften von Menschen ist die Soziologie bestimmt, den obersten Platz einzunehmen, denn sie ist die Zusammenfassung der Angaben, welche die übrigen Wissenschaften liefern; sie ist der Schlusstein, der ihre Wölbung hält und krönt; sie ist die Ergänzung der Anthropologie nach der geistigen Seite hin." Such a desirable end, however, is hardly to be attained by confusing two distinct approaches to the essential problem of man and culture. If, to paraphrase Wundt, we call sociology or social science the being, anthropology is the becoming and is thereby historical. The one cannot exist without the other.

[13] Queries, AA, n.s., 35:293–296, 1933. Equally to the point are Lesser's comments, "that cultural understanding is a manifold and that the more content we put into it the profounder it becomes.... The historical record is instrumental, and so too is any psychological record which can be validated. But, and here I think the primary principle of our methodology must lie, the fact of historicity is neither an end nor by itself a means but a condition which must be recognized at every step. Lip service alone will not do" (The Pawnee Ghost Dance Hand Game, p. 336, Columbia Univ. Press, 1933).

[14] See R. B. Dixon, Some Aspects of North American Archeology, AA, n.s., 15, no. 4, Remarks by Berthold Laufer, pp. 573–577.

BUREAU OF AMERICAN ETHNOLOGY,
WASHINGTON, D. C.

EARLY HISTORY OF THE EASTERN SIOUAN TRIBES*

By John R. Swanton

THE SIOUAN linguistic stock was given its place and name in the Powellian classification mainly on the basis of papers by Albert Gallatin published in 1836 and 1848.[1]† Gallatin made four subdivisions in the family: (1) the Winnebago, (2) the Sioux proper and Assiniboin, (3) the Minnetare group, and (4) the Osage and their southern kindred. The Cheyenne were doubtfully, and of course erroneously, assigned to it, but it is to be noted that Gallatin does not give them the Siouan color on his map. By a curious accident the Catawba Indians of South Carolina are given the same color as the Siouan tribes generally, though Gallatin does not appear to have recognized any connection between them, and states, indeed, that he seemed to discern some affinities between Catawba and Muskogee or even Choctaw. Ultimately, it will probably be shown that he was not entirely astray here though considerably ahead of his time. On the other hand, he does note the resemblance between Catawba and the Woccon language as indicated in Lawson's vocabulary, and suggests, correctly enough, that Catawba was very likely spoken by the Congaree, Cheraw, and other small tribes of the region.

Horatio Hale, the Canadian linguist, was first to suggest the existence of a Siouan dialect east of the Appalachians. In 1870 he interviewed an old Tutelo man living among the Cayuga Indians and obtained a vocabulary from him which "showed, beyond question ... that it was closely allied to the languages of the Dacotan family." The discovery was so unexpected that Hale at first thought this individual might have been a Dakota captive. A second visit, however, in October of the same year, removed all doubts and the language was recognized as that of the old Tutelo of Virginia. On December 19, 1879, Hale set forth his conclusions briefly at a meeting of the American Philosophical Society, and at a later meeting, March 2, 1883, made a complete presentation accompanied by a historical account of the tribe, a grammatical sketch, and comparisons between Tutelo words and corresponding terms in Dakota and Hidatsa. This paper placed the relationship of the Tutelo beyond question, and it was further confirmed through material collected by Howitt, Sapir, and Frachtenberg.[2]

Meanwhile, in 1881, Dr. A. S. Gatschet, of the Bureau of American Ethnology, had been struck by the Siouan resemblances of many words used by the Catawba Indians among whom he had been working, and more careful

---

* The present paper was prepared before the appearance of F. G. Speck's article, entitled Siouan Tribes of the Carolinas as Known from Catawba, Tutelo, and Documentary Sources (AA 37:201–225, 1935). Speck's intimate knowledge of the Catawba language and his acquaintance with the remnants of the Catawba and Tutelo people make his contribution of exceptional value and it should not be missed by students interested in the subject. Fortunately, Professor Speck's treatment of these tribes and my own make the articles complementary rather than antagonistic.

† Superior figures refer to notes at the end of this essay, p. 381.

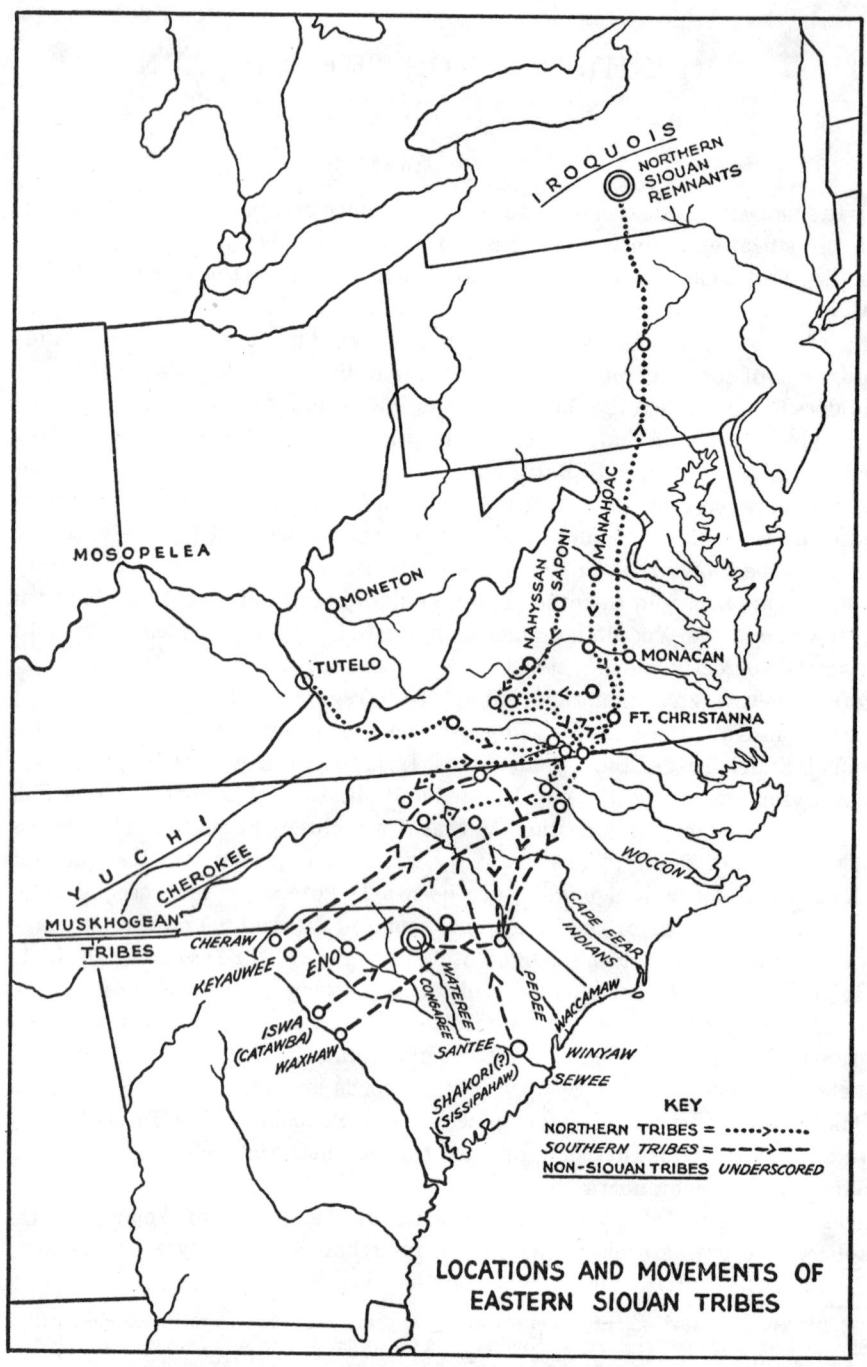

Map 1. Locations and movements of Eastern Siouan tribes.

comparisons instituted by him and the Siouan specialist, James Owen Dorsey, placed this connection also beyond reasonable doubt.[3]

As has already been noted, Gallatin, as far back as 1836, had suggested that the Woccon and several other tribes of the Carolinas were perhaps connected with Catawba, and Hale had been told by his old informant Nikonha that the Tutelo and Saponi could understand each other's speech. Nikonha knew of another tribe associated with these which he called Patshenins or Botshenins, and which Hale was probably right in identifying with the Occaneechi. He also assumed that the speech of these last was connected with the two others, though unfortunately he neglected to ask Nikonha about it.[4]

In 1886 Dr. Gatschet had the good fortune to come upon a small group of Biloxi Indians living near Lamourie Bridge, Louisiana, and he obtained a vocabulary from them which established their Siouan connections beyond question. Dr. Dorsey visited them in 1892 and 1893 and collected a large amount of material, including both texts and vocabulary, which was published in 1912 in Bulletin 47 of the Bureau of American Ethnology, under the editorship of the present writer.[5] Finally, in 1908, the writer discovered at Marksville, Louisiana, living among the Tunica Indians, a single survivor of the Ofo or Offagoula tribe and found to his astonishment that this was another Siouan dialect. Subsequent researches identified this tribe with the Mosopelea or Monsouperea, known to have lived in or near southern Ohio shortly before the end of the seventeenth century, and showed that their removal to the south had been very late.[6]

The results of the work of Hale, Gatschet, and Dorsey, and further information derived from a careful study of historical sources, were incorporated by James Mooney into a small, and now classic, bulletin which appeared in 1895.[7] In this paper Mooney demonstrated very satisfactorily the Siouan connection of the following tribes: the Indians of the Manahoac and Monacan confederations, including the Tutelo and Saponi, the Occaneechi, Eno, Shakori or Shaccoree, Sissipahaw, Keyauwee, Woccon, Catawba, Sugeree, Waxhaw, Cheraw or Sara, Wateree, Congaree, Santee, Sewee, Pedee, Winyaw, Waccamaw, Cape Fear Indians, and a tribe he called Mohetan. He suggested, indeed, that the Eno and Shakori might not be Siouan and admitted that the relationship of several others rested on rather tenuous circumstantial evidence, but, as we shall see presently, the peculiarities of the Eno and Shakori may be otherwise explained, and all additional evidence has tended to confirm the correctness of Mooney's classification.

The word Mohetan, however, is now known to be a misprint of Monetan, a tribe located much farther toward the northwest than the position Mooney assigns to it, probably on the Kanawha river. To the west of these again were the Ofo or Mosopelea; farther down the Ohio, according to tradition, was the former home of the Quapaw; and there is evidence of an ancient residence of the Biloxi and Osage in adjoining territories. Modern research has, therefore, tended to extend the domain of "the Siouan tribes of the east" farther west and that of the Siouan tribes of the west farther east at a not remote period.

This, of course, is merely confirmatory of the evidence furnished by community in language and current traditions.[8]

We now come to a point of particular significance regarding the eastern Siouans, but one upon which insufficient emphasis has hitherto been placed. Because, when first known to Europeans, they occupied one continuous geographical area, and were separated by a considerable interval from those in the west, it has naturally been assumed that the former were all more closely related to one another than to any of the trans-Mississippi Siouans. On the contrary, the eastern Siouans must be sharply separated into two groups, the Virginia Siouans, including the Manahoac, Monacan, Nahyssan, Saponi, Tutelo, Occaneechi, and Moneton, and the Carolina Siouans embracing all the rest.

Even a superficial comparison of the Tutelo and Catawba vocabularies on one hand and the western dialects on the other is sufficient to show that Catawba stands clearly apart from all of them, and that Tutelo is nearer Dakota, Hidatsa, and other of the western languages than it is to Catawba. Indeed, Catawba may prove to have been more closely connected with one or more of the western and southern dialects than with Tutelo. In this conclusion I am supported by the leading Catawba specialist of today, Professor F. G. Speck.

The evidence of language is furthermore strikingly borne out by the evidence of history. We find that, although associated from time to time with Siouan groups from the Carolinas, the Virginia tribes always held together and ultimately migrated toward the north and settled among the Iroquois, whereas the Carolina Siouans, without an exception, gravitated in the opposite direction and most of them ultimately coalesced with the Catawba.

Bushnell has called attention to the fact that the Rechahecrians who came to the falls of the James in 1654 or 1656, to the terror of the Virginia colonists, and defeated a combined force of whites and Powhatan Indians, were really the Nahyssan and a tribe called "Mahocks," evidently the Manahoac. This information is preserved by John Lederer.[9] Mooney assumes that these tribes were merely allied with the Rechahecrians, but the latter term is evidently a general name for inhabitants of a cave country.[10] One may guess that the Manahoac and Nahyssan had been pushed out of their earlier homes by the Susquehanna or other northern Indians. In 1670 John Lederer found them on the Staunton, and he calls both tribes Nahyssan, their eastern town being called Sapon and their western town apparently Pintahae. The next year Batts and Fallam visited two "Sapiny" or "Sapong" towns and a town of the Hanathaskies or Hanahaskies, evidently the Nahyssan proper.[11] This movement was probably caused by the same pressure from the north, and we may assume that it was instrumental in inducing both to leave these sites about 1675 and move to the junction of the Staunton and the Dan, where they settled together on an island below the supposedly cognate Occaneechi.

In the meantime another Siouan tribe, known as Tutelo or Totero, which, near the end of the seventeenth century,[12] seems to have been on the Big Sandy, and which Fallam and Batts had visited in a town somewhere near the present

Salem, Virginia, moved to an island just above that of the Occaneechi at the junction of the Staunton and the Dan. Before 1701 all of them had abandoned that region in turn and retired into North Carolina, where the Saponi and Tutelo were found by Lawson on the headwaters of the Yadkin and the Occaneechi on Eno river near the present Hillsboro. Shortly afterward, accompanied by the Keyauwee and Shakori, they moved in toward the white settlements, but in 1714 Governor Spotswood established Fort Christanna on Meherrin river, near the present Gholsonville, Virginia, and summoned thither several Siouan tribes in order by their means to protect his southern frontier. How many tribes were invited we do not know, but it is interesting to observe that, with a single possible exception, the only ones which actually settled there were Virginia Siouans. Those mentioned are the Meipontsky, Occaneechi, Saponi, Stegaraki, and Tutelo. The Stegaraki were a division or town of the Manahoac, and the Meipontsky were probably identical with the Ontponea of the same group. At least no such name occurs among the Carolina Siouans. After 1722, when peace was made between the Iroquois and the Virginia tribes, the Fort Christanna Indians moved north, first to Shamokin, Pennsylvania, and later into the Iroquois country proper. The remnant of Monacan, who seem to have retained a settlement of their own above the falls of the James, probably went along with them. One band of Saponi remained in the south, however, in all likelihood a body which had never been at Fort Christanna. They were reported from Granville county, North Carolina, until after the middle of the eighteenth century,[13] and may still be represented among the "Croatan Indians" reported from Person county in that state, which formerly was part of Granville.

A temporary association of the Siouan tribes of Virginia with the Keyauwee and Shakori has been mentioned above, with the further fact that they did not accompany the former to Fort Christanna. Governor Spotswood, probably in consequence of this failure, suggested the establishment of another town to include the Cheraw, Keyauwee, Eno, and evidently the Shakori, on the frontiers of North Carolina, a plan which did not materialize.[14]

The Cheraw, who here appear on the scene, were immigrants whose successive movements may be traced from the northwestern corner of the present South Carolina where they lived in De Soto's time. They drifted first to the neighborhood of Swannanoa Gap, east of Asheville, then to the Yadkin, and sometime before 1700 they had established themselves on the river Dan, near the southern boundary of Virginia, where they occupied two towns, "Upper and Lower Saura." In 1710 they moved southeast and joined the Keyauwee, but later the two tribes seem to have separated, the Cheraw moving lower down the Pedee to the present Cheraw district in South Carolina, where they proved a thorn in the flesh to the South Carolina colonists. In 1733 the Keyauwee, probably accompanied by the Eno and Shakori, are said to have gone south to join the Cheraw. Another tribe which must have united with them at this period was the Sissipahaw, whose fields were on Haw river. Barnwell says, indeed, that the Sissipahaw were the same tribe as the Shakori, but apparently this means that they were a branch of that tribe. Before 1739 the united tribes removed to the Catawba country, and Eno and Cheraw are mentioned by Adair as dialects spoken in the Catawba confederation about 1743. The Cheraw constituted a distinct body as late as 1768.

In the meantime, remnants of the more southern Siouans had also gathered about the Catawba. Adair asserts this of the Wateree and Congaree. Some, however, seem to have died out in their home territories, and a part of the Cheraw and their allies left mixed-blood descendants near their former homes on the Pedee in the misnamed "Croatan Indians" of Lumber river.[15]

It should be noted that there are some evidences of a deeper penetration of the Carolina Siouans into Virginia in the first half of the seventeenth century. Edward Blande and his companions in the Discovery of New Brittaine reported that on their expedition they had come upon "Schockoores old fields" close to old fields of the Nottoway Indians and there is even a Shockoe creek near Richmond, Virginia.[16] The origin of this last, however, has been traced by Bushnell with much greater probability to the Shackaconia, a division of the Manahoac.[17]

On the other hand, there is good evidence that most of the Siouan tribes found in North Carolina by Lederer, Lawson, and their successors were relatively late immigrants from territories farther south. The Cheraw, whose movements have just been sketched, constitute one historically documented example of this trend.

Let us now consider the Eno and Shakori, which are almost always coupled and usually lived close together. In 1653 Governor Yeardley of Virginia says that his emissaries had visited the Tuscarora Indians and found them at war with "a great nation called the Cacores (Shakori), a very little people in stature, not exceeding youths of thirteen or fourteen years, but extremely valiant and fierce in fight, and above belief swift in retirement and flight, whereby they resist the puissance of this potent, rich, and numerous people. There is another great nation by these, called the Haynokes (Eno), who valiantly resist the Spaniards further northern attempts."[18] The meaning of this last sentence we shall see in a moment. Lederer met these Indians in 1670 and agrees in the assertion that they were of low stature. He says: "These and the mountain-Indians build not their houses of bark, but of watling and plaister." From these statements Mooney was led to suspect that the two tribes might not have been Siouan. However their peculiarities will be satisfactorily explained if we suppose that, like the Cheraw at a somewhat later time, they had removed from farther south. Mooney himself gives one bit of evidence for such a removal in noting that Enoree river in South Carolina bears a name identical with that of the Eno tribe except for the addition of a characteristic Catawba termination -ree.[19] It can hardly be regarded as a result of the subsequent removal of this tribe southward, Enoree river being too far west of the Catawba country.

The Keyauwee make their appearance in 1701 when Lawson found them in a village south of the present High Point, North Carolina. They were then on intimate terms with the Saponi and Tutelo but, as we have seen, they later followed the fortunes of the Cheraw and other southern Siouans. Besides this association there are two items that would suggest a southern origin. One is the fact that their chief in Lawson's time was by birth a Congaree.[20] The second is the close resemblance of their name to that of the Keowee river, in northwestern South Carolina, also borne by two Cherokee towns. To be sure, Mooney's informant Wafford asserted that this word was a white corruption of Cherokee Kuwâhi'yĭ, "Mulberry-grove place," but reinterpretations are well known in the history of nomenclature, and it is also possible that the Keyauwee may have got their name from the Cherokee term.[21] At least it is interesting to note that this name appears in the same part of South Carolina as Enoree, the very part from which the Cheraw are known to have migrated.

Probability of a general tribal movement toward the northeast is also greatly strengthened by a study of earlier contacts between the Siouan tribes and the Spaniards. These go back to 1521 when two Spanish vessels touched upon the coast of what is now South Carolina and carried away a great number of Indians to be enslaved in the West Indies. One of these was taken to Spain, received the name of Francisco of Chicora, and supplied the historian Peter Martyr with considerable information regarding the country and people which is of value to us today in spite of a number of misunderstandings and miscopyings.

In another place I have given reasons for the belief that this Indian was carried off from the neighborhood of Winyaw bay. I have also made an attempt to identify the names of some of the provinces given by him with those of Siouan and Muskhogean tribes found thereabouts in later times. The results are meager, yielding, so far as the Siouan tribes are concerned, only a possible identification of Xapira (Shapira) with Sampit, a Santee subdivision, Guacaya (Wakaya) with Waccamaw, Xoxi (Shoshi) with Sewee, Yenyohol with Winyaw. But, if the Shakori once lived farther south, as I have suggested, the name Chicora actually may be the earliest form of their name which has come down to us. The main objection to this, hitherto, has been the great distance between Winyaw bay and central North Carolina, where the Shakori lived when first discovered; but I think this difficulty is not insurmountable.[22]

In 1540 De Soto passed through the westernmost parts of South Carolina and, as we have seen, visited the Cheraw town, the name of which, since he had Muskhogean interpreters who transposed Catawba r's into l's, his chroniclers record as Xuala or Xualla. Only one other Siouan place name appears in the De Soto narratives, Guaquili, the Aguaquiri of Pardo, which proves to be of great importance to us in trying to lay down the route of the latter Spanish officer.[23]

In 1566, Captain Juan Pardo, under orders from Pedro Menendez, Governor of Florida, left the Spanish post of Santa Elena, the modern Beaufort, South Carolina, proceeded inland to the Cheraw town, which he calls Xuada and Xuara, and on his return made a circuit toward the east as far as "Guatari," in which we unquestionably find the later Wateree, and then returned to Santa Elena, picking up his out-trail at a point called Gueza. The following year he was sent to the Cheraw again, and beyond through the Appalachians, evidently on the trail marked out by De Soto, as far as Chiaha and some points beyond on Tennessee river. This time, however, he swung eastward from Gueza as far as Guatariatiqui on the road to Guatari and went to the Cheraw via Aguaquiri. On his return he seems to have reached Guatari from the Cheraw by a more direct route than on the first occasion and to have returned from Guatari to Santa Elena by the same trail as on his first journey.[24]

The itinerary given proves without question that Aguaquiri or Guaquili lay east of the route followed by Pardo on his first journey to the Cheraw, and, furthermore, Pardo's account of that first journey seems to indicate that he was following a river most of the way. This river can only have been the Savannah and his narrative serves to confirm a conclusion independently arrived at that De Soto went north from Cofitachequi upon a trail along the watershed between the Savannah and the Saluda. Some of the data supplied by Pardo and Vandera, another chronicler of the route, are almost irreconcilable, but, checking them off as well as we can, it would seem as though Guatariatiqui—probably the Wateree Chickanee ("Little Wateree") of Lawson—were on the Saluda river near Dyson and the Guatari on the Broad river somewhere near the mouth of Indian creek. If the figures could be stretched somewhat, Guatariatiqui might be placed on the Broad river and Guatari would then be on Wateree creek, an affluent of the Wateree river, the later historic seat of the tribe. Thus the Wateree were found in 1566–1567 west, if anything, of their later habitat.

On his first journey northward, at a point which I conjecture to have been in the neighborhood of the mouth of the Broad river, where there is a notable archaeological site, Pardo came upon a town called Isa (Ysa), whose chief was very powerful, and he spent the following night at a smaller town subject to him. There is little doubt that this word is identical with the Catawba term Iswa, which means "river," and which was later applied to one of the great divisions of the Catawba Indians. Farther south was a town called Gueza, thought by some to signify the Waxhaw.

Besides the places actually visited by Pardo, mention is made of two others which might be reached by means of the river passing through Guatari. These are called Usi and Sauxpa or Sauapa and are said to have been near the sea "where salt was made." In these it is possible that we have Sewee and Sissipahaw, supposing that Sauxpa is the proper spelling of the second word, Spanish x of the period being equivalent to English sh. It would then be in the neighborhood of Chicora and lend strength to the supposition that Chicora is a synonym of Shakori which, as we have seen, Barnwell equates with Sissipahaw.

Our information is so meager and tenuous that we have to grope our way doubtfully much of the time in this investigation, but at least we have *certain* historical proof derived from the De Soto and Pardo chroniclers that Siouan peoples connected with the Catawba once occupied all of northwestern South Carolina to the Savannah river. We have further proof that one of these tribes, the Cheraw, migrated from the northwestern corner of that state to the Dan in Virginia and indications that the Eno and Keyauwee did the same. In the Spanish narratives, moreover, we find grounds for thinking that the Catawba, Wateree, and perhaps the Waxhaw were farther west in 1566–1567 than their historic seats, and that the Shakori and Sissipahaw may have been much farther south.

The movement of these tribes toward the northeast may have been due in part to Pardo himself. Although he represents his contacts with most of them to have been peaceful, he established small garrisons among the Cheraw and Wateree, and we learn that these, along with two planted in the Appalachians, were afterward destroyed by the Indians. There is no record of Spanish reprisals, but some tribes concerned in the uprising may well have feared such and removed farther from the coast and from the Spanish settlements in consequence. This general movement might also help to explain the apparent displacement of the Wateree in Lederer's time, since they appear to have been on the upper Yadkin in 1670 when he visited them.[25] Yeardley's remark regarding the Eno may also be recalled at this point.

A second reason for this movement, and one in operation previous to the arrival of the Spaniards, was the southward trek of the Cherokee Nation, which, from some point on the upper Ohio or its branches, was evidently working down along the great war trail from the head of the New river to Chattanooga. They seem to have found some Muskhogean tribes pretty well to the south, but above them the Appalachian mountain section appears to have been divided between Catawba-speaking people toward the south and Yuchi toward the west and north.[26] There is evidence, too, that some place names of the southern flank of the mountains here are Catawba in origin—Toxaway, Toccoa, Kituhwa—while the migration legend of the Catawba, however much it may be distorted, brings them from the northwest, logically the quarter in which their other kinsmen were to be found.[27] Evidence of wars between the Yuchi and the Siouans antedating the irruption of the Cherokee is found in Gabriel Arthur's statement that "all ye wesocks children they take are brought up with them (the Tamahittans or Yuchi) as ye Ianesaryes are a mongst ye Turkes."[28] Wesock seems to be Waxhaw plus an Algonquian termination.

Conclusions

The Siouan tribes of the east consisted of two very distinct dialectic groups, divided in historic times very nearly by the line which now separates Virginia from North Carolina. The former were related most closely with the Dakota, Hidatsa, and other Siouans of the northwest, while the latter, typically represented by the Catawba, stood apart from all other Siouan groups. Their language was the most aberrant of all Siouan dialects. Both groups had probably come into their historic seats from points farther toward the west and north. As the Earl of Bellomont, in 1699, says the "Shateras" were "supposed to be the Toteras, on Big Sandy River, Va.,"[29] it may be that the Virginia Siouans had advanced up that stream, but it is more likely that most of them came by the great trail along the Kanawha. The Catawba and their allies, on the other hand, probably made their way through the southern Appalachians or around their lower end, and may have been followed by the Yuchi, trailed in turn by the Shawnee. If the Westo were Yuchi, as I have supposed, the bitter war in progress in 1670 between them and the Catawba[30] may have been a continuation of a longer struggle begun very much farther toward the north, of which the presence of Wesock children among the Yuchi on the upper Tennessee river is one indication. This contest, however, was somewhat interrupted by the advance of the Cherokee along the war trail from the northeast, themselves very likely urged on by their kindred, the Iroquois. This would have tended, and perhaps did tend, to push the Siouans south, but the expeditions of Pardo and subsequent disagreements may have deflected it toward the northeast. As we know, Spain did not follow up her initial attempts at conquest, and in the gap created by Siouan emigration the Cherokee now poured across the mountains into northwestern South Carolina, which became the home of the Underhill branch of the nation. As we know, they also pushed the Creeks out of northern Georgia and part of northern Alabama but were defeated and halted by the Chickasaw. The Yuchi, already separated into several bands, were partly driven south, and partly incorporated with the invaders.

Meanwhile, the Carolina Siouans who emigrated farthest northeast came in contact with their remote cousins in Virginia for the first time, at least the first time for several hundred years. The pressure of the English and Iroquois and subsequent events, however, separated them again, the Virginians migrating north to the hospitable Five Nations, while the bulk of the southern Siouans gathered in about their largest single tribe, the Catawba.

But one item need be added. There is evidence, which has not yet been thoroughly marshaled, that the Siouan and Muskhogean linguistic families are related and that the Catawba tongue occupies an intermediate position between the extreme branches of each.[31]

NOTES TO "EARLY HISTORY OF THE EASTERN SIOUAN TRIBES"

[1] Trans. and Coll. Am. Antiq. Soc., 2:121, 306, 1836; Trans. Am. Ethn. Soc., 2: xcix, 77, 1848.

[2] Horatio Hale in Proc. Am. Philos. Soc., 21:1–47, 1883–84; J. N. B. Hewitt, MS., Bur. Am. Ethn., and, AA 15:295, 477.

[3] McGee, The Siouan Indians, BAE-R 15:159, 1897.

[4] Hale, op. cit., 10.

[5] A Dictionary of the Biloxi and Ofo Languages, BAE-B 47:4, 9, 10.

[6] Swanton, J. R., New Light on the Early History of the Siouan Peoples, Jour. Wash. Acad. of Sci., 13:33–43, 1923; same author, BAE-B 47.

[7] Mooney, James, The Siouan Tribes of the East, BAE-B 22, 1895.

[8] For Moneton, see The Journeys of Needham and Arthur *in* First Explorations of the Trans-Allegheny Region, by C. L. Alvord and Lee Bidgood, p. 221 (Cleveland, 1910). The interpretation of the name given here shows their close connection with the Tutelo and Dakota. The same proof is yielded for Saponi in words recorded by Byrd (see Mooney, op. cit., 46).

[9] Bushnell, Jr., D. I., The Five Monacan Towns in Virginia, 1607, SI-MC 82:16 (cited hereafter Monacan Towns). John Lederer *in* Alvord and Bidgood, op. cit., 146. Also see Bushnell, The Manahoac Tribes in Virginia, 1608, SI-MC 94, no. 8 (cited hereafter: Manahoac Tribes).

[10] Mooney, op. cit., 36.

[11] Alvord and Bidgood, op. cit., 152–153, 185. For the earliest known locations of the Monacan, including the Tutelo and Saponi, see Bushnell, Monacan Towns.

[12] Docs. Col. Hist. New York, 4:488, 1854.

[13] Mooney, op. cit., 37–55. Articles Manahoac, Monacan, Tutelo, Saponi, Ft. Christanna, Handbook of Am. Ind., BAE-B 30; Bushnell, Monacan Towns, 9.

[14] Colonial Records of North Carolina, 5:320–21.

[15] Mooney, op. cit., 64.

[16] Mooney, op. cit., 56–60. Article, Cheraw, BAE-B 30.

[17] Bushnell, Manahoac Tribes, 14.

[18] Alvord and Bidgood, op. cit., 129; Mooney, op. cit., 64.

[19] Narratives of Early Carolina, 27–28 (*in* Original Narratives of Early American History, editor, A. S. Salley, Jr.).

[20] Mooney, op. cit., 62, 64.

[21] Mooney, op. cit., 61, 62.

[22] Mooney, Myths of the Cherokee, BAE-R 19:525.

[23] Swanton, John R., Early History of the Creek Indians, BAE-B 73:31–48.

[24] Narratives of De Soto, The Trailmakers Series (ed. E. G. Bourne), 2:103.

[25] E. Ruidiaz y Caravia, La Florida, 2:465–473, 481–486 (Madrid), 1894.

[26] Alvord and Bidgood, op. cit., 157.

[27] Mooney, BAE-R 19.

[28] Speck, F. G., personal communication. Schoolcraft, History of Indian Tribes, 3:293–296.

[29] Alvord and Bidgood, op. cit., 218.

[30] Docs. Col. Hist. New York, 4:488, 1854.

[31] Alvord and Bidgood, op. cit., 159–160.

Bureau of American Ethnology,
Washington, D. C.

SOZIALPSYCHISCHE ABLÄUFE IM VÖLKERLEBEN

By Richard C. Thurnwald

Eine analyse der Kulturphänomene und ihre Vergleichung führen zur Unterscheidung zweier verschiedener Kräfte. Die eine wirkt im Sinne einer Mehrung an Fertigkeiten und Kenntnissen, sie führt zu erhöhter Beherrschung der Natur und zu erweitertem Wissen um Zusammenhänge des Geschehens. Unter dem Eindruck dieser Vorgänge reden wir von "Fortschritt," oder unter besonderem Gesichtspunkt von "Entwicklung." Eine anders wirkende Kraft scheint die Wiederkehr von mit einander verketteten Situationen herbeizuführen. Während die Richtung der ersten Kraft im Sinne einer Geraden "aufwärts" weist, scheint die zweite Kraft, die eine Rückkehr zu ähnlichen Situationen bewirkt, sich in einem Kreis zu bewegen. Mit Rücksicht darauf spricht man von "Zyklen" sozialer Gestaltungen und damit verbundener "Kultur." Dabei handelt es sich nicht allein um die Wiederkehr bestimmter sozialpsychischer Verfassungen, sondern auch um die Wiederholung von miteinander verketteten Folgeerscheinungen, um "Abläufe." Im folgenden soll nur von diesen zyklischen Vorgängen die Rede sein.

Die Abfolge von Aristokratie, Demokratie, und Tyrannis hat bekanntlich Aristoteles zur Aufstellung einer Art "Gesetzmässigkeit der Wiederkehr des Gleichen" veranlasst. Chinesische Staatsphilosophen haben auf ähnliche Zyklen hingewiesen, deren Ablauf sie mit etwa 300 bis 500 Jahren ansetzten. In der modernen europäischen Literatur wurde der Wiederkehr ähnlicher sozialer Gestaltungen und sozialpsychischer Situationen von verschiedenen Seiten Beachtung zugewendet und hat mitunter zu abstrusen Hypothesen verleitet. Sie hat vor allem dazu geführt, dass infolge emotioneller oder kurzsichtiger Ueberbewertung der Aehnlichkeit von wiederkehrenden Situationen eine Analyse der komplexen Kulturphänomene unterlassen und die Aufmerksamkeit auf diese Komponente allein eingeengt wurde. Die Folge war ein Uebersehen der anderen eingangs erwähnten Komponente, die als fortschreitender Akkumulationsprozess von wachsender Naturbeherrschung und Einsicht in die Bedingtheiten des Lebens gekennzeichnet wurde.[1] Wenn wir uns hier den Zyklen zuwenden, so geschieht das unter Anerkennung des Akkumulationsprozesses und unter Berücksichtigung der Tatsache, es nur mit einer Komponente der Kulturgestaltung zu tun zu haben.

I

Zunächst sei an verschiedene Formen der Familiengestaltung erinnert. Aus der Fülle der Erscheinungen lässt sich überall (1) ein Grundverhältnis von *Mutter zu Kind* herauslösen. Die Mutter hat ihre eigene Feuerstelle, an der sie kocht und für das Kind sorgt. Dies stellt den "Kern" der Familie dar. Daran schliesst sich (2) der *Schutz der Frau durch den Mann*. Diese Beziehung

---

[1] Ausführlich erläutert auf S. 266 ff. von Bd. IV von "Die menschliche Gesellschaft," Verlag de Gruyter, Berlin, 1935.

variiert entsprechend der Männergesellschaft und den dort geltenden Auffassungen. Eine unendliche Zahl von Varianten regelt nach Brauch und Sitte die Beziehungen unter den Geschlechtern in den verschiedenen Lebensaltern, die Dauerpaarungen, damit verknüpfte Zeremonien, die Ansichten über den Anspruch der Familien oder Sippen an die Kinder, usw.

Die weibliche Lebenssphäre mit ihrer physiologischen Bedingtheit und ihrer psychischen Auswirkung auf dem Gebiete der Mütterlichkeit und alles dessen was weiterhin damit zusammenhängt, vor allem die Notwendigkeit regelmässiger Versorgung mit, wenn auch geringer Nahrungsmenge, bestimmt in erster Linie die Situation. Die Art, durch die von männlicher Seite Schutz der einzelnen Mutter zu Teil wird, hängt von der jeweiligen Gestaltung der Männergesellschaft ab. Während das Mutter- Kind Verhältnis trotz allem was sich drum und dran findet, biologisch fundiert und darum verhältnismässig stabil ist, werden die Formen der Männergesellschaft durch viel mehr und durch andere Faktoren bestimmt. In der Männergesellschaft macht sich der akkumulative Vorgang des technischen Fortschritts geltend, also die eingangs erwähnte erste Kraftkomponente. Dadurch werden die Grundlagen für die Nahrungsgewinnung geschaffen und die Voraussetzungen für die soziale Organisation und die Formen des "Wirtschaftens" hervorgerufen. Deshalb sind die Gestaltungen der Männergesellschaft viel schwankender, sind der "Entwicklung" unterworfen und, wie wir sehen werden, auch zyklischen Serien ausgesetzt.

Was ergibt sich daraus für die Formung der Familie? Der *stabile Kern* bestimmt die Ruhehaltung. Um diesen schwanken, "pendeln," die Beziehungen der Männer gemäss den Gestaltungen ihrer Gesellschaft. Eine herrschaftliche Organisation des politischen Verbandes wirkt sich im Familienleben als "Patriarchat" aus und führt in vielen Fällen zur Sohnesfolge. Die Bedeutung welche die Frau als Bestellerin der Felder erlangte, sicherte ihr Anerkennung und Einfluss in der Männergesellschaft, weil sie Einwirkung auf den akkumulativen Prozess erlangte. Als Folge sehen wir Ausbildung "mutterrechtlicher" Züge. Irgendwo entstandene Wertungen werden natürlich ebenso verbreitet oder nachgeahmt wie materielle Objekte. Als Folge stellen sich die verschiedensten örtlichen Besonderheiten ein, die aber unsern Blick nicht verwirren dürfen.

Keinerlei Gestaltung ist etwas "Ewiges," sondern jede ist Aenderungen ausgesetzt. Das zeigt sich auf dem Boden der ethnographischen Forschung dort, wo genaue historische Einzeluntersuchungen vorgenommen wurden, ebenso wie auf allen anderen Gebieten menschlichen Soziallebens.

Die Kraft, die auf dem Gebiete der Familiengestaltung immer wieder zu einer Grundhaltung des Pendels zurückdrängt, liegt im stabilen Kern des Grundverhältnisses von Mutter zu Kind. Die äusserlichen Formveränderungen werden durch das Hereinspielen des akkumulativen Faktors bedingt, an dem die Frauen entweder aktiv teilnehmen (Feldbau, Töpferei, Hauseinrichtung, usw.) oder durch die veränderten Existenzbedingungen der Männergesellschaft (Form der Nahrungsgewinnung, Ueberschichtung, usw.) in

Mitleidenschaft gezogen werden. Die Vorgänge, die das Ergebnis aus beiden wiederholt erwähnten Komponenten darstellen, scheinen jeweils teils etwas neues zu bieten, teils nach schon dagewesenen zurückzuweisen. Der Beobachter verzeichnet, je nach seinem voreingenommenen Standpunkt, bald die eine Komponente, bald die andere. Nur eine Analyse der Vorgänge nach beiden Richtungen gewährt ein Abwägen, und ein Urteil darüber, wie weit an einem Phänomen die ersterwähnte, oder die letzterwähnte Kraft mehr beteiligt ist, und wie beide ineinander wirken.

II

Ganz ähnliches vollzieht sich innerhalb der sozialen Gestaltungen der Männergesellschaft. Bei der Wiederkehr ähnlicher Formen der Familie bestimmen die biologischen Kräfte und deren psychische Auswirkungen eine Grundhaltung des Pendels. In der Männergesellschaft ist es anders. Obwohl dahingestellt bleibt, wie sich die in die Augen springenden "biologischen" Faktoren, die bei der Verzahnung des Familienlebens wirksam werden, von den gleich zu erörternden "Emotionen" unterscheiden. Denn in der Männergesellschaft führen gewisse *Emotionen,* die als *"elementar"* bezeichnet werden können, zur Wiederkehr ähnlicher Situationen. *Persönliche* müssen aber von kollektiven Elementaremotionen unterschieden werden. Setzt sich die Emotion einer Person bei ihr, unabhängig von den Mitmenschen, in eine abreagierende Handlung um, so liegt der erstere Fall vor. Das gilt, auch wenn weiterhin Gruppen davon betroffen und in Bewegung und Handlung gesetzt werden. Hat z.B. eine Emotion einen Mann veranlasst, einen anderen tot zu schlagen, so werden in einer primitiven Gesellschaft eine jede der beiden Sippen, denen der Totschläger und der Erschlagene angehört, davon in Mitleidenschaft gezogen und wahrscheinlich in Blutrache verwickelt. Andere Gesellschaften ziehen einen solchen Fall vor Gericht. Sitten, Vorschriften, Gesetze regeln durch solche und ähnliche Emotionen hervorgerufene Situationen in jedem Volk zu jeder Zeit, und lassen sie je nach Tradition und Wertung ausklingen. Die Männergesellschaft versucht daher die Auswirkungen von sie störenden persönlichen Emotionen durch unbewusst entstandene (politische Gemeinde, Staat) oder bewusste und klar formulierte Ordnungen einzudammen, damit sie sich nicht in Kollektivemotionen (z. B. in Kämpfen und Kriegen) auswirken.

Besondere Verflechtungen kommen den *Kollektivemotionen* zu. Die Ausgangsreize rühren von gemeinsamen Erlebnissen einer Gruppe her. Diese Erlebnisse können in Witterungsphänomenen bestehen: in ungewöhnlicher Dürre, oder Feuchtigkeit, Hitze oder Kälte; oder in ansteckenden Krankheiten, die Menschen, Haus-oder Beutetiere dahinraffen; oder endlich in Kampzuständen, die oft wie eine mystische Seuche leidenschaftlichen Massenwahns die Gruppen in Bann schlagen. Die Folge solcher Reize sind Emotionen bei allen Menschen der leidenden Gruppe. Durch Gemeinsamkeit der Emotionsrichtung werden sie verstärkt und bringen oft Paniken mit sich, wenn intelligente Führung fehlt. So wurden immer wieder Wanderbewegungen als

Situationsfolgen ausgelöst, Kriegspsychosen, Massendepressionen, die sich als Selbstaufopferung oder in Hoffnung auf Erlösung auswirkten. Umgekehrt reizt die gute Ernte, Erfolg in Politik oder Wirtschaft zu Festen, zu Ueppigkeit des Lebens, und Ueberheblichkeit. Streifen wir durch die Völkerschicksale so fallen uns Belege für solche Zusammenhänge zu, wir sehen wie gelegentlich ähnliche Erscheinungen als Folge ähnlicher Kollektivemotionen wiederkehren, ohne dass der Grad zivilisatorischer Ausrüstung dabei entscheidend ins Gewicht fällt.

Es wäre nicht wert, an alle diese Zusammenhänge zu mahnen, wenn man nicht in jedem einzelnen Fall vergessen würde zu fragen, welche sozialpsychischen Reize die Voraussetzung für persönliche Emotionen und kollektive Stimmungen bilden, die Einzel-Aktionen und Gesamtsituationen veranlassen. Es scheint manchmal, als würde man sonst zwar überall nach Ursache und Wirkung forschen, nur auf dem Gebiete sozialer Vorgänge davor zurückzuschrecken. Gewöhnlich begnügt man sich mit egozentrisch befangenen Anklagen oder Beschuldigungen gegen Personen oder Gruppen, denen man "Bösartigkeit" oder "schlechten Charakter" vorwirft. Wenn zwei streitende Teile die gleiche Haltung in der gegenseitigen Beurteilung einnehmen, wird die subjektive Befangenheit eines jeden offenbar. Allein wir müssen gerade durch ethno-soziologische Vertiefung lernen, die Vorgänge im Völkerleben wie Naturgeschehnisse zu betrachten, nach deren verzweigten Zusammenhängen wir zu forschen haben. Nur daraus kann ein "Verstehen" quellen, und können vielleicht sogar "Lösungen" sich finden lassen. So eröffnen sich praktische Perspektiven aus der Sphäre objektiver Betrachtung. Die Emotionalität und die Kurzsichtigkeit menschlichen Planens und Handelns vermag dieses nicht aus seiner "Natur"-gebundenheit herauszuheben und zur vollen Selbstbestimmung des eigenen Schicksals zu führen. Wohl aber vermögen wir vielleicht gelegentlich durch vertiefte Erkenntnis der Zusammenhänge in erregten Zeitläuften zur Klärung und Beruhigung beizutragen, wenn es gelingt die Aufmerksamkeit auf die Verknüpfung von Ursache und Wirkung zu lenken.

III

Solche Zusammenhänge zeigen sich besonders in der Verkettung von Emotionen und Handlungsweisen, die, bei verschiedenen Völkern und unter sonst sehr andersartigen Umständen, zu ähnlichen Situationsreihen führen. Deren Abfolge erstreckt sich in den einzelnen Fällen gewöhnlich über Jahrhunderte. Das tritt am deutlichsten in sich ablösenden Organisationsformen der politischen Struktur zu Tage. Diese Beobachtung hat, wie in der Einleitung bemerkt, bereits im Altertum die Aufmerksamkeit soziologischer Denker auf sich gezogen. Inzwischen ist das verfügbare Material nicht nur vermehrt, sondern durch die Ethnologie auch tiefer zurück ergänzt worden.[2] Der Schlüs-

---

[2] Näheres darüber auf S. 286 ff. und 301 ff. von Bd. IV "Die menschliche Gesellschaft"; und in "Analyse von Entwicklung und Zyklus" in "Mensch en Maatschappij" IX/1–2, 1933. Ein Sonderfall wird berichtet in des Verf's "Black and White in East Africa" (London: Routledge and Sons, 1935), p. 20 (27); vgl. dazu auch pp. 16–17 (7, 9, 10, 11).

sel aber für die Klärung und Begründung der sich wiederholenden Erscheinungsreihen muss auf psychologischem Gebiet gesucht werden.

Die erwähnten Abfolgen beginnen mit einer "ethnischen Ueberschichtung." Diese findet sich hauptsächlich in dem Sonderfall, dass Sippen oder Sippensplitter von Hirtenvölkern (oder Jägern) zwischen den Siedlungen von Feldbauern herumstreifen und mit ihnen Tauschbeziehungen anknüpfen. (Berührungen von anderen Völkern seien hier der Kürze und Einfachheit wegen ausser Acht gelassen.) Obwohl sich dabei verschiedene Situationen ergeben können, je nach dem Zahlenverhältnis der beiden Hauptbeteiligten, je nach sonstigen Schicksalswendungen, Eigenschaften, und Umständen, sei hier nur *ein* typisches Muster herausgegriffen.

Dem anfänglichen Neben- oder Durcheinander- Wohnen (wie in Teilen Zentral- oder Ost-Afrikas und anderwärts) folgt eine Periode von Streitigkeiten und Kämpfen, in denen das gegenseitige Verhältnis zivilisatorischer Ausrüstung, moralischer Kraft, und sonstiger Hilfsmittel auf die Probe gestellt wird. Infolge der Besonderheit der Lebensführung und des Wirtschaftsertrages (auf Grund eines Austausches von Getreide gegen Kühe) findet auf jeder Seite eine wechselseitige Ergänzung statt, die mit der Zeit Gewohnheit wird und zu einer beiderseitigen Verzahnung in der Weise führt, dass jede ethnische Gruppe der anderen für ein zivilisatorisch bereichertes Leben bedarf (dass Getreide für die Hirten "Bedürfnis," und Kuhbesitz, Milch und vielleicht auch Butter, für die Feldbauer "Bedürfnis" geworden). Zwischen einzelnen Feldbauer Siedlungen und einzelnen Sippen von Hirten kommt es zu einer mit der Zeit sich festigenden Symbiose. Dabei fällt den unternehmenderen und aktiveren Hirten die politische Führung zu, während die manchmal zivilisatorisch reicher ausgestatteten Feldbauer sich oft kulturell durchsetzen. So spalten sich symbiotisch verbundene Hirten-Feldbauer-Einheiten ab. Diese treten unter Führung von Hirten-Sippen in *Rivalität* miteinander. Die Feldbauer werden in diesen Rivalitätskämpfen Gefolgsleute der Hirten. Aus den Rivalitätskämpfen geht schliesslich *eine* Hirten-Sippe als endgiltiger Sieger hervor. Auf diese Weise kommt es zur Entstehung grosser Gemeinwesen. Ein solches bezeichnen wir als *Staat*. Zunächst hält die Scheidung von Feldbauer Tradition und von Tradition der Hirten an. Mit der Zeit aber fliessen beide ineinander. Wir sagen : die ethnische Schichtung wird von einer sozialen verdrängt.

Das sind aufs Knappste reduziert, die Vorgänge, die in weit auseinander liegenden Gegenden und Zeiten sich wiederholt zugetragen haben. Den einzelnen Vorgängen liegen jeweils die gleichen Geisteshaltungen zu Grunde, die aus ähnlichen Emotionen abzuleiten sind. Diese wiederum finden ihre Begründung in analogen Reizen der sozialen Situationen. Die Situation, die eine Weile (viele Jahrzehnte oder Jahrhunderte) lang andauert, tritt uns als "Sozialverfassung" eines Gemeinwesens oder Volkes, entgegen. Da aus gewissen Situationen Emotionen entspringen, die sich in Geisteshaltungen ausdrücken und schliesslich in Handlungen umsetzen, ergibt sich eine Kausalkette, die eine neue soziale Situation aus einer vorhergehenden schafft.

Es ist nicht möglich, in dieser Skizze auf eine Kennzeichnung der einzelnen Emotionen und Geisteshaltungen einzugehen. Noch weniger auf die mit Hörigkeit oder Sklaverei verbundenen Ueberlegenheits- und Unterlegenheitskomplexe und deren Auswirkung. Die Verwicklung mit der zivilisatorischen Ausrüstung der einzelnen in Betracht kommenden Gruppen konnte nicht berücksichtigt werden, obwol dadurch der Einzellfall seine Prägung und Ablaufsrichtung erhält. Nur an einem Beispiel sollte gezeigt werden, wie die Abfolge von Erscheinungen auf die Wiederkehr von ähnlichen Emotionen zurückzuführen ist, die sich ihrerseits aus bestimmten Situationen ergibt.

Diese Emotionen, die bei allen Menschen wesentlich gleich sind, entscheiden die Wiederkehr ähnlicher Gestaltungen des Zusammenlebens. Das Gefolgschaftsverhältnis verleitet zur Ausnützung der Gefolgsleute und Ueberspannung der Forderungen. Auf diese Weise entspringt aus der politischen Führung der Hirten ein *Herrschaftsverhältnis* über die Feldbauern. Das dadurch gehobene Selbstgefühl der Hirten (Superioritätskomplex) leitet die Rivalitätskämpfe unter den Sippen ein. Deren Führer werden in wachsendem Ausmass von der Zahl und dem guten Willen der Gefolgsleute abhängig. Wie ja Führung immer in einem Komplementärverhältnis zur Gefolgschaft steht wenn sie andauern soll. Als Folge stellt sich ein zunehmendes Durchbrechen der Heiratsschranken und des Monopolbesitzes an Kühen ein. Dadurch vollzieht sich eine soziale und kulturelle Angleichung. Der schliessliche Sieg einer der rivalisierenden Sippen, führt zur Anerkennung von Einzelherrschaft als "Despotie." Deren Aufrichtung wurde durch das scharfe Zugreifen der Sippenführer während der Rivalitätskämpfe vorbereitet. Das Bestreben des "Despoten," seine Herrschaft zu sichern, lässt ihn Leute um sich sammeln, die keinen anderen Rückhalt haben als ihn. Das sind rationale Erwägungen. Sie wurden aber wohl nie bewusst ausgeklügelt, sondern sind begabten Führern jeweils "intuitiv eingefallen." Die starke Persönlichkeit mit Einbildungskraft macht sich von den Schranken der aristokratischen Ueberlieferung und von den sakralen Bindungen frei. Der sich davon emanzipierende Despot fängt an, sich auf Sklaven oder fremde Söldner zu stützen. So wird, von oben und von unten her, die Bedeutung der Sippe untergraben. Deshalb wird die Gesellschaft individualisiert, Sippeneigentum wird durch Privateigentum ersetzt. Nur in Gilden, in Dörfern, oder in lose angegliederten ethnisch verschiedenen Gruppen lebt noch die Sippe weiter und kann, in Verbindung mit Staffelungs-Gedanken, zur Bildung von Kasten führen.

Die geschilderten Zustände begegnen uns, z. B. in den altorientalischen Gemeinwesen. Diesen Typ kann man als "archaische" Staatsbildung bezeichnen. Gelegentlich gelingt es anderen "adligen" Sippen die Herrscherfamilie zu verdrängen. "Dynastien" folgen aufeinander wie wir sagen. Bei zunehmender Vermischung und Vereinheitlichung der Kultur gelangen mehr und mehr Leute anderer Schichten und Gruppen zur Macht, ja zur obersten Führung. Der Typus der "Tyrannis" ergibt sich daraus. Das Nilland, Mesopotamien, Indien, China liefern sicheres Zeugnis für ganz ähnliche Reihen. Die griechische und römische Geschichte bietet ähnliche Belege. Auch viele sozialpsychologische Situationen und politische Gestaltungen von "Naturvölkern" dürften unter dem Gesichtspunkt der geschilderten Abfolgen Deutung finden. Allerdings wurde hier nur ein einzelner Ablauf zu schildern versucht. Andere Verkettungen gehen von anderen Anfangssituationen aus. Die Form anfänglichen Zusammentreffens, besondere Ereignisse, die ethnischen Verschiedenheiten der in Betracht kommenden Stämme, usw., bestimmen die Verkettungsrichtung, ebenso davon unbeeinflusste, von aussen her, einstürmende Vorfälle, wie etwa feindliche Angriffe.

Die Struktur einer Gesellschaft wird erst aus solchen Zusammenhängen und Abfolgen verständlich. Hier kommt die Bedeutung sozialpsychischer Dynamik zur Geltung. Auch eine Handhabe für die Erkundung der Aenderungsrichtung in den Gesellungsgestaltungen und Tendenzen einer Zeit ergibt sich aus solcher Betrachtungsweise.

Schliesslich kann die Frage der "Uebertragung" nicht übergangen werden. Bekanntlich wird aus der Menge von "angebotenen" Dingen vom annehmenden Volk nur "passendes" ausgewählt und seiner Kultur eingefügt. Gerade auf sozialpsychologischem Gebiet vermag sich Annahme fremder Einrichtungen auf die Dauer nur im begrenzten Rahmen des eigenen Traditionsmomentums zu halten. Dazu gehören auch die erörterten Verkettungen. Bei deren Ablauf werden willig Sitten oder Zeremonien von anderen aufgenommen, aber nur so weit als sie mit der gerade zur Geltung kommenden Phase in Einklang stehen. Diese Phase aber entspringt den eigenen Erlebnissen des Volks.

UNIVERSITY OF BERLIN,
BERLIN, GERMANY.

PRODUCTIVE PARADIGMS IN SHAWNEE

By C. F. Voegelin

SHAWNEE represents the most southerly language of the Central Algonkin division of the Algonkin stock, and like other members of its family is characterized by an unbelievably great number of morphological formations. Something will have been gained, obviously, when these numerous formations are subdivided into types which contain less bewildering variety. As a contribution to this end, paradigmatic formation as a type is herewith presented, while other aspects of Shawnee morphology and questions of phonology[1] are reserved for future discussions; but a general preliminary statement of these matters must precede the specific analysis of paradigms in order to show the relation between paradigmatic affixes and the word theme.

Since Jones made a scientific study of his native language (Fox), other Algonkinists have on the whole followed the type of stem classification which Jones, as has been said, instinctively guaranteed. This classification makes a fundamental distinction between numerous primary stems (sometimes called initial stems) which occur singly or in compounds, and relatively few secondary stems (sometimes called second-position stems) which never occur alone. The essential distinction certainly serves well for Shawnee, but the subclasses of Jones are here dispensed with. When a primary stem enters into composition, it is desirable to know whether the stem is bound (found only in composition) or free (found either in composition or independently); all secondary stems are, by definition, bound. Frequently a given primary stem will be bound in numerous words, text after text, and then suddenly appear free. The stem, mehči-, is an example in point. It is used to express the notion of completed action or action in the past (e.g., nimehčiwihθeni I have eaten; nimehčihalwihkaala I stepped over him; nimehčihaškami after I had stayed here). One might be tempted to regard mehči- as a tense prefix. But compare nimečto<*ni-mehči-hto I finished it, and nimečha<*ni-mehči-hh-a I finished him, in which mehči- is the only stem, followed by a transitive animate or a transitive inanimate suffix. Primary bound stems should be regarded as originally free elements which are losing their independence now preserved, if at all, only in sporadic and infrequent usages; secondary stems have already lost their independence. However, there are good reasons why bound stems may not be treated as affixes even if they express a semiformal meaning. Perhaps the most eloquent is the possibility of forming a verbal theme with a secondary stem (bound) preceded by a bound primary stem; if the bound stems were regarded as affixes, we should have the absurd situation of a word composed of prefix+suffix without stem (e.g., yaašilawiiwaači when they do so).

Despite the excellent linguistic attention which Algonkin languages have

---

[1] A description of Shawnee phonemes is to be found in Language 11:23–37. The glottalic phoneme is here written as h. I am experiencing some difficulty in finding suitable formulae for Shawnee morphophonemes. Instances of phonological analyses in this paper should be regarded as merely experimental.

received, an adequate generalization concerning semantic types of stems is yet to be made. The validity of such a generalization will probably be its success in anticipating the relative order of stems within a class. As matters stand, it is only possible to give lists of stems and indicate their relative order in known compounds (e.g., of the two primary bound stems, -ih- precedes wii- in nihwiiteemaaki<*ni-ih-wii-teemaaki I should have gone with them). The relative order of stems in general is in no sense given to undisturbed regularity. It has, for example, been said that incorporated nouns follow verbal stems in Algonkin, and this order is doubtless favored in Shawnee (e.g., ni-θake-hšee-n-a I pulled his ear [lit., I—seize hold of—ear—by hand—him]. -hšee- is a secondary stem having a doublet for independent usage: hohtawaka his ear. Compare niθakičaaleena I pulled his nose, ni-pehša-nowe-hšine I—touch—cheek—an. subj. intr. at rest; in these instances the incorporated nouns are primary stems: ninowa my cheek, hočaaši<*hočaali his nose). But a nominal stem may also precede a verbal stem in composition (e.g., ni-mhkwa-lawi I am bear-hunting [lit., I—bear—enter into activity in respect to]) perhaps because the verbal stem is secondary in the noun-verb order, or possibly because the verb-noun order is contingent upon the employment of a verbal stem which requires a formative suffix.

The most productive formatives are instrumental and transitivizing suffixes. The latter regularly occur in correlative pairs for animate and inanimate object. Comparable but less productive pairs of intransitive suffixes are sometimes employed for animate and inanimate subject. An instrumental suffix is always followed by a transitivizing suffix but a transitive suffix is not necessarily preceded by an instrumental suffix. The relationship between transitive and instrumental suffixes is as follows:

Transitive type	Transitive animate	Transitive inanimate
1	hh	hto
2	l	to
3	l	ta
4	m	ta
5	Zero	ta
6	Zero	a
7	w	a
8	aw	a

Instrumental suffix		Precedes transitive type
pw	by mouth	5
n	by hand	6
(h)θ	by heat	7
hh	by mechanical instrument	7
l	by projectile	8
(h)t	by vocal noise	8
šk	by feet in locomotion	8
hšk	by feet as agent	8
lhk	by legs	8
hk	by body	8

The pair of transitive suffixes which a given verb takes is determined by the instrumental suffix (if the verbal theme has an instr. suff.) or by the last stem in the theme. This stem may, for example, require suffixes of transitive type 4 (nikčitaweele-m-a I regard him with care; nikčitaweele-ta I regard it carefully); if however the final stem in composition is omitted, the stem before the last, now final, may require another pair of transitive suffixes (tr. type 1 in this instance, nikčitawa-h-a I guard him, nikčitawa-hto I guard it). Only occasional stems tolerate both instrumental suffix and also transitive suffix without instrumental suffix (e.g., instr. suff. -θ- followed by tr. type 7, nitepowaa-θ-w-a I debate him heatedly; cf. tr. type 3 without instr. suff., nitepowaa-l-a I debate about him, nitepowaa-ta I debate about it). Some stems tolerate only one instrumental suffix which is then apt to be empty of meaning (e.g., in Absentee Shawnee, nikki-θ-w-a I hide him, nikki-θ-a I hide it; in Cherokee Shawnee the stem kki- does not tolerate the instr. suff. -θ- but requires tr. type 2, nikki-l-a I hide him, nikki-to I hide it). Notions of instrumentality are emphasized when a stem tolerates several instrumental suffixes (e.g., nipehše-n-a I touch it by hand, nipešha<*nipehše-hh-a I touch it with mechanical instrument, nipehše-l-aw-a I touch him by projectile, by shooting, nipešška<*nipehše-hšk-a I touch it by feet).

In function, all formative suffixes make paradigmatic suffixes possible. Formative suffixes are obligatory when paradigmatic suffixes cannot be appended directly to a stem, but when formative suffixes are not necessarily required by the stem they may nevertheless be tolerated. An optional formative is in a sense merely a derivative suffix, but a formative-derivative distinction cannot be maintained, because it is the stem and not the suffix which determines the necessity of the formatives. Of the more derivative type of formative, the reciprocal suffix is a good example. In a paper concerning itself with formatives, it is only necessary to say that when a verbal theme ends with a reciprocal, it may be inflected as any animate intransitive theme. In the case of diminutive suffixes, those employed with animate verbs and nouns are formatives, but different diminutive suffixes are employed with inanimate nouns; the latter enter into the inflection and are accordingly classified as paradigmatic suffixes.

The order of elements in the word complex of Shawnee is as follows (± symbolizes plus or minus; +, always necessary):

± personal pronoun prefix
+ primary stem(s) ⎫
± secondary stem(s) ⎬ THEME
± formative suffix(es) ⎭
± paradigmatic suffix(es): these with the personal pronoun prefixes constitute the paradigmatic affixes.

An irregularity is found in an uncommon type of loose compound in which a stem appears in composition with its inflective affix(es) pleonastically retained (e.g., nimhšinhθeeθa my big older brother<*ni-mhši-ni-hhθeeθa my—big—my—older brother).

Before plunging into the paradigms (which are given alphabetic tags, A to N), the paradigmatic affixes (arabic numbers for suffixes, roman numerals for prefixes) will be listed. These affixes are of the mixed relational type, but in the following list they are assigned their most prominent meanings, with alphabetic letters referring to the paradigms in which they occur. Affixes followed by hyphens are never found in final position; those followed by hyphens in parentheses may be used either medially or finally; those not followed by hyphens occur only in final position.

Suffixes expressing number, with numerical surrogates below twenty:

1	-pe	Plural of 1st pers. subj. (A, B, C), obj. (A), psychol. subj. (F).
2	-pwa	Plural of 2d pers. subj. (A, C), obj. (A), psychol. subj. (F).
3	-pi	Plural indefinite of implied 3d pers. subj. (C), agentive actor (F).
4	-ki	Plural of 3d pers. obj. (A); of implied 3d pers. subj. (C), agentive actor (F); of an. noun (D), inan. noun (E).
5	-hke -hki	Plural of part. mode 3d pers. subj. (J, M), psychol. subj. (N), possible p. (F); of 3d pers. obj. of sub. mode (L).
6	-ko	Plural of pers. addressed in imperative (G, H); of 2d pers. obj. of sub. mode (L).
7	-lo	Singular of pers. addressed in imp. (G, H).
8	-no (-n-)	Singular of pers. addressed in imp. (H), possible s. (G).
9	-naa(-)	Plural of implied inan. obj. (B), inan. agentive actor (F); of 1st pers. possessor (D, E), psychol. subj. (F).
10	-waa(-)	Plural of 2d pers. subj. (A, B), possessor (D, E), psychol. subj. (F); of 3d pers. subj. (A, B, K, L), possessor (E), psychol. subj. (F); agentive actor (K, N); of an. noun (D); enters in formation of 2d pers. p. obj. (L, M).
11	-i	Singular of inan. noun (E), inan. intr. verb (I).
12	-a	Plural of inan. noun (E), inan. intr. verb (I).
13	-ti	Vocative p. of an. noun (D).
14	-hi	Voc. s. of an. noun (D).
15	-hhi	Diminutive s. of inan. noun (E).
16	-θa(-)	Dim. p. of inan. noun (E).
17	-li	Plural of inan. noun (E).

Suffixes expressing 1st and 2d person, with numerical surrogates in the twenties:

20	-i(-)	1st pers. obj. (A, G, L, M); enters in formation of 1st pers. ex. obj. (L, M).
21	-a(-)	1st pers. subj. (K, L), agentive actor (K, N); 2d pers. subj. (L), agentive actor (N); enters in formation of 1st pers. ex. obj. (L, M), agentive actor (N).
22	-aake	1st pers. ex. obj. (G), subj. (K, L), agentive actor (K).
23	-akwe	1st pers. inc. subj. (K, L), agentive actor (K, N); enters in formation of 1st pers. inc. obj. (L, M), 2d pers. p. obj. (L, M).
24	-ane -ani	2d pers. s. subj. (K, L), agentive actor (K).
25	-eekwe	2d pers. p. subj. (K, L), agentive actor (K, N).
26	-i (-eh-)	2d pers. subj. in ref. to 3d pers. implied obj. (G); 2d pers. obj. in ref. to 3d pers. subj. (L, M).
27	-ele(-) (-el-)	1st pers. subj. in ref. to 2d pers. obj. (A); 2d pers. obj. in ref. to 1st pers. subj. (A); enters in formation of 1st pers. inc. obj. (L, M), 2d pers. obj. (L, M).

Suffixes expressing 3d person, with numerical surrogates in the thirties:

30	-ka(-)	3d pers. subj. (J, M), psychol. subj. (N).
31	-ke(-)	Inan. 3d pers. subj. (I); an. 3d pers. subj. (L), obj. (L); enters in forma-
	-ki(-)	tion of 1st pers. ex. agentive actor (N).
32	-ta(-)	3d pers. subj. (J, M), psychol. subj. (N).
33	-te	3d pers. subj. (K, L), psychol. subj. (F), obj. (L), agentive actor (N).
	-či	
34	-aa(-)	3d pers. obj. (A, L, M), agentive actor (F), psychol. subj. (N).
35	-li	Obviative (less important of two 3d persons, explicit or implied) as s. obj. (A), subj. (C), possessor (D), agentive actor (F); as s. or p. subj. (J, K), agentive actor (K).
36	-hhi	Obv. as p. obj. (A), subj. (C), possessor (D), agentive actor (F).
37	-ii(-)	3d pers. agentive actor specifically not obv. (F).
	(-i(-))	

Suffixes expressing other notions and personal pronoun prefixes:

40	-y-	Indeterminate meaning (K, L, M).
41	-mV-	Indeterminate meaning (H, K, L, M).
42	-ki	Locative case (E).
43	-w(-)	Static voice (I). This suffix is also employed sporadically with animate verbs, but not in productive paradigms.
I	ni-	1st pers. subj. (A, B, C), psychol. subj. (F), possessor (D, E).
II	ki-	2d pers. subj. (A, B, C), psychol. subj. (F), possessor (D, E), obj. (or psychol. subj. if the ki-ele type is translated "you—by me") (A); enters in formation of 1st pers. inc. (A, B, C, D, E, F).
III	hw-	3d pers. subj. (A, B), psychol. subj. (F), possessor (D, E).

Identical and similar suffixes in the list given above may be distinguished or further distinguished by morphophonemic formulae of vocalic initials which are reflected in fusion with preceding elements.

Subordinate-mode paradigms may express conditional or other subordinating notions, depending on the subordinating stem in the verbal theme, but the conditional notion of subordination is pleonastically expressed by suffixes 5, 24, 31, 33 ending in -e in contrast to the -i ending in other types of subordination.

Most illustrative themes in the following paradigms represent types to which all paradigmatic suffixes may be appended without change in the theme. There are in addition pleomorphic themes: e.g., in one such theme the stem final vowel is -a in the expression of 1st and 2d persons, and -e in the expression of 3d person. The theory of presentation here followed is that the theme generally accommodates itself to the paradigm; accordingly, a description of these accommodations (pleomorphism) should be included in a study of themes rather than in a study of paradigms. Essentially, all that remains to be done is to classify themes into a few classes sharing characteristic changes in reference to paradigms.

As will be noted in the illustrative themes, subordinate modes are characteristically initiated by a subordinating primary stem; participial verbs usually show internal stem modification in the initial syllable of the theme.

The paradigms express some meanings which are not formally explicit. For example, the inanimate object of the transitive inanimate verbal themes is implied while the animate object of the transitive animate verbal themes is not only implied but is also as a general rule made explicit by paradigmatic suffixes.

Paradigm A, independent mode with transitive animate verbal theme: -kkil- TO HIDE ANIMATE OBJECT.

I—him	ni-kkil-a	(I-34)
you s—him	ki-kkil-a	(II-34)
I—them	ni-kkil-aaki	(I-34, 4)
you s—them	ki-kkil-aaki	(II-34, 4)
we ex—him, them	ni-kkil-aape	(I-34, 1)
we inc—him, them	ki-kkil-aape	(II-34, 1)
you p—him	ki-kkil-aawa	(II-34, 10)
you p—them	ki-kkil-aawaaki	(II-34, 10, 4)
I—you s	ki-kkil-ele	(II-27)
you s—me	ki-kkiš-i	(II-20)
we ex—you	ni-kkil-elepe	(I-27, 1)
you—us ex	ki-kkiš-ipe	(II-20, 1)
I—you p	ki-kkil-elepwa	(II-27, 2)
you p—me	ki-kkiš-ipwa	(II-20, 2)
he—him obviative	ho-kkil-aali	(III-34, 35)
he—them obv	ho-kkil-ahi	(III-34, 36)
they—him obv	ho-kkil-aawaali	(III-34, 10, 35)
they—them obv	ho-kkil-aawahi	(III-34, 10, 36)

Paradigm B, independent mode with transitive inanimate verbal theme: -kkitoo- TO HIDE INANIMATE OBJECT.

I—it	ni-kkito	(I-)
you s—it	ki-kkito	(II-)
he—it	ho-kkito	(III-)
I—them	ni-kkitoo-na	(I-9)
you s—them	ki-kkitoo-na	(II-9)
we ex—it, them	ni-kkitoo-pe	(I-1)
we inc—it, them	ki-kkitoo-pe	(II-1)
you p—it, them	ki-kkitoo-naawa	(II-9, 10)
they—it, them	ho-kkitoo-naawa	(III-9, 10)

Paradigm C, independent mode with animate intransitive verbal theme: hkawehšee- TO LISTEN.

I	ni-tkawehše	(I-)
you s	ki-tkawehše	(II-)
he	hkawehše	( )
we ex	ni-tkawehšee-pe	(I-1)
we inc	ki-tkawehšee-pe	(II-1)
you p	ki-tkawehšee-pwa	(II-2)
they	hkawehšee-ki	(-4)
they indefinite	hkawehšee-pi	(-3)
he obv	hkawehšee-li	(-35)
they obv	hkawehše-hi	(-36)

Paradigm D, possessive and absolute of animate noun. The illustrative themes are -čeeninaa- SIBLING, which does not occur vocatively; -kwihθa- SON; and since kinship terms occur only in possessed form, čiipaa- GHOST, for absolute forms.

vocative, noun s	ni-kwihθe-hi	(I–14)
vocative, noun p	ni-kwihθe-ti	(I–13)
my, noun s	ni-čeenina	(I–)
your s, noun s	ki-čeenina	(II–)
his, noun s	ho-čeenina	(III–)
my, noun p	ni-čeeninaa-ki	(I–4)
your s, noun p	ki-čeeninaa-ki	(II–4)
his, noun p	ho-čeeninaa-ki	(III–4)
our ex, noun s	ni-čeeninaa-na	(I–9)
our inc, noun s	ki-čeeninaa-na	(II–9)
our ex, noun p	ni-čeeninaa-naaki	(I–9, 4)
our inc, noun p	ki-čeeninaa-naaki	(II–9, 4)
your p, noun s	ki-čeeninaa-wa	(II–10)
your p, noun p	ki-čeeninaa-waaki	(II–10, 4)
obv his, noun s	ho-čeeninaa-li	(III–35)
obv their, noun s	ho-čeenina-hi	(III–36)
obv. his, noun p	ho-čeeninaa-waali	(III–10, 35)
obv their, noun p	ho-čeeninaa-wahi	(III–10, 36)
absolute, noun s	čiipa	( )
absolute, noun p	čiipaa-ki	(–4)

Paradigm E, possessive and absolute of inanimate noun. Most inanimate nouns have pleomorphic themes. We meet here also the phenomenon of subparadigms wherein certain classes of themes require one paradigm while other themes require an altered paradigm. The illustrative themes are tθani, tθaniwa- BED, for paradigm Ea; mahkiθe, mahkiθen(a) SHOE, for paradigm Eb (the long bases of themes of this type express dual number when no suffixes are added); hahpaši(i)-, hahpaše(e)-, and with intimate-possessive formative, hahpašim- STICK, for paradigm Ec. Themes requiring paradigm Eb are peculiar in that they do not tolerate the intimate-possessive suffix which is optional for other themes.

	Paradigm Ea	Paradigm Eb	Paradigm Ec
noun s:			
my	ni-tθani (I)	ni-mahkiθe (I)	ni-tahpašim-i (I 11)
you s	ki-tθani (II–)	ki-mahkiθe (II–)	ki-tahpašim-i (II–11)
his	ho-tθani (III–)	ho-mahkiθa (III–)	ho-tahpašim-i (III–11)
noun p:			
my	ni-tθaniwa-li (I–17)	ni-mahkiθena-ki (I–4)	ni-tahpašim-a (I–12)
you s	ki-tθaniwa-li (II–17)	ki-mahkiθena-ki (II–4)	ki-tahpašim-a (II–12)
his	ho-tθaniwa-li (III–17)	ho-mahkiθena-ki (III–4)	ho-tahpašim-a (III–12)

	Paradigm Ea	*Paradigm Eb*	*Paradigm Ec*
noun s or p:			
our ex	ni-tθane-na (I–9)	ni-mahkiθene-na (I–9)	ni-tahpašim-e-na (I–12?–9)
our inc	ki-tθane-na (II–9)	ki-mahkiθene-na (II–9)	ki-tahpašim-e-na (II–12?–9)
your p	ki-tθani-wa (II–10)	ki-mahkiθen-wa (II–10)	ki-tahpašim-wa (II–10)
their	ho-tθani-wa (III–10)	ho-mahkiθen-wa (III–10)	ho-tahpašim-wa (III–10)
absolute:			
locative	tθane-ki (–42)	mahkiθene-ki (–42)	hahpašii-ki (–42)
diminutive s	tθane-hi (–15)	mahkiθene-hi (–15)	hahpaši-hi (–15)
diminutive p	tθanee-θali (–16, 17)	mahkiθenee-θa (–16)	hahpašee-θa (–16)
noun s	tθani ( )	mahkiθe ( )	hahpaši ( )
noun p	tθaniwa-li (–17)	mahkiθena-ki (–4)	hahpaše ( )

Paradigm F, passive definite of independent mode and of participial mode (one form) and of subordinate mode (three forms). The passive definite is a passive in which the agentive actor as well as the psychological subject is specified (e.g., kikkilekwa you, psychological subject, are concealed by him, agentive actor) in contrast to the passive indefinite in which only the psychological subject is specified. Both types of passives are formed by formative suffixes. But passive indefinite suffixes form intransitive themes which are inflected in intransitive theme paradigms while the passive definite formative forms a theme which requires a special paradigm.

The first eight forms of paradigm F are noteworthy because the agentive actor is an inanimate object despite the fact that the passive definite verbal theme includes a transitive animate suffix which officially implies an animate object; however, the animate object is usually made explicit paradigmatically but in the eight forms in question neither animate nor inanimate object is paradigmatically explicit.

Compare the animate personal relations of the independent mode of paradigm F with those of paradigm A: 1st or 2d person subjective with 1st or 2d person objective is expressed by paradigm A and not by paradigm F; 1st or 2d person subjective with 3d person objective is expressed by paradigm A but paradigm A lacks expression of 3d person subjective with 1st or 2d person objective while precisely this relationship is expressed by paradigm F, i.e., 3d person agentive actor with 1st or 2d person psychological subject; only when both terms of the predication are 3d persons do paradigms A and F duplicate each other: paradigm A expresses 3d person subjective with 3d person objective and paradigm F expresses 3d person agentive actor with 3d person psychological subject.

The illustrative themes for paradigm F are -kkilekw- TO BE CONCEALED BY

AGENTIVE ACTOR, for independent mode; kekkilekw- for participial mode; yekkilekw- for subordinate mode.

I—by inan actor	ni-kkileko	(I-)
you s—by inan actor	ki-kkileko	(II-)
he, they—by inan actor	ho-kkileko	(III-)
we ex—by inan actor	ni-kkileko-pe	(I-1)
we inc—by inan actor	ki-kkileko-pe	(II-1)
you p—by inan actor	ki-kkileko-pwa	(II-2)
alternative for above	ki-kkileko-naawa	(II-9, 10)
they—by inan actor	ho-kkileko-naawa	(III-9, 10)
I—by him	ni-kkilekw-a	(I-34)
you s—by him	ki-kkilekw-a	(II-34)
I—by them	ni-kkilekoo-ki	(I-4)
you s—by them	ki-kkilekoo-ki	(II-4)
I—by them indefinite	ni-kkilekoo-pi	(I-3)
you s—by them indefinite	ki-kkilekoo-pi	(II-3)
we ex—by him	ni-kkileko-na	(I-9)
we inc—by him	ki-kkileko-na	(II-9)
we ex—by them	ni-kkileko-naaki	(I-9, 4)
we inc—by them	ki-kkileko-naaki	(II-9, 4)
you p—by him	ki-kkileko-wa	(II-10)
you p—by them	ki-kkileko—waaki	(II-10, 4)
he—by him obviative	ho-kkilekoo-li	(III-35)
he—by them obv	ho-kkileko-hi	(III-36)
they—by him obv	ho-kkileko-waali	(III-10, 35)
they—by them obv	ho-kkileko-wahi	(III-10, 36)
he, they—by him	ho-kkilekw-i	(III-37)
he, they—by them	ho-kkilekw-iiki	(III-37, 4)
One(s) who—by him, them	kekkilekw-ki	(-37, 5)
he—by him, them obv	yekkileko-či	(-33)
they—by him, them obv	yekkileko-waači	(-10, 33)
he, they—by him, them	yekkilekw-iči	(-37, 33)

Paradigm G, imperative mode with transitive animate verbal theme: kkil- TO HIDE ANIMATE OBJECT.

you s—him, them	kkiš-i	(-26)
you p—him, them	kkil-ehko	(-26, 6)
you s—me	kkiš-ilo	(-20, 7)
you p—me	kkiš-iko	(-20, 6)
you—us ex	kkiš-inaake	(-20, 8, 22)

Paradigm H, imperative mode with animate intransitive or transitive inanimate verbal theme. All animate intransitive themes and transitive inanimate themes in $o, e, e/i, i$ require subparadigm Ha; transitive inanimate themes in a require subparadigm Hb. The illustrative themes are kkitoo- TO HIDE INANIMATE OBJECT, for Ha; mkaweeleta- TO REMEMBER INANIMATE OBJECT for Hb.

	Paradigm Ha	Paradigm Hb
you s—it, them	kkitoo-lo (-7)	mkaweeleta-no (-8)
you p—it, them	kkitoo-ko (-6)	mkaweeleta-moko (-41, 6)

Paradigm I, independent, subordinate, and participial modes with inanimate intransitive verbal theme. The illustrative themes are kinwaa- IT IS LONG, for Ia, weškalet-, weškaleh- (pleomorphic theme) IT IS ROTTEN, for Ib, waapškiyaa- IT IS WHITISH, for Ic.

	Paradigm Ia	Paradigm Ib	Paradigm Ic
indep s	kinwaa-wi (-43, 11)	weškalet-wi (-43, 11)	waapškiya ( )
indep p	kinwaa-wa (-43, 12)	weškalet-o (-43)	waapškiya ( )
subordinate or part mode	kinwaa-ki (-31)	weškaleh-ki (-31)	waapškiyaa-ki (-31)

The subordinate mode may be distinguished in theme from the participial, or the forms for the two modes may be identical as in the examples cited.

Paradigm J, participial mode with animate intransitive or transitive inanimate verbal theme. Certain animate intransitive themes and transitive inanimate themes in *o, i, e/i* require subparadigm Ja; other animate intransitive themes and transitive inanimate themes in *e* and *a* require subparadigm Jb. Subparadigm Ja alone tolerates the obviative. The illustrative themes are kekkitoo- ONE WHO HIDES INANIMATE OBJECT, for Ja, and meemhkaweeleta- ONE WHO REMEMBERS INANIMATE OBJECT, for Jb.

	Paradigm Ja	Paradigm Jb
One who—it, them	kekkitoo-ta (-32)	meemhkaweeleta-ka (-30)
Ones who—it, them	kekkitoo-čki (-32, 5)	meemhkaweeleta-kki (-30, 5)
obv one who—it, them	kekkitoo-lita (-35, 32)	
obv ones who—it, them	kekkitoo-lički (-35, 32, 5)	

Paradigm K, subordinate mode with animate intransitive theme, or transitive inanimate theme having an initial subordinating stem in composition; if a transitive inanimate theme shows participial stem modification, the resulting verb receives a participial translation suggestive of paradigm J; however, the implied inanimate object of the verbal theme functions as psychological subject while the persons expressed by the paradigm function as agentive actors, suggestive of paradigm F (e.g., kekkitooya the thing which is concealed by me. Cf. the same paradigmatic form but with theme having initial subordinating stem in composition, yekkitooya when I concealed it). The illustrative themes are yehpenhšin-, yehpenhši- (pleomorphic) TO FALL OFF, for subparadigm Ka, and kekkitoo- (participial-passive type) INANIMATE OBJECT IMPLIED CONCEALED BY AGENTIVE ACTOR, for subparadigm Kb.

Paradigm Ka	Paradigm Kb	Paradigm Ka	Paradigm Kb
I,	-by me	yehpenhšin-a (-21)	kekkitoo-ya (-40, 21)
we ex,	-by us ex	yehpenhšin-aake (-22)	kekkitoo-yaake (-40, 22)
we inc,	-by us inc	yehpenhšin-akwe (-23)	kekkitoo-yakwe (-40, 23)

Paradigm Ka	Paradigm Kb	Paradigm Ka	Paradigm Kb
you s,	-by you s	yehpenhšin-ani (–24)	kekkitoo-yani (–40, 24)
you p,	-by you p	yehpenhšin-eekwe (–25)	kekkitoo-yeekwe (–40, 25)
he,	-by him	yehpenhši-ki (–31)	kekkitoo-či (–33)
they,	-by them	yehpenhši-waači (–10, 33)	kekkitoo-waači (–10, 33)
he or they obv,	-by him or them obv	yehpenhši-liči (–35, 33)	kekkitoo-liči (–35, 33)

Certain types of animate intransitive themes and transitive inanimate themes in *e* require subparadigm Kc, which differs from subparadigm Kb only in that the expression of "he -by him" employs suffix 31 (as in Ka) instead of suffix 33. Transitive inanimate themes in *a* require subparadigm Kd, which differs from Ka only in that suffix 41 precedes all the Ka suffixes except suffix 31.

Paradigm L, subordinate mode with transitive animate verbal theme: yekkil- TO HIDE ANIMATE OBJECT.

he—him, them	yekkil-aači	(–34, 33)
they—him, them	yekkil-aawaači	(–34, 10, 33)
he—me	yekkiš-iči	(–20, 33)
he, they—us ex	yekkiš-iyameči	(–20, 40, 21, 41, 33)
he, they—you s	yekkil-ehki	(–26, 31)
he, they—us inc	yekkil-elakwe	(–27, 23)
he, they—you p	yekkil-elwaakwe	(–27, 10, 23)
we inc—him, them	yekkil-akwe	(–23)
you p—him, them	yekkil-eekwe	(–25)
you s—him, them	yekkil-ači	(–21, 33)
we ex—him, them	yekkil-akiči	(–21, 31, 33)
I—him	yekkil-aki	(–21, 31)
I—them	yekkil-akki	(–21, 31, 5)
you s—me	yekkiš-iyani	(–20, 40, 24)
you p—me	yekkiš-iyeekwe	(–20, 40, 25)
you—us ex	yekkiš-iyaake	(–20, 40, 22)
I—you s	yekkil-ela	(–27, 21)
I—you p	yekkil-elako	(–27, 21, 6)
we ex—you	yekkil-elaake	(–27, 22)

Paradigm M, participial mode with transitive animate verbal theme: kekkil- ONE WHO HIDES ANIMATE OBJECT.

One who—him, them	kekkil-aata	(–34, 32)
Ones who—him, them	kekkil-aački	(–34, 32, 5)
One who—me	kekkiš-ita	(–20, 32)
Ones who—me	kekkiš-ički	(–20, 32, 5)
One who—us ex	kekkiš-iyameta	(–20, 40, 21, 41, 32)
Ones who—us ex	kekkiš-iyamečki	(–20, 40, 21, 41, 32, 5)
One who—you s	kekkil-ehka	(–26, 30)
Ones who—you s	kekkil-ekki	(–26, 30, 5)
One(s) who—us inc	kekkil-elakwe	(–27, 23)
One(s) who—you p	kekkil-elwaakwe	(–27, 10, 23)

Paradigm N, participial mode of transitive animate verbal theme with the implied animate object of the verbal theme functioning as a psychological subject and the paradigmatically expressed persons functioning as agentive actors. This is comparable to the alternative possibility in paradigm K. The illustrative theme here is kekkil- ONE WHO IS CONCEALED BY AGENTIVE ACTOR.

One(s) who—by him	kekkil-aači	(–34, 33)
One(s) who—by them	kekkil-aawaači	(–34, 10, 33)
One(s) who—by us inc	kekkil-akwe	(–23)
One(s) who—by you p	kekkil-eekwe	(–25)
One who—by you s	kekkil-ata	(–21, 32)
Ones who—by you s	kekkil-ački	(–21, 32, 5)
One who—by us ex	kekkil-akita	(–21, 31, 32)
Ones who—by us ex	kekkil-akički	(–21, 31, 32, 5)
One who—by me	kekkil-aka	(–21, 30)
Ones who—by me	kekkil-akki	(–21, 30, 5)

Paradigms in L, M, and N are paradigmatically comparable. When paradigm L has 3d person subjective and 3d person objective, corresponding forms are found in paradigms M and N. When paradigm L has 3d person subjective with 1st or 2d person objective, corresponding forms are found in paradigm M but not in paradigm N. When paradigm L has 3d person objective with 1st or 2d person subjective, corresponding forms are found in paradigm N but not in paradigm M. When paradigm L has 1st or 2d person subjective with 1st or 2d person objective, corresponding forms are found neither in paradigm M nor in paradigm N. A schematic table of number surrogates shows these relationships:

Paradigm L	Paradigm M	Paradigm N
(34, 33)	(34, 32)	(34, 33)
(34, 10, 33)	(34, 32, 5)	(34, 10, 33)
(20, 33)	(20, 32)	
	(20, 32, 5)	
(20, 40, 21, 41, 33)	(20, 40, 21, 41, 32)	
	(20, 40, 21, 41, 32, 5)	
(26, 31)	(26, 30)	
	(26, 30, 5)	
(27, 23)	(27, 23)	
(27, 10, 23)	(27, 10, 23)	
(23)		(23)
(25)		(25)
(21, 33)		(21, 32)
		(21, 32, 5)
(21, 31, 33)		(21, 31, 32)
		(21, 31, 32, 5)
(21, 31)		(21, 30)
(21, 31, 5)		(21, 30, 5)
(20, 40, 24)		
(20, 40, 25)		
(20, 40, 22)		
(27, 21)		
(27, 21, 6)		
(27, 22)		

I take these paradigms to be sets of forms which show a certain variety within an empirically limited morphological and semantic framework, and try to avoid so far as possible the conveniences of linguistic fictions. The sets given above (A–N) include all productive paradigms (Algonkinists will note that the so-called reflexive is here thought of as two paradigms, a transitive inanimate verb, e.g., I SEE, followed by an inflected noun, e.g., MYSELF), and also include all forms within any one paradigm, as given by informants paradigmatically conscious. Paradigms established in this way were checked by the everyday speech of informants, but not by textual material; or rather, textual material reflecting obsolete speech shows certain slight extensions of what informants expressed as live paradigms. Thus, if the obsolete in addition to the present-day status of the language were to be accounted for, the passive theme in -(e)kw- would be regarded as employing most of the forms of paradigm K instead of only two forms which are in present-day speech felt to be a part of or an extension of paradigm F; the obviative would be employed a little more freely with animate nouns; and the same nouns would occasionally tolerate the locative, a toleration which is frowned upon by informants when considered in the abstract.

YALE UNIVERSITY,
NEW HAVEN, CONNECTICUT.

THE SOCIAL CONFIGURATION OF MAGICAL BEHAVIOR: A STUDY OF THE NATURE OF MAGIC

By W. Lloyd Warner

THE EIGHT MURNGIN TRIBES, whose social data are used as the materials for the demonstration of the theory of magic offered in this paper, are located west of the Gulf of Carpentaria and south of the Sea of Arafura in north Australia. They conform physically and socially to the general type of Australian aborigine. They possess a complex kinship system, patrilineal clans and moieties, and an age-graded structure which separates males and females and divides the men into several grades based on initiation into the ritual mysteries. They are totemic and have a large number of very elaborate rituals associated with the clan and moiety totems.

I. DESCRIPTION OF MURNGIN MAGIC WITH DETAILED DATA

Among all the clans of the eight tribes and all the members of the groups there is a profound belief in magic. The effects of its power are twofold: it can harm and destroy, or it can benefit and cure. Among the northern clans of the Murngin and Yaernungo there is a belief in magic, but there are no magicians of any kind, while among the southern and more western tribes magicians both evil and good are found everywhere. The "black" magician, to use the common ethnographic designation, can kill or injure his victim, and the "white" magician can cure him or restore his lost powers. All deaths, sicknesses, certain types of bad luck, and in general all those cases where the individual is seriously out of adjustment with his community, physically, mentally, or socially, are looked upon as the effects of black magic, while in almost every case except that of soul stealing the white magician is called in to remedy the situation. There is here a kind of warfare between the forces which do good and those which do harm to man. The latter are related to an organized set of concrete techniques embodied in the person of the black magician, while those forces which control the effects of black magic have an entirely different set to give them practical expression as part of the personality of the white magician. The struggle then becomes a warfare between these two types of magical personalities. This does not mean that they are necessarily enemies, though they usually are; further, a black magician is not looked upon by all men as fearsome, because to his own group he is a constant source of strength since its members seek his aid in repaying a wrong done to them by another group.

Occasionally, when a very old person dies, the diagnosis is: "It was nothing, just old age"—but this is very rare. Among some of the magical causes are: (1) the machinations of an evil magician; (2) possession by an evil ghost (mokoi); and (3) ritual uncleanliness. Their effects can be cured by: (1) ritual; (2) white magic; and (3) very occasionally, natural remedies. In the following pages devoted to Murngin magic we shall first describe black magic and the sorcerer, then white magic and the healer, and finally analyze these concrete data in order to determine the nature of Murngin magic. To do this we shall first examine the internal evidence presented by the activities of the black and white magicians in the southern areas in the hope that we shall thus illuminate our understanding of the functions of magic. We shall next consider the northern area without magicians, comparing it with the southern area to ascertain if this test situation throws any light upon the nature of magic and its possible relation to ritual and religion. After this we shall apply our findings to the theories held by Hubert, Mauss, and Durkheim[1]—particularly to their theory that magic is an individualistic technique without a church, therefore different from and antithetical to religion, the fundamental basis of which is its church organization. The last section of this essay will present a sociological interpretation of black and white magic that will take account of all the Murngin magical data, demonstrating that magic is a part of religion and, exactly like it, has its church.

Black Magic and the Sorcerer

The Murngin believe in a number of methods by which sorcerers can kill their victims. One of the more popular ideas is that the magician goes into the bush and makes a long turtle rope. When it is completed he brings it near the camp and hides it in preparation for the magical slaying of a tribesman. This is all done in secrecy. In this type of killing two people participate. In the middle of the night or early morning the two approach the camp where the one they intend killing is asleep. They crawl up near him. One man takes the rope, makes a loop in it, and slides it over the victim's head. While doing this he lies down beside him so as not to be observed by anyone who might be awake; or, if the victim should waken, to make him believe he is one of the man's wives. If all goes well he pushes the rope around the sleeping man's neck. Meanwhile the accomplice holds the opposite end of the rope some few paces away from the main camp. He has been told before that as soon as the killer gives a pull on the rope the cord will be properly placed. The helper starts twisting the rope while the other man sneaks away. He continues to twist it until he starts to choke the sleeper. The two then pull the struggling man toward them, pick him up and carry him to a safe place in the jungle. The one who has crawled into the camp lies beside the man's wives with whom he is supposed to copulate in the perfect killing.

The other magician, meanwhile, opens the left side of the man, who is now presumed to be in a dead faint, slits the skin between two ribs, somewhat

---

[1] Emile Durkheim, Elementary Forms of the Religious Life. (Transl. J. W. Swain.) New York, Macmillan, 1926. Hubert and Mauss, Théorie Générale de la Magie, Année Sociologique, vol. 7 (Paris).

below the heart, pulls the two ribs back, then covers his arm and hand with orchid juice and places a small sharpened hardwood stick in the palm with the sharpened end in his fingers. The victim is breathing heavily; when he inhales the magician pushes his hand upward, when he exhales the magician holds his hand. When the sorcerer reaches the heart he thrusts the killing stick into it and withdraws his hand from the body.

The victim's body is now held so that the trunk is leaning down and the blood is allowed to run into a paper bark receptacle or a waterproof basket. When the heart stops beating this is supposed to let the soul out, because in the native thinking the heart's blood is different from the body's blood, the home of the soul being in the heart. The basket of blood is carried away by the killer and hidden some distance away. The magician returns, puts the ribs in their places, and smooths the flesh upon them. He then builds a small fire. He heats his spear thrower in the fire, and rubs it against the wound. Previous to the killing he has gathered a nest of green ants and a small lizard, which are mashed together. The juice is taken from them and rubbed on the wound. The heating and rubbing continues until the opening is completely closed and all traces of the wound are gone.

When this part of the operation is completed the magician turns the body on its back. The large intestine protrudes several feet because of the magical death. A few green ants are shaken on the cut. They bite the flesh and the intestine retreats within the hole very much like a snake.

The spear thrower is then dipped in the heart's blood and whirled around the victim's head. The body quivers. The weapon is once more dipped into the heart's blood and waved again. He breathes heavily. This occurs several times until the man who lost his soul sits up and looks very much as before the magical "killing."

The operator now hits him on the head and tells him he will not remember what has happened to him. He is ordered to open his mouth and the magician twists his tongue so that the top of it lies on the bottom of the mouth and the reverse side faces the palate. He is told that in three days—but there is no particular set time or magical number—he will die: "The first day you will be very happy, the next day you will be sick, and the third day you will die." He goes back to his camp.

The magician sneaks away in the bush and returns to his own camp. The man who has lost his soul feels very weak. His wives ask if he has had his soul stolen, and he says, "Oh, no, I have had dysentery and I am very sick from it." The first day he feels very well, finds an abundance of food, and seems very cheerful; the second day he sickens, and the third day he dies. A "white" magician is then called by the relatives to ascertain who has been responsible for the death. He looks at the dead man to see what spirits are standing beside him, for the spirits of the killers are nearly always to be found by their victim's corpse, but only medicine men can see them. The doctor then announces who has done the deed and the relatives then start to discuss the best way of avenging the death.

A Case History of the Sorcerer Laindjura

One of the most noted killers in the southeastern Murngin country was Laindjura, who had destroyed many victims by black magic. As an individual he was not very different from the ordinary man in the tribe, although possibly a bit more alert. He was a good hunter as well as an excellent wood carver, and had several wives and a number of children. There was nothing sinister, peculiar, or psychopathic about him, for he was perfectly normal in all of his behavior. Among his own people the attitudes were no different toward him than toward any other man in the clan. It was extremely difficult, however, to obtain Laindjura's confidence to the point where he would talk about his activities as a sorcerer. Although he and I were on very friendly terms it was not until my second field trip into the area that he gave me long accounts of his various killings.

It is impossible definitely to evaluate how much Laindjura and other killers believed the case histories which they gave me. There was no doubt in my own thinking that Laindjura believed a great part of them. Since he was constantly credited and blamed by friends and enemies for certain deaths, he may at first have taken an attitude "as if" he had done these things and ultimately come to believe that he had actually performed the operations he claimed he had. A black sorcerer who is credited with many killings has a rather difficult time among the people surrounding his own group, and under most circumstances it is more difficult and unpleasant to be so classed than as an ordinary man; hence a man would not practice such complete duplicity as these stories might indicate unless the setting were extraordinary from our point of view.

The killing of Bom-li-tjir-i-li's wife.—"All of us were camping at Marunga Island. We were looking for oysters. This woman I was about to kill was hunting for lilies that day, for the other women had gone another way to search for oysters. I carried a hatchet with me and watched her. The woman gathered her lily bulbs, then left the swamp, went back on the sandy land and lay down in the shade. She covered herself with paper bark to keep warm because she had been in the lily pond and felt cold. Only her head came out from the bark. She could not see me.

"I sneaked up and hit her between the eyes with the head of a tomahawk. She kicked, and tried to rise up but couldn't. Her eyes turned up as if she was dead. I picked her up under the arms and dragged her to a mangrove jungle and laid her down. She was a young girl.

"I split a mangrove stick from off a tree and sharpened it. I took some djel-kurk (orchid bulb) first and got it ready. I did not have my spear thrower with me, so I took the handle off my tomahawk and jabbed about the skin on her mons veneris which was attached to her vagina and pushed it back. I pushed the skin up to her navel.

"Her large intestine protruded as though it were red calico. I covered my arm with orchid juice. I covered the killing stick with it, too. I put the stick in the palm of my hand so that I could push the point upward with my thumb. When she inhaled I pushed my arm in a little. When she exhaled I stopped. Little by little I got my hand inside her. Finally I touched her heart. I pushed the killing stick with my thumb up over the palm, which pressed the stick against my fingers, into her heart. She had a very large heart and I had to push harder than usual.

"I pulled the stick out. I stood behind her and held her up with her breasts in my hands. She was in a squatting position.

"Her heart's blood ran out into the paper-bark basket I had left to catch it in. It ran slower and slower and then stopped. I laid her down and took the blood away. I hid it. I came back and broke a nest of green ants off a tree. I laid it near her. I put the live ants on her skin. I did not squeeze them, for I was in a hurry because I was afraid her relatives would come looking for her. The skin, when bitten by the ants, moved by itself downward from her navel and covered her bones over her mons veneris.

"I then took some dry mud from an old lily pond. I put my sweat on the mud and warmed it over the fire. I put it against her to heal the wound so that no trace would be felt of what I had done. I was careful that none of her pubic hair should be left inside her uterus so that it would be felt by her husband or seen by the women. I kept up the mud applications until the vagina looked as it did before. I put blood and sweat in the mud and warmed it and put it inside the uterus. I did this again, using the mud, sweat, and blood. I did this six or eight times. The inside now was as it was before.

"I turned her over. Her large intestine stuck out several feet. I shook some green ants on it. It went in some little way. I shook some more on, and a little receded. I shook some more, and all of it went in. Everything was all right now. There was no trace of the wound.

"I took the tomahawk handle which had her heart's blood on it. I whirled it around her head. Her head moved slowly. I whirled it again. She moved some more. The spirit that belonged to that dead woman went into my heart then. I felt it go in. I whirled the stick again and she gasped for breath. I jumped over her and straightened her toes and fingers. She blew some breath out of her mouth and was all right.

"It was noontime. I said to her: 'You go eat some lilies.' The woman got up and walked away. She went around another way. I said to that woman: 'You will live two days. One day you will be happy, the next day you will be sick.' The woman went to the place where I had found her. She went to sleep. I took her blood and went away. The other women came from where they had been gathering oysters. They were laughing and talking. They awakened the girl. She picked up her lily bulbs and went to the camp with the women.

"The next day she walked around and played, laughed, talked, and made fun and gathered a lot of oysters and lilies. She came back to camp that night. She brought the things she had gathered into camp. She lay down and died that night."

White Magic and the Healer

White magic is an effective force used to cure sickness, heal wounds, remove the malignant effect of a snakebite, and, in general, to remove from the individual a feeling of dysphoria, giving him a sense of well-being and an adjustment to his community.

The white magician usually performs this function and applies this power. He can remove foreign objects which have been shot into the body of the sick man and diagnose on the principle that the patient can live if the cause of illness is only a foreign object, but must die if his soul is stolen.

II. A SOCIOLOGICAL INTERPRETATION OF BLACK AND WHITE MAGIC

Statement of the Problem

Durkheim's "church" among the Arunta is a clan organization. Each clan celebrates its spiritual unity through the unifying concept of the totem and with such objective symbols as the totemic emblem, its ritual and myths. Magic and the magician, on the other hand, fail to become part of religion and are antithetical to it because they have no church, says Durkheim. It is the thesis of this essay that the essential nature of magic and ritual is the same, both expressing a fundamental unity and primarily functioning alike for the individual and for the group, at least in Murngin society.

The analysis of Murngin magic to determine its nature is divided into the following attempts at proof: (1) testing the magical beliefs of the North, which does not possess magical "techniques," by comparing them with those of the South, which does; (2) examining the social configuration of magic, not only in the North but also in the South, to see how the individual and the society behave when magic is put into effect.

THE TEST OF THE NORTHERN AND SOUTHERN AREAS

The Murgin offer an excellent opportunity to study the nature of magic in relation to the social organization and society generally, particularly in relation to religion. The northern and eastern clans lack the medicine men of the southern and western clans, and depend on one of the rituals for healing. The social organization of both groups is identical, the kinship system, moiety divisions, and so forth, being the same even in minute detail. We can thus observe what elements are found in the nonpersonalized magic of the north and how they operate in the area of the southern shamans. From this we can possibly find what generalized elements of the culture are organized into the social personality of the medicine man. As our analysis develops it may be possible to determine whether ritual and magic are essentially different in their fundamentals. In the north the therapeutic magic is a curative ritual; the two are one. The ritual used here is part of the mourning ceremony belonging to the ordinary garma variety. This curing ritual may serve as a circumcision rite if the group needs a short ceremony to circumcise a boy before the wet season starts.

The society goes through a prophylactic performance at its yearly totemic ritual; at the death of a member there is a prophylactic ceremony in the mourning rite for the recently dead, which, in that aspect of its expression, is as much magical as it is religious, the purposes and social forces behind it being both. If the mourning ceremony were not held the soul would linger with the living, causing sickness and possible death. The leaf ceremony in the mourning rite chases the dead soul away. The various communions exclude the soul from the group, the entire mourning ceremony forcing it out of the society and into the totemic well. The sacred cannot remain with the profane; as Durkheim has pointed out, sacredness is contagious, hence dangerous (a lingering soul might make the living ill), and the two realms must be kept separate.

The medicine man who removes the hard object from within the organism caused by a malignant mokoi (trickster or evil spirit), or the bone injected by an outraged totemic being or another sorcerer, is doing the same thing for the society and its individuals as the mourning rite. The magician too is performing a ritual which has no validity, as he has no position or power, unless the group sanctions it. The medicine man's social personality and the sources of his power are located within the group. The white magician is but the reverse of the coin on whose other surface appears the black sorcerer. The white magician through his personal mana helps the sick individual to readjust himself to his social environment.

A prerequisite of social conditioning and adjustment is a normal organism, normal not only in biological fact but also in the values of the group. The normal human being, not only among the savage Murngin but in any society, according to the evaluations of the group, is the "well" person. Sickness is felt by civilized man to be expectable but not normal, largely because sickness interferes with his ordinary participation in his culture. Both the savage and civilized man consider sickness out of the ordinary, even though all organisms experience it, not only because of the lack of physical well-being, but also because the individual's daily social life is changed.

The effect of black magic is found only when the social personality of the victim is out of adjustment with its environment and fails to keep a satisfactory equilibrium. The victim is sick, he fails in the hunt or in fishing, he has his women taken from him, he is wounded in a spear fight or falls from a tree, and, in general, he is not in a state of well-being. His physical energy is not sufficient to keep up the multiple activities of his social personality, he feels himself on the debit side, with his individual mana inadequate for adjustment, his social personality dysphoric and maladjusted. While feeling the effects of black magic his condition greatly resembles the condition of an obsessive psychotic individual in our Euro-American culture, since both the individual and his society recognize his inadequate adaptation. The extreme of this maladjustment is the person whose soul has been stolen—the ultimate in black magic. The soul, the sacred individualization of power and the epitome of the social participation of the organism, seems lost to the individual owner and under the control of another, that is, the human part of the man has been stolen and lost to him.

The white shaman functions as one who reëstablishes the victim's social equilibrium. The society positively sanctions his actions by placing its belief in the magical and social mana under his control. The ceremonial leader in the north performs these same functions. Even here a man can be killed or made ill by magic: by black magicians, mokois, and so forth, who are outside the society, by the magicians to the south, and by the mokois, the asocial trickster spirits of the jungles.

The ailing member of society in the north must also be cured and regain his vigor and feeling of power. There being no medicine man here, herbs are used, but the native considers them insufficient. In this area the curative technique is the well ritual—a "secret" thing caused the sickness and a sacred ritual is to remove it. The individual is placed in the well, sung over, ritually cleaned, and regarded as cured by the ceremonial leader in the clan exactly as the tribe is purified and sickness prevented by ritual, and exactly as the victim of magic is healed by the magical technique of the medicine man in the south and in the Murngin country. In the north the ceremonial leader directs the healing ritual when the solidarity of the clan and the group is felt at its greatest strength. The whole of the social forces are focused on the individual through the totems, the totem well, and the attitudes and beliefs of the participants. The leader merely expresses through his direction of the ritual the social mana of the ritual in the group. This power is believed to go into the individual and remove his weakness. The leader functions here as in the Djungguan ceremony when he directs the ritual over the python totemic emblem to sing power into it, or at the bloodletting in this same ceremony when he places the power of the python spirit into the individual and his blood, which is to be used in the circumcision ritual. It is not the leader who has this power, but the ritual of his group. The power and efficacy of the ritual come from the mana of the entire group, organized into a society of clans. The leader, then, in the north cures by ritual and performs those functions carried out by the medicine man in the south. His activities are organized by his clan, he represents his church in the Durkheim sense, not only as a religious ritual leader but also in the functions of a magician. The clan, however, in both cases is the "church" behind him. In the south the leader's powers are divided. The well ritual may still be used, but there is also the white magician here. His social personality is little different from that of another member of the clan. He differs inasmuch as it is recognized that he has a special power. He is sought by the afflicted, however, exactly as a ceremonial leader in this area is sought by the relatives of the dead or by the parents of a boy who is to be circumcised. The relatives of a sick man send for the shaman to cure and diagnose the illness of their ailing kinsman and either to restore him to his normal participation in the group or to pronounce his death sentence. *The medicine man then helps organize and direct the community's attitudes toward the sick man.* He directs the community's attitudes and fundamentally organizes the community, like the ceremonial leader. He examines his patient, says that he will die because his soul has been stolen, and the community at once recognizes that death is near. The society organizes itself then into a group which in effect excommunicates the patient, trying to force his soul into the realm of the dead and the sacred. If the magician diagnoses the case as curable and removes the cause, he reëstablishes the individual's equilibrium, making him believe he can once more participate in his usual manner in the group. He can do this because he organizes group attitude, since the belief in the curative power of this ritual unifies the point of view of all the members. The magician, while healing, is usually watched by a number of the near and far kinsmen. They all express great satisfaction in his removal of the sickness (the foreign object) and an affirmation of the victim's cure, as do the magician and the victim.

The Behavior of the Individual and the Society When Magic Is Put Into Effect

The isolation of the various elements in the particular social configuration surrounding the death of a victim of black magic may help to illuminate the fundamental nature of Murngin magic and explain its potency and unusual effectiveness, and a general analysis of the group behavior under such a situation will be profitable.

When the supposed theft of a man's soul becomes general knowledge, the sustaining social fabric pulls away from the victim. The familial attitudes of the kinship personalities change, the collaboration of the victim and his society, in which his social personality has always been an integral part, ceases. The group now acts with all the ramifications of its organization and with the countless stimuli positively to suggest death to a suggestible individual. The ordinary daily activity of the victim's social life is removed. The society itself creates a situation which, if unchanged, makes it impossible for the individual to adjust himself to it even though he should try, but in addition to such pressure he usually not only makes no effort to live and to remain a part of his group but actually, through the multiple suggestions from it, coöperates in his withdrawal therefrom. He becomes what his society's attitudes make him, committing a kind of *suicide*. The social configuration in which he finds himself operating at this time is one of anomia[3] for him. His ordinary social personality is removed, his part of the social structure having not only disintegrated but also in large part disappeared. Such a man is neither in the world of the ordinary nor in that of the sacred. He is, to use the literal Murngin expression, "half dead." Partly sacred, since his soul is not in this world, he is in a position of danger, not only to himself as a spiritual entity, since his soul is neither in this world nor in its proper place in the totemic well, but also to his group, because a soul not properly ritualized and placed in the sacred well with the totemic spirits and sacred ancestors is likely to cause illnesses and death to those near to him in kinship. Before death takes place the group, then, begins the mourning ritual, the object of which is to transmute the social personality into a spiritual being, that is, to make the soul safely enter the totem well. Even before death the soul starts behaving like the sacred totem; the ancestors and dead relatives come for him and enter his heart; the soul "ceases" reciprocal relations with the profane living, relating itself to the sacred dead; and the living cease acting their everyday rôles and become virtually related to the sacred part of the dying person.

The personality of the victim thus has the ordinary attitudes of society removed from him, the taboo attitude of the sacred being substituted. He responds by recognizing his change of status: the wounded feudist killed by magic dances his totem dance to make himself like his totem and insure his immediate passage to the totem well; the man dying of an illness moves his hands convulsively like his crab totem or flaps his hands like his black duck

[3] Emile Durkheim, Le Suicide (Paris, Librairie Félix Alcan, 1930; nouvelle édition). In general, anomic suicide is a type supposed to be due to the change in the society which surrounds the individual and gives him a feeling of maladjustment and of being "lost." The change here, however, is more dynamic than one of process; that is, the society as a functioning structure regularly performs this act upon individuals whose souls have been stolen, rather than that the society changes in a structural way and becomes something different from what it was before and by so doing causes the individual to become maladjusted and suicidal. Since this is true, there are in this situation some of the elements of the type Durkheim calls the altruistic type of suicide, in which the individual destroys himself because of the perfect working of the society.

totem, listening for the sounds of his ancestors' approach as he follows the suggestive sequence of the mourning song and ritual wailingly sung and danced over his body. His effort is not to live but to die.

There are two definite movements of the social group in the process by which black magic becomes effective. In the first movement the community contracts; all the victim's kin withdraw their sustaining support—all in his entire community completely change their attitudes and place him in a new category. He is no longer seen as the ordinary living being like all the other people, but as an abnormal person who is more nearly in the realm of the sacred and taboo. This movement of withdrawal by the society means that his place in the general social fabric has been taken away from him so that he now stands in an entirely different relationship to all of his kin, his clan, and the general tribal grouping. The organization of his social life has collapsed so that he is alone and isolated.

The second movement of the group is its return toward the victim under the integrating force of the mourning rite. The "half dead" man whose soul is in the dangerous position to the community of being neither sacred nor profane must be removed by ritual from any contact with his community; and its purpose now as an organized group with its ceremonial leader, a close relative of the victim's, is finally to cut him off entirely from the ordinary world and ultimately place him in his proper position in the sacred totemic world, that of the dead. The victim, on his part, reciprocates this feeling, behaving in the manner of his totem, with which he attempts to identify himself. The mourning rite is truly a *rite de passage*.

The effect of this double movement, first away from the victim and then back with all the compulsive force of one of its most powerful rituals, is obviously drastic. An analogous situation in our society is hard to imagine. If all a man's near kin, his father, mother, brothers and sisters, wife, children, business associates, friends and all the other members of the society, should suddenly withdraw themselves because of some dramatic circumstance, refusing to take any attitude but one of taboo and looking at the man as one already dead, then after some little time perform over him a sacred ceremony believed with certainty to guide him out of the land of the living into that of the dead, the enormous suggestive power of this twofold movement of the community after it has had its attitudes crystallized can be somewhat understood by ourselves.

The magicians are the leaders who crystallize this group attitude. By the power of their rituals they organize social opinion and attitudes just as effectively and certainly as the ceremonial leader does by the sacred totemic ritual. Both depend upon the group's participation to make their power effective. It is a group situation, not an individual one, that is operative in both circumstances. It is the power of the "church" or community which integrates the total group, directed by the ceremonial leader in the totemic ceremonies, and it is the power of the church (the clan group) which destroys a man under the guidance and leadership of its magicians.

Black magic is a force expressed through the dysphoric condition of an individual member or members of a social group and an ever-present possible danger to all the members of Murngin society.

The attitude of the kinsmen of the man they believe to have been killed by black magic is most illuminating. The sorcerer always belongs to a hostile group or what is equivalent in the Murngin mind to one so far away that it is unknown and strange. A sorcerer of one's own clan is not asked to kill any member of it or of completely friendly clans, but to destroy outsiders who are looked upon as enemies and who reciprocate. The source of the enemy sorcerer's power lies within the known antagonisms which connect one's group with the foreign groups. Probably it is the foreign group's mana, as thought of by the victim and his group, which attacks a member of one's own clan through the magician's ritual. It is the enemy's magician, it must be remembered, who helps to organize this community's attitudes toward the death of its own clansman and it is likely that he also is an organizer of the outside clan's feelings. One's own sorcerer is equally feared by his clan's enemies and the deaths in their clans ascribed by them to the evil worked by him. The local sorcerer is not feared by his kinsmen; rather they go to him in times of trouble and weakness since his power can reëstablish their and their clan's sense of well-being by killing the enemy in retaliation for the slaying of their own kinsman.

The power of the black magician then comes (1) from the very nature of the clan itself because of its antagonism and at times open warfare with the people of the victim; (2) from being associated with the dead; and (3) ultimately from the action of the victim's people because of their earlier withdrawal of support from him and later thrusting him from the society.

The power of the white magician but reverses that of the black, for the healer is ordinarily a member of his own or a friendly group and is made effective by the positive attitude of the victim's people.

The mana of the ceremonial leader comes from his oral and ceremonial ritual, which in turn gains its power ultimately from a society or church, namely, the clan. The mana of the medicine man comes from his ritual, in which the group must participate by its belief if his technique is to be effective, which means that his source of power is in the group. He too must have and does have his church, which in Murngin society is the group of clans.

UNIVERSITY OF CHICAGO,
CHICAGO, ILLINOIS.

THE GREAT WORLD THEATER

By T. T. Waterman[*]

A GOOD WAY to get an impression of the lands in the world is to examine a globe, looking down upon its North Pole. The most cursory glance at the globe will show the land masses in their proper places and will give the observer an impression of three great peninsulas or "continental radii" diverging from the center.

The map which goes with this essay actually shows these radii in relation to each other, and in relation to the center, in some detail. On the globe, the proper relation of these masses is obscured by the curvature of the globe itself. There is an undoubted advantage in having the masses spread out on a flat surface.

This arrangement of lands has caused certain observers to look upon the whole earth as a tetrahedron, and to speak of the tetrahedral *form* of the earth, looking upon our planet, especially from the standpoint of living populations, plant and animal, as a tetrahedron, instead of a sphere.

A tetrahedron, as the name implies, is a four-sided solid, each face being a triangle. Thus a tetrahedron has *three* sides and a base, while a pyramid, for example, has *four* sides and a base. A pyramid is a five-sided figure.

A great deal has been said about this so-called "tetrahedral theory." The real point, perhaps, is not a tetrahedral "form of the earth," but the tetrahedral *arrangement* of the continents.

Philosophers have even pointed out that a tetrahedron has the least possible cubic content for a given amount or extent of surface, while a sphere has the greatest cubic content. That is, if a mechanic were constructing a tin can to hold the greatest possible amount of milk for a given number of square feet of sheet tin, the sphere would be the form he would choose, or *ought* to choose.

If a tinsmith were constructing a container to hold the *least* amount of milk for a square yard of tin (supposing such an enterprise likely), the tetrahedron would be the logical form, for by mathematical laws a tetrahedron is the form containing the least *content* for a given amount of *surface*.

These facts long ago associated themselves with the old theory that the earth was originally a sphere, that it took form from primeval chaos, and was at one time very hot.

When a rigid surface was once formed, any further cooling and shrinking would result in an evolution toward a tetrahedron.

The amount of surface being fixed while the inside shrank, wrinkles would be thrown up which ought logically to show, in more or less a dim way, an accommodation to the idea of tetrahedral form. To express the matter in commonplace terms, the tetrahedron is ideal when a solid has *too much surface*.

---

[*] Deceased, January, 1936.

Whether or not the earth has actually been shrinking through long periods, is another matter. The point is that while the so-called "nebular hypothesis" has, so to speak, gone somewhat out of style, and while, again, to speak of a tetrahedral form of the earth is rather pushing things to extremes, the earth today being quite as perfect a sphere as a billiard ball is, and probably much more nearly perfect, the arrangement of continents still suggests a tetrahedral plan, or tendency.

If this is in any measure true, the terrestrial globe should show a series of great wrinkles, tracing on its surface a sort of tetrahedral figure. In this case, the base of the tetrahedron is "at the top," as the earth is usually drawn, the region around the North Pole being the base of the figure, the apex lying at the South Pole. If now we split the tetrahedron apart, sacrificing the South Polar regions, the result will be something like the earth drawn on Goode's North Polar projection.

In sober fact, we do find a great area of emerged land around the North Pole. Radiating off from this central mass, we do find three great radii, which we call the "continents" of South America, Africa, and Malayo-Australia, but which on the map (and to some extent in actual fact) are really peninsulas. The rest of the habitable lands consist of islands.

This arrangement seems to be a very permanent one. That the number of islands existing, and the heights of mountains, and the depths of the shallower parts of the oceans have been altered from time to time, and from the human point of view very radically altered, is quite beyond question.

Some recent critics have even set the continents adrift, and have pictured Africa or South America as floating about on a sort of fluid base. Without trying to deny the changes in the earth's surface parts, which from our limited human viewpoint have been on a majestic scale, we may safely conclude that the continents are where they belong, and where they have always been.

Thus if one island is removed from the scene, or another island emerges from the deeps, if continents are actually connected at one time by a land bridge, which in later ages is sunk beneath the waves (and all of these things have apparently happened), we can borrow a cosmic viewpoint, and dismiss such changes as incidental. They may be regarded as relatively trifling, in view of the great, solid, majestic, and permanent land masses on which the drama of history has been acted out.

Thus we arrive at what we may call the "drama of existence." In a very real sense it *is* a drama. We are unable to sense its opening act, and we know nothing, or less than nothing, about its concluding tableau, but its individual acts are dramatic in the extreme.

Even a hasty glance at the books on palaeontology, otherwise called "historical geology," will convince any reader that the slow changes which altered a primitive animal more or less the size of a rabbit, into a towering modern horse, would be a sensation if they could be introduced into a pageant on the stage. The gradual alteration of reptiles into flying birds would thrill any audience, if it could be shown on the screen.

The transmogrification of monkey into man, now accepted quite generally, in spite of pope and parson, as an established fact, is in many ways the most dramatic of all the episodes of existence.

The point of view of this present essay with which we, author and reader, are now working, is that practically all of this "acting" has been done on one rather limited stage. Considering the enormous expanse of the lands, it has been performed on a very limited and quite definite stage. Out of a thousand acts or "scenes" of the drama, at least nine hundred and fifty have been staged on the lands immediately around the North Pole.

This matter is important enough to deserve a commonplace illustration. Let us draw a line which encircles the North Pole, at a distance of sixty-seven and a half degrees, coinciding with what we call the Tropic of Cancer. There is no particular reason for choosing the Tropic of Cancer, except that it is already on the map, and nearly every well-informed person knows more or less dimly where it is. If then we draw this circle around the North Pole, inclosing a *relatively* small part of the earth's surface, it will be interesting to see what relation it has to human history.

It is necessary to say *human* history, for the sciences of geology and palaeontology have gone so far that we can actually speak today of the "history" of events which happened long before human history began at all.

Thus we can speak of the history of the elephants, or the early history of flowering plants, dealing with events so ancient that man's entire history is by comparison a mere moment. We may well ask ourselves, first, which part of man's history has transpired in this circumpolar area.

The briefest answer is, that it has all occurred there.

Let us ask, for example, where the great men of history have been born. This is a relatively simple matter, easily worked out. To make the point more clear, let us ask where the great religious leaders of the human race have been born. It might be equally appropriate to ask where they died, or where they were first married, or where they lived, but the question of birthplace is simpler.

As a matter of fact, the religious leader most familiar to most of us is Jesus, and our accounts say that he was born in Bethlehem of Judah, which lies well within the circle we just drew on the map. Buddha, who started another great world religion, was born near Kapilavastu, in northwestern India, also inside the circle. Mohammed was born at Mecca, near the coast of Arabia, a few miles outside of the circle, but near it. Zoroaster (Zarathustra) was born nobody knows where, except that the event took place somewhere on the plateau of Iran, far inside the circle. He founded the wisdom of the Magi, and invented or discovered the Devil (speaking again quite seriously), and he is undoubtedly one of the world's great religious leaders, though his teachings are less popular than formerly.

Speaking briefly, an examination of any good encyclopedia will convince almost anybody that all the religious and semireligious leaders, from Confucius to Joseph Smith, have been born in the same region. To increase the catalogue would be a waste of time.

A point of criticism suggests itself here. Most of us were also born within the circle, and there is a chance that these religious leaders are known to us, and considered "great," because they, after all, are *our* people.

If somebody were to come down from Mars, perhaps his verdict as to who is great in human religious history might not correspond with the verdict of history.

Not coming from Mars, we can hardly go back of the human record, and if the entire historical record was composed by people within the circle, that is another important point, tending to the same conclusion. That is, if anyone questions me about the religious leaders in history, my only retort would be to turn to the question of who made the written documents of history. Out of a hundred such documents, ninety-nine were set down within the circle, including the written history volumes of Egypt, India, and China.

The limits set down by the circle we just drew, in imagination, just about coincides with the limits of Holarctica or Arctogaea, or whatever we choose to name the great northern land mass. There seems little doubt that it is a remarkable region, a point well illustrated by the events of military history.

All the great commanders who have figured in the pages of history, were born within this circle. This includes Alexander and Scipio and Robert E. Lee, Hannibal, Wallenstein, Foch, von Mackensen, Napoleon, and Sitting Bull. Every man who has ever made a resounding name for himself on the field of battle, saw the light of day in this limited area, along with all the military women, for example, Semiramis, Boadicea, and Joan of Arc.

All the great men of science, like Newton and Galileo, every famous tailor and dressmaker even, and all the famous cooks, have sprung from this circumpolar soil. Every epoch-marking invention, like every inventor in the worldwide hall of fame, arose to fame in the same neighborhood. This statement includes the nameless inventor of the bow and arrow, the inventor of pottery, the man who designed the alphabet, and the first tamer of horses. Every master sculptor, from Praxiteles to Rodin, every painter, poet, and dramatist who has charmed the race, was born and lived in this environment around the North Pole.

It may be well to turn from individuals, around whom a world of more or less obscuring folklore congregates, and consider the more objective matter of culture, as contrasted with feats and marvels. If one is interested in great things, rather than great personages, the general history of inventions may be worth looking at. There is no question that certain inventions have had a great deal to do with the progress of human nature.

To say where these discoveries were first made would require an enormous erudition, and vast knowledge. It is possible to say where these inventions made their first appearance *in history*, with the proviso that all of history has not been written yet, and future discoveries may change the facts, or change our impression about the facts. It is possible to draw interesting conclusions, however, from the mere examination of the textbooks, especially from certain textbooks. Thus the writings of James Henry Breasted, of the University of

Chicago, are outstanding from his interest in everyday things. The present list is based, shall we say primarily, on a book by Breasted and another book by A. L. Kroeber.

It seems that the facts concerning great inventions and great discoveries are in some ways more significant than the "facts" about great men. The lives of great men lend themselves to folklore, and the growing of myths, while the discovery of butter, or the invention of mail service, is likely, shall we say, to be more significant because it is less picturesque.

The greatness of Alexander may thus be a matter of debate, while the fact that quinine came to us from a certain region, is not debatable if the facts are really known. Thus the relative greatness of Alexander compared with the greatness of Napoleon might be debated forever, while the origin of quinine, if our records are any good, can be settled once and for all.

It may be refreshing at this point to turn to a chart or sketch showing when some of our basic discoveries and inventions came into existence. Here are the facts, briefly presented. If they do not altogether confirm what has just been said about the Tropic of Cancer, nevertheless, they are facts.

TABULATION SHOWING THE FIRST HISTORICAL APPEARANCE OF CERTAIN INVENTIONS

Men of Lower Palaeolithic Europe: Fire, stone tools

Men of Upper Palaeolithic Europe: The bow and arrow, clothing, the earliest art, first traces of religion, houses

Egyptians: Copper, bronze, wheat, the plow, donkeys, paper, ink, the alphabet, glass, barley, millet, bricks, playing-cards, checkers, chess

Sumerians: Wheels, a scale of weights, steeples, the spread-eagle design

Babylonians: Codified law, coined money, the arch

Hittites: Horses as draft animals, iron

Assyrians: Cotton, banks, postal system

Chaldeans: Astronomy, the Zodiac, the week, degrees of the circle, names of the days in the week

Persians: Monotheism, Satan, chickens (the barnyard fowl), trousers, moustaches

Arabs: Camels, the use of milk, calculus, algebra, the Arabic numerals, zero, coffee

Greeks: Euclidian geometry, the screw, the perfected column in architecture

Chinese: Tea, porcelain, gunpowder, silk, rice, parasols and umbrellas, spectacles (eyeglasses), pepper, the printing press, the mariner's compass, asbestos, paper money, watertight compartments in ships, the fingerprint system of identification, kites

American Indians: Maize, tobacco, potato, sweet potato, hammocks, quinine, cassava, toboggans, snowshoes, the tipi (original of the Sibley tent), the "cocaine" plant, zero (independently discovered, before its discovery by the Arabs), cocaine, the Scuppernong grape, vanilla, chocolate, cochineal, guinea pigs, peanuts

This tabulation indicates that "civilization," as we know it, came to us from various sources. The American Indians and the Chinese, two people that we rarely think of as civilized at all, have apparently made their full contribution to human culture. The American Indian has, in fact, made more numerous *original* contributions than the classical Greeks made. What bearing this fact has on the question of genius and intelligence in the "races," it would be difficult to say.

The tropical habitats of certain of these peoples is also noteworthy. The "tropical" Indian tribes gave us the potato, cassaba (from which household tapioca is made), the hammock, tobacco, maize, quinine, and cocaine. These would be a great contribution from any people, whatever their habitat.

It is fair to remark, at this point, that the Negro, existing in various parts of the world, under any number of varying conditions of soil and climate, following various modes of life, has never made any contribution of any sort of importance to culture.

1340 High View Place,
Honolulu, Hawaii.

BIBLIOGRAPHY OF ALFRED L. KROEBER

I. Chronological List*

1898
1. Animal Tales of the Eskimo, JAFL 12:17–23, 1898.

1899
2. Tales of the Smith Sound Eskimo, JAFL 12:166–182, 1899.

1900
3. Cheyenne Tales, JAFL 13:161–190, 1900.
4. The Eskimo of Smith Sound, AMNH–B 12:265–327, 1900.
5. Symbolism of the Arapaho Indians, AMNH–B 13:69–86, 1900.

1901
6. Decorative Symbolism of the Arapaho, AA 3:308–336, 1901.
7. Ute Tales, JAFL 14:252–285, 1901.

1902
8. The Arapaho, part I, AMNH–B 18:1–150, 1902.
9. Preliminary Sketch of the Mohave Indians, AA 4:276–285, 1902.
10. Review of B. Laufer's The Decorative Art of the Amur Tribes, AA 4:532–534, 1902.

1903
11. The Coast Yuki of California, AA 4:729–730, 1903.
12. The Native Languages of California (with R. B. Dixon), AA 4:1–26, 1903.
13. Traditions of the Arapaho (with G. A. Dorsey), FMNH–PAS 5:1–475, 1903.

1904
14. The Arapaho, part II, AMNH–B 18:151–230, 1904.
15. Dr. Uhle's Researches in Peru, AA 6:576–577, 1904.
16. A Ghost Dance in California, JAFL 17:32–35, 1904.
17. The Languages of the Coast of California South of San Francisco, UC–PAAE 2:29–80, 1904.
18. Types of Indian Culture in California, UC–PAAE 2:81–103, 1904.

1905
19. Basket Designs of the Indians of Northwestern California, UC–PAAE 2:104–164, 1905.
20. The Department of Anthropology of the University of California (with F. W. Putnam), UC Miscellaneous, 1 35, 1905.
21. Notes in H. N. Rust's The Obsidian Blades of California, AA 7:690–695, 1905.
22. Supposed Shoshoneans in Lower California, AA 7:570–571, 1905.
23. Systematic Nomenclature in Ethnology, AA 7:579–593, 1905.
24. Wishosk Myths, JAFL 18:85–107, 1905.

1906
25. Article: Anthropological Societies in California, in Recent Progress in American Anthropology, AA 8:483–495, 1906.
26. Measurements of Igorots, AA 8:194, 1906.
27. Notes on California Folk-lore, in Proceedings California Branch of American Folklore Society, JAFL 1906–1908.
28. Notes in H. N. Rust's A Puberty Ceremony of the Mission Indians, AA 8:28–32, 1906.
29. Recent Researches by the University of California, AA 8:606, 1906.

---
* See p. 433 for List of Abbreviations.

30. Progress in Anthropology at the University of California, AA 8:652–663, 1906.
31. The Dialectic Divisions of the Moquelumnan Family, etc., AA 8:483–494, 1906.
32. University of California, *in* Recent Progress in American Anthropology, AA 8:483–495, 1906.
33. Two Myths of the Mission Indians of California, JAFL 19:309–321, 1906.
34. Guide to the Collections of the Department of Anthropology, University of California, UC–Miscellaneous, 1–15, 1906.
35. The Yokuts and Yuki Languages, Boas Anniversary Volume, 64–79, 1906.

1907

36. The Arapaho, part III (Religion), AMNH–B 18:279–454, 1907.
37. Articles: California (Indians of), Chimariko, Chumashan Family, Esselen, Gabrielino, Karok, Kawia, Luiseño, Mariposan Family, Mission Indians of California, Mono-Paviotso, and smaller articles, *in* Handbook of American Indians, BAE–B 30 (part I), 1907.
38. The Ceremonial Organization of the Plains Indians of North America, ICA, 15th Session, Quebec, 2:53–65, 1907.
39. Gros Ventre Myths and Tales, AMNH–AP 1:56–139, 1907.
40. Horatio N. Rust, JAFL 20:153, 1907.
41. Indian Myths of South Central California, UC–PAAE 4:167–250, 1907.
42. Numeral Systems of the Languages of California (with R. B. Dixon), AA 9:663–690, 1907.
43. The Religion of the Indians of California, UC–PAAE 4:319–356, 1907.
44. Shoshonean Dialects of California, UC–PAAE 4:66–165, 1907.
45. The Washo Language of East Central California and Nevada, UC–PAAE 4:251–317, 1907.
46. Yokuts Names, JAFL 20:142–143, 1907.
47. The Yokuts Language of South Central California, UC–PAAE 2:169–377, 1907.

1908

48. The Anthropology of California, Science, n.s., 27:281–290, 1908.
49. Articles: California Indians; Zuñi, *in* Hastings' Encyclopaedia of Religion and Ethics, 1908–22.
50. Catchwords in American Mythology, JAFL 21:222–227, 1908.
51. Ethnography of the Cahuilla Indians, UC–PAAE 8:29–69, 1908.
52. Ethnology of the Gros Ventre, AMNH–AP 1:141–281, 1908.
53. A Mission Record of the California Indians, UC–PAAE 8:1–27, 1908.
54. Notes on the Luiseño, UC–PAAE 8:174–185, 1908.
55. Editor of C. G. Du Bois, The Religion of the Luiseño Indians of Southern California, UC–PAAE 8:68–173, 1908.
56. Notes on the Ute Language, AA 19:74–87, 1908.
57. On the Evidences of the Occupation of Certain Regions by the Miwok Indians, UC–PAAE 6:369–380, 1908.
58. Origin Traditions of the Chemehuevi Indians, JAFL 21:240–242, 1908.
59. A Southern California Ceremony, JAFL 21:40, 1908.
60. Wiyot Folk-lore, JAFL 21:37–39, 1908.

1909

61. The Archaeology of California, Putnam Anniversary Volume, 1–49, 1909.
62. The Bannock and Shoshoni Languages, AA 2:266–277, 1909.
63. California Basketry and the Pomo, AA 2:233–249, 1909.
64. Classificatory Systems of Relationship, JRAI 39:77–84, 1909.
65. Measurements of Chukchis, AA 2:531–533, 1909.
66. Notes on Shoshonean Dialects of Southern California, UC–PAAE 8:235–269, 1909.
67. Noun Incorporation in American Languages, ICA, 16th Session, Wien, 569–576, 1909.

1910

68. At the Bedrock of History, Sunset Magazine 25:255–260, 1910.
69. The Chumash and Costanoan Languages, UC–PAAE 19:237–271, 1910.
70. The Morals of Uncivilized People, AA 12:437–447, 1910.

1911

71. Articles: Salinan, Yokuts, Wiyot, Yuki, Yurok, etc., in Handbook of American Indians, BAE–B 30 (part II), 1911.
72. The Elusive Mill Creeks, Travel 17:510–513, 548, 550, 1911.
73. Incorporation as a Linguistic Process, AA 13:577–584, 1911.
74. The Languages of the American Indians, Science Monthly, 500–515, 1911.
75. The Languages of the Coast of California North of San Francisco, UC–PAAE 9:273–435, 1911.
76. Phonetic Constituents of the Native Languages of California, UC–PAAE 10:1–12, 1911.
77. Phonetic Elements of the Mohave Language, UC–PAAE 10:45–96, 1911.
78. Phonetics of the Micronesian Language of the Marshall Islands, AA 13:380–393, 1911.
79. Shellmounds at San Francisco and San Mateo, Records of the Past 10:227–228, 1911.

1912

80. The Indians of San Diego, California Topics 2:8, 1912.
81. Ishi, the Last Aborigine, World's Work Magazine 24:304–308, 1912.

1913

82. The California Academy of Sciences, Science, n.s., 37:833–835, 1913.
83. The Determination of Linguistic Relationship, A 8:389–401, 1913.
84. New Linguistic Families in California (with R. B. Dixon), AA 15:647–655, 1913.
85. Relationship of the Indian Languages of California (with R. B. Dixon), Science, n.s., 37:225, 1913.

1914

86. Chontal, Seri, and Yuman, Science 40:448, 1914.
87. Phonetic Elements of the Diegueño Language (with J. P. Harrington), UC–PAAE 11:177–188, 1914.

1915

88. A California Indian Hunting Legend, California Fish and Game 1:52–59, 1915.
89. Eighteen Professions, AA 17:283–288, 1915.
90. Frederick Ward Putnam, AA 17:712–718, 1915.
91. A New Shoshonean Tribe in California, AA 17:773–775, 1915.
92. Serian, Tequistlatecan, and Hokan, UC–PAAE 11:279–290, 1915.
93. Visible Speech, Scientific American 112:471, 1915.
94. Zuñi Culture Sequences, Proceedings of the National Academy of Sciences 2:42, 1915.

1916

95. Arapaho Dialects, UC–PAAE 12:71–138, 1916.
96. California Place Names of Indian Origin, UC–PAAE 12:31–69, 1916.
97. The Cause of the Belief in Use Inheritance, American Naturalist 50:367–370, 1916.
98. Floral Relations Among the Galapagos Islands, UC–P in Botany, 6:199–222, 1916.
99. Heredity Without Magic, AA 18:294–296, 1916.
100. Inheritance by Magic, AA 18:19–40, 1916.
101. The Oldest Town in America and Its People, AMNH–Journal 16:81–85, 1916.
102. The Speech of a Zuñi Child, AA 18:529–534, 1916.
103. Thoughts on Zuñi Religion, Holmes Anniversary Volume, 269–277, 1916.
104. What an American Saw in Germany, The Outlook 112:92–95, 1916.
105. Zuñi Potsherds, AMNH–AP 18:3–37, 1916.

1917

106. California Kinship Systems, UC–PAAE 12:339–396, 1917.
107. The Matrilineate Again, AA 19:571–579, 1917.
108. Review of F. J. Teggart's Prolegomena to History, AA 19:68–70, 1917.
109. The Superorganic, AA 19:163–213, 1917.
110. The Tribes of the Pacific Coast of North America, ICA, 19th Session, Washington, 385–401, 1917.
111. Zuñi Kin and Clan, AMNH–AP 18:47–204, 1917.

1918

112. The History of Philippine Civilization as Reflected in Religious Nomenclature, AMNH–AP 19:35–67, 1918.
113. The Possibility of a Social Psychology, The American Journal of Sociology 23:633–650, 1918.

1919

114. Kinship in the Philippines, AMNH–AP 19:69–84, 1919.
115. The Linguistic Families of California (with R. B. Dixon), UC–PAAE 16:47–118, 1919.
116. Nabaloi Songs (with C. R. Moss), UC–PAAE 15:187–206, 1919.
117. On the Principle of Order in Civilization as Exemplified by Changes of Fashion, AA 21:235–263, 1919.
118. Peoples of the Philippines, AMNH–Handbook Series, 1–224, 1919.
119. Sinkyone Tales, JAFL 32:346–351, 1919.

1920

120. California Culture Provinces, UC–PAAE 17:151–169, 1920.
121. Games of the California Indians, AA 22:272–277, 1920.
122. Source Book in Anthropology (with T. T. Waterman), UC–Syllabus No. 118:1–565, 1920.
123. Three Essays on the Antiquity and Races of Man, UC–Syllabus No. 119:1–80, 1920.
124. Totem and Taboo: an Ethnologic Psychoanalysis, AA 22:48–55, 1920.
125. Yuman Tribes of the Lower Colorado, UC–PAAE 16:475–485, 1920.

1921

126. The Aboriginal Population of California, Science 54:162, 1921.
127. Indians of Yosemite, Handbook of Yosemite National Park, 49–73, 1921.
128. Observations on the Anthropology of Hawaii, AA 23:129–137, 1921.

1922

129. Basket Designs of the Mission Indians of California, AMNH–AP 20:149–183, 1922.
130. Elements of Culture in Native California, UC–PAAE 13:259–328, 1922.
131. Introduction, in E. C. Parsons' (ed.) American Indian Life, 5–16, 1922. New York: Huebsch.
132. Earth-Tongue, A Mohave, in E. C. Parsons' (ed.) American Indian Life, 189–202, 1922. New York: Huebsch.
133. Review of Edward Sapir's Language, The Dial, 314–317, 1922.

1923

134. American Culture and the Northwest Coast, AA 25:1–20, 1923.
135. Anthropology. New York: Harcourt, Brace & Company, 522 pp., 1923.
136. Historical Introduction, in Phoebe Apperson Hearst Memorial Volume, UC–PAAE 20:ix–xiv, 1923.
137. The History of Native Culture in California, in Phoebe Apperson Hearst Memorial Volume, UC–PAAE 20:125–142, 1923.
138. Relationship of the Australian Languages, Journal and Proceedings of the Royal Society of New South Wales 57:101–117, 1923.

1924

139. The Uhle Collections from Chincha (with W. D. Strong), UC–PAAE 21:1–54, 1924.
140. The Uhle Pottery Collections from Ica (with W. D. Strong; and three appendices by Max Uhle), UC–PAAE 21:95–133, 1924.

1925

141. Archaic Culture Horizons in the Valley of Mexico, UC–PAAE 17:373–408, 1925.
142. Handbook of the Indians of California, BAE–B 78:1–995, 1925.
143. The Uhle Pottery Collections from Moche, UC–PAAE 21:191–234, 1925.
144. The Uhle Pottery Collections from Supe, UC–PAAE 21:235–264, 1925.

1926

145. Archaeological Explorations in Peru. Part I, Ancient Pottery from Trujillo, FMNH–M 2 (no. 1), 1926.
146. Culture Stratifications in Peru, AA 28:331–351, 1926.
147. The Uhle Pottery Collections from Chancay, UC–PAAE 21:265–304, 1926.
148. Yurok Law, ICA, 22nd Session, Rome, 1926.

1927

149. Arrow Release Distributions, UC–PAAE 23:283–296, 1927.
150. Coast and Highland in Peru, AA 29:625–654, 1927.
151. Disposal of the Dead, AA 29:308–315, 1927.
152. The Uhle Pottery Collections from Nazca (with A. H. Gayton), UC–PAAE 24:1–46, 1927.

1928

153. A Kato War. Schmidt Anniversary Volume, 394–400, 1928.
154. Cultural Relations between North and South America, ICA, 23rd Session, New York, 5–22, 1928.
155. Native Culture in the Southwest, UC–PAAE 23:375–398, 1928.
156. Peoples of the Philippines, AMNH–Handbook Series 8, 1–230, 1928.
157. Sub-Human Culture Beginnings, Quart. Review of Biology 3:325–342, 1928.

1929

158. Pliny Earle Goddard, AA 31:1–8, 1929.
159. The Valley Nisenan, UC–PAAE 24:253–290, 1929.

1930

160. Archaeological Explorations in Peru. Part II, The Northern Coast, FMNH–M 2:53–116, 1930.
161. Article: Archaeology, Encyclopaedia of the Social Sciences 2:163–166, 1930.
162. Article: Caste, Encyclopaedia of the Social Sciences 3:254–256, 1930.
163. Article: Primitive Art, Encyclopaedia of the Social Sciences 2:226–229, 1930.
164. Textile Periods in Ancient Peru (with Lila M. O'Neale), UC–PAAE 28:23–56, 1930.

1931

165. Historical Reconstruction of Culture Growths and Organic Evolution, AA 33:149–156, 1931.
166. The Seri, Southwest Museum Papers, No. 6:1–60, 1931.

1932

167. Quantitative Expression of Culture Relationships (with H. Driver), UC–PAAE 31:211–256, 1932.
168. Yuki Myths, A 27:905–939, 1932.

1933

169. Process in the Chinese Kinship System, AA 35:151–157, 1933.
170. A Supplement to "Anthropology." New York: Harcourt Brace & Company, 32 pp., 1933.

1934

171. Blood-group Classification, American Journal of Physical Anthropology 18:377–393, 1934.
172. Native American Population, AA 36:25, 1934.
173. Yurok Marriages (with T. T. Waterman), UC–PAAE 35:1–14, 1934.
174. Yurok and Neighboring Kin Term Systems, UC–PAAE 35:15–22, 1934.

1935

175. History and Science in Anthropology, AA 37:539–569, 1935.

Editor of—

Proceedings of the California Branch of the American Folk-Lore Society. Published in JAFL 1906–1908.

University of California Publications in American Archaeology and Ethnology. Vols. 1 through 36. Published by University of California.

II. Subject Index*

Anthropological societies, 25, 48
Anthropology Department (U. of C.), 20, 29, 30, 32, 34, 48
Antiquity of Man, 123
Arapaho Indians, 5, 6, 8, 13, 14, 36, 95
Archaeology, 61, 105, 145, 160, 161
Arrow release, 149
Art, 163. *See also* Decorative art, Designs, Symbolism
Australian languages, 138

Bannock Indians, 62
Basketry, 19, 63, 129

Cahuilla Indians, 51
California
    Anthropological societies, 25, 48
    Archaeology, 61
    Basketry, 19, 63, 129
    Cahuilla Indians, 51
    Ceremony, 159
    Chemehuevi Indians, 58
    Chimariko Indians, 37
    Chumash Indians, 37, 69
    Costanoan Indians, 69
    Culture, elements, 130, history, 137, provinces, 120, types, 18
    Diegueño Indians, 87
    East Central Indians, 45
    Esselen Indians, 37
    Folk-Lore, 27. *See also* Mythologies
    Gabrielino Indians, 37
    Games, 121
    Ghost Dance, 16
    Handbook, 42
    Indians of, 37, 49, 53, 59, 142
    Karok Indians, 37
    Kato Indians, 153
    Kawia Indians, 37
    Kinship, 106, 174
    Languages, 12, 17, 31, 35, 42, 44, 45, 47, 66, 67, 75, 84, 85, 115
    Luiseño Indians, 37, 54
    Mariposa Indians, 37
    Marriage, 173
    Mission Indians, 33, 37, 129
    Miwok Indians, 57
    Mohave Indians, 9, 77
    Mono Indians, 37
    Moquelumnan family, 31

Mythology, 41, 88
Names. *See* Place names, below
Nisenan Indians, 159
Northwest Indians, 19, 75
Numeral systems, 42
Paviotso Indians, 37
Place names, 96
Pomo Indians, 63
Population, 126
Religion, 43
Salinan Indians, 71
San Diego Indians, 80
Shoshonean Indians, 22, 44, 66, 91
South Central Coast Indians, 17, 41, 47
University of California Department of Anthropology, 20, 29, 30, 32, 34
Washo Indians, 45
Wiyot Indians, 60, 71
Yokuts Indians, 35, 46, 47, 71
Yosemite Indians, 127
Yuki Indians, 11, 35, 71, 168
Yurok Indians, 71, 148, 173, 174
California Academy of Sciences, 82
Caste, 162
Catchwords, 50
Ceremonial, 38, 59
Chancay, 147
Chemehuevi Indians, 58
Cheyenne Indians, 3
Chimariko Indians, 37
Chincha, 139
Chinese, 169
Chontal Indians, 86
Chukchi, 65
Chumash Indians, 37
Clan, 111
Classification, blood-group, 171
Classificatory systems, 64
Costanoan Indians, 69
Culture, American, 134, Californian, 137, elements, 130, growths, Mexico, 141, relations, 154, 167, Southwest, 155, stratifications, 146, subhuman, 157, Zuñi, 94

Dances. *See* Ghost Dance
Decorative art, of Arapaho, 6
Designs, basketry, 19
Dialects. *See* Languages
Diegueño Indians, 87

---
* Numbers refer to those in the Chronological List.

Earth-Tongue, a Mohave Indian, 132
Eskimo, tales of, 1, 2, 4
Esselen Indians, 37
Evolution, organic, 165

Fashion, 117
Floral relations, 98
Folk-lore. *See* Mythologies

Gabrielino Indians, 37
Galapagos Islands, 98
Games, 121
Germany, 104
Ghost Dance, 16
Goddard, Pliny Earle, 158
Gros Ventre Indians, 39, 52

Hawaii, 128
Heredity, 99
History and Science in Anthropology, 175
Hokan, 92
Hunting legend, 88

Ica, 140
Igorot Indians, 26
Incorporation, noun, 67, 73
Inheritance, 100. *See also* Use inheritance
Ishi, an Indian, 81

Karok Indians, 37
Kato Indians, 153
Kawia Indians, 37
Kinship, 64, 106, 111, 114, 169, 174

Languages, 12, 17, 31, 35, 42, 44, 45, 47, 50, 56, 62, 66, 67, 73, 74, 75, 76, 77, 78, 83, 84, 85, 87, 93, 95, 102, 115, 138
Laufer, B., review of, 10
Law, 148
Luiseño Indians, 37

Magic, 99, 100
Marriages, 173
Mariposan family, 37
Marshall Islands, 78
Matrilineate, 107
Measurements, 26, 65
Mexico. *See* Valley of Mexico
Micronesian language, 78
Mill Creek Indians, 72
Mission Indians, 33, 37, 129
Miwok Indians, 57
Moche, 143
Mohave Indians, 9, 77, 132

Mono Indians, 37
Moquelumnan family, 31
Morals, 70
Mythologies, 1, 2, 3, 7, 13, 24, 27, 33, 39, 41, 58, 60, 88, 119, 168

Nabaloi, 116
Names, 46, 112
Nazca, 152
Nevada, 45
Nisenan Indians, 159
Nomenclature. *See* Names
North Pacific Coast Indians, 110, 134
Nouns, 67
Numeral systems, 42

Obsidian blades, 21
Oldest town, 101
Organization, ceremonial, 38
Origins, 58

Paviotso Indians, 37
Peru, 15, 139, 140, 143, 144–147, 150, 152, 160, 164
Philippines, 112, 114, 118, 156
Physical anthropology, 26, 65, 171
Place names, California, 96
Plains Indians, 38
Pomo Indians, 63
Population, 101, 126, 172
Pottery, 105, 139, 140, 143–5, 147, 152
Professions, eighteen, 89
Psychology, 113, 124
Puberty, 28
Putnam, Frederick Ward, 90

Quantitative expression, 167

Races, 123
Relationships. *See* Kinship
Religion, 36, 43, 103, 112
Reviews, 10, 108, 133
Rust, H. N., 21, 28, 40

Salinan Indians, 71
San Diego Indians, 80
Sapir, review of, 133
Science in Anthropology, History and, 175
Seri Indians, 86, 92, 166
Shellmounds, 79
Shoshonean Indians, 22, 44, 62, 66, 91
Sinkyone Indians, 119
Smith Sound Eskimo, tales of, 2, 4
Songs, 116

Source Book, 122
Southwest, 155
Styles. *See* Fashion
Supe, 144
Superorganic, 109
Symbolism, of Arapaho, 5, 6

Taboos, 124
Tales. *See* Mythologies
Teggart, review of, 108
Tequistlatecan Indians, 92
Textiles, 164
Totem, 124
Trujillo, 145

Uhle, Max, collections of, 139, 140, 143, 144, 147, 152, researches of, 15
University of California Department of Anthropology. See Anthropology Department

Use inheritance, 97
Ute Indians, tales of, 7, language of, 56

Valley of Mexico, 141

War, 153
Washo Indians, 45
Wishosk Indians, 24
Wiyot Indians, 60, 71

Yokuts Indians, 35, 46, 47, 71
Yosemite Indians, 127
Yuki Indians, 11, 35, 71, 168
Yuman Indians, 86, 125
Yurok Indians, 71, 148

Zuñi Indians, 49, 94, 102, 103, 105, 111

III. Periodicals, or Other, Index*

American Anthropologist, 6, 9, 10, 11, 12, 15, 21, 22, 23, 25, 28–32, 42, 56, 62, 63, 65, 70, 73, 78, 84, 89–91, 99, 100, 102, 107–109, 117, 121, 124, 128, 134, 146, 150, 151, 158, 165, 169, 172, 175

American Journal of Physical Anthropology, 171

American Journal of Sociology, 113

American Museum of Natural History, 4, 5, 8, 14, 36, 39, 52, 101, 105, 111, 112, 114, 118, 129, 156

American Naturalist, 97

American Scientific Journals. *See* Science; Science Monthly; Proceedings of the National Academy of Science; American Naturalist; American Journal of Sociology; Scientific American; Records of the Past; Quarterly Review of Biology

Anniversary Volumes, *Boas*, 35, *Putnam*, 61, *Holmes*, 103, *Hearst*, 136, 137, *Schmidt*, 153

Anthropos, 83, 168

Biology. *See* Quarterly Review of Biology

Books, 135, 170

Bureau of American Ethnology, 37, 71, 142

Encyclopaedia of the Social Sciences, 161–163

European Journals. *See* Anthropos; Journal of the Royal Anthropological Institute (of Great Britain and Ireland); Journal and Proceedings of the Royal Society of New South Wales

Field (Columbian) Museum of Natural History, 13, 145, 160

Folk-Lore Journals. *See* Journal of American Folk-Lore

Hastings' Encyclopaedia of Religion and Ethics, 49

International Congress of Americanists, 38, 67, 110, 148, 154

Journal and Proceedings of the Royal Society of New South Wales, 138

Journal of American Folk-Lore, 1–3, 7, 16, 24, 27, 33, 40, 46, 50, 58–60, 119

Journal of the Royal Anthropological Institute (of Great Britain and Ireland), 64

Miscellaneous
  American Indian Life (ed., Elsie Clews Parsons), 131, 132

National Academy of Science. *See* Proceedings of

Physical Anthropology Journals. *See* American Journal of Physical Anthropology

Popular Magazines and Nonscientific Articles, 68, 72, 80, 81, 88, 104, 133

Proceedings of the National Academy of Science, 94

Quarterly Review of Biology, 157

Records of the Past, 79

Science, 48, 82, 85, 86, 126

Science Monthly, 74

Scientific American, 93

Southwest Museum Papers, 166

University of California
  Publications in American Archaeology and Ethnology, 17–19, 41, 43–45, 47, 51, 53–55, 57, 66, 69, 75–77, 87, 92, 95, 96, 106, 115, 116, 120, 125, 130, 139–141, 143, 144, 147, 149, 152, 155, 159, 164, 167, 173, 174
  Publications in Botany, 98
  Syllabuses, 122, 123
  Miscellaneous, 20, 34

Yosemite National Park, Handbook of, 127

---

* Numbers refer to those in the Chronological List.

ABBREVIATIONS USED

A	Anthropos
l'A	L'Anthropologie
AA	American Anthropologist
AAA-M	American Anthropological Association, Memoirs
ArA	Archiv für Anthropologie
AES-P	American Ethnological Society, Publications
AGW-M	Anthropologische Gesellschaft in Wien, Mitteilungen
AJPA	American Journal of Physical Anthropology
AMNH	American Museum of Natural History—
-AP	Anthropological Papers
-B	Bulletin
-M	Memoirs
-MA	Memoirs, Anthropological Series
-MJ	Memoirs, Jesup Expedition
BAE	Bureau of American Ethnology—
-B	Bulletins
-R	(Annual) Reports
CNAE	Contributions to North American Ethnology
CU-CA	Columbia University, Contributions to Anthropology
FL	Folk-Lore
FMNH	Field Museum of Natural History—
-M	Memoirs
-PAS	Publications, Anthropological Series
IAE	Internationales Archiv für Ethnographie
ICA	International Congress of Americanists (Comptes Rendus, Proceedings)
IJAL	International Journal of American Linguistics
JAFL	Journal of American Folk-Lore
JRAI	Journal of the Royal Anthropological Institute
MAIHF	Museum of the American Indian, Heye Foundation—
-C	Contributions
-IN	Indian Notes
-INM	Indian Notes and Monographs
PM	Peabody Museum (of Harvard University)—
-M	Memoirs
-P	Papers
-R	Reports
PMM-B	Public Museum (of the City) of Milwaukee, Bulletin
SAP-J	Société des Américanistes de Paris, Journal
SI	Smithsonian Institution—
-AR	Annual Reports
-CK	Contributions to Knowledge
-MC	Miscellaneous Collections
UC-PAAE	University of California, Publications in American Archaeology and Ethnology
UPM-AP	University of Pennsylvania Museum, Anthropological Publications
USNM	United States National Museum—
-R	Reports
-P	Proceedings
UW-PA	University of Washington, Publications in Anthropology
ZE	Zeitschrift für Ethnologie